Towards a 'Natural' Narratology

'Monika Fludernik takes narratology by the scruff of the neck and gives it a vigorous shaking ... this radical reorientation of narrative theory empowers her not only to elaborate a set of fresh theoretical categories but also to trace the career of these categories through a historical sequence of texts. No one will come away from this book feeling under-nourished.'
Brian McHale, Distinguished Professor of American Literature, West Virginia University and co-editor of *Poetics Today*

Towards a 'Natural' Narratology makes an intervention into ongoing debates in literary theory and criticism. In this book, Monika Fludernik argues for a new narrative theory which builds on insights from conversational narrative while touching on key issues of poststructuralist theorizing.

Drawing on insights from cognitive linguistics, discourse analysis and structuralist narratology, the author examines narrative structures as they have developed from oral storytelling to the realist novel and beyond. Narrative, it is argued, need not be defined in terms of plot, but can also be aligned with what Fludernik terms 'experientiality'. This reconceptualization of narrative and the crucial notion of narrativity allows for an inclusive re-analysis of central narratological issues and prepares the way for a redefinition of narrative in relation to other literary and non-literary genres.

Towards a 'Natural' Narratology is a ground-breaking work of synthesis which makes a significant contribution to fundamental issues in literary theory. Fludernik's new model entails a radical reconceptualization of current narratological thinking and integrates narrative theory within a wider range of topical debates in literary studies.

The book will be of interest to advanced undergraduate and graduate students of English Literature, Literary Theory and Historical Linguistics.

Monika Fludernik is Professor of English at Freiburg University in Germany. Her previous publications include *The Fictions of Language and the Languages of Fiction* (1993) and essays on a wide range of topics in English and American literature.

Towards a 'Natural' Narratology

Monika Fludernik

London and New York

First published 1996
by Routledge
2 Park Square, Milton Park, Abingdon, Oxon, OX14 4RN

Simultaneously published in the USA and Canada
by Routledge
270 Madison Ave, New York NY 10016

Reprinted 2001 (twice), 2002

Transferred to Digital Printing 2005

Routledge is an imprint of the Taylor & Francis Group

© 1996 Monika Fludernik

Typeset in Times by
Florencetype Limited, Stoodleigh, Devon

All rights reserved. No part of this book may be reprinted or
reproduced or utilized in any form or by any electronic,
mechanical, or other means, now known or hereafter
invented, including photocopying and recording, or in any
information storage or retrieval system, without permission
in writing from the publishers.

British Library Cataloguing in Publication Data
A catalogue record for this book is available from the British Library

Library of Congress Cataloguing in Publication Data
Fludernik, Monika.
Towards a 'natural' narratology / Monika Fludernik.
    p.   cm.
Includes bibliographical references and index.
1. Narration (Rhetoric)   2. Criticism   I. Title
PN212.F58 1996
801.95–dc20
95-36357

ISBN   0–415–12482–4 (hbk)
ISBN   978-0-415-58563-7 (pbk)

For Dorrit and Paul

Contents

Preface   xi
Acknowledgements   xv

Prologue in the wilderness   1

1 Towards a 'natural' narratology   12
  1.1 Linguistic concepts of the natural   13
    1.1.1 Natural narrative   13
    1.1.2 The linguistic theory of naturalness: from frames to prototypes   17
  1.2 A redefinition of narrativity   20
    1.2.1 History vs. experientiality   20
    1.2.2 Narrativity   26
    1.2.3 Narrativization   31
    1.2.4 Realism and mimesis   35
    1.2.5 Fictionality   38
  1.3 Towards a 'natural' narratology   43

2 Natural narrative and other oral modes   53
  2.1 Oral types of storytelling: a generic overview   57
  2.2 Natural narrative: the creation of story meaning   60
    2.2.1 The features of conversational storytelling: the experiential mode   63
    2.2.2 Report, observational narrative and the vicarious mode   71
    2.2.3 Institutionalized storytelling and the link with written narrative   77
  2.3 Humorous and didactic short forms   81
    2.3.1 The joke   81
    2.3.2 Exemplum and/or anecdote   85

3 From the oral to the written: narrative structure before the novel ... 92
3.1 Middle English prose ... 94
3.2 Middle English verse narrative ... 107
   3.2.1 Saints' legends ... 107
   3.2.2 Romance ... 115
3.3 Renaissance prose and popular writing before Behn ... 120

4 The realist paradigm: consciousness, mimesis and the reading of the 'real' ... 129
4.1 Aphra Behn, or: from drama to fiction ... 131
   4.1.1 The orientation: development of report structure ... 131
   4.1.2 The narrative episode and the dramatic scene ... 142
   4.1.3 The consciousness scene ... 153
4.2 The natural parameters of realism ... 159
   4.2.1 Verisimilitude and effet de réel ... 159
   4.2.2 Natural parameters ... 163
   4.2.3 Authorial narrative, omniscience and reliability ... 165
4.3 The consciousness novel: the English novel from Behn to Woolf ... 168
4.4 The unimpassioned observer: neutral narrative ... 172

5 Reflectorization and figuralization: the malleability of language ... 178
5.1 Reflectorization ... 179
   5.1.1 Original proposals ... 179
   5.1.2 Lawrence and Weldon: a case study ... 184
5.2 The 'empty centre' or figuralization ... 192
   5.2.1 Original proposals ... 192
   5.2.2 Mansfield's 'At the Bay': another case study ... 198
   5.2.3 Reflectorization and figuralization contrasted ... 201
5.3 Observers, narrators and reflectors ... 207
   5.3.1 The anonymous witness position ... 207
   5.3.2 Embodiment, skaz, unreliability: cognitive parameters reintroduced ... 211
   5.3.3 Consonant reflectorization ... 213
5.4 Summary ... 217

6 Virgin territories: the strategic expansion of deictic options ... 222
6.1 The deictic centre extended: 'odd' personal pronouns and the presentation of consciousness ... 223
   6.1.1 'Odd' pronouns: multiple subjects, impossible protagonists and invented pronominal morphology ... 224
   6.1.2 Alternation ... 236

6.2 *Person as a narratological category reconsidered*	244
6.3 *Tense and narration: undermining deixis as usual*	249
6.3.1 *The narrative present*	249
6.3.2 *'Odd' narrative tenses*	256
6.3.3 *Non-finite verb forms*	260
6.3.4 *Tense alternation*	262
6.4 *Deixis in action*	266

7 Games with tellers, telling and told   269

7.1 *Narratological postmodernisms*	271
7.2 *The narrativization of the teller: narration as reflective consciousness*	274
7.3 *The usurpation of telling by competing discourses*	278
7.4 *Reading a story where there is none: against the grain of the text*	288
7.5 *Hermetic writing: the deconstruction of the referential function of language. Where even the most intrepid reader fears to tread*	294
7.5.1 *Plenitude and multiplicity*	294
7.5.2 *Language disassembled into words*	299
7.6 *Narrative and poetry: the condition of writing as* écriture	304

8 Natural Narratology   311

8.1 *What is Natural Narratology? A theoretical outline*	312
8.1.1 *The historical side of things: narrativization and its limits*	315
8.1.2 *What is narrative? (Part one)*	318
8.1.3 *Degrees of narrativity, non-narrative texts and the question of historicity*	323
8.2 *Standard models reviewed: how to square the circle*	330
8.3 *Narratological categories and cognitive parameters*	333
8.3.1 *Story vs. discourse reconsidered*	333
8.3.2 *Tellers vs. reflectors, agents and readers: the dramatis personae of narratology*	337
8.3.3 *Throwing out the baby and preserving the bath water: typological categories reconceptualized*	341
8.4 *The medium of narrative: genre revisited (What is narrative? Part two)*	347
8.5 *The politics of narrative: feminism, postcolonialism and the discourse of authorial power*	358
8.5.1 Écriture féminine *and the place of narratology in feminist studies*	359
8.5.2 *Ideology and power*	366
8.6 *Pulling the threads together: finishing touches to the design of Natural Narratology*	371

In lieu of an epilogue	376
Notes	379
References	407
Texts	407
Criticism	418
Author index	443
Subject index	448

Preface

This book began its life during my stay at the National Humanities Center (Research Triangle Park, North Carolina), where I was completing a book on speech and thought representation. *Towards a 'Natural' Narratology* grew from material that was too unwieldy to be included in *The Fictions of Language and the Languages of Fiction* since I found that the larger narratological issues that I was broaching required nothing short of a radical reconceptualization of narratology, indeed required the creation of a new narrative paradigm. In the meantime I had also started on a project examining narrative structure in late medieval and early modern English narrative on which I continued work during a sojourn at Freiburg on a Humboldt fellowship. In this way my earlier (pre)occupation with the representation of consciousness, my long-time narratological interests and training, and this new project dealing with early English texts all came together to produce what for some people may remain a very diversified bill of fare, featuring conversational storytelling and Literature (with a capital L), linguistics and narratology, postmodernist issues and questions of literary theory.

Towards a 'Natural' Narratology proposes to redefine narrativity in terms of cognitive ('natural') parameters, moving beyond formal narratology into the realm of pragmatics, reception theory and constructivism. Unlike traditional narratology, this new model attempts to institute organic frames of reading rather than formal concepts or categories that are defined in terms of binary oppositions. Unlike most other narrative theories, moreover, the new paradigm is explicitly and deliberately *historical*. The *towards* in the title reflects not merely the preliminary nature of the proposed cognitive and organicist model; it also refers to the chronological path which individual chapters trace from storytelling in the oral language to medieval, early modern, realist, Modernist and postmodernist types of writing. It is only by means of this diachronic journey through English literature that the conceptual tools which are requisite for a 'natural' narratology could be developed.

In contrast to the 'classic' narratologies of Bal, Chatman, Genette, Prince or Stanzel, this model sets out to discuss narrativity, *not* from the vantage point of the realist and Modernist novel or short story, but from the perspective of those discourse types which have hitherto attracted comparatively little sustained analysis: oral and pseudo-oral types of storytelling, including conversational narrative and oral history; historical writing; early forms of written narrative (the medieval verse epic, medieval histories and saints' lives, storytelling in early letters from the fourteenth to the sixteenth centuries, narratives of the Elizabethan age up to Aphra Behn); and, at the other end of the spectrum, postmodernist literature. The latter field includes fairly well-known modes of writing such as neutral narrative and the present-tense novel, but additionally embraces fiction in the second person and in the *we* form, or texts employing *it, one* as well as the German *man* or French *on*; *skaz*-type narratives; and experimental writing from Beckett to Maurice Roche, by Clarice Lispector, Kazuo Ishiguro or Christa Wolf. Such an emphasis on what I am tempted to call the non-canonical forms of narrative (non-canonical, that is, within present-day theoretical discussions of the novel) triggers a number of modifications of current narratological paradigms as well as raising some serious methodological issues about the basic presuppositions of the classic typologies. An analysis of non-canonical narrative therefore prepares the way for fresh reconceptualizations of the storytelling mode, resulting in the proposal of a new narratological paradigm that is based on cognitive parameters and a reader-response framework, and it also accommodates fictional and non-fictional types of narrative. From this perspective, the realist underpinnings of classical narratology can be transcended in the direction of an analysis that posits realism as the special case of the model, namely as that context which allows the fullest application of mimetic interpretative reading strategies.

As explained more fully in Chapter 1, the term '*natural*' in the title feeds from three separate disciplines and areas of knowledge. It acknowledges a fundamental inspiration from natural narrative, i.e. unelicited conversational storytelling, and relies on the results of much research in discourse analysis in the Labovian tradition. Second, there is an allusion to natural linguistics which in one manifestation (the Austrian school linked with the name of Wolfgang Dressler) deals with cognitive parameters that relate to a theory of naturalness. Finally, the reception-oriented approach in which I engage enlists Jonathan Culler's concept of naturalization and redeploys it for the purpose of narrative *re-cognization* during the reading process. My proposal renames and redefines Culler's concept and introduces the term *narrativization*.

Fed from these three sources (natural narrative, the linguistics of naturalness, Culler's naturalization), the new model centrally incorporates findings about natural narrative, situating conversational storytelling at the very heart of 'natural' narratology. By attempting to cover as many different kinds of narrative as possible, the methodology followed in this book parallels my approach in *The Fictions of Language and the Languages of Fiction*, where I deliberately concentrated on non-canonical examples of free indirect discourse. Thus, readers will find novels from the eighteenth to the early twentieth centuries underrepresented in comparison with earlier and later writing, which receives much more extensive coverage. Moreover, texts discussed in this book are almost exclusively drawn from literatures in the English language because my training and expertise are in English studies, and because I rely on much language-specific linguistic groundwork relating to discourse markers, tense usage and syntactic structures which would make a cross-linguistic comparison difficult to handle. Nevertheless, in the later chapters dealing with experimental writing there are some excursions into German, French and Spanish territory in an attempt to complete the general picture. For easy reference translations have been provided for the medieval material and for the French and German quotations.

This book is primarily conceived as a contribution to narratology, yet I hope that its historical aspects will also make it accessible to a wider audience of scholars in the field of English literature. With this double interest group in mind, I may perhaps suggest that narratologists concentrate on the framing theoretical Chapters 1 and 8, with forays into Chapters 5, 6 and 7, which (especially Chapter 5) deal with specifically narratological issues. Literary critics with more general interests may perhaps want to browse through Chapter 1 and concentrate on the historical presentation in Chapters 3, 4 and 7. Chapter 2 provides an introduction to various kinds of oral storytelling and will be of interest mainly to the non-linguist trying to get her bearings in unknown territory.

The structure which I have chosen for this study is circular. After a playful reflection on the liminality of the 'natural' I start with an introduction to the theory of Natural Narratology and close the circle at the end by trying to integrate this new model with the traditional typologies. In the central chapters (Chapters 2 to 7) I proceed chronologically, starting with oral types of narrative (Chapter 2), and continue with a chapter on medieval and early modern texts (Chapter 3). Chapter 4 argues that from a perspective of narrative structure the fiction of Aphra Behn was crucial to the invention of the novel. The second half of Chapter 4 provides a rough outline of the relevant stages in the development of the novel from realist to Modernist fiction. The chapter closes with a discussion of neutral narrative which serves as an example of fiction that begins to move away from the automatic institution of natural parameters. Chapter 5 concerns itself with late nineteenth- and early twentieth-century texts that employ unexpected perspectival combinations and require a reshuffling of cognitive resources. With Chapters 6 and 7 the book moves into its postmodernist phase. Chapter 6 deals with superficially formal aspects of narrative: the use of pronouns and tense. These topics in turn have quite serious implications for several central areas in narrative theory. Chapter 7 examines the narrativization of various kinds of recalcitrant material, mostly radical linguistic experiments. The chapter tests the applicability of the concept of narrativization and documents the limits of this reading strategy. Chapter 8, finally, closes the circle and returns to theoretical and narratological subjects, rounding off the model as projected in Chapter 1. Among other issues, Chapter 8 considers at length how the boundaries between the different genres might be redrawn in the wake of my redefinition of narrativity. It also provides a discussion of the status of ideology within a narratological model.

TYPOGRAPHICAL CONVENTIONS

The following quotational and typographical conventions are observed in this book.

In all quotations from both literary and non-literary sources, emphasis in the original text is rendered in italics, and my own emphases are given in bold italics. Documentation in quotations from literary sources includes: the title of the work cited; the volume, part or book number in capital roman numerals; the relevant chapter in small roman numerals; author's name and publication date of edition quoted; page and/or line numbers. Volume and chapter information has been provided to facilitate the tracing of passages in different editions.

Acknowledgements

As a consequence of its rather involved history, this book has in the past four years significantly affected my life and that of people around me. Many friends and colleagues have given me invaluable feedback on earlier versions of individual chapters. I would particularly like to thank Dorrit Cohn, Marcel Cornis-Pope, Hilary Dannenberg, Andrew Gibson, Paul Goetsch, Manfred Jahn, Brian McHale, Ansgar Nünning, Brian Richardson and Gudrun Rogge-Wiest, all of whose perceptive remarks and patience with the imperfections of early drafts I greatly appreciated.

This study could not have been completed had I not had the necessary funding as well as dispensation from departmental duties. I would like to thank the Andrew W. Mellon Foundation and the American Council of Learned Societies for making possible my year at the National Humanities Center in 1990–91, where first drafts of Chapters 1 and 5 were produced, and the Alexander von Humboldt Foundation for awarding me a fellowship at the research centre for orality and literacy issues here in Freiburg in 1993–94. Both the National Humanities Center and the Freiburg *Sonderforschungsbereich* 321 have been wonderful host institutions and have made my sojourns at Chapel Hill and Freiburg pleasant and productive ones. I would particularly like to register my gratitude to the staff of the National Humanities Center and, at the *Sonderforschungsbereich*, to Wolfgang Raible, whose personal commitment and courtesy have transformed this research institution into something akin to a warm and lively family gathering.

Help with the typing of early versions of the text has come from Karen Carroll and Linda Morgan at the National Humanities Center. I also wish to thank Nóirín Veselaj for extensive typing assistance both during my Humboldt fellowship and at the final redaction of the text. My greatest obligation, however, is to Luise Lohmann, whose expert handling of the manuscript and uncomplaining patience with my numerous extensive revisions were greatly appreciated. For editorial assistance and help with the proofreading and indexing I wish to thank my team at Freiburg, Vera Alexander, Hilary Dannenberg, Stefan Jeanjour, Bettina Krukemeyer, Christopher Mischke and Gudrun Rogge-Wiest.

Grateful acknowledgement is made to Stephen Greenblatt for permission to quote extensively from 'Towards a Poetics of Culture' (1989) and to Charles Tomlinson for allowing me to reprint sections of 'The Request' and 'The Castle' (from Tomlinson 1985). Permission to quote from Fay Weldon's 'Weekend' in *Watching Me, Watching You* (1981) has been granted by Fay Weldon and by Sheil Land Associates Ltd and is herewith acknowledged with thanks. I am also grateful to the Suhrkamp Verlag for allowing me to print an extract from E.Y. Meyer's novel *In Trubschachen* (1973/1974), and to the Rotbuch Verlag for granting permission to quote passages from Heiner Müller's 'Bildbeschreibung' (1985). Special thanks go to Elizabeth Couper-Kuhlen for having given me access to her collection of transcribed conversational narratives and for allowing me to quote from them.

Prologue in the wilderness

Let us consider, for example, not the President's Hollywood career but a far more innocent California pastime, a trip to Yosemite National Park. One of the most popular walks at Yosemite is the Nevada Falls Trail. So popular, indeed, is this walk that the Park Service has had to pave the first miles of the trail in order to keep them from being dug into trenches by the heavy traffic. At a certain point the asphalt stops, and you encounter a sign that tells you that you are entering the wilderness. You have passed then from the National Forests that surround the park – forests that serve principally as state-subsidized nurseries for large timber companies and hence are not visibly distinguishable from the tracts of privately owned forest with which they are contiguous – to the park itself, marked by the payment of admission to the uniformed ranger at the entrance kiosk, and finally to a third and privileged zone of publicly demarcated Nature. This zone, called the wilderness, is marked by the abrupt termination of the asphalt and by a sign that lists the rules of behaviour that you must now observe: no dogs, no littering, no fires, no camping without a permit, and so forth. The wilderness then is signalled by an intensification of the rules, an intensification that serves as the condition of an escape from the asphalt.

You can continue on this trail then until you reach a steep cliff on to which the guardians of the wilderness have thoughtfully bolted a cast-iron stairway. The stairway leads to a bridge that spans a rushing torrent, and from the middle of the bridge you are rewarded with a splendid view of Nevada Falls. On the railing that keeps you from falling to your death as you enjoy your vision of the wilderness, there are signs – information about the dimensions of the falls, warnings against attempting to climb the treacherous, mist-slickened rocks, trail markers for those who wish to walk further – and an anodyzed aluminium plaque on which are inscribed inspirational, vaguely Wordsworthian sentiments by the California environmentalist John Muir. The passage, as best I can recall, assures you that in years to come you will treasure the image you have before you. And next to these words, also etched into the aluminium, is precisely an image: a photograph of Nevada Falls taken from the very spot on which you stand.

2 *Prologue in the wilderness*

> *The pleasure of this moment – beyond the pleasure of the mountain air and the waterfall and the great boulders and the deep forest of Lodgepole and Jeffrey pine – arises from the unusually candid glimpse of the process of circulation that shapes the whole experience of the park. The wilderness is at once secured and obliterated by the official gestures that establish its boundaries; the natural is set over against the artificial through means that render such an opposition meaningless. The eye passes from the 'natural' image of the waterfall to the aluminium image, as if to secure a difference (for why else bother to go to the park at all? Why not simply look at a book of pictures?), even as that difference is effaced. The effacement is by no means complete – on the contrary, parks like Yosemite are one of the ways in which the distinction between nature and artifice is constituted in our society – and yet the Park Service's plaque on the Nevada Falls bridge conveniently calls attention to the interpenetration of nature and artifice that makes the distinction possible.*
>
> *What is missing from this exemplary fable of capitalist aesthetics is the question of property relations, since the National Parks exist precisely to suspend or marginalize that question through the ideology of protected public space. Everyone owns the parks. That ideology is somewhat bruised by the actual development of a park like Yosemite, with its expensive hotel, a restaurant that has a dress code, fancy gift shops and the like, but it is not entirely emptied out; even the administration of the right-wing Secretary of the Interior James Watt stopped short of permitting a private golf course to be constructed on parkgrounds, and there was public outrage when a television production company that had contracted to film a series in Yosemite decided to paint the rocks to make them look more realistic. What we need is an example that combines recreation or entertainment, aesthetics, the public sphere, and private property. The example most compelling to a literary critic like myself is not a political career or a national park but a novel.*
>
> (Greenblatt 1989: 8–10)

Stephen Greenblatt's humorous anecdote about a trip to Yosemite National Park provides a perfect illustration of some of the issues with which I will be dealing in this book, while at the same time marking a limit to my own enquiry into fiction and the novel. Where Greenblatt's story serves as an exemplum of the ideology of representation and opens up into an analysis of the capitalist underpinnings of the supposedly 'natural', my own enquiry will be directed towards narration, narrativity and fictionality, with the question of ideological underpinnings relegated to the horizons of the analysis. It is my contention that, paradoxically, we still know much too little about narrative to indulge in any easy generalizations about its commitments to, and ensnarements by, its political, societal and ideological embedding. At the same time, I maintain, it is only in the light of recent deconstructivist, Lacanian and New Historicist insights into the workings of the symbolic that one could dare tackle the concept of the natural in both its complexity and intrinsic paradoxicality. No immediate access to the natural nor a naïve reduction of the natural to pure undiluted Otherness can any longer claim legitimacy so that a theoretical approach that exploits the concept of the natural needs to clarify its own position from the very start.

Like Baudrillard's America, Greenblatt's Yosemite Park appears to the eyes of the beholder as a structure of signs that traces a significant trajectory and culminates in a paradoxical deconstruction of these signs' canvassed meaning. The hypothetical nature enthusiast follows the officially designed trail of signifiers to their ever denser and allegedly epiphanic source only to find, with the reader, that the promised reward, on reaching the destination of the visitor's semiotic quest, deconstructs itself by symbolic overkill. The natural quite brazenly displays itself as a mere representation of the real thing which, across the abyss, continues to haunt the quester's imagination and eludes the grasp of the explorer. In this tale of frustrated mastery over the symbolic 'other' the natural thus operates both as the prime signifier and the elusive signified. Its function can be compared to that of the textual 'real' in the realist novel with its paradoxical relation to the 'Real' of human cognition. Greenblatt's anecdote not only illustrates the short-circuit of signification in the symbolic code which keeps projecting an imaginary other but fails to grasp the Real; it additionally mirrors the perplexities of fictional writing, of trying to constitute an imaginary world, which is the 'real' world in yet a different shape. Greenblatt's 'exemplary fable', like the fictional detail in Barthes's arguments about the *effet de réel*, attests to the trustworthiness of its own discourse. Not only is this an anecdote *about* the effects of the real in the guise of the natural; the story of this trip, generalized and ahistorical as it may be, additionally invites the reader's active collusion so that she comes to share the various facets of the experience apostrophized in the fable. This applies no doubt most forcefully to those numerous readers who can compare Greenblatt's narrative description with their own personal experience of visiting the Nevada Falls Trail.

Greenblatt's utilization of the anecdote as a marker of the real within his own critical discourse moreover instantiates the late Joel Fineman's characterization of the function of the anecdote in historical writing (Fineman 1989). According to Fineman, in historical discourse anecdotes serve as the prime signifiers of the historical real. At the same time anecdotes paradoxically tend to flaunt their literacy. As Fineman emphasizes, most anecdotes consist of an entirely fictional dialogue that is said to have taken place between the historical protagonists. The very constructedness of fictional dialogue which I noted in connection with my thesis of schematic language representation in *The Fictions of Language and the Languages of Fiction* can therefore be found to obtain also in the realm of the historical anecdote and to perform a crucial function within the

4   *Prologue in the wilderness*

semiotic economy of the historiographical discourse. Just as all language representation is sheer invention but projects an illusion of veracity in accordance with familiar schemas of utterance and expression, the historical anecdote serves to attest to historical truth by inventing a fictional scene that is meant to highlight the specificity of the historical *in actu*. Greenblatt's anecdote, fittingly in the second-person present-tense mode of imaginary projection, ascribes to the real of the story an at best fictional (i.e. verisimilar) status: it is an 'exemplary fable', part of an instructional discourse whose moral advertises itself in the appealing form of a poststructuralist exemplum.

Let us consider the narrative shape of this exemplary tale. Unlike the historical anecdote and unlike the typically anecdotal form of jokes, Greenblatt's story exceeds the familiar structure of the anecdote in both functional and formal respects. On the formal side, this story of an imaginary trip through Yosemite National Park lacks the typically anecdotal climax of a dialogue with a punch line or a similarly climactic focus. Functionally, the hypothetical setup of this purely fictive 'fable' marks the experience as repeatable (on the lines of Derrida's *iterable*)[1] so that, through its very ability of being reiterated, i.e. re-experienced, the fictive comes to acquire the connotations of the real. (Barthes's *effet de réel*, on the other hand, has no truck with iterability.) Greenblatt is here able to combine two very disparate modes of discourse, the oral tale (the anecdote) and the decidedly experimental technique of second-person fiction with its realist substratum of the guidebook text (a prototypically iterative genre describing acts of sightseeing to be repeated by each reader-tourist). It is on account of this combination that the passage so admirably lends itself to the purposes of the present study, informing my conception of the 'natural' of storytelling in its most mundane as well as most artificial, i.e. experimental, incarnations. The natural, as Greenblatt implies, is that which requires the most insistent signification by means of (artificial) signifiers – just as the supposedly mimetic representation of direct discourse is constituted by a maximum of artificial markers of alterity.[2] Man's 'natural' environment is the asphalt; the domain of the natural, which through symbolic or ideological intervention has acquired the connotation of originarity, therefore only gradually moves towards and develops into the 'real' natural as that area which requires additional marking and where the asphalt abruptly ceases. On similar lines the textual real, although supposedly accessible through a naturalistic reading of the discourse, in fact requires a sophisticated deployment of rhetoric (the rhetoric of the verisimilar) to mark its realism, and in historical discourse: its historicity.

Greenblatt's excursion into the officially demarcated realm of the wilderness defines nature in opposition to culture and then deconstructs this dichotomy by exposing the cultural embeddedness of the very notion of the wilderness: the wilderness needs to be delimited by means of cultural signifiers; progress towards the heart of the wilderness involves an intensification of these signifying strategies; and contact with the real wilderness is repeatedly deferred to the point where Nature at last comes into view but at the same time remains off limits across the abyss of the bridge, framed by the iron rail and labelled by scriptoral and visual representations.[3] This understanding of the term *natural*, and of its inherent self-deconstruction, can be contrasted with the more familiar dichotomy of the natural as opposed to the unnatural, perverse or 'deviant'. In that dichotomy, the natural occupies the unmarked pole and constitutes the privileged term of the opposition. This structure of signification can be linked with insights from linguistic markedness theory, which contrasts default values with specifically marked options that are foregrounded. Such oppositional markedness relations are liable to deconstructionist treatment, especially from the perspective of their ideological (ab)uses. Thus, the dichotomy between the natural and the unnatural can be analysed very much in terms of deconstructionist arguments about margin vs. centre, or in relation to the insidious workings of the supplement. The natural/unnatural dichotomy also lends itself to illustrating the dialectic between a number of binary oppositions of major cultural and ideological import. Just as the *self* can be said to be constituted by its opposition to an *other*, the so-called *normal* or natural likewise emerges from its opposition to that which is experienced in terms of extra-ordinariness, or of deviation from expected norms. Such norms and conventions are cognized precisely in comparison with the unconventional and abnormal. Inversely, the constitution of the self by means of the other frequently serves to extrapolate those aspects of the self which one wishes to deny – shifting the blame onto the victims. (For instance, one could argue that conquistadores' repeated tales about natives' cannibalism serve to provide a cover for the fact that European explorers may have had to take recourse to human flesh in order to survive when cut off from their supplies.)

Theoretical accounts on these lines have become the stock-in-trade of cultural criticism and provide a convincing analysis of the societal constitution of, for instance, heterosexuality or whiteness as the default value against which one then tends to define ethnic and orientational minorities in terms of their inherent (but really constructed) 'otherness'. This clearly marked observable other, however, is not at all homogeneous (including a host of diverse ethnicities and orientations), and the default term itself is liable to embrace a number of national and patriotic selves as well as some potential others: white foreigners, middle-class third generation immigrants, etc. The dialectic of self-constitution therefore operates with great facility even where the position of the Other consists in a heterogeneous collection of differentiated others. It also thrives upon the inherent indeterminacy of the concept of the normal and the natural, supporting a variety of discriminatory discourses by moulding the denotations and connotations of the normal at its discretion.

Whereas the mechanics of opposing self and other is fairly clear-cut, the case is much less well defined when it comes to the opposition between the natural and the unnatural. In cultural contexts like those invoked above the natural comes to double the function of the self, that of supposed normality, of the cultural default value. However, in contrast to the self/other dichotomy, there appears to be no generally accepted oppositional term that will inevitably provide an antithesis to the natural. Except in the ethnic and sexological realm where the barbaric and the perverse figure as standard opposites, the natural can in fact be contrasted with a variety of quite dissimilar others. The 'unnatural' can be conceived of in terms of the abnormal, but it is also conceptualized in terms of the cultural, the artificial, the civilized, the fictional, the contrived or – most generally – the human. Although some of these opposites should clearly be identified as negative foils (the artificial and the fictional being prime examples), the blanket terms 'civilized' or 'human', on the contrary, easily support an inversion of the evaluative poles: the natural may be imagined as the uncultured, and the barbaric as a kind of savage substratum of civilization. Indeed, historically speaking, the positive connotations of the wilderness have been with us for only a fairly brief period; after all, they derive from a proto-romantic critique of civilization as being intrinsically more inhuman(e) than the natural society of the (now 'noble') savages outside the civilized world. In fact, the opposition of nature vs. civilization, and particularly nature vs. technology, has remained an arena of ideological strife with fluctuating alliances. (Much topical political argument in this area is triggered precisely by a general lack of consensus on what exactly is 'natural' and to what extent a curtailment of, or improvement upon, nature would be legally and morally justified. Contested areas of application include, for instance, the issues of artificial insemination and genetic manipulation.) My first point is, therefore, that – unlike the *normal* – the counterpoint of the *natural* tends to disperse into quite incompatible oppositions with differing evaluations not only *between* the individual dichotomies but even *within* any one opposition. Thus, when opposing the *natural* and the *artificial*, the natural is coded positively; whereas in the opposition *natural* vs. *human*, the positive evaluation tends to fall on the human end of the scale. Conversely, the *natural* vs. *human* dichotomy can equally operate with an evaluative inversion of these terms. Ecologists (and Romantics) tend to evaluate the natural in positive terms, whereas farmers may well panic about the distressing aspects of Nature (e.g. natural disasters). That such a lack of consensus should attach to the concept of the natural follows directly from the fact that *all* of these oppositional terms are directly or indirectly linked to the position of mankind; civilization, technology, mind and imagination are all human attributes supposedly absent in nature. Humans are therefore typically imaged in two contrastive ways: as standing in opposition to nature (or even as being 'better than' nature); and – from a biological and theological perspective

– as *part* of nature. The peculiar vagaries of the concept of the natural can hence be explained as deriving from the basic position of man in his biologically conditioned habitat, from man's 'immundation' so to speak. This inescapable embodiment in the natural has recently provided a major metaphor for 'natural' linguistics; in the theoretical framework of natural linguistics man's enmeshment or engagement with his environment operates as a central constitutive feature and as a fundamental cognitive frame.

Above I noted two very different uses of the term *natural*: one in which the natural paradoxically turns out to be constituted by semiotic overkill and therefore emerges as the result of (artificial) signifying structures; and one in which the natural is dichotomously opposed to a number of 'unnatural' *others* that take a variety of different and incompatible shapes. The first use is Greenblatt's, the second belongs with a wider field of sociology and gender studies. Both uses of the term are informed by the potential for deconstruction: most clearly in Greenblatt's case, but centrally so also in the current treatments of the no longer innocent deployment of the natural/unnatural dichotomy. Before placing my own understanding and differentiated uses of the term *natural* against these two perspectives – and it will be seen that the cognitive viewpoint which I adopt needs to be set in relation to *both* Greenblatt's *and* the standard sociological paradigm of the natural – I would briefly like to remark on the terms 'contrived', 'artificial', and 'fictional' as they occur in Greenblatt's little fable, where they operate as major constituents in the dialectic of the natural. It has to be observed, to start with, that Greenblatt's 'natural' is set in explicit opposition to the tarmac of civilization which encloses as well as invades the wilderness much as the privately owned forests encroach upon the territory of the publicly owned national park. The tarmac and civilization therefore de-fine, i.e. delimit, the wilderness at the same time as they erase the demarcation. It is of course no coincidence, indeed it is one of the implicit ironies of Greenblatt's tale, that he conceives of the wilderness in terms of ownership. This immediately invokes the background of historical invasion and conquest of the wilderness in the history of native American subjugation, decimation and extermination. Although nowhere alluded to explicitly, Greenblatt's research on the Spanish Conquest in *Marvellous Possessions* (1991/1992) suggests just such a parallel. The colonial background invokes a definition of the wilderness in which possession and exploration are crucially at stake. Whereas Native Americans saw the earth as belonging in equal measure to all creatures (including mankind) and therefore believed nature to be sacrosanct from human appropriation, the colonists' ideology, on the contrary, was one of private property and the civilizing mission of Manifest Destiny. Greenblatt's characterization of the wilderness as designated symbolically, i.e. linguistically, by the intensification of demarcational and behavioural rules therefore seems to mirror Nature's complete subjection to the code of civilization. In Yosemite, Nature appears to be part of, or an inset within, civilization and is therefore suitably conceptualized in purely symbolic terms: prohibitions against trespassing, in the institutionalized language of authority; the privileged discourse of poetic effusion (the Muir quotation); and the image of the waterfall with its denotational superscription. The waterfall itself remains off limits, with human access coming to an abrupt halt on the bridge which spans but does not erase the dwindling gulf beneath. The bridge and its railing constitute the boundary between the linguistic (or symbolic) realm and the ostensive domain of the natural in its unadulterated alterity. The wilderness proper, although labelled, depicted and interpreted for the viewer, eludes *physical* appropriation and thereby constructs the natural as signified within the symbolic realm of civilization. The natural signifies the privileged experience of that which has been lost irretrievably and now has to be called into existence by fictional means: through symbolic denomination and, non-coincidentally, by means of poetic invocation.

Greenblatt's account of this adventure concentrates on the process of circulation, on the symbolic economy of one's experience of the park. It is within this frame that one needs to place the ironical and paradoxical observations which punctuate his text. The bridge, as we have noted, constitutes the limit of the symbolic realm, and it is therefore fitting that the enjoyment of one's vision of the wilderness (note that it is merely a *vision* and no real *experience*!) should be secured by a railing (the symbol of paternalistic authority) which benevolently (but prohibitively) 'keeps you from falling to your death'. The intensification of the rules as one approaches the heart of the wilderness is therefore motivated not so much by the *preservation* of nature as by the (benevolent but prohibitive) attempt to evade its dangers, dangers which apparently require symbolic and institutional overkill. As Baudrillard puts it: '[...] it is dangerous to unmask images, since they dissimulate the fact that there is nothing behind them' (1988: 169). Another ironic touch of Greenblatt's can be noted in the appended anecdote – this time a 'real' historical anecdote – about the film company's painting of the rocks 'to make them look more realistic' (i.e. 'more natural').[4] Whereas all previous encroachments on nature had been in terms of framing, the constitutive gulf between the natural and the artificial is here mimetically erased, violating the most basic rule of the symbolic economy. The paradox itself of course offers little surprise to the reader who is familiar with the tricks of eighteenth-century landscape gardens with their fake ruins, or with Oscar Wilde's reflections on the influence of art on life. It is, not surprisingly, a *film* company that requires cosmetic touches to ensure its audience's access to the 'real': film is the medium that pretends to the greatest possible mimeticism while at the same time being constrained to deploy the most sophisticated technology to fake that effect of the real.

Prologue in the wilderness 9

The anecdote about the painted rocks not only darkly hints that art requires major tampering with the real if it wants to signify that real on its symbolic plane, but additionally refers us back to a somewhat obscure passage in Greenblatt's previous paragraph where he argued that 'the natural is set over against the artificial through means that render such an opposition meaningless'. The opposition between the natural and the artificial comes to be meaningless because it is a difference at the same time marked symbolically and deictically and erased by the process of designatory identification. (The waterfall is pointed out but also represented pictorially.) What Greenblatt appears to suggest is that on the bridge the very oppositions that constitute the natural (as that which does not 'naturally' exist within the human realm of civilization) are candidly deconstructed by putting the waterfall and its image in metonymic proximity. As a result the difference and identity of image and waterfall become unmasterable, uncontrollable within the opposition's symbolic economy.

> The simulacrum is never that which conceals the truth – it is the truth which conceals that there is none.
> The simulacrum is true.
> (Baudrillard 1988: 166)[5]

Like the film company's realization that viewers will prefer painted rocks to the real thing, this constellation paves the way for Greenblatt's acute observation, summarizing Muir's words, that one will, in the wake of one's visit to Yosemite, treasure this 'image'. That image, surely, refers to the photo on the plaque next to Muir's 'inspirational' words. The diagnosis proves correct for Greenblatt's own experience of the park, since he remembers the photograph but only vaguely recalls the message of Muir's 'sentiments'. Like a good tourist, Greenblatt therefore zooms in on the 'image', not on the *view* (a second-hand experience of the wilderness in any case), and he does so by means of a fable that traces the fictional (he says 'artificial') nature of the national park's 'distinction between nature and artifice'. The exercise reveals that it is the deconstruction of that distinction (the 'interpenetration of nature and artifice') that makes the distinction possible in the first place.

It is here, then, that we finally reach the question of mimesis and of fictional contrivance. There is no doubt that the image of the waterfall is meant to mirror the natural model. In fact the image is specified to be a *photograph*, thus suggesting an even closer affinity to the film company's concern about real rockscape. Moreover, visitors are likely to take a picture from this very spot, reproducing simulacra of the image on the plaque. The 'vaguely Wordsworthian' hope that tourists will treasure this image in years to come, from this perspective, evokes the very mundane (unintended?) reading of photo albums, displacing the inspirational sentiments which are both the medium and the message of the Muir quotation. The natural therefore comes to be situated on the same level as the mimetic, namely as the product of an illusion generated and engineered by the narrative to evoke that which cannot be imitated or reproduced but merely represented by means of suitable ('objective') correlatives of linguistic or pictorial shape. The natural, such as we encounter it in discourse, has always already been reshaped symbolically and is therefore an interpretative effect, a discourse rather than a referent beyond the proverbial abyss of language and mind. Whatever we encounter as natural within the national park (up to the railing on the bridge) is necessarily prestructured symbolically (contrived), man-made (artificial), and fictional (art). Narrative structure, artifice and fictionality in Greenblatt's tale mirror the extent to which these properties are foregrounded; they are not deviations from a natural pregiven that is unstructured, self-generating and real, but are instead deliberate barings of the constitutive narrative economy.

My own uses of the term *natural* cut across the distinction made so far between Greenblatt's informed de-aestheticization of the wilderness and the standard natural vs. unnatural opposition, although I also re-enact the inherent deconstructionist potential of both approaches. *Towards a 'Natural' Narratology* continues the direction taken in *The Fictions of Language and the Languages of Fiction* (Fludernik 1993a) by firmly reiterating my insights about the artificial nature, inventedness and fictionality of the mimetic. In my previous study I illustrated this basic tenet with the example of speech and thought representation, arguing that the most patently mimetic, apparently verbatim rendering of another's speech act in fact needed to be marked most extensively by means of expressive features whose relation to an actual pre-existing utterance was entirely fictive. I now extend this insight on the lines of Greenblatt's analysis of the natural to cover, quite generally, all mimetic representation. Fictionality, I maintain, is located precisely in the evocation of such representational mimesis (also called realism). In contrast to the poststructuralist analyses of this paradox in deconstructionist research, however, I locate this dialectic – as in *The Fictions of Language and the Languages of Fiction* – in the realm of conversational storytelling, in the oral language, incorporating and creatively redeploying insights from discourse analysis and the study of natural narrative. This empirical basis provides me with a link to cognitive parameters of storytelling and story appreciation. Representational mimesis, it is argued, constitutes a primary cognitive strategy of reading (interpreting) narrative whether oral or literary. Alternative worlds in fiction, just like the supposedly real world of conversational storytelling, depend for their readability on natural, i.e. cognitive, parameters. The natural in my own theoretical setup is therefore *both* a construction (in terms of being a reading effect) *and* a pre-given frame of human cognization. To the extent that the natural relates to an effect of mimesis or realism, it is a constructed entity, a reading *effect*; in so far as the natural relies on, or reflects, basic cognitive processes which relate to human 'immundation', as I earlier called it, it can be opposed to what I will term the *non-natural* (rather than *un*natural). The non-natural here refers to strategies or aspects of discourse that do not have a natural grounding in familiar cognitive parameters or in familiar real-life situations.

My definition of the natural therefore combines the constructivist (and deconstructional) features of Greenblatt's analysis with the more standard dichotomies deployed in the sociological realm, and it sets these two approaches into perspective by aligning them with two different levels of the cognitive process: the level of basic cognitive parameters on the one hand and the level of significational processes on the other. Just as Greenblatt's fable documents that the cultural discourse about the pristine virtues of the wilderness serves manifestly capitalist purposes, my own appropriation of his trip up the Nevada Falls Trail exploits the narrative economy of the text in the interests of a narratological reconceptualization of the cognitive reading process. The railing which keeps you from falling to your death as you enjoy this stunning prospect is a linguistic and empirical rather than a semiotic or deconstructivist one, and the fundamental structure of signification outlined in this book persists into the more mundane realm of narratology which is regrettably devoid of exotic wildernesses and pseudo-Wordsworthian poetry. Except, of course, for the fanciful vagaries of this initial prologue and its exceptionally candid glimpse of the processes of mimesis that shape the reader's experience of the narratological wilderness.

1 Towards a 'natural' narratology

Let me start with an *apologia* for the title of this book. Three sources of inspiration have fed into the term *'natural' narratology*. For the moment I propose to keep the inverted commas on *'natural'* as an indication that I am very much aware of naïve and evaluative readings of that term and intend to eschew any prescriptive or moralistic interpretations. My espousal of this controversial label, as the prologue was meant to demonstrate, occurs at some level of sophistication. My own uses of the *'natural'* do not, however, merely reflect poststructuralist tenets. On the contrary, I attempt to cut through the threads of the deconstructionist and sociological debate and to institute a reconceptualization of the term within a more specifically cognitive perspective. My use of the concept of the *'natural'* relates to a framework of human embodiedness. It is from this angle that some cognitive parameters can be regarded as *'natural'* in the sense of 'naturally occurring' or 'constitutive of prototypical human experience'. The term *'natural'* is not applied to texts or textual techniques but exclusively to the *cognitive frames* by means of which texts are interpreted. Nor will the *'natural'* in these pages be opposed to the *unnatural*. Fictional experiments that manifestly exceed the boundaries of naturally occurring story(telling) situations are, instead, said to employ *non-natural* schemata.

The general framework for the theory is a constructivist one (Nünning 1989b, 1990a; Sternberg 1992; Jahn [under review]).[1] Readers actively construct meanings and impose frames on their interpretations of texts just as people have to interpret real-life experience in terms of available schemata. It will be argued that oral narratives (more precisely: narratives of spontaneous conversational storytelling) cognitively correlate with perceptual parameters of human experience and that these parameters remain in force even in more sophisticated written narratives, although the textual make-up of these stories changes drastically over time. Unlike the traditional models of narratology, narrativity (i.e. the quality of *narrativehood* in Gerald Prince's terminology[2]) is here constituted by what I call experientiality, namely by the quasi-mimetic evocation of 'real-life experience'. Experientiality can be aligned with actantial frames, but it also correlates with the evocation of consciousness or with the representation of a speaker role. Experientiality, as everything else in narrative, reflects a cognitive schema of embodiedness that relates to human existence and human concerns. The anthropomorphic bias of narratives and its correlation with the fundamental story parameters of personhood, identity, actionality, etc., have long been noted by theoreticians of narrative and have been recognized as constituting the rock-bottom level of story matter (G. Prince 1982; M.-L. Ryan 1991). Where the current proposal supersedes this setup is in the redefinition of narrativity *qua* experientiality *without* the necessity of any actantial groundwork. In my model there can therefore be narratives without plot, but there cannot be any narratives without a human (anthropomorphic) experiencer of some sort at some narrative level. This radical elimination of plot from my definition of narrativity is based on the results of research into oral narrative, where, as I will illustrate, the emotional involvement with the experience and its evaluation provide cognitive anchor points for the constitution of narrativity. Merely plot-oriented narratives are therefore here argued to represent a zero degree of narrativity even though they are traditionally endowed with proto-typical narrativity.

In Chapter 1 the basic ingredients for the new model and its general structure are laid out. A discussion of my precise theoretical position in comparison with current typologies, and an explanation of the full significance of the proposed reconceptualizations, particularly of my redefinition of *narrativity*, will be postponed until Chapter 8. At that stage the reader will have had the experience of observing how the model works in practice. I have also left an engagement with some other theoretical key issues to the end of the book. Narratological discussions frequently rely on a fairly slim realist corpus of texts, and I have therefore felt the need to broach these issues only after the reader has been introduced to a wide range of non-canonical narratives and is able to weigh competing theses against that evidence. Whereas Chapter 1 provides a guideline to the framework of the new theory, the final chapter closes the narrative and argumentative bracket by supplying some more in-depth treatments for professional narratologists. Chapters 1 and 8 are thus designed to mirror one another and frame the historical chapters which they embrace.

1.1 LINGUISTIC CONCEPTS OF THE NATURAL

1.1.1 Natural narrative

Natural narrative is a term that has come to define 'naturally occurring' storytelling in the linguistic literature of discourse analysis (Labov 1972). What will be called *natural narrative* in this book includes, mainly, spontaneous conversational storytelling, a term which would be more appropriate but is rather unwieldy. *Natural* narrative, in contradistinction to the wider area of *oral* narrative, comprises only spontaneous forms of (therefore conversational) storytelling but excludes oral poetry and folktale traditions of oral storytelling as they still exist, for instance, among Acadians in Nova Scotia.[3] Although oral poetry and its non-verse 'equivalents' will not be entirely neglected, they are considered to constitute a more literary (i.e. institutionalized) form of storytelling that cannot lay claim to being 'natural' in the same manner or to the same extent as conversational narration. Oral poetry, *qua* 'elaborated orality' (Koch and Österreicher 1985), although signally affected by the cognitive constraints of oral discourse production (and reception), requires quite different kinds of competence and performance levels from those sufficient for everyday spontaneous conversation.

Two points need to be stressed. On the one hand, oral storytelling comes in a great variety of forms and shapes (see Chapter 2), from spontaneous narration of personal experiences (natural narrative proper) to the telling of jokes and anecdotes, the retelling of *other* people's experience (narrative of vicarious experience), bare reports and summaries of events, the 'telling' of imaginary scenarios, all the way to the longer and culturally institutionalized forms which eventually developed into the epic and the folk tale. Within this range one needs to distinguish not only the quite different institutional settings of these various text and discourse types, allowing for a scale of formal and thematic structures that impinge on the production and shaping of such texts (note, for instance, the very strict formal and thematic requirements for jokes);[4] one should also examine the varying personal involvement of the teller, the range of linguistic, structural and thematic creativity allowed for each oral genre and the interaction between these institutional constraints and the personal performance features.

Besides the variety of oral discourse forms, I would like to emphasize, as a second major point, the tensions between orality, performativity and narrativity. Discussions of narrativity, even though they have partly relied on conceptually[5] oral texts (the folk tales of Vladimir Propp, the Greek myths analysed by Lévi-Strauss), have predominantly taken written and especially fictional texts as their object of demonstration. By moving both historical (i.e. non-fictional) and oral (non-written) forms into the centre of my enquiry, I radically depart from this tradition. Taking my bearings from E.M. Forster's *The king died and then the queen died of grief* (1974: 60), which has never convinced me of its exemplary narrativity[6] (and that not only on account of its lack of discursivity),[7] I wish to analyse literary narrative against the foil of naturally occurring forms of storytelling, arguing that natural narrative and jokes tell us more about the workings of narrativity even in more complex texts than do the pseudo-oral stories (fairy tales) and constructed example sentences (E.M. Forster's paradigm) on which narratologists have so frequently relied.

The narrativity which can be observed to emerge from spontaneous conversational storytelling is a holistic or organic as well as dialectically constituted phenomenon. Taking natural narrative as my departure point, I concentrate on the structural properties of conversational storytelling (its episodic structure) and on the dynamic interaction or dialectic between the news value of the tale and its impact on the experiencer's retrospective evaluation (reportability vs. narrative 'point'). Chapter 2 presents a full discussion of the basic types of natural narrative and their formal and experiential variations. A connection will be established between a number of formal points (linguistic markers) and episodic narrative structure, and it will be argued that cognitive parameters correlate with these formal aspects of natural narrative. Second, the entire frame of storytelling itself operates as a cognitively grounded frame. Natural narrative therefore supplies key conceptualizations for the study of all types of narrative.

In this book natural narrative is conceived as 'natural' exclusively in terms of its quality of spontaneous (re)production, and on the basis of its universality, its transcultural existence and significance. Natural narrative will not be considered in any way more 'normal' or 'non-artificial' than the written language; both oral and written forms of discourse are coequal, structurally determined symbolic media which operate within specific generic, cultural and contextual frames. Neither written nor oral forms of discourse can be produced or understood outside such a frame, and since such frames are determined by cultural, i.e. societal and ideological, circumstances, they cannot lay claim to any mythic 'naturalness'. Results from the analysis of even prototypically natural storytelling in spontaneous conversational settings indeed document the entirely structured nature of that discourse much on the lines of Derrida's insights into the basically 'written' (i.e. formal) nature of the spoken language. Thus, despite the use of the term '*natural*', any mythic or originary concepts of naturalness will here be decidedly repudiated.[8] As long as one starts out from a consideration of orality, and specifically of natural narrative, in terms of pure otherness or of an unstructured natural pre-existence and self-emergence, no significant similarities and influences can be observed between the oral and the literary language; which may, in fact, account for the near-complete silence on natural narrative within classic narratology. Interaction between the oral and the written, the spontaneous and the consciously structured, or between the apparently non-institutionalized and the societally determined generic (the legal, the theologico-moralistic, the literary, etc.), becomes possible only on the basis of comparable cognitive structurations which then prepare the ground for processes of intertextuality and cross-fertilization. My methodology therefore fully endorses the analyses of the deconstructionist debate, although I then move on to more pragmatic exploitations of these insights.

My approach moreover complements recent results regarding other aspects of the oral language such as oral syntax (Halford and Pilch 1990;

Chafe 1994) which have decisively put to rest any previous notions of conversational language as unstructured, ungrammatical, pure performance, or pure unreflected naturalness.[9] The discovery of oral syntax and of the existence of discourse strategies which display a wide range of converging structural and dynamic configurations has entirely discredited such earlier snobbery and is forcing us to rethink completely our formal models of linguistics. Although the *practical* result of discourse analysis has been to carve out new research areas and to put traditional, particularly generative, approaches in their place, the eventual upshot of this development is likely to be a formalization of language within a new paradigm of linguistics, this time from the point of view of oral discourse, a paradigm that incorporates the written language as one of several particularly complex discourse modes.

The use of the term '*natural*' in *natural narrative* also needs to be distinguished from Barbara Herrnstein Smith's concept of *natural discourse* (B. Smith 1978/1983), which she contrasts with *fictive* discourse. Smith defines natural discourse as 'all utterances, spoken or inscribed, that can be taken as someone's saying something, sometime, somewhere' (1983: 47)[10] in the sense that this then constitutes a non-fictive speech act. Smith here relies on Searle's definition of the fictional speech act, a model that (I think, illegitimately) transfers a communicative structure on to literary discourse and is then constrained to define the literary speech act as make-believe.[11] For instance, Smith argues that at the beginning of Tolstoy's *Death of Ivan Ilyich* the text pretends to belong to the genre of the biography: 'Tolstoy is, if you like, pretending to be *writing* a biography while actually *fabricating* one' (ibid.: 329–30). Smith's prototype for fictive discourse is poetry which is said to be about language. Since I am concerned with narrative only, which is not a speech act in the ordinary sense of the term, my own definitions in fact cut across those of Smith's. Indeed, my understanding of natural narrative counteracts a distinction between fiction and non-fiction on her lines.[12] Issues of truth and referentiality are bracketed in my account. Discourse analysis, one can note, lends itself to very diverse literary appropriations.

The major theoretical function of natural narrative in this study consists in supplying a prototype for the constitution of narrativity. Moreover, natural narrative, it is argued, operates as one central productive pattern of cognitive origin which regulates the textual production and reception of new naturally non-occurring discourse types and modes (Chapter 6). The term *natural* here, as elsewhere, serves less as a referential marker of essentialist meaning than as a functional operator that makes it possible to discuss similarities and distinctions between observable discourse types. Although natural narrative is taken to be cognitively prior to, and more basic than, other types of narrative, this priority will be of a typological and prototypical kind and cannot simply be equated with arguments of diachronic precedence or of a privileged generic status. Natural narrative not only serves as a prototype in my theory; within my argumentative discourse the concept of the natural itself displays prototype effects.[13] Prototypicality and embodiment are not reducible to idealist positions, but instead lend themselves to metaphoric extensions and transfers that increase the potential applicability of the new paradigm. My recourse to natural narrative therefore resembles Alfred Schütz's sociological recourse to everyday experience as a prototype of human relations.[14]

1.1.2 The linguistic theory of naturalness: from frames to prototypes

In recent years new developments in linguistics have introduced the term 'natural' to designate aspects of language which appear to be regulated or motivated by cognitive parameters based on man's experience of embodiedness in a real-world context. The term features as a label in the Austrian linguistic school of *Natürlichkeitstheorie*[15] ('theory of naturalness'). Similar phenomena, though not necessarily dubbed '*natural*', emerge from research in the area of cognitive linguistics, particularly prototype theory,[16] and from many of the contributions to the journal *Cognitive Linguistics*. Recent studies in iconicity likewise deploy a cognitive framework.[17] A third, largely independent current (which prototype theory claims to embrace) is the older discipline called *frame theory* as initiated by Schank and Abelson (1977). Frame theory (now at its MOP stage)[18] attempts to explain the cognitive comprehension of real-life situations in terms of holistic situation schemata. Such schemata (whether frames, scripts or schemas)[19] are of a prototype nature; they lend themselves to metonymic and metaphoric extension and can be used as points of reference and comparison, thereby helping users to master new contexts.

The above attempts to situate language and human understanding in relation to holistic cognitive parameters have been developed by so-called cognitive linguistics. Cognitive linguistics tries to locate linguistic processes within more general processes of cognitive comprehension. These cognitive processes, it is argued, relate to human embodiedness in a natural environment and are essentially motivated by metaphors of embodiment. To take some simple examples. Categorization of entities in the world depends on people's practical *use* of them and on people's *expectations*. For this reason so-called basic-level concepts (*horse, tree, flower*) are immediately useful in terms of everyday interaction with our environment, whereas superordinates (*animal, flora*) do not figure as prominently in practical use, and subordinates (*Highland pony, birch*) – although available for special occasions – cannot claim immediate cognitive relevance.[20] Much of what happens cognitively when humans try to come to terms with new situations can be explained as relying on extrapolation from known situations. Situations tend to be comprehended holistically on the lines of frames and scripts with underlying understandings about participants' goals or intentions feeding into the process. Thus, in Schank and Abelson's famous restaurant script, which is a cognitive device available to speakers of most languages,[21] a culturally determined set of props (tables, chairs, cutlery, table cloths, flowers, candle on table, menu, waiter, etc.) holistically interconnects with a series of actions (entering, sitting down, ordering, eating, paying), participants' goals (satisfying one's hunger, fighting boredom, social occasions such as business meetings, courting, celebrating) and cause-and-effect patterns that in turn derive from human basic-level body experience (food is eaten and then plates are empty, stomach feels full).[22] Much of frame theory, since it spells out these pre-understandings, sounds ridiculously babyish, but that is the point of the exercise. Such connections are in fact taken for granted as part of one's bodily enmeshment in the world. Similarly, the concept of frames explains how one interacts with objects in a cognitively adequate fashion: houses are preunderstood to have doors, windows, roofs and gardens, and all of these parts of the object 'house' interrelate with human needs and actions in a 'natural' way. Prototype theory stresses how whole/part relationships and back/front, right/left, up/down orientations (as well as a host of other concepts)[23] not only play a crucial role for our immediate body experience but from there are apt to infect our categorial thinking and effect repercussions even on the level of entirely 'abstract' areas of reasoning. In particular, lexicalization can be argued to rely on natural parameters of various kinds.[24]

Natural linguistics (as I'll dub the *Natürlichkeitstheorie* school) attempts to analyse a number of areas in linguistics by outlining natural factors affecting or motivating linguistic forms and functions. Such analyses have concentrated on phonetics and phonology as well as morphology (Dressler *et al.* 1987; Dziubalska-Kołaczyk forthcoming) with a natural syntax theory being developed by Mayerthaler and his team in Klagenfurt (Mayerthaler 1992; Maratschniger 1992), and the approach – at least in principle – also embraces semantics (the area most fully covered by prototype theory). In the syntactic realm, which has recently come into more particular focus, iconicity relations and the influence of cognitive parameters (agent roles etc.) on word order are crucially at issue.[25] Diagrammatic iconicity[26] in fact needs to be treated as one of the central features of linguistic motivation. As Linda R. Waugh (1993) demonstrates, Saussurian arbitrariness is now well on its way to being replaced by models that centre on iconicity relations which are perceived to be more 'natural': 'the **natural** condition of language is to preserve one form for one meaning, and one meaning for one form' (Bolinger 1977: x; my emphasis).

It is not my intention in these pages to apply frame theory or prototype theory in a detailed linguistic fashion. The entities with which I will be concerned – narrative texts of fairly considerable size (at least when discussing literary fiction) – will be conceived in terms of generic frames. These in turn allude to frames from both literary and non-literary backgrounds, and it will be argued that they do so both in their formal make-up and in their functional workings. The central insight that I have adopted from the linguistics of naturalness is that of the *embodiment* of cognitive categories and of the reliance of higher-level symbolic categories on such embodied schemata. It will be proposed that the reading process and the reading experience can be defined in relation to readers' cognitive reliance on such embodied schemata and parameters, and that this applies on a number of interacting and interdependent levels. As a consequence of this cognitive orientation, a specific viewpoint in relation to the issues of narrativity, fictionality and narrative causality will evolve in the course of my argument. Perhaps most importantly, schema theory and cognitive linguistics lay the foundation for a discussion of the crucial concept of mimesis which can now be situated in relation to cognitive constraints and parameters.

My brief introduction to two areas of linguistic research that use the term '*natural*' has attempted to clarify in what sense, and for what kinds of connotations, I am employing the concept of the natural. On the basis of these frames 'natural' narratology provides a model that pays particular attention to the inherent structures of natural narrative, while at the same time describing the cognitive parameters that define both natural narratives and more complex (and literary) forms. In this way I hope to specify more precisely what is 'natural' about natural narrative and how this quality of naturalness can become operative for production and reception purposes in other kinds of narrative. Natural narrative is here not presented as 'more natural' than, say, the novel or the short story. Rather than relating to a myth of naturalness with ideological functions, the concept of the natural as here proposed operates as a definable category whose functions demonstrate its viability and usefulness in concrete textual terms. In particular, by relating the natural to its anchorings in human everyday experience, evaluative connotations of a discriminatory cast should be kept at bay. The natural in this study corresponds to the human. As that which exists on earth, the human is both *part of* nature and *constitutive of* civilization. Anything concerning man in his civilized habitat and his living-acting-working conditions thus inevitably discredits the nature–culture dichotomy and the very artificial opposition between the natural and the contrived.[27] In fact the artificial is not a graft on the human–natural but its natural by-product. If one defines the natural in terms of the human (as is after all entirely appropriate from a human perspective), one should not be surprised to find products of human invention such as narratives proliferate on a scale from the more immediately spontaneous enactment of conversational storytelling to increasingly more deliberate and reflexive manifestations in the creative shapings of literature. In relation to such a scale, spontaneous forms of storytelling can be imaged as natural and prototypical since they provide a generic and typological resource for more subtly and complexly textured artifacts of creative structuration.

1.2 A REDEFINITION OF NARRATIVITY

Before I turn to the third element which has fed into my model of a 'natural' narratology, Jonathan Culler's concept of *naturalization* (Culler 1975), I need to explain in what ways the new paradigm redefines the notion of narrativity. It is on the basis of this reinterpretation that Culler's strategy of naturalization will be redeployed and redefined as *narrativization*, i.e. as the reading of texts *as narrative*, as constituting narrativity in the reading process. I will return to the concept of narrativity and narrativization in Chapter 8. There I also discuss more fully what use other critics have made of the term *narrativity* in the framework of their definitions of narrative, and I will demonstrate how, within my own paradigm, these prior conceptualizations can be integrated.

1.2.1 History vs. experientiality

Definitions of narrative have traditionally made (a series of) action(s) the prime constituent of narrativity. According to these definitions at least two, sometimes three, events need to be told, and plot is then construed as the logical and chronological concatenation of these two or three events on the level of the *fabula* (event sequence) transformed into a *sjuzhet*.[28] The traditional definitions of narrative are all incipiently teleological since they situate narrative dynamics in the tension between the initial situation and the final outcome which is supposed to provide a suitable endpoint to the course of events bracketed by this frame.

> A *simple narrative* is a series of episodes collected as a focused chain. Not only are the parts themselves in each episode linked by cause and effect, but the continuing center is allowed to develop, progress and interact from episode to episode. A narrative ends when its cause and effect chains are judged to be totally delineated. There is a reversibility in that the ending situation can be traced back to the beginning; or, to state it another way, the ending is seemingly entailed by the beginning. This is the feature of narrative often referred to as *closure*.
> (Branigan 1992: 20)

Although thus centrally installing actionality and event sequences in their definition of narrative, most narratological paradigms actually treat of narrative in a categorizing, descriptive mode, with the result that narrative in these typologies appears to be static, spatial. This paradox can be resolved if one observes that sequentiality *per se*, even if it provides cause-and-effect patterns of interpretation (*post hoc propter hoc*), is ultimately unable to embody narrative dynamics. *The king died and then the queen died of grief* may be a 'plot' as well as good story material in the sense of a *fabula* for the purposes of rewriting into another plot; as narrative, however, it holds little or no interest. The problem does not seem to lie in the observance of chronology, either. On the contrary, chronological reshuffling of the kind we have come to appreciate so much in Modernist fiction increases a narrative's static quality since all stages of the development have to be viewed simultaneously as a kind of mosaic or puzzle before one can start to establish the vital (relative) chronology of the *fabula*. It is not temporality *per se* that 'makes' narrative; or if so, that temporality relates more to the reading process than to the context of the story.

Besides the events-in-succession theory of narrative (from Aristotle to E.M. Forster) another more sophisticated model has been proposed by Claude Bremond (1973), who employs a schema of successive stages of decisions about alternative courses of action among which the protagonist needs to choose. What I would like to preserve from Bremond's model is the acknowledgement of dynamic movement, even if that movement, in Bremond, ends up reverting to a sequential mode, with alternative choices always propelling one new stage of sequentiality at a time. Where the traditional chronological model has a clear view of the starting-points and endpoints of the plot, with a description of logico-chronological development in between, Bremond seems to lose sight of this overall frame in the nitty-gritty detail of documentary material from the intervening stages. This is especially sad because Bremond's model *does* introduce implicit cognitive categories which could have provided some more extended in-depth analyses of narrative dynamics had their role been thematized instead of merely presupposed. For instance, the heroic adventure story, which is the model plot for both Propp and Bremond, invariably entails the hero's departure in search of adventure (whether to obey higher orders or indulge in restlessness is of no immediate concern). The hero always encounters obstacles which have to be overcome, and he eventually returns victorious. From the structuralist point of view, which favours chronological reshuffling, such a sequential accumulation of episodes resulting in the eventual glorification of the hero appears to be fairly uninteresting: after all, episodes succeed one another chronologically and are lined up in directly causal chains (resulting, in fact, from the deliberate choices which the hero makes in reaction to events, with other junctures determined by coincidence). The teleology operative in the story, in its overall pattern, appears to be immediately present to us, an almost inevitable semantic structure produced by the chronology of causally linked plot items.

If Bremond, on the level of theoretical discussion, appears to lose sight of this overall teleology (which is after all implicit in his schema), he makes an important contribution by incorporating in his sequential model the crucial experience of unresolved direction. Bremond therefore allows an insight into the peculiar micro-textual dynamics of plot episodes in which reader expectations are apt to be upset at each and every turn, just as the protagonist's intentions and goals are likely to be interfered with, requiring continual reorientation relative to the character's overall aims and needs. Bremond very aptly characterizes this continual reshuffling and manages to foreground the provisional nature of narrative episodes.[29] Such provisionality is in fact a constitutive part of human action schemata such as we experience them in practice in daily life. This experience includes also a recognition of the interaction between short-term and long-term goals as regulating one's choices in relation to immediate action, and it covers the recurring situation of an encounter with external forces that intrude upon premeditated plans. Such external forces manifest themselves, for instance, in the interactional limitations that the conflict with other people's interests and goals may impose on an agent, or in the shape of environmental constraints which are beyond personal control. (For the latter case I am thinking of exposure to natural disasters, political and institutional dictates, or of the confrontation with other people's unfathomable motives.)

While Bremond by this very important redrawing of cognitively relevant aspects of human agency almost loses sight of teleological parameters, the traditional chronological approach (which does incorporate teleology) is an experiential blank since the goals of agents never enter the picture at all. Neither model approaches narrative teleology from a higher-level semantic perspective which one could picture as the narrative's overall structure. Such logic is best described in terms of the function of the plot in the constitution of an entirely different kind of teleology, one identifiable not with the plot level *per se*, but with the 'implied author's shaping intentions'.[30] It is this logic which determines the interplay between the characters' plotting on the level of the fictional world and the narrative's overall counter-plotting, as illustrated so forcefully in Jonathan Culler's stimulating discussion of *Oedipus Rex* (1980) and the function of Destiny in that play. As Sturgess (1992) has perceptively pointed out, that function closely corresponds to an implied author position.[31] Such double teleology does not show up in folk tales, which is why there is no mention of this dynamic in the Proppian and Bremondian accounts of narrative structure. Duplicitous teleology of this sophisticated type does, however, become particularly relevant for the novel, especially the novel with a central puzzle. It is no coincidence that Culler's second example besides *Oedipus Rex* is *Daniel Deronda* as discussed by Cynthia Chase (1978).

So far I have alluded to three major constituents of narrativity – bounded sequentiality (Forster), experiential intentionality (Bremond), and dynamic teleology (Culler). In his monumental *Time and Narrative* (1983–85/1984–88) Paul Ricoeur has aptly characterized this triadic viewpoint in terms of configurality and emplotment with appropriate reference to the cognitive make-up of story comprehension. Whereas emplotment relates to the chronological sequencing under the aspect of teleological resolution, configurality describes the holistic comprehension of plot experience in its totality as well as in its parts. Story experience is configured on the level of *Mimesis I* where it relates to people's cognitive experience of human action in the world (involving recognition of one's own experience of being human and one's intuitive grasp of frames, schemata and scripts). This level is a pre-textual and indeed pre-narrative one, providing the cognitive basis for story comprehension at its most elemental level. Ricoeur's *Mimesis I* really corresponds to the action-oriented parameters of frame theory.

> The intelligibility engendered by emplotment finds a first anchorage in our competence to utilize in a significant manner the conceptual network that structurally distinguishes the domain of action from that of physical movement. [...] *Actions* imply *goals*, the anticipation of which is not confused with some foreseen or predicted result, but which commit the one on whom the action depends. Actions, moreover, refer to *motives*, which explain why someone does or did something, in a way that we clearly distinguish from the way one physical event leads to another. Actions also have *agents*, who do and can do things which are taken as *their* work, or *their* deed. As a result these agents can be held *responsible* for certain consequences of their actions. In this network, the infinite regression opened by the question 'Why?' is not incompatible with the finite regression opened by the question 'Who?' To identify an agent and to recognize this agent's motives are complementary operations. We also understand that these agents act and suffer in circumstances they did not make that nevertheless do belong to the practical field, precisely inasmuch as they circumscribe the intervention of historical agents in the course of physical events and offer favorable or unfavorable occasions for their action. [...] Moreover, to act is always to act 'with' others. Interaction can take the form of cooperation or competition or struggle.
>
> (Ricoeur 1984b: 54–5)

On the level of *Mimesis II*, configuration takes the shape of emplotment in the standard form of chronological rearrangement with a view towards ulterior teleological resolution. A configuration is 'extracted' from simple succession (ibid.: 65–6). Such a 'grasping together' (ibid.: 66) transforms the succession of (chronologically ordered) events of the *fabula* into 'one meaningful whole', into the narrative's 'point' or 'theme' (ibid.: 67) and imposes a 'sense of an ending' (ibid.) which retroactively defines previous stages as (inevitably) contributing to the endpoint:

> [...] to follow the story is not so much to enclose its surprises and discoveries within our recognition of the meaning attached to the story, as to apprehend the episodes which are themselves well known as leading to this end. A new quality of time emerges from this understanding.
>
> (ibid.)

This quality I would identify with teleology, as Ricoeur's brief mention of Culler (1980) corroborates. Teleology therefore also appears to invert the arrow of time by dynamically interrelating ending and beginning (Ricoeur 1984b: 67–8). Ricoeur moreover proposes a third level of *Mimesis III* which relates to the reader's or auditor's interpretative interaction with the narrative. Configurality on that level is crucially determined by active interpretation (teasing out the teleological perspectives inherent on level II) and the reconstruction of the story as a thematic and semantic whole. It is on this level III of Ricoeur's schema that questions of (historical) reference are resolved in the course of interpretation (ibid.: 71).

Ricoeur's model, which combines the aspects of sequentiality and emplotment with their experiential and teleological perspectives, is based on the constitutive concept of temporality, both in its sequential and experiential nature. Nevertheless the peculiar dynamic of narrative *experience* somehow never enters the picture. This is, I believe, particularly detrimental to Ricoeur's otherwise so insightful discussion of historiographic narrative. The major constitutive factor of historical narrative for Ricoeur remains its emplotment of historical evidence into a story – and that story is then shown to be fictionalized in quite blatently literary terms.[32] Ricoeur, curiously, fails to draw the crucial distinction between the different kinds of agenthood of a fictional protagonist and that of a quasi-agent[33] in historical discourse. Such a distinction would be based not on the cognitive issues of intentionality or the fulfilment of goals, but on the essential *experience* of the events which the necessarily human agents undergo in fictional texts and which is lacking for historical agents in historical discourse. To clarify: historical protagonists are of course also perceived as ordinary human agents who have goals, harbour unacknowledged intentions, evince weaknesses of character, engage in duplicitous dealings, etc.; what their personal *experience* was like (their hopes and fears, their loves and hates, their suffering) becomes noteworthy only in so far as it relates to the historical plot. It is therefore no coincidence that history is frequently bare of personal interest, that it is so difficult to make historical characters come alive; after all, their consciousness, their life *qua* personal experience, needs to be pressed into the service of larger historical relevancies. This is obviously less true of historical *biography* whose topic is, precisely, an historical figure's life. Recent historical attempts to describe the everyday experience of common people have, likewise, reconquered a territory long reserved for the writer of historical novels. History of the *Annales* type, on the other hand, which treats of quasi-characters such as the Mediterranean or presents the history of institutions, completely refrains from using experiential schemata since neither the Mediterranean nor, say, the Exchequer can have feelings or experiences of a personal nature.

The type of experiential quality that is typical of fiction invariably links up with the emphasis on a protagonist such that the tellability of the story consists in, or derives from, the extraordinary achievements, adventures or sufferings of that character, foregrounding this person's shrewdness, courage, heroic stature or tragic downfall, especially in combination with an upward or downward trajectory of Fortune's wheel. This should not be surprising in view of narrative's task of providing reading patterns for typically human predicaments. The writing of history, on the other hand, observes quite different tasks. Most historical writing appears to emerge from two needs: the necessity of fixing in writing what is fast receding from common memory; and the conscious interpretation of past events in the light of present-day concerns. Such present-day concerns may be didactic, and it is here that the functions of historical writing overlap with those of fiction, at least of literature written prior to the general acceptance of a Modernist aesthetics. Much earlier writing had to justify its existence in terms of moral teaching or other utilitarian purposes. But whereas literary didacticism concerns itself with the individual, with the complexities of moral decisions, or with (philosophically relevant) essentials of humanity in their typical manifestations, historical knowledge of necessity tends to concentrate on political rather than personal morality, on *patterns* of decision-making and on elusive historical truths. Not that these aspects need be incompatible. As soon as history started to become more narrative, improving on the early forms of the annals and chronicles[34] with their unrelated presentation of 'one thing after another', it was the pattern of the great life, and hence of regal biography, that flourished with much success, and this was a pattern that allowed for a skilful combination of the personal and the historical (i.e. political). Kings' decisions in this discourse are seen in terms of personal morality, such as justice, mercy, wisdom, truthfulness and the like, and relations to subjects are conceived of in similar terms (loyalty, disloyalty, flattery, fealty). Such personal relationships were not mere rhetoric as long as the feudal system was in place, and they later continued to be employed as useful ideological fictions. *Historia rerum gestarum* and kings' lives were therefore influential models of writing about past events.

The narrative schemata of experientiality operative in fiction also constitute an important anticipation of later historiographical attempts at reincorporating experientiality, attempts that became necessary as politics ceased to be comprehensible in terms of regal biography. Whereas fiction's solution to the problem of an adequate representation of the historical resulted in the invention of the historical novel, historiography in turn developed a novelistic historical *écriture* (Rigney 1990) which spawned the classic writings of nineteenth-century French, German and English historiography linked with the 'great' names of Macaulay, Michelet or Ranke. It is therefore *prototypical* historiography and *prototypical* fiction which are at odds on the issue of experientiality, and individual novels or histories may obey rules of their own.

1.2.2 Narrativity

> [...] *narrative is a perceptual activity that organizes data into a special pattern which represents and explains experience.* More specifically, narrative is a way of organizing spatial and temporal data into a cause–effect chain of events with a beginning, middle and end that embodies a judgment about the nature of the events as well as demonstrates how it is possible to know, and hence to narrate, the events.
>
> (Branigan 1992: 3)

I now return to the notions of narrative and of narrativity and hence to the proper subject matter of narratology. I here argue that *narrativity is a function of narrative texts and centres on experientiality of an anthropomorphic nature*. This definition divides the traditional area of enquiry (i.e. narratives) along unexpected lines, claiming narrativity for natural narrative (the term *text* is therefore employed in its structuralist sense) as well as drama and film (*narrative* is therefore a deep structural concept and is not restricted to prose and epic verse). On the other hand, the definition tentatively excludes historical writing from the central realm of prototypical narrativity, namely to the extent that historiography consists in a mere calibration of events which are then reported as historical facts.

The concept of *the narrative* defined in this manner cuts across standard divisions and restructures the territory in significant ways. Narrativity, although divorced from the requirements of *form* and *medium* (no teller is necessary, nor is drama excluded), cannot be equated with the category in Chatman's definition (1978, 1990) since, in contrast to Chatman, I exclude some traditional forms of narrative, and I emphatically refuse to locate narrativity in the existence of a narrator (even if implicit, implied or covert). Like Chatman, however, I do welcome film and drama into the realm of potential narrativity. In my argument, historical writing and action report are not actually narrative in the fullest sense. However, since all narrative includes non-experiential sequences, I will allow a place in the model for such forms of narrative, categorizing historical writing as narrative with restricted narrativity, narrative that has not quite come into its own.

My distinctions furthermore disqualify the criteria of mere sequentiality and logical connectedness from playing the central role that they usually hold in most discussions of narrative. I do, however, acknowledge that they are still a necessary ingredient for most narrative texts in the traditional understanding of that term. Actants in my model are not defined, primarily, by their involvement in a plot but, simply, by their fictional *existence* (their status as *existents*). Since they are prototypically human, existents can perform acts of physical movement, speech acts, and thought acts, and their acting necessarily revolves around their consciousness, their mental centre of self-awareness, intellection, perception and emotionality.

My rewriting of the traditional definitions crucially relates to the dominant position of the portrayal of consciousness in the literature of the past century. In the wake of this reconceptualization, I hold that action belongs to narrative as a consequence of the fact that experience is imaged as typically human and therefore involves the presence of existents who act; I therefore maintain that existence takes priority over action parameters, rather than treating consciousness as an incidental side effect of human action. In my view narrative thus properly comes into its own in the twentieth century when the rise of the consciousness novel starts to foreground fictional consciousness. As Käte Hamburger first suggested (1973/1993; Cohn 1978), narrative is the one and only form of discourse that can portray consciousness, particularly *another's* consciousness, from the inside,[35] and it is this capacity (which in many ways constitutes a *negative capability* of sorts)[36] that provides narrative with a niche in the field of competing discourses, historical or otherwise. Narrative is as alive as ever, much to the shame of apocalyptic prophets whose prognostications about the 'death of the author' (Roland Barthes) or 'the literature of exhaustion' (John Barth) have thus turned out to be quite fallible. The (post)structuralist obituary on narrative of course conceptualizes narrative as plot. It is only by redefining narrative on the basis of consciousness that its continuing relevance can be maintained.

My definition of narrativity also stands in radical opposition to F.K. Stanzel's tenets, although it eventually both supersedes and integrates them within 'natural' narratology. Stanzel centrally aligns narrativity with *mediation*.[37] Mediation in Stanzel's *A Theory of Narrative* (1979/1984b) comes in two modes, teller and reflector mode. In the teller mode a narrator relays the information, in the reflector mode it is from the reflector character's perspective that events appear to surface, as if by themselves. In both cases a story (a series of linked events) is prototypically considered to be the signified of narrative, with telling or reflecting as the medium of transmission. Although I will not discard Stanzel's model but rather integrate it as a basically metaphorical construct of possible ways of reading narrative texts, his definition of *narrativity as mediated story* cannot be preserved in my own model. Not only is Stanzel's paradigm predicated on the exclusion of the dramatic from the realm of narrativity – a stance which I reject much as I would like to adhere to it for reasons of tradition and nostalgia; Stanzel's implicit reliance on a presupposed action chain is likewise unacceptable within my own terms of the definition. The very concept of mediacy, since it supposedly mediates story material (plot) in the linguistic shape of narrative, needs to be reconceptualized. Like the concepts of action or plot (chain of events), narrating as a personal act of telling or writing can no longer claim primacy or priority. Both acting and telling are facets of a real-world model most forcefully present in natural narrative but nevertheless disposable on a theoretical level. Likewise, reflector mode narrative is already firmly constituted by the natural parameter of human consciousness, of experientiality. Experiencing, just like telling, viewing or thinking, are holistic schemata known from real life and therefore can be used as building stones for the mimetic evocation of a fictional world. People experience the world in their capacity as agents, tellers and auditors and also as observers, viewers and experiencers.

If the model which I am proposing goes beyond Stanzel's dichotomy, it is in the sense of reversing the emphasis in the teller-vs.-reflector mode dichotomy, by grounding narrativity in the representation of experientiality. Fictional representation can be clothed in the traditional form of telling or in the by now firmly established form of reflector-mode narrative. Additional formal alternatives are also possible, including neutral narrative and all kinds of traditionally non-narrative modes (among which one can number drama and film). These additional alternatives appear to derive from, or correlate with, another natural parameter, that of *visual experience*, or, one can also say, perception and observation. Whereas in reflector mode narratives we appear to experience reality from within another's psyche, neutral narrative and some types of film seem to be constituted on a schema of visual, sometimes even voyeuristic experience (cp. under 4.4). Drama, it needs to be observed, can vary quite surprisingly in the combination of such possibilities, ranging from the teller mode with a dramatic narrator figure on stage (cp. Richardson 1988) all the way to identificational and voyeuristic techniques.

There is another area in which Stanzel's proposals with regard to mediacy can be integrated with the present model. It may be recalled that Stanzel distinguishes grades of mediacy, with the summary or chapter argument format (which comes in the present tense) constituting zero degree of mediacy (1984b: Chapter 2). If one uses a past tense rather than the present, such summaries transform themselves into report, but – I argue – are no more 'narrative' in the restricted sense in which I use the term. What I would therefore like to propose is for some summaries to show degree zero of *narrativity*, with the present tense cancelling not sequentiality *per se* (or logical connections) – these do definitely survive into such summaries – but *cancelling the dynamics of experientiality*. This accounts for the well-known effect of 'freezing' (Casparis 1975) in summaries and other passages employing the (historical)[38] present. I note additionally that the absence of experiential dynamics correlates with an absence of explicit mediating interpretative instances (teller, reflector, viewer). Summaries and reportative passages are mere bare backbones of stories, and they therefore lack narrativity as well as mediacy.

What, then, is narrative experientiality?

Experientiality first of all needs to be distinguished from the Heideggerian notion of *Geworfensein*, the interminable succession of *nows* as subjected to the concerns of Care (Ricoeur 1984b: 62–5). It therefore has to be distinguished from the flux of temporality, the prototypical experience of *nows* as they recede into the past while anticipating that which will be past after having briefly become *now*. Experientiality *includes* this sense of moving with time, of the *now* of experience, but this almost static level of temporal experience is supplemented by more dynamic and evaluative factors.

I have noted earlier that Bremond's notion of choice – related to cognitive goals and plans – is a great advance on merely sequential models of narrative. Human experience typically embraces goal-oriented behaviour and activity, with its reaction to obstacles encountered on the way. The appearance of such an obstacle in one's path also constitutes a major event, and one which is reflected in the central incidence schema (Pollak 1988) of oral narratives (Quasthoff 1980; Fludernik 1991, 1992a, 1992c). This unexpected occurrence indeed dynamically triggers the reaction of the protagonist, and it is this three-part schema of 'situation–event (incidence)–reaction to event' which constitutes the core of all human action experience.

In narrating such experience, however, after-the-fact evaluations become important as a means of making narrative experience relevant to oneself and to others. All experience is therefore stored as emotionally charged remembrance, and it is reproduced in narrative form because it was memorable, funny, scary, or exciting. Whereas, in oral narrative, narrated experience always tends to be related to incidence, more extended narrative ventures (already in oral history interviews, as in Studs Terkel's work) frequently reproduce quite uneventful experiences and already tend to centre on interviewees' mental situations. The dynamics of experientiality as it surfaces in the narrativity of natural narratives reposes not solely on the *changes* brought about by external developments or effected through the self-monitored (goal-oriented) actions of a central intelligence or consciousness. On the contrary, this dynamic is related particularly to the resolution effect of the narrative endpoint of the tale and to the tension between tellability and narrative 'point' (Labov 1972; Fludernik 1991). Pure sequentiality and even causality do not figure at all from a cognitive perspective, although temporality and specificity do. Thus, timeless or habitual situations do not trigger narrative dynamics,[39] just as narratives cannot have everybody (or no one in particular) as their protagonist.

Specificity has of course also figured in definitions of literary *realism*, which in the standard definition consists in having the text project 'a record of the vicissitudes of human existence under the given circumstances of a particular place at a particular time' (Furst 1988: 103). It was Ian Watt who contrasted 'neo-classical generality' with 'realistic particularity' (1957: 17), thus historicizing the novel and its immanent realism. As we will see below, realism and experientiality do very much overlap in the frame of my model, and specificity – whether a characteristic of *realism* or of *narrative* in general – certainly plays an important role in the constitution of narrativity. The feature that is, however, most basic to experientiality is *embodiment* rather than specificity or individuality because these can in fact be subsumed under it. Embodiedness evokes all the parameters of a real-life schema of existence which always has to be situated in a specific time and space frame, and the motivational and experiential aspects of human actionality likewise relate to the knowledge about one's physical presence in the world. Embodiment and existence in human terms are indeed the same thing, which explains why some postmodernist texts that refuse the reader the consolation of an embodied protagonist (as in Beckett's scenarios of a disembodied voice) touch on the one most vital parameter of narrative experientiality, with baffling and disorienting effects for the reader.

Experientiality in narrative as reflected in narrativity can therefore be said to combine a number of cognitively relevant factors, most importantly those of the presence of a human protagonist and her experience of events as they impinge on her situation or activities. The most crucial factor is that of the protagonist's emotional and physical reaction to this constellation, which introduces a basic dynamic feature into the structure. Second, since humans are conscious thinking beings, (narrative) experientiality always implies – and sometimes emphatically foregrounds – the protagonist's consciousness. Narrativity can emerge from the experiential portrayal of dynamic event sequences which are already configured emotively and evaluatively, but it can also consist in the experiential depiction of human consciousness *tout court*. Any extended piece of narrative relies on both of these building stones. Most basic forms of narrative are exclusively built on an action schema, but acting and thinking are equally part and parcel of the dynamic human predicament of living in a world with which one inevitably interacts. The specific aesthetic effect of narrative need not rely on the teleology of plot, on how all the episodes and motives contribute to the final outcome, but can be produced also by the mimetically motivated evocation of human consciousness and of its (sometimes chaotic) experience of being in the world. Such processual chaos is always resolved aesthetically by the way in which episodes are read as configured between an initial and a final state, and even a narrative's explicit refusal to interpret or evaluate manages to 'resolve' such chaos implicitly by proclaiming itself to be a-teleological, deliberately evading narrative responsibility.

What this is supposed to suggest is that narrative experientiality, which is typically of a dynamic kind, can endure quite extensive pruning in the interests of overall narrativity – narrativity, that is, which is primarily based on a consciousness factor rather than on actantial dynamics or teleological directedness. Teleology and dynamics in many experimental texts are constituted not on the level of emplotment (with its emphasis on suspense) but on the interpretative level where the reader imposes a generic aesthetics on recalcitrant textual givens.

1.2.3 Narrativization

Having redefined narrativity in more holistic and dynamic terms, I now need to bring in the diachronic perspective, and I do this under the aegis of a reception-oriented model of establishing narrativity in the course of the reading process.

I here also come to the third area of inspiration for my term *natural narratology*. In 1975 Jonathan Culler proposed the concept of *naturalization* to account for readers' interpretative strategies when confronting textual or semantic inconsistencies (1975: 134–60). Culler's naturalization in particular embraces the familiarization of the strange:[40]

> The strange, the formal, the fictional, must be recuperated or naturalized, brought within our ken, if we do not want to remain gaping before monumental inscriptions. And the first step in the process of naturalizing or restoring literature to a communicative function is to make *écriture* itself a period and generic concept.
>
> (ibid.: 134)

Where Todorov links one of his three definitions of the verisimilar to the evocation of the *real* (1968: 2–3), Gérard Genette in his famous essay 'Vraisemblance et motivation' (1969: 73–99) connects verisimilitude with the establishment of narrative *realism*, with a text's correlation with a body of maxims held to be true by received opinion, conformance to which signifies the familiar, the readable, the verisimilar. Culler, on the other hand, links the process of naturalization with that of the Russian Formalists' notion of *motivation* – the disclosure of the non-arbitrary nature of textual elements (and therefore the very reverse of Roland Barthes's *effet de réel*) – and the French structuralists' notion of *making verisimilar*, what Culler calls *vraisemblablisation*:[41]

> 'Naturalization' emphasizes the fact that the strange or deviant is brought within a discursive order and thus made to seem natural. 'Motivation', which was the Russian formalists' term, is the process of justifying items within the work itself by showing that they are not arbitrary or incoherent but quite comprehensible in terms of functions which we can name. *Vraisemblablisation* stresses the importance of cultural models of the *vraisemblable* as sources of meaning and coherence.
>
> (Culler 1975: 137–8)

Culler's process of naturalization is therefore closely bound up with the framing textual and generic conventions as well as with the general philosophical and ideological reading models current at the time of a text's composition. If readers encounter initially odd, inexplicable elements, they will attempt to recuperate these items by taking recourse to available interpretative patterns. Characters who behave contrary to expectation may be capricious or mad or unconventional, but their behaviour will be recuperated within a frame that re-familiarizes the initial oddity. Culler therefore defuses the radicality of Genette's Barthesian definition of the real, refamiliarizing that which apparently refuses to be an instantiation of a maxim,[42] of the classical code of decorum, of how one *should* and *must* act. Whereas Genette and Barthes paradoxically locate the real (or its signifier, rather) on the site of that which is unverisimilar and therefore resists easy semiotic recuperation, Culler reinvites the unfamiliar, the strange and the unbelievable back into the realm of the *vraisemblable* by showing how readers refuse to allow this intrusion of the Other into their neat picture of the world, preferring to invent additional strategies of defusion and refamiliarization, naturalizing the oddity by means of a recourse to other frames, other explanatory patterns. Naturalization thus serves to reintegrate the unfamiliar with the known and the familiar, operating on the basis of a higher-level *vraisemblance* that introduces a plurality of frames of reference in order to recuperate one consistent model of the fictional world.

In Barthes's concept of the *effet de réel*, on the other hand, the unfamiliar or inexplicable has been promoted to the position of the prime signifier of the real. The realistic detail which serves no observable function[43] constitutes reality since it appears to be that which is not controlled by the artistry of the text. That argument is, however, paradoxical. By aligning the apparently afunctional detail with the text's significational strategies of evoking the real, the realistic detail in fact *does* acquire a function, if only the function of the inexplicable which – by its very recalcitrance to rules and maxims – accredits itself as the 'real real', as a kind of transcendental signified (the Real). Life, as one knows, is messy and disorderly, so that literature must not present too neat, too artistic a picture of it. The unexpected in oral narrative not only constitutes the life blood of narrative, its tellability; it is structurally central to the shape of experience. Verisimilitude and coincidence are indeed two poles of an opposition that need to be kept in precarious balance. Barthes himself, as Furst notes with great perspicacity, involved himself in apparent contradictions when refusing realism a 'code of accreditation' (*code d'accréditement*).[44] Whereas Barthes defines this code of accreditation as a self-reflexive baring of the text's fictionality (Furst 1988: 102), realism's protestations of veracity and asseverations of the norms of the real do in fact constitute such a code of accreditation and disclose the realist text to be metafictionally aware of its storification. By contrast, Barthes's *effet de réel* eludes the grasp of accrediting mechanisms whether of the self-reflexive or the rule-related kind, but the very positing of the realistic detail as yielding direct access to the Real in turn generates yet a third category of accreditation: that of the apparent authenticity of the afunctional, atypical and non-contrived. Barthes's *effet de réel* therefore falls into the trap of mimetic immediacy, he has 'learned what the artist must always keep in mind, that one must transcend "realism" for truth' (Kearns 1992: 861). This knowledge, however, like all mimesis, is illusory.

Todorov's study of the *fantastic* (Todorov 1970/1993) develops these insights further by sketching the tensions between the realistic and the otherworldly (and therefore realistically non-recuperable) in the ambivalence of the fantastic. Unlike the *uncanny*, which ultimately turns out to yield to logical explication, and unlike the *magical* (which remains off limits), the *fantastic* resides in the area of indeterminacy where neither a realistic nor a transcendental reading can be proved correct. The fantastic therefore eludes naturalization, but it does *not* operate as the Other. The most interesting structural property of Todorov's schema lies precisely in the position that he proposes for the *Other*. Unlike Roland Barthes, he recuperates the otherworldly within a matrix that posits the magical as equally real and true. In contrast to Culler's familiarization of the unfamiliar, therefore, Todorov's approach allows the unfamiliar to preserve its status as magic, as the non-realistic, the inexplicable. In the realist novel, which is Genette's (and in this particular chapter also Culler's) chosen demonstration area, the mimetic frame eliminates the fantastic except for those stories that explicitly thematize a magic otherworldly realm (as in the ghost story). It is a measure of the realist novel's secularization that direct contact with the otherworldly no longer counts as realistically verisimilar.

To return to Culler's concept of naturalization: Culler does not simply mean to eliminate the strange; naturalization *either* integrates the unfamiliar within a larger frame that explains the strange as quite familiar within a different perspective (religious non-conformity, for instance, is recuperated not as sanctity, which would be incomprehensible from a secular viewpoint, but as sheer mental derangement[45]), *or* it proposes a more embracing frame that is able to explain inconsistencies as functions within its own setup. Most human prototypes applicable to larger frames include discordant elements which are then resolved within the explicatory workings of the frame. Such explanation may be logical, psychological, biological, institutional and so on, and the resolution of opposites has both moral and political, that is to say ideological, dimensions. Thus the well-known topos of appearance vs. reality resolves an irreconcilable dichotomy by downgrading appearance as illusion (the Buddhist version), or as deliberate deception, dissimulation and duplicity in ontological (Christianity) or psychological (secular humanism) form. The prototype is exploitable for a variety of quite disparate purposes. It can, for instance, identify arrogance as a mask for shyness or provide a psychological explanation (in terms of latent envy or jealousy) for an otherwise inexplicable murderous outbreak, for instance when a seemingly peaceful and harmless husband or neighbour suddenly goes berserk.

I have been inspired by Culler's naturalization to coin the term narrativization, which I now introduce into the discussion. It needs to be noted at the outset that my conception of narrativization needs to be set apart from Hayden White's use of this term. Whereas I use narrativization to describe a reading strategy that naturalizes texts by recourse to narrative schemata, Hayden White uses the term in the sense of storification, a transformation of historical material into narrative shape (H. White 1981: 2–3). White's narrativization therefore corresponds to Ricoeur's establishment of an *intrigue*, a plot. According to White, the masters of modern historiography (Braudel or LeRoi Ladurie)

> [...] refused to tell a story about the past, or, rather, they did not tell a story with well-marked beginning, middle, and end phases; they did not impose upon the processes that interested them the *form* that we normally associate with storytelling. While they certainly *narrated* their accounts of the reality that they perceived, or thought they perceived, to exist within or behind the evidence they had examined, they did not *narrativize* that reality, did not impose upon it the form of a story.
> (ibid.: 2)

White's understanding of storification, as he should perhaps have called this process, therefore relies exclusively on the establishment of a plot.

My own approach is quite different, if only because storification does not play a crucial role within the framework of 'natural' narratology. In my reading, which is based on Culler's process of naturalization, narrativization applies one specific macro-frame, namely that of *narrativity*, to a text. When readers are confronted with potentially unreadable narratives, texts that are radically inconsistent, they cast about for ways and means of recuperating these texts as narratives – motivated by the generic markers that go with the book. They therefore attempt to re-cognize what they find in the text in terms of the natural telling or experiencing or viewing parameters, or they try to recuperate the inconsistencies in terms of actions and event structures at the most minimal level. This process of narrativization, of making something a narrative by the sheer act of imposing narrativity on it, needs to be located in the dynamic reading process where such interpretative recuperations hold sway.

Besides being a synchronic feature, narrativization can, however, also be extended to the diachronic realm. In the long history of narrative forms and modes one can observe extensions of existing genres, particularly on the basis of familiar cognitive parameters and frames. This applies to the complex process of transcoding oral into written narratives – a path which will be traced in Chapter 3 – and equally concerns the establishment of more modern types of narration such as second-person fiction (treated in Chapter 6). Narrativization can therefore ultimately feed into diachronic change, in the incorporation of new options into the realm of familiar genres or discourse types. These newly available frames are generic and narratological rather than natural categories of a cognitive quality, but they are at least partly based on cognitive parameters, which they utilize to produce new combinations and new insights. Narrativization thus constitutes a processual boundary between the reader and the text, and between the text and its historicization. I will take up the significance of narrativization in my summary in Chapter 8 after I have had the opportunity of illustrating narrativization in its historical manifestations in Chapters 5 to 7.

1.2.4 Realism and mimesis

One major aspect of narrative texts has so far remained unaccounted for: the position of mimesis within 'natural' narratology. Mimesis is indeed to be located at the very core of a 'natural' narratology. Culler's naturalization, as we have seen, fundamentally correlates with *vraisemblance* (1975: 137–40). However, the concept of mimesis as I am utilizing it here requires careful definition. As I have already suggested in *The Fictions of Language and the Languages of Fiction*, mimesis must NOT be identified as imitation but needs to be treated as the artificial and illusionary projection of a semiotic structure which the reader recuperates in terms of a fictional reality. This recuperation, since it is based on cognitive parameters gleaned from real-world experience, inevitably results in an implicit though incomplete homologization of the fictional and the real worlds. As Iser puts it:

> It is evident [...] that the attempt to translate fiction back into reality involves the undoing of the 'as-if' dimension. [...] second thoughts begin to arise as to whether representation can really be equated with mimesis. Since the world represented is bracketed, it cannot take on a determinate form of its own but must find it through its relatedness to something else.
>
> (Iser 1993: 15)

Since much material in fictional narrative resists realistic recuperation, alternative world-building strategies and interpretative naturalizations come into play at several levels. Experimental fiction can be read as intertextual play with language and with generic modes, and this – since it projects an intentional meta-narrative function – is a mimetic strategy just like any other. Reading experience in terms of making sense of the text can be conceptualized as a deliberately anti-narrative discourse which is then recuperated as the product of rhetorical strategy on the part of the author. Such experimental texts are therefore not mimetic in terms of reproducing, if in a different medium, a prototypical version of narrative experience, but are mimetic in their structured anticipation of readers' attempts at reinterpreting them mimetically if only at a meta-meta-realist level of a self-reflexive, explicitly anti-mimetic language game. Phenomenology and language critique need not therefore be at odds but can be subsumed under the one cognitive faculty of sense-making, and that sense-making, since it always relies on natural categories of cognition, is by definition mimetic. Experimental fiction is in fact read against its grain since readers, in so far as they read such texts *as narrative*, supply the inexplicit narrativity of the text by extrapolation from its anti-narrative surface.[46] There are texts where such a strategy comes to an abrupt halt and falters on their non-narrativity. Where no consistent fictional world is recuperable, narrativity ceases to operate and mediation through self-reflective consciousness can only be of itself, of language and semiosis in action.

'Natural' narratology, as I envisage it, relies on a definition of narrativity as mediated human experientiality (which can be plotted on the level of action or on the level of fictional consciousness). Mediation occurs through a consciousness parameter which comes in various shapes (actantial, reflective, observational or self-reflective consciousness). Narrativity is then established by readers in the reading process on the basis of four levels of natural categories (see below under 1.3) which are combined to 'project' the fictional world. Recuperation of narrativity from non-naturally coded texts in turn becomes possible through recourse to a variety of natural cognitive parameters, with self-reflexive language-gaming a last-ditch scenario.[47] Where narrativity can no longer be recuperated by any means at all, the narrative genre merges with poetry (see under 8.6).

Mimesis and narrative fictionality are therefore, to all intents and purposes, here employed as synonyms. In fact, in the prologue I identified narrative with the fictional *par excellence*. Narrative is a category of human behaviour that occupies a very special place among behavioural modes. Its functions seem to serve a deep-seated human need to cognize oneself in projected semiotic models of a narrative cast.[48] That these semiotic models used to be the only available cultural *epistèmai* before the advent of writing[49] cannot be overemphasized. Writing made available a completely different kind of cognition which resulted in the development of scientific rationalism and the historical recuperation of the past.[50]

> To raise the question of the nature of narrative is to invite reflection on the very nature of culture and, possibly, even on the nature of humanity itself. So natural is the impulse to narrate, so inevitable is the form of narrative for any report of the way things really happened, that narrativity could appear problematical only in a culture in which it was absent – absent or, as in some domains of contemporary Western intellectual and artistic culture, programmatically refused. [...] Far from being a problem, then, narrative might well be considered a solution to a problem of general human concern, namely, the problem of how to translate *knowing* into *telling*, the problem of fashioning human experience into a form assimilable to structures of meaning that are generally human rather than culture-specific.
>
> (H. White 1981: 1)

If one takes the oral model to be the basic incarnation of storytelling, as I do, one cannot then consider narrative beyond its oral frame without paying attention to the process by which writing absorbed and remodelled narrative in its own interests while preserving at least some of the original cultural functions of oral storytelling. And one of the most prominent features of natural narrative is its fictionality, which nevertheless links up very closely with oral narrative's referential mimetic code. Narrative mimesis evokes a world, whether that world is identical to the interlocutors' shared environment, to a historical reality or to an invented fictional fantasy. And in so far as all reading is interpreting along the lines of a represented world, it necessarily relies on the parameters and frames of real-world experience and their underlying cognitive understandings. Mimesis is therefore here conceived in radically constructivist terms.

At this point the notion of *realism* requires some clarification. I will be using the term *realism* and the *realist novel* extensively in this book, and a definition is therefore very much in order. In particular, it needs to be noted at the outset that my understanding of the term *realist* is a broad one that cannot be limited to the *nineteenth-century* realist novel.

Since Ian Watt's pioneering study (Watt 1957) the realist novel has been conceived as starting with Defoe. In this book I argue that it is actually Aphra Behn who was the first[51] real novelist, but – like Watt – I use the term *realist* to apply to the novel from its earliest times, linking the notion of *realism* not to the nineteenth-century movement of Realism but to the novel's mimetic evocation of reality both from a sociological and psychological perspective.[52] Verisimilitude and realism in fact correlate very closely. *Realism* refers to a realistic portrayal of the fictional world in the sense that secular non-fantastic explanations can be provided for the plot and seemingly fantastic experiences are eventually explained in 'realistic' terms. In contrast to other definitions *I do not*, however, reduce the setting and fictional personae of realism to the bourgeois milieu: realism can embrace the aristocracy as well, but it needs to do so in a non-Arcadian setting, eschewing the generic alignments of romance and pastoral. The motivational aspect of realism links with the novel's increased psychologism. Novels spend more space on explaining characters' motives, and they also portray characters' deep-seated emotions and fears, reflections and enthusiasms in verisimilar terms. Unlike the generally mannered and formalistic soliloquy of the Renaissance romance, novelistic renderings of characters' minds move away from the rhetorical set piece to a representation that evokes more individualistic emotions. Realism therefore links up with an individual's very personal experience and the verisimilar rendering of it in the text. Realistic elements in narrative such as the pregnant repartee in dialogue, or the description of gestures, the adding of the odd detail with an *effet de réel* function – all of these can be traced back to the thirteenth-century legendaries and have been particularly noted in Chaucer's oeuvre. They do not, however, constitute overall realism, which had its breakthrough in the wake of the picaresque novel. Brinkmann's (1977) distinction between external and internal realism well reflects the two major types of novelistic illusionism: the deployment of an *effet de réel* on the one hand and the instantiation of psychological verisimilitude on the other.

Although my views correspond well to received ideas about realism, I have felt it incumbent on me to specify more particularly how I wish to employ this term, distancing myself from the too restrictive generic definition of realism as a late nineteenth-century literary style and movement, and at the same time limiting my own usage to the psychological realm by excluding the mere occurrence of realistic detail as a distinguishing feature. Realism in the sense in which I am using the term therefore closely corresponds to a mimetic representation of individual experience that cognitively and epistemically relies on real-world knowledge. That realism is a significational effect, however: the result, that is, of the mimetic illusion that is transported into the reading process by readers' urge for narrativization. The representation of experientiality in narrative and the effect of mimetic realism therefore correlate with one another. As we will see in the following section, both, moreover, coincide with the notion of fictionality as I define it in contradistinction to the fictive (imaginary, hypothetical) and the historical (referential).

1.2.5 Fictionality

A final remark is here due regarding the relation between my concept of narrativity and that of fictionality. It needs to be most emphatically noted, to start with, that narrativity can be constituted both in fictional and in non-fictional texts. Autobiographies are perfect instances of narrative but are not necessarily *fictional* in the received definition of that term. Inversely, a great deal of early fiction is not yet fully *narrative* in my understanding of the concept. If 'natural' narratology excludes historical writing from its core set of texts, it does so also on account of the *thematic emphasis* (non-specificity) and the implicit purposes of historiography, and not merely because historical narrative belongs with non-fictional texts or consists of report structures. The original purposes of historical writing may indeed be stalled by a reader's decision to ignore them, as happens so frequently when originally historical writings are reinterpreted as historical novels or even pure fiction.

The relationship between narrativity and fictionality in my model turns out to be very close and it cuts across the fictional vs. non-fictional boundary. Narrativity, I have argued, is based on the attempt to portray human experientiality in exemplary fashion. However, in our real-life experience human experientiality consists of that which eludes our immediate grasp, it is something non-objective, non-definable precisely on account of its holistic gestalt-perceptional shape. Historical writing, by contrast, does not seek such elusive signifieds, and instead attempts to weigh documentary evidence, to deliberate between causality patterns and explanatory proposals, to sift the wealth of detail for configurational possibilities. There is therefore a sense in which fictionality inheres in my restricted definition of narrativity since the experience portrayed in narrative is typically non-historical (non-documentary, non-argumentational). However, in making this statement, it is important to insist immediately that fictionality in this understanding cannot be contrasted with truth or reality. Historical writing is *fictional* (H. White 1978), i.e. *fictive*, precisely to the extent that it produces a configured relation (in Ricoeur's sense) of an elusive historical 'reality' – but such fictivity is to be distinguished from fictionality in the more literary sense. It is this literary kind of fictionality, the subjective experience of imaginary human beings in an imaginary human space, that correlates with narrativity since the emphasis on human experientiality can be manifested most perfectly in the ideal realm (as Aristotle knew very well).

> En définitive, ce réalisme subjectif, non objectif, est peut-être la grande force du texte, puisque, comme y insiste le narrateur de la *Recherche* dans *Le Temps retrouvé*, une littérature qui limiterait son domaine à la seule surface de la réalité n'aurait aucune raison d'être, le réel, à proprement parler, se situant au-delà de l'univers physique et de ses conditions d'existence.
>
> (Viègnes 1990: 24)
>
> All things considered, this subjective, not objective, type of realism is perhaps the great force of the text since, as insists the narrator of the *Recherche* in the final volume *Le Temps retrouvé*, literature that only limited itself to the surface of reality would have no right to exist for the real is actually situated beyond the physical universe and its existential conditions.
>
> (My translation)

My proposals therefore tend towards entirely discarding the concept of fictionality or of the fictional, and this for two reasons. One needs to distinguish carefully between the fictional, on the one hand, and the fictive or hypothetical, on the other. Fictionality and narrativity appear to collocate in roughly the same generic contexts. Fictionality typically surfaces in narrative form (including narrative poetry, drama and film); it is not generally employed to define poetry,[53] sculpture or music, and in painting is restricted to specifically narrative representations. Of course, fictional elements do begin to emerge when one considers the poetic persona as a kind of fictional character or observes sculptural representations of characters from mythology. Nevertheless, as the current linguistic usage illustrates, the application of the term fictionality usually exceeds the denotations of mere external existence (sculpture) or mere disembodied voice (poetry). (See also under 8.4 below.) One can observe this very well in the collocations of the lexeme *fictional*: a story may be fictional, and a fictional persona is one that is part of a fiction or fictional situation, indeed a (fictional) *character*. The imagined and the hypothetical, on the other hand, are *fictive* or invented, but not necessarily *fictional*. Note also that poetry's truth value interferes with a categorization of poetry as fiction: after all, most poetic statements are of a philosophical cast and may therefore be interpreted as referring to real-world entities, even if these are abstracts like *love* or *honour*, or are represented implicitly and metaphorically. In its requirements for narrative embodiment, fictionality correlates precisely with the kind of narrative experience that I have made the basis of the concept of narrativity.[54]

Second, fictionality is here explicitly divorced from its traditional *referential* reading in the familiar opposition of fiction vs. historical (rather than *logical* or *literal*) truth. I completely endorse Lamarque and Olsen's argument that fictionality must not be linked to a failure of reference. Lamarque and Olsen reject

> [...] certain persistent misconceptions about fiction: for example, the association of fiction with 'reference-failure', or the 'intransitivity of writing', or the suggestion that fiction is 'cut off' from the world, or lacks 'correspondence' with the facts. The perspective also undermines the more refined post-structuralist theory that fictional discourse is somehow paradigmatic of all discourse, that the deliberate flouting of the link between language and reality, which is supposedly definitive of fiction, shows that that link itself is unstable or untenable.
>
> (1994: 33)

As I have attempted to show, the distinction between fact and fiction is taken care of by extratextual parameters and expectations. This is not to say, of course, that the historicity of *some* fiction is not frequently made the object of explicit comment and even lengthy reflection, or that historical writing may not easily slide into fictionalizing techniques. In so far as such techniques are fictional they are narrative, and in so far as fiction pretends to be historiography it attempts to shift its notional emphases away from narrativity and towards documentary reliability and argumentative prose. Lamarque and Olsen are quite correct in emphasizing the processual and constructivist aspects of fiction:

> [...] the fictive dimension of stories (or narratives) is explicable only in terms of a rule-governed practice, central to which are a certain mode of utterance (fictive utterance) and a certain complex of attitudes (the fictive stance).
>
> (ibid.: 32)

Finally, in my usage the term fictionality has absolutely no truck with *construction* or *configuration*, whether historical or novelistic. *All* narrative (even on its minimal level of sequential report) is a fictive construct, a representation, and cannot reproduce 'reality' in any mimetic fashion. Stories, lives, the products of conversation are all concepts of the human mind, the result of cognitive parameters which we bring to bear upon the flux of unknowable and indivisible being, upon our exposure to the world. The recent catch phrase which exposes historiography as 'also fiction' since it employs 'fictional techniques' – though important as an illustration of a developing historiographical self-awareness – needs to be handled with great care lest it result in an indiscriminate equation of historical and novelistic texts.[55] History is a constructed discourse, and this discourse may 'lapse' into fictionalizing tendencies,[56] for instance by inventing items based on a construction of sequentiality unwarranted by documentary evidence. However, in so far as historical prose attempts to write 'history' and not 'specific human experience', it will tend to remain non-fictional in the framework that I have outlined. History, by definition, is that area of study which interprets, orders, analyses and attempts to *explain* human experience, but it does not set out to *represent* such experience. Human experience as stored in fictional texts indeed frequently provides history with its quotational source material: most historical 'events' are reconstructed from oral or written witness reports which usually display a high degree of narrativity (Rigney 1990: 36–62). For reasons of space I here eliminate a discussion of Genette (1990) and Cohn (1990) on the fiction vs. history controversy. My own position is closer to Cohn's than to Genette's, and it is no coincidence that what I call narrativity corresponds to what Cohn treats under the heading of fictionality.

Lamarque and Olsen, by contrast, have proposed to make a major distinction between fiction and narrative, where their use of narrative refers exclusively to the presence of event sequences.

> Once it is recognized that narrative and fiction are separate concepts, and, most importantly, that narrative *per se* is merely a formal feature of a text without referential or ontological implications, the pervasiveness of narrative comes to seem quite unsurprising. Furthermore, the metaphysical connection is severed when the narrative form is seen to be neutral on questions of truth, reference, and 'correspondence with reality'.
> (1994: 224–5)

They go on to quote Prince's definition of narrative to document this 'formal feature' of narrativity. Lamarque and Olsen also create a major discontinuity between the notions of fiction on the one hand and literature on the other. Literature appears to come in writing only, whereas fiction includes film, drama and other media (ibid.: 255).

> 'Fiction', in the relevant sense, covers a large subclass of all invented stories, which can be realized in a number of media. It covers *Dynasty*

as well as *The Tempest*. 'Literature', on the other hand, covers only a small subclass of *linguistic* expressions: the majority of linguistic expressions, even those in the fictive mode, do not fall under the concept 'literature'. Furthermore, even if the concepts of 'fiction' and 'literature' had the same extension, they would still be different concepts with different meanings. For 'fiction' is a descriptive concept while 'literature' is an evaluative concept. This does not mean that works of literature and works of fiction are different *kinds of text*. It has been a main contention of the argument so far that fiction is not a type of text at all but a mode of utterance which can only be identified with reference to the utterer's intention, i.e. the intention to invoke the fictive response, to invite the audience to adopt what we have called the *fictive stance* to the text produced.

(ibid.)

It is obvious from my approach that I cannot concur with Lamarque and Olsen but have moved in an entirely different direction. Fictionality, in my own framework, exists outside the purview of an evaluative definition of literature, and narratives are, precisely, prototypical instances of the fictional. We do, however, agree with regard to the reader's active construction of fictionaliy, i.e. narrativity.

To conclude. It is here argued that for narratologists the crucial distinction is not that between the fictional and the historical or between the hypothetical and the real, but that between the narrative and the non-narrative, with historical discourse situated ambiguously on the borderline between these two fundamental types of discourse. Fictionality and narrativity largely overlap, but only if the fictional is not completely reduced to the traditional sense of the non-historical and a-referential. Referential concerns may determine generic categorization, but they do not affect a text's or utterance's narrativity. Eliminating the term fictionality helps to avoid confusion between the fictional and the *fictive*. One needs to distinguish, therefore, between three aspects that are traditionally treated under the heading of the fictional: historical truth vs. invention (*fiction proper*); the *hypothetical* imaging of situations, lies, etc. vs. the real (or, the counterfactual vs. the factual in *logical* terms[57]); and the *fictive* as that which has been fabricated or constructed but can be contrasted neither with the historical (*that*, too, shows the feature of constructedness) nor with the factual (the hypothetical is usually fictive).

It is important to emphasize at once that I am using these terms in contexts radically divorced from the terminology of Wolfgang Iser (1993). Iser's distinction between the fictional and its sources, the fictive and the imaginary, is based on a quite different arrangement of these elements and moreover situates itself on a discourse level (the *fictive* shows up in fictive discourses). Iser's *imaginary* appears to be particularly problematic from my own perspective: it seems to provide the emotional matter for experientiality but – to judge from Iser's examples – cannot be equated with it; indeed it shares features with imaginary projection as in dream visions which I would prefer to treat under my category of the hypothetical. Iser's speech act of *fabrication* (das *Fingieren*), on the other hand, corresponds both to my concept of the counterfactual or hypothetical and to the constructional aspect of what I have dubbed the *fictive*. No doubt Iser has quite different purposes in mind, so that – in view of my own preoccupations – I have ended up rearranging the field in an entirely different manner. For the purposes of this book – and this section – however, it should suffice to note that within the frame of 'natural narratology' the term *fictional* can be dispensed with. The basic dichotomy for my model is that between the narrative and the non-narrative.

1.3 TOWARDS A 'NATURAL' NARRATOLOGY

> An important consequence of this conceptualization of 'empirical' and 'scientific' is that it principally and fundamentally relates knowledge to man and not to 'the reality.'
>
> (S.J. Schmidt 1989: 323)

It is now time to outline the model which I am here proposing and which will form the basis of the detailed analyses of *Towards a 'Natural' Narratology*. In this model cognitive parameters enter at several levels, in a manner that generalizes the term '*natural*' over a number of alternative as well as combined applications. Besides the obviously synchronic cognitive parameters, the model is meant to allow for historical analysis, providing diachronic perspectives on narrative texts.

The model operates on four levels. The axiomatic natural parameters of real-life experience form the most basic experiential and cognitive level. On this level are situated the core schemata from frame theory, which accommodate presupposed understandings of agency, goals, intellection, emotions, motivation, and so on. My *level I* – parameters of real-life experience – is therefore identical with Ricoeur's *Mimesis I*. It comprises the schema of agency as goal-oriented process or reaction to the unexpected, the configuration of experienced and evaluated occurrence, and the natural comprehension of observed event processes including their supposed cause-and-effect explanations. In this schema teleology (i.e. temporal directedness and inevitable plotting) combines with the goal-orientedness of acting subjects and with the narrator's after-the-fact evaluation of narrative experience. Such a pattern is typical of natural narrative, as we will see in Chapter 2.

On *level II* I locate four basic viewpoints which are available as explanatory schemas of *access* to the story. All four relate to narrative mediation, to narrativity. I distinguish between the real-world 'script' of TELLING; the real-world schema of perception (VIEWING); and the access to one's own narrativizable experience (EXPERIENCING). These storytelling schemata are macrostructural and comprise the basic frames of telling, viewing, experiencing and cultural knowing.

A fourth schema that I will be using a great deal is that of ACTION or ACTING. Properly speaking, this fourth frame really belongs with level I since it refers to the *what* and not to the *how* of narrative experience. However, as will become clear in a moment, in terms of the interpretative *use* made of frames located on level II, ACTING also is one of the frames that readers resort to in the process of narrativization, and this schema – visualized at level II – does not merely comprise understandings about goal-oriented human action but additionally invokes the entire processuality of event and action series. When readers attempt minimally to narrativize texts that are highly inconsistent they may have to rely on the rock-bottom schema of actionality to tease out a rudimentary sense in story-referential terms.

Furthermore, the frame of TELLING can be extended to incorporate what I call REFLECTING, i.e. the mental activities outside utterance which turn the act of telling into a process of recollection and self-reflective introspection. Whereas the TELLING frame invokes a situation of enunciation and hence an addressee persona, REFLECTING tends to project a reflecting consciousness in the process of rumination. I will return to the applications of level II on level IV below.

My *level III* of cognitive parameters comprises well-known naturally recurring story-telling situations. Since storytelling is a general and spontaneous human activity observable in all cultures, it provides individuals with culturally discrete patterns of storytelling. These patterns include not only a knowledge about storytelling situations and the structure of that situation (who is telling what to whom, interaction or non-interaction with listeners, etc.), but also an understanding of performed narrative and particularly an ability to distinguish between different *kinds* or *types* of stories. As genres proliferate and written texts appear on the scene, the relevant competence increases accordingly and also changes in kind. In the process of acculturation, particularly *literary* acculturation, potential audiences acquire generic models which decisively influence their reading experience. Genres, after all, are large-scale cognitive frames. Such models are different only in degree from the simple text types or 'genres' encountered in oral storytelling in which the basic parameters are context-bound. These consist of the relationship of the teller to the audience and to the told; institutionalization (private vs. public narrative); tradition as a memory trace; performance as the most important constitutive feature of natural narrative; and the distinction between elaborated and simple oral storytelling. On level III relevant parameters additionally include narratological concepts: the concept of the narrator, of chronological reordering (e.g. flashback), of authorial omniscience (both in the meaning of access to protagonists' internal states and in the sense of the narrator's temporal and spatial release from the limitations of human embodiedness). Level III also features the more precisely generic parameters of literary narratives – the readers' concepts of *the historical novel*, *the Bildungsroman*, etc., as they are acquired through exposure to literature.

My levels II and III do *not* reproduce Ricoeur's *Mimesis II* (which concerns the immediate textual level of discourse), but characterize features which are partially relevant for Ricoeur's level of *Mimesis III*, the level of reconfiguration. Whereas cognitive parameters on levels I and II are decidedly transcultural, basic-level experiential frames, categories on level III are culture-specific and to a large extent acquired, in fact even taught, as abstract categories. One has to distinguish, for instance, between knowledge about the dynamics of conversational exchanges, such as one can participate in on a bus or at parties, and knowledge about the dynamics of written narratives. Thus, as a kind of fine-tuning of the more basic frames of ACTION, TELLING, VIEWING, and EXPERIENCING from level II, one can add, on level III, the practical generic knowledge of what jokes, anecdotes, witness-box reports, conversations with doctors (telling the history of one's illness), etc., are like. Such practical *awareness* need not always entail a conscious knowledge of abstract categories. Cognitive parameters on level III are 'natural' precisely because they operate in a non-reflective manner and relate to one's pragmatic experience of hearing and reading stories. It is important to emphasize most forcefully that these categories are not (yet) *constituted by the reader's immediate interpretation* but provide – like categories situated on levels I and II – cognitive tools *for* the interpretation of narrative texts or discourses. Yet, as I will argue below, parameters on level III are already the result of a metaphorical extension of concepts from levels I and II to the level of a more abstract instrumentarium employed in the apperception of *written* narratives. Due to our long history of exposure to written narratives, generic parameters on level III have simply turned into available cognitive schemata and are no longer the result of a conscious process of interpretation and naturalization.

This brings me to the fourth and final level of my model of natural storytelling parameters, the level which concerns the interpretative abilities by which people link unknown and unfamiliar material with what they are already familiar with, thereby rendering the unfamiliar interpretable and 'readable'. On *level IV* readers utilize conceptual categories from levels I to III in order to grasp, and usually transform, textual irregularities and oddities. Level IV constitutes an all-embracing *dynamic* process engendered by the reading experience. In correlation with Jonathan Culler's more general concept of *naturalization* (Culler 1975) I have called this process *narrativization*. (Compare above under 1.2.3.) Culler's naturalization is concerned with the *interpretation* of literary texts (including, in particular, poetry). According to Culler, readers, faced with initially inconsistent or incomprehensible texts, attempt to find a frame that can naturalize the inconsistencies or oddities in a meaningful way. In contrast to Culler's more general process of naturalization, narrativization on level IV is exclusively concerned with *narrative* parameters. It circumscribes readers' attempts at making sense of texts, particularly of texts which resist easy recuperation on the basis of parameters from levels I to III. Narrativization is that process of naturalization which enables readers to re-cognize as narrative those kinds of texts that appear to be non-narrative according to either the natural parameters of levels I and II or the cultural parameters of level III. Such interpretative strategies serve to naturalize texts in the direction of natural paradigms, for instance by providing a realistic motivation that helps to ensure readability. Thus, Alain Robbe-Grillet's novel *La Jalousie* (1957) has frequently been narrativized as the jealous husband's observations of his wife through the window shutters.[58] In like manner readers also narrativize discourse that seems to have no perceptible origin. The very term 'camera-eye' technique, for instance, betrays another such narrativization which attempts to correlate the text with a frame from recognizable experience (the VIEWING frame from my level II). When dealing with storytelling in the second person, and with impersonal *one*, *it* and (French) *on* (Chapter 6), I argue that such texts are indeed read, not as a series of actions in the traditional story sense, but as narratives portraying human experience and a human story-world. Readers narrativize such texts by resorting to the EXPERIENCING frame, overruling the oddity in pronominal usage that makes such texts difficult to narrativize within a TELLING frame.

How do natural parameters interrelate with narrativization? '*Natural*' parameters and frames on levels I to III are only indirectly responsible for narrativization. Natural parameters do not *effect* narrativization, but narrativization utilizes natural parameters as *part of* the larger process of naturalization applied by readers to the unfamiliar. Naturalization processes are reading strategies which familiarize the unfamiliar, and they therefore reduce the unexpected to more manageable proportions, aligning it with the familiar. Whereas naturalization and narrativization are interpretative processes, natural parameters or frames are *cognitive* categories of a *synchronic* kind which correlate with real-world knowledge. Narrativization needs to be conceptualized as a cultural and literary process, one in which the concept of the natural plays a crucial structuring role without ever becoming part of the cultural product itself. Although narrativization can ultimately result in the establishment of new genres and new narrative modes, these do not thereby become 'natural'; they merely become recuperable from a semantic and interpretative perspective, and they do so through readers having recourse to natural categories. However, once new texts appear on the scene in massive numbers, as has been the case with the novel of internal focalization or with second-person fiction, they may institute a new genre or a new narrative mode and have to be included as a reference model on level III.

What the above outline yields is an explanation of types of narrative as based on simple cognitive parameters. Thus, one can now comprehend Stanzel's narrative situations as a direct development from natural categories. Fiction with a teller figure evokes situational real-life equivalents of telling and their characteristic constellations. If there is a personalized narrator, for example, a certain cognitive, ideological, linguistic and sometimes even spatio-temporal position may become attributed to that narrator, and she becomes a 'speaker' on the model of the standard communication script. One can thereby explain the entire communicative analysis of fiction as an (illicit) transfer of the frame of real-life conversational narrative onto literary personae and constructed entities (such as that of the notorious 'implied author'). Second, and even more important, one can trace the recurrent personalizations of the narrative function which regularly results in the ontology of a 'narrator' to the influence of the very same schema, namely that of the typical storytelling situation: if there is a story, somebody needs must tell it. Even more absurd, since the earlier (script-logical) tendency to identify the non-personalized narrator with the (historical) author has become untenable in the wake of the Modernist aesthetic, the responsibility for the telling has now been transferred to the (covert) narrator, or the implied author, and that even in narratological circles. The persistence of this preconceived notion that *somebody* (hence a human agent) must be telling the story seems to derive directly from the frame conception of storytelling rather than from any necessary textual evidence.[59]

First-person narrative of course relates back to narratives of personal experience, a model from oral storytelling that has developed into autobiographical proportions. Autobiography itself is actually a fairly late development, long preceded by the third-person form of the *Life*. This is not surprising, after all, since people may easily tell of their adventures, their particular experiences at one point or another, but to write one's own life requires a sustained Augustinian effort to construct from the random succession of remembered scenes (the material of narratives of personal experience) that well-structured tale with teleological shape. *Other* people's lives, paradoxically, are knowable and tellable much more easily, and therefore surface as a genre soon after prose takes over.[60] Likewise, literary third-person narrative, of the authorial type, can now be discussed in terms of storytelling models that derive from the institution of the oral poet and from the shape of the folk tale. The figure of the authorial narrator can then be seen to replace the visible and audible *jongleur* (Kittay and Godzich 1987) and becomes a textual function in its own right with its own subsequent developments in form and function. In so far as literary texts pretend to historical truth and mimetic realism, these functions of the authorial narrator remain linked to actual situations of telling and writing. First-person and authorial narrative are, however, only subtypes of the TELLING frame (level II) and constitute themselves generically (in reference to level III) rather than by direct recourse to natural parameters from levels I and II.

By contrast, the third major narrative situation according to Stanzel, the figural, develops from two quite different directions. On the one hand there is an increased interest in consciousness, usually third-person consciousness, on the part of writers, resulting in an extended portrayal of the mind: early examples are Aphra Behn, Horace Walpole, Ann Radcliffe, and Jane Austen, and – for the first person – Charles Brockden Brown and William Godwin. (Epistolary narrative participates in this emphasis on consciousness.) As long as there is also a continued interest in realism and history, the portrayal of consciousness results in the omniscient type of novel. That is to say, fiction at one point discovers that it can not only present another's mind by conjecture and a little bit of invention (by a stretching of the imagination, so to speak), but can present consciousness extensively as if reading people's minds. This was not yet an available option in the sixteenth-century novel. The willing suspension of disbelief is precisely the attitude that becomes necessary for this quite non-natural narratorial feat (cp. Cohn 1990: 790–1). Once one has been inside people's minds, however, one can dispense with the omniscient narrator convention since 'he' is neither more nor less 'real' than a position from which you look directly inside your characters' minds. From the all-knowing narrator[61] who interferes less and less with the fictional personae it is therefore a brief step towards a textual model that visualizes narrative as directly presenting characters' consciousness. Telling can be dispensed with, readers simply orient themselves to a position within the fictional world; they are no longer constrained to experience the story as something that happened to another person and which they must relate to their own life by means of a conscious effort of empathy and understanding. Figural or reflectoral narrative allows them, instead, to experience the fictional world from within, as if looking out at it from the protagonist's consciousness. Such a reading experience is structured in terms of the natural frame of EXPERIENCING, which includes the experiences of perception, sentiment and cognition. Real-life parameters are transcended. Instead of merely observing and guessing at other people's experiences, frames naturally available only for one's own experience become accessible for application to a third person.

Nevertheless, part of our own everyday experience is still our curiosity about others, and this lack of knowledge has its own charms of a detective and/or voyeuristic kind. In what has been termed neutral narrative the refusal to allow the reader access to consciousness harks back to the real-life experience of observation as much as it self-reflexively refuses expected meanings to the reader, thereby constituting a deliberate literary strategy. Historically, it is no coincidence that neutral narrative was invented precisely at that point in time when readers had come to expect full access to protagonists' consciousness. Such expectation would make the refusal to provide inside views all the more frustrating and therefore spur readers on to attempt to fill the resultant vacuum interpretatively – aligning the deliberate lack of information about characters' emotions and motives with these characters' indifference, inability to face their emotions, incomprehension of actual circumstances, etc. In the absence of a fully fledged evaluative narrator figure the lack of inside view is therefore immediately linked with (mimetic) psychological motivation on the part of a character, and this is especially true for neutral first-person texts. Camera-eye narration has of course also profited from the example of the film, which – as a new experience for readers – provided an interesting aesthetic model. In texts such as Muriel Spark's *The Driver's Seat* (1970) the novel's thematic concerns – the incomprehensibility of a psychopath's mind – become a metaphor for the reader's bewilderment at the narrative presentation which situates her in the position of an uncomprehending observer of compulsive behaviour.

This leaves us with narrative texts that appear to espouse entirely non-narrative models – non-narrative, that is, in the traditional sense of the term. Narratives in the form of drama (the 'Circe' episode of Joyce's *Ulysses*), dialogue (work by Ivy Compton-Burnett and Christine Brooke-Rose, Gabriel Josipovici's *In a Hotel Garden* [1993] or Nathalie Sarraute's *Tu ne t'aimes pas* [1989]), or in question-and-answer format (the 'Ithaca' episode in *Ulysses*) – these all lack narrativity from a merely formal rather than essentially narrative perspective since they can still be read as portraying human experience, even if the reader has to read between the lines to discover the story and/or experience which are buried under the non-narrative cloak. Such readerly ingenuity is called for in even greater measure in experimental texts like Beckett's late prose fiction, in which narrativity appears to be something constituted entirely in the reading process with little notional help from the referential potential of the language. Successful narrative readings of 'Ping' and comparable texts become possible only in so far as one imagines a human agent or experiencer in a situation of radical extremity. Readings that see such texts as wordplay with no existential (fictional) situation attached to it are, I maintain, readings that – *en fin de compte* – refuse the constitutive property of narrativity to these texts.

What does this model 'do' in comparison to the standard paradigms of Genette and Stanzel? As I have illustrated at length in my discussion of narrativity, 'natural' narratology bases itself on a very specific definition of narrative which is thematically identified as the presentation of experientiality. Formally, and I have only hinted this so far, one can now claim that all narrative is built on the mediating function of consciousness. This consciousness can surface on several levels and in different shapes. Consciousness comprises both lived experientiality and intellectual attempts to deal with experience, and it includes the comprehension of actancy just as it necessarily embraces an understanding of mental processes. Narrative modes are therefore all 'resolved' or mediated on the basis of cognitive categories which can be identified as categories of human consciousness. Teller-mode narrative employs the prototype of the human teller, the ruling consciousness of a narrator, to mediate story experience. Figural or reflectoral narrative, on the other hand, makes use of protagonists' consciousness and from that anchorpoint orders narrative experience, relying on a protagonist's consciousness for its centre of cognition, intellection and subjectivity. Neutral narrative and texts that conform to Banfield's 'empty centre' definition (Banfield 1987) place the ordering consciousness in a surrogate figure, that of the reader who 'views' and thereby constructs narrative experience. (For more extensive argument on that score see Chapter 5.)

The four levels of my cognitive model are therefore the operative reader-oriented side of that deep-structural mediation of narrative which employs consciousness as its cognitive structure. It is this cognitive base structure which allows the integration of non-natural forms of storytelling and of all self-reflexive experimental writing into the model of 'natural' narratology. Not only are reflectivity and self-reflexiveness simply facets of human intellection and, in spite of their meta-theoretical character, *part* of the ruling consciousness of the textual producer (intuited in many postmodernist texts as the so-called 'implied author'); meta-reflection itself, as an activity relative to a (meta-)consciousness, can be treated as a level of fictional mediation. The proposed paradigm for 'natural' narratology can now be represented in diagram as follows:

human experientiality = topic of narrative
⇓
mediation (narrativization) by means of consciousness
(a complex natural category with several available frames to choose from)
⇓
narrativity = mediated experientiality

Different forms of constituting consciousness:

(a) protagonist's consciousness (EXPERIENCING) reflector-mode narrative

(b) teller's consciousness   (TELLING)   teller-mode narrative
                                              (REFLECTING)   much experimental
                                                                        self-reflexive fiction

(c) viewer's consciousness   (VIEWING)   neutral narrative;
                                                                         Banfield's empty centre;
                                                                         reflectorization

Towards a 'natural' narratology 51

These options are not categories that apply exclusively to specific texts; they can be combined and extended in the manner that prototypes allow themselves to be extended, and can be applied to new situations. Thus, self-reflective consciousness, based on REFLECTING, is an extension of the frame applied for more standard teller-mode narrative. These most abstract cognitive parameters come into play in the process of reading and interpreting narrative experience.

The proposals that I am sketching here in preliminary form constitute a multi-layered model of the reading process which relies on a combination of cognitive models on each and every level. The most comprehensive prototypes that roughly correspond with narrative situations in Stanzelian terms are in fact describable as metaphorical applications of typical real-world strategies of sense-making: the telling model (with personal experience occupying a privileged position), the experiencing model, the viewing/observation model. Seen in diachronic succession, these patterns allow an excellent insight into the extension of natural parameters, an extension that made possible the development of entirely non-natural models such as that of omniscient and, later, reflector-mode narration. Cognitive models interact with one another creatively so that they cannot be reduced to one simple metaphor applicable at all times and in all places. However, if one allows for the interplay with deliberate writing strategies of the metafictional and self-reflexive kind which have always enhanced as well as subverted prototypical narrative realism, one can broaden the reach of narratological enquiry beyond its present limitations. The above sketch obviously requires some fine-tuning, which will be performed in Chapter 8 after we have taken the applications of the theory in our diachronic stride.

What the present model therefore attempts to do is to rescue diachronic considerations for the study of narrative and to make possible a discussion of narrativity and narrative structure that spans the entire range of available narrative discourses. Hence, not only do I intend to reintroduce those texts which standard paradigms have tended to ignore; I also want to establish a theoretical framework which transforms the standard narratological paradigms into prototypical special cases which can be extended in radial[62] fashion. Such an approach would tend to explain one's intuitive perception that there exists a lack of sufficient and even necessary conditions defining the text-type *narrative*. The representation of human experience is the central aim of narrative, and it can be achieved both by means of the low-level narrativity of action report and by a variety of telling, viewing and experiencing patterns in sophisticated combination. Reading, interpreting and comprehension processes are therefore in this model structured organically or 'naturally' on the basis of prototypicality just as they rely on 'natural' cognitive parameters for their more specific detail. The paramount use of this model, besides that of 'explaining' narrative situations as cognitively relevant categories, would therefore appear to lie in its ability to trace the development of new narrative types – tracing, that is, the active deployment of cognitive strategies which are based on cognitive schemata drawn from real-world experience and prior textual and generic models. Additionally and no less importantly, I attempt to bring together both the most neglected type of narrative – oral storytelling – and the most egregiously playful experimental texts into one project of narratological analysis, illustrating that narrative even of widely disparate forms reposes on the same definable core of narrativity. By these means narratology should finally be provided with a definition of its subject matter, a definition curiously ambiguous in most standard treatments.[63] Naturally, my suggestions will fail to exhaust the subject. After all, this new paradigm is aptly entitled *Towards a 'Natural' Narratology*, leaving ample space for extension and improvement, or even falsification, by those responding to it.

2 Natural narrative and other oral modes

The relationship between the practice of everyday storytelling, on the one hand, and the writing of novels, on the other, has on the whole eluded narratological research. There are various reasons for this state of affairs. For one, there exists a plural consensus that oral narrative and the novel have nothing or very little in common.[1] Narratology, except for its structuralist origins in folk-tale analysis (Propp 1968), has concentrated on *fictional* narrative, mostly on the eighteenth- to twentieth-century *novel*, with some subsidiary consideration of the short story.[2] Recently, there has been a new trend to consider medieval narrative, and narratological insights are currently being brought to bear on the epic.[3] The novel and the epic, as *art* forms, seem to be considerably more sophisticated than conversational narrative, although work on oral poetry suggests a close link between oral literature and the *chansons de geste*, the early German verse epic, and equivalent English forms (Bäuml 1985; J.H. Fisher 1985; J.M. Foley 1985a). To exclude the analysis of oral narrative from narratology is therefore quite unjustified. Formulaic oral poetry, it has been demonstrated, frequently preserves some of the formulaic features and many of the structural and compositional aspects of the oral language on its way from orality to written composition (which originally entailed oral performance). On the other hand, the status of epic formulae in the *written* epic is arguably different from their original function in the still entirely oral literature. Whereas the formulae in oral poetry *enable* composition in performance, in the (written) epic an imperceptible and gradual shift has occurred from the status of an intrinsically compositional factor to that of a stylistic or literary device.[4] One must therefore conceptualize the move from orality to literacy as a continuum that affords the narratologist interesting insights into different functions of narrative elements within their narrative patterns.

Research into the epic and into forms of medieval narrative has so far still left open the basic questions of the precise relation between naturally occurring narrative and folk tales at one end of the literary spectrum and our present-day sophisticated novelistic genre at the other. Structuralist analyses of the folk tale and other 'simple forms'[5] have proved very recalcitrant to adaptation for the novel and the short story, except on a very special thematic-semantic level of deep structure (Greimas 1983). There seems to be a wide gap, a major discontinuity, between simple fairy tales and the novel in its familiar shape. This discontinuity becomes even more marked when one compares, not epic poetry, but everyday conversational stories with fully fledged narrative literature. It is therefore no wonder that this apparent incompatibility between oral and literary narratives has so far stood in the way of a serious analysis of possible structural and functional similarities between oral and written narratives.

Linguistic studies have recently demonstrated more and more interest in the so-called oral structure of medieval texts. The most influential recent work in that area has been Suzanne Fleischman's *Tense and Narrativity* (1990). Fleischman starts out from the thesis that the medieval French epic, which is the endpoint of an oral tradition that came to be formalized in writing at some point, displays a number of features typical of present-day conversational narrative. These features include the structure of narrative episodes describable on the basis of the Labovian model (Labov and Waletzky 1967; Labov 1972), and the occurrence of the 'performative' historical present. (Fleischman relies on the work of Schiffrin [1981] and Wolfson [1982], both of whom work in the Labovian tradition.) Independently from Fleischman, a research group in Freiburg im Breisgau, Germany, has concentrated on the transitional features between the oral and the literary media and on the dialectics between orality and literacy within a continuum of genres and texts.[6] Work done in this research group includes analyses of the medieval contexts for the orality–literacy spectrum and the examination of present-day intertextuality and 'inter-orality.' The theoretical framework on which these projects rely is that of Koch and Österreicher (1985). A fundamental distinction is made between *medium-related* orality and literacy (*mediale Mündlichkeit/Schriftlichkeit*) and *conceptual* orality and literacy, i.e. the description of the *linguistic features typical of* the oral or written language respectively (*konzeptionelle Mündlichkeit/Schriftlichkeit*). That these latter features are not exclusive attributes of either oral or written discourse but need to be arranged on a scale between typical orality and typical literacy is evident from the necessity of accommodating the interaction of such features: only a proportionally higher use of, say, oral features across *several* categories will push a text into the 'oral' end of the scale.[7] I will return to the difficult question of what 'oral features' in written discourse might consist of at a later point. The Freiburg model has recently introduced another pair of processual concepts, those of *Verschriftung* (medial transcoding) and *Verschriftlichung* (conceptual transcoding), which designate aspects of the transition from the oral to the written realm.[8] Conceptual transcoding characterizes the refunctionalization of oral material within the written genre, and it is therefore the process that is most relevant to my own concerns.

Before one can tackle this problem and the questions of origin (if there are supposedly 'oral features' in written discourse, can they be argued to derive directly from the oral language?), it will be well to study the oral by itself by way of a prior exposure to the functioning of oral discourse. Only after a thorough analysis of the spoken language can one legitimately start to compare early written texts with the oral system and attempt to elucidate the existence of an oral substratum in the written medium. Recent accounts of epic poetry (Goody 1987 is a case in point) have again undermined earlier confident pronouncements on the essential orality of the Homeric oeuvre, and the simple equation of parataxis with underlying orality is just as problematic (see Stempel 1964). The proposals that I am offering in this study therefore attempt to elude a purely linguistic argument based on 'oral' features (parataxis, discourse particles) and to substitute for it a narratological cognitive *frame* related to discourse *structure*. In so far as structural patterns typical of oral types of narration can be observed to survive in written texts, I will suggest that they can then legitimately be called reflexes of oral structures of storytelling, with the immediate proviso that oral structures *function differently* in the written medium and are subject to quite extensive remodelling for the various purposes of the more literary genres.

Conversational narrative and other forms of naturally occurring narrative have been dismissed too hastily as being (supposedly) irrelevant to the study of the novel and other more literary types of narration. By ignoring the common narrative essence underlying both natural and literary storytelling, narratology has effectively failed to come into its own as a comprehensive discipline: it has remained entrenched in the purely literary camp of fiction and/or the novel. More recent trends in narratology that have started to deal with *non-fiction* genres (biography, history, faction)[9] have, I believe, helped to point the way towards a more adequate representation of narrative in all its manifestations. Although these approaches (Cohn 1989, 1990; Genette 1990) still concentrate on highly complex narrative forms and indeed posit very abstract criteria of differentiation between the fictional and the non-fictional (the identities of author, narrator and character; the representation of consciousness), they nevertheless in their own way develop the insights from Ricoeur's trilogy on time and narrative (Ricoeur 1983–85/1984–88) which so signally attempts to bridge the gap between the literary and the historical.

What other literary narrative forms are there besides these historical, non-fictional book-length texts? There is, first, the *epic*, which has been treated as a predecessor of the novel and has therefore already received quite extensive treatment from literary narratologists, as well as, more recently, from oral poetry scholars, inspired by the work of Milman Parry. In Chapter 3, when considering medieval and early modern narrative, I will therefore concentrate instead on the romance and on the shorter forms: the tale (including its medieval avatars such as the *fabliau*), the saint's legend, the homiletic exemplum, and on the pre-eighteenth-century novelistic romance. The anecdote, another short oral form, is discussed at the end of this chapter (2.3.2). Among *oral* forms to be considered in the present chapter I will concentrate on conversational storytelling (experiential narrative) and on the joke. All these types of narrative, written and oral – with the exception of the avatars of the short story (from the *Decameron* to Aphra Behn) – share one prominent feature: they are structured on an episodic pattern that operates in a recursive manner, whereby a series of episodes is strung together one after the other (Ermarth 1981; Fludernik 1991). Episodic narrative structure will therefore have to be presented in some detail below. Classic analyses of narrative plot have concentrated precisely on what are generally regarded to be episodic tales: the Proppian corpus of Russian fairy tales, Bremond's folk tales, and Todorov's example-stories from the *Decameron*.[10] The standard narratological typologies, on the other hand, have tended to analyse plot in terms of the interaction of the discourse and story levels of the narrative and have concentrated on the textual rearrangement of the story chronology. Important as this aspect is for the understanding of the novel, it neglects to consider the dynamics of the reading process[11] and downplays the similarities between different types of episodic narrative. An interesting proposal that significantly develops the analysis of plotting is Marie-Laure Ryan's (1987) essay on the window structure of narrative, in which she attempts to do justice to the dynamic factor in plot architecture. Ryan stresses characters' intentions and plans as well as their wishes and hopes, and the effect of these on possible plot development. Incorporating these several layers of fictional virtualities, the model provides for a more complex account of narrative in process than traditional plot analysis allows. Yet even Ryan's account uses a simple text, a fairy tale, as its object of analysis – a move that helps to upgrade the fairy tale but puts in doubt a possible application to the novel.[12]

Narratological approaches therefore interact with critics' historical agendas: the fairy-tale approach can be appropriate also for the sixteenth-century novel – which is, however, usually treated in novelistic terms – and much medieval episodic narrative can be analysed profitably in terms of the story/discourse opposition which is generally applied only to the novel. What is therefore needed is a much clearer sense of the narrative properties of non-literary or non-fictional genres and of their (dis)similarities in relation to one another. Once such a survey has been carried out, it becomes clear that fiction, or what has hitherto been analysed *qua* fiction, can no longer remain the same when seen in the light of its debts to natural narrative and the earlier episodic tale. In particular, it is then possible to analyse much more precisely in what ways the prototype of the novel departs from earlier narrative genres. There appears to be an almost unbridgeable gap between the episodic and the non-episodic, yet one can also discover a good number of features which survive from natural narrative well into the most recent novel on the market. Such features include the functions of the narrator figure, which can involve address to a listener (or to a fictional narratee); moralizing and evaluative commentary; explicit distancing from the story-events as well as empathetic identification with the protagonists; quite deliberate structural trimming of the story in the process of producing a plot; as well as mimetic impersonation on the basis of discourse representation (including the attribution of typical mental responses to narrative agents).[13] Although literary fictions can *in principle* dispense with all of these features (except, arguably, story configuration and speech and thought representation), many of them recur with great frequency in standard literary prose. Commentary, for instance, is a common ingredient of most literary narrative, excepting only reflector-mode narration.[14] Yet, as I will argue below in Chapters 4 and 5, even narratives that seemingly allow us a view through the window of a character's mind do not institute an entirely new type of narrative incompatible with the structure of conversational storytelling. Quite on the contrary, they radicalize the story core of human experience that is already present at the heart of oral episodic narrative.

In the following I will describe some of the basic features of various types of natural narrative and attempt to document how written narratives refunctionalized features of the oral tale for their own purposes. This is a speculative and preliminary survey; a definitive historical treatment would presuppose access to a wide spectrum of data that are not yet fully accessible. Since my ulterior purpose in this book is to reinterpret theoretical positions in narratology, I will here merely sketch the outline of such historical research.[15]

2.1 ORAL TYPES OF STORYTELLING: A GENERIC OVERVIEW

There are at least three major naturally occurring types of conversational storytelling with related genres and subcategories, besides a number of other oral modes which occur 'naturally' – that is to say, cross-culturally – but exceed the frame of a spontaneous conversational setting. Boundaries may be fluid between the various types, as for instance in TV discussions and documentary features on the radio, in some of which spontaneous narration may emerge despite the inherently formal, elicitational aspects of the setting.[16]

In the area of spontaneous conversation I will distinguish between the following three genres:

(a) *Experiential conversational storytelling* – the prototype of natural narrative. Conversational storytelling concentrates on story experience: one's own (*stories of personal experience*) or another's (*stories of vicarious experience*). This type of narrative has received extensive analysis in linguistic circles (Labov, Harweg, Schiffrin, H. Sacks, Johnstone, Jefferson,

Wolfson, Tannen, Quasthoff) and we therefore have accumulated a fair amount of information about this familiar oral genre. Under 2.2.2 below I distinguish one further category – that of *observational narrative*.

(b) **Narrative report**. Much narrative in conversation does not develop into a proper 'story' but simply provides a summary of the speaker's doings, of certain events or developments. In so far as this type of narration can be analysed in terms of 'narrative clauses' (Labov 1972), it is necessarily *narrative*. However, since no experiential quality can be attributed to the subject matter of the narrative (which is, precisely, a report and not a *story*), the discourse structure and narrative patterns observable in narrative report are demonstrably different from those in experiential narrative.

(c) A third type of spontaneous conversational storytelling is that of the *joke* and/or the *anecdote*. Although there exists some quite extensive literature on the humour of jokes (see, e.g. Preisendanz and Warning 1976, or M.T. Goldsmith 1991), I know of only one excellent discourse-analytic study of jokes (Euler 1991). Jokes, which are only imperfectly distinguishable from anecdotes,[17] are structured in close affinity to experiential tales but – for obvious reasons – handle the 'point' of the story differently from most experiential narratives. Jokes frequently conclude with a punch line (which may or may not hinge on a pun), and – unlike conversational narratives of personal or vicarious experience – they play with the generic expectations of the listener, manipulating two levels of story understanding which then converge in the punch line. In one common type of joke a seemingly quasi-realistic situation is presented which, in the punch line, is then radically undermined and requires the reconstruction of an alternative (realistic or absurd) account of events. The 'point' of the joke, as a consequence, tends to lie in the *conjunction* of, on the one hand, the disparities between the two versions of the events and, on the other hand, the unexpectedness (absurdity) of the belated recognition of the 'true' explanation of the 'plot'. This concluding high point already constitutes a major departure from the story pattern of experiential narrative. Experiential narratives, by contrast, tend to deal with an unexpected turn of events which frustrates the experiencer's expectations. Jokes, in addition, simplify or elide the initial segments of the experiential story pattern since no elaborate real-world pre-understandings need to be invoked for the listener. They can not only dispense with the initial abstract and orientation sections (if one adheres to the Labovian schema) but also elide practically all orientational and evaluative commentary on what I call the off-plotline level of the narrative (see below).

I now turn to types of storytelling which have a non-spontaneous setting. They are either elicited or situate themselves in a storytelling frame of cross-individual cultural tradition. The following genres should be distinguished.

(a) *Folkloristic oral storytelling (prose)*. Such storytelling continues to exist in Canada, for instance in Nova Scotia among Acadians, and no doubt widely among Native Americans and in Africa.[18] The characteristic features of such storytelling events include their culturally determined setting (tale tellers are invited as guest performers; the telling observes structural and organizational formats), their performative and communal quality (tale tellers hold the floor for considerable periods of time; storytelling may alternate with prescribed responses from the audience in ritualistic fashion), the professional status of the storyteller (not everybody has the talent to become a narrator or is allowed to perform as a storyteller), and the thematic restriction of the subject matter of such tales (incorporating what one would define as mythology or folklore).

(b) *Epic poetry (verse)*. In its cultural *setting* epic poetry is indistinguishable from (a), but tends to confine itself to heroic deeds of the distant past and to the verse form. In contrast to the folk tale, which has received little *linguistic* analysis (although ethnologists and folklorists have studied such tales in great detail), oral poetry is one of the most extensively discussed oral forms, although the results in this area have been far from satisfactory. Oral poetry research suffers from an intrinsic lack of reliable data and from the cultural disparity between the few available recordings. Thus the Homeric epics exist only in *written* form and their comparison to Yugoslav *guslar* poetry is at best speculative. Second, researchers are usually conversant in only *one* cultural environment (and language), and evaluations about the similarities or dissimilarities between, say, the Homeric epics and *guslar* poetry or the Ghanaian epics (Goody 1987) are therefore self-confessedly imprecise, having to rely on other people's descriptions of the characteristics of the oral performance, on translations of an unfamiliar language and on second-hand explanations of the cultural context. Recent research appears to suggest that, at least for oral poetry, the famous thesis of Milman Parry and Albert B. Lord (Lord 1960) can no longer be maintained in its original version: formulaic language, although arguably a remnant of oral structures, cannot in and of itself have been the main structuring factor of oral delivery. As an alternative Goody (1987) proposes a cognitive model of bards' retention of the text in units of narrative episodes (with recurring formulae), and suggests that the formulaic language such as we observe it in Homer is already the *result* of written composition.[19]

(c) *The life story*. This also is a longer type of narrative. It may occur in spontaneous conversation ('Granny, I've always wanted to ask you what happened to you during the war'), but more recently has been the hunting ground of oral historians, who have tried to elicit life stories in fairly non-spontaneous settings (tape recorder, interview format, etc.). The life story obviously is no complete autobiography. Very rarely indeed is there a situation in which people will be led to narrate their entire life from their

60 Natural narrative and other oral modes

birth to the present moment. Exceptions may be initial sections of interviews ('Well, to start with, tell me something about yourself') or – perhaps a rather exceptional situation – meeting a new partner and catching up on one's respective background. Life stories, as I have called them, tend to be focused thematically, for instance on the narrator's childhood, war experience, career (cultural environment) – e.g. 'your life in the theatre' – and participation in historical or political events/movements (again: war experiences, 'your membership of the Communist Party', 'your life as a suffragette'). These days interviews conducted in an oral-history framework, however, additionally attempt to elicit less event-oriented experience and more of the implicit *mentalité* of their subjects so that questions about people's *opinions, attitudes* and *superstitions* figure prominently. Leading questions on such topics frequently trigger spontaneous conversational narratives since interviewees will illustrate their opinions by reference to personal experience.[20] TV and radio discussions, although embedded in a structural setting that is very different from the above, usually combine a variety of storytelling forms that emerge in a spontaneous manner. Some radio and television programmes have narrational output that corresponds to the life story model[21] (feature programmes), some encourage the life-story pattern even in discussion, some cultivate a relaxed atmosphere which allows for experiential narrative and even jokes, and some are very formal and tend to bar anything more lengthy or more personal than narrative report.

In the following I will concentrate on experiential narrative and on the joke as the two most common types of natural narrative.

2.2 NATURAL NARRATIVE: THE CREATION OF STORY MEANING

Recent work in discourse analysis has helped to define the properties of oral discourse in unprecedented detail. The mass of scholarship on oral discourse has indeed become difficult to sift, and van Dijk's four-volume handbook (van Dijk 1985) can be recommended as a general introduction to the diversity of methods and approaches now observable in the field.

When dealing with natural *narrative* one needs to distinguish carefully between characteristics of oral discourse *in general* and the specific uses to which these are put for narrative purposes in a storytelling context. For instance, main and subsidiary clauses have to be distinguished on a formal level; foreground and background, on the other hand, are *functional* concepts, as are the concepts *rheme/theme* and *topic/focus*. Thus, if one considers the text-type *argument*, background and foreground are realized in terms of presupposition and new information (the given/new distinction),[22] whereas, in the text-type *narrative*, foreground and background tend to be conceptualized in terms of plot structure (foreground) and supernumerary information (background). Neither functional distribution can be correlated with syntax in any simple one-to-one relation. Moreover, the general given/new or theme/rheme distribution is of course relevant to narrative, too, and not only in terms of plot: narrative cannot be treated as entirely divorced from 'ordinary' conversation or 'ordinary' oral discourse. Not only do general discourse features such as topic/focus distribution impinge on narrative; natural narrative also has a noticeable *communicative* text level which, in its potential for incorporating all types of discursive and addressee-oriented discourse features, immediately refutes a strict theoretical dichotomy between 'ordinary' discourse and narrative. Nevertheless narratives may also be argued to employ discourse features for specifically narrative ends.

The most striking examples of the narrative appropriation and reinterpretation of general discourse elements are perhaps the narrative use of repetition and the narrative exploitation of intonational factors. Repetition in conversation is a topic that has been widely studied.[23] One key analysis of repetition in narrative is Polanyi's (1978) study which demonstrates the use of repetition to mark re-entry onto the plotline after digressive asides of an explicatory or commentatory nature. Here is a brief example of this type:

B: {...} he said could you come now so he. described where it was and *off I went* — {...} frightfully expansive collection of flats set in {...} gardens {...} very well kept and everything you know
A: m
B: m - so *off I went*. the flat was {...}

(Bublitz 1989, handout)[24]

In 'ordinary' conversation, however, repetition occurs in a variety of different functions, such as the signalling of agreement, or for emphasis, hesitation, emotional foregrounding, and so on.

WA: could ha / I thought / it was very nice
BE: oh
MA: oh it *really* - it *really* was (.) it was super

('Yum Chow'; Couper-Kuhlen 1994)

Similarly, in everyday communication one will observe that pitch levels, pauses, intonation structures and volume levels are used for a variety of different functions, emphatic or emotional. Moreover, they interact to mark off prosodic units such as the basic tone unit (see below) as well as more extensive semantic or thematic blocks of discourse. In narrative, as I have argued (Fludernik 1991, 1992a), the interaction of pitch and volume serves to relieve the plot foreground against the orientational background structure, a contrast that can additionally be marked by means of syntactic or temporal (tense-alternation) signals.

Another crucial factor to be taken into consideration in natural narrative is that of the circumstances or setting of the production of discourse. In particular, spontaneous conversational storytelling differs greatly from storytelling performed in interviews or narration in storytelling sessions. In both of the latter cases, the stories are usually longer, which can result in a looser structure (drifting from one memory to another) or in complex, even 'literary' techniques (see, for instance, some of the interviews in Studs Terkel's collections), and in the repetitive many-layered structure of much oral folk narrative. These longer forms do not have to contend with the problems of the narrator's having to hold the floor. The conversational narrator, by contrast, needs to make great efforts to hold the floor, for instance by coming to the point right away and then backtracking for vital background information – all manoeuvres which result in an apparently random and 'urgent' structure and produce the multi-levelled economy of the conversational tale. I will come back to these differences below. Genre and narrational context (the setting of the storytelling) therefore impinge crucially on how many features of ordinary conversation can be preserved in the storytelling format.

Besides these framing conditions one also has to note the structural properties of conversational language itself. As Chafe (1977a, 1977b) has noted with great acuity, the oral language is structured as a succession of what he calls *idea units* which allow one to produce or process only one major idea at a time. Chafe links the notion of the idea unit with that of recall and activation, measuring pauses before the onset of individual words and phrases as indicative of the required time of recall. Chafe's analysis of the spoken language, which is in large measure corroborated by the transcripts of Svartvik and Quirk (1979), has serious consequences for syntactic theories of language.[25] The oral language is structured much more loosely than written discourse (Halford and Pilch 1990), and many idea units are not complete sentences, although they frequently consist of constituents and can include complete basic sentences or subordinate/coordinate clauses.

One interesting conclusion to be drawn from conversational analysis, for example, concerns the status of subsidiary clauses. Only brief restrictive relative clauses can be included within one idea unit (such as *the man I paid yesterday*); subsidiary and coordinate clauses all go into a separate idea unit, and this renders them *intonationally* equivalent. It is therefore rare to find an introductory subsidiary clause except for *when, if,* or *while* clauses, and the common subsidiary *because, though,* or *when* clauses emerge as intonationally coordinative rather than subordinated. This is most obvious for *when* clauses, which frequently initiate plotline action.[26] Conjunctions in the oral language, in fact, largely appear to operate on the lines of discourse markers such as *so, well, now* and the like. Indeed, the difference between discourse markers and conjunctions seems to be quite fluid. *So,* for instance, can do multiple duty, signalling a return to the plotline, performing as a causal conjunction as well as an adverb of manner ('therefore', 'then', 'in this manner'). As I will note below, these discourse markers fulfill important roles as signals of structural points in narrative. They can mark the story's return to the plotline after a digression (such as embedded orientation, commentary), signal the result section of the narrative, and they also serve to flag new episode beginnings.

2.2.1 The features of conversational storytelling: the experiential mode

Conversational narrative is characterized above all by its framing. It occurs in separate conversational sequences that are set off from the surrounding discourse. The primary feature – highlighted in Mary L. Pratt's (1977) study – is that of *turn-taking*. As a consequence, conversational narratives are almost always announced or invited explicitly, to ensure that the audience will yield the floor for a lengthier period of time.

(a) What are the . . the strangest things that've . . . happened to . . . you during your career as a public analyst?
('The Missing Sparrow'; Couper-Kuhlen 1994)

(b) I'll never forget this one time I went to play (.) uh miniature golf
('Miniature Golf'; ibid.)

(c) I'll tell you a story now about nuns
(Fludernik 1991: 383)

(d) Somebody told me you almost got in a punch-out at a gas station
(Wolfson 1982: 38)

Conversational narratives therefore share a common abstract pattern with the initiating sequences of jokes and anecdotes.

In naturally occurring storytelling situations storytellers are awarded turns which they attempt to hold. Narrators operate under the constraint to meet *tellability* or *reportability* requirements; they have to ward off a listener's potential threatening 'so what?' (Labov 1972). This constraint can be interpreted as the source of the observable structural properties of conversational storytelling. The speaker must attempt to get to the point as fast as possible, postponing background information to a later point (when it is supplied as embedded orientation), and she has to evaluate the *significance* of the experience recounted, clarifying the story's 'point' (Labov and Waletzky 1967). The resulting structure can be split into a plotline and an off-plotline level of the story, in which the plotline includes the initial orientation, the story episodes and the final result and evaluation, whereas the off-plotline level combines embedded orientation and interspersed evaluative or explicatory commentary (Fludernik 1991, 1992a).

A third important factor connected with framing is the constant interaction between interlocutors even during turn-taking time. This feature of conversational storytelling has received ample analysis. Thus, it has been found that listeners signal their continuing interest in the story by *mnh* etc., nodding and other gestural indications (Goodwin 1981; Goodwin and Goodwin 1987), the gist of which is: 'please proceed'. Listeners also may get very involved in a story, supplying their own lines. As Tannen (1989: 115–26, 119–21) demonstrates, listeners sometimes hazard a guess as to what a story protagonist said, elaborate on the ongoing story by supplying protagonists' verisimilar discourse, draw moral or other conventional maxims from the narrative. And, of course, they continually interrupt to ask questions, and register their surprise, solidarity, empathetic anger, etc., by a number of exclamatory devices:

M: I don't know if I'll ever run another one [Marathon] or not (.) I had such a bad experience in the last one and- what with M. almost getting killed (.) I'm afraid to ask anybody to come
M: ⎰ with me
B: ⎱ What happened?
M: he got run over by a car
    ⎰ when he came with me
B: ⎱ **are you kidding**

('Marathon Race'; Couper-Kuhlen 1994)

Duncan (1974), Sacks (1986, 1987) and Bublitz (1988) have also documented how the listener's reaction or non-reaction directly influences the storytelling, as, for instance, when the narrator mentions somebody's name, and continues to elaborate on that person's identity until she receives a recognition signal (*o yea*, etc.) from the listener.

Moreover, storytelling fulfils discourse-related functions. It is not just gratuitous, non-serious 'play'. Tannen has, for instance, demonstrated very perspicaciously how storytelling is conducted, not in the spirit of truth or information, but in order to create or preserve face. Narratives in spontaneous conversation are frequently told to demonstrate that one is a 'good' and 'reliable' person, or they attempt to create emotional solidarity with the listener. For example, people often try to gain somebody's approval or attention by narrating a story about a topic of interest to that person. As Tannen notes, much 'behind somebody's back' discussion, although seemingly treacherous, derives from an attempt to appease one's immediate listener or to ingratiate oneself with him/her (Tannen 1990). I still remember how my mother, who is as a rule quite proud of my academic achievements, in a conversation with my British landlady went out of her way to lament my unnatural interest in books (and my then disinterest in cooking), and how furious I was about this, interpreting this as her having changed over to the 'enemy side' of those wishing to see women behind the proverbial stove. Since, as Tannen suggests, the main objective of women's conversation is to create mutual trust and friendship (what she calls intimacy), such temporary swaying from one's real position on certain issues can be seen as a natural consequence of this general attempt to create an atmosphere of solidarity in ongoing conversational interaction. My mother, for instance, in my own best interests was trying to ingratiate herself with my landlady, who, being a traditional housewife, had little sympathy for my academic leanings.

I now come to the more particularly *narrative properties* of natural storytelling. As I have suggested elsewhere (Fludernik 1991, 1992a), the structure of oral narrative can be described in terms of two interacting levels which are set apart from one another by means of intonational features and tense usage.

(a) *The off-plotline level*. The major off-plotline category is that of embedded orientation. In contrast to William Labov's narrative structure, I reanalyse embedded orientation to include much that Labov situates on the plotline. Embedded orientation in my concept therefore comprises all background information that relates to the current story extension (what Harweg [1975a] calls the *endogenic situative*) as well as all background information that extends temporally beyond the immediate story frame (Harweg's *exogenic situative*), and it also includes intonationally marked 'asides'. For instance, in l. 22 of the story quoted below ('but it was a very very large campground') the embedded orientation relates to an external existential factor that temporally exceeds the time limits of the adventure, whereas l. 68 ('so there was this large stick we had in the tent') refers to the time-frame of the story. An example of an aside is l. 73 ('not knowing exactly what I was gonna do'). The second important off-plotline category is current commentary, whether evaluative or explicatory. See, for instance, l. 30 ('I don't know what time it was').

(b) *The on-plotline level*. Whereas off-plotline units, as asides, are subordinated intonationally, the on-plotline units are merged with the framing conversation by preserving pitch and volume levels (usually markedly decreased – and sometimes increased – for the off-plotline). The basic

---

Abstract – Orientation – {[episode 1][episode 2][...][episode n]} – evaluation – coda

↑ initial incipit ↑ final resolution

Episode pattern:
   incipit – (narrative clauses) – setting – incidence(s) – situative – result(s) [27]

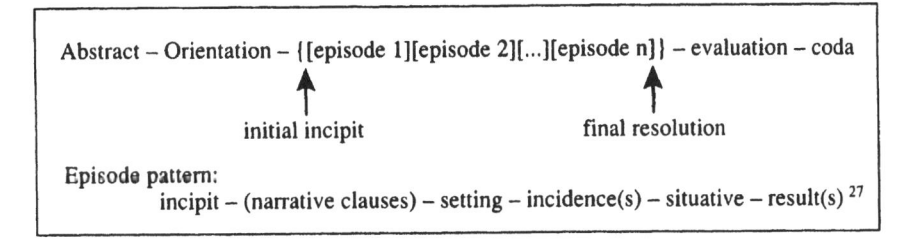

Figure 1 Basic story structure for experiential narrative

story structure therefore consists of the following sequence, – a schema developed further from Labov (1972) and Harweg (1975a) in Figure 1 (see p.65). In this diagram the initial *incipit*, which introduces the story proper as well as its first episode, is frequently marked by a temporal specifier (*one day, that afternoon*, a specific date) and triggers a narrative past tense. The central part of each story is taken up by a series of narrative episodes. Each episode culminates in an *incidence* that occurs on the background of a state or ongoing activity which I have called the *setting*. This incidence is an event that impinges from outside onto the setting (Pollak 1988; Harweg's exogenic progredient [Harweg 1975a]). The episode concludes on a *result* slot which provides closure and serves as a transition to the next incipit of the following episode. It should be noted right away that I differ from Labov in placing the setting *on* the plotline (he classifies it as embedded orientation) and in arguing for the presence of *incipit* and *incidence* points in the schema. I additionally depart from Labov by arguing that the incidence is invariably followed by a *result* slot – an insight I owe to the temporal markers uncovered by Harweg (1975a). Although the functions of the result and evaluation sections became clear to Labov's follower Schiffrin, the important distinction between the result/reaction point and the final evaluation was never made explicit (Schiffrin 1981). An unexpected corroboration of this functional difference can be noted in the use of verb tenses in Italian conversational narrative (Centineo 1991; cp. Fludernik 1994e), where the result and evaluation sections are set off against each other by means of temporal choices.

Here is an example of a conversational story, a narrative of personal experience, with all the categories marked appropriately:

1	P:	a couple of years ago	**orientation**
2		I was working in Banff /	
3		driving a taxi /	
4		when the summer was over /	
5		I acquired a car	**orientation/abstract**
6		from a rental company↕	
7		and drove it back to Toronto	
8		< from Banff > //	
9		and I went back↕	**delayed orientation/off-plot**
10		I drove back with this girl I knew //	
11	I:	Catherine //	
12	P:	and yeah //	
13		and the second day of driving /	**incipit: Episode 1**
14		the second night we stopped↕	
15		we were only in Saskatchewan	
16		< that's as far as we got > //	**off-plot comment**
17		and we stopped at this campground	**narrative clause**

Natural narrative and other oral modes 67

18	< I forget the name of the campground > /	**comment**
19	but since it was the first week in September ↕	**setting**
20	there was no other campers /	
21	or maybe one or two other campers //	
22	but it was a very very large campground //	**embedded orientation**
23	*and so* we set up our tent /	**narrative clauses/incidences**
24	and had hot dogs and beans /	
25	and marshmallows over the fire /	
26	and all those other Canadian treats //	
27	*and then* uh it got dark↕	**closure of Episode 1**
28	and we went to bed //	

29	and uh perhaps about one or two in the morning	**incipit: Episode 2**
30	< I don't know what time it was >	**comment**
31	I was sort of half awake /	**setting**
32	and uh uh the girl Catherine woke me up↕	**incidence**
33	+ Paul / Paul / Paul /	
34	there's something outside /	
35	there's something outside + //	
36	< and I thought >	**result/evaluation**
37	[ts] yeah yeah //	
38	girls' imagination //	
39	there's nothing outside //	

40	*but* uh sure enough ↕	**Episode 3**
41	there was something outside //	**incidence (perception)**
42	I heard it a little later too //	
43	and uh 't was footsteps //	
44	actually quite a [f] quite a lot of footsteps	
45	< and I was thinking	**setting**
46	oh / >	
47	what the hell could that be //	
48	like there was no other campers around us //	**delayed orientation, but**
49	and it was 's dark /	**really comment on setting**
50	and it's quiet /	
51	and it's in the woods ↕	
52	and you started to get scared /	
53	and started to worry //	
54	and I was listening	**setting**
55	and it was like there was more than /	**perceptions (incidence)**
56	there was more than /	

57	one set of footsteps //	
58	and there was quite a few sets of footsteps /	
59	and they were sort of circling the tent //	
60	and I thought	**result/evaluation**
61	oh God (laughs)	
62	this is it //	
63	you know my time has come //	**comment**
64	*but* I thought	**result 2**
65	well since I am the uh the man in the tent /	
66	I'll have to uh stay calm /	
67	and uh protect the female /	
68	*so* there was this large stick we had in the tent /	**delayed orientation**
69	and I said to the girl	**result 3**
70	< I said you know > ↕	
71	+ don't worry + //	
72	I'll take care of it //	
73	not knowing exactly what I was gonna do //	**comment**

74		*but anyways* I picked up the stick /	**incipit: Episode 4**
75		put my head to the door /	**narrative clause**
76		and I couldn't see anything /	
77		and I stepped out //	**narrative clause**
78		then ↕	
79		(laughs) I was confronted by the footsteps //	**incidence**
			result missing for reasons of suspense
80		it turned out to be	**summary**
81		< you know I thought perhaps it had been wolves or something	**comment**
82		but it just turned out that they were Wiener dogs //	**summary**
83		don't ask me /	**comment**
84		what Wiener dogs were doing in the woods /	
85		I have no idea /	
86		I don't know who owned them //	
87		but I I maybe one Wiener dog may may have made sense /	**comment**
88		but there was maybe five or six Wiener dogs /	
89		little tiny Wiener dogs circling the tent //	
90		*and* I just	
91	I:	(laughs)	
92	P:	started laughing //	**result 1**
93		no threat there //	**evaluation/thought**
94		*so* I went back to bed /	**result 2**
95		told the girl that we were just surrounded by Wiener dogs /	**narrative clauses**

96	she couldn't believe it //	**comment**
97	she checked too /	**comment**
98	and and she started to laugh ↕	**result 3**
99	and then we went to sleep /	**final resolution 4**
100	no problem //	**story-internal evaluation**
101	our lives were not in danger //	

(Halford 1993: 343–4; Hoffbauer 1991: 84–6;[28] Halford's notations)

I've deliberately picked an 'ordinary' messy story. The narrator tells us how he was camping on a campground in Saskatchewan and how he and his girlfriend were surprised by what sounded like footsteps and how, harmlessly, it turned out to be Wiener dogs. The central two episodes of the story are therefore the moments of fear inside the tent and the heroic effort of checking, which is followed by (comic) relief. The 'point' of the story is both the scary nature of the experience and – a face-projecting feature – the protagonist's courage in adversity. In contrast to the idealized schema for narratives of personal experience, this story does not have any incidences proper besides the ones mentioned already: the storyteller being woken up and hearing the 'footsteps'. On the contrary much is made of the *actions* of the campers. In the first episode, for instance, marked clearly by intonational features, there is merely an establishment of 'scene', installing oneself on the campground and having a good time, the central 'point' of which is setting up tent (l. 23), and which is concluded by the couple retiring for the night. The second central episode then starts right into the setting – 'in the middle of the night' – and the experiencer's first incidence is being woken up, which is followed by his first, as yet unconcerned, reaction.

At this point the speaker's evaluation of events takes over to such an extent that one can either speak of an elaboration of episode 2 or posit a new episode (without incipit): the central realization of the protagonist that somebody or something (a bear?) *is* circling the tent constitutes an experiential core which closely resembles an incidence. Alternatively, following Harweg's model (1975a), the first part of episode 3 could be handled as a postincidental *situative* (exogenic situative): the protagonist's *perception* of events and states connected with the incidence. Episode 3 elaborates on the situation of the protagonist, performatively highlighting his predicament by means of elaborate 'quotations' from his thoughts (already in the previous episode). Lines 49–53 are particularly 'involving' (Wolfson 1982) or empathy-creating: they switch from the summary comment (it *was* dark) to a historical present emphasizing the protagonist's realization of being enclosed by darkness, and then implicitly motivate the storyteller's fear by recourse to a general *topos* of natural human fear in darkness and isolation. This involvement of the listener is underlined by the use of the second-person pronoun *you* (in the meaning of 'one'). It marks the special status of this passage, which is *both* story material (what the protagonist felt) *and* an appeal to the listener on common grounds of humanity, asking for empathy.

Episode 4, much more straightforwardly, details the protagonist's resolution to do something and the enaction of this decision. Episode 4 is action-oriented, concentrating as its topic on the confrontation with the dogs. The incidence (what the narrator eventually encounters on exiting from the tent) is in fact delayed and replaced by the commentary and evaluation, another trick to emphasize the disorientation of the protagonist and the reportability (i.e. weirdness) of the experience.

The final repetitious result-events constitute a report on how the narrator got back to 'bed', noting the woman's disbelief and her checking up on the dogs, incidences that are mentioned rather than elaborately told (as they might have been from *her* perspective). The tale concludes on a note of story-internal evaluation, portraying what the couple must have been thinking as they settled back to sleep (the last line can characteristically be read as free indirect discourse).

Incipit and result points in this tale are the most marked units or slots in the story schema: observe the discourse markers *and so* (l. 23), *and then* (l. 27), *but* (l. 40/l. 64), *so* (l. 68),[29] *but anyways* (l. 74), *so* (l. 94). This observation is crucial in terms of the development of narrative structure in written texts. As we will see in the next chapter, medieval and early modern narratives emphasize episode beginnings and endings by similar discourse markers (*so, well*) and additionally employ inversion and preposing patterns to emphasize the episodic structure. Moreover, one can already observe in this oral tale how the purely experiential model is always already flanked by reportative sequences and how these (at first) affect the centre of episodes rather than their circumference. The incidences at these points are increasingly – to use Harweg's terminology – endogenic progredients rather than exogenic progredients: things no longer happen to the protagonist; he (or she) becomes active instead. The shift is from what happens to the protagonist to what the protagonist himself achieves out of cunning or adventurousness. Experientiality in narratives of personal experience consists in the dynamic interrelation between the description of personal experience on the one hand (the setting-plus-incidence core of the narrative episode) and the evaluative and rememorative transformation of this experience in the storytelling process: tellability and point of the story dialectically constitute each other. The narrative is a narrative, not because it tells a story, but because the story that it tells is reportable and has been reinterpreted by the narrating I, the personal storyteller. Oral narratives of personal experience do not obey a teleological pattern except in so far as the story has an endpoint, an ulterior point of reference from which it is told retrospectively. A complex organic unity is established which balances experience in the raw and the storyteller's re-evaluation of it. Stories of personal experience epitomize typically human experience by representing it in the shape of an objective correlative that is organic in form and function.

2.2.2 Report, observational narrative and the vicarious mode

As we have noted there are several kinds of natural storytelling, taken in the minimal sense of spontaneous oral narration of past events. Although people tell each other stories all day long, some of these narratives are quite different from others, both in their purpose and in their structure and make-up (for instance in the use of tense), and they differ also in their contextual grounding. In particular, one needs to distinguish between the minimal form of a mere *report* of events and *narrative storytelling* on an extended scale. The latter comprises narratives of personal experience, narratives of vicarious experience and observational narratives.

Report is used simply to summarize or present the facts of the case, to provide *information*. This is signalled, as Weinrich (1964/1985) already noted, by the use of the *discussing tenses*, in particular the French *passé composé* and the German perfect. Some of the examples given by Harweg (1975a: 157–8) emphasize this very clearly. When yesterday's meeting of Uncle Paul is reported (rather than narrated) to the family, the tenses are all in the German perfect, and there is a marked tendency for this narrative to come to a halt. New information has to be elicited by repeated queries: 'And what did you do then?' These queries also take the perfect tense in German. In English, on the other hand, the perfect tense is used much more restrictively, because of the well-known grammatical fact that 'past' events have to be expressed in the past tense as soon as a specific time frame has been mentioned. The distinction between narrative and report is therefore less clear cut in English, although it can be traced in the analysis of episodic structure.

Report is predicated on second-hand experience or on a summary of first-hand experience rendered non-experientially. It therefore fully correlates with objectivity, distance, and the 'point' of the story. Its aim is to provide *information*, not to tell a story. The most striking structural facet of report lies in its lack of the schema of incidence which constitutes the core of experiential episodic narrative, whether of personal or vicarious experience. Thus reports frequently consist of a series of actions or events and a final result, and there is a noticeable preponderance of *then* clauses – whereas in experiential stories *so* would be by far the most pervasive discourse marker. Also, since reports do not have to perform aesthetic gymnastics, balancing tellability with narrative point, evaluative and commentatory asides are rare, and the whole intonational differentiation of narrative levels is rendered functionally irrelevant. Even more interestingly, intonational contours on the plotline are decisively different. Whereas experiential narratives employ extreme pitch variation – naturally so because changes in pitch operate as discursive markers – reports have comparatively level pitch and volume contours.

The following example of a report sequence comes from a passage of conversational exchange:

B: [...] where did she
A: she went to OXFORD
B: [m]
A: - then she did - - MS C at OXFORD - - - because of there was a particular man there she wanted to WORK with - and then she got a - research fellowship at GLASGOW - then she got this assistant lectureship at QM - - but in the meantime got
B: [m]
A: MARRIED - - - and at HOME. she's not a BIT the way she is at COLLEGE at home she's very much the little WOMAN - - she gets flatly contradicted by Bernard every time she opens her MOUTH
B: [m]
A: - and she never PROTESTS . and she always AGREES with him [...]

(Svartvik and Quirk 1979: 104)[30]

Report here blends with generalizing description of this woman's married life. Note, in particular, the typical 'and then' pattern of the report sequence. The following passage also consists basically of one incidence (what the woman did out of frustration with all these foreign loan-words), but this incidence is not part of a holistic narrative schema.

C: we have this girl I'm sure I told you who chooses the HEAD words for the DICTIONARY and. after she'd waded through - a lot of - she was doing K she did all those words like KRIS and KUKRI and then she drew a HALT and wrote a note at the BOTTOM saying ENOUGH already with the IMPERIAL KNIVES and we all GIGGLED very much but (laughs - -) the POINT is that sort of these are the WORDS
A: (laughs - -) YES
C: whether or not WE'RE there - - -
A: YES I mean they're words for SOMETHING of which there is no exact English equivalent or we wouldn't have BORROWED them . PRESUMABLY [...]

(ibid.: 736)

Unlike narrative report, which may occur at any point within a conversation, whether of personal or vicarious experience, full-blown natural narrative is characterized by the feature of turn-taking and the accompanying dynamic between on-plot and off-plot levels of discourse. Among such narratives, one can again distinguish several kinds. The two most basic cases are *narratives of personal experience* and *narratives of vicarious experience* – a distinction roughly corresponding to the narratological concepts of first- and third-person texts. This distinction is also reflected in Alfred Schütz's sociological work where an *I–you* (*we*) relationship of a personal sphere is contrasted with an increasingly anonymized relationship of the *I* to *others*. Schütz's original terms are *Wirbeziehung* and *Ihrbeziehung* (Schütz 1960: 202–7). In discourse analysis it was Labov and Waletzky (1967) who first discovered stories of vicarious experience and distinguished them from tales of personal experience. However, it needs to be noted that the stories quoted by Labov always involve an *observer-I*, in the sense that the narrator, though not the main protagonist of the story, was nevertheless physically present at the scene of events and watched the goings-on. (See the story about the braggart who stole the glove [Labov and Waletzky 1967: 18–19] as well as the story about the murder triggered by an insult [ibid.: 16].) Wolfson (1982) cites two truly vicarious narratives. Here the speaker has apparently received the information by hearsay rather than direct observation. The first is the story of the bra-buyer who nearly gets arrested; the second the story of the woman who fell down the stairs (Wolfson 1982: 94–5). Couper-Kuhlen's corpus of conversational stories (1994), which she has kindly made available to me, also has a restricted number of narratives of vicarious experience. In one ('Kerb crawler') a mother tells of her daughter's frightful encounter with a man who invites her into his car, and in another story ('Baby formula scandal') an employee of a drug firm tells of a professional problem with which he was not personally involved. In both cases the narrator is not present when things happen but hears about it from the daughter, other staff, or in the case of the funny 'Door handle', from the lodger. Stories of truly vicarious experience are fairly rare, and there tends to be a connection between the storyteller and the experiencer which explains how the narrator came to learn of the experience and came to empathize with it.

Although stories that render what the speaker has observed as a *witness* are usually treated as a subsidiary narrative category within narratology (only Stanzel seriously concerns himself with the 'I as witness' or the 'peripheral first-person storyteller'),[31] in terms of natural narrative (and, therefore, 'natural' narratology) this is a central and basic story category, as has been noted also by Quasthoff (1980) from a linguistic perspective. In observational experience, it is the narrator's surprise, dismay, shock, fear or frustrated expectation that constitutes the tellability of the story. Truly vicarious narrative, on the other hand, operates as narrative by hearsay. Its tellability depends on the interest afforded by the described experience, which needs to have been especially funny, weird, exotic or outrageous. The emphasis is therefore on the effect of this experience, which has been undergone by another person, on narrator and listener alike. The rendering can be empathetic towards the story protagonist (for example in tales that relate how somebody managed 'to get away with murder', for instance when cheating the (tax) authorities, and thereby eliciting the narrator's and listeners' admiration). Alternatively, the protagonist of the vicarious story may be passive, in the sense that things *happen to him/her*, and these events may be tellable because they are particularly sad, lucky, awesome or weird. In fact in vicarious narrative the two basic schemata available for tales of personal experience operate in a comparable manner: there is either an agent who achieves certain things or an experiencer to whom things happen.

We can now define *observational narrative* in more precise terms. In observational narrative the observer is a passive experiencer of events that usually do not concern him/herself directly. However, if the story is one that centres on agency rather than passive experience, the observer – like the vicarious narrator – identifies with the perspective of the agent and her agential intentions. The foregrounding of *agency* therefore shifts the centre of attention to the agent rather than concentrating on empathetic suffering.

This schematic constitution of agency is a matter of perception, too. Thus, if the observer sees a mugger jump out of a car and attack an unsuspecting pedestrian, she is likely to identify with the pedestrian because the pedestrian has been in visual focus prior to the arrival of the mugger and the observer's emotional reaction therefore reflects the pedestrian's surprise and dismay. By contrast, had the observer noted a curious person hovering about in front of a bank and then seen this person put on a mask and rush into the bank waving a gun, the perspective would have been that of agency. Such a concentration on the agent is fully compatible with the observer's disapproval of the actions involved. In fact, the crucial factor here is the *observer's perception of incidence*. If the incidence is noted as originating with an already established proto-agent, then the agency pattern is triggered; if the incidence is produced by a previously unfocused agent, this agent will be perceived as intruding upon a perceptional-experiential sphere, and the observer will identify experientially with the object affected by the intrusion or will interpret the intrusion to affect him/herself should no specific object be visualized. (For instance, if the robber jumps out of a passing car and starts to shoot wildly in all directions, this incidence cannot be conceptualized in terms of the experiences of a formerly focused pedestrian but touches on the observer directly since she is physically present on the scene and within the range of the weapon.)

The above remarks go beyond current discourse analysis and current narratology in that they posit a core of experience as narrative substratum which can be explicated only from within a frame notion of human situatedness. I will outline more fully what the consequences of such an approach are for the status of human consciousness within narrative (see Chapter 5), yet even at this point one can note how the very notions of agency and experience are set within a 'script' of intentional human activity on the one hand and passive submission to impinging contingency on the other. What this means for narrative theory is that one can construct basic 'scripts' for tellable stories, and these scripts can be analysed structurally as incorporating the central notions of intentional action and incidence (extraneous occurrence).

To contrast this with narrative of *personal experience*: the central part of a story of personal experience, in contradistinction to observational stories, it can now be argued, balances the incidence of events over which we have no control and the experiencer's intentional agency. Whereas the agency of another remains for the observer a largely unmotivated activity requiring interpretation, one's own activities are of course conceptualized as both intentional and intensional. Agency for oneself is determined by one's goals, by *mind*, but since others' state of mind remains inaccessible from the viewpoint of an external observer, agency in and by itself seems to become the prime motor controlling others' activities and actions. This basic dissymmetry in human cognition and experience has far-reaching consequences for subjective experience and the narrative representation thereof, including – most signally – the linguistic expression of subjectivity (Langacker 1985, 1990). In particular, the dynamics of perception on the one hand and of memory on the other deserve analysis. I have noted above that the empathetic identification of the observer with the agent or experiencer who is focused on, directly correlates with the given *perceptual* focalization and with the cognization of what therefore constitutes itself as an incidence. In narratives of personal experience, on the other hand, memory is the crucial perceptional equivalent. In experiential narrative the process of rememorization comprises the past experience *qua* quasi-present experience, activating the perceptional and experiential elements – the consciousness of acting and experiencing – that were the substance of one's experience and are now recreated in the story.

Narratives of personal experience – the most common type of natural narrative – can be characterized by their central incorporation of the incidence schema. This schema of incidence has *experiential value* since it is based on actual 'insider' experience on the part of the narrator. By extension, a structural employment of the schema of incidence allows a storyteller to incorporate the story agent's intentions and motives even into tales of vicarious experience – a factor that enriches the experiential qualities of the story as well as increasing the story's explanatory power ('point'). Whereas the observer-narrator can only describe what an agent does and how this action affects him/herself, the experiencer is in the unique position to present his/her own case – the very factor that correlates with the face-projecting or face-preserving objectives of natural storytelling. Hence the immediate attractiveness of using the experiential schema in vicarious narrative. On the other hand, a personalized narrator does not have access to other people's minds, and this dissymmetry of information (particularly in regard to others' motivations) mirrors precisely the dissymmetry of our individual human experience. As Langacker (1990) has demonstrated, perception is predicated on an egocentric deictic centre that from the fullness of its self-experience moves outwards in ever-decreasing degree of objective knowledge or (self-reflectively) inward in an increasing measure of reflective awareness (see also Fludernik 1993a: Chapter 7). In so far as vicarious storytelling remains 'realistic' and does not adopt an 'omniscient' stance, vicariousness is therefore hampered in its insights into protagonists' experience in the same way as is the narrator of personal experience in relation to her co-protagonists' experience.

Likewise the *narrator-observer*, situated halfway between an actual experiencer and a vicarious hearsay narrator, is severely constrained in her cognitive presentation of the story. Like the narrator of personal experience, the narrator-observer can only relate events from an outside perspective and lacks the knowledge about other people's motives and aims. However, as with the narrator of personal experience, this deficiency is in some measure offset by the narrator's faculty of speculation and surmise. Oral narrative consistently attributes to its story protagonists typical and appropriate reactions, thoughts and motives, and it does so in order to make the story more easily accessible, more meaningful. A tale of a mere sequence of events holds little narrative interest unless its effect on the observer is of note or the events themselves drastically depart from normal expectations. Access to the ideational domain of the teller or character is therefore a prerequisite for the generation of tellable narrative.

Solicited and lengthy narratives observe entirely different patterns of structure and intonation and they even have some specific temporal peculiarities. This cannot be taken too seriously. Many tales that have been analysed in studies of discourse analysis have been elicited in interviewing sessions, and there is little or no spontaneity about them. (A laudable exception is the interview stories collected in Quasthoff [1980] and the material from Couper-Kuhlen's corpus [1994].) In particular, the different structure of long, elicited stories appears to relate to the fact that no real turn-taking frame is in place, with the consequence that the speaker does not necessarily feel the need to be relevant, or to be brief, or to provide a really good story. Elicitation therefore easily slides into a report scenario. Quite a few of Labov's informants actually took the request to tell about a scary experience as a demand for information,[32] which explains the report shape of some of these stories. The absence of an interactive listener and, therefore, of a turn-taking routine, has, for instance, a major import on the stories collected by Studs Terkel. There are a large number of present tenses that resemble *literary* uses of the historical present tense (1990: 38–9, 283) and do not match the pattern of the oral historic present tense (Fludernik 1991) in stories of personal experience. Terkel's stories also employ free indirect discourse (e.g. 1990: 503) in a particularly 'literary' manner. In addition, elicited stories such as Terkel's frequently reflect (on) the interviewee's diffidence about what will interest the interviewer. Such uneasiness then results in structural unevenness, with the

Natural narrative and other oral modes 77

storyteller jumping from a report to a scene and then retracing her steps ('Is that what you wanted to hear?').[33] Solicited narrative therefore skews the patterns observable in spontaneous storytelling and is no reliable guide for their analysis.

2.2.3 Institutionalized storytelling and the link with written narrative

Institutionalized narrative (oral poetry, oral storytelling) depends on, and at the same time elaborates, the structure of natural narrative. One of the most important conditions of institutionalization is the functional status awarded the bard – in the medieval French tradition, the *jongleur*. Even when audience and bard interact, the bard occupies a hierarchically higher, more powerful position and is able to exert control over the narration and manipulate its parameters. The second very important feature of institutionalized narrative concerns the *subject* of the tale, which is invariably traditional. In contrast to real-world reports of battles, espionage, etc., institutionalized narrative *repeats* (if in adorned form) mythic, ritual, religious or national key events rather than *inventing* new stories or retailing the extraordinary, the original, the *new* (as conversational narrative certainly does). Storytelling in the tradition of the tall tale (Bauman 1986) likewise tends to repeat well-known plots, as does, of course, the genre of the joke. Although such tall tales are *fictional* (they cannot possibly be true), there also is a noticeable tendency to *repeat*. The telling does not satisfy a news value but is understood to derive its entertainment value from the fact of having become a proven 'success', of having 'survived' through numerous retellings. Like the songs of folksingers or bards' oral poetry, tall tales are of course embellished and restructured in the course of time, as indeed are jokes, anecdotes and many stories of personal experience.

This takes me to the next important point. Institutionalized narrative is also – almost by definition – vicarious narrative: the story is about the heroic and mythic past and not about the bard's own experience. Except in the spiritual realm (following St Augustine's *Confessions*) narratives of personal experience did not become 'productive' in literature until fairly late in literary history. There are witness reports and historical first-person narratives of course, but few autobiographical tales.[34] Neither Boccaccio nor Chaucer or Gower use first-person tales, although Chaucer's frame narrative in *The Canterbury Tales* is quasi-autobiographical. This absence of first-person narrative correlates with the putative pre-modern lack of interest in 'the individual'. According to the standard view of an 'invention' of the self in the Renaissance and the consequent 'birth' of the individual, personal self could not be seen except in relation to God. Vicarious experience prevails as a model for self-understanding from More to Defoe in spite of the significant social and societal changes which did indeed allow for nonconformist individuality to be enacted against the pressures of tradition and religious orthodoxies. It is only with the replacement of religion by morality (a redefinition of virtue in *social* terms)[35] that *self* becomes an independent concept available for active deployment, and it appears as such with Behn and Richardson rather than Defoe or Fielding. Much of the predominance of heterodiegetic narrative until well into the sixteenth century can additionally be explained in relation to the cultural, political and societal function of institutionalized narrative and is intimately bound up with narrative's investment in the current political and ideological power structure. As long as performed narrative remained the predominant means of popular instruction, it could only with difficulty allow personal narratives to take over. The moralistic tone of much early narrative (a quality that apparently first emerged in the fourteenth century, where it became noticeable in the saints' legends) is observable even in the unlikely texts of Nashe's *The Unfortunate Traveller* or the work of Defoe, and it correlates directly with the claim that early autobiography in fact served the purposes of institutionalized storytelling. Whence also the disruptive effect of radical Protestant writings with their emphasis on Nonconformist individual faith and belief.[36]

The specific changes that occurred in oral poetry's linguistic and structural make-up all relate to the bard's right to assume control, which allows him the privilege of long turns. Rather than telling events in a series of some five or six brief episodes, therefore, epic narrative concatenates a significantly larger number of episodes, and the problem of how to structure this series becomes acute. We are therefore at the point where Ermarth (1981) locates the initiation of the dramatic structure in narrative, the point of the invention of the scene. By unifying series of episodes under the general denominator of a continuity of setting or on the basis of a continuity in the protagonists, a dramatic ground-pattern is set up. The resultant 'scenes' are usually connected by narratorial summary or comment. Chafe's analysis of the pear stories[37] (Chafe 1980) suggests that one can explain the connecting of larger episodes (i.e. scenes) by means of commentary as a feature deriving directly from natural narrative where every change of scene (new setting, new set of characters) potentially produces a problem of reorientation and causes difficulties of recall. The extent of such additional processing can be gauged by the length of pauses and by the proliferation of fillers (*ah, so, mn, uh*). At these points narrators also find themselves constrained to make the shift of scene in their stories explicit:

> And you see him riding away ... and then .. into the screen .. comes [.55] just the girl - [.4] riding [.55] on another bicycle [.55] in an opposite direction
>
> (Chafe 1980: 312)[38]

> the little .. boy that fell off the bicycle gives him [.45] three- ... pears, ... and they went back, [1.55] [.95] a-nd [.15] then you switch back to the man that's [.4] climbing down out of the tree
>
> (ibid.: 314)

and you just know that old man's going to see [.45] these little boys coming and say 'Ha .. You're the ones who stole the pears.' [1.9] [.7] But u—h [.35] still ... It comes back to the old man [.3] up in the pear tree

(ibid.: 303)

In Chaucer, for instance, comparable connecting passages of commentary are frequently narratorial vignettes – raised to a level above the story progression – and come in the present tense.[39]

I wol no lenger tarien in this cas,
But to kyng Alla, which I spak of yoore,
That for his wyf wepeth and siketh soore,
I wol retourne, and lete I wol Custance
Under the senatoures governance.

('The Man of Law's Tale' B[1] 983–7; 1987: 101)

The most important factors in the orality–literacy continuum appear to be the very simple ones of textual *length* and of the proliferation of settings and actants made possible through this increase in length. Complexity, even in the epic or in oral poetry, invariably connects with elaboration and a multiplication of plots, whereas in conversational narratives, owing to the constraints on length, it is, rather, density of information compressed into the smallest units of utterance that makes for the complexity of natural narrative. We will have to go over this terrain in much more detail in the next chapter. Suffice it to note for the moment that institutionalized forms of oral narrative have had a decisive shaping effect on the avatars of the novelistic genre. Nevertheless, as I hope to outline in Chapter 3, there are no simple one-to-one relations between observable oral forms and early written documents. Not only is this the case simply because written discourse works differently in conceptual terms, so that, by the very fact of being indited on paper, previously oral discourse becomes restructured (Stock 1983; Goody 1987). In addition different types of oral patterns interact in the emergence of early written discourse and genres, which may then be observed to adopt contradictory patterns: experiential structures for historical writing (which is vicarious in its deep structure); report-like narrative structure for (experiential) first-person stories. Thus, many Elizabethan criminal biographies, even in the first-person mode, have practically no experiential value since they concatenate chunks of incidence with one another but do not detail the characters' motives, reactions to incidences or their evaluation of past actions. Some third-person texts, on the other hand, start to present their characters' psyche in great detail, transferring the quality of experientiality onto vicarious narration.

Before turning to the 'oral' genres of the joke, the anecdote, and the exemplum – all three of which typically occur in written versions – I would briefly like to anticipate here how natural narrative (excluding institutionalized oral poetry and prose folk narrative) *functionally* differs from written forms of post-Renaissance narrative. (I leave open for the moment the extent to which medieval genres of narrative belong or do not belong to the oral or the written pattern.) Jokes, anecdotes, and presumably exempla, it can be argued, share these features of natural narrative.

We have seen above that natural narrative in its prototypical shape of the story of personal experience is structured by means of an interaction between a narrative frame, a plotline level of the story proper, and an off-plotline level of embedded orientation and narrational evaluative or explicatory commentary. In this structure the frame connects with ongoing conversational exchange within which the story is embedded. The story incipit marks the entry into the world of the narrated events and experiences. It therefore constitutes a marker of fictionality comparable in its function to Weinrich's shift into the narrating mode (*erzählende Tempora*[40]). The resolution point at the end of the story functions as another bracket which provides a transition back into the ongoing conversational exchange. Although the novel frequently replicates such framing on a macro-structural level, this explicit framing tends to relate to the interaction between narrator and narratee rather than to a communicational act affecting reader and author in their historical identities.

A second major feature of natural narrative concerns the distribution of commentary and embedded orientation within or between episodes. Within the dynamic pattern of natural narrative, narrative commentary and description show up precisely in the slots for comment and embedded orientation. Since these belong to separate intonational levels, they are very clearly set off from narrative clauses in the plotline. As a result, natural narrative never blurs the boundary between narrative content and descriptive background information or evaluative commentary. In written narratives, by contrast, no equivalent foregrounding or backgrounding exists, and the levelling of episodes into continuous text likewise tends to unify the discourse into one amorphous and uni-level structure. As a result, description becomes a discourse type in its own right which may merge with narrative clauses referring to the plot as well as usurp entire sections of great textual length. The modern terminological inventory which contrasts narrative with description (or enumerates report, scene [speech], description and comment as the basic modes of narrative discourse),[41] reflects precisely this loss of the natural storytelling pattern observable in conversational narrative. Description no longer operates as that functional entity which occurs in the slot reserved for embedded orientation[42] but becomes an extendable and separate discourse type in its own right.

What this implies for the interpretation of written narrative is that the holistic or organicist cognition which is a constitutive element of natural narrative dissolves in the transcoding process from oral to written narrative. As a consequence, entirely different functional parameters develop. However, it won't do simply to ignore oral discourse. Only by concentrating on oral narrative can one hope to come by some answers about the properties of narrative as a transcultural phenomenon. In the present study natural narrative is therefore examined alongside literary types of narrative with a view towards assessing their functional similarities as well as their differences.

I now turn to those oral genres which even today flourish in oral performance but are also frequently transmitted in books. Jokes and anecdotes occupy a position on the borderline between the written and oral genres.

2.3 HUMOROUS AND DIDACTIC SHORT FORMS

2.3.1 The joke

Jokes appear to share some of the characteristic patterns of experiential narrative in a condensed form. They can help to illustrate the workings of those kinds of experiential narrative where the central incidence is constituted by an exchange of words (a *débat*) rather than by the observation or experience of extraneous events impinging on the setting. A conversational exchange, to be sure, is frequently structured in terms of a basic sequence of 'incidences', too – in the sense that the 'point' of the story lies in the protagonist's successful rhetorical reaction to her antagonist's linguistic moves. The narrator's retorts to figures of authority are a recurring type.[43] As noted above, the face-projecting 'point' of most experiential narratives consists precisely in the illustration of the teller's acumen, shrewdness, courage, etc. – all attributes that emerge from the protagonist's *reaction* to the incidence. Thus, whereas the 'performative' (Wolfson 1982) presentation of the incidence links up with the empathy factor of the experiential story, the 'point' of a story resides in the teller's (the experiencing self's) mastery of such unexpected coincidences, a mastery that is meant to project a positive autostereotype. In a different type of story the narrative structure is designed not to elicit admiration or respect, but to invite sympathy, and in these tales the experiencing self may be portrayed as overwhelmed by the experience. This constellation frequently correlates with the lack of a 'result' section in the narrative, which may be replaced by an 'and finally X happened'-plus-evaluation unit. Jokes and anecdotes, on the other hand, belong to the first story type and foreground the 'point', whether by means of witty repartee, a punch line or an unexpected resolution.

Narratological analysis reveals that jokes can be analysed in terms of condensed stories. They frequently reduce the frame elements to the mere announcement of the genre (*Do you know the one . . .*) and elide the abstract section, replacing it by a characterization of the setting: *You know the one where the cowboy sits in the bar and a blue Indian comes in?* Nor do jokes generally have initial orientation sections – a feature that highlights their acknowledged fictionality: the 'story' of the joke is not embedded in a realistic context. (This characteristic applies only to jokes. Anecdotes, by contrast, frequently have both initial and embedded orientation sections.) The central part of the joke also observes the structure of experiential narrative, since it usually has a (non-obligatory) incipit, setting and incidence slot and there is frequently a developing (linguistic) interaction between the protagonists. Most jokes conclude with the punch line, which may or may not correlate with the 'victory' of one protagonist over the other, but definitely provides closure (result/resolution slot) for the audience. As part of their condensation of the narrative pattern, jokes moreover tend to eliminate the evaluation section which is so prominent in the experiential tale. Sometimes there may, however, be an appended 'appreciation' tag (*That's a good one, isn't it*), or narrators may repeat the punch line or even comment on it. By contrast, anecdotes and exempla, the (mostly) written equivalents of the joke in historical and didactic discourse, tend to expand the evaluation section into lengthy commentary, providing an exegesis of the story. Such evaluation may range from a simple 'moral' all the way to an allegorical commentary that turns the anecdote into a simile. (See, for instance, the pericope from the life of St Nicholas discussed below under 3.1.)

I now turn to two jokes from the useful collection by Euler (1991):

COLIN 2

Colin:	1	//	< do you know about the Welshman and he's
	2		and he's
Eric:	3		< about what >
Colin:	4		< the Welshman and he's
	5		he wanted to be a signalman > //
Eric:	6		no
Colin:	7	//	< so
	8	//	< so he ha'
	9		he goes up before this board
	10		and they say to him now then Digh > /
	11	/	< the express train from Cardiff is coming up the line
	12		and the express train from Glasgow is coming down the line > //
	13	/	< what are you going to do > //
	14	//	< and he said oh I take my little flag > /
	15		and I run up the line and I wave my little flag until the express train from Cardiff stops
	16		and then I run back up the line and wave my little flag
	17		until the express train from Glasgow stops > //
	18	//	< and he says

Natural narrative and other oral modes 83

19		Digh you've forgotten your little flag > /
20	/ <	what did you do > //
21	// <	and he said
22		I take my little lamp
23		and I run up the line and I wave my little lamp until the express train from Cardiff stops
24		and then I run up the line and wave my little flag eh my little lamp
25		so the express train from Glasgow stops > //
26	// <	they say Digh
27		you've forgotten your little lamp > /
28	/ <	what are you going to do /
29	// <	he said
30		oh
31		I phone my wife Blodwyn > //
32	// <	and they say
33		why do you do that //
34	// <	well I phone my wife Blodwyn and I say Blodwyn
35		get on your little bicycle and come over there's gonna be the biggest fucking accident you ever saw > //

COLIN 3

1	// <	I think my favourite Jewish one
2		is
3		the two Jewish guys
4		who meet on the street
5		and one of them says
6		Abraham
7		how are you > //
8	// <	he says very good Isaac how are you //
9	// <	good > //
10	// <	and how's the family he says
11		wonderful > /
12	/ <	the doctors' [sic] three and the lawyers' [sic] four > //

(Euler 1991: 173–4; notations refer to intonational parameters)

Colin 2 illustrates the initial framing sequence and the request for proceeding with the joke. It then has a brief orientation section (Welshman, wants to become a signalman, has to take a test) followed by the incipit (note the *so* in line 8) and the triple exchange which has the joke in the final answer. In fact one can analyse this joke as consisting of three narrative episodes of roughly equivalent structure, and the punch line comes with the third incompatible answer/reaction.[44] As is typical of most jokes, there is no final evaluation – the punch line concludes the text. *Colin 3*, which is here quoted as a 'minimal joke', relies on a non-dramatic exchange between the two protagonists, in which the dialogue serves as a kind of *effet de réel* painting of the scene. There is no earthly reason why the two characters should be *named* except to emphasize their 'Jewish' background. This is appropriate in so far as the joke turns precisely on a typically Jewish characteristic, i.e. on the stereotype of Jewish parents' excessive concern for education and career-planning. At ages three and four Abraham's boys are already marked out for their prospective professions. The second joke is therefore closer to the structure of an anecdote since it introduces a more specific setting (names, recognizable ethnic background). In the anecdote this kind of setting is generally extended to a historical presentation of sorts.

Note also the temporal features in both jokes. The central parts of the joke are predominantly in the present tense and this underlines both the hypothetical or fictional character of the joke as well as the condensed structural pattern: since jokes display incipit plus incidence sequences, there is an overwhelming opportunity to use the historical present tense. (In the two jokes the presents are: in *Colin 2*, so *he goes up* [incipit] and *they say, he says, they say, they say*; in *Colin 3*: *who meet* [setting], *one of them says*; *he says*.) *Colin 2* interestingly has a past tense both for the initial orientation and for the prospective signalman's responses. In *Colin 3*, on the other hand, the teller dispenses with inquit tags and ends on a juxtaposed exchange that 'speaks for itself'. The temporal features therefore also corroborate the preservation of the natural narrative pattern in jokes and document how the pattern is condensed.

Jokes, although they inevitably present vicarious experiences, are therefore not much different from the standard types of natural narrative. In contrast to conversational stories, jokes are announced explicitly, but then most stories of personal or vicarious experience likewise have a very explicit framing mode. If quite a number of stories rely on the protagonists' rhetorical victory over their antagonists, so do a number of jokes, even though the discourse *effect* is, of course, unrelated to the speaker's (joke teller's) current discourse behaviour. (Jokes may be told to present oneself as a humorous person, but they are not usually employed to corroborate one's current argument or to project face.) The joke functions on the pattern of a minimal episodic unit, a minimal narrative structure that also applies to the exemplum and the anecdote. More elaborate versions of jokes can add extensive background information and lively dialogue or concatenate several episodes, and therefore look like stories.[45] Like exempla, similes or anecdotes, jokes are basic-level types of vicarious narrative that have survived in nearly unmodified form in written manifestations of storytelling. In the case of exempla and anecdotes, the genre was preserved via such semi-oral texts as the sermon or the grand rhetorical set speech; in the case of the joke, collections of jokes have helped to introduce this oral genre into literature.

Not *all* jokes, however, tell a story. A good many jokes and anecdotes consist of witty repartee or simply of a pun. For instance, the following joke consists of one utterance, which evokes a *double-entendre* between the literal meaning of the utterance and the implied innuendo.

> Says the Tower of Pisa to Big Ben, 'If you've got the time, I've got the inclination.'

An entire love story can be projected from this one line. That story is *not* present in the text but a construction on the part of the eager reader who pictures a stereotypical female act of seduction. Again, many of the jokes that Freud quotes in his study on the joke are equally non-narrative and observe a different set of patterns. For instance, some jokes outline an ever more absurd line of argument by one of the joke 'characters'. A famous instance of this is the kettle sequence: a man, accused of having returned a borrowed kettle with a hole in it, defends himself by arguing, first, that he returned the kettle intact; second, that the kettle already had a hole in it when he borrowed it; and, third, that he never borrowed the kettle in the first place.[46] Another type of joke situates its absurdity on the metalinguistic plane of the characters' argument, as does the joke about the traveller who accuses his friend of lying about his destination.[47] There is thus a huge variety of different types of jokes, only some of which actually follow a story pattern. And among the jokes *with* a story pattern one can again distinguish between a great number of different types. Narratological analyses of the joke therefore promise to be a fruitful area of research.

2.3.2 Exemplum and/or anecdote

I will now turn to an anecdote from William Roper's *Life of Sir Thomas More*, an anecdote which, in its narrative structure, lends itself to an identification with the exemplum pattern and which will allow me additionally to take up Joel Fineman's thought-provoking remarks about anecdotal discourse as that which constitutes the illusion of the real within the historiographical text (Fineman 1989). Indeed, in my example text the anecdote cannot be distinguished from another genre, that of the parable on biblical lines. Current terminology regarding 'simple forms' such as the anecdote, the exemplum or the parable (not to mention the novella and the short story, the fable, the fairy tale or the folk tale) is very imprecise indeed. André Jolles's proposals about the 'inner form' of the various genres that he discusses in his book *Einfache Formen* (1969) are highly idiosyncratic and have not found many followers. Recent research, however, has not fared much better. Weber's (1993) definition of the anecdote fails to distinguish the anecdote from the joke because he downplays the historical factor. Most of his examples are quite humorous and rely on a punch line. Similarly, Bremond *et al.*'s (1982) definitions of the exemplum characterize that genre as, more or less, a brief story. In the light of the examples provided, however, this is really an echo of current definitions of the anecdote. Even the newest contributions to the *exempla* discussion (Haug and Wachinger 1991, Koch 1994) fail to provide any really trenchant definitions. Haug and Wachinger even include discussions of the *Pañcatantra*, which most scholars would tend to categorize as a collection of fables or tales. Even a recent collection of essays on the exemplum (Engler and Müller 1995b) of a more theoretical cast, which addresses a number of exciting functional issues, still has to accommodate the anecdote and Boccaccio in its fold. On account of these inconsistencies even within the standard literature I will here desist from attempting to separate the anecdote from the exemplum or the parable.

The following passage takes the form of a parable integrated within one of Roper's many anecdotes about More. These anecdotes serve to authenticate More's life (biography) and the historical truth of events (historiography), and they also – most importantly – present More as a saint.[48]

> It fortuned not longe before the cominge of Queene Anne throughe the streetes of London from the Tower to Westminster to her coronation, that he [More] receyved a letter from the Bishoppes of Durham, Bathe, and Winchester, requestinge him bothe to keepe them company from the Tower to the coronation, and alsoe to take twenty pounds that by the bearer therof they had sente him to buy him a gowne withe; which he thankfully receyvinge, and at home still tarrieinge, at their next meetinge sayed merrilye unto them; My Lordes, in the letters which you lately sente me, you required two thinges of me; the tone wherof, sithe I was soe well contented to grante you, the tother therfore I thoughte I mighte be the boulder to denye you. And like as the tone, because I tooke you for noe beggers, and myselfe I knewe to be noe very ryche man, I thoughte I mighte the rather fullfill, soe the tother did put me in remembrance of an Emperour, that had ordeyned a lawe that whosoever committed a certeyne offence, which I nowe remember not, excepte it were a virgine, shoulde suffer the paynes of death, such a reverence had he to virginitie. Nowe soe happened it, that the first committer of that offence was a virgine, wherof the Emperour hearinge was in no small perplexetye, as he that by some ensample wolde fayne have had that lawe put in execution. Wherupon when his councell had satt longe, solempnly debatinge this case, sodeynly rose there uppe one of his councell, a good playne manne amonge them, and sayd, Whye make ye soe much adoe, my Lordes, about soe small a matter. Lette her first be deflowered, and then after maye she be devowered. And soe though your Lordshippes have in the matter of the matrymonye hytherto kept yourselves pure virgines, yet take good heede, my Lordes, that you keepe your virginities still. For some there be that by procuringe your Lordshippes first at the coronacion to be presente, and nexte to preach for the setting forth of

it, and fiynally to wryte bookes to all the worlde in defence thereof, are desierous to deflower you, and when they have deflowered you, then will they not fayle soone after to devower you. Nowe, my Lordes, quothe he, it lyeth not in my powre but that they maye devower me; but God beinge my good Lorde, I will provide they shall never deflower me.

(More 1910: 240–1).

Roper's anecdote of More's playful answer to his friends the bishops deals with an episode that occurs after More's resignation from the office of Lord Chancellor and proleptically (as well as prophetically) inscribes the saint's destiny for us. This anecdote serves a number of functions within the biographical discourse which Roper is recording. Like most historical anecdotes it is of course meant to illuminate the character of More the protagonist. For one, the anecdote presents More as a shrewd politician who recognizes the trap of opportunism for the very real dangers it entails: opportunism may lead from small compromises to the committing of more vital compromises and finally to acting against one's conscience. Second, and no less important, More's noted integrity (a theme on which Roper harps repeatedly) is painted in no uncertain terms. Roper anticipates the main theme of More's letters from the Tower: his willingness to put down his life rather than swear an oath against his conscience. More's uncompromising probity contrasts with the easy corruptibility of his friends the bishops. On a third level, the anecdote provides one more example of More's wit, showing how he bests his tempters by means of an exemplum which turns the tables on them and completely confounds their argument. The situation therefore constitutes a precise parallel to More's famous parable about the integrity of 'Cumpanye', which he explicated in a letter to his daughter. In that parable the twelfth member of a jury, a 'poore honest man of the countrey, that was called Cumpanye', asks the other members of the jury whether they would be willing to go to hell with him 'for companionship sake' (More 1910: 298–300[49]). In More's anecdote losing one's virginity is indeed tantamount to succumbing to mortal sin and thereby incurring eternal damnation. From a fourth perspective, Roper's anecdote about More operates as a *mise-en-abîme* for More's Passion; it is in fact structurally equivalent to other stories (which are also anecdotes) elsewhere in Roper's hagiographical text. Moreover, More's own invented exemplum (the story of the king and the virgin) constitutes a *mise-en-abîme* within Roper's anecdote, redefining it on the basis of characteristically allegorical revaluations.

Roper's discourse, which employs a significant sequence of hagiographical anecdotes, constitutes itself as historiography (biography) precisely through the repeated enunciation of anecdotal material: history operates by means of anecdote as Fineman (1989) suggested. These anecdotes are meant to throw a significant light not only simply on More's character and personality, but also on these scenes' hagiographic significance. In so far as many of these anecdotes anticipate or reflect the ulterior story of More's martyrdom (his willingness to sacrifice his life for the preservation of the purity of his conscience, i.e. for his soul), typological and hagiographical considerations come into play. Indeed, Roper's biography, like Foxe's *Actes and Monuments*, reiterates the one typological frame which is in excess of realistic requirements: whereas Foxe parades one martyr after the other, Roper keeps returning to one anecdote after the other, all of which have a christological subtext meant to illustrate More's sanctity even before the time of his tribulations. (In this respect Roper erases the Thomas à Becket parallel in which 'conversion' is a significant story moment.) More's sacrificial meekness and voluntary suffering, for instance, are dwelled on in one anecdote after the other: More's willingness to be drowned if that sacrifice could save the world (1910: 218); More's exemplary poverty (ibid.: 232–4) and ascetic practices (219–20, 234, 268); More's refusal to blame anybody (the king or others) for swearing the oath.[50] In the present context Roper's anecdotes are therefore less crucial to a realistic evocation of historical truth, although a number of them certainly operate in this way (as, for instance, the scene of his daughter's, Margaret's, final goodbye to More on his way to the Tower, a scene explicitly witnessed and evaluated by the bystanders[51]). More importantly, Roper's anecdotes stress the religious significance of More's sanctity (the prime signified of the anecdotes) as a recurrent hagiographical theme of didactic impact. It is therefore a spiritual truth, an exemplary model of behaviour, which is being illustrated in these anecdotes, and they impart an insistent positive evaluation of death and the afterlife, and a consequent devaluation of earthly life and goods.

To return to more structural concerns. The anecdote, like most anecdotes, starts with a specific historical setting and, by way of incipit, More's receipt of the fatal invitation. Thereafter More's response (including his parable) constitutes the point of the text – a more elaborate one than would be customary in oral form. More's parable, in turn, is structured in the familiar episodic shape: orientation ('there was an Emperor'), incipit ('now it so happened'), setting (perplexity), incidence (happy turn of events: the unexpected contribution from the 'good playne manne'), and resolution (his advice). Like a good allegory, this is followed by the moral, identifying the bishops and More as virgins in danger of being deflowered and, in consequence thereof, devoured, that is to say, executed by the king, *undone* physically as well as spiritually. Where this anecdote exceeds the simplicity of an exemplum or an oral story is, however, not in the formal structure of the tale but in its framing (parable within anecdote) and the complex effects of thematic and structural mirroring that this framing generates. In particular, certain key terms and metaphors influence the argument in the parable and in sophisticated ways connect with the frame story and, on a third level, with More's biography. In the anecdote, the martyr is likened to the virgin lamb to be devoured by the wolf. Violence is active. The virgin, who is entirely passive in the parable itself – an *object* of the discourse – becomes activized only in the allegorical exegesis. The bishops (*qua* virgins) are accused of potentially succumbing to their 'deflowerment' by, first, *going to* the coronation, then by actively *preaching* and finally *defending* the indefensible, thus losing their orthodoxy (virginity). Likewise, More, *qua* virgin, is also portrayed as actively 'provid[ing] they shall never deflower' him. More's implicit invective – in spite of his apparent desire not to blame anybody – crucially inculpates his friends the bishops, who are indeed among those 'some there be' that 'by procuringe' the allegorical virgin are soliciting More's connivance at their own opportunism – a hint that is even more apposite if we remember that the letter which More received contained *money* to buy *clothing* with. The bishops were thus, quite literally, attempting to 'procure' More, nor is the 'gowne', as temporal and fleshly wrapping of the spiritual soul/virginity, an entirely incidental element within this significational economy. More's humour and rhetorical dexterity therefore emerge forcefully from the text, which turns out to be much more sophisticated than a first appreciation of the parable might have suggested. More behaves like a wolf in lamb's clothing, disguising his underhand incriminatory subtext by resorting to metaphor and innuendo in the shape of parables.

More's irony (or should one say sarcasm?) can be traced to the content of the exemplum. In the parable, the story is presented from the king's political perspective. Except for the automatic identification of the typological virgin with spotless purity and innocence, the discourse centres on the vexing predicament of a 'poor' king who finds that the first offender against his newly proclaimed law cannot legally be prosecuted under its terms. The king therefore finds himself in a situation of acute embarrassment (he is threatened with a loss of 'face'). The king's councillors, who share this perspective, debate the problematic situation at length until a good playne manne' provides the solution for so 'small' a matter. In the parable the good plain man's solution is to do violence (necessarily illegal) to the virgin – i.e. to implicate her, to 'procure' her – and by these means to withdraw from her her one claim to exemption from mortal punishment. This situation reflects in emblematic fashion attempts on the part of More's interrogators to force him to explain his reasons for *not* swearing the oath, although his frank answer would immediately have exposed him to the mortal charge of treason (ibid.: 278). The correlation between the anecdote and More's situation is even more explicit in More's argument with his interrogators concerning this deadlock, a deadlock which they try to break by threatening him with torture (ibid.: 325–6, 329). More's replies (ibid.: 326) indicate that he considers the application of torture illegal since it would either force him to commit perjury (in terms of the parable, force him to prostitute himself, sell his soul for the preservation of his body), or it would inflict violence on his body (the rape of the exemplum).

It is a major ironic conceit in More's parable that the evil councillor is characterized as a 'good' man of common sense. Not only does this – in a superficial tactic of flattery – suggest an implicit identification of the teller with his good friends the bishops of Durham, Bath and Winchester,[52] seemingly condoning the contemplated violence to the virgin; the locution additionally reflects the 'commonsense' attitude of More's contemporaries, who believed that he (More) was acting against all reason and sound sense and that taking the oath would have been a little matter of no importance. And do we not perhaps also detect an allusion to the Becket story and to another king's similar 'embarrassment', of which he is 'rid' by an overzealous group of knights? That this little matter of no importance is bound to result in the execution of the anecdotal virgin characterizes the little matter as one of mortal significance and reveals the good plain man to be the Tempter in person. More, as he said explicitly in his letters, was indeed forcing the king (or his advisors) to take illegal and unethical measures if they wanted to convict him of treason according to the law.

There is one final inconsistency in this parable, an inconsistency typical of metaphorical discourse in general. Not all attributes of a rose can be fruitfully applied to one's beloved: she has no thorns, does not need to be watered daily, nor does she grow in flowerbeds or on hedges. The good plain man's advice is to deflower the virgin – obviously by means of violence. The exegesis provided by More, however, shifts the emphasis away from rape or the direct infliction of violence. Instead it reverts to the procurement situation of the frame, thus introducing the image of the virgin's connivance at her own undoing. More's exegesis therefore at first brackets the logical argument of the parable (rape) and substitutes for it a reading that is more appropriate to the bishops' invitation to him (persuasion and procurement). The parable and its interpretation thus contain a forboding which will later be realized in its application to More's biography: having exhausted all means of persuasion under duress (no longer *offering* money and temporal goods for his connivance but *threatening* and *performing* More's deprival of them), the good plain man's advice is finally taken in its original literal impact and violence is inscribed on More's body. That this violence – happily for More – was unleashed as a consequence of perjury and false accusation and not, as the parable would suggest, by means of torture or murder, does not change the basic constellation and proleptic truth enunciated in the parable. More was lucky, too, in escaping the full rigour of the treason law by having the sentence converted to a beheading instead of the constitutional hanging, drawing, mutilating and quartering – a punishment which in contemporary terms signified the most shameful and degrading death that could be inflicted on a criminal's body. Such a death meant that the victim was being conspicuously and effectively 'undone'.

More's parable and Roper's anecdote which frames it are sophisticated literary artifacts. Nevertheless, even in the anecdote, orality has a crucial symbolic function in projecting the illusion of unfeigned, spontaneous storytelling, an illusion of historical immediacy. In Roper's case this historical dimension comes to be backgrounded against the prominent hagiographical overtones, and More's own parable, although operating precisely in the form of an *historical* anecdote, refrains from extensive historical identification (indeed, his parable is an invented story designed to serve his argument). Nevertheless, both texts employ the shape of the anecdote at least deep-structurally as an historical authentification device, an historical *effet de réel* in Fineman's (1989) sense. But More and Roper both go beyond this by highlighting the paradoxes and ambiguities of the story, emphasizing the pretended lesson to be learned from the tale and uncovering the implicit subversive reinterpretation of lesson and story in the light of More's own predicament. The anecdote therefore opens itself to all the virtualities of signification that merely lie dormant in natural narratives. As soon as a specific historical situation – a larger 'frame' – is introduced and the anecdote is incorporated in a complex written text, its simplicity becomes an artificial illusion of oral spontaneity, and the tale generates all sorts of complexities when attempts are made to control its meanings. The anecdote, by generic attribution a *historical* text-type, therefore epitomizes that interesting area of orality absorbed by the workings of the written text. It provides a window into literature, into textuality and into the realm of that slippery signifier – the historical Real – whose elusiveness triggers a multiplicity of discursive manoeuvers and interpretative strategies. The anecdote, that most natural form of oral history, therefore marks the threshold into the symbolic realm of *écriture*, and it defines that threshold at its most treacherous.

3 From the oral to the written
Narrative structure before the novel

This chapter is designed to provide a transition between the discussion of narrative experientiality in oral narrative in Chapter 2 and the presentation, in Chapter 4, of experiential modes of narration from the realist to the Modernist novel. The chapter will therefore trace a complex set of developments on several levels of analysis.

To start with, the texts that will be discussed (medieval and early modern prose, verse narrative) are *written* texts, some of which, however, are considered to have been transmitted orally before getting fixed in a written mould. The chapter therefore traces a development from what are traditionally believed to be oral kinds of narrative to texts allegedly modelled on the oral pattern to texts which have become emancipated from the oral tradition and have initiated a new (written) mode of *écriture*.

Second, the literature treated in this chapter comprises a great variety of genres. No argument is here proffered that would claim a direct development from one genre into another, but an interdependence and mutual fertilization will be acknowledged to exist between some generic traditions. No complete account can be provided in the space of one brief chapter, so that whatever I have to say in these pages will necessarily need to remain sketchy and impressionistic.[1] The situation in Middle English literature is complicated by a number of frame conditions which in their intricacy exceed even the complexities of the French circumstances. For instance, the existence has to be noted of an Old English tradition (both prose and verse) which 'breaks off' at the time of the Norman conquest and results in a resumption of Latin writing (in prose) even for those genres where the vernacular had already been in use before, as for instance in the Anglo-Saxon chronicles (Tristram 1988). Middle English 'resumes' its formal circulation only in the thirteenth century, and it does so in both verse and prose, although prose is present less generally and does not really become widely used for narrative until the fifteenth century.

The comparison of narrative structure in prose and verse genres and texts is a further crucial aspect to be dealt with in these pages. In my opinion, in the formal analysis the development of prose has to be strictly separated from the developments in the verse epic. With one curiously early exception (the saintly literature of the Katherine Group dated in the 1230s),[2] literary prose throughout the medieval period appears to have required additional effort on the part of writers, and frequently – well into the late fifteenth century, including the work of Malory and Caxton – displays a number of aesthetic infelicities (repetitiveness, problems of reference) which are absent from even the earliest instances of verse narration from the thirteenth century. Early Middle English verse as in the saints' legends or early romances may be drastic, vulgar and crude from the perspective of sophistication afforded by Chaucer, but its repetitiveness serves observably useful purposes in the narrational structure, and it never descends to the depths of bungling which are so annoying in some of the writing of Caxton and Malory. These evaluative remarks relate to presentational qualities, they do not mean to denigrate the *literary* quality of any of these texts. Structural infelicities can be observed also in Renaissance writing, and some of my remarks about criminal biographies in Chapter 4 will likewise be critical of writers' lack of lucidity.

It is usually argued (quite convincingly) that prose is always a latecomer in vernacular literatures and that the earliest kind of documents of national languages always belong to the genre of epic poetry. Epic poetry, it is frequently maintained, preserves features from the oral language, such as formulaicity or various structural kinds of repetition (e.g. stanzas with refrains), which are designed to afford a mnemonic aid to the singer as well as facilitating the easy appreciation of merely *heard* material on the part of the audience. The very same syntactic structures, in prose texts, give the impression of being undoctored, ill-at-ease attempts at linguistic expression. The development of an elegant prose style therefore needs to break away from verse composition. At the same time, vernacular prose in the Middle Ages also had the ever-present example of Latin prose to imitate and measure itself against. Indeed, much of vernacular prose was a direct or indirect translation from Latin (and French) sources, and its indigenous qualities can best be gauged in relation to these sources. The great achievement of the three saints' lives in the thirteenth-century Katherine Group, for instance, becomes all the more formidable in comparison with their Latin sources; such a comparison documents a complete recomposition of the source material into an episodic alliterative prose of great clarity and structural simplicity, a prose style which does not lack an eloquence and grandeur arguably absent from the convoluted prose of the Latin originals. English prose does not try to imitate the syntactic complexity of these Latin originals (which consists of an interweaving of numerous subsidiary clauses) until the sixteenth-century humanist writing of authors like Bishop John Fisher or Sir Thomas More. A comparison of these early English prose lives with French instances of *dérimage* (unrhyming, *Prosa-Umsetzungen*), as discussed in Cerquiglini (1981) and – superlatively – in Kittay and Godzich (1987), is instructive.

In the French examples, too, the exigencies of composition in prose require a complete rearrangement of the narrative propositions.[3]

A further central aspect of narrative development in the late medieval and early modern periods concerns the fate of experientiality. Experientiality, in the oral mode, was intimately linked with the mould of narrative of personal experience. The pattern of episodic narrative, with its incidences and evaluative result sections, provided a formal correlative to the dialectics of reportability and point which, I maintained, constitute (oral) experientiality. In the following I will trace the fate of the formal oral pattern (on a level of linguistic analysis) and outline the decline, fall and resurrection of the experiential mode in various types of third-person (vicarious) forms of narration. The majority of narrative genres in this period belong to third-person narrative. Indeed, with the exception of the dream narrative (a late development) and a few rare exceptions,[4] first-person narratives occur only as frame narratives (the prologue to *The Canterbury Tales*) or as witness reports (in legal documents and, sometimes, in contemplative writing). It can now be observed how the epic and the verse romance, which are by generic definition prototypically third-person forms, have adopted some of the linguistic patterns from oral first-person stories, and how they have adopted an experiential (though vicarious) content along with the formal pattern. Other genres, like the saints' legend, on the other hand, continue to rely on the linguistic models of experiential narrative but have lost all experiential quality and, despite the formal markings that recall oral experientiality, they function very much like narrative report.

In tracing developments of the experiential pattern in early narratives one therefore needs to distinguish between texts that preserve the pattern only *formally* and those that additionally preserve the experiential quality. Formal departures from the oral model which occurred in the wake of the conceptual transcoding (Habermalz, forthcoming) of performed oral narrative into the written medium also require analysis. And finally one will need to discuss the crucial revalorization of third-person narrative which correlates with its adoption of the experiential mode. The results from material examined in this chapter will determine the presentation in Chapter 4, where the beginnings of the novel and the realist tradition are at issue. The invention of what is traditionally called the novel can then be described as the outcome of a confluence of writing modes which became available in the process of the narrative transformations in the late medieval and early modern periods.

3.1 MIDDLE ENGLISH PROSE

Middle English prose narrative does not exist in great abundance. Basically, the following discourse types or genres are available.

(a) **Prose legends**. After the early collection of texts called the Katherine Group (*c.* 1230), written in *alliterative* prose, saints' lives occur in various kinds of verse (from *The South English Legendary* and the *Northern Homily Cycle* of the thirteenth century all the way to Bokenham, Lydgate and Capgrave in the fifteenth), and prose texts emerge only in the fifteenth century with the *Gilte Legende* and Caxton's *Golden Legend*. The genre continues in prose until the early seventeenth century (see *The Lives of Women Saints of our Contrie of England 1610–1615*). All these texts are, naturally, third-person narratives. Saintly (auto)biography (Margery Kempe's *Book*) occurs very rarely indeed. The tradition also comprises hagiographical literature of a historical nature, as in the lives of prominent Catholic martyrs[5] and in Foxe's *Actes and Monuments*. Although hagiography proper disappears in the wake of its discrediting by Protestant polemicists, the hagiographical form survives until the time of Defoe (Rosenwasser 1986). There was a notable hagiographical tradition that supplemented Foxe's writing by incorporating it with the Puritan, and particularly Quaker narratives of tribulation (Knott 1993), but recusant hagiography (e.g. John Mush's *Life of Margaret Clitherow*), and even autobiography (Gerard's account of his persecution [1609]), can be found in nearly equal number.

(b) **Letters**. The first few letters are available in the late fourteenth century and there are major collections for the fifteenth and sixteenth centuries (see, especially, *The Cely Letters* and *Paston Letters*).

(c) **Legal depositions** – not a particularly fruitful ground for narrative analysis. Chancery documents from the fifteenth century, for instance, do have numerous narrative passages – i.e. they frequently *report* the events which have necessitated the petition or ruling of the document. There is, however, no feature of experientiality observable in these reports. Even in two petitions where husbands ask Parliament to prosecute the rapist of their wives (Fisher *et al.* 1984: 227–9, 244–5) there is an account of the rape that merely decries the deed, but without any sympathy for the wife or an insight into her possible emotions. In fact, in one case, the petition goes on at great length to ask for the restitution of stolen goods, without once returning to the fate of the woman.

(d) **Sermons**. These do not generally have a great selection of long narratives but include a large number of exempla and brief retellings of different parts of the Bible.[6] (For a discussion of an example, see below.)

(e) **Translations**, most notably of the Bible (Wyclif, Tyndale). Much of the translation material, however, goes into *verse* translation, even from what are originally *prose* sources (e.g. most Middle English legendaries).

(f) **Prose romance**. In the fifteenth century, Arthurian legends and chivalric romances, formerly written in verse, appear for the first time in prose.

(g) **Historical texts**. These also used to be in verse (Laʒamon's *Brut*) or in Latin. Besides Mandeville's *Travels* (fourteenth century), first examples of travellers' stories and histories occur as late as the sixteenth century. The *Cambridge Bibliography* also lists a great number of kings' lives, most of which appear to be in Latin.

In the following I will concentrate on the sermon and the saints' legend. I will start with simple forms,[7] which are typically related to the exempla literature and proceed to more extensive works. Let me consider the following paragraph from Caxton's 'The Life of S. Erkenwold':

> In a day of summer as this blessed saint Erkenwold rode in his chair for to preach the word of God, it fortuned that the one wheel of the chair fell off from the axletree, and that notwithstanding the chair went forthright without falling, which was against nature and reason, and a fair miracle, for God guided the chair and it was a marvel to all them that saw it. O merciful god and marvellous above all things, to whom all brute beasts be made meek, and wild things be obedient, who vouchsafest to call to thy mercy thy blessed servant, to make him partable of thy excellent joy, give thou us grace by his prayer, which knew by revelation that his soul should be loosed from the body by temporal death, to be preserved from all manner evil and everlasting death.
> (Caxton 1900: VII, 68)

Most saints' legends are studded with the enumeration of one miracle after the other. Caxton's *Golden Legend* (1483), although it somewhat abbreviates the even more extensive passages of the Voragine text, preserves a fair amount of such reiteration. The narration of miracles was a central point in saints' lives (albeit less crucial for martyrologies) since canonization depended on the certification of miracles (Vauchez 1981). It was therefore in episodes, structured at their briefest much like the one before us, that miracles were authenticated in terms of 'historical' truth (and therefore operated as historical anecdotes), and miracle episodes additionally epitomized the hero's sanctity on a symbolic level. Such sanctity, of course, directly correlates with the *spiritual* Truth preached by the saint, and this Truth is in turn indirectly signified by the stories of performed miracles. That in our passage this Truth should, typically, be one 'against nature and reason' reflects the basic typology of hagiographical literature: the saint represents the otherwordly in pure essence, against sublunar rules and expectations.

The chosen passage is remarkable above all for its triviality. In contrast to the preceding paragraph, in which we learn that the chair – built for the dying St Erkenwold so that he could still go out and preach – became a relic for people after his death and helped believers to be cured of their sickness (VII, 68–9), the miracle here is defined *ex negativo*: the wheel breaks off, which might have endangered Erkenwold's life, but this – rather unspectacularly – has no immediate visible consequences. (Miracles, by their very nature, have to be seen and wondered at so that they can cause their typical visible effects on the bystanders.) Such insignificant miracle scenes must have served as the source for the parodic treatment of miracles in Reformation legendaries such as Hieronymous Rauscher's *One hundred selected gross impudent fat well-fattened stinking papal lies* (1562).[8] Protestant tracts like these use the triviality of the 'miracle' as their target and lampoon the depth of theological exegesis bestowed on such trivia. In our example, the homiletic second half of the paragraph is out of all proportion in relation to the preceding 'miracle'. It really constitutes a general address to the audience, dwelling on a repeated invocation of *memento mori* and the message of Redemption through Christ.

As has been variously observed, moral commentary became much more prominent in fourteenth-century prose (and verse), perhaps in an attempt to balance the increasing entertainment value of religious stories. (Horstmann [1881] notes correctly that *The South English Legendary*, as well as most of the thirteenth-century saints' lives which he collected and edited, were popularizations catering to what are arguably crude and vulgar tastes.[9]) In our example passage the moral is particularly prominent, taking up as much space as the narrative episode itself. The story proper in the first part can be reduced to the basic minimal points of experiential storytelling: St Erkenwold sets out on a journey (incipit), and as he is travelling along (setting), the wheel suddenly drops from the axle of his vehicle (incidence), but – owing to God's intervention – nothing happens (result). The letdown of 'no result' triggers the 'evaluation' section of the narrative, which is really the 'moral' of this tale and of all miracle stories in their generic structure. In our story the 'experience' – the unexpected emergency – is not linked to St Erkenwold's emotional involvement with it, but (as in stories of vicarious experience from natural narrative) it does involve the audience, and this audience – via the mediation of the bystanders who observe the miracle – is meant to evince dismay at St Erkenwold's danger and subsequent surprise and relief at his rescue. It is the audience, too, that would tend to interpret real-world events in terms of *nature* and *reason*. Religious belief (in miracles particularly) reposes precisely on the bracketing of nature and reason, and it is this central recognition of divine otherness (and of the intervention of God in this world) that constitutes the message of saints' legends. Not only is realism compatible with fantasy in this genre, but the hagiographic message in fact *requires* the presence of realistic elements and their inherent incompatibility with the spiritual/religious version of the story. From this perspective, the audience as vicarious experiencer of the observed clash between *the wisdom of this world* and the *Truth residing in God* is preprogrammed to adopt the position of an informed witness for whom the contradictions resolve themselves at the moment when the saint's life 'makes sense'. This then also helps to explain why saints' lives do not centre on the personal experience of the saint herself, on her physical and emotional suffering and on the agonies of her moral choice. The saint provides a *spectacle* for the audience, an exterior without psychological interiority, and this scenario corresponds to, and is constituted by, a *spectator's* point of view. The saint's comportment (the signifier) is a symbolic representation of idealized behaviour and attitude (the signified). Realist elements in saints' vitae emerge in the realism of the story background and circumstances, and they receive support from the audience's emphatic projection of themselves into a recognizable social environment. The saint, by contrast, stands out from this environment as an alien with an otherworldly (and therefore, in a measure, unknowable) mentality. She has a recognizably frail human body, a body which provides the receptacle (and *retable*) for the operations of divinity in what the audience and viewers perceive to be a realm contiguous with their own human sphere of existence. The more fantastic the saint's otherworldliness becomes, the more persuasiveness it acquires through the paradoxes of the economy of Truth: the more outrageously 'unrealistic', the truer it will be to the standards of sanctity whose wellspring lies precisely beyond the powers of the flesh. The saint's body therefore operates as a vellum on which divinity inscribes itself to be read by the human audience witnessing the miracle which is incarnated in the saint's resistance to human inscription (torture). The witnesses' conversion, effected through their vicarious experience of divinity in and through the body of the saint, can then be mediated iconically in the hagiographic text, with a view towards effecting conversion in the contemporary audience listening to the narrative.

What we can observe in the saints' lives is therefore a very deliberate exploitation of natural storytelling parameters in the service of a didactic and ideological policy. The central incidence of the miracle maximizes tellability, and the didactic point recuperates the intrusions of the otherworldly as a spiritual intervention from beyond that naturalizes the miracle as divine rather than human verisimilitude. If saints' lives never become 'novels' (with Capgrave a remarkable exception), this is precisely because they rigorously displace the experience of a human internal perspective. That such a refusal to see the martyr as a recognizable fellow human being should undermine the chances of a realistic *imitatio Christi* on the part of the audience (as has frequently been argued in support of the thesis that saints' lives were 'merely' moral tales and had no perceptible influence on the audience's real lives – see, e.g. McMahon 1992: 18) is not necessarily the only conclusion that can be drawn from the noted firm didactic control of the hagiographer and the standard typological interpretation of hagiographical literature. On the contrary, one can argue that the saint's psychology is missing from the record because it has already been sufficiently signified by the external trappings in their full symbolic, allegorical and typological significance. The audience is at no loss to supply the missing emotional and mental interiority because that interiority is already inscribed in the external gestures and words of the saint. Imitation (of Christ, as illustrated in the story of the saint) consists, precisely, in that leap of faith which will conquer sublunar weakness and fear by extirpating any remnants of care for this world. This leap of faith hinges on the concept of purity of soul – symbolically signified by and realized in chastity and virginity – a purity that has such a firm anchoring in faith that it can no longer be upset by temptation. Since it is only by God's grace that such purity can acquire the concomitant strength of faith and physical heroism to resist temptation and to endure the ultimate in physical suffering, the faithful *are* indeed encouraged to identify with the saint. What they are encouraged to imitate, however, is the saint's absolute surrender to the will of God and not, primarily, her superhuman moral strength or ability to suffer. *That* is an ability awarded only by God's grace, through the workings of *parousia*, of divine presence in the body of the saint in this world. As has been remarked (see, e.g. Jankofsky 1991: 92), the practical application of hagiographical teaching in the British Isles produced hosts of Protestant and Catholic martyrs when religion once more became a political issue of major proportions in the fifteenth century.

Hagiography provides an example of erased central experientiality, where the erasure operates in the familiar pattern of an absent presence, and where the surface manifestation of experientiality has been transferred to the observational and reflective stance of the witness and listener/reader. Such a pattern employs the trope of vicariousness on more than a formal level: the central narrative experience is represented by the saint but experienced vicariously by the audience; the saint is a representative of God in this world, the witness a representative of the ideal human reaction to miracles. I will return to the formal pattern in the verse legends below (3.2.1). The status of experientiality as a mediated effect on the bystanders, however, is observable even in the earlier verse literature.

My second example is from a sermon from MS Royal 18 B. xxiii from the fourteenth century.

> Now to þis matere acordynge I fynde a tale þat þer was somtyme a man þat had iiij frendes. And in þre of hem specially he leid grett affeccion in, but in þe iiij he had but litill affeccion in. So it befell on a tyme þat he had trespased aȝeyns þe kynge of þe londe, and so had forffette aȝeyns þe lawe þat he was vurthye to die. And whan þat he was take and shuld be brouthe to þe dome, he prayed to hem þat toke hym þat he myght speke with is frendes or þat he died.
>
> He com to is firste frende, þat he trusted most in, and preid hym of is helpe and succour aȝeyns þe kynge. And þis firste frend answered hym on þis wyze: 'The kynges felone I will not hold ne mayntene, for þou art wurthy to die; and þer-fore raþur I will bie þe a clothe to berye þe in.' Oþur answere he myght noon haue. þan full sorefully he toke

is leue and vent to aseye is second frend, besechynge hym of is helpe aʒeyns þe kynge, þat he wold graunte hym is liff. And he answerd hym and seid þat þe kynges felone shold haue no noþur fauour of hym but þat he wold helpe hym-selfe to lede þe kynges tratoure vn-to þe dethe. Than whan he myght not spede at þe second, he vente to a-sey þe þride frende, and com to hym and preyd hym þat he wold goye with hym and helpe hym aʒeyns þe kynge þat he wold forʒeue hym is trespase. And he answerd heym and seid þat he wold not helpe hym, but sethe þat he was þe kynges traytour, he wold helpe to hange hym. Than he vent to aseye is iiij frende, þe wiche he trusted leste vppon, and preyd hym þat he wold goye with hym and preye for hym to þe kynge þat he wold forʒeue him is trespasse. And þan he answerd hym and seid, 'In-asmuch as þou preyste me faire, þowʒ þou haue but litill deserued it, ʒitt I will goy with þe to þe kynge and preye þe kynge to forʒeue þe þi trespasse; and raþur þan þou shuld be dede, I will die for þe my-selfe.'

(*Middle English Sermons* 1940: 86–7;
editorial italics eliminated)[10]

The 'tale' that is here propounded at length has a typical recursive structure: a similar situation is reapplied to three or four different characters. This well-known folkloristic motif (cp. the three caskets in *The Merchant of Venice* and Freud's analysis of the scene)[11] occurs prominently in jokes[12] and is here exploited for allegorical exegesis. In the terms of the sermon the first friend represents the world, the second the family, the third the devil, and the fourth Jesus Christ.[13] The tale uses an oral structure of storytelling. The four episodes in which the doomed man visits each of his four friends are framed by an initial announcement (or abstract) that 'a tale' is going to be told, which is followed by an orientation section and a typical story incipit: 'So it befell'. The preliminary episode – the protagonist's sentencing (damnation for his sins) and request to talk to his friends (which is obviously granted) – does not yet reflect the structure of experiential narrative (personal, vicarious or perceptional) since it contains no central incidence. That is, one could read 'And whan þat he was take' as an *incipit*, 'and shuld be brouthe to þe dome' as *setting*, but then one encounters the protagonist's *reaction* (the request) as the next step, with the pronouncement of the death sentence elided and merely implied.

The three succeeding episodes observe a similar reportative pattern of clearly marked incipits ('he com to is firste frende'; 'þan full sorefully he toke is leue and vent to aseye is second frend'; 'Than whan he myght not spede at þe second, he vente to a-sey þe þride frende'), followed by the requests for help and the (ever-increasing hardheartedness of the) answers. In the first request episode there is a brief resolution point: 'Oþur answere he myght noon haue', whereas the end of the second episode merges with the incipit of the third ('Than whan he myght not spede'). The third episode ends on the drastic excess of the third friend's unfeeling answer, and the final fourth episode again obeys the same pattern: the protagonist 'goes and says' ('vent', 'preyd') and receives an answer. In contrast to prototypical experiential narrative, this is an episodic structure of bipartite moves (incipit and protagonist's request) followed by the reaction or result brought about by this request. The incidence already consists in the (negative) outcome of the supplicant's ventures. Unlike a story structure in which the experiencer has something befall him/her and then *reacts* to the incidence, thereby displaying his/her ability to master the situation (and to evaluate it retrospectively), the present setup has an active agent (in his role of petitioner) confronted with the limits of his ability to determine his own life. Such a setup suits the religious doctrine in perfect manner: humans can 'do' but only up to a point. By contrast, other types of episodic structure, such as those of the typical rogue story in the Elizabethan literature (see below), observe a pattern in which the actions of the protagonist do bring forth results: the rogues win out over their victims. In the rogues' biographies the double structure of *incipit/ action-result* epitomizes domination and control on the part of the actor-experiencer whose deliberate actions and their success constitute the narrative core experience.

The third type of narrative structure that I wish to discuss in this section is the *and then* style, which has sparked extensive discussion for the early texts of English and German prose.[14] According to Enkvist and Wårvik (1987), Old English narrative clauses of plot-propelling function are marked by the use of initial *þa*. Riehl (1993) notices a similarly pervasive use of Middle High German *do* in the texts which she analyses. In Middle English (ME) prose this clause-initial adverb (or, really, discourse marker) appears only rarely in the three early prose lives of the Katherine Group (early thirteenth century), although it can be found quite regularly in some of the popular *verse* renderings (Horstmann 1881) from the late thirteenth century. Of the three lives in the Katherine Group only the legends of St Margaret and St Katherine preserve the traditional *þa* + V + S pattern, and the instances are extremely rare.[15] *þo* (the ME form) occurs in non-initial sentence position in some of the verse lives of *The South English Legendary* and in the thirteenth-century *Of þe Vox and of þe Wolf* (in both of which the predominant use is still in the clause-initial position), but in the *Northern Homily Cycle* (Horstmann 1881) it disappears from practically all sentence-initial positions and occurs only in post-verbal locations. In the sermon literature, which (as we have seen) employs a highly condensed kind of storytelling, *þan(ne)* comes to replace earlier *þo* (compare the twelfth-century *Early English Homilies* with the fourteenth-century *Middle English Sermons*). In these texts *thanne* clearly serves to mark the onset of a narrative episode rather than highlighting a narrative clause *per se*. Finally, in the fifteenth century, especially in Malory, *þan* occurs with astonishing frequency, before practically disappearing in sixteenth-century prose.

As a conclusion to this section I will briefly analyse some passages from *The Gilte Legende* and *Morte D'Arthur* to illustrate the excessive use of *than* in these texts and to document the relation of this use of *than* to the creation of a fluid episode structure. Malory's work can be argued to illustrate the *malaises* of sixteenth-century prose *in nuce*: the problem is that of establishing a long continuous text on the basis of an episodic conception of storytelling. As we will see below under 3.3, these problems persist in similar form in late sixteenth-century and early seventeenth-century English narrative. However, where Malory and Caxton had little in the vernacular to model themselves on and inevitably echoed their French example texts, the early sixteenth century had already developed a humanistically inspired prose style. The rogues' literature *qua* the avatar of the novel reacted *against* this humanistic prose as much as it espoused a structural simplicity related to (but not consciously imitative of) the religious discourse of the Bible translations, Foxe's *Actes and Monuments*, the style of popular preaching and of the oral language in general.

Let me start with a passage from *The Gilte Legende*:

> In a tyme *it befelle* that all the province of Seint Nicholas suffered gret peyne for hunger, for mete failed allmost to all the peple. *And thanne* the servaunt of God herde saye that there were schippes charged with whete and were ariued atte the port. *And thanne anone* he went thedir and preied the schipmen that thei wold helpe the peple that pershid for hunger of eueri schip an C buschels of whete. *And thanne* thei saiden: 'Holy fader, we dur not, for it is deliuered to vs by mesure, and we most yelde the same mesure into the emperours garners in Alisaundre.' *And thanne* the holi man saide to hem: 'Dothe as I haue preied you, and I behete you in [the] vertue of God that it schall not be lessid whanne ye come to the garners.' And whanne thei hadd deliuered hym, thei come into Alisaundre and deliuered the fulle mesure that thei hadd resseived. *And thanne* thei told this miracle to the servauntes of the emperour, and thei all preised gretly God and his servaunt. *And thanne* this holi man departed this whete to eueri man after his nede, so that it suffisid two yeres not onli for to liue by but [also] for to sowe.
>
> (*Three Lives from the Gilte Legende* 1978: 54)[16]

In this miracle episode, the *thanne* occurrences mark St Nicholas's and the shipmen's important actions much in the manner of Old English *þa*. The paragraph starts with a clear episodic narrative marker ('it befelle'), and the famine provides a kind of setting on the background of which St Nicholas hears about the wheat ship in the harbour. The 'thanne anone' clause constitutes Nicholas's immediate reaction as well as the incipit of the next sub-episode, in which he goes to the ship, asks for the wheat, is answered and promises a miracle and has the wheat delivered to him.

From the oral to the written 103

Two sequences of result episodes are appended to this: the accounts of the merchants' arrival in Alexandria and of the miracle of the multiplying of the wheat, which is followed by the shipmen's praise of God (in the evaluation slot). The second appended result section returns to St Nicholas, increasing the effects of the miracle even further.

The paragraph thus has a cyclical structure: famine – miraculous intervention through God's providence – famine ended. Likewise, the shipmen arrive in port and arrive in Alexandria[17] in a frame-like bracketing of the oral exchange with St Nicholas. Through the intervention of St Nicholas and the miracle, life returns to its original state or condition: Nicholas's province (Myra) is rid of the famine, and the ships arrive in Alexandria in the same condition in which they left their original port. The paragraph also illustrates how the overall cyclical pattern lends unity to the miracle episode within which sub-episodes become mere 'scenes': initial predicament with news of help; the dialogue with the merchants; the miracle in Alexandria; the miracle in Myra.[18] Nicholas's persuasion of the merchants by a mere verbal promise in God's name is as much a miracle as is the providential arrival of the ships in the initial sub-episode. The paragraph therefore runs together a series of miracle scenes in a manner that enhances their miraculous qualities or effects and reiterates the basic message. Episodes one and three record passive receptions of the events, episodes two and four highlight Nicholas's active involvement but with the clear indication that he can produce beneficial effects only by proxy and not of his own accord.

These (sub-)episodes are no longer clearly marked. The *thanne* clauses apply equally to all types of events (incipits; incidences and results) and the above analysis in terms of four sub-episodes relies on cognitive rather than linguistic analysis. A more correct description of the circumstances would be in terms of a linear description, of a sequence with an overall initial marker (*it befelle*), followed by a simple series of dynamic occurrences and actions, with a final resolution that is not marked formally. The passage from *The Gilte Legende* therefore anticipates a narrative discourse which lacks experientiality (no incidences, no evaluation) and begins to level narrative episodes into a continuous sequence of 'new steps' and 'result' points. Such a structure prefigures much of the picaresque and criminal literature from the late sixteenth and early seventeenth centuries.

Let me now turn to Malory. I will discuss two passages from the first chapter ('Merlin') of *Morte D'Arthur, The Tale of King Arthur*. The first passage has recurring instances of *so* and *thanne*, the second makes use of more varied discourse markers.

So whan the duke and his wyf were comyn unto the kynge, by the meanes of grete lordes they were accorded bothe: the kynge lyked and loved this lady wel, and he made them grete chere out of mesure and desyred to have lyen by her. But she was a passyng good woman and wold not assente unto the kynge.

104 *From the oral to the written*

And ***thenne*** she told the duke her husband and said,

'I suppose that we were sente for that I shold be dishonoured. Wherfor, husband, I counceille yow that we departe from hens sodenly, that we maye ryde all nyghte unto oure owne castell.'

And in lyke wyse as she saide ***so*** they departed, that neyther the kynge nor none of his counceill were ware of their departyng. ***Also soone as*** kyng Uther knewe of theire departyng soo sodenly, he was wonderly wrothe; ***thenne*** he called to hym his pryvy counceille and told them of the sodeyne departyng of the duke and his wyf. ***Thenne*** they avysed the kynge to send for the duke and his wyf by a grete charge:

'And yf he wille not come at your somons, thenne may ye do your best; thenne have ye cause to make myghty werre upon hym.'

Soo that was done, and the messengers hadde their ansuers; and that was thys, shortly, that neyther he nor his wyf wold not come at hym. ***Thenne*** was the kyng wonderly wroth, and ***thenne*** the kyng sente hym playne word ageyne and badde hym be redy and stuffe hym and garnysshe hym, for within forty dayes he wold fetche hym oute of the byggest castell that he hath. ***Whanne*** the duke hadde thys warnynge ***anone*** he wente and furnysshed and garnysshed two stronge castels of his, of the whiche the one hyght Tyntagil and the other castel hyght Terrabyl.

(Malory 1971: 3)[19]

I have quoted the passage in full in order to compare the three episodes which it contains. The first episode coincides with the duke's arrival at the king's court, his lady's counsel, and the duke's clandestine departure. Note how this episode finishes in the middle of a paragraph according to the cited (Vinaver's) edition. The first episode starts with the discourse marker *so*, the major reaction of Igrayne is introduced by 'And thenne', and the result and closure is achieved by means of '*so* they departed'.

The second episode concerns the king's discovery that he has been tricked. Again the episode is initiated by a temporal *so*-combination ('Also soone as'), and the two actions are introduced by *thenne* – the king's calling of his council, and the answer given to him.

In the final episode, again initiated by a temporal *so*, the king's commands are repelled by the duke, and the king is therefore angry and threatens to make war on the duke (both steps highlighted by *thenne*). There is a final result section that describes the duke's preparations for the impending siege. This section is particularly noteworthy since it starts with a *whanne* clause – a type of clause very frequently employed at episode *beginnings*. (The locution 'anone he wente' also collocates with incipits.) However, in the present instance no new episode is necessarily initiated in this place since the following paragraph (not quoted above) initiates a new episode and has the earlier structure of a *so ... thenne ... thenne ...* sequence (ibid.: 3–4). The passage starting with the *whanne* clause ('Whanne the duke hadde thys warnynge') therefore seems to serve both as a macro-structural marking of the final consequences of the king's lust for the lady Igrayne and as a setting and orientation for the ensuing war over her between king and duke.

The text therefore displays a recurring pattern in which an initial *so* clause (frequently with a temporal 'as soon as' meaning) marks the incipit, and the episode-internal important developments and concluding result clauses are emphasized by means of *thenne*.

At the end of chapter one of the text this initial structure has been extended in two directions. Episodes have considerably increased, to triple length (or breadth), and discourse marker *so* is starting to usurp positions hitherto reserved for *thenne*, which has also acquired the alternative (allolexeme) *than*.

I will only quote the final passage of a more extended section (ibid.: 35-7). This three-page extract starts with an episode in which Merlin and Arthur go out on the lake ('*So* kynge Arthure and Merlion alyght'), get the sword ('*than* kynge Arthure toke hit up') and return to the shore ('And *so* he com unto the londe and rode forthe' – all ibid.: 35). This conflates with the next – much longer – episode, in which Arthur is saved from another battle with king Pellinore. There is an incipit using *and* ('*And* kynge Arthure saw a ryche pavilion' – ibid.) followed by extended dialogue with Merlin, in the course of which Arthur, for his acquiescence in not fighting Pellinore, receives the sword and the scabbard – a scene interrupting the dialogue and highlighted by two *than* clauses: '*Than* kynge Arthure loked on the swerde and lyked hit passynge well. *Than* seyde Merlion [. . .]' (ibid.: 36). This is followed by more of Merlin's advice (and prophecy) and a new sub-episode occurs which starts and ends with *so* ('*So* they rode unto Carlion [. . .]'): '*But* Merlion had done suche a crauffte unto kynge Pellinore saw nat kynge Arthure, and *so* passed by withoute ony wordis' (ibid.).[20] Arthur's arrival at Carlion is again marked by *so* but the remainder of the paragraph has *and whan* and *but*.

The chapter ends with Arthur taking two fatal decisions. The first is his engagement to fight king Royns. This reverts to the original pattern from the beginning of the chapter: '*So* [. . .] com a messyngere', followed twice by *than* (ibid.: 36-7). However, not only is the dialogue much longer than usual; the *than* also marks the messenger's departure and the final advice given to king Arthur, but Arthur's response is not marked in the same way and therefore falls flat of its expected decisiveness. The very final passage of the initial chapter (Arthur's replication of the slaughtering of the innocents and king Royns's preparations for war) significantly departs from the *so . . . thenne/than* pattern and is therefore now quoted in full:

'Well,' seyde Arthure, 'I shall ordayne for hym in shorte tyme.'
   Than kynge Arthure lette sende for all the children that were borne in May-day, begotyn of lordis and borne of ladyes; for Merlyon tolde

kynge Arthure that he that sholde destroy hym and all the londe sholde be borne on May-day. Wherefore he sente for hem all in payne of dethe, and so there were founde many lordis sonnys and many knyghtes sonnes, and all were sente unto the kynge. And *so* was Mordred sente by kynge Lottis wyff. And all were putte in a shyppe to the se; and som were four wekis olde and som lesse. And *so* by fortune the shyppe drove unto a castelle, and was all to-ryven and destroyed the moste party, save that Mordred was cast up, and a good man founde hym, and fostird hym tylle he was fourtene yere of age, and *than* brought hym to the courte, as hit rehersith aftirward and towarde the ende of the MORTE ARTHURE.

So, many lordys and barownes of thys realme were displeased for hir children were so loste; and many putte the wyght on Merlion more than o[n] Arthure. *So* what for drede and for love, they helde their pece.

But whan the messynge com to the kynge Royns, *than was he woode* oute of mesure, and purveyde hym for a grete oste, as hit rehersith aftir in the BOOKE OF BALYNE LE SAVEAGE that folowith nexte aftir: that was the adventure how Balyne gate the swerde.

(ibid.: 37)[21]

The episode starts with *than* and provides the reason for the king's action only in an appended *for* clause. The most important development regards Mordred and is highlighted by a *so*-plus-inversion structure: 'And so was Mordred sente'. The account of the ship's destruction is again introduced by a *so*, and the final result (in a coordinated sentence structure) has a *than* which I hesitate to define in terms of a discourse marker. (*Than* here appears to mean 'and later' or even 'and eventually' rather than 'as a result'.) The final two paragraphs are even odder, however, since they employ *so* twice in what are obviously characterizations of the *result* of Arthur's (mis)doings. The chapter moreover closes on a *but whan ... than* (plus inversion) construction, which according to the earlier pattern belongs in the *middle* part of an episode. The final paragraph therefore looks as if it should have been appended after Arthur's decision about king Royns or after the 'departure of the messenger' sentence.

What can be observed from the above is a rampant undermining of episode structure in terms of a developing interchangeability of *so*, *and*, *but* and *than*. *So* and *but* become more frequent, whereas *thenne* and *than* lose ground. The text has obvious problems with the marking of large-scale units and tries to highlight such macro-structural incipits by means of *thenne* and macro-structural 'resultant states' by means of *so* (as in the last passage). Whereas the writer of *The Gilte Legende* has the advantage of a model which basically consists of a series of independent episodes strung together, Malory has to manage his plot on several levels of hierarchical order and

From the oral to the written 107

this causes a number of conceptual difficulties. Malory appears to have attempted the introduction of the small-scale episode structure from natural narrative (as would be suggested from the sudden appearance of *so* at the beginning of episodes – a particle not found in *The Gilte Legende*), and is modifying this pattern as he goes along, with messy results but also some workable solutions.

I have here assumed the existence of a prior oral pattern based on the recurrence of *so* and on a comparable development in late Elizabethan prose. This argument will, I hope, derive some corroboration from remarks in the next two sections where the development of narrative structure in both the Middle English verse literature and Elizabethan narrative will be discussed. Whereas Malory has formal problems but preserves the experiential core and evaluative endpoint, the two prose passages which I analysed earlier document content-related departures from the experientiality of the oral tale but preserve the structural format intact. I now turn to the verse genres for a structural comparison and will return to prose below under 3.3 and again in Chapter 4.

3.2 MIDDLE ENGLISH VERSE NARRATIVE

3.2.1 Saints' legends

Middle English verse narrative, at first sight, appears to be structured in entirely different ways from the examples of prose discussed so far. This imprecision is partly superficial – verse, particularly the short verse line, simply 'sounds' different, and it requires a fairly simple, i.e. short, sentence structure, particularly when the verse is rhymed, as is the case with many of the legends from the thirteenth and early fourteenth centuries. Most rhymed verse, especially of the couplet type, tends to correlate the verse line and the clause in parallel syntax, which calls for a narrative structure that is very similar to that of natural narrative and its concatenation of idea units into successive episodes. The simplicity of such verse does not necessarily derive from the basic *paratactic* structure of oral storytelling which resurfaces in these instances of verse narrative; paratactic effects can in fact be achieved by what is – definitionally – subordination.[22] This is true even for prose narrative, as in Caxton's style, where relative *the which* functions as a paratactic marker in the meaning of 'and which'. The simplicity and 'oral' nature of Middle English verse is therefore constituted not by the syntactic properties of the verse but, rather, by the *brevity* of the verse line – corresponding to the five to seven words' frame of oral idea units. Second, the verse narratives preserve episodic narrative structure, as is instanced by their use of discourse markers, particularly those relating to the onset of narrative episodes (the *incipit*). In the following passage from a popular vita the episode incipits are marked by *þenne* and *and* respectively.

> Þenne bad Maxcence hys gayler
> þat he scholde þe mayden take
> And laden here in-to presoun þer,
> þe whyles he scholde þe wheles make.
> And or þe þrydde day were gon,
> þey weren Iwrouʒt al for here sake;
> So grym þey were to loke vpon,
> þat many a man þey garte quake.
> ('Seynt Katerine' ll. 465–72; Horstmann 1881: 253)[23]

These popular legends also have oral-mode abstracts embedded in extensive addresses and exhortations to the reader:

> Olde ant yonge, i preie ou . oure folies for to lete;
> þenchet on god þat yef ou wit . oure sunnes to bete!
> Here i mai tellen ou . wid wordes feire ant swete
> þe vie of one meidan, . was hoten Maregrete.
> ('Meidan Maregrete' ll. 1–4; Horstmann 1881: 489)[24]

Although the short verse line comes closest to the enunciative unit observable in natural narrative, it should be emphasized that real natural narrative sounds very different. Whereas idea units are introduced by *and* and other discourse markers 80–90 per cent of the time, discourse markers in the early verse narratives are fairly rare by comparison: of the two examples quoted above only the first has two instances of what one might be justified in calling a discourse marker. The second example, indeed, entirely departs from the structure of the oral line since, instead of proceeding from less significant to more significant sense items, it starts the lines (or half-lines) with 'new' (E. Prince 1979, 1981), important material. The second half-line is much less emphasized, whereas first half-lines serve to raise the audience's attention level. Although such long lines are still structured on the example of the short line (a long line is frequently made up from two short lines), they already allow a significant weighting between foreground and background information, a factor that was difficult to establish in the short line since the oral equivalent – intonation – could only be imperfectly transferred into the stanza scheme.

The first example passage is also very instructive with regard to the paratactic properties of the verse line. Although each line starts with an unstressed function word (a conjunction, article, modifier or personal pronoun) and thereby easily fulfills the iambic rhythm, the overall structure, i.e. of the stanza, is one of two sentences with a fairly complex syntactic pattern. Thus, the first sentence has a construction that depends on *bad* in the first line, a coordinate *scholde ... take and laden* in lines 2–3, and a temporal *þe whyles* clause which *logically* cannot refer to any of the previous verbs (*bad, scholde ... take and laden*) but of course implies an unstated 'and while she was there'. Even the simpler construction in the second sentence is much more sophisticated in its balancing of the result of the command (*bad*), i.e. the completion of the wheels, and their effect on bystanders. Note also the consummate artistry of the rhyme, in which *for here sake* rhymes with *garte quake* (i.e. 'made them shudder'), which is precisely the intended effect on the sympathetic listener, who shudders to think of Margaret's imminent ordeal.

Medieval verse narrative, besides its episodic structure, also employs a fairly prominent allocutive meta-narrative discourse which serves to introduce the tale (and provide an abstract), to 'shift' between changes of scene, to interpret the events and to supply a final conclusion (moral). For this reason medieval narrators are much more extensively present in the discourse than even the garrulous narrators of some nineteenth-century novels. The comparison with Trollope offers itself, but the prominence of the medieval narrator lies less in the number or length of authorial intrusions than in their handling. Where Trollope's use of the intrusive narrative comment would be a sign of sophistication (echoing earlier anti-illusionist masters such as Diderot), medieval tales refer the function of a real teller back to the familiar real-life experience of the bard which can be resuscitated schematically in each oral performance of the tale. Such narratorial manipulation does not detract from the story but promotes its effective transmission.

Addresses to the audience such as the one in the second example above are of course unthinkable in nineteenth-century fiction with its groundings in a *written* discourse. The medieval narrator figure is also notable for the prevailing tendency to shift scenes, a characteristic already prominent in oral narrative.[25] Whereas later novelistic locutions such as 'while X is singing, I will use the time to tell you about her trip to London' are highly anti-realistic and constitute a deliberate metafictional[26] technique, this is not the case for the medieval texts, where the active narrator persona is required from a structural point of view as a means to effect the articulation and alignment of macro-episodes. The same kind of gear-shifting occurs also in prose. I quote a brief passage from the story of 'St. Katharine' in Caxton's *Golden Legend*:

> But now I leave this young queen in her contemplation, and shall say you as far as God will give me grace, how that our Lord by his special miracle, called her unto baptism in a special manner, such as hath not been heard of before ne sith, and also how she was visibly married to our Lord, in showing to her sovereign tokens of singular love.
> (Caxton 1900: VII, 8–9)

Compare the following two examples from Chaucer's 'The Man of Law's Tale', in the second of which the narrative commentary marks the return to the plotline after what – in a natural narrative pattern – would be delayed orientation:

The sorwe that this Alla nyght and day
Maketh for his wyf, and for his child also,
Ther is no tonge that it telle may.
But now wol I unto Custance go,
That fleteth in the see, in peyne and wo,
Fyve yeer and moore, as liked Cristes sonde,
Er that hir ship approched unto londe.
(B¹ 897–903; Chaucer 1987: 100)[27]

This constable was nothyng lord of this place
Of which I speke, ther he Custance fond,
But kepte it strongly many a wyntres space
Under Alla, kyng of al Northhumbrelond,
That was ful wys, and worthy of his hond
Agayn the Scottes, as men may wel heere;
But turne I wole agayn to my mateere.
(B¹ 575–81; ibid.: 95)[28]

In the first passage the narrator leaves King Alla to his grief and lamentation to shift the scene to Custance floating in the sea, exposed to the elements. In the second passage the narrator, in like manner after an orientation section, shifts back to the plot level of the narrative. Such elaborate strategies are obviously motivated and justified in a situation where different strands of narrative have to be joined in a manner that should help the audience to follow such shifting. Again, where structures of this type occur in verse, they are geared towards the needs of an audience, considering particularly their ability to process aural information; they are not a sign of the speaker's problems with articulation or enunciation, as is the case in the examples from natural narrative (Chafe 1980).

A final consideration in this section is awarded to the status and shape of the narrative episode in the verse literature, concentrating in particular on early uses of þo and on the development of the episode in late fourteenth- and early fifteenth-century verse.[29]

Besides some 'popular' vitae designed, as Horstmann believes, for recital at fairs and church festivals, the fourteenth- and early fifteenth-century English legends come in two collections, *The South English Legendary*[30] and the *Northern Homily Cycle* (edited in Horstmann 1881). Narrative structure in the verse legends is obviously greatly dependent on the rhyme and stanza patterns. Thus Bokenham's collection of vitae displays a rigid stanza structure in which each stanza corresponds to an episode.

Whan þis yung man had herd þe answere
  Of blyssyd Anneys, he wex ful heuy,
  And so sore blynd loue hym anoon dede dere
  þat in soule both anguysshyd & in body
  He syknyd, & in hys bede he doun dede ly;

> But by hys greth syhys aspyid he was
>   Of lechys, wych told his fadyr þe caas.
> And **whan** he sey þat þe affeccyoun
>   Of his sone to anneys was set sore,
> Of alle hys profyrs he made iteracyoun
>   In euery degre & rathere more;
> But sekyr his labour was but lore,
>   For pleynly she seyd þat in no wyse
> Hir fyrst sposys profyrs she nold despyse.
> And for he þat tym of þe prefecture
>   In þe hey astate stode & dygnyte,
> Hym þoht þat noon oþir creature
>   To-forn hym in worshepe preferryd myht be,
> Wherefore he wundryd who shuld ben he
>   Be whom þus anneys hir dede enhaunce,
> And of his treasoure made swych auaunce.
> ('Lyf of S. Anneys', ll. 4190–210; Bokenham 1938: 115)[31]

The *whan* clauses in this passage mark new incipits, but the episodes themselves lack a central incident. Instead, the son's and then the prefect's reaction to Agnes's refusals (in the *when* clauses) is narrated, and the resolution (the involvement of the father) entails further results. The *Scottish Legendary* also employs a fast-paced enchaining of sub-episodes with an *as*-clause that marks the onset.

> & **as** he saw þat hurt hir nocht,
> chennys of yrne son var wrocht;
> þar-vith stratly scho ves bundine,
> & syne in a pressone thrungine.
> & **as** scho ves þar alane,
> for to fand hir þe feynd has tane
> þe schape of angel, of his mycht,
> & come til hir, schenand ly[ch]t,
> & sad til hir: 'Iulyane,
> of god ane angel I ame ane,
> & send me for to monest þe
> þat, or þu forthire torment be,
> þat þu til god[is] sacryfy.'
> ('St Julienne', ll. 41–53; *Legends of the Saints in the Scottish Dialect* 1891: 425)[32]

The first episode again lacks an experiential core. It merely has an incipit (which conflates with the result of the previous episode) and two actions of the judge which are reactions to this initial state of affairs. The second episode, on the other hand, does have an incidence, the arrival of the false angel, and it highlights this event performatively by means of quoted speech.

The following quotations from the *South English Legendary* (*SEL*) and the *Northern Homily Cycle* (*NHC*), by contrast, are free from the recurrence of temporal *when* clauses[33] and instead use the traditional *þo* and *þan*. (Not all the lives in the *SEL* have a recurring *þo* pattern, whereas most of the 'popular' individual vitae edited by Horstmann do.) In the first passage from the *SEL* the individual stages in the justice's increasing frustration are marked by a series of *þo* clauses.

¶ *þo* þis fur was strong ymaked . he sat amidde wel stille
Nemiȝte þat fur hire enes brenne . ne harmi worþ a fille
þo nomen hi & walde pich . & brimston wel faste
& vpe hire tendre bodi naked . al seoþinge gonne hit caste
& euere sat þis maide stille . hit negreuede hire noþing
Ac prechede euere wiþ glade hurte . of Iesu heuene king
¶ *þo* nuste þe liþere Iustise . what he miȝte do more
Whan he nimiȝte þis clene þing . ouercome mid his lore
A scherp swerd he let & kene . þurf out hire þrote do
To bynyme hire speche . & hire holi lyf also
þo heo was þurfout þe þrote ismyte . þe bet heo spac ynouȝ
& prechede ȝurne of Iesu Crist . & wel smere louȝ
¶ Ȝe heo seide þat Cristene beoþ . glade & bliþe ȝe beo [...]
('St. Lucy', ll. 141–152; *SEL* 1956: 570)[34]

þo need not necessarily coincide with an episode beginning. In the first two occurrences (the trials by fire and pitch) the *þo* does indeed emphasize the onset of the next sub-episode. However, the third *þo* appears to emphasize the effect of St Lucy's indestructibility on the judge: he is at a loss. Significantly, this information is taken up again in the next line with the *whan* clause, which – from a cognitive perspective – appears to correlate with the incipit point of the subsequent (final) attempt to shut up the maiden's preaching. The last *þo* in the quoted passage is a marker of the final stage of St Lucy's passion. *þo* occurs only one more time in that particular vita, as a temporal conjunction, not as an adverb or discourse marker: 'þo heo hit hadde vnderfonge' ('When she had received it [the host]' – l. 169). In fact *þo* here comes very close to the later productive *whan* and *as* pattern, with a shift from the 'and then' to an integrative and anaphoric 'and when this was done' reading. As with the Bokenham passage there is no central incidence in these episodes. The tortures provide a starting point for the episode, which then exhausts itself in the description of their lack of effect. This non-result constitutes both the core of the episode and the negative outcome of the initiating actions. The saint's lack of response triggers the next round of tortures, so that the incipits combine the resolution section of the previous episode with the incipit point of the following episode. This condensation of narrative episodes also occurs in *The Gilte Legende*, as we have seen, and becomes a standard feature in the picaresque literature. (See below under 3.3.)

A final set of examples comes from the *Northern Homily Cycle*.

When þe Emperoure þis sight had sene,
In hert he had ful mekill tene;
He cumand þat þe mayden bright
Suld sone be broght bifor his sight.
And all-if he in hert war tende,
He spac to hir with wordes hende:
'A, worthi maydin mikel of prise [...]'
('De sancta Katerina historia' ll. 307–312; Horstmann 1881: 168)[35]

þan þat terant was ful tene
& ordand Katerin paynes kene:
He gert his men tite in þat tyde
Naken hir both bac and side,
With scorpions *þan* he did hir bete,
& mani oþer paines grete;
Bot al he saw might noght auale
In hir fait(h) to ger hir faile.
þan in a preson þai hir did
Whare scho was all in mirkenis hid,
And wight men set he hir to gete,
þat scho sul haue no drink ne mete,
Se sustinance suld scho haue nane,
Till twelue daies war cumen & gane.
Bot angels ilk day come hir till:
Of gastly fude scho had hir fill.
þus in þat preson gan scho dwell.
And in þat same tyme *so bifell*:
(ll. 345–362; ibid.: 168–9)[36]

The text mostly relies on a recurrent use of *þan* (as an analysis of Horstmann's text shows), but *þan* can be supplemented with *whan ... þan* instances in many of the popular saints' lives collected by Horstmann. The first two episodes are fairly complete, with an incipit (l. 307, l. 345), a series of actions and a resolution (ll. 351–2), but none of the episodes have an experiential core. A particularly interesting case of episode management can be observed in the latter half of the quoted passage. *þan* in line 353 ('þan in a preson þai hir did') opens a new episode, the next trial of St Katherine, whereas the *þus* clause completing the episode provides an end point to the first stage of the saint's passion.[37] The saint's worldly antagonist is away on a trip and thus makes room for the interlude of Katherine's second feat of conversion (converting the queen). That this point in the story corresponds to a major structural juncture is underlined by the next line: 'And in þat same tyme so bifell' (l. 362) – a phrasing usually reserved for story-initial incipits. The quite openly marked re-entry onto a new macro-structural story segment (which is also on a new level of seriousness) can therefore be argued to have imposed a more formal emphasis on the closure process as well, resulting in the use of *þus*.

What conclusions can be drawn from this analysis of the saints' legends? As is true of most texts from Middle English, the stories told in these legends are heterodiegetic: we learn *about* the saint's trials but not from her own perspective or in her own words. The structural pattern of this genre, however, still reflects the oral model of experiential episodes, with successive new incipits, the incidences of what is done to the martyr, and usually an extended reaction block which describes the saint's imperturbability and her victory over the tyrant's attempts to break down her resistance. This imperturbability, for the judge, corresponds to a *lack* of reaction, and duly triggers the next round of verbal *agon* or the next stage of yet more gruelling torture.

One can therefore argue that the saint's legend closely follows oral models by preserving an episodic succession of scenes of verbal combat or physical oppression. The very extra-linguistic structure of the events themselves corresponds with the narrative schema. What already changes in the typology of the saints' legend is the location of experientiality. Contrary to what one would expect, the experiential centre of the legend pertains to the tyrant and his vain attempts at subduing the martyr. He is the one to voice exasperation and rage and, eventually, to acknowledge defeat, and he is the agent who tries to inscribe his will on the virgin's body. Thus, although the legend depicts a frame in which the martyr has things done to her (incidence) and reacts by non-action, the narrative interest also focuses on the perpetrator of the violence and on his ingenuity and persistence. The 'incidences' are planned strategies which emanate from one source of determined action and compete with the schema of a dynamic interaction of saint and tyrant. The overall pattern of violence traces a course of exponential escalation and eventual deflation into pathetic failure, a frame that enlists our sympathies. The tyrant's reactions to his failure are depicted in great detail: he foams at the mouth, he utters curses, he tears his hair – and orders a new round of tortures. The saint's legend can therefore be conceptualized *both* as a series of incidences befalling the martyr *and* as a series of intentional actions manipulated by the judge or tyrant. To put this differently, one can image the structure of the saints' legend in terms of the ACTION pattern and in terms of the EXPERIENCING pattern, and this duplicity or ambivalence then helps to preserve the dynamics of natural narrative, where evaluation and experience have been integrated within one holistic (or organic) experiential frame. At the same time, the formal structure undergoes a marked development towards levelling, since the absence of a central incidence tends to condense incipits and resolutions into a series of 'and then and then' sequences.

3.2.2 Romance

Before turning to *Troilus and Criseyde* for an exemplification of the later romance style, I wish briefly to review two of the classic romances, *King Horn* and *Floris and Blancheflour* (both from the thirteenth century). I will also consider John Capgrave's fifteenth-century vita *The Life of St. Katharine of Alexandria*, which in its length and narrative structure belongs with the romance genre rather than with the standard type of saint's legend.

King Horn (c. 1225), in its metrical and syntactic outlay, can be compared to the early saints' legends. The verse line closely resembles oral idea units. Structurally, too, this romance preserves the episodic pattern from the oral language. The first episode telling of King Murry's death, for instance, has the incipit 'Hit was upon a someres day' (l. 31; Sands 1993: 18), and the text then goes on to describe Murry's encounter with the 'Sarazins', which results in their fight and his death (ll. 31–62). What is particularly noteworthy in *King Horn* is the involvement of the narrator with the story and its protagonists. Not only does the narrator directly talk to the audience ('Alle beon hi blithe / That to my song lithe!' – ll. 1–2; ibid.: 18); the narrator also, with the benefit of hindsight, alerts the reader to imminent tragedy, mourning the disaster before it occurs: 'With him riden bute two – /All too fewe ware tho!' (ll. 37–8; cp. also l. 54; ibid.). The narrator also emphatically presents Horn's mishaps by means of expressive exclamation: 'Ofte hadde Horn beo wo,/Ac nevre wurs than him was tho!' (ll. 119–20; ibid.: 20). This can be argued to echo oral patterns of evaluation.

A later romance, the famous *Floris and Blancheflour*, already departs from the pattern of the experiential episode. *Floris and Blancheflour* also employs some of the shifting mechanisms that I pointed out earlier: 'Now let we of Blancheflour be/And speke of Floris in his contree.' (ll. 203–4; ibid.: 287). The narrator is here more of an arranger than an active bardic voice, and he frequently presents report sequences which have an episodic structure (in the sense of an incipit and a conclusion) but no central point of incidence. For instance, when the merchants sell Blancheflour in Babylon, this is narrated in a marked-off episode (ll. 183–202; ibid.) which starts with the recurrent discourse marker *now* and a historical present tense ('Now these marchaundes sailen over the see' – l. 187) and closes on their contentment with the bargain: 'Now these merchaundes that may belete/And been glad of hur biyete' (ll. 201–2) – again marked by means of the *now* and the historical present. The narrative also runs one episode into another without delimitation, for instance when Floris arrives back from his trip and starts looking for Blancheflour:

Now Floris hath undernome
And to his fader he is coome;
In his fader halle he is light.

> His fader him grette anoon right
> And his moder, the Queene also,
> But unnethes might he that do
> That he ne asked where his leman be;
> Nonskins answere chargeth he,
> So longe he is forth noome
> In to chamber he is coome.
> The maidenis moder he asked right,
> 'Where is Blauncheflour, my swete wight?'
> 'Sir,' she saide, 'forsothe y-wis,
> I ne woot where she is.'
> She bethought hur on that lesing
> That was ordained bifoore the King.
> 'Thou gabbest me,' he said tho;
> 'Thy gabbing doth me muche wo!
> Tell me where my leman be!'
> All weeping saide thenne she,
> 'Sir,' she saide, 'deede.' 'Deed!' saide he.
> 'Sir,' she saide, 'for sothe, ye.'
> 'Allas, when died that swete wight?'
> 'Sir, withinne this fourtenight
> The erth was laide hur about
> And deed she was for thy love.'
> Flores, that was so faire and gent,
> Sounid there, verament.
> The Christen woman began to crye
> To Jesu Christ and Saint Marye.
> The King and the Queene herde that crye;
> Into the chamber they ronne on hye,
> And the Queene seye her biforne
> On sowne the childe that she had borne.
> The Kinges hert was all in care,
> That sawe his sone for love so fare.
>
> (ll. 219-54; ibid.: 287-8)[38]

The onset of this scene is marked by a triple historical present, but after that no clear episode boundaries can be made out between a series of dynamic moments: Floris's impetuosity in immediately running off to Blancheflour's room, the heated exchange with her mother (his nurse) and his falling into a faint, the nurse crying out, the parents running in, the king's consternation. All these are mirrored formally in the breakneck speed of the syntax and in the refusal of a central incident. What is developing here anticipates the structure of action scenes in the picaresque novel.

Throughout *Floris and Blancheflour* the episodic pattern structure is awry. Incipits and closures abound, mostly marked doubly and triply with *now*, *thus* and historical present tenses, with subject–verb inversion or the syntax of topicalization. And yet one episode seems to run into the other because the central incidences remain elusive and indefinable. The narrative is also extremely innovative in the prominence it awards to pyschological motivation and in its concentration on characters' states of mind. (The latter aspect connects with the uncannily pervasive use of the historical present in this romance: descriptions of Floris's or Blancheflour's grief are cast in set scenes, employing a series of static historical presents)[39].

The modification of the episode is less drastic in Capgrave's *Life of St. Katharine*. Episodic narrative here disappears simply because what would be dealt with in one oral episode is here expanded into two cantos. Thus the orientational material alone encompasses some 200 lines which provide an in-depth presentation of Costus's (Katharine's father's) character, a description of Antioch and Alexandria and a historio-political introduction. The story of the king's childless marriage and the miracle of Katharine's conception and birth take up much less space. Many of the central episodes of the saint's life are swelled to epic proportions, as when her dialogue with the scholars is developed as an exercise in theological argument which takes up all of Book IV.

It is therefore instructive to compare these developments with *Troilus and Criseyde*. Like the Capgrave text, *Troilus* frequently runs several stanzas together, particularly in the presentation of long speeches or prolonged meditations. Indeed, even in the narrative report, sentences sometimes continue from one stanza to the other:

This Troilus was present in the place
whan axed was for Antenor Criseyde,
for which ful soone chaungen gan his face,
As he that with tho wordes wel neigh deyde.
But natheles he no word to it seyde,
Lest men sholde his affeccioun espye;
With mannes herte he gan his sorwes drye,

And ful of angwissh and of grisly drede
Abod what lordes wolde unto it seye;
And if they wolde graunte – as God forbede –
Th'eschaunge of hire, than thoughte he thynges tweye:
First, how to save hire honour, and what weye
He myghte best th' eschaunge of hire withstonde.
Ful faste he caste how al this myghte stonde.
    (*Troilus and Criseyde* IV, ll. 148–61; Chaucer 1987: 540)[40]

Although it is not the rule, this manner of writing easily accommodates continuity beyond the story distribution. We have seen earlier that the narratives from *The Canterbury Tales* are still very much structured on the episode pattern. *Troilus* is different no doubt also because this is a long story and not a series of tales, a long story with ample space for extended passages of direct speech and interior (quoted) monologue. In contrast to the tales, too, nothing much 'happens' in *Troilus* – characters' perceptions, thoughts and dialogue are prominent; it is mostly Pandarus who takes the initiative. Unlike Malory and his obvious difficulties with a long piece of prose, Chaucer moves gracefully along without any major hitches, and this despite the formidable task of doing so without the benefit of episodic structure. Indeed, Chaucer here anticipates a writing style in verse that, in prose, did not fully come into its own until the novel. One of the reasons why the narrative of *Troilus* is so very modern appears to derive directly from its emphasis on characters' feelings and thoughts. Such an emphasis immediately undermines the foregrounding of *action* or *incidence* (which is basic to the episodic structure) and uses action merely to *link* 'scenes' in which characters engage in conversation with themselves or among each other.

To illustrate this analysis, I will here briefly rehearse the structure of Book IV of *Troilus*, a book in which quite a few things can be said to 'happen': Calchas is to receive his daughter back in exchange for Antenor, all three characters learn of this and react accordingly, with Troilus moping about at home until Pandarus visits him and Criseyde receiving a visit from her friends telling her about the council's decision. Finally Troilus visits Criseyde and they debate a possible elopement but eventually decide to comply with the exchange of Criseyde and to rejoin one another after a set term of days.

Book IV starts with a proem. It then sets the scene for Antenor's capture by a macro-structural incipit ('byfel' l. 31, Chaucer 1987: 538) and a relation of the fight, the capture of prisoners and the negotiations for an exchange of prisoners. In this initial sequence, despite the incipit marking *byfel*, there is little left of the old episodic structure.

> Liggyng in oost, as I have seyd er this,
> The Grekes stronge aboute Troie town,
> Byfel that, whan that Phebus shynyng is
> Upon the brest of Hercules lyoun,
> That Ector, with ful many a bold baroun,
> Caste on a day with Grekis for to fighte,
> As he was wont, to greve hem what he myghte.

> Not I how longe or short it was bitwene
> This purpos and that day they issen mente,
> But on a day, wel armed, brighte, and shene,
> Ector and many a worthi wight out wente,
> With spere in honde and bigge bowes bente;
> And in the berd, withouten lenger lette,
> Hire fomen in the feld hem faste mette.

The longe day, with speres sharpe igrounde,
With arwes, dartes, swerdes, maces felle,
They fighte and bringen hors and man to grounde,
And with hire axes out the braynes quelle.
But in the laste shour, soth for to telle,
The folk of Troie hemselven so mysledden
That with the worse at nyght homward they fledden.
    (*Troilus and Criseyde* IV, ll. 29–49; Chaucer 1987: 538)[41]

Stanza 5 elaborates on the scene of preparation for the fight, and stanza 6 twice refers to the onset of the battle (*out wente, hem faste mette*). In stanza 7 the battle itself is described in one of those typical a-dynamic presents which provide a static summary[42] or picture of the fighting, and the stanza closes on the conclusion (significantly with a change into the past tense): *mysledden, fledden*. It can of course be argued that these are remnants of the episode (incipit: *out wente*; incidences: *hem faste mette, fighte, bringen ... to grounde, quelle*; results: *mysledden, fledden*). However, this pattern has been changed to apply, not to a protagonist's perceptions and experiences, but to a general description of the Trojans' and Greeks' conflict. It is only in the results that the Trojans emerge as *different from* the Greeks. The perspective on these events is not that of a protagonist or of a neutral observer but the Olympian slightly bemused perspective of the latter-day historian who summarizes events at his pleasure and, *qua* historian, can easily admit to ignorance on historical details ('Not I' – l. 36; ibid.).

That the narrative is clearly intent on stringing together a series of scenes becomes nowhere so apparent as in Pandarus' and Troilus' (non) reactions to the council meeting which determines the exchange of Criseyde. Troilus rushes to his room in order to indulge in breast-beating and lamentation (st. 38–48) and is unable to move for woe. Pandarus is nearly demented with concern and has to come looking for Troilus (st. 50). If Pandarus was in the same meeting, why did he not contact Troilus there and then, accompanying him home? After a lengthy lamentatory dialogue between the two, Pandarus utters his treacherous advice, suggesting to Troilus that he get himself a new lover. Stanza 75 is typical of the spirit of the narrative:

This Troylus in teris gan distille,
As licour out of a lambyc ful faste;
And Pandarus gan holde his tunge stille,
And to the ground his eyen doun he caste.
But natheles, thus thought he at the laste:
'What! Parde, rather than my felawe deye,
Yet shal I somwhat more unto hym seye.'
    (*Troilus and Criseyde* IV: 519–25; ibid.: 545)[43]

One may want to note the initial 'This Troylus' – a new marker of incipits[44] – and the following series of actions, mostly linguistic and mental, which occur in its wake. Where, as we will see, sixteenth-century prose moves towards an elimination of the episode as a consequence of larger *action* sequences, Chaucer has to forgo the episodic pattern because he concentrates on characters' internal experience, not on action sequences.

What we can learn from this brief excursion into Middle English romance can be summarized as follows: The romance starts out with an episodic pattern but soon begins to string episodes together in order to create larger units which are less fast-paced and allow for a more detailed presentation of characters' psychology. Action sequences become less important, and characters' dialogue and psychological meditations are foregrounded. *Troilus* and Capgrave's *St. Katharine* have solved the problems of this process of condensation by evolving a macro-structural pattern in which larger scenes (consisting of dialogues or soliloquies) are strung together. The earlier romances are still battling with the exigencies of overcoming the episodic pattern. One consequence of eliminating the central incidence and of running episodes together, as we have seen, is the increasing afunctionality of incipits and result sections, which continue to mark new directions (changes of scene, for instance) but veil rather than clarify the macro-structural patterns in the story. We will observe a similar tendency in narrative prose, where the shift from episodic to scenic storytelling requires an interim stage at which incipits remain in prominent focus yet episodes have all but disappeared from the text.

Romance and epic, moreover, document the crucial transference of the experiential core from action-oriented parameters to a presentation of the protagonists' consciousness which starts to take up more and more space. This is most pronounced in *Troilus*, where one is nearly at the stage of the eighteenth-century novel, but *in nuce* this can be observed also in the later romances and in Capgrave's novelistic vita. Rather than abiding with the pattern of incidence within an action-oriented frame, the Middle English romance already starts to replace action by consciousness, and it clearly anchors such experientiality in the third-person subject.

3.3 RENAISSANCE PROSE AND POPULAR WRITING BEFORE BEHN

In the sixteenth and seventeenth centuries two competing narrative styles can be observed to coexist, and it is the second of these, the popular type of writing, which eventually feeds into the development of a new genre, the novel.[45] The two major strands of writing that I will be concerned with are, on the one hand, humanistically inspired prose with its views on stylistic decorum and its sophisticated syntactic balancing and, on the other, the popular genres which sprang up in the sixteenth century: the rogue's story, the travelogue, the pamphlet, Protestant hagiography (Foxe), diaries, autobiographies, as well as vernacular and popular historiography (Holinshed). This is a wide field, and I will therefore limit myself to some few examples which, for the moment, will have to serve as representative specimens.

We have already discussed one example of humanistic prose, in More's parable of the virgin, at the end of Chapter 2. One can observe in particular that the writings of More, Fisher, Ascham, Sidney or Lyly all employ a sentence pattern in which an almost architectural balancing act is performed between various arguments and counter-arguments, between causes and effects, external action and internal intentions or reactions. Such complexity obviously derives from the Latin model of *amplificatio*, which the more humanistically schooled authors tried to emulate in the vernacular. A second source, however, can be traced in Caxton's translations, which already tended to string together a series of relative clauses in loose adjunction on the lines of *the which, thereof*, or *after which*. Humanistic prose builds on a similar basis but reworks the clauses to integrate them as parts of a logically structured overall argument. Sixteenth-century prose carefully balances oppositional terms in parallelism and antithesis, employing series of concessive clauses and their positive counterparts, arguments and counter-arguments, or by accumulative exemplification, using different types of similies or comparisons.

In the realm of narrative the high style goes with classic breadth of treatment and a discourse of the same: most of the plots are openly aligned with standard plots from the classics, rewriting romance from a variety of schematic situations which are then employed in alternating constellations. In spite of their (Renaissance) emphasis on the active individual, these texts frequently highlight the exemplary nature of the protagonists, not their singularity or idiosyncrasy. In this, sixteenth-century Renaissance narrative not only prefigures the classicism of *Rasselas*; it also sharply contrasts with the popular literature of its time. The major argument of the travel literature and criminal stories is that they are *true* even if they are fantastic, an argument that is later amended to 'the more fantastic the truer' since one can supposedly invent the known but not the hitherto unthinkable (McKeon 1987). Whereas popular writing mostly relied on the witness report, with mediated personal experience a second-best option, the elaborate inventions of Lyly or Sidney classically situated themselves in the chronologically and geographically removed countries of Greek antiquity or in a fairyland version of pastoral France (Lodge's *Rosalynde*). Popular literature tended to be marketed in terms of its recent history value, with contemporary life as its point of reference. This is true even for the presentation of exotic travel in such writing: accounts of travel into foreign parts echo the witness quality of travelogues (e.g. the accounts of the Spanish Conquest) rather than the serenity of a Claude Lorrain. (The latter appears to be more on the lines of the pastoral settings in Sidney or Lyly.) The romance – unlike the travelogues and popular writing – remains within the tradition of third-person omniscient narration, with the leisureliness of the narrational process inscribed even within first-person narrative insets (as in the *New Arcadia*'s lengthy reports in Book I which rewrite the omniscient presentation of the *Old Arcadia*).

One therefore observes a first very important difference between popular narrative written in the first-person mode (or in peripheral first-person narrative)[46] and the distanced third-person narrative of the Renaissance 'novel'. There is a great measure of playfulness in the latter[47] and a prevalent note of seriousness and moralistic urgency in the former. Nothing could be further from the humanistic taste than the incipient confessional stridency of some of the rogues' literature. Whereas the popular writing is closely linked to the actual narrative experience – what kind of events befell the protagonist or how shrewdly she managed to trick her enemies – Sidney's much less mundane interest is in the exercise of political, courtly and moral virtues which the story is meant to foreground. In effect the plot in Sidney, as in Spenser, has become an allegorical demonstration of a more general didactic message. In the popular writing, of course, plot is the focal point of the tale; the moral argument which it ostensibly serves is frequently undermined by the 'truth' of the story. The rogue's real success obscures his later (feigned?) act of repentance.

Let us now look at a specific example from Sidney:

> And *so*, getting on their horses, they travelled but a little way *when*, in the opening of the mouth of the valley into a fair field, they met with a coach drawn with four milk-white horses furnished all in black, with a blackamoor boy upon every horse – they all apparelled in white, the coach itself very richly furnished in black and white. But before they could come so near as to discern what was within, *there came running upon them* above a dozen horsemen who cried to them to yield themselves prisoners, or else they should die. But Palladius, not accustomed to grant over the possession of himself upon so unjust titles, with sword drawn gave them so rude an answer that divers of them never had breath to reply again; for being well-backed by Clitophon, and having an excellent horse under him, when he was overpressed by some he avoided them; and ere the other thought of it, punished in him his fellow's faults; and so, either with cunning or with force, or rather with a cunning force, left none of them either living, or able to make his life serve to other's hurt; *which being done*, he approached the coach, assuring the black boys they should have no hurt (who were else ready to have run away), and looking into the coach, he found in the one end a lady of great beauty, and such a beauty as showed forth the beams of both wisdom and good nature, but all as much darkened as might be with sorrow; in the other, two ladies who by their demeanour showed well they were but her servants, holding before them a picture in which was a goodly gentleman – whom he knew not

– painted, having in their faces a certain waiting sorrow, their eyes being infected with their mistress's weeping.
(*Arcadia* I, x; Sidney 1987: 119–20)

Although this paragraph has some exciting events, the entire scene is incidental to the main plotline. It only serves as an introduction to Palladius's meeting with the lady. The passage is noteworthy from a different perspective, too. For one, it introduces Palladius as the experiencer of the events, a fact that emerges for instance from the linguistic shape of the incidence of the episode: 'there *came* running upon them above a dozen horsemen'. At the beginning of the paragraph there is an incipit ('when [...] they met with'), and later the reactions of the protagonist ('gave them so rude an answer') and a result ('that divers of them never had breath to reply again') are given. This result is reiterated after a long explanatory clause ('for being well-backed by Clitophon [...]'): 'left none of them either living, or able to make his life serve to other's hurt'. What is particularly instructive in comparison with the oral pattern is not only the lengthy description of the particulars of the hero's actions but also the further development of the paragraph. This continues with what one might well have regarded as another episode incipit: 'Which being done, he approached the coach', and is followed by another incidence ('he found'). However, instead of *resulting* in any action on Palladius's part, the text then provides a description of the lady, and it is *she* who finally addresses *him*, mistaking him for Amphialus, as the narrative omnisciently anticipated in the previous paragraph.

Two conclusions can be drawn from this. The narrative empathizes with a protagonist's experience and continues to use the episode pattern of experiential narrative. Rather than quickly going over the main steps of incipit-incidence-result, however, the narrative here is able to dwell on details – no constraints as they would operate in oral production apply, and the story is infinitely expandable to include description as well as extended presentations of consciousness. The second part of the paragraph, as we noted, begins like another episode, but, after the incidence, lingers on the perceptions of the protagonist, from where it moves into the background information provided by the narrator, and from there into dialogue. What one can observe in this passage is in fact the incipient constitution of a *scene*, following slyly on an initial 'real' narrative episode which provides a kind of macro-structural signal for the scene's onset. As we will see in Chapter 4, such initial scene markers are quite common in nineteenth-century fiction, particularly at the beginnings of narratives. I pointed out earlier how the Middle English romance went through a phase of an inflationary use of the incipit structure. A similar development can be observed in Renaissance prose. To the extent that the narrative episode breaks down because its central incident or its dynamic incidence-reaction pattern dissolves, the incipit remains as a distinct cognitive element which helps to monitor the linear developmental structure of the narrative. Sidney, one can argue, moves from an elaboration of the experiential narrative episode into a departure from it, and towards a more fully presented scene than Chaucer could provide within the epic genre.

In the following I want to illustrate how Renaissance popular literature, which relies on a much closer observance of the oral pattern, increasingly comes to dissolve the episode structure and how it merges with the experiential and scenic pattern to produce the kind of narrative structure which we have come to associate with 'the novel'.

Most Elizabethan and Jacobean popular literature is predicated on the adventure story. Protagonists travel to distant countries and see magnificent sights; they roam the streets of London or the highways and have a series of encounters. The main action structure of such writings is therefore one of brisk movement from one place to the next with a series of either experiences that befall the protagonist or actions of special bravery and trickery that he performs to the detriment of other characters. In fact no unitary perspective is ever adhered to from a cognitive standpoint: criminal biographies frequently present the experience of the victims, and the triumph of the robbers is merely implied, or it is limited to the initial outline of the excellent plan that they have conceived. Let us look at a late example from Elkanah Settle's *William Morrell* (1694):

> And thereupon both the father and bride *take* a whisper privately together, and immediately the closets and cabinets were rummaged, and near a hundred guineas mustered up and stowed in a small casket to carry with her to London, to rig her in all ample manner accordingly [end of episode]. As they merrily *travel* along [setting], the father, bride and brother in the coach, and the bridegroom *en cavalier* riding by, taking a little start before 'em upon Hounslow Heath, he *comes* [incidence] back furiously galloping to the coach-side and with much concern *bids* 'em have a care, for he was certain there were highwaymen before in the road, and he much feared the coach would be robbed [indirect discourse]. This put [result] the travelers into some small fright, and all of 'em (for the coach was full) into a very great care how to preserve the small treasure they had about them. 'Nay, gentlemen,' *replies* [incidence, new sub-episode] the spark [i.e. William Morrell, the supposed bridegroom], 'for that small matter I have about me, I fear not all the thieves in Christendom [...] or [...] I have a horse has such a pair of heels as I defy any man in England [...] to outride me.' This hint made [reaction] the poor bride immediately **request** his securing some small things of hers [...]. In short, some other small matters were presently entrusted to his protection and preservation; and so being desired to troop off with all speed and to meet them at the general rendezvous aforesaid, our merchant [i.e. the bridegroom] *puts spurs* to his steed, and the coach *trundles* leisurely after him [concluding result].

> At Brentford they *arrive* [incipit] safely in some little time after, and making a halt at the Red Lion, inquiry *is* made [incidence] if a gentleman so mounted and so dressed was there. No, answer <u>was</u> [result] made, no such man was there; [...]
> (Settle, in Peterson 1961: 326–7)⁴⁸

Such *pudeur* is in keeping with the confessional nature of these writings. The criminal who narrates his (or her) exploits cannot openly exult in the brilliance of his perfidy since he is supposed to be contrite. Nor is the criminal biographer allowed to praise the rogue's ingenuity. In both cases an implicit hint at the shrewdness and creativity of the criminal mind is used to vouchsafe the cloak of moral integrity and ensure the moral lesson. As a consequence, these stories frequently depict a situation on which the robber intrudes, rather than outlining a pattern of active purposeful action on the highwayman's part. Nashe's *The Unfortunate Traveller* (1594), incidentally, is an exception to this rule since his protagonist Jack Wilton remains unrepentant and can therefore gloat over his ill deeds. Texts that are based on such an experiential storytelling pattern do, however, have difficulties dealing with story matter located in the interim of exciting and purposeful action. The length of such texts alone requires longer passages of orientation, biographical information and the like. In so far as the criminal protagonist does himself experience success or failure, is acted upon or for once fails to trick a particular victim whose perspective might have been adopted, the experiential episode becomes less accommodating to the narrative purpose. The central incidence is then replaced by a progredient (Harweg 1975a), i.e. the protagonist's active participation in events. In the following example from the anonymous⁴⁹ *Don Tomazo* this development from a central incidence into an action on the part of the protagonist can be observed at leisure:

> Thereupon the two Dons turned [incipit] their horses' heads; but as they rode by [setting] a goldsmith's shop, Don Tomazo's counterfeit pieces began to ferment in his pocket, so that at their instigation Don Tomazo, deeming it a foul shame that he should come into such a town as Plymouth and leave no monument of his fame behind him, *alights* [progredient] at the goldsmith's shop and *desires* silver for as much gold as amounted to £14/10s/9d. The goldsmith, satisfied with the trial he made, *delivers* [reaction] the silver demanded; and so the two Dons, having given that great town a small taste of their ingenuity, <u>steered</u> [result] directly for the county of Cornwall where they <u>found</u> great opportunities of business, <u>played</u> several pranks, and among the rest, this in particular.
> (Anon., *Don Tomazo*; Peterson 1961: 244)

As already in the verse legends, incidences then tend to merge with the result section of the episode since results, too, are protagonists' actions.

Such a syncopated episode structure additionally marks the unpremeditated and obsessive nature of criminal exploits: the highwaymen or forgers rush from one exploit to another without reasoned evaluation of their actions – a pattern that easily fits a recursive incipit-plus-incidence (= result) schema.

> Now by that he [Tomazo] had remained there for some time meditating upon his misfortune in chill-blood, Jemmy *gets* [incipit] up and, *perceiving* his master gone, *runs* into the back side where he *finds* [incidence] the horse in a cold trance, *wondering* what was become of the grass that used to grow in England, but <u>could</u> [result] not imagine where Tomazo should be. In that amaze he *flies* [incipit] about to seek him, but not *succeeding* in his search, *away he posts* [result] to Moffat. In the meanwhile the old man *rises* [incipit], who *finding* [incidence] both his son and Don Tomazo absent, yet *seeing* their horses, <u>could</u> [result] not conjecture what the De'il should be become of 'em. He waited for some hours with patience, expecting their return, but neither *appearing*, *away goes he also* [result] to draw dryfoot after both.
>
> (ibid.: 196)[50]

In particular, one can here observe how changes of scene are thematically both onsets of action and their conclusion, since there is no evaluative closure to the single episodes, which operate much like a chain of signifiers indefinitely deferring narrative meaning. Thus, 'away he posts' is a result of Jeremy's fruitless search for Tomazo, but it also initiates a change in scene, and the same is true for the final 'away goes he also'.

Even more drastically, episodic structure in the seventeenth century gets undermined by the recurring use of *present participle constructions* (as already in the previous example). These were fairly infrequent in late Middle English prose and early sixteenth-century writing, where, instead, one had a preponderance of relative *the which* constructions and other sentence-initial relatives.[51] In the context, these present participles attempt to smooth episodes into long event sequences rather than the basic episodic three-fold configuration which characteristically moves from incipit to incidence to result and again into a next incipit-incidence-result unit, thus foregrounding a series of episodes in loose succession. Present participles come to provide a narrative background (including all former turns of the narrative episode – i.e. incipits, incidences or results) and to prepare the way for the unitary marking of key events by means of either the historical present or the past tense.

This can be observed with even greater adequacy in the passage quoted below from the 'Life of St. Wenefride'. Here an entirely new argument structure surfaces from the foregrounded present and past tenses, highlighting above all the murder of Winifred and the death of the murderer by divine intervention.

But she as soone as she was gone from him, secretlie by a posterne gate stale away, and ran with all speede she could towards the Churche. The impious Prince hearing that she was so slipt away, **runneth** [incipit] presentlie after her, and ***ouertaketh*** [incidence] the innocent lambe, and he ***renewing*** his former filthie suite, but she ***denying*** him, affirming that she was ioyned vnto Christ, wherefore she could not, neither would euer couple herself with man, the furious youth ***raging*** at her answer, with his sword ***cuttes of*** [incidence] her head: which ***falling*** [result] to the earth, ***deserued*** of god to haue a fountaine of water to spring in the place, which to this day continueth, and the head still ***tumbling*** downe the hill, ***came*** rowlling into the Churche, where her maister and parents were: who ***being astonished*** at that sighte BEUNO ***tooke*** vp the head, and with it he ***goeth*** out to the homicide, moste sharplie ***reprouing*** him for the fact, and ***calling*** on god for punishment of so heynous a crime. Whereupon the yong man ***fell dedd*** [result] to the ground [...]
(*The Lives of Women Saints of our Contrie of England* 1886: 90)

We are here on the very threshold of the constitution of the narrative scene, which emerges from episodic popular narrative rather than the Sidneyan romance schema. My discussion of Behn in the next chapter will be geared towards documenting in more detail how such scenes develop. In the above text present participles completely obstruct any (cognitive) action structure, running events together in a series that builds up into two scenes: Winifred's 'martyrdom' at the hands of her infatuated lover, and the scene in (front of) the church which is the setting for the murderer's punishment. In accordance with the text's hagiographical frame, Winifred conforms to the type of the passive victim. Experientiality in these episodes cannot be aligned with the woman's perspective, though, but – as in hagiographic discourse generally – appears to be related to the viewer who has to be instructed by means of the miracle.

The passive victim configuration recurs also in Foxean hagiography: martyrs for the Protestant faith have things happen to them. However, these victims also become very active since they militantly resist their spiritual victimization by responding to their interrogators' questions, and because they eventually actively accept their own death. Unlike the passive and unsuspecting victims which people the pages of criminal biographies and provide a foil to the attractive, forceful, intelligent rogue, the protagonists of Protestant martyrologies purposefully connive at their victimization. An episodic structure with a central incidence followed by a strong result/resolution section (the repelling of the interrogators' doctrinal stance) serves an eminently useful function in this context, and Foxe is therefore able to exploit the tradition of the oral narrative pattern. However, the simplicity of medieval saints' legends cannot be replicated in full where historical detail and theological argument have to be included in the account, and much incidental realistic detail also obstructs the basic episode structure.⁵² At other points Foxe's accounts are more sparse and follow the episode structure of oral narrative. In the following two passages the essential incipit-incidence-result pattern is preserved unmodified, but one can already see how this is due to the brevity of the presentation: no such succinctness occurs in the vita of William Tyndale or any of the other major Protestant martyrs.

> They then bound him with the chains, and having set up the fagots, one Warwick cruelly cast a fagot at him, which struck him on his head, and cut his face, so that the blood ran down. Then said Dr. Taylor, 'O friend, I have harm enough; what needed that?'
> (Foxe 1967: 219)

> Then the bishop, calling William, asked him if he would recant, and finding he was unchangeable, pronounced sentence upon him, that he should go from that place to Newgate for a time, and thence to Brentwood, there to be burned.
> (ibid.: 220)

What these examples are meant to demonstrate is the gradual *formal* shift from the oral pattern of episodic narrative which still survives in Renaissance prose to the creation of more complex and lengthy forms of narration which are either modelled on the Middle English epic verse tradition and Latin prose (Sidney) or transcend the limitations of the oral pattern by creating macro-structural incipit points and by levelling the dynamics of the oral episode into a succession of events.

None of these formal developments occurs for merely formal reasons. They become possible in the wake of a shift in narrational emphasis. Where conversational narrative and its literary successors presented a pattern in which protagonists encounter dangers and parry these challenges, the picaresque tradition reflects a quite different narrative schema of intentional action in which the protagonist tries to leave his mark on his surroundings or drifts from one set of exploits to the other. In the romance, on the other hand, action becomes backgrounded against the protagonists' thoughts and impressions. Characters' moral decisions and their emotional turmoil become much more important than the actions they perform in accordance with these deliberations.

In the following chapter I will illustrate how these two lines of development come together to create that new genre of storytelling which has since acquired the label of the novel. That new mould emerges equally from the traditions of formal structures and from the poetic or conceptual frames impinging on storytelling. It also provides a conclusion to a long process of narrative transformations from oral to written modes of cognizing narrative. The two traditions of popular writing and romance join hands, as we will see, to produce that genre which goes beyond mere reporting to produce new holistic shapes of experiential narrative and new formal conceptualizations of narrative discourse.

4 The realist paradigm
Consciousness, mimesis and the reading of the 'real'

I have indicated at the end of the previous chapter how the episodic pattern of narrative structure breaks down in sixteenth-century prose writing as a consequence of the pressures from the themes and the requirements of length. The medieval epic romance, as a form that grew out of the oral medium, had managed to extend episodic structure by elaborating and concatenating one 'scene' after the other, and its overall comprehensibility was guaranteed by readers' reliance on a holistic story schema accessible on the basis of their familiarity with the story material (French romance). Significantly, episodic structure disappeared first in texts which departed from these traditional forms – as witness Chaucer's *Troilus and Criseyde* which relies on Boccaccio rather than myth or national history (the staple of epic poetry) – and in narratives of reduced experientiality episodic structure soon became levelled (as in the verse legends). In new recensions of great length episodic structure became particularly difficult to handle, as in the work of Malory who had to condense a new storyline from a vast literature of Arthurian legends whose sources had quite different plot arrangements (and were written in the verse medium). One can immediately see how Malory's attempt to fall back on the episodic pattern available from the oral tradition results in diffuseness and in a lack of overall narrative movement.

On the thematic level, too, episodic narrative proved to be an embarrassment for Renaissance writers. No longer is narrative experience tied to the protagonist's confrontation with the unexpected, miraculous or absurd; on the contrary, fictional characters increasingly become autonomous agents whose wit, sophistication and resourcefulness propel the action forward: it is their intervention into the lives of others, into the circumstances in which they find themselves, which 'makes' the story, not their encounter of unexpected strokes of fate to which they react. Whereas the medieval mind saw man as acted upon by divine intervention, Renaissance man takes the burden of agency on himself, creates his own circumstances and field of action and masters the world around him. The unexpected occurrence therefore moves from the centre of narrative experience to its periphery, providing an excuse for the protagonist to move into action and to demonstrate his skill, his courage, his control. Since most of these picaresque heroes are fairly spontaneous and unreflective agents, narrative evaluation is frequently elided or postponed, and one gets a series of incipits (now merged with the incidence function) followed by reaction-events in a staccato rhythm of unabated 'doing'. Such series typically lack a higher-level narrative shape; our present-day aesthetic disappointment with the picaresque text stems precisely from this lack of an overall narrative structure that would transform 'mere' sequences of events into larger significant units that, in their turn, build up into a story-whole of balanced proportions.

In this chapter I will first trace the development of a new holistic pattern of narrative which supplants the episodic structure of the epic (and the oral tale), replacing it with a teleologic shape which reposes on a substructure of scenes. The deadlock, aesthetically speaking, in which picaresque writing finds itself is overcome by the invention of the narrative scene, which allows for concatenation by means of interlinking units of narrative report. The episode, as will be remembered, likewise had a recursive structure. The realist novel's series of scenes concatenated by means of report sections allows for the establishment of a larger compositional structure of narrative *intrigue* (Ricoeur 1983: 17-48) which typically relates to a *teleological* pattern (Ermarth 1981). Holistic shape, a constitutive factor of the oral episodic structure, re-emerges as a characteristic of the teleologic framework as well, but it is of course an entirely different holistic shape. Such a new pattern of narrative became necessary since fiction was now no longer able to rely on pre-patterned discourses (French romances, Latin models or traditional storytelling schemata) but, by inventing new stories, had to invent their holistic shape along with them. In this, I will argue, narrative prose was greatly aided by the drama, which provided just such a neat teleological structure of scenes arranged in balanced proportion. Indeed, the first author/ess who produced the new narrative schema in an uncanny anticipation of its later perfections was Aphra Behn, herself a playwright of major accomplishment. Behn experiments with prose structure in a wide range, from what we would now call the tale or novella (e.g. 'The Lucky Mistake'), to the brief novel (*Oroonoko*), and a full-blown 'three-decker', *Love-Letters Between a Nobleman and his Sister* (1684-87). In these she can be observed to have perfected the new narrative structure. Behn additionally should be credited with the introduction into English literature of the consciousness novel, anticipating in surprising detail some of the features noted for *Clarissa, The Castle of Otranto* and the writings of Jane Austen. Finally, by experimenting with the (French) novel of letters[1] – and superseding this model in the direction of the realist psychological novel[2] – Behn prefigures in *Love-Letters* the history of the novel from the time of Richardson to the mid-nineteenth century,[3] an anticipation that is also reflected in her attitude towards history as a pre(-)text of/for her fiction. Behn's main claim to historical significance, however, is to having refined the *dramatic scene* for the purpose of narrative. This rests on two grounds: on the overall *structure* of her writing, and on the *invention of the 'consciousness' scene* which initiates what later in the history of the novel will develop into the tradition of the consciousness novel.

After discussing Behn's narrative oeuvre in detail, I will proceed to an analysis of the 'natural', i.e. cognitive, schemata in the realist novel, demonstrating how the Modernist consciousness novel constitutes the ultimate refinement and radicalization of the 'natural' parameters on which the paradigm of the realist novel reposes. A final section of this chapter will deal with neutral narrative and with the inherent limitations of 'realist' (natural) parameters. The practical consequences of these limitations will be illustrated in Chapter 5 in my analysis of reflectorization and figuralization. My line from Aphra Behn to Virginia Woolf as representing the great tradition of the English novel rewrites the history of English fiction from a narratological perspective, engendering the paradigm of the realist novel from natural parameters which ultimately can be correlated with the three *narrative situations* proposed by Stanzel in 1955 (Stanzel 1969), although these are also extended. As I will argue under 8.3.3, standard narrative theories typically relate to this 'realist' paradigm, and they do so because their very theoretical terms are shaped by the 'natural' schemata that realist fiction deploys, actualizes, and elaborates. The term *realist novel* is here used in the more general sense given to it since Ian Watt's seminal *The Rise of the Novel* (1957), a definition that Michael McKeon has basically corroborated though also refined in terms of his own complex schema (1987). I have presented my own perspective above under 1.2.4. Realism, in this study, therefore refers to the illusionistic evocation of a verisimilar fictional reality whose convincing presentation correlates particularly with psychological or motivational verisimilitude. Realism, in the sense of descriptive realism or an *effet de réel* on the lines of ekphrastic ornamentation, on the other hand, is a feature of much medieval and early modern writing and affects the development of the novel as a supplementary rather than constitutive factor.[4]

4.1 APHRA BEHN, OR: FROM DRAMA TO FICTION

4.1.1 The orientation: development of report structure

What precisely is it that makes Aphra Behn the first practitioner of the novel, the first 'modern'? As I will argue, the work of Behn constitutes a key point in the development of the novel mainly in three areas: in the elaboration of orientational sections; in the restructuring of narrative discourse such that (scenic) macro-episodes emerge to replace the earlier episodic pattern of narrative; and, finally, in the invention of the consciousness scene.

The sea change undergone between Caxton, the picaresque novel and Behn's tales can be illustrated best by comparing three text beginnings. The initial section of Caxton's *Paris and Vienne* (1485), a translation from the French, still reflects a more oral pattern of narrative structure, but it also represents a clear instance of self-conscious *écriture*: the text is avowedly an exercise in *writing*, and it attempts a markedly literary prose. This, as we will see below, is not the case with Elkanah Settle, who in some sense is even closer to the oral tradition of storytelling than was Caxton. Caxton's prose, despite its writerly orientation, however, does not even begin to display the *raffinement* of Behn's simplicity since it indulges in the Renaissance predilection for excessively elaborate syntax.

However, Caxton's beginning of *Paris and Vienne* is extremely well balanced. It manages an elegant period with a sequence of subordinated clauses which are co-ordinated on the first subordinate level, and proceeds to a presentation of major background information in a hierarchical sequence of coordinative clauses. Nevertheless the opening paragraph still attempts to fit too much information into one overarching syntactic frame. That habit can be explained by the tendency in oral narrative to pack background information into orientational off-plot segments. These, since set off from the main story line by means of intonational and rhythmic signals, allow for a flexible open-ended supply of addenda and comments by the narrator without in any way impairing the dynamics of the main story line. Caxton's unconscious attempt to transfer this structure to the written medium – and this transfer already appears to have been adopted from a French model of *écriture* – encounters its limits, which are precisely the limits of the syntax of Renaissance prose, in the complexity of temporal and descriptive information which it combines on interacting levels and trajectories. Behn, as we shall see, starts out from the less complex sentence structure of picaresque narrative and from this manages to build temporally and logically linked sequences into which flashbacks and descriptive asides are hierarchically integrated. Behn has a 'pre(liminary) history' (*Vorgeschichte*) to tell, and this is instantiated most clearly in her use of the past perfect tense. Caxton, by contrast, merely introduces the dramatis personae and subordinates decisive preliminary occurrences to the descriptive *incidentia* relating to the presentation of existents. Prototypical realist narrative, by contrast, uses description as a merely ornamental addition to the plot, inverting the proportion.[5]

> In the tyme of kynge Charles of Fraunce the yere of our lord Ihesu Cryst M CC lxxj / was in the londe of vyennoys a ryche baron daulphyn and lord of the lond that was named syr Godefroy of alaunson & was of the kynges kynrede of fraunce / the whiche daulphyn was ryȝt myghty and a grete lord bothe in hauoyr and in landes / & was a ryght wyse man / in so moche that for his grete wysedom he was moche made of / bothe of the kynge of fraunce & of al the lordes & barons of his

The realist paradigm 133

courte / soo that noo thynge was doon in the sayd royame but that he was called therto / & had to his wyf a moche fayre lady whiche cleped was dame dyane whyche was of so grete beaulte that she was wel worthy & dygne to be named after that fayre sterre þᵗ men calle dyane that appyereth & sheweth a lytel afore the day / and also she was replenysshed of all noblenes & gentylnes that a lady may or ought to haue / The sayd daulphyn thenne and this noble lady dyane were vij yere to gyder wythoute yssue that moche they desyred to haue / and prayed our lord bothe nyght & day that they myght haue chyldren playsaunt and redy to hys deuyne seruyce / and our lord thorugh hys benygnyte herede theyr prayer / and after hys playsyr gaf vnto them the viij yere of theyr maryage a ryght fayr doughter for the whyche / grete gladnes & Ioye was made thorugh all the daulphyns londe / and the chylde was baptysed with grete honour & Ioye / & in token of grete loue they named hyr vyenne by cause the cyte where she was borne in was called vyenne / and thys doughter was delyuerd vnto a noble lady for to be nourysshed wyth hyr / the whyche lady was of the sayd cyte and had a lytel doughter of the age of vyenne the whyche was named ysabel / & so the fayre vyenne was nourysshed wyth the same ysabel from hyr tender age vnto many yere after / & soo grete loue was betwene them bothe that they called eche other systers / & the fayre vyenne grewe and encreaced euer in souerayn beawte & gentylnesse / so that the renomee of hyr excellent beawte flourysshed not onely thurgh al fraunce but also thurgh al the Royame [a jʳ] of englond & other contrees / It happed after she was xv yere of age that she was desyred to maryage of many knyʒtes & grete lordes [. . .][incipit]
(Caxton 1957: 1–2)

I have below spaced out the syntactic construction of this passage in order to clarify the relationship between its interbraided subordinate and coordinate clauses. The text begins with a temporal specification followed by the locality of the setting and only then introduces Sir Godefroy as 'a ryche baron daulphyn'. The sentence continues with a series of further details about this character; telling of his status, his wealth, his wisdom and the esteem in which he is therefore held at court. A second coordinate clause on the second level introduces Sir Godefroy's wife. Again we first hear of her name in the first relative clause, then of her beauty, which is elaborated hyperbolically in another relative-clause cluster, and she is finally also described as noble and gentle. (Like that of Sir Godefroy's wisdom, the characterization of Dame Dyane's qualities goes last on the list of descriptive parameters.) Only then does the second sentence (marked typographically by the capital T in 'The sayd daulphyn') proceed with some facts about story matter – the couple's inability to conceive an heir, their prayers, the birth of the daughter and her naming, her nurture and the eventual acquisition of a faithful companion. The actual onset of

134 *The realist paradigm*

the plot begins with the incipit section: 'It happed ... that she was desyred to maryage'.

>   *In the tyme of kynge Charles ... was in the londe ... a ryche baron ... /that was named syr Godefroy*
>   the whiche daulphyn was ryʒt myghty and a grete lord ...
>   & was a ryght wyse man
>   in so moche that ... he was moche made of
>   soo that noo thynge was doon ...
>   but that he was called therto
>   & had to his wyf a moche fayre lady
>   whiche *cleped was* dame dyane
>   whyche was of so grete beaulte
>   that she was wel worthy ... to be named after that fayre sterre
>   that men calle dyane
>   that appyereth & sheweth ...
>   and also she was replenysshed of ... gentylnes
>   that a lady may ... haue
>   *The sayd daulphyn thenne* ... were wythoute issue
>   that moche they desyred to haue/
>   and prayed our lord ...
>   that they myght haue chyldren
>   *and our lord ... herede theyr prayer/*
>   and ... gaf vnto them ... a ryght fayr doughter
>   for the whyche ... was made
>   *and the chylde was baptysed ...*
>   in token of grete loue they named hyr vyenne
>   by cause the cyte
>   where she was borne in
>   was called vyenne/
>   *and thys doughter* was delyuerd into a noble lady ... for to be nourysshed ...
>   the whyche lady was ...
>   and had a lytel doughter ...
>   the whyche was named ysabel
>   *& so the fayre vyenne* was nourysshed ...
>   *& soo grete loue* was betwene them bothe
>   that they called eche other systers/
>   *& the fayre vyenne grewe ...*
>   so that the renomee of hyr ... beawte flourysshed not onely ...
>   but also ..
>   *It happed* ... [incipit]

There is a clearly marked hiatus between the first and the second half of this orientational section. In the first half, which concentrates on the dramatis personae and habitual elements of the background, the syntactic structure is heavily subordinative, employing a large number of hierarchical levels; the second half presents the pre-history of Vienne's contracted marriage and the story onset with her clandestine love affair, and it does so by a much more coordinative syntactic structure. Description in the first half is structured circularly around the figure of Sir Godefroy and his satellites, whereas the first developments on the story level in the second half of the passage are rendered in sequential report-like units. These are not conceptualized in terms of narrative episodes, nor do they consist in a mere enumeration of one action after the other. On the contrary, a teleological progression is traced from the couple's wish for a child to the conception, baptism and education of the daughter up until the time of her eventual development into marriageable property.

The pattern which we noted in Caxton is preserved in the Elizabethan romance literature. For instance, Gascoigne's bowdlerized version of *The Adventures of Master F.J.* (1593), *The Pleasant Fable of Ferdinando Jeron[i]mi and Leonora de Valasco* (1575), starts with an orientation that in many points evokes Caxton's informational structure.

> In the pleasant Countrie of *Lombardie*, (and not farre from the Citie of *Florence*) there was dwelling sometimes a Lorde of many riche Seignories and dominions, who neverthelesse bare his name of the Castle of *Valasco*: this Lord had one only sonne and two daughters: his sonne was called (during the life of his father) the heyre of *Valasco*, who married a faire Gentlewoman of the house of *Bellavista* named *Leonora*: the elder daughter of the Lord of *Valasco* was called *Francischina*, a young woman very toward, bothe in capacitie and other active qualities. Nowe the Lord of *Valasco* having already maried his sonne & heyre, and himselfe drawing in age, was desirous to see his daughters also bestowed before his death, and especially the eldest, who both for beutie and ripenesse of age might often put him in remembrance that shee was a collop of his owne fleshe: and therefore sought meanes to draw unto his house *Ferdinando Jeronimi* a yong gentleman of *Venice*, who delighting more in hawking, hunting, and such other pastimes than he did in studie, had left his owne house in *Venice*, and was come into *Lombardie* to take the pleasures of the countrie. So that the Lorde of *Valasco* knowing him to be of a very good parentage, and therewithall not onely riche but adorned with sundrie good qualities, was desirous (as is sayd) to drawe him home to his house (under pretence of hunting and hawking) to the end he might beholde his fayre daughter *Francischina*: who both for parentage and other worldly respects, might no lesse content his minde, than hir beautie was likely to have allured his liking
>
> (Gascoigne 1907: 383)

In contrast to the Caxton passage, the hypotactic element here persists throughout the entire introduction, a fact that may be linked to the nature of the events related: these are mostly mental, concentrating on the Count of Valasco's intentions and plans rather than exclusively on his actions. We will see below that Behn manages to offer a much clearer presentation of such deliberations in her opening of 'The History of the Nun; or, The Fair Vow-Breaker' (1689). There is here a clear line of development from Caxton to Behn. The protagonists of these narratives are introduced in their social setting, with dependents (wives, daughters) enumerated and described in superlative terms, and the initial situation of lack (of a daughter in Caxton's text; of a husband for Francischina in Gascoigne's) then gives rise to the first steps of the plot.

Let me now turn to a different sort of text, a late picaresque novel which chronologically comes *after* Behn but perfectly epitomizes the characteristics of this sixteenth- and seventeenth-century genre. Elkanah Settle's *The Complete Memoirs of the Life of That Notorious Impostor Will. Morrell* (1694) starts with a lengthy abstract characterizing William Morrell and briefly summarizing his career. It then immediately moves into Morrell's first criminal exploit. By contrast, Aphra Behn's 'The History of the Nun' (1689), and – even more perspicuously – 'The Lucky Mistake' (1689), one of the last things she wrote before her death, operate on a much more 'modern' pattern of introduction which foregrounds the circumstances of a few chosen characters, sometimes prefacing them with a passage of philosophical speculation (as in 'The History of the Nun').

Elkanah Settle's account starts with a long paragraph which packs what is practically the biography of Morrell into six sentences with several subordinate clauses each.

> This famous rover, from the multitude of his titles, to begin with his right name William Morrell, was by profession a chirurgeon, and more than twenty years ago, for many years together, a practitioner of good credit in Banbury, where his industry honestly got him by his practice a comfortable subsistence, with which he maintained himself, his wife and family very handsomely, till about twenty years ago he began to be very lazy and much addicted to hanker after the conversation of the gentry thereabouts. And being a person very facetious, and his company not disacceptable, he screwed himself into the society of the best quality round about and would be a month or two a guest at several great men's houses. More particularly he some time since insinuated himself into the favour of a worthy gentleman near Banbury, viz., Humphrey Wickham of Swalcliffe, Esq., whose person and character he pretended to represent, and in which imposture he made his last exit. His original, it was very obscure, and his first start into the world was in no higher a post than a journeyman shoemaker, in which character he lived some considerable time at Worcester, understanding so little of what he professed at Banbury, viz., chirurgery, that he knew the virtue

The realist paradigm 137

of no other plaister than his own cobbler's wax. From that employment, he took a frolic to sea; from whence returned, he came to Swalcliffe with the true privilege of a traveler, his authority unquestionable; he talked miracles both of his voyages and adventures, for example, that he had made a voyage to Constantinople and Barbados (for east and west were all one in his geography), and so amused the country-people with his rodomontades that they looked upon him as a prodigy of a man. His great art he professed was chirurgery (the little he had of it being indeed gotten on shipboard), and what with promised wonders and great words, the common crutch of little abilities, together with some favours and countenance received from Captain Wickham (a common charity from so worthy a gentleman), which very much heightened his reception, he made shift to rub through the world.

(Peterson 1961: 302–3)

One can note a number of interesting aspects in this introductory section. To start with, the text clearly presupposes contemporary knowledge of 'this famous rover', and it therefore markets itself as a *historical* narrative. The reader's status of information also explains some of the structural features of the paragraph. To our modern intuitions, the discourse appears unpleasantly rambling and illogical. This impression derives, above all, from the way Settle structures (or fails to structure) this paragraph. For instance, the first sentence telescopes Morrell's profession, his original family circumstances before the outset of his criminal career, as well as the reason for his lapse (moral laziness), into one and the same discourse unit. The second sentence then goes on to mention his strategy for getting into society, leaving the all-important fact of his doing so under a false title to be supplied only in the third sentence, where it is temporally anchored to an indefinite 'some time since'. The fourth sentence retraces its steps to Morrell's first (false?) identity as a shoemaker and the fifth sentence runs together his trip to sea and the conversational benefits he derives from it after his return. The last, sixth, sentence finally returns to Morrell's profession as a chirurgeon, which is now, however, exposed as one more fake identity. The paragraph (and its last sentence) signals the conclusion of this biographical abstract by reverting to Morrell's status as an impostor who 'made shift to rub through the world'.

The most disorientating aspect of this paragraph touches on the chronology of Morell's life. It remains unclear in this account how far removed from the narrator's present are the individual stages of Morrell's career. Thus there is a clear line from shoemaker to sailor to traveller-chirurgeon, but this fails to connect chronologically with the 'real surgeon'-to-'imposture of Wickham' line. Only on a rereading of the paragraph does it emerge that the second half of the passage seems to be filling in on this prior frame. The crucial step from Morrell's being befriended by Wickham to his fraudulent impersonation of that gentleman remains unanchored chronologically and is not even mentioned at the end of this first paragraph, where it logically should have gone. In addition, visualizing the circumstances of Morrell's life causes further problems. How could Morrell have been a chirurgeon 'by profession' if he learned that trade on shipboard after he left his 'comfortable subsistence'? Or are we to understand the chronology of this paragraph as saying that Morrell was *originally* a shoemaker, then went to sea, then established himself and his family as a chirurgeon in Banbury and, twenty years before Settle starts to write up his account of Morrell's life, became lazy and sought out the company of gentlemen? This chronology somewhat conflicts with the impression one gains of the connection between Morrell's life as a doctor and the facilitation of his later impostures. Morrell's entry into the company of gentlemen seems to depend on his faculty for entertaining company with the stories of his adventures at sea. (The extent of these voyages remains in fact tantalizingly inexplicit.) If Morrell came off board and then straight away went to Swalcliffe, entertained company and ingratiated himself with Captain Wickham, this is difficult to link with his practice 'of good credit' which he conducted 'for many years together'. The moral explanation that is provided at the beginning of the paragraph, on the contrary, has it that it was his laziness that first drove him into the company of the gentry. What one therefore sorely misses as a modern reader – and, I wish to add, a reader unfamiliar with Morrell's notoriety – is a clear account on the lines of: 'Morrell was born in the year X/Y years ago in the town of Z and brought up a shoemaker. When he was twelve years of age, he ran off to sea, where he continued for so-and-so many years, journeying all the way to Barbados etc., until he settled in Banbury, established himself as a chirurgeon and led a respectable existence with his wife and family. Around twenty years ago Morrell suddenly became lazy, and forsaking his professional duties, started to ...' The entire passage smacks of a deliberate refusal to situate events chronologically, what Genette has termed *achrony* (1980: 84), and one could even draw a parallel to the eighteenth-century novel's preference for *aperspectivism* (Stanzel 1984b: 12–13, 117–25). In contrast to visual presentation, however, early texts generally have a fairly lucid presentation of the chronology since they tend to dispense with the complicating factor of a pre-history. I therefore remain wary of the comparison.

Settle's introductory paragraph is unsatisfactory from another perspective as well, this time a motivational or logical one. Morrell's moral lapse is characteristically attributed to laziness, but this – within the first paragraph – explains merely his societal extravagances, failing to add that these inevitably led to Morrell's financial ruin and the need to procure money some other way: which finally takes us to his criminal activities as an impostor. That connection is made explicit only in the subsequent second paragraph of the text, which, frustratingly, starts with 'But to begin our history in order' (Peterson 1961: 303), and then explicitly relates how

The realist paradigm 139

Morrell's business fell off since he was unavailable when patients needed him, and points out how he devised 'several tricks and frauds to hold his head aboveboard' (ibid.).

Our passage from *William Morrell* can fruitfully be contrasted with the beginning of Aphra Behn's 'The Unfortunate Happy Lady: A True History' (posthumous), where the chronology is already firmly in place. Yet on account of the overlong sentential pattern, the passage shares some of the breathlessness of the first paragraph of Gascoigne's *The Adventures of Master F.J.*:

> I cannot omit giving the World an account, of the uncommon Villany of a Gentleman of a good Family in *England* practis'd upon his Sister, which was attested to me by one who liv'd in the Family, and from whom I had the whole Truth of the Story. I shall conceal the unhappy Gentleman's own, under the borrow'd Names of Sir *William Wilding*, who succeeded his father Sir *Edward*, in an Estate of near 4000*l.* a Year, inheriting all that belong'd to him, except his Virtues. 'Tis true, he was oblig'd to pay his only Sister a Portion of 6000*l.* which he might have very easily have done of his Patrimony in a little Time, the Estate being not in the least incumbred. But the Death of his good Father gave a loose to the Extravagancy of his Inclinations, which till then were hardly observable. The first Discovery he made of his Humour was in the extraordinary rich Equipage he prepar'd for his journey to *London*, which was much greater than his fair and plentiful Fortune cou'd maintain, nor were his Expences any way inferior to the Figure he made here in Town; insomuch, that in less than a Twelve-Month, he was forc'd to return to his Seat in the Country, to Mortgage a part of his Estate of a Thousand Pounds a Year, to satisfy the Debts he had already contracted in his profuse Treats, Gaming and Women, which in a few Weeks he effected, to the great Affliction of his Sister *Philadelphia*, a young lady of excellent Beauty, Education and Virtue; who, fore-seeing the utter Ruin of the Estate; if not timely prevented, daily begg'd of him, with Prayers and Tears, that might have mov'd a *Scythian* or wild *Arab*, or indeed anything but him, to pay her her Portion. To which, however, he seemingly consented, and promis'd to take her to Town with him, and there give her all the Satisfaction she cou'd expect.
>
> (Behn 1967: 37–8)[6]

The logical connections in this orientation are perfectly clear; what causes some ambiguity is the experiential moment of the tale. Philadelphia's plight, on which the story centres, is here merely stated rather than described in psychological detail. In fact, it appears to be appended as a kind of afterthought to the sweeping account of her brother's vice-ridden carousing. Both protagonists' situations are presented as if from outside, allowing little empathy with their motives or consciousness. Philadelphia becomes a proper character of the story only when the narrative starts to focus on her experiences, her near-rape by a customer of the brothel in which her brother places her against her knowledge. Empathy with Philadelphia emerges therefore primarily from the dialogue scenes in which the beautiful and virtuous innocent defends her virginity and from the disclosure of the intrigue itself, which is designed to provoke the reader's outrage at her brother's base and criminal behaviour. Although the relative chronology causes us no problems at all, there is some imbalance in the contraction of what must be several months' profligacy on the part of the brother into one paragraph and the move to Philadelphia's precipitate arrival at the brothel in the next. Since the brother's evil plans remain a secret in the transition (although they soon become apparent enough), the fast-paced rhythm of the beginning seems to come to an initially unmotivated halt. Since the story then proceeds at a more verisimilar pace, this early imbalance does not cause any major disruptions of meaning.

A second, nearly 'perfect', example of an orientational section comes from Behn's 'History of the Nun' (1689). This tale starts with a lengthy philosophical discussion in perfectly logical sequence. The first paragraph argues that the greatest sin on earth is that of the violated vow and then illustrates this point by reference to jilted women and men. The text then proceeds to a distinction between various kinds of promises and oaths, highlighting the sacredness of religious vows. In the third paragraph some injunctions are proposed for 'the young Beauty' who is upon the threshold of devoting herself to God, and this advice is supported in the fourth paragraph by reference to the narrator's own experience of having wisely desisted a religious calling, albeit (she claims) she still harbours some wistful nostalgia for the seclusion and safety of the religious life. The fifth paragraph then initiates the setting in the following words:

> In *Iper*, a Town, not long since, in the Dominions of the King of *Spain*, and now in possession of the King of *France*, there liv'd a Man of Quality, of a considerable Fortune, call'd, Count *Henrick de Vallary*, who had a very beautiful Lady, by whom, he had one Daughter, call'd *Isabella*, whose Mother dying when she was about two years old to the unspeakable Grief of the Count, her Husband, he resolv'd never to partake of any Pleasure more, that this transitory World could court him with, but determin'd, with himself, to dedicate his Youth, and future Days, to Heaven, and to take upon him Holy Orders; and, without considering, that, possibly, the young *Isabella*, when she grew to Woman might have Sentiments contrary to those that now possest him, he design'd she should also become a Nun; However, he was not so positive in that Resolution, as to put the matter wholly out of her Choice, but divided his Estate; one half he carried with him to the Monastery of *Jesuits*, of which number, he became one; and the other half, he gave with *Isabella*, to the Monastery, of which, his only Sister was Lady

Abbess, of the order of St. Augustine; but so he ordered the matter, that if, at the Age of Thirteen, *Isabella* had not a mind to take Orders, or that the Lady *Abbess* found her Inclination averse to a Monastick Life, she should have such a proportion of the Revenue, as should be fit to marry her to a Noble Man, and left it to the discretion of the Lady *Abbess*, who was a Lady of known Piety, and admirable strictness of Life, and so nearly related to *Isabella*, that there was no doubt made of her Integrity and Justice.

(Behn 1967: 265-6)

This paragraph provides a very clear outline of the chronology, placing Iper (Ypres) and the protagonists in their relation to the contemporary reader's spatio-temporal coordinates (although there is no precise dating of the story time), and then presents us with the major facts in their strict chronology: the mother's death, the father taking holy orders, the arrangements for his daughter. This is complemented by a relation of the father's motives and aims, his weighing of the implications of his decision, and the eventual realization of his plans. It also introduces the Lady Abbess into the tale and explains her function within the father's arrangements.

Unlike the exposition for the life story of William Morrell, this paragraph manifests great clarity, even though – as we should also note – the *syntactic* structure of the writing is even more convoluted, much on the lines of Caxton's page-long first paragraph of *Paris and Vienne*. In contrast to the passages from Caxton and Settle, however, the hypotactic clauses are here balanced by a highly sophisticated deployment of parataxis which helps to highlight the progressive stages of the father's motives, decisions, weighing of counter-arguments and final arrangements. In fact the paragraph, like Caxton's *Paris and Vienne*, falls into precisely two blocks, the first introducing the father – providing for a narrative agent whose subjective individuality in his bereavement is portrayed in the circumstantial plenitude of descriptive prose – , the second detailing a series of (partly mental) actions on his part. In the first half the syntax is highly hypotactic, filling the reader in on Count Henrick's wife, daughter, bereavement, grief and decision to take vows, welding these points together in one series of relative clauses; in the second half, which continues paratactically after 'he resolv'd', we get a series of deliberate steps in succession: 'and, without considering [...], he design'd [...]. However, he was not so positive [...] but divided [...] but so he ordered the matter, that [...] she should have [...] and left it to the discretion of [...].' These paratactic elements are, however, modified by hypotactic qualifications and specifications which outline the extent or practical application of the Count's arrangements, paying attention both to the supplying of 'delayed orientation' (such as the fact that the Abbess is his sister, and the report on her good reputation) and to the possible effects or consequences which would need to be taken into account (outlined in conditional and consecutive clauses).

To recapitulate: from Caxton and the picaresque novel to Behn the narrative becomes more logically stringent, chronologically and spatially concrete (although Caxton does not have a problem with that), and it begins to centre on *one* major protagonist and his experiences, deliberations, goals, decisions and actions (who then puts these decisions and actions into effect). The orientation therefore starts to acquire that leisurely tone and extended particularity which under the pens of Balzac or Zola becomes the hallmark of the typical nineteenth-century introduction to the novel's world.

4.1.2 The narrative episode and the dramatic scene

In the above I have frequently mentioned the word *scene*. One primary reference of *scene* is the dramatic scene from the dramatic genre. We have already noted, for instance, how Elkanah Settle's exploits can be visualized as a stageable engagement of wits. Dramatic influence on Elizabethan prose writing is certainly no big news. As Aercke (1988: 132 footnote 3) points out, not only Behn but also many of her contemporaries and earlier colleagues, such as William Congreve, Thomas Dekker, Thomas Deloney, Robert Greene, Richard Head, Francis Kirkman, Thomas Lodge, John Lyly, Thomas Nashe, Henry Neville and Elkanah Settle, wrote both for the stage and for the reading public who were consuming pamphlets, romances and criminal biographies. Dramatic scenes abound in the fiction of the time, and the *intrigues* in the picaresque novel echo trickery scenes from the stage literature. The machinations set in gear in Greene's *A Groats-worth of Wit* (1592–96) in order to cheat the brother out of his inheritance resemble the tricks we observe in the comedies of Ben Jonson, Aphra Behn, William Wycherley or William Congreve. The novel also employs typically 'dramatic' (i.e. sensational) scenes for instance that of the rape which Jack Wilton witnesses in Nashe's *The Unfortunate Traveller* ([1594] 1964: 248–54). Equally reminiscent of Elizabethan and Jacobean stage plots is the comedy enacted between Sylvia and Brilliard in Behn's *Love-Letters*. Sylvia exchanges clothes with her maid and has her welcome the ardent Brilliard. This gives rise to further complications as the jealous Octavio watches Brilliard being admitted to 'Sylvia' by the 'maid' (who is of course Sylvia in disguise). Or, to take another example, there is the seduction scene in Behn's 'The Fair Jilt' (1688) in which Miranda traps poor 'Father Henrick' in the confessional and then in melodramatic fashion accuses him of rape – a constellation reminiscent of a grand operatic scene.

The above uses of the words *scene* and *dramatic* are still of a fairly impressionistic nature and relate to stageability and the comparison of prose passages with similar scenes in drama. Another, more specific sense, is that of *dialogic exchange*. The increase in the 'direct' representation of conversational exchange in Elizabethan and seventeenth-century texts is truly astounding. Thus, the largest amount of the comedy (besides the tricking of dupes in the *plot*) develops from characters' linguistic duels, in which they revel in witty repartee. This is not yet a prominent factor in Nashe and Greene, although Jack Wilton documents his persuasive powers and the glibness of his tongue throughout. However, Settle's text or the anonymous *Don Tomazo* (1680)[7] already prefigure the dialogue scenes that are so prominent in, say, *Moll Flanders*.[8] Settle's story proper begins with a dialogue scene prefaced by a *medias in res* incipit:

> Accordingly, he **equips** himself with a sturdy, young country-fellow, a Ralpho to our Hudibras, and **takes** a knight-errantry one day to a fair at Brailes in Warwickshire, his habit between a grazier and a plain country gentleman, where sauntering about with his man Tom (for so his squire was titled), at last spying a knot of good likely kine (near a score of them). 'Ah, master,' *says* Tom, 'what a parcel of brave cattle are these?' 'Ay, Tom,' *replies* the master, 'I am sorry I saw them no sooner; these would do my business to a 'T,' but as the Devil and ill luck would have it, I have laid out my whole stock already, and so I'll e'en set my heart at rest.' The country-fellow, the owner of the cattle, seeing a gentleman of his honest appearance surveying his beasts, and hearing every word that passed between the man and master (for they took care to talk loud enough to be heard), <u>thought</u> he had got a good chapman and <u>desired</u> the gentleman to draw nearer and handle the cattle. 'Handle?' *answers* Tom. 'What for? You know, sir, you have laid out all your money already, and what should we handle cattle unless we had cole to buy 'em. I confess they are for your turn above any I have <u>zeen</u> in the whole <u>vair</u>, but that's nothing, the money, master, the money.' 'The money?' *replies* the countryman. 'Troth, that shall make no difference, nor break squares between us; if you and I can agree, the cattle are at your service. I suppose you are some honest gentleman hereabouts, and the money will do my work next market day. Pray, what may I call your name?' 'My name is Walters,' *replies* our cattle-merchant. 'Walters, master?' *answers* our countryman. 'What, any relation to his worship the noble Sir William Walters?' 'Ay, friend, a small relation, a brother of his.' 'A brother of Sir William's!' *Off goes* the countryman's bonnet at the next word, and a long scrape made, <u>**for no respect was too great for a brother to a person of such eminent quality**</u>. 'My cattle, noble squire, ay with all my heart.' In short, after much ado to make the countryman be covered before him, he <u>fell</u> to treat about the price of the cattle, in which he bargained so warily that they had almost parted for a single shilling in dispute between them. But at last the bargain and sale concluded, Tom *is* commanded to drive home the cattle, the money to be paid next market day, and the countryman *has* the honour to drink a pot at parting with his worshipful chapman, our Sir William's brother.
> (Peterson 1961: 303–5)[9]

The liveliness of this scene resides in the naturalistic dialogue which traces Morrell's ingenuity at deceiving the credulous farmer. The dialogue is notable also for its great vivacity and linguistic evocation of real-life speech patterns. Compare, for instance, the indication of Tom's social inferiority (or trustworthy naïvety?) as implied in his dialectal voicing of *zeen* and *vair*, and the narrator's appropriation of the countryman's deixis in 'our Sir William's brother' (last line). The entire paragraph prefigures a scene on stage; it could be stage-acted to a T. Whereas Elkanah Settle's first orientational paragraphs echo the structures of Caxton's laborious subordinate constructions, this third paragraph closely resembles those structures of Elizabethan prose that I illustrated earlier in Chapter 3.

The episodic pattern of narrative is here already used in an advanced stage of dissolution. Present participles (and one past participle) replace preterites, and there is an inflation of the historical present [in the following HP] which takes over most of the propelling narrative clauses, including the final rounding-off gag: '[...] the bargain and sale *concluded*, Tom *is commanded* [...], the money *to be paid* [...] and the countryman *has* the honour [...]' (ibid.: 305). The fundamental bracketing structure is, however, still in place. The onset of the episode at the country fair is marked by an HP (*equips* and *takes*) and – after two present participles (*sauntering*, *spying*) – we get a series of verbal exchanges which are rendered in the HP (with the deluded countryman's speculations supplied in the backgrounded *for* clause). The episode closes on a double resolution, the conclusion of the bargain 'fell to treat' and the crowning act of the imposture: pocketing the cattle and doing the farmer the 'honour' of drinking a pot of ale with him.

At the same time the vivacity of the dialogic exchange is already developing in the direction of the scenic mode, which Behn is the first to initiate. Behn employs dialogue with great skill, especially in *Love-Letters*. However, true to the Renaissance model, she also frequently presents the characters' discourse in indirect speech. Thus, in the scene of Miranda's pretended seduction in 'The Fair Jilt', the verbal exchange between 'Father Henrick' and the desperate woman is mostly rendered in *indirect discourse*, with direct speech reserved for Miranda's more outrageous statements and for her public accusation and testimony. (Henrick himself, characteristically, refuses to defend himself and remains silent.) What is perfectly visualizable as a scene on stage is here not rendered exclusively in the dramatic *form* of dialogue. One may wonder at Behn's practice: would it not have been easier for her to have Miranda re-enact a typical 'dramatic' monologue from her stage inventory? On the other hand, Behn may early on have come to realize the *advantages* of indirect presentation: rather than having to impersonate all their feelings and utterances, her characters can be allowed to deliver themselves only at the climaxes of emotional involvement, a technique that refines dramatic effect rather than vitiating it. Nevertheless, as in the latter half of *Love-Letters*, Behn does sometimes

The realist paradigm   145

approach a structure resembling the dialogue scene, though less for dramatic effect than in order to convey the full dexterity of Sylvia's witty bantering. Thus when Sylvia finally gets Don Alonzo to parley with her (Behn 1993: III, 418-9), their subtle sounding out of each other's attraction is rendered with great skill, echoing some of the finer moments in the dialogue of Shakespeare's comedies.

Dramatic structure on the Elizabethan and Jacobean stage used to be determined by change of place and/or change of characters. The entry of new participants usually creates a new situation, and a shift to a different setting implies a temporal lapse or the introduction of the sub-plot level. Drama – unlike prose – was able to accommodate frequent shifts in locale to simultaneous or subsequent events elsewhere. Such a shift in location, combining one set of events in one place with a set of events elsewhere constituted a difficult task for early narrative, as we saw in the previous chapter.[10] Picaresque narrative, in so far as it centres on the experience of the protagonist, frequently evades the problem because it moves *with* the hero from place to place. The question of structural handling only becomes acute if several strands of action need to be combined. Behn is extremely adept at transferring what is after all a dramatic model of the *intrigue* on to the narrative structure of the novel or tale. She manages to reproduce the felicitous uniting of two strands of action at the moment where these meet to effect mutual misunderstanding and result in dramatic conflict and its eventual resolution. The structure of 'The Lucky Mistake' – perhaps Behn's most refined and most 'modern' tale – brings two mismatched parties together outside the convent walls and reconciles the antagonists, effecting a happy resolution of their conflicts. In 'Agnes de Castro', 'The Dumb Virgin' and 'The Unfortunate Bride' narrative lines cross to produce disaster: Constantia comes to suspect Agnes of treachery; Maria learns that her lover is actually her lost brother; Frankwit reappears on the scene just when he has been given up for dead and Belvira has married Wildwell. So far the plotting echoes that of drama even if the successful handling in prose cannot be taken for granted.

Behn's major structural innovation, however, cannot be described in these large plot-related terms. It concerns Behn's move from the episodic plot arrangement to what I here call the report-cum-scene pattern. Behn does not fully achieve this move but she anticipates it in several places, most successfully in her late 'The Lucky Mistake'. In addition, Behn initiates a new way of integrating preliminary orientation, for the first time introducing the formal device of the past perfect tense.

As a first example let us look at the episode of the Prince's capture in *Oroonoko* (1688):

> *Oroonoko* was ***no sooner*** return'd from this last Conquest, and receiv'd at Court with all the Joy and Magnificence that culd be express'd to a

young Victor, who was not only return'd Triumphant, but belov'd like a Deity, ***than there arriv'd*** in the Port an *English* ship.

The Master of it ***had often before been*** in these Countries, and was very well-known to *Oroonoko*, with whom he ***had traffick'd*** for Slaves, and ***had us'd*** to do the same with his Predecessors.

(Behn 1967: 160–1)

The beginning of the new plot section is marked by the *no sooner ... than* construction, which echoes a setting-plus-incidence kernel (see below). The crucial innovation by Behn follows in the subsequent brief orientational section which explains the history of the Captain's relations with Oroonoko. This background is rendered by means of clauses in the *past perfect tense*. The use of the past perfect to narrate the 'pre-history' of the story proper constitutes an entirely new, and one could even say revolutionary, development. In earlier fiction such backtracking was usually managed by means of a hypodiegetic narrative (where characters that newly appear on the scene tell their life story up to that point). The same pattern was current in drama, and Behn's departure from this model is therefore all the more noteworthy.

After the above paragraph the text continues with a longish description of the trader's character and of the friendship which develops between him and Oroonoko. The trap is laid by a seemingly harmless invitation to Oroonoko and his crew to come aboard, and we get a description of all the preparations on both sides. (This material roughly corresponds to the orientation section of oral narrative.) The following paragraph then completes the treachery by detailing the manner in which the prince and his entourage were seized:

The Prince having drank hard of Punch, and several Sorts of Wine, as did all the rest, (for great Care was taken they should want nothing of that Part of the Entertainment) was very merry, and in great Admiration of the Ship, for he had never been in one before; so that he was curious of beholding every Place where he decently might descend. The rest, no less curious, who were not quite overcome with drinking, rambled at their Pleasure *Fore* and *Aft*, as their Fancies guided 'em: So that the Captain, who had well laid his Design before, gave the Word, and seiz'd on all his Guests; they clapping great Irons suddenly on the Prince, when he was leap'd down into the Hold, to view that Part of the Vessel; and locking him fast down, secur'd him. The same Treachery was used to all the rest; and all in one Instant, in several Places of the Ship, were lash'd fast in Irons, and betray'd to Slavery. That great Design over, they set all Hands at work to hoist Sail; and with as treacherous as fair a Wind they made from the Shore with this innocent and glorious Prize, who thought of nothing less than such an Entertainment.

(ibid.: 162)

The central part of this episode (the Prince's kidnapping: 'gave the Word, and seiz'd') can be seen as the equivalent of an oral incidence point; in fact the entire paragraph can be argued to represent the setting-plus-incidence core of the oral narrative episode. Note, however, in what ways it departs from this oral model. For one, it is the captain who initiates the crucial action of seizing his guests; the treachery is not related as if *experienced* by Oroonoko. The captain's actions are explicitly noted as having been premeditated, a circumstance rendered in another past perfect clause ('*who had* well *laid* his Design before'). One can here observe a parallel with the picaresque tradition where it is the exploits of the crook that hold the reader's attention and the victims' perspective is sometimes relegated to the margins of the discourse. Note also the extended portrayal of the background circumstances on which the incidence eventually intrudes. As we will see below, this also already anticipates the nineteenth-century format of scene onsets. The conclusion of the quoted paragraph rounds off the episode in a manner that is reminiscent of the oral pattern. Its triple insistence on the accomplishment of the kidnapping, however, yet again emphasizes a macro-structural point of resolution that has a functional correlation with more extended prose writing.

This narrative episode does not constitute the major event of this part of Behn's narrative. On the contrary, it is designed to *initiate* the following very lengthy scenes on board ship in which Oroonoko resolves to commit suicide by starvation and is then persuaded to make another deal with the treacherous captain (who tricks him once again). The outline of this negotiation is rendered in great detail. The dialogue to some extent echoes a dramatic model but has been rewritten to fit the purposes of the narrative. Thus, although the description of Oroonoko's state of mind, the very words uttered by him to the captain (via his intermediary), and the captain's answers are all rendered in great detail, the captain and Oroonoko do not exchange this dialogue in a standard face-to-face situation. The representation therefore needs to insert a number of narrative links which serve to move the messenger to and fro between the interlocutors. Half of the dialogue, moreover, is transmitted to the reader in *indirect* discourse, which does not, however, destroy the prominent effect of vivacity.

What Behn is doing here is trying to elaborate the episodic narrative pattern of the picaresque novel by expanding it to include dramatic highlights. Such highlights already exist in Elizabethan fiction. I have discussed a passage of this nature from Sidney's *Arcadia* in Chapter 3. Another instance would be Jack Wilton's lengthy dialogue with the publican early in Nashe's *The Unfortunate Traveller* (1594), and there are of course numerous soliloquies and public addresses in Thomas Lodge's *Rosalynde* (1590) or, again, in *The Arcadia*. From the start Behn emphasizes her characters' feelings and emotions, seizing on precisely that subject matter which cannot be represented in drama in the same elegant manner.[11] There is one and only one such passage in *The Unfortunate Traveller*, in the scene where Wilton believes they are coming to get him for vivisection (Nashe 1964: 262). Elsewhere in Elizabethan prose the representation of consciousness tends to be dramatic, in the form of soliloquies – a staple device of the romance. Where dramatis personae would have laboriously to explain their motives to others or to dramatize them in soliloquies, Behn simply drops a line or two such as:

> This did not a little vex the Captain, and the more so, because he found almost all of 'em of the same Humour; so that the Loss of so many brave Slaves, so tall and goodly to behold, would have been very considerable: He therefore order'd one to go from him [...] to *Oroonoko* [...]
>
> (Behn 1967: 163)

Narration in passages of this sort can be extremely economical, an aspect that Behn clearly recognized and used to full advantage. In other contexts, however, a dramatic stringing together of what I here call scenes can be entirely effective for the narrative, too. Thus, in 'The Fair Jilt', we can watch Behn combine the strong points of narrative (exposition, summary, shift of scene, motivation), with the advantages of visualization, as well as putting a marked emphasis on the representation of subjectivity, a feature that characterizes all of her narrative writing.

I now come to the third type of 'scene' that Behn provisionally institutes in her prose.[12] Behn does not yet employ a fully developed eighteenth-century 'scene' – in fact, Behn's oeuvre achieves the scene exclusively in the realm of the portrayal of consciousness. But what one can already observe here is how the brief narrative episode from the oral pattern which the picaresque novel had adopted in the course of narrative transcoding (*Verschriftlichung*)[13] is here already rewritten for the purposes of large-scale narrativity. Thus, where in the picaresque tradition the tale would have concatenated one micro-episode after the other (and the traces of this strategy are still in evidence in the Behn text), 'The Fair Jilt' creates a larger plot-unit which is structured, *not* on the dynamics between a central incidence and a result/reaction/resolution segment which follows it, but on a central scene flanked by an elaborate marking of the incipit and an equally decisive marking of the conclusion.

This shift in structure can be observed most clearly in the transposal of the *setting-plus-incidence unit* from the centre of the oral episode to the starting point of a scene. Incidences that obtrude on settings survive into Behn's narrative discourse. Indeed, these collocations are uncommonly emphasized:

> [...] while the poor innocent young *Henrick* **was** thus **languishing** in Prison, in a dark and dismal Dungeon, and *Miranda* [...] **was triumphing** [...] **there was a great Noise** about the Town, that a Prince of mighty Name [...] **was** arriv'd [...]
>
> ('The Fair Jilt'; Behn 1967: 97)

The realist paradigm 149

After Henrick has been condemned to die for his supposed attempt to rape Miranda, he is left languishing in prison, and the narrative turns to Miranda's ill-fated intrigue with Prince Tarquin, the outcome of which will save Henrick's life. This underlines the *onset* of the episode rather than constituting its climax; indeed, the central scene of Miranda's ensnarement of Tarquin, which consists of a *repeated* encountering of glances ('she never glanc'd that Way, but she met [his eyes]' – ibid.: 100), is managed in a descriptive passage that highlights the carefully contrived effect of Miranda's appearance as her chosen strategy of catching Tarquin's attention and notes the emotional tension experienced by both parties ('he was wholly ravished and charmed, and she over-joy'd to find he was so' – ibid.).

The scene for Miranda's conquest is set by noting the arrival of Prince Tarquin and by providing his background history for the reader. Unlike the earlier introduction of Henrick which had been narrated to Miranda by her maid in a story-within-the-story format, this briefing on Prince Tarquin is managed in a narrational paragraph and expanded to include the narrator's evaluative characterization of the man (ibid.: 97–8). Again, this information about Prince Tarquin is introduced by a *past perfect tense*: 'We had often heard of this great man' (ibid.: 97). In the following there is the report of Miranda's immediate infatuation with the very title of a 'prince', and an account of how she initiates contact by means of a *billet doux*. We then learn of their first meeting at church, and finally of the Prince's surrender against all his well-wishers' advice. This macro-segment ends with Miranda's marriage to the prince and the macro-structure is here very carefully signalled by a double closure which twice emphasizes the fatality of this marriage to the prince, noting the pity some felt for him and how others openly 'cut' the couple.

> At last, in spite of all that would have opposed it, he marry'd this famous Woman, possess'd by so many great Men and Strangers before,[14] while all the World was pitying his Shame and Misfortunes.
>
> Being marry'd, they took a great House; and as she was indeed a great Fortune, and now a great Princess, there was nothing wanting that was agreeable to their Quality; all was splendid and magnificent. But all this would not acquire them the World's Esteem; they had an Abhorrence for her former Life, and despised her; and for his espousing a Woman so infamous, they despised him. So that though they admir'd, and gazed upon their Equipage, and glorious Dress, they foresaw the Ruin that attended it, and paid her Quality little Respect.
>
> She was no sooner married, but her Uncle died; and dividing his Fortune between *Miranda* and her Sister, leaves the young Heiress, and all her Fortune, entirely in the Hands of the Princess.
>
> (ibid.: 100–1)

Note the triple anaphorically emphasized reference to the marriage as a conclusion to the drama of Miranda's conquest of the prince – a strategy that serves to round off one macro-episode before it initiates, in the third paragraph, the next macro-episode, which deals with Miranda's budding criminal inclinations, called forth by the temptations of the inheritance.

In contrast to the oral pattern, therefore, this macro-episode *starts* with what used to be the central part of the oral episode – the setting-plus-incidence pattern – and it concludes with a heavily emphasized resolution section. The macro-episode is thus flagged both front and back, achieving a marked effect of partitioning that prepares for the subsequent homogenization of the matter enclosed within these narrative brackets. This material includes the summarizing closure of gaps (Genette's analepses, 1980: 50) by means of background exposition in the past perfect tense, the presentational (and evaluative) setting for events, the narration of the plot and, most crucial of all, the detailed description of characters' motivations for these actions and of their feelings and experiences, decisions and evaluative judgements in the course of developments. This macro-episode also summarizes much off-scene action – as in the brief outline of advice which Tarquin receives from his well-wishers (but rejects) – *and* it begins the process of elaboration of realistic detail which will become the hallmark of the realist novel and enter the chronicles of narratology under the mellifluous name of Barthes's *effet de réel* (Barthes 1968).

Whereas the oral episode had to restrict its repertoire of realistic detail so as not to clutter the narrative's effectiveness, the picaresque novel tended to downplay extensive description, since its major concern lay in the plot-directed development of the action in relation to the wiles and ruses of the artful protagonist. In the wake of Elizabethan romance, description in Behn's prose starts to take up considerable space whether in the orientation section (for the background history) or within episodes where it details the characters' little stratagems, their doubts, illusions and, above all, aspirations – the desires which make them 'tick'. Note also how Behn's descriptions are frequently subjective rather than objective, rendering the characters' mutual *perception* of one another's qualities (as in Miranda's and the Prince's mutual appreciation of each other when they first meet) or proffering the narrator's enthusiastic and strongly evaluative presentation of characters whom she pretends to have met in person.[15] 'Behn's' (i.e. the narrator's) unhindered omniscient access to her characters' psyches – a legacy of the romance tradition of the tale rather than of her picaresque predecessors – is clearly contrasted with characters' false interpretations of their perceptions of each other on the story level, where such misinterpretations frequently determine the plot. Not only does glamorous appearance belie the dark iniquities it hides; appearances are also faked and artfully employed to achieve a calculated effect of interpretation. In the passage under discussion Miranda feigns modesty by casting down her eyes at encountering the Prince's; she blushes; and, when meeting him after the service, 'forc'd an innocent Look, and a modest Gratitude' (Behn 1967: 100). Description begins to burgeon, to acquire a status all by itself, and it also starts to turn subjective, rendering characters' perceptions rather than mere quasi-objective background information.

To recapitulate, Behn contrives to anticipate *in nuce* the central features of the realist tradition in the novel: the flashback, the report-cum-scene structure, the independence of description, authorial omniscience (though here still in the hands of a personalized narrator figure), reliable (evaluative) narration as a guideline to the textual meaning(s), and subjective presentation of consciousness. Behn moreover initiates woman and her virtue (or lack thereof) as the major *thematic* preoccupation of the novel (cp. McKeon 1987: Chapters 4–6), although she characteristically introduces a germ of 'double-speak' into her presentations of women as untrustworthy and fascinating to others.[16] I will return to the question of subjectivity in the next section when outlining Behn's anticipation of the consciousness novel; the point to be noted at present is that Behn is the first to set up a new structure, which will be refined in the eighteenth-century novel and become the paradigm of realist writing in the nineteenth century.

The repercussions of this invention of the macro-episode, which, I argue, prefigures the narrative scene, can be observed in the placing of the setting-plus-incidence module. This regularly recurs in eighteenth- and nineteenth-century novels at the introduction of 'scenic presentations' of dialogue or of heated interaction, where the incidence consists in the encounter with the interlocutor or combatant, and it also introduces scenes representing characters' psychological turmoil. To illustrate the point, let me adduce a few examples from canonical texts:

> It was now a pleasant Evening in the latter end of *June*, when our Heroe **was walking** in a most delicious Grove, where the gentle Breezes fanning the leaves, together with the sweet Trilling of a murmuring Stream, and the melodious Notes of Nightingales, formed altogether the most enchanting Harmony. In this *scene*, so sweetly accommodated to Love, he meditated on his dear *Sophia*. **While** his wanton Fancy *roved* unbounded over all her Beauties, and his lively Imagination painted the charming Maid in various ravishing Forms, his warm heart melted with tenderness; and at length, throwing himself on the Ground, by the Side of a gently murmuring Brook, he broke forth into the following Ejaculation.
> [...]
> At these words he **started up**, and beheld – not his Sophia – no, nor a *Circassian* Maid richly and elegantly attired for the Grand Signior's Seraglio. No; without a Gown in a Shift that was somewhat of the coarsest, and none of the cleanest, bedewed likewise with some odoriferous Effluvia, the produce of the day's labour, with a pitchfork in her Hand, Molly Seagrim approached.
>
> (*Tom Jones*, V, x; Fielding 1974: 255–6)

152 *The realist paradigm*

As she **was concluding** the last stanza, to which an interruption in her voice from sorrow gave peculiar softness, the appearance of Mr Thornhill's equipage at a distance **alarmed** us all, but particularly encreased the uneasiness of my eldest daughter, who, desirous of shunning her betrayer, returned to the house with her sister. In a few minutes he was alighted from his chariot, and making up to the place where I was still sitting, enquired after my health with his usual air of familiarity. 'Sir,' replied I, 'your present assurance only serves to aggravate the baseness of your character; and there was a time when I would have chastised your insolence, for presuming thus to appear before me. But now you are safe; for age has cooled my passions, and my calling restrains them.'
(*The Vicar of Wakefield*, xxiv; Goldsmith 1966: 136–7)

I **had now arrived** at that particular point of my walk where four roads met – the road to Hampstead, along which I had returned; the road to Finchley; the road to West End; and the road back to London. I had mechanically turned in this latter direction, and **was strolling** along the lonely high-road – idly wondering, I remember, what the Cumberland young ladies would look like – **when**, in one moment, every drop of blood in my body was brought to a stop by the touch of a hand laid lightly and suddenly on my shoulder from behind me.

I turned on the instant, with my fingers tightening round the handle of my stick.

There, in the middle of the broad, bright high-road – there, as if it had that moment sprung out of the earth or dropped from the heaven – stood the figure of a solitary Woman, dressed from head to foot in white garments; her face bent in grave inquiry on mine, her hand pointing to the dark cloud over London, as I faced her.
(*The Woman in White* I, iii; Collins 1975: 14–15)

One afternoon, when the chestnuts **were coming** into flower, Maggie had brought her chair outside the front door, and was seated there with a book on her knees. Her dark eyes had wandered from the book [...] they seemed rather to be searching for something that was not disclosed by the sunshine [...]

Suddenly she was roused by the sound of the opening gate and of footsteps on the gravel.
(*The Mill on the Floss* IV, iii; Eliot 1980: 245–6)

In each of these cases the incipit (in the structure of the incidence schema) is followed by a dialogue scene, least pronounced in Fielding, but very prominently so in George Eliot. The kind of scene which Behn's texts develop is therefore marked formally by a pattern of setting-plus-incidence which has been transferred from the centre of the narrative episode to the incipit position, where it now indicates the beginning of the subsequent

The realist paradigm 153

scene; in addition it is characterized thematically or presentationally by its topic as a unit including the location and time of action that echoes the constitution of the dramatic scene. Thus in 'The Fair Jilt' Miranda's first meeting with Prince Tarquin is at church, where she makes him fall in love with her; and in *Love-Letters* the scene where Sylvia first meets Don Alonzo also receives ample description as setting. Note additionally that the incidence is one that invariably triggers *perception* on the part of the experiencing character. Formally, the scene itself inside the narrative bracket can be either pure dialogue or description of consciousness. The evocation of a scene consists in providing the sense of a unit of spatial and temporal coordinates. This unit is marked off by the onset of the incipit and by a conclusion that serves to shift into a different time or location.

What I have tried to illustrate so far is the structural development of the realist novel's typical report vs. scene alternation that obtains from the eighteenth century onwards. This new structure is particularly suited to evoking both the figure of a summarizing and evaluating narrator persona and the illusion of mental or visual immediacy. Chronological spacing and narrative rhythm are much aided by the restructuring of brief narrative episodes that inevitably have to occur in quick succession and which are reorganized into much more extensive scenic units flanked by immensely flexible blocks of reporting discourse. I will turn to the cognitive relevance of this restructuring and to its significance for a paradigm of natural narratology below under 4.2.

4.1.3 The consciousness scene

Behn's third lasting impact on the development of novelistic discourse consists in the invention of the consciousness scene. Unlike later full-blown instantiations of reflectoral narrative (pure internal focalization), Behn's texts do not employ interior monologue or extensive free indirect discourse but tend to render the internal drama of her protagonists' minds chiefly by means of descriptive psycho-narration,[17] with very few clauses of free indirect discourse interspersed with this narratorial version of internal events. Let me illustrate this by the example of Isabella's final surrender to love from 'The History of the Nun'.

> [...] I have already said, she had try'd all that was possible in Human Strength to perform, in the design of quitting a Passion so injurious to her Honour and Virtue, and found no means possible to accomplish it: she had try'd Fasting long, Praying fervently, rigid Penances and Pains, severe Disciplines, all the Mortification, almost to the destruction of Life it self, to conquer the unruly Flame; but still it burnt and rag'd but the more; so, at last, she was forc'd to permit that to conquer her, she could not conquer, and submitted to her Fate, as a thing destin'd her by Heaven it self; and after all this opposition, she fancy'd it was

resisting even Divine Providence, to struggle any longer with her Heart; and this being her real Belief, she the more patiently gave way to all the Thoughts that pleas'd her.

As soon as she was laid, without discoursing (as she us'd to do) to *Katteriena*, after they were in Bed, she pretended to be sleepy, and turning from her, setled her self to profound Thinking, and was resolv'd to conclude the Matter, between her Heart, and her Vow of Devotion, that Night, and she, having no more to determine, might end the Affair accordingly, the first opportunity she should have to speak to *Henault*, which was, to fly, and marry him; or, to remain for ever fix'd to her Vow of Chastity. This was the Debate; she **brings** Reason on both sides: Against the first, she **sets** the Shame of a Violated Vow, and **considers**, where she shall shew her Face after such an Action; to the Vow, she **argues**, that she was born in Sin, and could not live without it; that she was Human, and no Angel, and that, possibly, that Sin might be as soon forgiven, as another; that since all her devout Endeavours could not defend her from the Cause, Heaven ought to execute the Effect; that as to shewing her Face, so she saw that of *Henault* always turned (Charming as it was) towards her with love; what had she to do with the World, or car'd to behold any other?

Some times, she thought, it would be more Brave and Pious to dye, than to break her Vow; but she soon answer'd that, as false Arguing, for Self-Murder was the worst of Sins, and in the Deadly Number. She could, after such an Action, live to repent, and, of two Evils, she ought to chuse the least; she **dreads** to think, since she had so great a Reputation for Virtue and Piety, both in the *Monastery*, and in the World, what they both would say, when she should commit an Action so contrary to both these, she posest; but, after a whole Night's Debate, Love was strongest, and gain'd the Victory.

('The History of the Nun'; Behn 1967: 295–6)

The passage starts with an iterative summary of Isabella's unsuccessful attempts to overcome her passion. The scene is then set for the internal argumentational dialogue at the conclusion of which Isabella finally decides to betray her religious vows. The intimacy of this scene is both external and internal: Isabella's decision is taken in bed, which she shares with her companion Katteriena – a setting that makes it impossible for her to soliloquize aloud in the manner of the Renaissance novel or stage.[18] Second, the reasons which she adduces on both sides of the issue are presented in a jumbled and realistically inconsequential manner. In circular fashion she keeps returning to the frightening prospect of the shame that she would incur for breaking her vows. At the conclusion of the paragraph, in a strong *non sequitur* she spontaneously comes to reassert her passion: 'but, after a whole Night's debate, Love was strongest, and gain'd the Victory'. This neatly echoes the emotionality and spontaneity of her final surrender.

The realist paradigm   155

In the central paragraph Isabella's arguments against the shame and scorn that she will bring on herself are clearly weak from a theological and logical perspective. Their emotionality surfaces very prominently in the final clause, which is an instance of free indirect discourse: 'What had she to do with the World, or car'd to behold any other?' Behn is – to my knowledge – the *first* English writer to employ free indirect discourse for the representation of consciousness – excepting, that is, ambiguous Middle English examples.[19] Previous use of this form had been restricted to the representation of speech acts (Fludernik 1993a: 94–6, 107 footnote 46). The incipient internal focalization is additionally underlined by Behn's peculiar use of the historical present tense. (I have highlighted the relevant forms in the quotation.) Wright (1992) has argued that Behn's use of the present is later replaced by the subjective past progressive in free indirect discourse, but the function that it seems to observe in Behn's work appears to be entirely different, and diverse at that. At the beginning of the passage the presents echo a 'discussing mode' present on Weinrich's lines: they *summarize* the points of Isabella's internal debate. The present tense *dreads* in the final paragraph, on the other hand, has a clearly subjective function (although it could not be replaced by a past progressive form): Isabella's anxiety for her good reputation here resurfaces after she has contemplated the option of suicide and rejected it as even more shameful than vow-breaking.

There is a touch of irony in this for the reader who already knows the story: Isabella will eventually succumb to the impulse of double murder, thus committing a crime even more heinous than suicide. It may also strike the reader as odd that Isabella should not have sought guidance with her aunt the abbess. This argues for Isabella's fundamental dishonesty with herself. The abbess would presumably have imposed prolonged incarceration on her niece, a strategy that would eventually have succeeded in quenching her niece's passion by intercepting her contact with Henault, which kept feeding it. Isabella's secretiveness therefore serves the unhindered spreading of the disease, where the aunt's policy would have curbed the passion, nipped it in the bud. The insistence on Isabella's dread of losing her good reputation therefore implies, it seems to me, a very acute diagnosis of the constraints under which she labours: had Isabella sought refuge with her aunt she would have been subjected to the unalleviated contempt of her community without gaining anything in exchange. By eloping with Henault she will, it is true, lose her good reputation in the eyes of the world, but at least, she will in exchange gain Henault's affectionate glance[20] (in metonymy for his passionate embraces). Isabella's battle is one between love and duty, with duty firmly grounded in the external trappings of self-esteem; there is no mention of her love of God at all in these deliberations, surely an indication that for all her virtues Isabella's vocation has always been misplaced, the result of her father's decree rather than of her own developing inclinations.[21]

As I have already noted, the establishment of (at first intermittent) internal focalization in Behn's work does not rely on the extensive use of free indirect discourse (FID). It is of course true that Behn employs FID with surprising facility and felicity, not only for the presentation of speech (where the use of FID was an accepted strategy throughout the Renaissance[22]), but also for the portrayal of consciousness. However, Behn's claim to have initiated the consciousness novel cannot repose on her use of FID alone since no extensive continuous passages are to be found in her work. Most of Behn's instances of FID consist merely of a line or a phrase or two; however, this usually marks the climax of a detailed presentation of the protagonist's efforts to come to a decision, tracing a character's developing passion, grief or other emotion:

> She was eternally thinking on him, how handsome his Face, how delicate every Feature, how charming his Air, how graceful his Mein, how soft and good his Disposition, and how witty and entertaining his Conversation, she *now fancy'd*, she was at the *Grate*, talking to him as she us'd to be, and blest those happy Hours she past then, and bewail'd her Misfortune, that she *is* no more destin'd to be so Happy, then *gives* a loose to Grief; Griefs, at which, no Mortals, but Despairing Lovers, can guess, or how tormenting they are; where the most easie Moments are, those, wherein one resolves to kill ones self, and the happiest Thought is Damnation; but from these Imaginations, she *endeavours* to fly, all frighted with horror; but, alas! whither would she fly, but to a Life more full of horror? She *considers* well, she *cannot* bear Despairing Love, and *finds* it impossible to cure her Despair; she *cannot* fly from the Thoughts of the Charming *Henault*, and *'tis* impossible to quit 'em; and, at this rate, she found, Life could not long support it self, but would either reduce her to Madness, and so render her an hated Object of Scorn to the Censuring World, or force her Hand to commit a Murder upon her self.
>
> ('The History of the Nun'; Behn 1967: 281–2)

In this passage Isabella's battle against love is portrayed in the most vivid colours. As early as the first sentence the anaphoric *how* constructions syntactically highlight Isabella's emotional involvement. A second typical feature of the deictic centre is the use of *now* as in 'she now fancy'd' (ibid.: 281) to indicate the experiencing self's temporal perspective. Behn's most striking linguistic device for the transmission of internal focalization, however, is her use of the historical present tense. Behn's historical presents are not all of one cast, indeed the first two ('she is no more destin'd to be so Happy, then gives a loose to Grief') provide a kind of initial summary of the state of mind in which Isabella finds herself and which we see described in more detail below. A brief gnomic analysis of the kind of griefs that Isabella has to grapple with is followed by what appears to be a snapshot of her immediate perplexities. Although the verbs in the present tense are all descriptive, part of (consonant)[23] psycho-narration, the effect is one of seeing with Isabella's mind, an effect underlined by the expressively marked 'but, alas! whither would she fly, but to a Life more full of horror?' (ibid.: 282) – the only part of the passage which is formally recuperable as free indirect discourse. None of the lexical features in and by itself allows an unambiguous reading as definitely linked to Isabella's perspective, yet the net effect clearly is a portrayal of her subjectivity. Henault is *charming* for the narrator as well as for Isabella, and it did of course eventually prove impossible for her to forget him (as the continuation of the story documents). In the context, one will therefore tend to empathize with Isabella's predicament and read the *charming* and the *impossible* as echoes of her impressions and thoughts.

Behn often approaches the form of free indirect discourse without fully meeting the syntactic criteria, as she does in the *how* construction of the previous quotation. In the following passage from *Love-Letters*, Octavio jealously observes Sylvia being courted by his uncle (who is well past the prime of life):

> While he was thus considering he saw his Uncle's Coach coming, and Sylvia with that doting Lover in it, who was that day dressed in all the Fopperies of Youth, and every-thing was young and gay about him but his Person; that was Winter it self, disguised in artificial Spring; and he was altogether a meer Contradiction: But who can guess the Disorders and Pantings of *Octavio's* Heart at the Sight; ***and tho' he had resolved before he would not to save his Life lay violent Hands on his old Parent; yet at their Approach, at their presenting themselves together before his Eyes, as two Lovers going to betray him to all the Miseries, Pangs, and Confusions of Love, going to possess – her, the dear Object and certain Life of his Soul, and she the Parent of him, to whom she had disposed of herself so intirely already, he was provok'd to break from all his Resolutions, and with one of those Pistols he had in his Pockets, to have sent unerring Death to his old amorous Heart*** [...]
> (*Love-Letters* III; Behn 1993: 300)

Octavio's emotions and evaluations encompass the entire paragraph: the phrase 'that doting Lover' and the image of winter dressed up as spring both render Octavio's impressions and the narrator's depiction of them; Octavio's *feelings* are left implicit and declared to lie outside the competence of the narrator's art. The relevant passage, which I have bold-italicized for easy reference, syntactically breaks the period of logical presentation ('yet at their Approach [...] he was provok'd') by an excessive accumulation of clauses rendering what Octavio sees as the imagined result of his sensual perceptions: 'presenting themselves [ ] as two Lovers', 'going to betray him to all the Miseries [...]', 'going to possess – her'. This last construction constitutes an even more noticeable syntactic break; the syntax here seems to evoke Octavio's loss of articulation at the mere thought of Sylvia's possession by his rival. There is one more break, at the critical and emotionally delicate point where Ocatavio's thoughts move from the object of his desire, Sylvia, to the status of his rival: 'and she the Parent of him'. This is a typical expressive construction of exclamatory import of the type noted in Banfield (1982: 38)[24] as a direct discourse syntagm which also recurs in free indirect discourse. Behn here provides a window on Octavio's mind, iconically mirroring his seething emotions in the deliberate unruliness of her syntax. Yet Behn also controls this subjectivity firmly by means of the bracketing syntactic structure just as her novels bracket internal focalization within a pervasively authorial mode of presentation.

A word or two is also due here on the history of the soliloquy in Renaissance writing. The sixteenth- and seventeenth-century romance employed extensive soliloquy for passages of internal debate. Gynecia and Philoclea, Cleophila (Zelmane) and Dorus in Sidney's *Arcadia* all pour forth their lamentations, weigh the pros and cons of their urgings and the possible course of action in lengthy self-analysis. These soliloquies are, however, of an intensely rhetorical nature, with much self-address in the second person (Müller 1982, 1991). They are also not particularly verisimilar as renderings of thought processes. Rosader's debate with himself in Thomas Lodge's *Rosalynde* (1590) on whether or not he should help his evil brother against the lion that is threatening to devour him cannot be called a convincing representation of consciousness. Behn's portrayals of internal debate are more verisimilar in terms of the represented anguish and indecision, yet formally different from the Renaissance type of soliloquy since they integrate the mental subject matter with the narrative discourse rather than framing it as an inset in the form of a soliloquy. Behn therefore anticipates the later novel of consciousness with its increasing deployment of free indirect discourse, although she herself has not yet advanced FID to its later pervasive status but depends instead on narrative report with extensive consonant psycho-narration.

Behn's writing, as I have tried to illustrate, departs from previous models, and nowhere more radically than in the invention of the consciousness scene. It is apparent from the above examples how the consciousness scene develops from what could structurally have been a soliloquy; it is therefore initially a dramatic feature rather than a narrative one. However, as I will argue under 4.3, the increasing use of this kind of mind-reading shifts the textual emphasis to a more narrative function and helps to reshape its structure and the manner of its reception, anticipating the novel's eventual wholehearted espousal of internal experientiality. In collocation with Behn's restructurings of the episodic pattern of narrative, her initiating of the flashback and the straightening out of orientational material, the invention of the consciousness scene marks a crucial step in the shift from 'early' narrative to 'the novel'.

I will return to the further developments of the consciousness novel below. Before this, it will, however, be useful to recapitulate in major outline how the classic realist novel came into being. Particular emphasis will be placed on the cognitive parameters that are brought into play in the textual manifestations of realism.

4.2 THE NATURAL PARAMETERS OF REALISM

4.2.1 Verisimilitude and *effet de réel*

Realism is a term used both loosely and restrictively, and it has acquired a number of prominent connotations in relation to the English novel (and, one should note, an entirely different set of connotations when applied to the French novel). I will here use realism in the sense in which it has been employed by Ian Watt in *The Rise of the Novel* (1957), as the key characteristic of the novel as a genre, and in the sense in which Genette and Riffaterre, Barthes and Todorov define the realist tradition (if only by its contraventions). This understanding of the novel as an intrinsically, or at least originally, realist genre has meanwhile been corroborated by Michael McKeon in his seminal *The Origins of the English Novel* (1987), in which he very carefully traces the concept of the *real* as it develops from what one might consider as fairly unpromising sources. More recent work on documentary fiction (L.J. Davis 1983; Ray 1990; Hunter 1990) likewise concentrates on the elaboration of the concepts of the 'real' vs. the 'historical' in the early novel, discussing the *how* of representation on the basis of the *agencement* of the concepts of verisimilitude, mimesis and higher-order Truth. It has also been noted that the realist novel is 'realist' simply from a socio-historical perspective in that its dramatis personae cease to be kings and princes and become 'people like you and me', reflecting the social status of its bourgeois readership (Watt 1957: Chapter 2). Although there is obviously some justification in this view, and evidence for it can be adduced from the lack of chivalric settings in seventeenth- and eighteenth-century novels,[25] the equation does not come out quite right since it implicitly makes the bourgeois readership directly responsible for a shift in taste that promotes its own status and interests to the centre of literary representation. Not only can one counter that *any* readership typically wants to read not about themselves but about the *Other* (whether from more exalted or from thrillingly degraded walks of life); one can even argue that the absence of the romance cast of characters from the novel derives from the eighteenth-century novel's deliberate concentration on *contemporaneous* life rather than from its fixation on a bourgeois cast of characters: much as the public might have liked to read about their sovereigns and higher nobility, such curiosity could not be indulged in except in allegorical garb (Sidney, Spenser) or in historically displaced representation. In fact, it has been noted that the eighteenth-century novel typically avoided a historio-political thematics, whereas the nineteenth-century historical novel frequently dealt with the eighteenth century in terms of a historical *sujet*.[26] Nevertheless the trappings of romance return to the novel in the late eighteenth century, since idyllic, pastoral settings and fantastic events set in far-off places or in the distant past are typical of the age's Gothic themes. One can observe this in the (re-)emergence of the characters of romance and chivalry in the Romantic tradition. If one includes the historical novel in the category of realist fiction, the feature 'contemporaneity' can therefore only be cited as a historical characteristic of the *beginnings* of the genre, since the novel had to write *against* forms of *romance* and was forced to establish its pretended truthfulness and historicity in contradistinction to the alleged spuriousness of the romance. However, for the genre of the novel as a whole, contemporaneity is not as binding a feature as the requirement of a 'truthful' and 'convincing' representation of life. The precise locality of novelistic settings, their temporal relation to the reader's placing in time, and the social status of the dramatis personae figure as merely incidental side effects.

The key notion for the realist novel is therefore that of verisimilitude, which in turn involves the concept of typicality. Realist fiction prototypically sets its action in a historical and geographical space which overlaps with readers' spatio-temporal coordinates of real life: *thirty years ago, in this country of ours, in London*, or: *recently in Surinam*. This contiguity tends to be marked in a denotational manner, by means of the *naming* of familiar towns, of countries and areas recoverable from a map, and it explicitly invokes the reader's knowledge of these geographical entities.[27] Historical personae, especially in the historical novel, serve the same function. Everyday reality is moreover projected from realist detail engendered by the novelistic text. This corresponds to Barthes's famous *effet de réel*: the descriptions of dresses, furniture, housefronts and so on project an illusion of referentiality. These, besides their specific social significance, also signal real-life verisimilitude, calling to mind the abundance of objects surrounding us in everyday life and thereby supporting the effect of well-observed faithful representation of the world that the text attempts to achieve. (I here skip over Barthes's link of the more spectacular realist detail with the uncanny, the unexpected or the seemingly afunctional.)[28]

Traditionally, realism has also been treated in terms of verisimilar behaviour. Whereas *naming* necessarily involves objects and people in their existential or referential aspects, the prototypical verisimilar touches on human *agency* and *motivation*, on the likelihood of certain developments or reactions, and on readers' establishment or projection of the characters' mind-frame. This kind of realism very much relies on a folk theory of psychological explanations: (re)actions are verisimilar if and only if they fit a recognizable type. As Michael Riffaterre points out at length, argument in the realist novel frequently operates on the basis of proverbial wisdom: *The marquise, being extravagant as are all marquises, ordered her carriage and then went to bed* (Riffaterre 1990: 5–11). Another common argumentational ploy is the one involving familiarizing *that* in a construction like 'that familiar propensity of the feminine mind'.[29] Observe the following examples from a novel chosen at random:

> Tito felt that Romola was a more unforgiving woman than he had imagined; her love was not **that** sweet clinging instinct, stronger than all judgment, which, he began to see now, made the great charm of a wife.
> (*Romola*, xxxvi; Eliot 1993: 323).

> [...] they were in keeping with her new scorn of **that** thing called pleasure which made men base – **that** dexterous contrivance for selfish ease, that shrinking from endurance and strain [...]
> (ibid.: 324)

> Romola was feeling the full force of **that** sympathy with the individual lot that is continually opposing itself to the formulæ by which actions and parties are judged.
> (ibid.: lx; 504)

Such tricks of referential innuendo invoke the reader's world knowledge of human psychology and refer to the reader's sophisticated evaluation of common motivation and inclination patterns, and they underline the illusion of the 'real' in the text, allowing readers to re-cognize plot developments and fictional motivation on the basis of the psychology by means of which they themselves operate in their own lives.

Psychology – the tracing of people's emotions, supposed inclinations, the establishment of their *character* – therefore becomes a primary focus of the realist novel. This feature is only incipiently present in Behn, who still partly clings to the intrinsically evil or good nature of her dramatis personae, or tends to vacillate between presenting their good and evil actions in alternation without managing entirely to balance these diverse traits into a consistent (if complex) portrayal of their character. Thus, Behn's fair jilt, Miranda, is a coquette, a liar, even a murderess; yet when her lover has been arrested for attempted murder (to which she incited him), she surprisingly follows him to prison, is faithful to him and keeps him company.[30] Judging from her earlier deceitfulness, one would have expected differently. Inversely, Sylvia, in *Love-Letters*, starts out as a virtuous soul whose way to hell is paved with good intentions as she gradually transforms herself into an experienced liar and deceiver. Oroonoko, by way of contrast, acts in a consistently heroic manner, and the characters in 'The Lucky Mistake', one of Behn's most polished pieces, entirely succeed in capturing our fancy as fully portrayed individual beings. Behn's psychology may not be up to the mark of Fielding (Defoe and Swift actually share some of her problems as far as the realistic presentation of characters is concerned), but it is a great advance over Bunyan and the picaresque novel, over allegory and the popular literature's unreflecting immersion in action and intrigue. Where Behn clearly goes beyond allegory and romance is in her identificational potential (protagonists in allegorical discourse cannot be identified with) and in her critique (even if implicit) of idealization: non-parodic romance rarely includes its own critique.

Behn's exclusion from the canon may additionally have been motivated by her adoption of the fantastic and the coincidental as one of the propelling features of her plots. Her plot repertoire includes all kinds of unbelievable events and a great number of outrageous coincidences: Oroonoko's capture by the captain; the meeting of brother and sister in 'The Dumb Virgin'; the intrigue of the black lady who manages to ruin the lovers' marriage in 'The Unfortunate Bride'. Yet fortuitous events can be argued to constitute one of the hallmarks of the realist novel, cluttering not only the pages of eighteenth-century texts (where the novel's antecedents of fantasy and romance could be cited as intertextual precedents) but also determining much of the incontrovertible core of realist fiction in the mid- and late nineteenth-century novel. Thus, coincidental (though perfectly 'realistic') events result in the tragedy of Maggie Tulliver, and *Daniel Deronda* turns on quite a few fortuitous encounters which prove to be of crucial significance for the plot. Hardy is another well-known instance, with the letter lost under the doormat in *Tess* or, in *Jude the Obscure*, Jude's drunken submission to his ex-wife. Here the unexpected coincidence acquires the character of a fatality, whereas in the beginning of the novel it still smacked of divine intervention.[31]

This finally takes me to the crucial notion of *mimesis*. Realist texts are, in the standard definitions, mimetic texts: they re-present a fictional reality which iconically reflects our image of what is real. Yet our understanding of what is real derives precisely from well-worn clichés of what should happen, has been known to happen, conventionally does happen, reflecting an array of frames and scripts, conventionalized expectations, moral attitudes and commonsense notions of the agentially and psychologically verisimilar.[32] For this reason verisimilitude and mimesis not only go hand in hand, but representations of the real are mimetic only in so far as they are typicalized and conventional, the one proviso to this argument being that the mimetic also claims to represent that Real which seems to lie beyond its grasp: the surprising, fantastic,[33] otherworldly and demonic, that which by definition seems to be unspeakable and unrepresentable. If the known can be signified by means of the typical, so paradoxically can the unknown. Where the unrepresentable has to be represented, the text reverts to images of the known which are exaggerated (ultimate good, ultimate evil) or combined in unheard-of constellations: travellers see natives with three heads and one eye; native customs are presented as a combination of known practices, yielding oddities which reinforce the reader's expectation of the marvellous.[34] Verisimilitude, and the lack

The realist paradigm 163

thereof, lies in the eyes of the beholder. Fictional realism, therefore, is as much a function of interpretation as the construction of plot or the evocation of fictional character.

4.2.2 Natural parameters

I will now turn to the question of natural story parameters and their development in the novel. I have already outlined how the surface structure of the narrative episode is rearranged to shift the cognitively salient setting-plus-incidence point to the beginning, the onset of what then becomes a 'scene'. Such scenes are initially extended narrative episodes that eventually eliminate the prominence of plot (action, events) in favour of confrontational dialogue, dynamic soliloquy or scenic description, where the last consists of interaction that goes beyond physical struggle. The report-cum-scene replaces the oral concatenation of narrative episodes but echoes the episodic base structure. Scenes flanked by report are concatenated just as episodes used to be; the onset and conclusion points are equally salient; and the setting-plus-incidence core of the oral episode is transferred to the macro-structural incipit point of the scene. The originally oral structure of episodic narrative, I argued in Chapter 2, can be related to the cognitive parameters of storytelling, of actionality, experientiality and perception, all of which combine to reflect natural human embodiedness and subjection to the constraints of human experience.

The oral storytelling schema can be constituted as a frame, and in Chapter 2 I distinguished between two basic types of storytelling as they are observable in spontaneous narrative – stories of personal and stories of vicarious experience. Storytelling, it was argued, occurs in well-known settings, such as remembering one's own experiences, the retelling of hearsay (what others have told us), and the witnessing of others' experience as we happened to observe it. These frames combine the various aspects of that experience in a holistic or organic fashion. Such holistic frames embrace the intrusion of incidences, actions which were performed or observed, the reception of events which suddenly materialized and impinged on the observer and the protagonist's reactions to developments which originated outside herself. In the oral tale the parameters of telling and those of the story experience were integrated in the dynamic multi-level construct of episodic narrative, with its balance between reportability and point, between the experientiality of the story on the one hand and its significance for the present situation of narration on the other. It was further argued that, during the process of transcoding oral genres into written ones (*Verschriftlichung*), hearsay narrative developed into the genres of historical writing and epic discourse and monopolized narrative production on account of its privileged societal, political and ideological status. Most medieval and early modern narrative operates on the reporting model which does not thematize experientiality at all.

164 *The realist paradigm*

Paradoxically, the experiential model first occurs in the standard third-person mode of the epic, where the protagonists' (necessarily vicarious) experience acquires central importance. (First-person narrative, as we have seen, hardly exists in the early period.) Medieval narrative, moreover, preserves one other crucial feature of the oral model: the narrator is a personalized teller, a child of his own time, somebody who frequently involves himself with the sources of his narration, pointing out where he heard or read the story he is about to tell.

With the Renaissance, a different kind of text comes into being, that of the travel literature in which the authenticating claim of personal witness becomes significant. In spite of this reliance on personal witness, the episodic pattern of personal narrative with its core of experientiality is, however, displaced in favour of a more action-orientated schema as soon as we turn to the genre of the picaresque novel. As one arrives on the threshold of the novel, reanalysing Behn's work in the light of natural frames, one can note both continuity – the narrator is frequently involved in the tale as a witness and bystander with a privileged access to hearsay information – and discontinuity. Behn's emphasis on characters' emotional experience re-emphasizes experientiality but locates it, not in the narrative incidence (the plot function), but in the significance of external and internal occurrences: Behn's heroines and heroes are strikingly prone to self-analysis, reflecting both on what has happened to them (in an extended notion of incidence) and on what they are supposed to do in response to it (extending the resolution/reaction point), and they are also crucially concerned with the analysis of their own feelings. In spite of the fairly romance-like intrigue plot that occupies most of Behn's texts, the narrative emphasis has shifted from the report of external machinations to their significance for the protagonists and to the moral and ethical conundrums which they have to face as a consequence of these intrigues and their emotional reactions to them.

Behn preserves the traditional storytelling frame (her narrators are all personalized, even if not consistently so). Her narrators tell a true story, and frequently even claim to have witnessed it in part. Since this truth claim rests precisely on the alleged biographical identification of the narrator with the historical author, Aphra Behn-the-famous-playwright, the traditional distinction between the author and the narrator figure – invaluable as it is for the sophisticated theoretical analysis of the novel – has to be suspended if one wants to capture contemporary readers' historical access to the narrative. This access operates precisely on the basis of real-life authentication through witness report and therefore undermines the theoretically necessary distinction between Behn-the-historical-person and Behn-the-narrator. As regards the natural paradigm for the story level, Behn does not yet fully exploit the frame of VIEWING (which will become the major frame for the consciousness novel and so-called neutral narrative), but complements the frame of personal experience with the report and action-orientated frame which was prevalent in the picaresque tradition, thus wedding romance to the picaresque and enriching it with one more experiential frame, the experience of reflective or ruminative ideation. Just as we are familiar, as humans, with the enactment of our goals and plans, with how we act on others and interact with them, we are also familiar with our mental enactments of ideas, plans, goals; our battle against temptation, illicit desire and the imp of the perverse; our struggle against irrationality and aggression. We are, that is to say, aware of our own mental experience of deliberation and argument, as we experience our own emotional turmoil. THINKING, or REFLECTING, just like ACTING, EXPERIENCING and VIEWING, constitutes a fourth unit on the fundamental level of cognitive parameters of human experientiality, and with Behn it begins to emerge as a central natural frame in the constitution of narrativity. These frames have their structural counterparts on the linguistic level of narration, with the consciousness scene recuperating EXPERIENCING from the oral mode, and combining the VIEWING frame with the former setting-plus-incidence points which now serve to introduce scenes.

All such parameters are realistic in that they evoke real-life experience, but they need not necessarily remain within the world of natural storytelling situations. Traditional epic discourse already starts to depart from a strict adherence to a verisimilar distribution of knowledge: what the heroes experienced when they fell in love,[35] unlike their feats in battle with the enemy, cannot but be invented and elaborated, and that despite the foregrounding of its hearsay quality, of its alleged transmission in oral song. The epic, which constitutes an entirely respectable tradition, therefore already displays narratorial omniscience, but it does so in muted form. The singer of the traditional tale is a *persona* of salient textual status (and the *jongleur* or the bard were, of course, a physical presence to their audience). This setup precluded the kind of anonymous omniscience associated with the realist novel. Moreover, the epic story, although it contains extended descriptions of heroes' feelings and combines several strands of action as well as extensive shifts between different story locations, can still lay claim to being authenticated by the historical mode of oral transmission, thus camouflaging its own constructedness and artificiality. Which takes us to the issue how 'natural' is omniscient narrative, and what is the status of natural parameters in the narrative situations of the realist and modernist novel.

4.2.3 Authorial narrative, omniscience and reliability

Authorial narrative is most familiar to us in the form of a reliable guide to human affairs. There is a consoling ability to know, to see into characters' minds, to grasp the why, how and wherefore of life, and to uncover life's rules and regularities *sub specie aeternitatis et mundi*. As first properly realized in Fielding's historiographical metaphor, authorial narrative makes possible what is naturally impossible. It combines the historian's and traditional storyteller's breadth of story matter (presenting the full range of *contemporary* rather than bygone reality) and the romance writer's concern for the inner life of his protagonists. It effects a new combination between the analysis of the external course of events – regulated by the rules of human agency and the laws of Nature – and the examination of protagonists' internal motivations; the latter, too, determined by the laws of Nature, namely 'human nature'. Authorial omniscience naturalizes the Renaissance discourses of the strange and spectacular by subsuming the unexpected within its rhetoric of confident anticipation, explanation and categorization of humanity and the world around it (McKeon 1987). One can observe this already in Behn, who, in the interests of moral Truth, exploits the *exempla* quality of her moralistic tracts about characters' motivation, yet subtly deconstructs this truth by engaging our sympathies with the protagonists' plight. Thus, in *Love-Letters*, Sylvia's deceitfulness, which is denounced at several points by the narrator, contrasts with the perfidy of her lover Philander, who has no qualms about betraying her nor about seducing the fair and virtuous Calista. In nigh-Shakespearian manner evil breeds evil, so that Sylvia, who suffers at the hands of Philander and the contemptible Brilliard, ends up ruining the noble Octavio, who, had she first met him rather than Philander, might have assured them both a haven of bliss. Likewise, in 'The History of the Nun', Isabella is initially more sinned against than sinning but ultimately falls prey to infamy of abysmal proportions.[36] The authorial rhetoric, which at the outset of the tale had sought to impose a message of vow-breaking as the root of all evil, later fails to implement this interpretation and provides the reader with an empathetic recognition of Isabella's very real plight. Behn therefore moves in the direction of the realist claim (explicit in Fielding, though less so elsewhere) that narrative can provide an adequate explanation and illustration of human affairs.

Such an aim is of course highly suspect from a present-day perspective, and the much-talked about 'death of the author' (which also, to some extent, reflects a 'death' of the narrator persona)[37] traces precisely the loss of this illusion of knowability anchored in the figure of the authorial narrator. The invention of the authorial narrator goes back at least as far as Chaucer's *Troilus and Criseyde*, but it does not become foregrounded until Behn and Fielding because the romance tradition structured narratorial omniscience on the pattern of *topoi* of emotions. Thus, although Chaucer and Caxton can apparently 'look into' their protagonists' minds, what they then observe and represent for us are highly rhetorical set pieces of schematized emotions: love, despair, grief, passion or bliss. And, as we have seen, they tend to portray these minds by means of soliloquial discourse rather than in narrativized shape. It is only with Behn, and certainly in the wake of the action-oriented picaresque tradition, that the crucial processes of pragmatic deliberation and reflection, emotional self-analysis and decision-making come to the fore, and with them the entire question of psychological (motivational) verisimilitude. Such verisimilitude then highlights the 'impossible possibility' of authorial discourse. Authorial narration performs the naturally impossible by yielding to the human narrator the authority of a quasi-godlike historian of human affairs. This contradiction, the very non-naturalness of the historian's omniscience, is, however, naturalized in the frame of empirical enquiry which authenticates a scientific metaphor for the narrator's exercise of omniscience. To the extent that the authorial narrator exemplifies the laws of human nature on the basis of illustrative case studies of a few chosen human subjects (the protagonists), 'his' uncanny ability to know other people's minds becomes backgrounded and hardly noticeable as an infraction of real-life frames.

I have here been using the term *omniscience* as it correlates with zero focalization (Genette) or the non-natural property of knowing others' minds.[38] The authorial narrator's more extended omniscience regarding the space and time of the action does not pose any problems in relation to natural parameters: it can be accounted for easily within the traditional function of the historian as a compiler and accumulator of traditional lore and a recensor of earlier versions of the story. Knowing what happened at the same time in a different place or what events led up to a specific situation does not violate expected natural frames to the same extent as reading people's minds, and it is for this reason that this aspect looms so large in the discussion about authorial omniscience, which is then frequently equated with the issue of access to internal subject matter and the whole complex of focalization. Mind-reading in the realist authorial novel is not yet a major break with real-life conventions, or only guardedly so. The real break with natural parameters occurs in the invention of preponderantly figural narrative, of internal focalization, where narratorial knowledge can no longer be anchored in the pieties of received morality and serves to replicate well-proven psychological insights relying on everyday experience and guesswork.

Authorial narrative of the Fielding type reposes on the telling mode, extending this natural paradigm beyond the limits of real-life storytelling. I have noted in Chapter 2 that even in oral narrative there is ample attribution of speech and thought acts to the protagonists, whether these are people with whom the narrator had actually interacted or the dramatis personae of a vicarious narrative. Bearing the dramatic genre in mind as well – where soliloquies typically abound – the extension of narratorial privilege into the authorial mode can therefore be conceptualized as a gradual process of broadening the narrator's grasp on the story matter, rather than as a revolutionary deviation from expected norms. Narratorial omniscience in the authorial mode is certainly unavailable to real narrators in natural interaction; yet it is the kind of privilege that one most wishes a narrator to have, since it affords the reader the comforting illusion of reliability, objectivity and absolute knowledge. To the extent that Fielding's narrator in *Tom Jones* or Thackeray's in *Vanity Fair* claim to present an account of humanity in action, they enact the oracular role of the wise man (if a wise man of satirical propensities) who acts as the repository of conventional wisdom.

Before turning to the first great instance of the non-natural in novelistic narrative, that of the consciousness novel, a word is due here on the first-person novel. Realism in narrative, although frequently identified with the work of Balzac, George Eliot or Trollope, nevertheless embraces a great number of works which use the first-person mode, including quite a few of Dickens's novels, some of the Brontës' work and even texts from the very beginnings of the canonical novelistic tradition, such as Defoe's masterpieces or Paltock's *Peter Wilkins* (1750), Goldsmith's *The Vicar of Wakefield* (1766), Godwin's *Caleb Williams* (1794) or Maria Edgeworth's *Castle Rackrent* (1800). The entire canon of epistolary narrative needs to be added to this canon of the first-person mode (with obvious caveats and qualifications). The first-person novel, a form that already flourished in the picaresque tradition, in the criminal autobiography and the confessional memoir, has so far remained outside the focus of this chapter for the simple reason that it constitutes fairly unproblematic fare: its authentication devices are anchored in the personal witness function of the narrator, and most narrators stay well within their limitations as regards narratorial access to information in other people's minds. Indeed, the first-person mode traditionally helps to transform unbelievable and hardly convincing accounts into trustworthy testimonies of the teller *qua* traveller, criminal or repentant sinner. It does so even in texts which have an unreliable narrator. In *Castle Rackrent*, as Edgeworth herself claims in the preface, Thady misrepresents the events because he is too naïve for this world, but this renders him doubly 'reliable' in respect of providing a truthful account of affairs, if with a false interpretation attached to them. That is to say, Thady fails to grasp the grim significance of what he tells us or to put the correct construction on his various masters' character. But, since he does not try to *deceive* us by artful rhetorical designs, we are easily able to see through his encomiums to the grim facts of the matter of which he appears to be so blissfully and blithely unaware. The authenticity of first-person report merely strengthens the realism of the realist novel from a subjective perspective, which, precisely on account of its subjectivity, provides all the more valid evidence of truth for the reader, who appears to have immediate access to an allegedly objective reality.

4.3 THE CONSCIOUSNESS NOVEL: THE ENGLISH NOVEL FROM BEHN TO WOOLF

Whereas what Stanzel calls the first-person and authorial narrative situations are predicated on a frame that hinges on a teller-mode visualization

The realist paradigm 169

of the narrative process and – in the case of authorial narrative – extends this process into less immediately reproducible realms of authorial control, fiction which centres on characters' consciousness by means of internal focalization appears to be clearly set apart from everyday modes of storytelling. The extended portrayal of others' minds – in fact even of one's own consciousness – in and by itself constitutes a signal of fictionality, as Käte Hamburger was the first to point out in her classic study of the logic of literature (1957/1968): it is only in literature that the I-originarity of another's self can be presented in the third person as if from their very own perspective. Interior monologue and extensive mind portrayal in the shape of free indirect discourse have therefore developed into markers of fictionality, particularly in historical and journalistic narrative, and are treated as a major criterion for the distinction between fiction and non-fiction, especially by Cohn in her recent work on the fiction/non-fiction boundary (1989, 1990).

Stanzel's own treatment of stream of consciousness, as I have pointed out elsewhere (Fludernik 1993a: 378–9), is actually ambiguous since the original conception of the figural narrative situation (*personale Erzählsituation*) was limited to the third-person mode but included autonomous interior monologue (zero degree of mediacy). In Stanzel's revised typology, however, the crucial distinction between teller and reflector mode supersedes that of the concept of narrative situation. Reflector mode texts are now defined as being based on a protagonist's deictic centre (Bühler 1934; Banfield 1982; Wiebe 1990). As a result first-, second- and third-person texts can be accommodated within reflector-mode narrative and the term *figural narrative* should be restricted to the historically prominent type of novel which, according to Stanzel's original formulation, is situated on the authorial–figural continuum of his typological circle (Fludernik 1993b, 1994a, 1994c). I will return to questions of typology in Chapter 8, and merely want to note this issue here in connection with the status of the consciousness novel for narrative theory. Stanzel's definition of reflector-mode narrative and Banfield's presentation of texts with a SELF rather than a SPEAKER overlap to a surprising degree, and they both rely on empirical linguistic evidence. It is in the light of this basis in deictic signals that internal focalization acquires the status of more than a merely theoretical category in narrative theory. In addition to the linguistic aspects of the presentation of consciousness, however, the question of its functional importance, as well as its quantitative presence, within the development of narrative writing in the late nineteenth-century and early twentieth-century novel requires consideration.

It is of course a noted fact that presentation of consciousness by means of internal focalization increases towards the end of the nineteenth century and becomes a constitutive feature of Modernist prose (Kahler 1973; Herget *et al.* 1986; Nünning 1992). Historically speaking, however, one can observe the makings of the consciousness novel in Aphra Behn and note its intermittent resurgence in much writing *before* Austen, who is usually credited with the first realizations of reflectoral narrative before the mid-nineteenth-century novel. Besides Richardson, the Gothic novel deserves explicit mention for its extensive portrayal of consciousness, whereas earlier texts of the now recovered female tradition, such as Charlotte Lennox's *The Female Quixote* (1752) or Eliza Haywood's *Betsy Thoughtless* (1751), still imitate the dramatic soliloquy or use brief summarizing psycho-narration. The history of the rise of the consciousness novel therefore encompasses two phases: a formal phase in which the linguistic foundations of reflectoral writing are already available, and a second phase in which the rendering of consciousness attains increasing structural prominence and results in a highly sophisticated use of this technique. In this second phase the use of internal focalization additionally comes to fulfil very specific ideological functions. If the consciousness novel is being discussed here in its relation to novelistic realism, and surprisingly so for some readers I should think, this reflects the very rhetoric of Modernist fiction, which claimed to be truer to life than the realist and naturalist novel could ever hope to be: truer, that is, to the very experientiality of people's subjective involvement with their environment. As I have stated in Chapter 1, I propose to treat the consciousness novel as the culmination point in the development of narrative realism rather than as its first regrettable lapse into idiosyncratic preoccupations with the non-typical and no-longer-verisimilar of human subjectivity. The Modernist novel as the paradigm of the consciousness novel also constitutes the climax of a technical achievement, namely that of the perfection of the VIEWING and EXPERIENCING frames which allow for the easy recuperation (naturalization) of story matter as if through the eyes of a fictional consciousness. Although reflectoral narrative, from one point of view, is the most 'unnatural' (Cohn 1990: 791) type of narration, from the cognitive perspective it recuperates one of the prime natural frames of human experiencing and therefore naturalizes the unnatural (or, as I would prefer to call it, the non-natural) to perfection.

Here is not the place to illustrate the long history of the novel of consciousness or to document its apogee in the work of Virginia Woolf. This is familiar ground and I will take it for granted, referring the reader to the literature.[39] Before closing this section, I will therefore briefly remark on the fate of the tradition which Behn initiates within the eighteenth century, that is to say before the recognized inception of the tradition by Jane Austen. In this context the work of Richardson, especially *Clarissa* (1747–48), earns pride of place, but one needs to note a few more novels written in the latter half of the eighteenth century which served as catalysts of the incipient tradition: Horace Walpole's *The Castle of Otranto* (1765), Ann Radcliffe's novels, for instance *The Mysteries of Udolpho* (1794), and William Godwin's *Caleb Williams* (1794), besides the fiction of Mary Wollstonecraft. One may also want to include Charles

Brockden Brown's *Edgar Huntly* (1799), the first classic American novel and one that already displays a remarkable quantity of free indirect discourse. Godwin's and Brown's books are first-person texts, and so are Clarissa's letters, in which the perplexities of the experiencing self are elaborated in unprecedented detail. Not only are these novels important in the history of free indirect discourse, providing the first instances of FID for the representation of consciousness *in a first-person context*[40] (Behn's examples of FID are all in third-person passages, and Defoe's first-person FID only represents *utterances*); they also initiate a development of poetic sensibility in the history of the novel which attains its appropriate perfection in Austen and Scott.

The rise of the consciousness novel would be unthinkable without *Clarissa* and the tradition of self-analysis which Richardson redeploys for secular rather than religious purposes. Richardson's feat of letterwriting *à l'instant* has been remarked on at length,[41] and the crucial importance of characters' consciousness in the story is also a commonplace of narrative criticism. In addition, Richardson to some extent anticipates the dramatic scene, although the frame structure of epistolary narrative does not allow for its full blossoming. In fact most of the story events of *Clarissa* (and Richardson's *Pamela*, for that matter) consist of confrontational dialogues, whence the easy development of scenic presentation in the unlikely context of first-person narrative. A good example of this is Clarissa's talk with her sister Arabella about Lovelace, a dialogue that is intermittently rendered in free indirect discourse (*Clarissa*, Letter iii; Richardson 1883: 11).[42] Or, a shorter passage:

> He smiled, and called himself *my servant*. – The occasion was too fair, he said, for Miss Howe, who never spared him, to let it pass. – *But, Lord help the shallow souls. Would I believe it of the Harlowes! they were for turning plotters upon him. They had best take care he did not pay them in their own coin. Their hearts were better turned for such works than their heads.*
>
> (Letter xii; ibid.: 66)

This is quite close to Austen's dialogues, which are, however, even more dramatic, usually involving several characters with their quite specific foibles and peculiarities. Besides Richardson, Eliza Haywood and Charlotte Lennox have recently been appropriated for the canon of eighteenth-century fiction. The standard treatments of these two authors (Löffler 1986; Spencer 1986; Todd 1989) emphasize the concentration on the protagonists' mind frame, and W.G. Müller (1979) even argues that Lennox anticipates the consciousness novel. It needs to be countered, however, that the presentation of Arabella's consciousness in *The Female Quixote* is definitely authorial, and ironic at that, and that the emphasis in the novel lies on the extensive presentation of dialogue rather than on the rendering of consciousness.

It is in connection with the Gothic novel that the representation of protagonists' (the heroines') minds moves to the forefront of technical innovation. Most of the eighteenth-century texts involve their characters in extreme and horrifying circumstances: physical confinement, fear of life, threat of physical punishment, encounter with wild beasts and Indians (*Edgar Huntly*), solitude, madness, guilt (*Caleb Williams*) and fear of the unknown or the otherworldly, the uncanny. The genre's concentration on consciousness is therefore supported thematically by plots which authenticate excessive emotion and render the depiction of such emotion necessary despite, or maybe because of, its very extremity. Not so in Behn, and certainly not so in the nineteenth-century tradition of the presentation of consciousness. The nineteenth-century novel tends to concentrate on reasonable feelings, deliberation, reactions to what one hears from one's interlocutor, etc.;[43] passages of extended presentation of consciousness therefore initially serve a motivational function, but extensions of this *effet de réel* occur in those novels which already shift towards reflectoral passages, in Eliot and Hardy in particular, and in Dickens's *The Mystery of Edwin Drood*. It is only with Modernism, with Joyce and Woolf, that the presentation of consciousness becomes independent, counting the atoms as they fall on the mind – though that, of course, is the most artificial effect of all. The natural parameters of EXPERIENCING and VIEWING therefore take a long time to produce a new type of writing, with the novel first passing through several stages of inside views *on* the characters. Internal focalization is originally conceived as *part of*, as well as abetting, authorial omniscience, foregrounding reflective thought rather than the mute registration of externalities as they come within the purview of the reflector's mind. Such a long history of gradual familiarization with the device accustomed readers to the Modernist exploitation of its full potentialities. By the time of Joyce's and Woolf's depiction of minds in their plenitude, these authors could build on cognitive parameters which were well in place and available for use: readers had considerable training in tuning in on such non-natural mind reading within a natural frame.

4.4 THE UNIMPASSIONED OBSERVER: NEUTRAL NARRATIVE

[...] la focalisation externe, grâce à laquelle le lecteur assiste en spectateur aux actes des personnages, mais sans qu'aucune autorité narrative lui expose leurs motivations, pensées, sentiments ou sensations.

(Husson 1991: 294)

External focalization helps the reader to observe the actions of the characters, but without a narrator's authoritatively revealing to him their motives, thoughts, feelings or sense perceptions.

(My translation)

Neutral or camera-eye narrative, as it is frequently called, in its setup appears to be even more non-natural than the uncanny access to others' mind afforded by the Modernist consciousness novel. Thus, narrativity (in my definition of 'experientiality') seems to be at a bare minimum in neutral narrative since the course of events is mediated neither through the experience of an agent nor through the evaluative eyes of a teller, and nobody's reflective or unreflective consciousness is involved. This description of neutral narrative, although adequate to most of its manifestations, fails to take account of the reader's active participation in the reading process. Although unimpassioned observation seems to characterize the non-experiential structure of neutral narrative, the majority of texts within the neutral mode trigger readings in which the protagonist's suppressed motivations, emotions or inclinations are adduced as implicitly signified by the narrative. In Alain Robbe-Grillet's novels *Le Voyeur* (1955) and *La Jalousie* (1957) the narrative discourse is read as reflecting visual impressions, i.e. perceptions, and these indicate the presence of a mind that insists on noting just these details, that insists on watching and – paradoxically – on suppressing its emotions.[44] As the theatre of Beckett or Pinter documents with equal force, a technique that frustrates the access to protagonists' internality by dwelling on the externalia of visual surface elements results in a desperate search for significance; it produces meaning(s) with a vengeance.

It is a commonplace of interpretation that detective Philip Marlowe in Chandler's *The Big Sleep* (1939) acts the tough guy and presents himself as a smart, cold, indifferent and uninvolved investigator of others' dirty business. For Marlowe emotions apparently threaten to evolve into sentimentality and to endanger the narrator's self-presentation. Likewise, in Hemingway, lack of explicitness comes across as much more suggestive than descriptional plenitude, implying unspeakable horror ('The Killers'), heroic suppression of pain and fear (in *For Whom the Bell Tolls* or *The Sun Also Rises*) and sometimes naïvety, a state of emotional shock, or fatalistic defeat (mostly in the Nick Adams stories). In *The Old Man and the Sea* lack of response is naturalized in a reading that attributes to the fisherman an accepting attitude of old age or a nearly religious submission to the powers of the elements.

Not only are many so-called neutral narratives naturalized in terms of a character's perceptions or suppressed emotions, many of the texts from the neutral canon on closer inspection turn out to be not so objective after all (Müller 1981). For instance, in Dashiell Hammett's *The Maltese Falcon* (1930/1974) descriptions of the various characters are far from non-evaluative. Thus, in the first paragraph of the novel, Samuel Spade is described as looking 'rather ***pleasantly*** like a blond Satan' (Hammett 1974: i, 5), and later we get: 'The smooth thickness of his arms, legs, and body, the sag of his big rounded shoulders, made his body like a bear's. It was like a shaved bear's: his chest was hairless. His skin was childishly soft and pink' (ibid.: ii, 12). The impression of neutrality in the text derives from the lack of information about Spade's feelings and from passages which describe visual effects that evoke a filmic rendering:

> A telephone bell rang in the darkness. When it had rung three times bed-springs creaked, fingers fumbled on wood, something small and hard thudded on a carpeted floor, the springs creaked again, and a man's voice said:
> 'Hello ... Yes, speaking ... Dead? ... Yes ... Fifteen minutes. Thanks.'
> A switch clicked and a white bowl hung on three gilded chains from the ceiling's centre filled the room with light. Spade, barefooted in green and white checked pyjamas, sat on the side of his bed.
> (ibid.: ii, 11–12)

Later when Spade kicks Cairo, the trajectory of his fist rather than Spade's intentional action receives narrative highlighting: 'The fist struck Cairo's face, covering for a moment one side of his chin, a corner of his mouth, and most of his cheek between cheek-bone and jaw-bone' (ibid.: v, 42). Whereas the first scene corresponds to what one might perceive in a film (darkness, sounds, light, recognition of Spade), the second passage involves a selective process by means of which a close-up of Spade's fist is foregrounded. If a neutral camera eye indeed were responsible for the text, there would not be the great number of close-ups of Spade's facial expressions and of other characters' mien, gestures and so on – the camera would remain firmly installed in one location and simply register what is going on. There is therefore manipulation which deliberately undercuts interpretation in terms of the parameters of intentional action and, particularly, refuses access to Spade's emotional experience. As a result, the reader feels transposed into the position of a viewer watching a film unroll with its various close-ups and other special effects. The impenetrability of Spade's mind here serves the purpose of suspense since it delays his recognition of the woman's guilt to the final showdown dialogue with her. In Robbe-Grillet's *La Jalousie*, on the other hand, narrativizations in terms of the husband's jealous fixation on a number of recurrent scenes suggest themselves from a thematic standpoint even if some of the perspectives may not be realistically feasible visual settings for the husband.

Neutral narrative may, moreover, be a misleading term because first- and third-person forms, at least in principle, lend themselves to quite different kinds of naturalization. First-person narrators in the neutral mode must be made responsible for their lack of 'natural' involvement with their experiences: the most prominent feature of first-person neutral narrative is the narrator's refusal or inability to inform about his own motivations, feelings or thoughts.

I would however maintain that this form of narration calls – better: *yells* for interpretation. More precisely, it forces the reader to seek a

plausible motivation in the psyche of the narrator: macho hard-boiledness in the case of Hammett or Hemingway, pathological removal of affect in the case of *L'Etranger*, mental vacancy in the case of Benjy.
(Cohn in Cohn and Genette 1992: 263)

In third-person neutral narrative, on the other hand, a scenario of things evolving as if by themselves can be observed, but since no narrator persona is at hand (signalled, in the first-person neutral mode, by the speaker's *I*, though without any personal or expressive features), one then has the typical 'camera-eye' effect of the mechanical shutter which registers incoming stimuli but does not interpret them, leaving it to the viewer of the film to make sense of the data transmitted.

Neutral narrative is also frequently identified with the dialogue novel because the mere transcription of dialogue seems to evoke an impassive or mechanical tape-recording of verbal events as they become observable and audible to the recording instance. In addition, the term 'neutral narrative' could also be applied to fictional work that uses non-personal syntactic and pronominal discourses. I discuss this case briefly under 6.3.3. Since such texts frequently lack a story as well as a perceivable teller figure, they belong with radical experimental texts such as the ones I deal with in Chapter 7. I am thinking of texts by Gertrude Stein, Beckett's 'Ping', or those passages in Maurice Roche's *Compact* that employ passive *il* constructions exclusively. Other examples might be the 'stories' by Gabriele Wohmann, as, for instance, 'Gegenangriff' or 'Selbstverteidigung', in which instruction-manual discourse and (pseudo-)scientific language are interspersed with a speaker's emotional discourse, none of which creates any consistent fictional reality.

Besides this diversity of possible applications of the term *neutral narrative*, its status as a category or mode in narrative theory has been fairly rocky. Genette, of course, subsumes neutral narrative under the concept of external focalization and therefore has no use for the term as such. Stanzel originally proposed a neutral narrative situation (1969: 23; 1978b: 566) but in later versions of his typology eliminated this narrative situation (1972: 5, 28–9; 1984b: 144, 263 footnote 12) and allowed for pockets of neutrality *qua* scenic presentation at practically all points of the typological circle. Since Stanzel's definition coincides with that of scenic presentation, this is no doubt an adequate solution, but it does not help with more descriptive neutral texts.[45] The latest important development in connection with camera-eye narration has been Ann Banfield's (1987) thesis that some sentences reflect Russellian notions of objectivity, recording impassively what goes on in a given scene. The position of the non-figural camera-eye viewpoint is indicated by means of a set of deictic features which are part of the repertory of expressive features elsewhere employed to signal SELF (i.e. subjectivity) in the absence of a SPEAKER. Banfield's proposal, as will be shown in Chapter 5 (see 5.2), actually describes a kind of discourse which is the very opposite of neutral recording since its latent expressivity frequently emerges to produce a speaker function.

There are, however, some texts that do indeed deserve the label *neutral narrative*, and these – in contrast to the current examples – are short texts of a descriptive nature. Alain Robbe-Grillet's collection *Instantanés* (1962) includes such 'stories'. 'La chambre secrète' and 'La plage' basically consist of description, and they metafictionally discuss the movements of the 'camera' as well. Both texts elude experientiality despite the rather pornographic (S&M) subject matter of 'La chambre secrète' (a description of various final stages of a murder in inverted chronological sequence); they elude experientiality not because there is no 'story' (in fact, there is the murder in 'La chambre secrète') but on account of the deliberately defocalized presentation, which rules out an anchor point for experientiality either on the level of the represented world (no experiencer is on stage) or on the level of the discourse and shifts the responsibility on the reader. In the case of 'La plage' the reading experience may then result in aesthetic evocations of walking along beaches, but with 'La chambre secrète' more sinister effects come into the critic's purview.

Neutral narrative, as narrative which renders a perfect representation of VIEWING, it seems, would appear to be a core frame of human experience: after all, observation, the witnessing of processes and events, constitutes one of our key experiences. However, as we have seen in our discussion of oral narrative in Chapter 2, observational parameters relate to the experiential factor of incidence and emotional involvement (even if it is only vicarious emotional involvement). As the term *camera-eye* so persuasively makes clear, unimpassioned viewing is the characteristic of a machine, an automaton (hence the derogatory implications about the voyeur's ethics or emotional warpedness). If natural frames and parameters relate to cognitive universals based on human body experience, then neutral narrative as the unreflective registering of impenetrable goings-on contravenes natural human experience. In so far, however, as readers re-interpret such impassivity to postulate the presence of a human viewer whose lack of involvement is taken to be of crucial semantic significance, neutral narrative, although an apparent representation of a non-natural frame, becomes naturalized, i.e. narritivized, and then again relates to human experiential parameters, even if these are implicitly, rather than explicitly, thematized. What we here encounter, then, is the first of a series of narrativizations. From initially unpromising fictional minutiae, such narrativizations recuperate for the reader, if not a plot, then at least the experiential quality of human agency, observation or reflection. I will trace a number of such narrativizations in Chapter 7 and discuss some of the limits set on the possible extension of this process. (Beckett's 'Ping' and Wohmann's work appear to constitute just such borderline cases, in which narrativity can be recuperated only imperfectly and whose status as narratives therefore relies almost exclusively on their marketing frame.)

The realist paradigm 177

This concludes my historical and typological remarks on the realist novel and its Modernist highlights. If realism stretches natural frames to breaking point, it does so in the interest of presenting us with an even truer picture of life. By getting an inside view of characters' minds we come to appreciate their motives and are more likely to find the story convincing and true to life. If we follow the meanderings of a mind as it observes the world, we are led to empathize with the protagonist and are apt to savour the privilege of mind-reading under the microscope. We ourselves may not have such interesting minds, or experience the same kind of epiphany, but we tend to recognize our own preoccupations in the symbolic images that are presented to us. Although we cannot read minds in real life, we end up taking interior monologues as being uncannily close to how real minds do actually operate. Finally, in the case of neutral narrative's radical refusal to give us such mind-reading, we tend to fall back on our real-life experience of opacity: the refusal to let us understand others better than they do themselves is clearly motivated by representational realism. Similarly, situations such as those described in *Le Voyeur* or *La Jalousie* immediately engage our detective perspicacity and we end up finding all sorts of verisimilar explanations for the observer's lack of emotional involvement, for his (or her) apparent inability to experience anything, even in reaction to external events. Neutral narrative no longer sets out to produce mimetic effect, channelling its resources into the signalling of expressivity as is so prominently the case with the consciousness novel. Instead, it can rely exclusively on the reader's inveterate wish to read fiction and to find, if not a story, at least a fictional protagonist worth the name.

The development of the realist novel therefore reflects a process of recuperation in the act of reading which starts out with a full instantiation of natural frames and ends with the narrativization of inherently non-natural frames. This process will be repeated again and again to apply to increasingly less recuperable kinds of texts, and the process of narrativization will become a highly sophisticated instrumentarium of cognitive adaptation. This is the story I wish to tell in Chapters 6 and 7. Before this we will, however, need to consider some types of discourse which require narrativization, but of a less radical kind. These texts pose some further interesting questions in relation to natural cognitive parameters and they also question some of the current theoretical positions within narratology. Realist frames still apply, but are distorted and yet again immediately recuperated by new realist frames. If, in the discussion of the great realist tradition, we traced the novel from Behn to Woolf, I here return to the nineteenth century to illustrate some of its more insidious techniques for undermining narrative realism, techniques which can be located at the very heart of realist *écriture*.

5 Reflectorization and figuralization
The malleability of language

This chapter will trace a complex of phenomena that have recently come to the attention of narratologists and which constitute a refinement of the realist technique while at the same time demolishing its realist bases. These phenomena centre on a number of crucial issues – crucial, that is, in narratology – and therefore radicalize tensions endemic to the realist narrative text: the operations of voice and perspective; the linguistic establishment of the deictic centre and its evocation of consciousness and/or speaker personae; and, finally, the entire complex relating to the issues of mimesis and invented (fictive) orality.

In the following I will introduce a distinction between *reflectorization* on the one hand and *figuralization* on the other and I will discuss how these two strategies – if that is what they are – converge in (post-) Modern(ist) writing techniques, particularly those that closely resemble the notorious Russian 'device' called *skaz*.[1] My argument is that fiction which displays a prominent speaker persona whose discourse is *reflectorized* in accordance with Stanzel's proposals (1984b: 168–84) yields a similar type of text to that of a narrative modelled on an empty deictic centre (Banfield 1987) which then allows that centre to develop a speaker function.[2] The *skaz* technique – a pseudo-oral type of narrative discourse – has recently started to be used pervasively not only in Afro-American writing (see Toni Morrison's *Sula* [1973] and *The Bluest Eye* [1970] as well as the third-person sections in Gloria Naylor's *Mama Day* [1988]) but also in a number of non-ethnic novels such as Adam Thorpe's *Ulverton* (1992), George Garrett's *The Succession* (1983) or Lawrence Norfolk's *Lemprière's Dictionary* (1991), with important anticipations in Thomas Pynchon's *Gravity's Rainbow* (1973) or Salman Rushdie's *Midnight's Children* (1981) and *Shame* (1983). Reflectorization and figuralization can therefore be argued to have anticipated the inception of a specific postmodernist style of writing which can even now claim a status of prominence equal to that of the better-known experiments in self-reflexive language play (as in the more familiar postmodernist *écriture* that goes under the name of surfiction). This massive deployment of pseudo-orality or *fingierte Mündlichkeit* ('simulated orality')[3] can be regarded as the ultimate endpoint in a conceptual development from oral storytelling into written forms of narrative and their eventual re-oralization[4] at the other end of the spectrum. It is certainly appropriate for ethnic literature in the recent past to have adopted this technique of pseudo-orality since such a move accommodates influences both from current postmodernist writing practices and from alleged ethnic oral traditions, thus tracing a circle that folds back to the oral roots of these cultures.

5.1 REFLECTORIZATION

5.1.1 Original proposals

In 1977 Stanzel published an essay entitled 'Die Personalisierung des Erzählaktes im *Ulysses*' in which he introduced the concept of *Personalisierung*, later translated as *reflectorization* (1984b: 168–84). The term was originally coined as a derivation from Stanzel's *figural* narrative situation, which in German is called *personale Erzählsituation* (hence: *Personalisierung*). In the English first draft of my doctoral dissertation I therefore translated the concept as 'figuralization', but Stanzel's (1984b) translation of his 1979 German *Theorie des Erzählens* then used the term *reflectorization* instead, which refers to the *reflector-mode* pole of one of his three basic narrative axes, that of the opposition *mode*. This change in terminology appears to have been determined by Stanzel's reconceptualization of his typology. In Stanzel's 1979 revised version of his narrative theory of 1955, it will be remembered, his three narrative situations are placed in relation to a structure of three intersecting axes, with the figural narrative situation now constituted by the reflector mode pole of the modal axis.

Reflectorization, in Stanzel's definition, is the 'assimilation of a teller-character to a reflector-character' (1984b: 169), or the result of 'making an authorial narrator think and speak as if he were one of the characters of the story' (ibid.: 172). The example on the basis of which he first illustrates this technique is a paragraph from Katherine Mansfield's 'The Garden Party' (1922):[5]

> 'But we can't possibly have a garden party with a man dead just outside the front gate.'
> That really was extravagant, for the little cottages were in a lane to themselves at the very bottom of a steep rise that led up to the house. A broad road ran between. True, they were far too near. They were the greatest possible eyesore, and they had no right to be in that neighbourhood at all. They were little mean dwellings painted a chocolate brown. In the garden patches there was nothing but cabbage stalks, sick hens and tomato cans. The very smoke coming out of their chimneys was poverty-stricken. Little rags and shreds of smoke, so unlike the great silvery plumes that uncurled from the Sheridans' chimneys.

Washerwomen lived in the lane and sweeps and a cobbler, and a man whose house-front was studded all over with minute bird-cages. Children swarmed. When the Sheridans were little they were forbidden to set foot there because of the revolting language and of what they might catch. But since they were grown up, Laura and Laurie on their prowls sometimes walked through. It was disgusting and sordid. They came out with a shudder. But still one must go everywhere: one must see everything. So through they went.

'And just think of what the band would sound like to that poor woman,' said Laura.

(Mansfield 1984: 493–4)

Stanzel comments with regard to the opinions expressed in the central narrative section:

Since this insertion supplies supplementary information for the reader, it must be regarded as part of a reader-oriented exposition by an authorial teller. These are not the words of a teller, who unwittingly discloses his own social prejudices and lack of understanding, but rather of someone who represents the Sheridans in his [own] manner of thinking and feeling. The character [i.e. this someone] in question is nameless, because he is not part of the fictional reality of the story. This anonymous reflector-character experiences these deliberations as an event in which earlier experiences and observations of individual members of the Sheridan family are reflected.

(Stanzel 1984b: 171)

In the passage quoted from 'The Garden Party,' the reflectorized teller-character temporarily becomes the collective voice of the members of the Sheridan family other than Laura, in which their lack of humanity and social conscience is audible.

(ibid.: 172)

The reflectorization of the authorial narrator is therefore here defined in terms of the narrator's taking on the personality (linguistic and ideological) of a character or, in this case, a group of characters whose views are presented as if 'through their minds'. This local disturbance cannot be explained as a brief snatch of free indirect discourse representing the thoughts of a reflector character (no individual character is available for this purpose), nor is it prima facie recuperable as the (authorial) narrator's personal language. Although Jose might have been the one to voice the disagreement with Laura's point of view – in fact, Jose just said 'Don't be so extravagant' – the continuation of the paragraph ('eyesore') is less clearly attributable to Jose, and the experience of Laurie and Laura noted at the end of the extract ('It was disgusting and sordid. They came out with a shudder. But still one must go everywhere: one must see everything. So through they went.') must be focalized by either Laura or Laurie.

Laurie is not present at the scene of this exchange, and Laura – from the evidence of her flanking sympathetic utterance ('"And just to think of what the band would sound like to that poor woman," said Laura.') – cannot be made responsible for 'disgusting and sordid' either.[6] Jose, of course, has not been present at these prowls. Stanzel therefore suggests that the only consciousness or perspective available at this point, that of the narrator, *mimes*, imitates, and assumes the characteristics of an intratextual reflector character as if the narrator had empathetically stepped down into the story and become one of the characters. In the ironic context of Stanzel's example passage there is a strong (though implicit) dissociation between the characters' 'false' values expressed in the passage and the values attributable to the 'implied author'[7] elsewhere in the text:

> [...] one cannot overlook the irony arising from the discrepancy between the opinions of the self-effacing narrator, whose presence can be inferred in other parts of the story, and the opinions announced by the reflectorized teller-character coinciding with those of the Sheridans. In this provocative way, the author evokes perhaps an even stronger rejection of these opinions in the reader than if they had been presented merely by individual characters, such as Mrs Sheridan.
>
> (ibid.)

The reflectorized teller character in this schema is a construct, combining the *knowledge* of the narrator with the focalization and language of a character present on the scene, but is identical to neither the narrator nor a specific identifiable character.

Indeed, the opinions voiced in the example passage cannot be unequivocally attributed to the Sheridans, nor are the Sheridans disclosed as the intended *object* of the passage's presentation. Although the expostulation against Laura's 'extravagance' is certainly in the spirit of Mrs Sheridan, who later on loses patience with Laura and calls her 'absurd' ('You are being very absurd, Laura' [Mansfield 1984: 495]), the context suggests, rather, that Laura's sister Jose is the source of the sentiments expressed in the paragraph. However, as Stanzel himself already pointed out, the paragraph cannot be a verbatim rendering of a remonstrance in these words by Laura's sister. This applies particularly to the description of the general condition of the cottages, which in no uncertain terms reflects a middle-class abhorrence of poverty that clearly belongs to a grown-up's perspective. The ending of the paragraph is even more noteworthy. We get a flashback to the Sheridan children's childhood ('when the Sheridans were little') and then a view of Laura's and Laurie's reactions to passing through the slum area, in which 'It was disgusting and sordid. [...] But still one must go everywhere [...]'. This is clearly an ironic free indirect discourse 'transcription' of the feelings of brother and sister. In contrast to the earlier evaluation of the cottages as 'the greatest possible eyesore', these opinions cannot be attributed to Mrs Sheridan, who would not have been likely to encourage Laura and Laurie's urge to 'go everywhere' and 'see everything'. Since the relevant paragraph cannot be read mimetically as Jose's continued expostulation with Laura (and Mrs Sheridan is not yet 'on the scene' – Laura runs to tell her of the dead man immediately *after* her exchange with Jose), there is therefore a good case for reading this story-internal perspective as belonging with the story's *narrator* (which is Stanzel's explanation). My own way of putting this would be to say that the passage's expressivity and evaluative slant need to be located on the level of the protagonists but that the failure to find a current onstage character to whom one might attribute an actual utterance or thought act (Jose is barred from this position since she would not remember Laura and Laurie's trip to the cottages) results, as a consequence, in the postulation of the narrator's (the only other available consciousness) ironic mimicry of typicalized story-internal opinions.

Another perspective from which to approach the phenomenon is by an analysis of reflectorized passages occurring in texts where they more clearly relate to a *specific character* who is 'on the scene' and whose point of view is being sarcastically presented by a seemingly approving (though implicitly recriminatory) narrator. I have myself characterized just such a collocation not only as implying the narrator's assumption of figural perspective but also, conversely, as the character's assumption of narratorial language and authority (Fludernik 1992c). The example I used was the presentation of Mrs Glegg in George Eliot's *The Mill on the Floss* (1860). Passages of reflectorization occur extensively in George Eliot. Another very rewarding passage comes from her *Romola* (1863). The topic of the following extract concerns Tito Melema's mindset, with psycho-narration[8] the dominant form of representation. The irony, if not sarcasm, directed against Tito depends on our knowledge of the values enunciated elsewhere in the book (and usually attributed to Romola). There is no explicit distancing from the self-justifications that Tito parades before his mind, and the final lines of free indirect discourse – in the past tense, which contrasts with the narrator's *in propria persona* pronouncements in the gnomic present tense earlier ('a mixed condition of things which is the sign, not of hopeless confusion, but of struggling order' – Eliot 1993: 482) – therefore appear as rationalizations of Tito's position that seem to be endorsed by the ostensible evaluative tenor of the paragraph.

> For Tito himself, he was not unaware that he had sunk a little in the estimate of the men who had accepted his services. He had that degree of self-contemplation which necessarily accompanies the habit of acting on well-considered reasons, of whatever quality; and if he could have chosen, he would have declined to see himself disapproved by men of the world. He had never meant to be disapproved; he had meant always to conduct himself so ably that if he acted in opposition to the standard of other men they should not be aware of it; and the barrier

between himself and Romola had been raised by the impossibility of such concealment with her. He shrank from condemnatory judgments as from a climate to which he could not adapt himself. But things were not so plastic in the hands of cleverness as could be wished, and events had turned out inconveniently. He had really no rancour against Messer Bernardo del Nero; he had a personal liking for Lorenzo Tornabuoni and Giannozzo Pucci. He had served them very ably, and in such a way that if their party had been winners he would have merited high reward; but was he to relinquish all the agreeable fruits of life because their party had failed? His proffer of a little additional proof against them would probably have no influence on their fate; in fact, he felt convinced they would escape any extreme consequences; but if he had not given it, his own fortunes, which made a promising fabric, would have been utterly ruined. And what motive could any man really have, except his own interest? [. . .] Men did not really care about these things, except when their personal spleen was touched. It was weakness only that was despised; power of any sort carried its immunity; and no man, unless by very rare good fortune, could mount high in the world without incurring a few unpleasant necessities which laid him open to enmity, and perhaps to a little hissing, when enmity wanted a pretext.
(*Romola*, lvii; Eliot 1993: 482–3)

Tito's conduct is explained in this passage as if the narrator were trying to condone Tito's harmless deceptions as necessary strategies of self-preservation under unfavourable political circumstances. The focalization is Tito's, and the mindset reflects Tito's struggle to disguise his ill deeds under the cloak of all too human expediency that, he believes, will not hurt anybody very much. Yet it is of course quite clear from the larger context that the passage constitutes a savage indictment of Tito Melema's morals, though this disapprobation can be detected only from the perspective of the entire novel's frame of values (Nünning's level N3 in Nünning [1989a], or the 'implied author' position). A close look at the style of this paragraph immediately reveals the rampant insincerity in the narrator's euphemistic designation of Tito's deceptions. Thus, Tito's opportunism and cunning parade under the labels of 'well-considered reasons' and 'conduct' whose 'opposition to the standard of other men' should remain concealed from them. Tito's rationalizations are cast in a style that weighs morality in the pros and cons of mercantile adventure ('agreeable fruits', 'his own interest') and that (rather than disclosing his calculating insensitivity and ethical obtuseness) projects a self-image of dispassionate objectivity by accusing his antagonists of 'spleen' and rejecting their hypothetical explanation of his actions in terms of their unjustified 'rancour'.

The viewpoint of this paragraph, then, is entirely that of Tito Melema, but the language, both stylistically and formally (most of the paragraph consists of psycho-narration), belongs to the narrator, 'who', however, appears to endorse Tito's exculpatory self-justifications. The two passages from 'The Garden Party' and *Romola* thus illustrate the phenomenon of reflectorization in its complex interrelating of an external viewpoint (the narrator's) and a specific character's or group of characters' point of view and language. Neither passage can be read as bona fide free indirect discourse, and that primarily on account of the descriptive and summarizing tenor of the texts. There is no realistic, i.e. mimetic, *vraisemblable* scenario on the lines of the Sheridans' performing of a specific thought act, nor does such a specific thought act present itself as likely to have occurred on Tito Melema's part either. It is in fact precisely this irresolvability of the textual evidence in terms of plot that introduces the necessity of an 'implied author' position: since the two texts so clearly refer to the *habitual* opinions of the Sheridans and of Tito Melema, respectively, there needs to be a source (i.e. a consciousness) on a higher textual level able to note the habitual nature of these characters' mindset and responsible for condensing their viewpoint into a typicalized representation of it. While the example from *Romola* is fairly distanced in tone, the Sheridans' possible locutions surface much more insistently, as is appropriate to the more figural mode of representation in 'The Garden Party'. I will come back to further distinctions between the two examples. The most prominent difference between them, of course, lies in the fact that the extract from *Romola* is *about* Tito Melema, whereas the passage from 'The Garden Party' ostensibly consists in a narratorial disquisition on the preposterousness of Laura's remark and additionally presents background information meant to help refute Laura's line of argument. Both texts preserve a strong narratorial presence and therefore differ in quality from passages adduced by Banfield to be instances of her 'empty deictic centre' (1987), which will be discussed below under the title of *figuralization* (5.2).

Before turning to a discussion of Banfield's empty centre I would like to discuss two further examples of reflectorization. In contrast to my example from *Romola*, Fay Weldon's 'Weekend' (1978) and D.H. Lawrence's 'England, My England' (1915) are problematic with regard to the possible attribution of point of view. They are therefore closer in tone to the Mansfield passage, where the origin of the opinions voiced in the discourse is never made explicit.

5.1.2 Lawrence and Weldon: a case study

D.H. Lawrence's 'England, My England' is a story with a conspicuous teller figure, yet it also has quite extensive passages of free indirect discourse and recurring stretches of figural/reflectoral narration. In this story the perspectives of Egbert, Winifred and her father are subtly intertwined. The text provides extended reflectoral presentations which alternate between Egbert and Winifred (with Egbert dominating as the main protagonist). Much background information is also supplied and one gets a description of the development of Egbert's and Winifred's attitudes and their mutual influence on each other. This juxtaposition of perspectives as well as, in particular, the clearly external analysis of Egbert's unacknowledged failings, the description of his appearance and of his face when dead – all these point to the existence of an external viewpoint and therefore of a not-so-covert teller in the tale, and this appears to be corroborated additionally by recurrent gnomic utterances like the following:

> Strange, that this sense of duty [towards the child] should go deeper than the love for her husband. But so it was. *And so it often is.*
> (Lawrence 1955: 309)

Why didn't Egbert do something, then? Why didn't he come to grips with life? Why wasn't he like Winifred's father, a pillar of society, even if a slender, exquisite column? Why didn't he go into harness of some sort? Why didn't he take *some* direction?

> *Well, you can bring an ass to the water, but you cannot make him drink.* The world was the water and Egbert was the ass. And he wasn't having any. He couldn't: he just couldn't. Since necessity did not force him to work for his bread and butter, he would not work for work's sake. *You can't make the columbine flowers nod in January, nor make the cuckoo sing in England at Christmas. Why? It isn't his season.* He doesn't want to. Nay, he *can't* want to.
> (ibid.: 312–13)

Much like George Eliot in *Romola* or *The Mill on the Floss*, Lawrence combines the various perspectives on the story by integrating both story-external (the narrator's) and story-internal points of view. In the following passage we move from a description of Egbert and Winifred through what appears to be their mutual appreciation of one another to a definitely external viewpoint on them both as a couple:

> Ah, how he had wanted her: Winifred! She was young and beautiful and strong with life, like a flame in sunshine. She moved with a slow grace of energy like a blossoming, red-flowered bush in motion. She, too, seemed to come out of the old England, ruddy, strong, with a certain crude, passionate quiescence and a hawthorn robustness. And he, he was tall and slim and agile, like an English archer with his long supple legs and fine movements. Her hair was nut-brown and all in energic curls and tendrils. Her eyes were nut-brown, too, like a robin's for brightness. And he was white-skinned with fine, silky hair that had darkened from fair, and a slightly arched nose of an old country family. They were a beautiful couple.
> (ibid.: 304)

'They were a beautiful couple' is unlikely to be Egbert's perspective. The passage moves from, first, a description of Winifred and, second, an appreciation of Egbert as an 'English archer' back to Winifred's brown hair and eyes, and returns to Egbert's good looks and prototypically 'English' physiognomic attractions. The discourse seems to utilize Egbert's and Winifred's perspectives of each other for a montage mounted by a story-internal observer of the family from within the fictional world. The evaluation of Winifred and Egbert as a beautiful couple therefore appears to relate to this narratorial identification with a story-internal position. The key term here is *observer*.[9] In this passage we also get a first indication of the narrator's ambivalent stance towards the characters. The exaggerated and emotionalized clichés of the discourse cannot belong to a truly objective narrator nor can they realistically be attributed to any one of the available characters either.

This interlocking of narrator's and character's opinions, language and expressive syntax can affect even single sentences:

> No, in all the *serious* matters she [Winifred] depended on her father.
> (ibid.: 308)

The syntactic signal of emotive 'No' – in refutation of Banfield's syntax of expressivity[10] – here has to be interpreted as belonging to the narrator's analysis of Winifred's reliance on her father. The 'No' therefore redounds on the teller. And yet: in the larger context of the story there remains the possibility that this just might be read as Godfrey Marshall's self-satisfied realization that he has not yet quite lost out to Egbert in his daughter's affection. This curious blend of internal and external perspective is even more conspicuous in the following passage:

> For Egbert had no intention of coming to grips with life. He had no ambition whatsoever. He came from a decent family, from a pleasant country home, from delightful surroundings. He should, of course, have had a profession. He should have studied law or entered business in some way. But no – that fatal three pounds a week would keep him from starving as long as he lived, and he did not want to give himself into bondage.
> (ibid.)

Egbert himself does not even conceive of 'coming to grips with life': he plainly refuses to countenance the very existence of inconvenient realities and the necessity of a struggle for survival against them. Phrases such as 'decent' family, 'pleasant' country home, and 'delightful' surroundings (as well as 'of course', 'in some way') all invoke a story-internal 'typical English middle class values' position which one might perhaps identify with Winifred's father. Yet in the immediate context of this particular passage we never explicitly hear of the father's disapproval of Egbert. As regards the word 'fatal', on the other hand, this can only be attributed to the omniscient teller-figure: Egbert, until his death, does not repent of having been firm in his rejection of 'bondage', as only he would call it. The paragraph goes on to indict Egbert for his 'amateurish' ways of doing things, for 'tampering':

> But often Winifred's father called her to London: for he loved to have his children round him. So Egbert and she must have a tiny flat in town, and the young couple must transfer themselves from time to time from the country to the city. In town Egbert had plenty of friends, of the same ineffectual sort as himself, tampering with the arts, literature, painting, sculpture, music. He was not bored.
>
> (ibid.: 308)

Here criticism of Egbert is even harsher, and his ineffectual position in the family, as an outsider doing what his father-in-law orders him to do, is hinted in the last sentence 'He was not bored'. This may be interpreted as Mr Marshall's belittling comment on Egbert's ineffectual manner of spending his visits to London, or it could reflect Egbert's resigned capitulation to his father-in-law's wishes: 'well, at least he was not bored'.

The story seems to repeat the old Lawrentian parable of man brought low by the contrivance of woman with her family-related priorities – a line of argument lifted from Nietzsche and here validated by means of a socioeconomic link with the industrial world, the world of money and politics to which Winifred is connected through her father. And yet, the story also insists, the tragedy of Egbert derives not from Winifred's or her father's insidious machinations but from Egbert's fatal flaw of aesthetic aloofness. Egbert fails to be the reliable, strong husband who is eventually expected to replace Godfrey Marshall as the authoritative male – and this is not only Winifred's unacknowledged interpretation of the situation but also, decidedly, the narrator's. Egbert's resistance to patriarchal expectations crumbles in the wake of his daughter's fatal accident, for which he was responsible, and his personality disintegrates to the point of absolute surrender: when he meekly joins the army against his will, he allows himself to succumb to the ultimate humiliation.

The narrator's criticism of Egbert is mitigated by the sustained inside presentation of Egbert's perception of the situation. True to the ambivalence rooted in Egbert himself, however, the narrative remains poised between story-internal evaluations and intermittent passages of narratorial incrimination. The concept of reflectorization is perfectly suited to describing this ambiguity because it characterizes the very blurring of the traces of voice in the text. In the following extract we move from Winifred's free indirect discourse into an evaluation *of* Winifred with intermediate echoes of Egbert's thoughts, and the passage ends on an omniscient(?) expression of sympathy for Winifred; or is this perhaps her father's evaluation of the situation? All of this has the appearance of a collage arranged by a story-internal teller figure who is speaking from Egbert's, Winifred's, Godfrey's (and maybe others') perspectives in succession:

But Egbert! What are you to do with a man like Egbert? He had no vices. He was really kind, nay, generous. And he was not weak. If he had been weak Winifred could have been kind to him. But he did not even give her that consolation. He was not weak, and he did not want her consolation or her kindness. No, thank you. He was of a fine passionate temper, and of a rarer steel than she. He knew it, and she knew it. Hence she was only the more baffled and maddened, poor thing.

(ibid.: 311)

All of this is ironical, yet the precise target of the irony remains elusive: both Winifred and Egbert are disparaged. The text refuses to pronounce authoritatively on the question, immersing the narrator in a mêlée of story-internal perspectives. The negative evaluation of Egbert – in this setup – comes across as equally unreliable as the positive, sympathetic ('poor thing') position on Winifred. The case is complicated by the stylistic properties of an entirely colloquial authorial narrative voice which, precisely on account of its colloquial and subjective nature, is no longer distinguishable from the characters' language or from that of potential story-internal observers. The narratorial discourse here abdicates from the duty of sustaining a stylistic norm such as used to apply in the realist novel, a norm frequently definable in terms of the neutrality of the narratorial idiom.

Let us now look at the second text, Fay Weldon's 'Weekend' (1978). This story describes the weekend experiences of Martha, wife, housewife and mother of three. The presentation is heavily tinged by a figural perspective – Martha's – but craftily supplemented by the narrator's voice. As in the Lawrence story, the narrator does not assume a story-external 'objective' position but mimes a set of simple and naïve views which are partly identical to those of Martha's husband Martin but also echo Martha's own obedient and uncritical acceptance of the values and expectations that her husband has imposed upon her. The pathos of the tale lies in Martha's unrewarded struggle to please everybody but herself, yet this pathos does not fully emerge until the end of the story since it is frequently covered up by the text's patently ironic slant. This heavy ironical slant is of a deadpan variety comparable to the one we have already encountered in *Romola*. The narrator, for instance, insists on Martha's good luck when the text clearly portrays her as being exploited, bullied and blackmailed by her husband, Martin, who embodies societal pressures and values inimical to his wife's development of self-esteem and self-confidence.

A deceptively idyllic vignette of middle class bliss is presented at the beginning of the story:

Weekend! Only two hours' drive down to the cottage on Friday evening: three hours' drive back on Sunday nights. The pleasures of greenery and guests in between. They reckoned themselves fortunate, how fortunate!

(Weldon 1993: 183)

This idyll, endorsed by a story-internal perspective apparently mimed by the narrator (note the exclamation marks; 'only'; 'how fortunate'), is undermined as soon as the routine of these weekends emerges: Martha does all the work, Martin enjoys himself and scolds Martha for 'making a fuss'. To make matters worse, Martha feels she has to efface herself and conceal her grievances for fear that Martin will leave her for a younger, more glamorous woman like Katie, their friend Colin's ineffectual but attractive wife.

The two paragraphs cited below, although technically free indirect discourse, present Martha's life from the perspective of others – the 'everyone' highlighted in the quotation. The style turns Martha – who may be the voice responsible for the final phrases ('before she knew where she was ...') – into a naïve and childlike person who unaccountably finds herself charged with drunken driving. This implication of naïvety is particularly pronounced in the second passage, which juxtaposes what must be Martha's incredulous recognition of her success (measured in generally recognizable status symbols) with an external observer's description of 'little earnest Martha with her shy ways and her penchant for passing boring exams':

> Martha's license had been suspended four months back for drunken driving. **Everyone** agreed that the suspension was unfair; Martha seldom drank to excess: she was for one thing usually too busy pouring drinks for other people or washing other people's glasses to get much inside herself. But Martin had taken her out to dinner on her birthday, as was his custom, and exhaustion and excitement mixed had made her imprudent, and before she knew where she was, why there she was, in the dock, with a distorted lamp-post to pay for and a new bonnet for the car and six months' suspension.

(ibid.: 184)

> Life now, by comparison, was wonderful for Martha. People, children, houses, conversations, food, drink, theatres – even, now, a career. Martin standing between her and the hostility of the world – popular, easy, funny Martin, beckoning the rest of the world into earshot.
>
> Ah, she was grateful: little earnest Martha, with her shy ways and her penchant for passing boring exams – how her life had blossomed out! Three children too – Jasper, Jenny and Jolyon – all with Martin's broad brow and open looks, and the confidence born of her love and care, and the work she had put into them since the dawning of their days.

(ibid.: 185)

This apparent idyll is undermined by a close appraisal of the situation. That Martin allows (forces?) Martha to drive the car on her birthday instead of himself foregoing the pleasure of too much drink – or instead of paying for a taxi – already casts a slur on Martin's character, and the negative picture of Martin is more than borne out once a full picture of Martha's marital predicament emerges.

The narrative continues by presenting Martha's weekend in terms of one scene of humiliation after another. Most of the paragraphs are from Martha's perspective, rendering her perceptions and feelings in the form of free indirect discourse and interior monologue. It is, however, Martin's views and wishes that are continually being quoted in Martha's thoughts, and her uncomplaining acceptance of these is a prominent source of the text's irony, all at the expense of Martha (indicating her naïvety) and – more insidiously – of Martin and his disguised marital tyranny. The narrative never explicitly exposes the inconsistencies between Martin's various precepts and injunctions, but the reader cannot help noticing these contradictions. Thus Martin insists on a Saturday lunch of fish and chips, but then, to please Katie, rebukes Martha 'You are funny with your fish-and-chip Saturdays! What could be nicer than this? Or simpler' (ibid.: 196) – all in reference to a salad Katie has made from the ingredients set aside for next day's buffet lunch for nine. Martin 'brings back flowers and chocolates' (ibid.: 187) for Martha, but prefers women to be slim (ibid.). When Katie throws a tantrum because her towel is wet,

> 'Oh dear,' cried Martha. 'Jenny must have washed her hair!' And Martha was obliged to rout Jenny out of bed to rebuke her, publicly, if only to demonstrate that she knew what was right and proper. That meant Jenny would sulk all weekend, and that meant a treat or an outing mid-week, or else by the following week she'd be having an asthma attack. 'You fuss the children too much,' said Martin. 'That's why Jenny has asthma.'
>
> (ibid.: 197)

The injustices of Martha's situation are even more glaring as regards the couple's financial arrangements. In the following description the final three clauses (highlighted below), again, cannot be attributed to any one of the characters – they must constitute the reflectorized narrator's perspective:

> Katie came back upset and crying. She sat in the kitchen while Martha worked and drank glass after glass of gin and bitter lemon. Katie liked ice and lemon in gin. Martha paid for all the drink out of her wages. It was part of the deal between her and Martin – the contract by which she went out to work. All things to cheer the spirit, otherwise depressed by a working wife and mother, were to be paid for by Martha. Drink, holidays, petrol, outings, puddings, electricity, heating: it was quite a joke between them. It didn't really make any difference: it was their

joint money, after all. ***Amazing how Martha's wages were creeping up, almost to the level of Martin's. One day they would overtake. Then what?***
Work, honestly, was a piece of cake.

(ibid.: 198)

Martha surely does not contemplate the scary moment when her salary might overtake Martin's, nor is Martin likely to *voice* these worries. The scenario, indeed, represents a moment that both characters fear, and the naïve presentation of this hypothetical situation echoes the idyllic and counterfactual viewpoint on Martha's marriage that has been predominant throughout the story.

'Weekend' climaxes with Martha's breakdown over her daughter's first period. For the first time Martha does not manage to do what is expected of her according to standard pedagogic lore – to be cheerful and 'joyous':

'Oh don't do that,' said Katie, 'do just sit down, Martha, you make us all feel bad,' and Martin glared at Martha who sat down and Jenny called out for her and Martha went upstairs and Jenny had started her first period and Martha cried and cried and knew she must stop because this must be a joyous occasion for Jenny or her whole future would be blighted, but for once, Martha couldn't.
Her daughter Jenny: wife, mother, friend.

(ibid.: 201)

The pressures on Martha to behave in accordance with a cliché of perfect motherhood are as diffuse as the voices in this text. Martin certainly is responsible for many of the rules of behaviour that Martha feels she has to obey, but Martin's expectations are also part of a more extensive frame of patriarchal values inimical to female self-realization. These precepts, mirrored in Martha's guilty conscience, build up a wall of ideologically determined discourse defining and containing Martha in a role which she is increasingly unable and unwilling to fulfil. Reflectorized narration is particularly suited to conveying just this indefinable omnipresence of discourses. Martha's predicament to some extent resembles the maze in which one finds oneself as a reader attempting to sort out the various voices cited and recited in this text. By refusing definite attributions of the discourse, the text iconically represents the pervasiveness of societal pressures on Martha and her dawning realization that her problems are in her marriage: 'Work, honestly, was a piece of cake' (ibid.: 198).

In this first section I have outlined a preliminary description of reflectorization as a phenomenon that occurs in texts with a more or less prominent narrator function and in which this narratorial voice intermittently (or, in the case of 'Weekend', continually) adopts either a character's mental habitus or the *mentalité* of a (usually unspecified) group of people (especially those representing a *communis opinio*). I will return to a closer examination of common opinion and communal perspective in section 5.3. I now turn to a related phenomenon which was also discussed under the heading of reflectorization by Stanzel (1977, 1984b), but actually corresponds more closely to Ann Banfield's concept of an 'empty centre' (Banfield 1987).

5.2 THE 'EMPTY CENTRE' OR FIGURALIZATION

5.2.1 Original proposals

Besides the proposal of a reflectorized authorial narrator, Stanzel (1984b), under the same title of reflectorization, has also discussed a related phenomenon, namely that of the implicit evocation of an observer figure on the story level. This particular feature correlates with Ann Banfield's category of the so-called 'empty deictic centre', which she proposed in 1987 in reference to Virginia Woolf's *The Waves* (1931).

Stanzel's discussion of the phenomenon is couched as a response to Roland Harweg's (1975b) analysis of deixis in Thomas Mann's short story 'Tristan'. The deictic features observable at the beginning of that story suggest the existence of a deictic centre which is located on the scene but cannot be identified with one of the main characters. Thus the protagonist of 'Tristan', the writer called Spinell, cannot be the reflecting consciousness at the beginning of the text[11] because he is there described as an eccentric and peculiar character, the *topic* of the narrative: Spinell does not focus on life around him; the text *focuses on* him. Since, in a reflectoral narrative, the existence of the reflectoral consciousness is a *presupposed* entity, it can never become the *topic* of the text. Later in the tale 'something' is described as 'com[ing] in' from 'back there'.[12] This seems to reflect the perspective of Mrs Klöterjahn, seated at the piano, yet the wording need not be attributable to her consciousness since elsewhere in the story the reader is not granted an inside view of Mrs Klöterjahn (Stanzel 1984b: 184). The thesis that it is the narrator who assumes an 'on the scene' perspective therefore directly reflects the critic's impasse in dealing with otherwise contradictory and uninterpretable linguistic signals in the text.[13]

As already noted, this type of reflectorization (in Stanzel's terminology) can be identified as an empty-deictic-centre phenomenon of the kind that Banfield proposed for Woolf's *The Waves* (Banfield 1987). As will be remembered, this novel is structured chronologically by a dual series of alternating sections: sections that describe the sea at various points between dawn and nightfall, and sections that document the progression of the characters' mental development by tuning in on their soliloquies at various points between childhood and death. The seascape descriptions of *The Waves* display the same deictic peculiarities noted in Thomas

Mann's 'Tristan'. In the following passages a centre of consciousness presumably located 'on the scene' is evoked by means of familiarizing articles (Bronzwaer 1970) and by the use of proximal deictics such as *here*, *now*, and *this*:

(i) In the garden the birds that *had sung* erratically and spasmodically in the dawn on that tree, on that bush, *now* sang together in chorus, shrill and sharp; now together, as if conscious of companionship, now alone as if to the pale blue sky. [...] Fear was in their song, and apprehension of pain, and joy to be snatched quickly *now at this instant*.

(Woolf 1963: 53)

(ii) And then tiring of pursuit and flight, lovelily they [the birds] came descending, delicately declining, dropped down and sat silent on *the* tree, on *the* wall, with their bright eyes glancing, and their heads turned this way, that way; aware, awake; intensely conscious of one thing, one object in particular.

Perhaps it was a snail shell, rising in the grass like a grey cathedral, a swelling building burnt with dark rings and shadowed green by the grass. *Or perhaps* they saw the splendour of the flowers making a light of flowing purple over the beds, through which dark tunnels of purple shade were driven between the stalks.

(ibid.)

(iii) Now, too, the rising sun *came in* at the window, touching *the red-edged curtain*, and began to bring out circles and lines. *Now* in the growing light its whiteness settled in *the* plate; the blade condensed its gleam. Chairs and cupboards loomed *behind* so that though each was separate they *seemed* inextricably involved. *The* looking-glass whitened its pool upon the wall. *The* real flower on the windowsill was attended by a phantom flower. Yet the phantom was part of the flower, for when a bud broke free the paler flower in the glass opened a bud too.

(ibid.: 54)

(iv) *The* land was so distant that no shining roof or glittering window *could be any longer seen*. The tremendous weight of the shadowed earth had engulfed such frail fetters, such snail-shell encumbrances. *Now* there was only the liquid shadow of the cloud, the buffeting of the rain, a single darting spear of sunshine, or the sudden bruise of the rainstorm. Solitary trees marked distant hills like obelisks.

The evening sun, whose heat *had gone out* of it and whose burning spot of intensity had been diffused, made chairs and tables mellower and inlaid them with lozenges of brown and yellow. Lined with shadows their weight *seemed* more ponderous, as if colour, tilted, had run to one side. *Here* lay knife, fork and glass, *but* lengthened, swollen, and made portentous. Rimmed in a gold circle *the* looking-glass held the scene immobile as if everlasting in its eye.

(ibid.: 148)

The markers of Banfield's 'Represented Speech and Thought' (her term for free indirect discourse) are clearly visible in these passages, and they project a deictic centre of observation on the scene as well as implying the presence of a consciousness that is the source of expressions like *seem* or *probably*. Observe also the many familiarizing articles, as in *the red-edged curtains, the looking glass, the real flower*. Even within a 'script' reading of the situation, it is precisely the use of the familiarizing article that serves to evoke a scene in the bedroom and dining room, inside the house. Yet earlier we have been at the seashore ('The sun rose. Bars of yellow and green fell on the shore gilding the ribs of *the* eaten-out boat [...]' – ibid.: 52), and then in the garden [i], finally in the house [iii]. Even though the construction of a consistent viewpoint of an observer situated inside the house is in principle possible, the feeling of immediate experience that is projected by these highlighted signals of consciousness effectively rules out a realistic scenario in which a fanciful observer might be located inside the darkened room. No mention is made in the text of physical movement away from the window (only somebody close to the windows could have observed the sea and the birds) to the inside of the room (the reflection in the mirror and of the flower against the window glass could have been perceived only from such a position farther inside).

In the passages I have quoted not only do the temporal and spatial deictics (*now*; *that tree*; *here*; *behind*, etc.) prominently signal a reflective consciousness; there are additionally some interesting uses of *verbal* deixis, i.e. tense. In the first passage the item *had sung* signifies anteriority in relation to *now sang*; in the specific context the past perfect therefore need not be an index of reflectoral consciousness. However, in the following two paragraphs, the past perfect tense does indeed relate to the perceptions of a reflectoral consciousness:

The sun **had now** sunk lower in the sky. The islands of cloud **had gained** in density [...] Some petals **had fallen** in the garden. They lay shell-shaped on the earth.

(ibid.: 129–30)

In neither passage does the past perfect explicitly relate an anterior event to an ongoing process (in which case it would be merely a 'shifted' past). On the contrary, the pluperfect signals the perception of a *current* state of affairs which is the result of a previous process. As a consequence the past perfect evokes a perceiving consciousness because the completion of the processes described becomes relevant only as a perception of their results (low sun, leaves scattered around). As with the spatial and temporal deictics, the use of such a past perfect points to a specific experiential position from which this process is cognized as both past and completed. From a general outside perspective two past tenses would do equally well: 'The sun sank lower, the islands of cloud gained in density [...] Some petals fell in the garden and lay shell-shaped on the earth.' The effect would, however, be the description of an ongoing process and no longer the perception of the results of such a process now completed and only reconstructed from the changes it has brought about.

When Banfield (1987) discussed this empty deictic centre phenomenon she talked about it in terms of

> [...] sentences with a deictic centre but without any explicit or implicit representation of an observer. Grammatically, such sentences would contain place and time deictics, *here* and *now* or their equivalents; they might also contain demonstratives designating sensibilia. But they would not contain those subjective elements and constructions implying the mental states of a personal subject. These would include embeddable subjective elements such as nouns or adjectives 'of quality' representing a subject's opinions, feelings or thoughts, as well as non-embeddable subjective elements such as exclamations. Nor would such sentences contain any third person pronoun representing a subjectivity or be interpretable, according to its linguistic context, as the perspective of a subject.
> (Banfield 1987: 273)

Banfield describes the quality of subjectivity in the sentences she quotes as dependent on the 'subjective past anchored to a *now*' (ibid.). In contrast to passages of reflective consciousness and represented speech and thought there is no character in the text with whom the deictic centre could be aligned. Banfield therefore speaks of an 'empty centre'.

> The sentences 1–7 [quoted by Banfield on p. 273], centred in an empty *here* and *now*, become then the appropriate linguistic representation of the unobserved, *here* and *now* defining the Russellian perspective, that physical subjectivity which may remain impersonal. *Here* and *now* name a private time and place which need not be occupied by a subject represented by a first or third person pronoun or other syntactically definable subjective elements which must be referred to a subject for interpretation. The deictic system is thus internally divided between those terms which represent the (personal) subject – *I* in speech, *he*, *she*, or a human *they* in the writing of the novel – and those which represent only a subjective centre – the deictic adverbials of time and place. Moreover, it is the personal pronouns which are defined in terms of the spatial and temporal deictics, and not vice-versa; it is *here-now* which is primary and not *I*. Around this empty centre, sensibilia, given a temporal dimension as events, group themselves. Structured by this spatio-temporal

centre, which encloses the space of perception or sensation, like the photographic plate 'frames' a portion of the visible world, they provide, so to speak, its content.

(ibid.: 274–5)

It is patently obvious that Banfield's example sentences – I have above supplied a fuller context for her passages from *The Waves* – coincide with the properties of the 'Tristan' sections noted by Stanzel. (Banfield, however, does not discuss any of the other related phenomena that Stanzel analyses.) The interpretations of this phenomenon according to Banfield and Stanzel are, however, diametrically opposed. Banfield attempts an explanation in terms of which written language (unspeakable sentences) – in an analogy with Barthes's (1981) photographic plate (from his *Camera Lucida*) – can project a consciousnessless deictic centre, a point of deictic observation, from whose perspective the text 'perceives' reality. Stanzel, on the other hand, in connection with the passages from 'Tristan', takes the absence of a character who might qualify for the deictically projected viewpoint as proof that the observed stylistic phenomena must be the narrator's antics. According to Stanzel, the narrator in such passages either identifies with an unspecified observer on the scene (for instance, at the beginning of 'Tristan', where the colloquial idiom suggests such a ploy), or simply himself takes an empathetic observation point on the story level, so that the deictic signals properly 'belong' with the narrator, who by means of transferential deixis (Bühler's *Deixis am Phantasma*)[14] assumes intradiegetic status.

The two interpretations could not be more different. They are both situated within the respective theoretic frameworks of Stanzel and Banfield. Banfield has to adduce some far-fetched philosophical analyses from Bertrand Russell (on egocentric particulars), Gilles Deleuze and Roland Barthes (on photography) to make palatable the concept of an egocentric empty centre in language. Stanzel, on the other hand, is constrained to undermine his useful teller/reflector distinction by having the narrator assume the characteristics of a reflector character or, alternatively, having the reflector character don narratorial garb (see his interpretation of the Father Conmee section from 'Wandering Rocks').[15]

Both solutions have equally important drawbacks. Stanzel has to posit a narrating persona in textual circumstances that do not warrant the existence of a teller figure. In fact his explanation of the Mansfield story relies on the positing of an implied author rather than a narrator in 'his' own right. Moreover, he introduces an additional phenomenon of *transfiguralization* (the narrator manipulates material from the characters' consciousness) which he illustrates as operating in the 'Circe' episode of *Ulysses* and in Thomas Mann's *The Magic Mountain* (Stanzel 1984b: 178–80), and this device likewise transforms the narrator persona from a distinct, embodied teller figure into a construct along the lines of Thomas

Mann's omnipotent 'spirit of narration'.[16] The purely linguistic functions of teller and reflector characters become again completely humanized as the narrator 'takes over' and impersonates reflector characters (reflectorization), or plays with the contents of characters' consciousness (transfiguralization). Such slippage from abstract terms to personalized narrative instances constitutes an ever-present danger as soon as one resorts to the postulation of narrator figures as narratological constructs on the theoretical plane.

Banfield's account is equally inconsistent, but for different reasons and in different respects. When presenting her new type of sentence, she quotes only seven example sentences from *The Waves*, and these are presented entirely out of context. Banfield, by these means, eschews the necessity of taking account of contradictory textual evidence. The passages from *The Waves* that I have quoted above help to sort out some of these misrepresentations. If one takes it for granted that the series of descriptive interludes in *The Waves* all belong to the same genre of text in which an empty deictic centre is posited by the language, there is then, as I have already noted, no explanation for a physical change in the position of this deictic centre. Banfield's metaphoric photographic plate borrowed from Barthes cannot accommodate such a change. If this camera-eye is stationary, it cannot reflect the different changes in its deictic position – from the seashore to the garden to inside the bedroom; if the camera is mobile, then this manipulation is motivated, intentional, the result of agency, and this agency cannot be ascribed to speakerless sentences in and of themselves. Additionally, Banfield fails to consider the occurrences of *perhaps* (see above under [ii]) and of the verb *seem* (under [iii] and [iv]), both of which, in her own model, require the presence of a reflective (not a non-reflective!) consciousness. Moreover, the use of *came* (in [ii] and [iii]) might be regarded as a further index of subjectivity beyond deictic positioning. This latter point is, however, arguable; *come*, like *this* and *that*, *here* and *there*, is frequently used for what Bühler (1934) has termed 'Deixis am Phantasma' (imaginary, or transferential deixis). Whether or not *came* here correlates with the perceptions of a reflective consciousness, it can be concluded that Banfield's 'empty centre' sentences include more features of a subjective nature than she allows for.

I will now introduce the term *figuralization* to describe the evocation of a deictic centre of subjectivity in a reflector-mode narrative that has no ruling figural consciousness attached to it. I use the word *figuralization* because the linguistic signals evoke a perceiver and experiencer, a consciousness (or SELF) on the story level. This figure (hence *figuralization*) operates as a reflector character in the sections from *The Waves*, but it can develop into a teller with speaker functions in its own right. The crucial switching point between the reflector figure and the emergence of a teller is the pronoun *you*. In figuralization, the second-person pronoun *you* occurs frequently and in a variety of applications ('one'; *you* = 'myself'). Examples of the development of such a teller stance are given below in reference to Katherine Mansfield's 'Feuille D'Album' (1917), and I will also briefly return to 'The Garden Party'. As I will argue, the empty centre, if it remains empty, a mere centre of perception, can induce reader identification, allowing a reading of the story through an empathetic projection of the reader into the figure of an observer 'on the scene'. In a sense this is the reflectoral equivalent of camera-eye narrative, and to this extent Banfield's metaphor of the photographic plate has some justification. If at all possible, figuralized narrative will, however, tend to be recuperated along the lines of the story-internal perspective of a bystander, a *vox communis*, and the like. I will trace the construal of this observer position more fully below under 5.3.

5.2.2 Mansfield's 'At the Bay': another case study

Let me now turn to further examples of the empty deictic centre from Katherine Mansfield's 'At the Bay' (1921), i.e. of passages in which no character can be located 'on stage' who might function as an observer or ruling consciousness and where no speaker or narrator position exists either. 'At the Bay' also comprises passages of reflectorization.

'At the Bay' is written in reflector-mode narrative, alternating[17] between the perspectives of Stanley Burnell, his wife Linda, his sister-in-law Beryl and other characters (the children, the maid Alice). Besides the dialogue, a fair amount of the story consists of free indirect discourse and narrated perception heavily tinged with the idiom of the current reflector character:

> And his [Pip's] hand opened; he held up to the light something that *flashed*, that *winked*, that was a most lovely green.
> 'It's a nemeral,' said Pip solemnly.
> 'Is it really, Pip?' *Even* Isabel was impressed.
> The *lovely green thing seemed* to dance in Pip's fingers. *Aunt* Beryl had a *nemeral* in a ring, but it was a very small one. This one was as big as a star and far more beautiful.
> (Mansfield 1984: 449)

I have highlighted the phrases that lexically signal the vocabulary of the children. The perspective appears to be located with Kezia and/or Lottie, since the locution 'even Isabel' suggests this is the younger girls' perspective on the older Isabel. Note also the adoption of 'nemeral' by the reflector character's free indirect discourse.[18] Throughout the story the attribution of perspective remains unclear with regard to the children. There are not sufficient textual clues to provide an unequivocal identification of the reflector as Kezia. It is true that in some parts of the story Kezia definitely functions as a reflector character (e.g. in section 3, p. 445, and in section 7). On the other hand, there are several passages that –

in the manner of the beginning of 'The Garden Party'[19] – appear to render the perspective of a collectivity, of all of the children. See, for instance, the paragraph about the Samuel Josephs (section 4, p. 448), or section 9, where the children are 'transformed' into animals in the inquit tags.

'At the Bay' is no simple case of (variable) reflectoral narrative, however. The story additionally has examples of *reflectorization* when the 'narrator' (using Stanzel's locutions for the moment) assumes a collective story-internal perspective, for instance in the women's views about Mrs Kember. This parallels Stanzel's example passage from 'The Garden Party' discussed earlier where we got the Sheridans' views about the poor and about Laura's 'extravagance'. The fact that the opinions voiced about Mrs Kember are collective gossip emerges towards the end of the passage ('Here the voices were always raised'), and we then shift into communal invented direct discourse. Note also the anticipatory free indirect discourse ('It was an absolute scandal!'):

> The women at the Bay thought she was very, very fast. Her lack of vanity, her slang, the way she treated men as though she was one of them, and the fact that she didn't care twopence about her house and called the servant Gladys 'Glad-eyes,' was disgraceful. Standing on the veranda steps Mrs. Kember would call in her indifferent, tired voice, 'I say, Glad-eyes, you might heave me a handkerchief if I've got one, will you?' And Glad-eyes, a red bow in her hair instead of a cap, and white shoes, came running with an impudent smile. ***It was an absolute scandal! True, she had no children, and her husband.* . . .** Here the voices were always raised; they became fervent. How can he have married her? How can he, how can he? It must have been money, of course, but even then!
>
> (ibid.: 450)

The most notable parts of 'At the Bay', however, are the descriptive passages[20] which – like the vignettes from *The Waves* – introduce an intradiegetic deictic viewpoint, one that is clearly evocative of a reflective consciousness although no character is 'on stage'. Section 1 is entirely taken up by this perspective. The shepherd – the only character on the scene – cannot function as the reflective consciousness because the narrative actually focuses *on* him: 'He was a grave, fine-looking old man' (ibid.: 442).

> ***There ahead*** was stretched the sandy road with shallow puddles, the same soaking bushes ***showed*** on either side and the same shadowy palings. Then ***something*** immense ***came into view***; an enormous shock-haired ***giant*** with his arms stretched out. It was the big gum-tree outside Mrs. Stubb's shop, and as they [shepherd and flock] passed by there was a strong whiff of eucalyptus. And ***now*** big spots of light ***gleamed*** in the mist. The shepherd stopped whistling; he rubbed his red nose

and wet beard on his wet sleeve and, screwing up his eyes, glanced in the direction of the sea. The sun *was rising*. It was *marvellous* how quickly the mist thinned, sped away, dissolved from the shallow plain, rolled up from the bush and was gone as if in a hurry to escape; big twists and curls jostled and shouldered each other as the silvery beams broadened. The far-away sky – a bright, pure blue – was reflected in the puddles, and the drops, swimming along the telegraph wires, flashed into points of light. *Now* the leaping, glittering sea was so bright it *made one's eyes ache to look at it*. The shepherd drew a pipe, the bowl as small as an acorn, out of his breast pocket, fumbled for a chunk of speckled tobacco, pared off a few shavings and stuffed the bowl. *He was a grave, fine-looking old man.* As he lit up and the blue smoke wreathed his head, the dog, watching, *looked* proud of him.

(ibid.: 442)

The text of section 1 is saturated with consciousness signals: character-deixis (*at the back; beyond; there ahead*); *come* and *appear* as indices of text-internal perception; *seem* and *look* to indicate a figural subjectivity; *something* to mark the perceiver's inability to recognize the perceived object; subjective evaluative lexis (*giant*, for a tree; *marvellous*; the *darling little woolly lambs*); temporal indicators of figural perception ('The sun was not yet risen'; 'The sun was rising'; 'now they had passed'); signals of actual perception ('out of sight', 'you could not see'); and – finally – even free indirect discourse ('rippling – how far?') and an address-pronoun:

It *looked* as though the sea had beaten up softly in the darkness, as though one immense wave had *come* rippling, rippling – *how far? Perhaps* if *you* had waked up in the middle of the night *you* might have seen a big fish flicking in at the window and gone again.

(ibid.: 441)

In this fantasia of section 1 the cat Florrie can talk(!),[21] and the dog in response 'saw, and thought her a silly young female' (ibid.: 443).[22] The perspective that permeates section 1 is deictically located inside the area taken up by the summer colony of bungalows. The deixis suggests that one perceives the shepherd appear on the horizon moving *towards* the colony and then sees him disappear again as he herds his sheep all the way through and out of the 'village'.

Round the corner of Crescent Bay, between the piled-up masses of broken rock, a flock of sheep *came* pattering.

(ibid.: 441)

Then pushing, nudging, hurrying, the sheep rounded the bend and the shepherd followed after *out of sight.*

(ibid.: 443)

Reflectorization and figuralization 201

Yet, within the boundaries of the summer colony, the perspective follows the shepherd and his flock,[23] for instance in the passage cited above where the tree outside Mrs Stubbs's shop looms into view. At this point the sun is described as rising, and – just as one had hoped to align these perceptions with the shepherd – he is described from an external perspective. Nor can one necessarily align the perspective with the children's impressions, or only in places where the idiom invokes a childlike naïvety. (The *giant* and the acorn-like bowl of the pipe perhaps suggest such an alignment.)

I will therefore, preliminarily, speak of an evocation of story-internal consciousness – much on the lines of Banfield's empty centre – but depart from both Stanzel and Banfield in positing that this technique is meant to evoke *not* the narrator's perceiving consciousness – the story has no narrator figure at all, at best an implied author who is responsible for the textual arrangements – but *the reader's*. Just as, in figural narrative, the reader is invited to see the fictional world through the eyes of a reflector character, in the present text the reader also reads through a text-internal consciousness, but since no character is available to whom one could attribute such consciousness, the reader directly identifies with a story-internal position. This text-internal reader position, naturally, is a *projection* into the empty deictic centre. Mansfield's use of the pronoun *you* is therefore doubly appropriate: as a possible signal of free indirect discourse[24] and as an inducement to reader empathy, banking on the *you*'s quality of address. In contrast to the putative impersonality of Banfield's empty centre I would therefore argue for a model of the reading process in which the reader takes an internal position with regard to the represented events, as if she were a witness rather than a mere camera eye. I will return to the important theoretical implications of this explanation which tie in with the proposed redefinition of narrativity in terms of experiential parameters.

5.2.3 Reflectorization and figuralization contrasted

After this analysis of 'At the Bay' it is worth returning briefly to the very beginning of 'The Garden Party', where one can observe the same technique of figuralization.

> And after all the weather was ideal. They could not have had a more perfect day for a garden-party if they had ordered it. Windless, warm, the sky without a cloud. Only the blue was veiled with a haze of light gold, as it is sometimes in early summer. The gardener had been up since dawn, mowing the lawns and sweeping them, until the grass and the dark flat rosettes where the daisy plants had been seemed to shine. As for the roses, **you** could not help *feeling* they understood that roses are the only flowers that impress people at garden parties; the only flowers that everybody is certain of knowing. Hundreds, yes, literally

hundreds, had come out in a single night; the green bushes bowed down as though they had been visited by archangels.

(Mansfield 1984: 487)

Like the opening of 'At the Bay' this contains a description from a story-internal perspective. However, this time the language additionally projects a prominent linguistic subjectivity, as witnessed by the large number of intensifiers and syntactic structures indicative of a figural consciousness.[25] Most of the passage can in fact be analysed as free indirect discourse or narrated perception. Thus, the initial two sentences are clearly free indirect discourse, with 'after all' pointing to a consciousness whose musings *in actu* the story opening intrudes upon. In the second sentence the figural perspective is given away by the idiomatic expression 'if they had ordered it'. There is no definite allocation of viewpoint except to the Sheridans, who are the organizers of the party, but since Laura later surfaces as the main reflector character one cannot exclude the possibility that this might also be read as already pertaining to Laura's childish perspective.

This situation is very different from the later passage of reflectorization quoted by Stanzel which we discussed in 5.1.1. In 'At the Bay', of course, there is no irony at all and one can therefore easily avoid the necessity of an imposed narratorial level, benefiting from the practice of Occam's razor. The major difference between reflectorization and figuralization therefore lies in the narratorial and (implicitly) dissonant tone of the former and the reflectoral and empathetic style of the latter. Both techniques employ free indirect discourse or expressive style to designate a specific viewpoint. In the case of figuralization that viewpoint cannot be aligned with a character on the story level, whereas in the case of reflectorization either there is a particular character available who is indeed the topic of the passage (Mrs Glegg, Tito) or the viewpoint relates to a complex of attitudes that may not be attributable to any one specific person but are characteristic of a fairly well-defined group of characters (the Sheridans). A final, third, crucial difference between figuralization and reflectorization therefore lies in the evocation of fictional personae. Figuralization renders perspectivizations of story matter that – within the reflectoral mode of narration – remain divorced from a specific focalizer; reflectorization, on the other hand, on account of the authorial mode of presentation, thematizes a clash between authorial language and a definite character's (or a group of characters') outlook and perspective.

The most important characteristic of figuralization seems to lie in the absence of a suitable character 'on stage'. A figure (who can be a speaker) is created, projected from the voice. The voice can be marked deictically, lexically and syntactically, as the case may be, but its recuperation as a story-*internal* SELF depends on semantic and story-schematic macro-textual features. This is definitely not what happens in *Romola* or *The Mill on the Floss*. Here we have a character well in place, and the reflectorized passages relate to this character. The original definition of reflectorization, i.e. the 'assumption by the authorial narrator of the features of a reflector character', does not seem to describe this phenomenon quite adequately. The clue to the question seems to lie instead with the problematics of irony. Irony is constitutive in these two texts – if there were no irony, there would not be a problem. Because there is an incompatibility with the trustworthy narrator figure of *The Mill on the Floss*, we know that the remarks must be tongue in cheek, must be similar to Mrs Glegg's own opinions of herself; because Romola's sense of honour is fundamental to *Romola*'s evaluative messages, Tito Melema's rationalizations must be seen as contravening these ethical precepts. The narrative echoes these opinions ironically – and it can echo them because these characters are plot existents. In the case of figuralization, no equivalent plot existent is on stage. Note also that *all* passages of reflectorization are passages about *habitual* thoughts and opinions, never about specific thought acts performed at a given point in the plot. This habituality is indeed one additional index of the external viewpoint afforded by passages of reflectorization, since the awareness of habituality always requires an external viewpoint of evaluation, a distancing from immediate experience. Note also that passages of reflectorization never deal with habitual *actions*. Even in 'Weekend', where one gets (at least initially) a presentation of the customary weekend Martha regularly has to 'undergo', the habitual turns into the specific with the visit of Martin's friends (still possibly a recurring experience) and, unambiguously, with the details of the dishes planned by Martha, and, at the very end, with the onset of Jenny's period. Passages of reflectorization in 'Weekend' never describe the initially habitual *actions* but only Martha's experiences and her opinions about her own happiness and good luck.

What is important to me here is the *mechanics* of such 'explanations'. Making sense of passages of this sort involves an arbitration between mimetic parameters (Is X likely to have thought something on those lines? – a question that, for instance, rules out the children as an observing reflectoral consciousness for section 1 of 'At the Bay') and the inevitable anthropomorphization of an observable deictic centre: is it the narrator or a character that is responsible for this discourse? The rationale of readerly interpretative strategies therefore depends heavily on the imposition of realist frames, on evoking an illusion of a fictional setting, and it naturalizes subjective data as relating to a narrator or character persona. It is no coincidence that reflectorization tends to collocate with the character's opinions and mindset, and that all the examples that I have quoted are clearly dissonant ones, with an implication of criticism in the frame of the text's values as a whole – something that is usually discussed in terms of the 'implied author' position.[26] Figuralization, on the other hand, is consonant in principle, there being no dissenting authorial position from which distancing might take its origin. Figuralization hence also tends to collocate with *perception*, with an observer position in the text, and acquires opinions only when there also emerges a strong evaluative stance, and ultimately a *you*. Perception and consciousness related to perception are therefore crucial issues. Of course, the terms focalization and point of view – the stock-in-trade of narratology – have always played a central role in the analysis of narrative. Nevertheless, the rationale for the perceptional metaphor in the discussion of point of view requires more extensive rethinking.

The major issue here is embodiment, or, rather, the lack thereof. As soon as no specific characters exist on the scene and one does not have to fall back on their specific thought acts or observation acts, one enters into a quite uncharted narratological no-man's-land in which traditional categories no longer work. In passages of reflectorization the story vs. discourse distinction is undermined in the sense that the discourse ceases to be attributable to either of the two levels exclusively: narrator personae and characters become merely implicit or potential sources of discourse, nor can these personifications simply be discarded on the model of 'objective' unspeakable sentences of the Banfieldian type, since expressivity and subjectivity are in fact rampant in such contexts. Figuralization and reflectorization therefore provide an excellent stepping stone (a double missing link that has never been missed) towards the even crasser experiments in postmodernist fiction, where the levels of story and discourse are dissolved and intertwined to an even more radical extent.

Reflectorization and figuralization become assimilated one to the other linguistically when the text starts to employ the generic second-person pronoun. At this intersection of expressivity teller and reflector-mode merge (Fludernik 1993a: 391–4). At the beginning of Mansfield's story 'Feuille D'Album' there is quite a prominent teller figure:

> He really was an impossible person. Too shy altogether. With absolutely nothing to say for himself. And such a weight. Once he was in *your* studio he never knew when to go, but would sit on and on until *you* nearly screamed, and burned to throw something enormous after him when he did finally blush his way out – something like the tortoise stove. The strange thing was that at first sight he looked most interesting. Everybody agreed about that. *You* would drift into the café one evening and there *you* would see, sitting in a corner, with a glass of coffee in front of him, a thin, dark boy, wearing a blue jersey with a little grey flannel jacket buttoned over it. And somehow that blue jersey and the grey jacket with the sleeves that were too short gave him the air of a boy that has made up his mind to run away to sea. Who has run away, in fact, and will get up in a moment and sling a knotted handkerchief containing his nightshirt and his mother's picture on the end of a stick, and walk out into the night and be drowned.... Stumble over the wharf edge on his way to the ship, even.... He had

black close-cropped hair, grey eyes with long lashes, white cheeks and a mouth pouting as though he were determined not to cry. ... How could *one* resist him? Oh, *one's* heart was wrung at sight. And, as if that were not enough, there was his trick of blushing. ... Whenever the waiter came near him he turned crimson – he might have been just out of prison and the waiter in the know. ...

(Mansfield 1984: 266–7)

'Feuille D'Album' then goes on to describe Ian French's (the 'boy's') love for the girl in the house across from his studio. It never returns to the concerns of the voice portrayed in the opening paragraphs. The initial passage mimes the perspective of a woman artist in Paris, but this does not refer to any specific character in the story (and certainly does not establish any first-person narrator, not even a narrator as witness). The text instead implies the narrator's appropriation of such women's (or such a woman's) opinions with regard to Ian. This viewpoint is corrected later on when the narrator discloses what Ian was really up to, providing an omniscient counterfoil to the initial voice of the engaging woman artist and her evocations of the naïve, harmless 'boy'. As in 'The Garden Party', the reader is thrown into the story rather than receiving any external information on the painter at the outset.

In the above we have again and again observed the emergence of *you* in passages of the empty deictic centre where it both enhances an internal perspective and potentially introduces a speaker function. The initial passage from 'Feuille D'Album' is noteworthy particularly for its insistent use of *you* and, later, *one* (which I have highlighted). This *you* here has an all-purpose function both of drawing the reader (*qua* narratee) into the story and of conveying the evaluative perspective of the woman painter, an internal perspective that can be read as both collective and individual. Taken out of context, separated from the central part of the story (which has a more prominent [authorial] narrator figure), this initial paragraph reads like a tirade, reads, that is, as *skaz* narration, as simulated oral discourse, and it leads the reader to expect that the narrator ultimately will turn out to be a first-person narrator. That, however, as we have seen, is precisely what does *not* happen.

Such a *you* can become even more problematic in texts where a character is 'on stage' but where there is also a competing narrative voice. Attribution of this discourse to a speaker (is somebody uttering something, thinking something?) or of the deictic centre to a character, then, frequently cannot be resolved on the basis of 'the story' or on the lines of verisimilar utterance or thought. (I have discussed a passage of this nature in Fludernik 1993a: 392–3.) In *Jacob's Room* Virginia Woolf has the narrator assume the expressive perspective of a young man about Athens and at the same time involves the narratee in the discourse by repeated allocutive use of *we* and *one*. The young man's experience of

Athens is thereby explicitly linked to anybody's, and therefore the implied reader's experience of Athens, and the recurrent mention of 'a young man' also hints that this typical experience must be Jacob's as well.

> Athens is still quite capable of striking *a young man* as the oddest combination, the most incongruous assortment. Now it is suburban; now immortal. [...] No form can *he* set on his sensations as *he strolls, one blazing afternoon*, along the Parisian boulevard and skips out of the way of the royal landau [...] and all the time the Acropolis surges into the air, raises itself above the town, like a large immobile wave with the yellow columns of the Parthenon firmly planted upon it. [...]
>
> *There they are* again, the pillars, the pediment, the Temple of Victory and the Erechtheum, set on a tawny rock cleft with shadows, directly *you* unlatch *your* shutters in the morning and, leaning out, hear the clatter, the clamour, the whip cracking in the street below. *There they are*.
>
> The extreme definiteness with which they stand, now a brilliant white, again yellow, and in some lights red, imposes ideas of durability, of the emergence through the earth of some spiritual energy elsewhere dissipated in elegant trifles. But this durability exists quite independently of *our* admiration. Although the beauty is sufficiently humane to weaken *us*, to stir the deep deposit of mud – memories, abandonments, regrets, sentimental devotions – the Parthenon is separate from all that; and if *you* consider how it has stood out all night, for centuries, *you* begin to connect the blaze (at midday the glare is dazzling and the frieze almost invisible) with the idea that *perhaps* it is beauty alone that is immortal.
>
> (*Jacob's Room*, xii; Woolf 1976: 146–8)

The narrative manages to erase definitive referential attributions and to merge narrator and reflector, character and addressee levels, as well as rendering the distinction between reflectorization and figuralization null and void.

Empty deictic centres and passages of figuralization can be considered 'empty' also because there are alternatives of attribution which remain irresolvable on a mimetic reading. For the moment I would like to note that the original distinction between reflectorization (clear authorial context) and figuralization (reflector-mode narrative without a reflector character) is liable to get deconstructed at those points of figuralized texts where a second-person pronoun surfaces in a clearly conative and gnomic function, with the result that such passages then appear to operate much on the lines of reflectorized texts, only without the possibility of verisimilar attribution of the discourse or deictic centre to a specific character. Had Jacob's figure become more prominent, we would again have had to talk of reflectorization. The prominent authorial voice here functions to create a story-internal focalization, drawing the explicitly ambiguous *you* into a position within the fictional world. The distinction between reflectorization and figuralization therefore ultimately does *not* lie in the presence or absence of a narrator figure alone, nor in the availability or non-availability of a reflector character either. On the contrary, these two coordinates combine to produce two types of paradoxical sites. On the one hand one gets the merging of a prominent narratorial perspective with the description of a specific character's outlook (reflectorization); on the other the merging of apparently unanchored deictic expressivity (which cannot be aligned to a narrator or a character) with a speaker position. In the latter case this speaker position then projects a narratorial voice or a figural perspective, or both – as in *Jacob's Room*.

Before attempting to provide some guidelines on how 'natural' narratology could deal with passages of the kind that we have just looked at, I would like to include in the discussion two further related phenomena which will round off this presentation of the possibilities of narrator–reflector interaction and the evocation of consciousness by means of a linguistic deictic centre (5.3.1 and 5.3.2). In 5.3.3 I will also consider *consonant* varieties of reflectorization – an approach which, as I will argue, may help to solve some of the conundra linked with Henry James's narrative art.

5.3 OBSERVERS, NARRATORS AND REFLECTORS

5.3.1 The anonymous witness position

In Chapter 48 ('Closing In') of *Bleak House* one comes across the following passage.[27]

(i) A fine night, and a bright large moon, and multitudes of stars. Mr. Tulkinghorn, in repairing to his cellar, and in opening and shutting those resounding doors, has to cross a little prison-like yard. He looks up casually, thinking what a fine night, what a bright large moon, what multitudes of stars! A quiet night, too.
[...]
(ii) What's that? Who fired a gun or pistol? Where was it?
(iii) The few foot-passengers start, stop, and stare about them. Some windows and doors are opened, and people come out to look. It was a loud report, and echoed and rattled heavily. It shook one house, or so a man says who was passing. It has aroused all the dogs in the neighbourhood, who bark vehemently. Terrified cats scamper across the road. While the dogs are yet barking and howling – there is one dog howling like a demon – the church-clocks, as if they were startled too, begin to strike. The hum from the streets, likewise, seems to swell into a shout. But it is soon over. Before the last clock begins to strike ten, there is a lull. When it has ceased, the fine night, the bright large moon, and multitudes of stars, are left in peace again.

(iv) Has Mr Tulkinghorn been disturbed? His windows are dark and quiet, and his door is shut. It must be something unusual indeed, to bring him out of his shell. Nothing is heard of him, nothing is seen of him. What power of cannon might it take to shake that rusty old man out of his immovable composure?

(*Bleak House*, xlviii; Dickens 1962: 663-4)

I will concentrate on two paragraphs[28] ('What's that?' [ii] and 'Has Mr Tulkinghorn been disturbed?' [iv]) but have also quoted the larger context to illustrate how the image of the quiet night is extended exhaustively in synonymic and metonymic fashion and how it is eventually superseded by its opposite in the series of exaggerations about the effects of the gunshot breaking in on that peaceful silence. That sudden change from an excess of quietude to pandemonium iconically represents the subjectivity of an experiencer, somebody lulled into a treacherous feeling of safety and then unexpectedly overwhelmed by the sudden explosion around him.

In what way do paragraphs (ii) and (iv) relate to the issue of reflectorization? The two passages – (ii) more clearly than (iv) – echo what passers-by might have exclaimed when hearing the shot. This interpretation is corroborated by (iii), which mentions 'foot-passengers' stopping in their tracks. Now although (ii) seems to echo pedestrians' exclamations, the wording cannot be a verbatim quote: 'Who fired a gun or pistol?' must be a condensation of several similar exclamations. As with the views put into the mouth of 'the Sheridans' (and presented in free indirect discourse), we here encounter a babble of voices condensed into three sentences of direct speech. In Fludernik (1993a: Chapter 8) I have illustrated the qualities of schematization and typification operative in free indirect discourse, pointing out how one frequently encounters contractions of several utterances of the same kind into one condensed and highly stylized passage of free indirect discourse. In the same place I also argued that even supposedly verbatim renderings of *direct* discourse are in fact highly stylized and potentially condensed forms of invented discourse, an analysis corroborated by recent findings of discourse analysis with regard to conversational storytelling (Tannen 1989). From this perspective, it is then no unwarranted conclusion to identify paragraph (ii) as an instance of typified direct discourse, as an evocation of minor characters' exclamations voiced on the scene of the crime.[29] Note also the schematic handling of interior monologue in (i) where Tulkinghorn's directly quoted thoughts ('A quiet night, too') give rise to a long paragraph (the one I have elided) that repeats these key phrases in subtle variation. Mr Tulkinghorn may not have uttered anything at all – it is well within the narrator's privileges to impute such words to Tulkinghorn in order to evoke his mute perceptions or thoughts.

The power of the authorial narrator is even more conspicuous in (iv). Although the direct question opening the paragraph and the sentence following it can be read as the speculations (and perceptions) of a passer-by, the clearly authorial idiom in the rest of the paragraph ('power of cannon', 'immovable', and – earlier – the odd 'bring him out of his shell') soon displaces the projected figure of an observer or passer-by, suggesting instead a reinterpretation along the lines of a series of rhetorical questions, or, more precisely, of reflectorization. These musings and inferences *about* Tulkinghorn are somewhat at odds with the narrative's presentation of Tulkinghorn earlier in the novel, where this character gives the impression of being an icy, implacable figure. The image of the mollusc in this passage and the attribution of rustiness to the lawyer here strike a note of naïvety, belittlement or harmlessness ('rusty old man') and are very much at odds with his known energetic disposition to ferret out secrets. Even 'immovable composure' seems a much too positive characterization of Tulkinghorn's unfeeling placidity and uncanny powers of self-control, which serve to mask his callous insensitivity. The paragraph indeed reverts to the false harmony and peacefulness encountered in the paragraphs before the shot is overheard, projecting a vignette of an uninitiated observer's speculations which appear to be designed to enhance the mystery and suspense at this juncture of the plot.

The whole passage, of course, counteracts such a pretense at ignorance since the suspense element inevitably leads one to expect a (re)solution of the puzzle. Like novelistic speculations about what *might have* happened (Riffaterre 1990: 29–33)[30] such protestations of ignorance serve two functions: on the one hand they expose the fictionality of the tale while, on the other, they reassert verisimilitude on the sly by introducing items of mimetic specificity. Mimetic recuperation is here effected through the evocation of an on-the-scene witness, whose bewilderment at the sound of the shot, like his speculations about Mr Tulkinghorn, sidetrack from the narrator's responsibilities of providing reliable information and evoke a verisimilar description of story-internal puzzlement. The reader, at this point, is not fooled as to the probable murder of Mr Tulkinghorn: after all, narrative significance, the building up of suspense, all these clamour for the shot to have been fired at him, or – possibly – *by* him in self-defence. However, the reader is just as frantically casting about for the possible identity of the murderer as the stander-by below Tulkinghorn's windows is casting about for explanations for the shot. At this very point in the story the reader is particularly tortured by suspense because the narrative has already suggested as a plausible murderer somebody with whom the reader has become involved empathetically: Lady Dedlock. In the final paragraph of Chapter 47, i.e. the paragraph preceding (i) above, we hear of Lady Dedlock taking a nocturnal walk in the garden in possession of the key that will allow her to slip away unobserved and, combining opportunity with her known motives of passion and despair (both applying to the relation between Tulkinghorn and her), enable her to do the deed.[31] The reader therefore cannot but make the inferences which the narrative slyly sets out to evoke. Not only does the narrative therefore craftily labour to suggest a hidden significance for this highlighted moment of the plot, spinning an elaborate poetic metaphor of quietude, pretending ignorance, heightening suspense: the reader is additionally fooled into misreading the clues (expecting and dreading to discover Lady Dedlock to be the murderer). It is only at the point when Detective Bucket manages to solve the murder case in Chapter liv ('Springing a Mine') that the reader is finally undeceived.

I turn now to paragraph (iii), which is remarkable in its descriptions of the effects of the shot. In the first few sentences these are harmless enough. Then we get 'a man's' report that is clearly exaggerated. Is this just the narrator's exaggeration, largely stylistic? Or are these rumours about the event on the streets, typically distorting the observable into the fantasized and portentous? Let us, preliminarily and simplistically, describe this stylistic ploy as the narrator's assumption of the superstitious mindset of the passers-by. If this is so, what we have here is a further instance of reflectorization. (It is reflectorization rather than figuralization on account of the authorial frame of the novel.) All the phenomena in this passage from *Bleak House* rely on an explicit or implicit miming of story-internal perspectives, either individual or collective. Some locutions suggest that there is some appropriation of figural idiom by the narrative (Fludernik 1993a: Chapter 6), for instance in '*those* resounding doors' in [i]. Whereas in (i) we seem to get an inside view of Tulkinghorn's mind – which before this chapter was resolutely and intriguingly closed to the reader – in paragraphs (ii) to (iv) the authorial narrator is clearly implicated, even though in (ii) more immediate miming of a story-internal position seems to be rendered.

In the above example passage one can therefore observe with great facility how the miming of an observer's position constitutes a mode of interaction between reflectoral and authorial readings. Verisimilitude, of both a linguistic and thematic kind, regulates what one reads into such passages. Thus it is the content of the questions that suggests this to be by-standers' words 'actually' uttered, even if in a less condensed shape, whereas several of the stylistic features and the speculation about Tulkinghorn's mindset imply an external and omniscient origin of the discourse. One can therefore observe how the line between the appropriation of figural idiom and its (verisimilarly illicit) extension into non-reflectoral regions becomes blurred. The observer position is the crucial (key) position which helps to mediate the transition from the reflectoral to the authorial realm and also – as we saw in the previous section – the position which emerges from the analysis of reflectoral passages without an available reflectoral character. The phenomena I have been presenting can be grouped around the observer position, which can be shown to serve as a passageway from narrator to character and vice versa. Moreover, this (harmless) observer

Reflectorization and figuralization 211

position itself can give rise to reflectorization if it develops towards a narrator position (adding a number of 'speaker' signals), and it can also initiate the reflectoral mode when developing into free indirect discourse.

5.3.2 Embodiment, *skaz*, unreliability: cognitive parameters reintroduced

I now turn to yet another example, this time a case of radical unreliability, to document the drawbacks of the traditional models and the reasons for their failure. The text is Thomas Mann's 'Death in Venice' (1912).

Cohn (1983) has perceptively suggested that the narrator of Mann's novella is an unreliable narrator since he blames Aschenbach when we as readers are – on the basis of his experiences rendered figurally – sympathetic to his motives, thoughts and feelings.[32] This discrepancy is even more visible at the very beginning of the tale, I feel, where the narrator praises Aschenbach in heavy-handed encomiums that, to a reader alert to their ironic potential, implies the distinctly ridiculous nature of Aschenbach's notorious self-sacrifice to Art. The narrator indeed adopts the voice of pompous morality that lauds art as long as it can be safely contained in its useful function of inculcating ethical precepts (such as duty) and can be controlled and manipulated through its status as a masterpiece. When Aschenbach strays from the path of reason and moderation – the all-time favourite of pedestrian art criticism that deals in the 'classic' – the narrator's sympathies wane rapidly, turning to harsh moral condemnation of the artist.

I will briefly discuss one passage in the earlier sections of the novella, in which the unreliability of this narrator – particularly his *laudatio* of Aschenbach's moral pre-eminence – comes across as the implied author's implicit criticism of Aschenbach's art. An ironic inconsistency is hinted as existing between, on the one hand, the praise of Aschenbach as the public figure representing discipline and *Tugend* (dutiful and measured self-restraint) and, on the other, Aschenbach's lack of real-life experience and hence of the playful, emotional and Dionysian qualities of art. This contradiction is thematized throughout the novella – in Aschenbach's own recognition that his mastery (as strict as the self-discipline that produced it) holds no pleasure for him (i; Mann 1989: 13/1936: 7) and, not least, in his musings about the connection between beauty and the 'abyss' ('Abgrund') of passion (v; 1989: 95/1936: 72). Aschenbach has been fleeing the beast in the jungle (repressed sexuality) all his life, and as his health wanes, the dangerous temptations of life increasingly assert themselves: the image of the tiger that both terrifies him and fills him with mysterious cravings ('fühlte sein Herz pochen vor Entsetzen und rätselhaftem Verlangen' – i; 1989: 10)[33] is closely linked to the later Dionysian nightmare (v; 1989: 88–90/1936: 67–8), and it is ironically juxtaposed with Aschenbach's 'courage', apostrophized earlier, which he requires for his morning's writing session: 'überreizt von der schwierigen und gefährlichen, eben jetzt eine höchste Behutsamkeit, Umsicht, Eindringlichkeit und Genauigkeit des Willens erfordernden Arbeit' (i; 1989: 7).[34] The narrator in the early parts of the novella is unreliable, *not* because he misrepresents Aschenbach's mental constitution, but because he fully and flatteringly endorses the repressive masochistic sham of the 'highest manly virtue' of proud suffering by the weak and the ugly (ii; 1989: 17–18/1936: 11–12). Although this narrator preserves a distance from his renowned subject (most clearly in the 'literary history' style of section ii), he identifies with Aschenbach's public role of the State educator, a role that Aschenbach himself comes to recognize for the sham it is in Chapter v (1989: 94–5/1936: 72); there he, in explicitly Socratic mode, denounces the artistic self-image of 'famous and honourable achievement', uncovering it as a lie and a travesty of real art. The narrator, in his insistent flattery, unwittingly suggests even deeper levels of irony:

> Gustav Aschenbach war der Dichter all derer, die am Rande der Erschöpfung arbeiten, der Überbürdeten, schon Aufgeriebenen, sich noch Aufrechterhaltenden, all dieser Moralisten der Leistung, die, schmächtig von Wuchs und spröde von Mitteln, durch Willensverzückung und kluge Verwaltung sich wenigstens eine Zeitlang die Wirkungen der Größe abgewinnen. Ihrer sind viele, sie sind die Helden des Zeitalters. Und sie alle erkannten sich wieder in seinem Werk, sie fanden sich bestätigt, erhoben, besungen darin, sie wußten ihm Dank, sie verkündeten seinen Namen.
>
> (ii; 1989: 18)[35]

This comes at the tail end of a long enthusiastic paragraph on Aschenbach's obsession with the figure of Saint Sebastian, of the 'heroism born of weakness' (ii; 1936: 12),[36] as the narrator calls it. Yet these words (which are ostensibly acclamatory) hint at a truer, subversive picture of Aschenbach's worship of courageous suffering. There is some inherent self-contradiction in 'Moralisten der Leistung', as if morality were dependent on will and achievement. Even more clearly, 'spröde von Mitteln' together with 'Willensverzückung' reveals the emptiness of the enthusiasm that Aschenbach's readers (and heroes?) apparently experience, with 'spröde' (ostensibly a synonym of sparsity) implying sexual prudery, an idea that likewise seems to attach to 'enthusiasm of the will' – *Verzückung* after all, like *spröde*, has clearly sexual connotations. The climax of irony comes with 'Wirkungen der Größe', which might translate as 'effects (or semblances) of greatness'. The locution not only unmasks the inanity and shallowness of Aschenbach's admirers but also helps to throw some insidious doubt on the greatness of Aschenbach himself. Aschenbach, the poet-hero, of frail health and delicate nerves, has pre-eminence thrust upon him in direct consequence of his popularity with the weak of his generation.[37]

Irony is a constitutive feature of this passage. The narrator assumes a mask, that of the gullible literary critic, and this mask is undermined, not because the narrator is untrustworthy – at the beginning of the tale Aschenbach's view of himself, though false (he is not a great artist), is quite in agreement with the narrator's eulogy of him – but because the exaggerated tone of praise and the almost oxymoronic inconsistencies in the narrator's encomium allow one to perceive his presentation to be inadequate. Only later in the text does the narrator become recognizably unreliable, namely when starting to indulge in the recriminatory labelling of his 'fallen' hero. In the earlier passages of unremitting praise the narrator's unreliability is still veiled, and it also seems to be aligned with a position of *communis opinio*. I therefore wonder whether this unreliability should not be interpreted as one more example of reflectorization. The narrator throughout continues unaware of the artistically positive aspects of what he persists in terming the 'Abgrund' ('abyss'). The irony must therefore lie with the text as a whole, with the notorious *implied author* of the novella. The limitations of the narrator figure are disclosed by the figural passages of the tale. The narrator's heavily incriminating discourse, on the other hand, like his earlier epideictic enthusiasmoi, projects a moralistic *communis opinio* that belongs with a certain *stance* rather than an individual's personal attitude. The difference between unreliability and reflectorization of the deadpan variety is therefore, one can contend, a gradual one. Only first-person narrators can be properly unreliable. Authorial narrators, when untrustworthy, acquire a personalized status that puts them in the same category with projected observer positions or reflectorized teller figures of the kind we have been looking at.

5.3.3 Consonant reflectorization

A very special case of reflectorization – one that is *consonant* – also exists, and it is particularly prominent in the work of Henry James. James's style constitutes one of the supreme puzzles of narrative theory. In his novels the narrator's and the characters' language and point of view are inextricably intertwined. Although James's language is frequently treated as the typical example of a marked split between 'who tells' and 'who sees', this categorization, as I will show, does not adequately render the characteristics of Jamesian prose, whose treatment of the voice factor is much more complex and much more sophisticated. I will argue that James is the consonant equivalent of reflectorization. James's irony, of which we get a generous deal, does not necessarily go against the reflector character (the notorious 'centre of consciousness'). On the contrary; in many passages the irony is directed against the reflector character's environment, against the *other* characters, whose motivations emerge between the lines through the (uncomprehending) eyes of the reflector figure.

214 *Reflectorization and figuralization*

Here is a passage from *What Maisie Knew*:[38]

> It was on account of these things that **mamma** got her for such low pay, really for nothing: so much, one day when Mrs Wix had accompanied her into the drawing-room and left her, **the child** heard one of the ladies she found there – a lady with eyebrows arched like skipping-ropes and thick black stitching, like ruled lines for musical notes, on beautiful white gloves – announce to another. She **knew** governesses were poor; Miss Overmore was unmentionably and Mrs Wix ever so publicly so. Neither this, however, nor the old brown frock nor the diadem nor the button, made a difference for Maisie in the charm put forth through everything, the charm of Mrs Wix's conveying that somehow, in her ugliness and her poverty, she was peculiarly and soothingly safe; *safer than anyone in the world, than papa, than mamma, than the lady with the arched eyebrows*; safer even, though so much less beautiful, than Miss Overmore, on whose loveliness, *as she supposed it, the little girl* was faintly conscious that one couldn't rest with quite the same *tucked-in and kissed-for-good-night feeling*. Mrs Wix was as safe as Clara Matilda, *who was in heaven* and yet, embarrassingly, also in Kensal Green, where *they* had been together to see her little huddled grave.
>
> [...]
>
> They dealt, *the governess* and *her pupil*, in 'subjects', but there were many the governess put off from week to week and that they never got to at all: she only used to say 'We'll take that in its proper order'. Her order was a circle as vast as the untravelled globe. She had not the spirit of adventure – *the child* could perfectly see how many subjects she was afraid of. She took refuge on *the firm ground of fiction, through which indeed there curled the blue river of truth*. She knew swarms of stories, mostly those of the novels she had read; relating them with a memory that never faltered and a wealth of detail that was Maisie's delight. They were all about *love and beauty and countesses and wickedness*. Her conversation was practically *an endless narrative, a great garden of romance, with sudden vistas* into her own life and *gushing fountains of homeliness*. These were the parts where they most lingered; she made the child take with her again every step of her long, lame course and think it beyond magic or monsters. *Her pupil* acquired a vivid vision of everyone who had ever, in her phrase, knocked against her – some of them oh so hard! – every one literally but Mr Wix, her husband, as to whom nothing was mentioned save that he had been dead for ages. He had been *rather remarkably* absent from his wife's career, and Maisie was never taken to see his grave.
>
> (James 1908: 26–8)

Both of these passages from Chapter 4 of the novel filter events through the experience of Maisie. Yet there is no single definable thought act or even a single occasion on which Maisie actually perceives these things on the plotline. She is (faintly, mutely) *aware* of things, and the narrative condenses (as James likes to make it quite frequently, very prominently for instance in *The Golden Bowl*) what may have been her feelings and thoughts on various occasions into one statement of the results, or the 'gist', of Maisie's musings. On account of this summarizing quality the passages are, incontrovertibly, psycho-narration. There is no doubt either that Maisie's idiom predominates in the first passage, as does the narrator's in the second. Genette's (and Bal's) explanations try to accommodate the peculiarities of this text in terms of the seeing vs. speaking dichotomy: the narrator speaks, and Maisie 'sees' (intuits, thinks). Yet because it is Maisie who 'sees', some of the language is bound to reflect her vision lexically and syntactically. The dichotomy of speaking and seeing can in fact only emerge in those textual areas where there is implicit contradiction or incompatibility. The occurrence of free indirect discourse has long been considered the locus classicus for such divergence. However, in the present case the syntax only rarely warrants the positing of free indirect discourse. One candidate is the sentence (highlighted above) about Clara Matilda, who is in heaven as well as in Kensal Green. Yet even in this sentence, *embarrassingly* and *little huddled grave* are not quite what one would expect as coming from Maisie, and the syntax itself displays no subjective root transformations on the lines required by Banfield. On the other hand, the tenses are clearly 'shifted', relating to a reference point in the past which can be aligned cohesively (Ehrlich 1990) with the plotline pasts of 'Maisie was faintly conscious' and 'drew this sense' and the earlier 'she knew'.[39]

That this style of writing is not the run-of-the-mill form of figural or reflectoral narrative can be verified by comparison with any passage from Flaubert, Hardy, Joyce's *Portrait*, D.H. Lawrence, Conrad or Woolf; and the difference is not merely one between irony and empathy. As I have stated above, irony is here pervasive, but of an empathetic mould. In 'pure' reflectoral narrative of the regular type, however, the narrator's voice is deliberately elusive, to the extent that irony cannot be attributed to the text in unequivocal fashion, as Booth lamented in his discussion of Joyce's *Portrait*. The James passage is also different from the famous technique used in William Golding's *The Inheritors* (1955), memorably analysed by M.A.K. Halliday (1981). In that novel, Lok's (the Neanderthal's) viewpoint is espoused so fully that it becomes difficult to recognize the bow and arrow as observed by him.[40] Although Lok's perspective is here complemented by a more reliable narratorial stance, the character's perceptions remain inviolate, a transparent window into the limited horizon of the protagonist. Not so in the James passage, where the mediation through a linguistic consciousness appreciably superior to Maisie's keeps clashing with her naïve evaluations and speculations and with the more colloquial idiom that one immediately attributes to

Maisie's own language or to what she has overheard from Mrs Wix. The narrator's linguistic signals are not all lexical, although in the second paragraph the rather precious descriptions of fiction's 'blue river of truth', the 'vistas' in the 'great garden of romance' and so forth foreground the narrator lexically as well as by means of the implied (ironic) stance vis-à-vis Mrs Wix's 'homely' storytelling. However, by *omitting to say* (clearly and unequivocally – in how un-Jamesian a manner!) that Mrs Wix broke her contract in not teaching Maisie anything at all, the narrative reflects Maisie's groping realization that Mrs Wix is not teaching her as she should, yet manages to convey at the same time that Maisie has become irresistibly enchanted by Mrs Wix's narrative proclivity.

To return to the linguistic signals of the narrative voice – beyond the complexity of the syntax with its many adjoined and subjoined modifying phrases – one notices in particular the crucial handling of character reference by means of descriptive noun phrases rather than pronouns. In particular, Maisie is quite frequently referred to by her name, as well as by 'the child', 'the little girl' and 'her [Mrs Wix's] pupil', whereas her parents consistently appear as 'mamma' (and 'her mother') and 'papa'. The technique thus combines a narratorial designation of Maisie with Maisie's childlike designation of other people. As in the opening paragraph of the novel the style here gives away some peculiarities of the narrative voice and the implied persona behind it who has a rather conspicuous penchant for precious upper-class vocabulary: 'rather remarkably absent', 'everyone literally but Mr Wix', 'practically an endless narrative', 'Miss Overmore was unmentionably and Mrs Wix ever so publicly [poor]'. The syntactic convolutedness – so very different from Virginia Woolf's loose paratactic and asyndetic style – of course most clearly bespeaks the presence of a narrative teller. This narrator does not *address* the narratee in a communicatory gesture, but performs instead as a conscious stylist, a *writer*.

How does the James passage link up with reflectorization? The first paragraph is the closest to reflectorization on the lines of Lawrence's 'England, My England', but with a much clearer sense of narratorial superiority over Maisie. Likewise, in the second passage, the narrator is prominent as a teller figure and assumes a clearly tongue-in-cheek definition of Mrs Wix's teaching. We here have *both* a clear narrator figure *and* a character on the scene. In correspondence with our example from *Romola*, a habitual, summary-like description is provided which centres on Maisie's experience and mind during a fairly long period of time and *not* on any specific actions or thought acts. One could therefore now start to distinguish between several kinds of reflectorization. Indeed, one could posit a scale of different types of reflectorization, from habitual (typicalized) contexts in novels with a prominent authorial narrator and intermittent reflector-mode narrative (James and Eliot) to more reflectoral texts with a less easily definable narrator function (Lawrence, Weldon) and to contexts with typicalized character positions (Dickens, Mansfield's 'Garden Party'), on into figuralization (Mansfield's 'At the Bay', Woolf's *The Waves*). The parameters for such an extension are typicalization both on the linguistic level (clichés) and on the level of plot, where the existence of characters and the specificity of particular thought or speech acts on the plotline are affected. Likewise, on the teller level, a clear authorial stance with remnants of at least potential embodiment and a Flaubertian stance of celestial omniscience start to merge, and the narratorial level additionally becomes dissolved through the linguistic typification of narratorial utterance that aligns itself with the style and opinions of the story-level existents, including those that are transindividual (*communis opinio*, bystanders, etc.).

5.4 SUMMARY

Starting out from Stanzel's reflectorization and Banfield's 'empty centre' we have moved a long way to consider related textual techniques. On the basis of my analyses, two different textual devices have been proposed to account for the various examples. The distinguishing criterion has been the presence or absence of a character 'on stage' to whom linguistic signals of consciousness can be attributed. If no such character is available, and there is also no narrator persona to whom these signals could be attributed, then the passage is one of *figuralization*. The text evokes a perceiving consciousness, whether of a mere observer or of a complete 'voice' on the story level. *Reflectorization*, on the other hand, can be defined as the *ironic* echoing of figural discourse well beyond free indirect discourse into the very opinions voiced by the narrative itself. The term reflectorization is therefore retained for cases where, besides a character whose consciousness is invoked, there is also a conspicuous narrative presence that triggers *either* the (ironic) assumption of the character's perspective by the narrator (Eliot), *or* the juxtaposition of narratorial and figural perspectives, resulting in a dual voice that can be both dissonant (Weldon) and empathetic (James), or may remain ambiguous between empathetic and ironic readings (Lawrence). Passages of reflectorization not only use typicalized language to convey stereotypical opinions and mindsets, they also restrict themselves to the presentation of *habitual* notions.

How does Natural Narratology go about dealing with these issues? In the examples that I have discussed there exists a graded scale between texts that employ only *here*, *now*, or *this/that* and texts that have instances of fully fledged free indirect discourse or of addressee-oriented direct discourse, both of which are established by their attendant linguistic signals. What are the reasons for the reader's decision to read these voices as belonging within the text rather than as an external narrator's speech act? Why, for instance, is there a clear hint of an external teller in 'The Garden Party'?

The answer to these questions cannot be grounded in the presence or absence of certain linguistic features alone. Banfield (1987) herself proposed that the oddity of the empty centre in *The Waves* depends on the absence of a character 'on the scene'. The empty centre is an empty centre because there is no clearly indicated SPEAKER (narrator) or a character's SELF to fill it. Stanzel's explanation (1977, 1984b), by way of the (re)introduction of a teller-figure also attempts to fill an empty slot by the closest available narrative instance: since there is a voice, it must emanate from somebody, and the evaluative stance of the 'implied author' then supports the construction of an apersonalized narrator figure who surfaces in precisely the two passages of reflectorization. The crucial conundrum is therefore a situation of non-attributable features of discourse, and – as I have argued – these can occur either in a reflector-mode narrative (Mansfield, Woolf) or in a teller mode narrative (Dickens, Eliot). Most of the quoted examples are reflector-mode texts or are situated on Stanzel's authorial–figural continuum. In a teller-mode narrative, which is more 'natural' and hence more 'realistic', unattributable discourse will immediately be naturalized as an echo of other characters' discourse. Such is the case with our example from Dickens. It is hardly likely that the narrator, in spite of his professed ignorance, will utter rhetorical questions from the level of the plot – note that the *that* in 'What's that?' (Dickens 1962: 663) has no anaphoric reference in the text and can only be explained from a story-internal deictic centre. It is in the same way that we intuit that the judgements ('that really was extravagant', etc.) in the 'Garden Party' passage (Mansfield 1984: 493) emanate from the story-internal perspective of the Sheridans and their like, even though the passage on account of its flashback to Laura's and Laurie's experiences also contains traces of a story-*external* stance. These traces are not linguistic, however, but need to be referred to semantic and macro-textual frames of reading.

Such recuperations are clearly *mimetic* on the level of narrative transmission. Readers and narratologists alike are in this way attempting to locate a realistic origin for the discourse and for the deictic centre. It is a moot point whether these recuperations are necessarily *intended* effects: the more clues there are for the presence of a bystander as observer, the more automatic such a recuperation will be and the more likely it is to have been an intended meaning effect. Instances of reflectorization and figuralization can be characterized as occurring precisely in those texts in which interpretative ploys founder since – as a consequence of the absence of the necessary character or narrator position – no realistic scenario of telling, observing or experiencing can be construed. One can see clearly, however, how such an 'absence' is really a gradual or graded one. At the beginning of 'Feuille D'Album' we appear to have an active narrator on *skaz* lines who has a close (embodied) connection with the protagonist and condenses her repeated experience of his visits into a subjective description. However, with the story's development into reflectoral narrative this realistic basis is undermined and narratological analysis has to fall back on reflectorization as an explanatory move – which, of course, does not really 'explain' anything. 'Feuille D'Album' also illustrates the meeting point of figuralization and reflectorization, the point at which a story-internal disembodied deictic centre has become a teller, a teller that is obviously located on the level of the characters.

Reflectorization should therefore be analysed in relation to speech and thought representation and to the empathy/irony scale. Once one looks at matters from this angle, the issue links up with the narrative and stylistic problems that one confronts in Mann's 'Death in Venice'. Unlike the presentations of (implied) consciousness that are current in neutral narrative (and which we have encountered at the end of the previous chapter), reflectorization and figuralization imply a very pronounced *agencement* of narrative voice. The two techniques, if this is what one wants to call them, rely on different narrativizations of the reading process. Whereas, in the case of figuralization, the text evokes a consciousness that the reader fills by projecting herself on the scene or by attributing the consciousness to common opinion and other loosely 'present' consciousness-carriers, in the case of reflectorization, by contrast, the problem is the conflicting presence of both a reflector *and* a narrator, both of whom behave against the rules.

I have not discovered any examples of either technique in the first- or second-person realm. This is, in a sense, logical. Figuralization rests on the absence of any character's consciousness *tout court*, and the existence of both an *I* and a *you* immediately supplies a teller and/or reflector figure. Reflectorization, on the other hand, seems to occur only on the 'authorial–figural' cline, and the identity of a first-person *I* (though split between a teller and a character) never quite achieves the effect of incompatibility required for the constitution of reflectorization. As for the *you* of a you-protagonist, unless the text is completely reflectoral the mere presence of the *you* inevitably suggests a very prominent situation of address irreconcilable with the ambiguities characteristic of reflectorization. However, it needs to be conceded that such pronouncements are premature at this stage of enquiry. Manfred Jahn has suggested (personal communication) that Dickens's famous 'My dream was out; my wild fancy was surpassed by sober reality; Miss Havisham was going to make my fortune on a grand scale' from *Great Expectations* (I, xviii; Dickens 1993: 137) might be a case of reflectorization. Primarily, I see this passage as simply a representation of Pip's thoughts at the time, as free indirect discourse. However, taking Jahn's proposal into full account would actually mean accepting distancing FID representations of characters' thought processes as textual points from which reflectorization might develop if this style continued for a longer passage. Only detailed analyses of many more texts can help resolve these issues.

Both reflectorization and figuralization are late developments in the history of the novel, but they are more widespread than one would expect. Both go back to the beginnings of extensive figural presentation in the mid-nineteenth century, since neither could occur without the reader's automatic interpretation of consciousness signals. Both are linked closely to the ever-increasing importance of free indirect discourse, yet neither requires the actual (formal) presence of all the linguistic markers signifying free indirect discourse. The two techniques become a fairly frequent device in Modernism, yet reflectorization is already prevalent in the Victorian novel, where it helps to maintain a cultured narratorial style even when treating of decidedly 'inferior' subjects. By means of reflectorization, the expected moralistic tone can be adhered to while the fascinations of the individual consciousness assert themselves despite this respectable linguistic frame.

It now appears that the teller/reflector dichotomy is not as impregnable a boundary as narratologists might tend to believe. However, the two phenomena under discussion are not a 'mere' mixing of teller and reflector mode that would prove their natural combinability and falsify Banfield's and Stanzel's contentions. On the contrary, readers register passages of this type as deviant and as requiring additional interpretative attention. One way of quickly disposing of the problem is to label such passages as ironic. Yet, as I have attempted to demonstrate, it is not necessarily irony (see the James example) but the incompatibility of linguistic and mostly non-linguistic features that causes the noted effects of defamiliarization. Incompatibility is resolved cognitively and ideologically by a number of reading strategies, foremost among which are the bystander/observer schemata for figuralization. Reflectorization resists even such harmless recuperation, but still subliminally allows the reader to link opinions and attitudes to typifications of recognizable stances by individual characters and/or a *communis opinio*, 'the villagers' and the like. Narrativization, and the frame of mimesis on which it relies, here encounter a first serious setback, a setback that will become more discomfiting still in the post-World War Two encounter of games with tales, tellers and told (Chapter 7). I will return to the crucial issues of observation, perception and focalization below under 8.3. These questions need to be fully sounded in all possible contexts before a proper drawing together of all the evidence can be effected.

One point may, however, deserve brief discussion at this early stage. Having disposed of Stanzel's and Banfield's terminology, my own distinction between reflectorization and figuralization may strike the reader as disappointing. Rather than aligning reflectorization with a simple category (frame, parameter) of 'natural' narratology, I have here made numerous distinctions which appear to have little connection with the model. True, I have emphasized the crucial status of perception in these deliberations, but where do we go from there? One important point in this chapter has been to note the diffuseness of the concept of consciousness – a notion that needs to be located on the interpretative level rather than merely on the level of linguistic signals. To the basic patterns of ACTING, TELLING, EXPERIENCING, VIEWING and REFLECTING I have here added a new angle: the possibility of empathetic projection by the reader in passages of figuralization and the proposal of the undefinable experiencer (bystander, *communis opinio*) for passages of reflectorization. I have hinted that in the narrative texts which I discussed the theoretical levels of discourse and story have come under siege, and that the distinction between the positions of teller and reflector characters – though I operate with them throughout – are starting to dissolve. These deconstructions of the standard dichotomies on which narratology has been built will be the focus of discussion below in Chapter 7. But even at this early stage it may be asked why I keep using the old terms and why I even create new ones whose applicability I immediately start to deconstruct in turn.

The central argument in the model of natural narratology is that tellers and reflectors, story and discourse are extended 'natural' categories, i.e. they are based on 'natural' macro-frames, and that readers (and literary critics) in the course of interpretation project these categories on to the text. Standard narratological categories can therefore be subsumed under the parameters of natural narratology. As regards the new schemata of reflectorization and figuralization, these I herewith humbly offer to the narratologist as provisional critical tools that may help to define and at least provisionally name phenomena that are only now being discovered. It is very likely that intensive research on figuralization and reflectorization will make these concepts unnecessary and cause them to be superseded by a different set of conceptual tools or that such research will eventually refocalize textual issues in entirely different ways. Until then what I have proposed here should serve as an interim language based on the admittedly fictive notions of stories and discourses, tellers and reflectors which have come into use as a result of persistent processes of narrativization on the theoretical plane of narratology.

6 Virgin territories
The strategic expansion of deictic options

In this chapter I will deal with two issues that have recently acquired some prominence in narratological discussions: person and tense. Person, classically the distinction between first- and third-person texts, has of course always been a hotly debated subject. Booth's pronouncement on this being 'the most overworked distinction' in narrative theory (Booth 1961/1983: 150) was later retracted by him (1983: 412), and Dorrit Cohn's recent work (especially her studies of the history vs. fiction problematics, and of first-person present tense narrative[1]) are perhaps the most insistent endorsement of the centrality of the concept *person*. The classical distinction between the first- and third-person realm, or between homo- and heterodiegesis (Genette 1980: 243–9), however, can no longer satisfy theoretical requirements of comprehensiveness and stringency. Experimental writing has meanwhile produced a broad spectrum of narrative texts employing different and frequently 'odd' personal pronouns, and this experimental work requires nothing short of an extensive and radical revision of the standard narratological treatment of person or voice.

In the first half of this chapter (6.1 and 6.2) I will discuss some of these recent fictional developments. Second-person fiction, due to its now fairly widespread occurrence, deserves pride of place on this list.[2] Besides the second person I will note the use of indefinite *one* (French *on*, German *man*) and even *it* in reference to a fictional protagonist, and I will discuss the invention by feminist writers of gender-nonspecific pronouns. These new options restructure the classic first- vs. third-person dichotomy in crucial ways, and they call our attention to an additional range of 'natural' pronouns such as *we* and *they* whose use in narratives has so far remained beyond the pale of narratological analysis.

The second (also deictic) issue dealt with in this chapter is that of the category of tense. Since the work of Hamburger (1957/1968) and her theory about the epic preterite, tense has been a favourite topic among narratologists, with work by Weinrich (1964/1985), Stanzel (1984b) and, more recently, Fleischman (1990) and Cohn (1993) significantly extending the scope and sophistication of the analysis of narrative tense. Again, this recent surge of interest is motivated by new textual preferences in experimental writing. Thus, the by now extensive use of the narrative present (i.e. the consistent replacement of the narrative past tense by the present tense on the main narrative level) is complemented by even more original experiments with the future tense, conditionals and even non-finite verb forms. Narration in the present tense has become extremely widespread in recent fiction, with interesting consequences for readers' (re-) conceptualization of the natural storytelling frame, where a story has to have happened in the past in order to become tellable.

In this chapter I will also broach the question of the apparent breakdown of realism in contemporary fiction. This issue will be discussed more extensively in Chapter 7, where I want to tackle it from the perspective of current narratological concepts. In this chapter I concentrate on aspects that are amenable to grammatical description and therefore allow me to document the great diversity of forms observable in recent writing and to specify and illustrate the very different kinds of naturalizations to which they give rise. In Chapter 7, on the other hand, the reader's construction of narrative out of disparate and increasingly recalcitrant materials will be at the centre of my analysis, in which I will then trace the triumphs and limits of narrativization.

6.1 THE DEICTIC CENTRE EXTENDED: 'ODD' PERSONAL PRONOUNS AND THE PRESENTATION OF CONSCIOUSNESS

In this section I wish to concentrate on the use of 'odd' personal pronouns in reference to fictional protagonists and illustrate how the imputation of a consciousness factor aids the reader's narrativization of such apparently unpromising linguistic structures. The possibility of reading such non-canonical pronouns as referring to a protagonist's internal SELF relies on an extended application of Banfield's theory of the deictic centre (Banfield 1982; Wiebe 1990) or of Stanzel's reflector mode. The experientiality of a SELF is extended to narrative subjects projectable from a surface structure *you*, *one* or *it*. The category person needs to be reanalysed in relation to readers' attempts to narrativize what they encounter in such texts – their attempt, that is, to re-cognize in terms of familiar natural parameters and frames what initially appears to contravene natural or commonsense expectations. Uses of *one* and *you*, especially, will be demonstrated to be inherently ambiguous and multi-functional, a factor which enhances the identificational potential of texts in the second person and with indefinite *one*. I will conclude with a consideration of texts which *alternate* between pronominal forms. In some fiction such alternation is fairly regular and unproblematic; in other texts one pronominal choice mutates into the other, creating referential instability.[3]

6.1.1 'Odd' pronouns: multiple subjects, impossible protagonists and invented pronominal morphology

I will start with the most realistic and natural kinds of unusual pronouns – *we* and *they*, excluding for the moment plural *you*.[4] Entire works written in the *we* form are rare: Pierre Silvain's *Les Éoliennes* (1971) is the only consistent *we* novel that I know of. Several *we* texts alternate between *we* and *I*: Zamyatin's *We* (1924), John Barth's *Sabbatical* (1982), Jean Echenoz's *Nous trois* (1992), or Gabriele Wohmann's 'Fahrplan' (1968). In most cases the *we* text represents an extended first-person narrative, for instance rendering the experience of childhood (as in Mauro Senesi's 'The Giraffe' [1963]) or of town/village life, and it therefore includes the first-person narrator in a larger community of playmates or village folk. *I* + *you* narratives (of which more below), on the other hand, usually background the *we* for very 'realistic' reasons: if both the narrator and the addressee have shared the experience, there is little motivation to evoke it narratively except in passing. In narrative clauses the second-person pronoun tends to dominate, with *we* occurring in orientational sections or comments by the narrator. Since second-person fiction frequently thematizes the relationship between the *I* and the *you*, the story focuses less on what *I* and *you* did *together* than on what *I* did and how *you* responded.[5]

We narrative is a fairly unproblematic case, or so it seems, and rare enough to have escaped much analysis so far.[6] *They* narratives are even rarer, at least in my own experience. They, too, appear to lend themselves to quite unproblematically realistic readings. Unlike *we*-narrative, however, *they* texts move into the purely fictional realm as soon as their multiple protagonists (a group of people, the citizens of a village) are presented as multiple experiencers whose consciousness, opinions and attitudes are represented in detail. Here reflectorization (as discussed in Chapter 5) sets in. Discourse and consciousness are attributed to a plural subject, a multiple SELF:

> you know the effects have been very bad especially on people wanting to go to university – and the attitude of their parents who have said ***no I don't want you to go to university ((or)) to places like that***
> (*Survey of English Usage* S. 5.10.65)[7]

The only consistent *they*-text that I know is Georges Perec's *Les Choses* (1965). The entire novel describes the experiences of a young couple, their poverty, aspirations and partial satisfaction of their (mostly pecuniary and aesthetic) needs. An extended literary instance of *they*-narrative in English is Mary McCarthy's *The Group* (1963), at least two chapters of which narrate the experiences of the Vassar girls as a group. Chapter 1 depicts their meeting at Kay's wedding, and the final chapter describes their reunion over Kay's funeral.

Kay would have been happy about that, *her friends knew*. They had worked with might and main to get her buried as an Episcopalian [...] It was amazing how sticky these ministers could be about burying a person who was not a church member.

Kay's father and mother would arrive too late for the ceremony; in this warm weather you could not wait too long. On the long-distance, they had told Helena to have their daughter cremated, and they would take her ashes home – they were very bitter. But Helena was certain that Kay would have hated that, and she had telephoned back to say that her friends would like to arrange a church ceremony for her, if her parents would agree. Whatever Kay would have wanted, her father said; probably her friends knew best. That was bitter too. Yet *the group* were sure they were doing the right thing. Kay had grown away from her parents; they had not seen eye to eye at all while she was out West, and it had hurt them when she had insisted on coming back to New York after the divorce, though she had a home with them. But they had staked her, which was sweet, just as now they had wired the funeral parlour with an authority for Helena to act. How sad that Kay had not found time – that was what her father said – to write them a single letter in the month before she 'went.' Naturally, if she had known, she would have.

(*The Group*, xv; McCarthy 1963: 355–6)

The latter part of this passage can be read as free indirect discourse from the perspective of the 'girls,'[8] but that is of course a completely unrealistic reading since the group's opinions and thoughts are unlikely to be synchronized in this manner. What we have, therefore, is a passage of reflectorization in which the group's impressions are artfully combined into unitary linguistic shape. The pronoun *they* here begins to function much like *he* or *she* in standard reflectoral narrative, acquiring a deictic centre and operating as a SELF (Banfield 1982).

Neither *we*- nor *they*-narratives constitute a prerogative of twentieth-century literature, except when they move into the reflectoral realm. I suspect that a dissertation on *we*- or *they*-novels before 1900 would be likely to unearth a considerable quantity of texts which have simply not stood out, so unremarkable have they seemed in their realistic setup. Narratives of expeditions or travelogues, for instance, might be a fruitful hunting ground for this type of text; narratives of military action, pilgrimages and spiritual quests of a closely-knit community, and the accounts of family-life among new settlers, immigrants or exiles also suggest themselves. *We*- and *they*-narratives therefore cannot claim to disrupt narrative realism and are not really 'odd' first- or third-person pronouns. Communal storytelling and narratives involving the experiences of communities, after all, belong to our cultural and historical heritage.

The case is quite different for **address pronouns**. The most outstanding oddity in the pronominal realm is what is usually called second-person fiction, narrative which employs an address pronoun in reference to the (main) fictional protagonist. Second-person fiction has recently risen to prominence; it is no longer limited merely to marginal, experimental texts written by unknown authors. Since its early avatars at the beginning of this century[9] second-person narrative has established itself as a highly competitive form, has moved into mainstream literature and is now being used by major authors.[10] Like first- and third-person texts, too, second-person fiction displays a large diversity of forms, ranging from the merely hortative mode (W.S. Merwin, 'Simple Test'; Lorrie Moore's *Self-Help*) to the predominantly reflectoral mode, where the *you*-protagonist is provided with a deictic centre of experientiality.[11] Second-person narrative also includes extremely complex setups such as peripheral second-person texts (where the narrator's past SELF, referred to by means of the first-person pronoun *I*, is peripherally involved with the *you*-protagonist's story, on which the narrative concentrates[12]) or a variety of interesting fictional situations of address (the narrator writing to a dead or imagined addressee whose story is evoked[13]). In particular, second-person narrative introduces great combinatory complexity by the fact that both the narrator and the current addressee of the narrational act can become involved on the story level, with the narrator's past self participating in the *you*-protagonist's experiences and the *you*-protagonist surviving into the time and situation of the narrative act. For this reason, second-person fiction destroys the easy assumption of the traditional dichotomous structures which the standard narratological models have proposed, especially the distinction between homo- and heterodiegetic narrative (Genette) or that of the identity or non-identity of the realms of existence between narrator and characters (Stanzel).[14]

As regards the establishment of experientiality in second-person texts, I would here like to concentrate on two issues: the initial ambiguity of reference in the majority of second-person narratives and its resolution in the evocation of a protagonist's consciousness; and, second, the projection of story experientiality on the narrational level – an aspect of second-person narrative which ties in with the use of the present tense in much second-person fiction. In particular, I will attempt to illustrate how both strategies allow a recuperation of not naturally occurring storytelling situations under the heading of implied experientiality: that is to say, by means of naturalizing and narrativizing what does not come naturally.

Most second-person texts initially seem to involve the reader directly, and this not only in prominently 'apostrophic' (Kacandes 1993, 1994) texts such as Italo Calvino's *If on a Winter's Night a Traveller* (1979). Observe the following two passages from the beginning of a story by Frederick Barthelme and from Robyn Sarah's 'Wrong Number':

You're stuck in traffic on the way home from work, counting blue cars, and when a blue-metallic Jetta pulls alongside, you count it – twenty-eight. You've seen the driver on other evenings; she looks strikingly like a young man – big, with dark, almost red hair clipped tight around her head. Her clear fingernails move slowly, like gears, on the black steering wheel. She watches you, expressionless, for a long second, then deliberately opens her mouth and circles her lips with the wet tip of her tongue. You look away, then back. Suddenly her lane moves ahead – two, three, four cars go by. You roll down the window and stick your head out, trying to see where she is, but she's gone. The car in front of you signals to change lanes. All the cars in your lane are moving into the other lane. There must be a wreck ahead, so you punch your blinker. You straighten your arm out the window, hoping to get in behind a van that has come up beside you, and you wait, trying to remember what the woman looked like.
('Moon Deluxe'; F. Barthelme 1983: 61)

The telephone rings. It's right beside you – you jump – reach for the receiver. 'Yes?'
A tiny instant's silence. Then: 'Jacqueline?' A man's voice – deep, civilized – with a somehow caressing intonation that is yet quiet and respectful.
Your heart beats. 'No,' you say, with a little apologetic laugh.
(Sarah 1975: 22)

You here at first seems to involve *me*, the reader, projecting an everyday situation with which one can identify. Yet the Barthelme-*you* immediately turns out to be male, the Sarah-*you* female – a conclusion that is not explicitly signalled in the text but which the reader infers on the basis of stereotypical heterosexual frames of behaviour: Barthelme's *you* is obviously attracted to the woman driver; and Sarah's *you* behaves in accordance with received clichés of female anxiety, titillation and romantic projection. As a consequence, even if it is conceived of as a generic *you*, some readers (those of the opposite sex) will already start to visualize this *you* as gendered differently from themselves. As second-person texts proceed to fill in more and more specific information about the *you*, with the *you* starting to acquire a job, a family, a specific age, idiosyncratic interests and attitudes, the status of this *you* as a fictional persona becomes increasingly clear. Although some texts may later reintroduce an address function[15] which suddenly puts a narrator on stage as well, in most second-person texts this address function (and its identificational effect on the reader) becomes muted as soon as the fictional protagonist takes centre stage, and the *you* becomes displaced from its communicational (deictic) relation to a possible (real) reader. Not entirely so, however, in texts which have a narratee who is also the story protagonist. Although that addressee-cum-protagonist frequently turns out to be dead (Carlos Fuentes, 'Alma

Pura') or even merely imaginary (Alice Munro, 'Tell Me Yes or No'), at the time when the narrator addresses him or her the *you* retains its full deictic significance since it is used by the narrative voice to address, exhort and appeal to someone in particular who belongs to the fictional world both on the story and the discourse levels. Although the theoretical distinction between communicative and noncommunicative types of narrative (Fludernik 1993b) is usually fairly clear, texts *in practice* tend to collapse these two categories, especially in recent fiction where the situation of story enunciation is frequently left ambiguous or unaccounted for. It may then initially become difficult to tell whether a specific addressee does or does not 'exist' on the enunciational plane.

Story and discourse are also under attack in second-person texts with a prominent address function, especially when it persists throughout the entire text. Such texts create a story *ex nihilo*, by the sheer force of exhortation and apostrophe. Reader involvement is maximized.

> Blindfold yourself with some suitable object. If time permits remain still for a moment. You may feel one or more of your senses begin to swim back toward you in the darkness, singly and without their names. Meanwhile have someone else arrange the products to be used in a row in front of you. It is preferable to have them in identical containers, though that is not necessary. Where possible, perform the test by having the other person feed you a portion – a spoonful – of each of the products in turn, without comment.
> ('Simple Test'; Merwin 1973: 245)

This guidebook format is soon undermined by further quite illogical instructions which the addressee receives:

> Guess again what you are eating or drinking in each case (if you can make the distinction). But this time do not stop there. Guess why you are eating or drinking it. Guess what it may do for you. Guess what it was meant to do for you. By whom. When. Where. Why. Guess which of your organs recognize it. Guess whether it is welcomed to their temples. Guess how it figures in their prayers. Guess how completely you become what you eat. Guess how soon. Guess at the taste of locusts and wild honey. Guess at the taste of water. Guess what the rivers see as they die. Guess why the babies are burning. Guess why there is silence in heaven. Guess why you were ever born.
> (ibid.: 246)

As in most of the stories written in the 'subjunctive' mode (Richardson 1991b) – for instance those in Lorrie Moore's collection *Self-Help* (1985) – the imperative, as if by fiat, creates a fictional (hypothetical) situation which then continues to be elaborated on, projecting a protagonist located in a very specific setup. Merwin's short story never fully fleshes out its protagonist, retaining its instructional mode, but much of Moore's work starts to add a significant number of little details to fictionalize the hypothetical frame.

> Meet in expensive beige raincoats, on a pea-soupy night. Like a detective movie. First, stand in front of Florsheim's Fiftyseventh Street window, press your face close to the glass, watch the fake velvet Hummels inside revolving around the wing tips; some white shoes, *like your father wears*, are propped up with garlands on a small mound of chemical snow.
>
> ('How to Be an Other Woman'; Moore 1986: 3)

Both *you*-texts with initial generic *you* that remains ambiguous and then progressively acquires the specificity required for a fictional narrative setup, *and* the exhortative texts of the 'subjunctive' mode establish experientiality by means of an active involvement by the potential reader. In the case of reflector-mode second-person fiction this empathy usually operates by means of initial generic *you*; in the case of the subjunctive mode, reader-address tends to modulate into address to, and the projection of, a fictional addressee-cum-protagonist.

If we return to the Frederick Barthelme passage quoted above, we can see that the fictionality of the situation becomes very pronounced as soon as we get the protagonist's thoughts in free indirect discourse: 'There must be a wreck ahead.' Such passages of free indirect discourse ease the reader's way into the perspective of the protagonist, preparing the ground for a reflectoral analysis of these stories. Thus, in the following passage from Rumer Godden's 'You Need to Go Upstairs', the blind girl who tries to go to the lavatory by herself becomes suddenly frightened of tripping over the family's pet turtle (named Schiff):

> This is the hyacinth bed; hyacinths are easy, strong in scent and shaped like little pagodas. [...] [A]nd these are crocuses and these are aconites – but Mother is not close and you remember that Schiff may be out on the path.
>
> Schiff! You stop. Schiff is so small that you might easily step on him, but Schiff is large enough for you to fall over. Mother ... but you must not call, you must go on. You think of falling, you can't help thinking of falling – down – into nothing until you get hit. Mother! Schiff! Mother! But you have not called and Mother is saying in what seems an ordinary voice to the visitor, but is her special loud voice for you. 'How strange! With all this sun, our tortoise has not come out on the path today.'
>
> (Godden 1968: 145–6)

Here the text manifests pure reflector mode narrative with the protagonist's exclusive perspective on things.

I have noted earlier that the generic use of *you* (that is to say, *you* in the meaning of 'one') is largely responsible for the easy move from implicit reader address to a reading that reduces its reference to a fictional character. Observe, for instance, the following passage from the beginning of William Styron's *Lie Down in Darkness* (1951) which appears to initiate second-person fiction, although the text later moves into more standard types of narration.

> Suddenly the train is burrowing through the pinewoods, and the conductor, who looks middle-aged and respectable like someone's favorite uncle, lurches through the car asking for tickets. If you are particularly alert at that unconscionable hour you notice his voice, which is somewhat guttural and negroid – oddly fatuous-sounding after the accents of Columbus or Detroit or wherever you came from – and when you ask him how far it is to Port Warwick and he says, 'Aboot eighty miles', you know for sure that you're in the Tidewater.
> (Styron 1951: 9)

Such opening gambits – as also in R.P. Warren's *All the King's Men* (1946) and Hawkes's *The Lime Twig* (1961) – pave the way for the establishment of internal focalization in the second person. Generic *you* cannot usually be upheld for very long without referentially attaching itself either to the real reader or to a protagonist. In the first case the real reader is swallowed up in the hypothetical situation and consents to the text's implications about herself; a good example of this is Jamaica Kincaid's *A Small Place* (1988). In the second case, the reference is ultimately aligned with a fictional protagonist, leaving the reader to withdraw from the referential circuit. An exception to this rule can be glimpsed in Max Frisch's sketch 'Burleske', which describes the hypothetical situation of a liberal-minded pharisee. The actual reader may or may not recognize herself in the role; in so far as the sketch is interpreted as an extended exercise in generic discourse, however, the *you* never acquires a purely fictional reference but remains deictically relevant for the current reader.

Besides the concept of generic *you*, *you* in the function of self-address constitutes a second type of second-person narrative. *You* as self-address in people's musings with themselves prominently serves to recuperate the second person for internal focalization. R.P. Warren's *All the King's Men* (see Fludernik 1995c) already employs self-address in conjunction with generic *you* and with the generic present tense (which then modulates into the present of interior monologue). Adumbrations of this technique can be found in Lillian Smith's novel *Strange Fruit* (1944) or in Radclyffe Hall's *The Well of Loneliness* (1928):

> Stephen [the female protagonist] flushed: 'No doubt she'll stick on by balance!' The words rankled, oh, very deeply they rankled. Violet was learning to ride side-saddle, that small, flabby lump who squealed if you pinched her; that terrified creature of muslins and ribbons and hair that curled over the nurse's finger! [...] She had fat, wobbly legs too, just

like a rag doll – and *you, Stephen*, had been compared to Violet! Ridiculous of course, and yet all of a sudden *you* felt less impressive in *your* fine riding breeches. *You* felt – well, not foolish exactly, but self-conscious – not quite at *your* ease, a little bit wrong. It was almost as though *you* were playing at young Nelson again, were only pretending.

But *you* said, 'I've got muscles, haven't I, Father? Williams says I've got riding muscles already!' Then *you* dug your heels sharply into the pony, so that he whisked round, bucking and rearing. As for *you, you* stuck to his back like a limpet. Wasn't that enough to convince them?

'Steady on, Stephen!' came Sir Philip's voice, warning.
(*The Well of Loneliness*, iv, 2; Hall 1982: 38)

Such interesting anticipations of second-person fiction are linked, as one can see, to the occurrence of free indirect discourse.[16] Self-address also lends itself to being extended into entire sections of interior monologue in the self- or hetero-apostrophic mode, as in Mario Vargas Llosa's three 'second-person' sections in Chapter 4 of *The Green Mansion*; these are all reminiscences of old Don Anselmo who relives his flight with Toñita.[17] As the case of Rex Stout's *How Like a God* (1929) demonstrates, the self-address function of such texts can be a matter of interpretation rather than empirical verification. It is only from the narrative context that one recognizes that the content of the three Don Anselmo sections must be memory, not current action or current thought. Likewise, in Carlos Fuentes's *The Death of Artemio Cruz* (1962), the monologic quality of the *you* sections is determinable mainly from their collocation with the *I* and *he* sections, particularly from the fact that the *you* sections never contain information other than that available to the dying protagonist Artemio Cruz. In Rex Stout's novel, on the other hand, the fact that these second-person sections are interpolated with the protagonist's ascent up the staircase prior to killing the woman to whom he has been in emotional bondage tends to corroborate a reading in terms of an evaluative flashback and at the same time undermines such an interpretation as unrealistic. Thus, the flashbacks help to motivate and explain the murder (Bill is completely obsessed with Millicent); on the other hand, the flashbacks take up considerably more time than does walking up a staircase. This is one of the cases where realistic frames grind to a halt, not because they are inapplicable (as they will turn out to be in some of the surfictionist texts which I will discuss in Chapter 7), but because the narrative is ambiguous between different frames – a storytelling frame (even if the story is written in second-person form) and a consciousness/reminiscence frame in which one has to read the *you* as self-address.

This immediately takes me to the question of natural frames in general. Although a highly conspicuous technique which initially strikes one as extremely odd, second-person fiction actually relies on previous frames or registers which help the reader to decode what is happening in such texts.

These frames do not necessarily refer directly to any of the cognitive setups that I have previously discussed: TELLING, VIEWING, EXPERIENCING. They usually have no connection with *narrative* at all, since most generally occurring uses of *you* are dialogic (including generic *you*), register- and text-specific (instructional discourse), or context-dependent (courtroom *you*).[18] Narrativization therefore has to occur on two separate levels. First, readers may be likely to recognize the instructional (guidebook etc.) frame as an invitation to their own involvement, realizing at the same time that such a frame *at the beginning of a novel* significantly reshapes the non-literary model and opens itself to possible narrativizations. Reflectoral *you* narrative therefore soon reinforces the standard VIEWING/EXPERIENCING pattern; in fact its force is significantly enhanced by the use of *you*. Generic *you* – like *one* – allows an easy transition into empathy[19] with the protagonist, much more so than either *I* or *s/he*, since these pronouns are both set apart from the addressee's/reader's deictic position.[20] Likewise, exhortative second-person modes (the examples from Merwin and Moore) also evoke a hypothetical and highly involving fictional scenario which – despite its present-tense shape – immediately lends itself to an invocation of narrative experience as it issues from the mind of the hypothesizing hortatory consciousness. Such texts frequently proceed from doing to thinking and feeling, exhorting the addressee to do something, and then providing an account of her subsequent thoughts and emotions. A (necessarily fictional) consciousness is therefore established early on, (re)producing the natural frame of a fictional experiencer.

The same tendencies can be observed to recur with the use of *one- (on, man)* narrative. Not only are these indefinite pronouns frequently replaceable with second-person forms (*you*; *tu* or *vous*; *du* or *Sie*); inversely, the indefinite pronoun is also frequently used in lieu of first- or second-person forms. Discourse situations that require politeness, reticence or deliberate ambiguity can be cited as pragmatic contexts for this usage. Thus, in the following exchange Stevens (who had earlier been guilty of dutifully accepting his employer's orders to dismiss the Jewish housemaids) pretends that he, like unnamed others (including Miss Kenton), had disapproved of His Lordship's orders. In actual fact, he had of course, in person, diligently hastened to execute His Lordship's commands and had reproved Miss Kenton for her criticism of Lord Darlington's decisions.

> 'Really, Miss Kenton ...' I picked up the tray on which I had gathered together the used crockery. 'Naturally, **one** disapproved of the dismissals. **One** would have thought that quite self-evident.'
> (*The Remains of the Day*; Ishiguro 1990: 154)

One has been known to occur with some frequency in passages of free indirect discourse, where the use of the indefinite pronoun helps to disguise the protagonist's responsibilities or to thematize her unwillingness to face up to her actions and feelings:[21]

> How could **one**, in any case, understand other people's motives and feelings, when **one's** own remained mysterious? Why did **one** look forward with irritation to the receipt of a letter on April 1st, and then feel alarmed and affronted when it did not arrive by the first post? Very likely the letter had been sent to Oxford. There was no possible urgency about it, since **one** knew what it would contain and how it had to be answered; but it was annoying to sit about, expecting it.
> (*Gaudy Night*, xi; Sayers 1968: 178)[22]

In English there is, however, no extended text employing *one* in reference to a fictional protagonist whose deictic center is thus being established; none, that is, except the translation of Maurice Roche's *Compact*, a work which includes some segments of *on* narration, translated by *one*.

> **On** se représente à l'intérieur de la cathédrale vide (et, dans le lit où l'**on** se trouve en réalité, recroquevillé sur le côté, **on** se met par la pensée à genoux. **On** a dans cette posture la forme d'un 2 . . .
> (Roche 1966: 22)

> **One** makes an appearance inside the empty cathedral (and, in the bed where **one** is in reality, curled up on one side, **one** mentally kneels down. In this position, **one** takes the form of a 2 . . .
> (Roche 1988: 10)

Monique Wittig's much more pervasive use of *on* in a reflectoral setting in *L'Opoponax* (1964) would have been the major test case, had not the English translator decided to render *on* consistently by means of *you*. This highly idiomatic choice again underlines the affinity between *one* and *you*, and it also documents the fact that the English pronoun *one* has a much more formal and idiolectically restricted application than does the French *on*. In fact, *on* is currently in the process of replacing *nous* ('we') in most contexts just as it is being replaced by *tu/vous* in its generic meaning (Söll 1969). German *man*, on the other hand, probably has the most restricted use among the three languages. It does, however, show up in literary texts much more extensively than does the English *one*. Elsewhere I discuss the extensive application of *man* in Joseph Roth's *Radetzkymarsch* (1932),[23] where it occurs in passages of internal focalization. Roth's *man* does not always survive translation into English (Fludernik 1995a), just as Wittig's *on*, though translated as *man* in the German version of *L'Opoponax*, never really establishes itself as a viable textual option since the German *man* has problems co-occurring with a present-tense verb in a reportative context. *Man* plus the present inevitably suggests a generic context or instructional prose. There are, however, at least two novels by Swiss-German authors that use *man* extensively.[24]

234 *Virgin territories*

In Gerhard Meier's *Der schnurgerade Kanal* (1977) extracts from Isidor's papers are rendered in the *man* form:

> Man denkt an Sacco und Vanzetti, Nicola Sacco und Bartolomeo Vancetti [sic]. Warum man gerade auf Sacco und Vanzetti kommt, läßt sich nicht erklären. Und wenn man an Sacco und Vanzetti denkt, denkt man sich, müßte man bedenken, daß im Augenblick auf dem Erdenrund vielleicht niemand an Sacco und Vanzetti denkt, daß sich niemand des frühen Films über sie erinnert [...] Und man fragt sich weiter: Ja, wie ist es denn gewesen mit diesem Sacco und Vanzetti? Und man hat sich als Knabe vor Augen, hat jene Nacht vor Augen, den Zirkus inmitten jener Nacht, jenen Zirkus, der diesen Film über Sacco und Vanzetti aufs Land gebracht hat am Anfang der großen Zeit des Films [...]
>
> (Meier 1987: 226, 227–8)[25]

In some passages the *man* is clearly identifiable as generic 'one':

> Man könne die böhmischen Landschaften Caspar David Friedrichs übrigens nicht betrachten, ohne über deren Himmel zu reden. Kaum je seien bei Friedrich stillere, unbewegtere ins Bild gekommen.
>
> (ibid.: 344)[26]

Not only are the subjects thus described predominantly mental (*man fühlt; man denkt*); Isidor's notes themselves are fantastic projections. For instance, the final section which is part of Isidor's diary describes the first and only extended physical movement on his part, and it traces his journey to the lake where he apparently drowns himself:

> Man bricht auf.
> Auf dem Weg zum Bahnhof fällt einem folgendes auf: [...]
> Mit der Lokalbahn überquert man die Ebene. Man stellt dabei fest, daß der Wildrosenstrauch, dem zuliebe man sich extra auf die rechte Seite gesetzt hat, abgeholzt worden ist [...]
> Man überquert Straßen, Wiesenmulden, fährt an abgebrochenen Liegenschaften vorbei, an Umbauten auch, erinnert sich der Geschicke deren Bewohner, deren Sippen.
> Auf der Fahrt durch den Wald wähnt man sich nach Rußland versetzt. [..]
> Man steigt in den Schnellzug um.
>
> (ibid.: 356–8)[27]

> Man wird ankommen.
> Die Anlagen werden noch Rosen haben, Kapuzinerkresse.
> Die Figur auf der Denkmalsäule wird nach der Bogenbrücke starren, von wo das Aufschlagen des Körpers nicht lauter zu hören sein wird als das Aufeinanderschlagen zweier Fingerknöchel. Über den Kanal wird der Südwind Duft von Kapuzinerkresse tragen.
>
> (ibid.: 360)[28]

On a realistic interpretation Isidor must have projected this scenario while still at the house – an interpretation corroborated by the fact that his notes are read by Dr Helene W., the female protagonist. A number of Gerhard Meier's other novels alternate between *ich* ('I') and *man* forms, with *man* operating as an allolexeme for 'we' much on the lines of the French *on*.[29]

In E.Y. Meyer's *In Trubschachen* (1973), on the other hand, the generic *man* is employed in a guidebook setting which closely resembles narrative uses of *you*. The specificity of the protagonist as a fictional character emerges only on the sly, by reference to the books he has packed, to what he has ordered to drink, etc. An extended passage from the novel is quoted under 6.3.2, where I discuss its use of the conditional tense.

The most striking pronominal oddity of all is the use of *it* in reference to a human subject. No text that I know of employs the impersonal pronoun in reference to its human protagonist in a consistent manner;[30] there are, however, at least two English texts which briefly introduce their protagonists by means of *it*, although they then both move on to the standard *he*. In both novels the uncanny conjunction of *it* with the protagonist is eased by means of a brief passage of free indirect discourse and narrated perception, and the use of *it* is authenticated by a realistic context: George is not yet quite awake, and Miles has just emerged from a coma.

> Waking up begins with saying *am* and *now*. That which has awoken then lies for a while staring up at the ceiling and down into **itself** until it has recognized *I* [...]
>
> Obediently the body levers **itself** out of bed [...] and shambles naked into the bathroom, where **its** bladder is emptied and **it** is weighed: *still a bit over 150 pounds, in spite of all that toiling at the gym!* Then to the mirror.
>
> What **it** sees there isn't so much a face as the expression of a predicament. *Here's what **it** has done to **itself**, here's the mess **it** has somehow managed to get **itself** into, during **its** fifty-eight years* [...]
> (*A Single Man*; Isherwood 1964: 7-8)[31]

> *It* was conscious of a luminous and infinite haze, as if *it* were floating, godlike, alpha and omega, over a sea of vapour and looking down; then less happily, after an interval of obscure duration, of murmured sounds and peripheral shadows, which reduced the impression of boundless space and empire to something much more contracted and unaccommodating. [...] *It* was conscious, **evidently**; but bereft of pronoun, all that distinguishes person from person; and bereft of time, all that distinguishes present from past and future.
> (*Mantissa*; Fowles 1982: 9)

In both passages the reader is likely to cognize the *it* as a human subject: in *A Single Man* the *it* can talk, and in *Mantissa* the *it* is very much aware of its surroundings even if it has lost the memory of 'who' it used to be. The attribution of consciousness, feelings and mental speculations therefore meets no obstacle, paving the way for a later identification of the two protagonists by means of a proper name. The most egregious contravention of standard parameters, therefore, must be that which does not even evoke the presence of a human subject.

Some feminist writing has attempted to provide ungendered morphological alternatives to the typically gendered personal pronouns (and to gender concord) in natural languages. Most of these experiments take the personal pronoun as their starting point. Since there is always a clearly human context in these novels, the reader usually has little difficulty in applying well-known cognitive frames to a fictional situation in which what are obviously human agents interact. In June Arnold's *The cook and the carpenter* (1973) these agents are referred to by means of the ungendered (invented) pronoun *na*. Such oddities bother the reader in one point only – that of the attribution of gender (and sex), since the constitutive indefiniteness of *na* makes it impossible to visualize characters' relationships. Arnold also employs *na* in passages of free indirect discourse, where this invented pronoun easily establishes a deictic centre.[32] By contrast, Marge Piercy's use of *per* in *Woman on the Edge of Time* (1976) is confined solely to passages of characters' dialogue and therefore never establishes internal focalization. Nor can one necessarily include Monique Wittig's *Le Corps lesbien* (1973) in this discussion of innovative morphology: *Le Corps lesbien* is, basically, a first-person novel; the *I* has merely been transformed into *j/e*, leaving the *toi* to operate with feminine (grammatical) concordance. In that book Wittig therefore radically undermines the gender of the speaking subject, but she does so by inventing a new morpheme for *I*, and leaves the second and third-person protagonists unaffected. *Le Corps lesbien* does not create a third-person deictic centre for the invented pronoun, and this setup is therefore not comparable to the other cases which I have discussed above.

6.1.2 Alternation

The above is a survey of a diversity of referential forms which can be encountered in (mostly recent) fiction. I have traced a scale of increasingly non-natural pronouns, which require considerable effort on the reader's part to be narrativized within the fictional context. Besides the existence of the documented diversity of these oddities, one must also pay close attention to the very important issue of pronoun (or person) *alternation*. The problem has recently been discussed by B. Richardson (1994), who provides the first in-depth treatment of the issue.[33] Two kinds of alternation have to be distinguished: successive alternation between pronominal choices referring to *different* protagonists, and alternation in reference to the *same* protagonist. An example of the former is Virgil

Virgin territories 237

Suarez's novel *Latin Jazz* (1989), in which each chapter has first-, second- and third-person sections which are aligned with specific protagonists. Alternation with regard to the *same* protagonist occurs, for instance, in John McGahern's *The Dark* (1965) and in Nuruddin Farah's *Maps* (1986). In the latter type of alternation, one can further distinguish between strategic alternation by segment or chapter, as in the McGahern text, and vacillating alternation, where the change in pronouns tends to be motivated psychologically rather than structurally.[34]

Pronouns, of course, alternate in narrative in a variety of quite different contexts. Not at issue in this connection is the alternation in pronominal reference between the narrative proper and direct discourse (or interior monologue) which it frames or embeds. In principle, the shift from quoting to quoted discourse does not provoke referential ambiguity since the shifting is meant, precisely, to alert the reader to the adoption of a new frame, that of characters' discourse. In some modern texts, however, the shift in and out of characters' referential anchoring can become obsessive, with the result that the narratorial presentation loses its plasticity and becomes submerged in the characters' discourse. Ingeborg Bachmann's story 'Paestum', which Stanzel has analysed with great verve (Stanzel 1981b), illustrates such a technique of radical ambiguity: one never knows precisely whether one is 'in the mind' of the female protagonist or not; the description of the journey, her exclamations and directions to the driver, and her internal comments all merge in one incessant stream of words which engulfs any subtle distinctions between the external and the internal, the objective and the subjective, the verbal and the non-verbal signified. In such texts a fusion of parameters occurs, and one cannot really speak of *alternation*. Nischik's concept of a *simultaneous* splitting of the narrative instance ('simultane Aufspaltung der Erzählinstanz') characterizes the effect of such writing very well, even though her own example illustrates the much more complex case of 'simultaneous' split reference to the same character on the *discourse* level (Nischik 1994: 240–4).

A clear distinction between referential parameters also persists in novels such as *Bleak House*, where, as has frequently been pointed out, the first- vs. third-person realms in the novel reflect complementary spheres of life, resulting in a *montage* of viewpoints rather than in a mere framenarrative (Esther's narrative as 'quoted by' the omniscient narrative). This version of montage remains fairly easy to absorb because it challenges no deep-seated preconceptions about the writing process, allowing one simply to see matters also from Esther's individual female perspective. If *Bleak House* provides a memorable reading experience, this is more due to the *tone* (and style) of the third-person sections than simply on account of the sweep of their omniscience (a range available to Dickens also in *A Tale of Two Cities* or to Thackeray in *Vanity Fair*). This technique of 'two novels thrown into one', as one might describe *Bleak House*, however, is not as widespread as one would expect. Postmodern examples of multi-perspectival alternating reference include Virgil Suarez's *Latin Jazz* (1989) or George Garrett's *The Succession* (1983). Suarez has different sections in first-, second- and third-person form with each form attributed to a different character. (The second-person strand is used for the Diego sections, Hugo's narrative uses the first-person mode, all other characters are aligned with the third person.) George Garrett's *The Succession* also alternates between first-person narrative (e.g. the old courtier) and third-person modes (the messenger), with one chapter in the second person ('Player') and a number of homodiegetic inserts (the letters of the priest, necessarily in the first person, the correspondence of Queen Elizabeth and James VI). Whereas works which include a diary, such as Daniel Defoe's *Robinson Crusoe* (1719) or Michel Tournier's *Vendredi ou les Limbes du Pacifique* (1967) neatly separate the narrative level from the quoted text, thereby producing a hierarchical frame structure rather than instituting segmentational alternation, *Bleak House* and *Latin Jazz* position their alternating discourses as coequal narratives on one and the same narrative level. The resultant effect is one of creative montage that does not seriously threaten readability.

Matters become much more threatening for the application of natural frames as soon as the different referential expressions refer to the *same* person, usually the main protagonist. This is, of course, already the case in frame narratives, but since these hierarchically bracket the first-person narrative by a natural situation of (frequently communal) storytelling (as in Henry James's *The Turn of the Screw*), no ambiguity or referential slippage occurs. Matters start to get much more complicated as soon as this storytelling frame is dropped and no realistic motivation for a framed first-person narrative can be supplied. Fay Weldon's *Female Friends* (1974), for instance, is unsettling precisely because we get Chloe's first-person account of her own unloved childhood side by side with the present tense third-person narrative which contrasts the three women's contemporary predicaments – a device which juxtaposes Chloe with Marjorie and Grace, opposes present and past, and provides both an external and an internal viewpoint on Chloe. Weldon's *The Cloning of Joanna May* (1989), too, juxtaposes Joanna's first-person sections with a third-person omniscient narrative that includes her as a story referent. Ellen Peel's essay on the alternation of first- and third-person sections also presents some interesting collocations of self-distancing (Peel 1989).

More unsettling still are the combinations in which one and the same protagonist shows up alternatively as a first-, second- and third-person referent. This is a typically postmodernist strategy, and there usually is no realistic frame which would mediate between these viewpoints. A notable example of this radical technique is B.S. Johnson's *Albert Angelo* (1964), a novel of considerable ingenuity in which one day in the life of the protagonist Albert Angelo is presented by means of his own account of his life (first-person narrative), in third-person sections, in sections of interior monologue (hence first person[35]), and in one second-person passage. Comparable, though less fanciful, uses of this technique can be found in John McGahern's *The Dark* (1965), which alternates between first-, second- and third-person sections, and in Gabriel Josipovici's story 'Second Person Looking Out' (1976). Some short story collections which may be short story cycles also have second-person chapters besides more common first- and third-person stories. Examples are Mary McCarthy's *The Company She Keeps* (1942; the second-person chapter is 'The Genial Host') or Tama Janowitz's *Slaves of New York* (1986; 'You and the Boss', 'Sun Poisoning'). In the Janowitz collection the female protagonist of the two second-person stories is definitely identical to the protagonist of some of the first- and third-person chapters. Pronominal alternation of this kind can be motivated very strongly in thematic terms, as in Nuruddin Farah's *Maps* (1986), where Askar's split personality and shifts in identification are reflected in the perspectives afforded by the first-, second- and third-person sections of the book.[36] Carlos Fuentes's *The Death of Artemio Cruz* (1962), on the other hand, provides, almost uncharacteristically, a realistic setup by means of which the first-person sections can be read as the interior monologue of the dying politician and the second-person sections can be naturalized as his reminiscences. The third-person segments, on the other hand, exceed Artemio's horizon of knowledge and present a more objectified and, at the same time, a more subjective account of Artemio's career.[37] By contrast, the rationale for the pronominal diversity of Carlos Fuentes's *Cambio de piel* (*A Change of Skin* [1967]) is much harder to grasp. The factuality of some narrative events in this novel is left radically in doubt, and the identity of the unnamed narrator, who appears to be responsible for the second-person sections, remains a puzzle: is there a specific occasion of address and narration? Are the second-person sections a kind of memory monologue during this narrator's confinement in prison?

All of the texts mentioned so far carefully alternate between blocks of first-, second- and third-person narrative. Even if the function and significance of the combination of perspectives for the narrative as a whole remains somewhat elusive (as in *Cambio de piel*), the reader can at least rely on a clear delimitation between alternating segments. This is no longer the case with Samuel Beckett's *Company* (1980) or Maurice Roche's *Compact* (1966). Roche alternates between first-, second- and third-person forms (and there are several varieties of each, with different typescripts and different tense usage), and he does so without any apparent plan: breaks or shifts occur in mid-paragraph and mid-sentence, and the rationale for the juxtaposing of so many perspectives cannot be guessed at by the text's 'story' either.[38] In fact, there is no story to speak of; or, rather, the one story that can be made out appears to be restricted to the 'Japanese' polite discourse strand. The protagonist's positioning in his room before his map merges with the depiction of his reminiscences and the reflections he engages in. These 'facts' fail to provide a 'realistic' frame for either the story of selling one's skin (told in the Japanese polite discourse strand) or for the descriptive passages of Kabuki stage directions and the extracts from instructional discourse. Samuel Beckett's *Company*, on the other hand, unlike the deliberate juxtapositions of Roche's text, does not employ pronominal alternation in the diffuse and seemingly afunctional manner of Roche's. Like many of Beckett's texts, *Company* traces one person's self-definition from a variety of contiguous perspectives. The alternation in person therefore reflects the prone protagonist's attempt at understanding himself, at approaching the centre from a number of only superficially contradictory directions. The protagonist's position of immobility correlates with his hearing in the dark a voice that must be the subject's merely fantasized interlocutor, the alter ego of his loneliness. The ambiguity and multi-perspectivism of the protagonist's self-conscious mirrorings are reflected formally by the various shifts between different pronominal constellations.

Even more disconcerting than Roche's chameleon-like transformations or Beckett's indeterminacies are texts like Juan Goytisolo's *The Virtues of the Solitary Bird* (1988) or Jean Thibaudeau's *Imaginez la nuit* (1968). In the latter, there exists a random sequence of passages rendering the experiences of protagonists referred to as *tu*, *vous*, *elle*, *ils*, *je* etc., which line up under one recurring '*je*', who can eventually be identified as the focalizer of the entire text (i.e. it is from *his* perspective that other characters are *tu*, *il* or *elles*). Goytisolo's technique is even more disorienting since there seems to be a plot, only one does not quite know what it is and how to link up the various segments of the text. Whereas Thibaudeau's random sequence of scenes can be explained in retrospect as a sequence of random associations on the part of the *je*, Goytisolo's novel requires the postulation of an 'arranger' (Hayman 1970), an instance responsible for the juxtaposing and sequencing of narrative segments. *The Virtues of the Solitary Bird* resists being naturalized as associative memory because no consistent situation is ever presented from which the protagonist (if, indeed, there is a consistent protagonist in the text) could remember things, nor is there a unitary consciousness which might be responsible for the text as fantasy. The comparison between these two novels also supports the problematic status of the category *person* on a theoretical level. One can only determine whether a narrative is homo- or heterodiegetic, or specify which category of 'person' a text belongs to, when one has defined what that text's story is, that is to say who is the protagonist. If one has no clear indication about the centrality of one character against another, it remains unclear whether first-person sections are inserts within a heterodiegetic frame or constitute the basic narrative discourse level, with *he* or *she* passages definable as distal deixis from that first person's deictic perspective. In the case of Thibaudeau's text, for instance, there initially appears to be an unstructured series of mini-stories about an 'I', a 'she', a 'he', etc. – all from the perspective of an arranger. This would constitute a radical alternation of person in the sense of a series of unconnected stories or presentations of a continuous story-world but in alternating configurations. That this conundrum relates to the question of realism, of focusing on a story schema, and is therefore ultimately a question of interpretation appears from the way in which such issues are determined in criticism: scenarios are constructed and their comparative verisimilitude is determined on the basis of holistic or organic plot schemata.

Whereas the pronouns in Goytisolo and Thibaudeau appear to be stable in their reference, even if it remains unclear which deictic centre they relate to, Julio Cortázar's novel *62: A Model Kit* (1968) performs even more disconcerting tricks. In this novel a number of characters are first referred to heterodiegetically (by means of pronouns or of a proper name), and *within the same paragraph* reference to these very same characters changes to the first person. Sometimes this move is camouflaged by a passage of interior (quoted) monologue (with first-person reference), after which the *récit* continues in the first person:

> The two of them barely fit into the ancient hydraulic elevator which, panting and moaning, carried them up to the fifth floor. **Celia** looked at the green linoleum floor, let herself be rocked by the vibration [...] Even though years passed, centuries, even though eternity passed, it was inconceivable for **her** to be going up to Hélène's place along with Hélène. 'No one really knows her', **she** thought when the elevator stopped with a kind of hiccup and **I** saw Hélène get out, pushing the suitcase, looking for the key in her purse. [...] Almost immediately Hélène decided to bathe first so that she could get dinner ready while **I** showered.
>
> (Cortázar 1994: 140)

Celia suddenly takes over as narrator in the middle of the paragraph, but no psychological motivation or explanation relating to a verisimilar move on the part of the heterodiegetic narrator is provided. At other times the switch from first- to third- or third- to first-person segment is abrupt and initially misleading; one only realizes belatedly that the reference of the pronouns has changed:

> 'An absurd gift', **Hélène** said, 'but that's where the charm lies, I suppose. [...]'
>
> 'This one is very pretty, quite different', **Celia** said, looking it [the doll] all over. 'It makes you want to be ten years younger so you can play with it, look at its underwear. It's completely dressed. Look at this slip, and it even has a bra. It's almost sinful if you think about it, because it has the face of a little girl.'
>
> Like **her**, of course, **I** have to swallow a smile when I hear **her** say: 'It makes you want to be ten years younger', she, who five years ago

must have been still playing at bathing and feeding a teddy bear and a doll.

(ibid.: 147)

On account of the previous passage one here surmises 'I' to refer to Celia, only to realize that it must be Hélène since it is Hélène from whose perspective Celia appears as a child. In the following passage the perspective changes with staggering speed: We move from Juan as a focalizer to Hélène's point of view, and immediately to a first-person narrative in which Hélène is the narrator.

It may have been the first time *she'd* [Hélène] said his [Juan's] name that night. She said it at the end of the sentence. The name came forth with a tone, with an inflection that it couldn't have had under other circumstances, loaded with something that went beyond the information and which *Hélène* seemed to lament, because *her* lips trembled and she slowly tried to get away from the fingers that were still digging into *her* shoulders, but *he* held *me* back with more force, and *I* almost cried out and *I* bit my mouth until he understood and with the confused sound of an excuse he suddenly let go and turned his back to me.

(ibid.: 242)

Since *62: A Model Kit* as a whole does not necessarily lend itself to being naturalized as Juan's interior monologue, such a passage cannot be explained as Juan's empathetic identification with Hélène when musing about her. Although Cortázar's pronominal experiment is stunning from a formal perspective, its functional significance for the novel remains unclear. Passages where proper names and the first-person pronouns alternate regularly belong to the reflector-mode so that there exists no juxtaposition between external and internal focalization on the macrostructural level. The technique is disruptive only because – unlike Beckett – a great number of characters are here presented in succession. In texts with uniform reflector-mode, as Stanzel was the first to point out (1984b: 227), the opposition person loses its significance: the *same* protagonist (reflector character) can be referred to by any number of pronouns. But in the texts that Stanzel cites there is only one reflector character 'on stage'. In Cortázar's novel, on the other hand, the reader is continually kept on the alert, having to thread her way through a labyrinth of referential expressions until she can hope to reconstruct a series of stories and, on repeated readings, the chronological and motivational relationship between these stories. Considerable effort is therefore spent on elucidating the referential applications of pronouns and proper names. As a consequence, deixis is foregrounded, unlike the typical case of reflector-mode narrative with pronominal alternation, where the adeictic alternation between first- and third-person pronouns is exploited fully for its potential of anchoring interiority.

Another very radical application of pronominal usage occurs in texts where the protagonist's self-definition is crucially at stake and the shift in pronoun reflects a shift in self-determination. Christa Wolf's novel *Kindheitsmuster* (*Patterns of Childhood*, 1976), for example, represents a fairly tame version of such a type of text since its first-, second- and third-person sections are kept neatly apart and they are clearly demarcated by the temporal and psychological distance to the narrating voice. Unlike Farah's *Maps* (1986), where first-, second- and third-person sections are separate coequal perspectives, Wolf's novel mirrors the narrator's self-division in the split self-reference that occurs in her autobiographical practice. The pronominal splitting serves radically to undermine referential continuity between her past and her present. Brian Richardson (1994) discusses a number of even more problematic texts and the ways in which *I* turns into *he*, *he* into *I*, or *I* into *you*. His examples include Nathalie Sarraute's *Tu ne t'aimes pas* (1989) and Clarice Lispector's *Água Viva* (*The Stream of Life*, 1989). Another famous text frequently noted in connection with pronominal alternation is Max Frisch's *Mein Name sei Gantenbein* (*A Wilderness of Mirrors*, 1964), another novel in which self-definition is crucially at stake.[39] Nischik (1994) discusses Atwood's 'The War in the Bathroom', in which a patently disturbed lodger tells her story from the perspective of her super-ego *I*, which controls her other self, referred to as *she:* 'I told her to close the door. She was upset so I let her lie down for a short rest. I will never allow her to live like that' (Atwood 1977: 17). Mental disturbances of a similar nature are also pointed out by Barbara Korte (1989) in reference to Erica Jong's *Fear of Flying* (1973) and John Updike's 'Flight' (1959). Another famous example of shifting pronominal usage devised to portray insanity is the last 'Darl' section in Faulkner's *As I Lay Dying* (1930).[40] An interesting case of *gender* alternation (*she/he*) occurs in one of the East German sex-change stories that created quite a sensation when they were published in 1980 (Finney 1992). In Sarah Kirsch's 'Blitz aus heiterm Himmel' (1980) the woman protagonist Anna metamorphoses into a man and renames herself Max. Anaphoric reference as a consequence changes from *she* to *he*.

I would here also like to note briefly the ending of Gabriele Wohmann's story 'Gegenangriff' ('Counter Attack', 1972), which is an exercise in similarly disorienting shifts, although initially the protagonists are kept separate. In this story a number of quite disparate building blocks are juxtaposed in a montage-like manner. One of these is in the newspaper sports cast type of register and concerns a boxing match in which the former champion challenges the new champion (hence the title). Juxtaposed with passages from this news story are passages in the second person which address a woman who is exhorted to be patient as if by a doctor in a closed institution or in an old people's home. Scientific discourse of diverse provenance completes the mosaic of juxtaposed passages. In the course of the text – there is no 'story' to speak of – the *you* (the exhorted person) becomes an *I*, the challenger is suddenly addressed as *you*, and the text ends with the challenger's victory, in a passage that uses the first-person pronoun. Not only are the two 'plots' or situations, which have no apparent connection with one another, combined uncannily and illogically in this final section of the text, but realistic readings of the piece cannot be provided either, except on a highly metaphorical level (the text as an illustration of verbal or physical aggression and of the provoking of counter-aggression). In fact, the story is non-narrativizable from a number of perspectives, and it anticipates some of the problems of radical experimental fiction that will be discussed in the next chapter. For the purpose of the present chapter I merely want to note the way in which a radical deconstruction of a text's pronominal setup affects the constructions of consistent dramatis personae.

A final text which I would like to mention in this section is Daphne Marlatt's novel *Ana Historic* (1988).[41] In this text the female protagonist and narrator Annie attempts to come to terms with her own past (especially in relation to her mother), with her present marriage to Richard, with her mother's life and with her writing. As for the latter, she is involved in tracing the history of a schoolteacher who emigrated to British Columbia in 1873 and, in gathering information about this woman, increasingly starts to fantasize about her, moving from the 'I' of her subject's diary and the 'she' of the historiographical discourse dealing with Mrs Richards, to the 'you' of empathetic re-experiencing. The narrator's stance towards her mother, her husband and herself is subjected to the same 'referential slither' (Bonheim 1983), and this results in rampant pronominal ambiguity and multivalency. The entire novel is a novel of flux, and the shifting alignments, thematically and otherwise, seem to reflect the protagonist's psychological instability, which is also mirrored in the novel's shifts and alternations between first-, second- and third-person forms. This instability is thematized in the address function of the second-person pronoun and ultimately resolved by the protagonist's interactive empathetic projection of self into other in the re-experiencing of an other's self.[42]

Having illustrated a wide range of experimentation with pronominal choices, I am now ready to tackle the theoretical issues that these texts raise – the status of *person* and its relation to a cognitively oriented 'natural' narratology.

6.2 PERSON AS A NARRATOLOGICAL CATEGORY RECONSIDERED

In this section I will deal with two separate issues. The first is the theoretical category *person*. As will be recalled, this is treated by Genette in terms of the dichotomy between homo- vs. heterodiegesis, and by Stanzel in terms of the identity vs. non-identity between the 'realms of existence' of narrator and characters respectively. The second issue concerns the cognitive frame of *personhood*. As I will argue, readers' visualizations of experientiality are necessarily linked to the existence of a human subject, the experiencer. That subject can realize experientiality as an agent, as a discursive or reflective instance (a teller or a 'mind' that cognizes), as an observer and as an experiencing consciousness. The narratological category of voice/person, as defined by Genette and Stanzel, relies on the prior positing of the figures of a narrator (or narratorial instance) and of the actants or characters, and – in Stanzel's case – the world(s) in which these are placed existentially.[43] Although these familiar narratological categories initially appear to be analytical, they emerge as being rooted in cognitive parameters and in a double conception of narrative texts. That double conception can best be described as a mutually interlocking concept in which the story/discourse (Chatman) distinction subtends a distinction between narrators as narrating agents (who may become fully anthropomorphized entities) and characters as actants. The dichotomy therefore correlates with the evocation of a story-world which relies on a realistic (pre)conception of story matter, in opposition to a conceptualization as a separate act of narration.

In the sample texts presented in the previous section the simple dichotomies of Genette and Stanzel[44] no longer easily apply. Second-person fiction radically undermines the binary opposition of the homo/heterodiegetic since second-person texts can be *homodiegetic* (in the sense of the narrator's sharing the fictional (story) world with the *you*-protagonist) as well as *heterodiegetic* (when the narrator, if there is one, remains confined to the act of narrating, addressing and enunciating).[45] The concept of 'realms of existence' is therefore a very valid and useful one, even for second-person fiction, but it needs to be redefined to accommodate also the communicational circuit, i.e. the evocation of a 'realistic' storytelling situation in which the speaker (narrator) addresses a narratee and recounts a sufficiently motivated story. Within such an extended model it then also becomes possible to characterize adequately the continuity obtaining between the realms of existence of a narratee and her earlier 'incarnation' as a *you*-protagonist. I have therefore proposed (Fludernik 1993b) a new set of terms combining these existential and descriptive parameters. In my terminology, an 'existential' continuity between the communicative (narrator–narratee) level and the story level is defined as *homocommunicative*, whereas a complete discontinuity between these existential levels is characterized as *heterocommunicative*. This dichotomy, however, does not apply as a rigid *either/or* option but necessarily lends itself to a conceptualization in terms of open scales. Figure 2 therefore accommodates peripheral types such as narratives in which the narrator is only an observer of the life of the protagonist of a third- or second-person text. In addition, *I + you* texts, *we-* and *they-* narratives, and plural *you-* texts allow themselves to be placed within this model. In so far as a communicative level can be established for the narrative, a scale of options becomes available that moves from various homocommunicative types of narrative (the narrator and/or narratee existentially straddle the story vs. discourse dichotomy) to a number of heterocommunicative narratives (narrator *and* narratee are divorced from the world of fiction). Both the homo- and the heterocommunicative realms have permeable boundaries, with the consequence that the model recuperates Stanzel's typological circle by projecting a comparable continuity of forms within the realm of communicative narratives. Unlike Stanzel, however, I have eliminated pure reflector-mode narratives from this circuit, arguing that distinctions of person do not apply at all in noncommunicative narrative (as I call it). Nor are the two areas of communicative and noncommunicative narration to be visualized in dichotomous terms, either. What Stanzel calls the authorial–figural continuum is indeed located precisely on the borderline of communication and noncommunication, and – I would argue – constitutes a separate category or type of text which I propose to call *figural* narrative (in contradistinction to the reflectoral narrative of noncommunicative texts).

Even this radically extended schema, however, fails adequately to represent such oddities as *one* (*on, man*) texts. It imperfectly subsumes these, along with texts deploying invented pronouns, under the category of third-person narratives. That subsumption has its problems, since *one* characteristically involves the reader or serves to camouflage its reference to an *I* or *you*. The typical ambiguity of *one* texts tends to locate these, rather, on the outskirts of the homocommunicative realm, even if such an attribution may remain implicit, ambiguous or fleeting. A typology, even in the revised shape of Figure 2, therefore provides some useful terminology to characterize certain setups, but its practicality extends little further than that. As a heuristic schema explicating how narrative works, it has little to offer, and it again runs aground in the attempt to deal with recent innovative devices. Nor is such a typology suited to dealing with any of the questions that I have raised in section 6.1.2 above – that of multiple or alternating reference, or of the possible *function*(s) of such referential shifts.

A matter that I have so far ignored concerns the *naming* of protagonists, a point that interacts with pronominal reference choices. As is well known, the realist novel, especially the eighteenth-century and nineteenth-century realist novel, employs a recurring set of denotational and descriptive referential phrases (cp. Halliday and Hasan 1976 and Leech and Short 1981), with anaphoric *he* or *she* accounting only for a portion of the referential noun phrases (NPs). Characters' first names and descriptive characterizations are prominently on display. The novel of reflectoral consciousness and, even more so, the experimental novel, on the other hand, have started to undermine this communicationally motivated distribution, either by reducing the number of NPs to a few shamefacedly

(A) Narrative with a Communicative Level (Teller Mode)

	homocommunicative narrative						heterocommunicative narrative	
	I + he/she	I	I + you	1 + you	you	you	you + he/she	you	he, she
	homodiegetic					homoconative			
		autodiegetic							
↙	peripheral homodiegetic (first-person in narrative) (including we-narratives of exclusive we): Mann, *Doctor Faustus*		peripheral homo- (i.e. auto)diegetic narrative with you-protagonist: Grass, *Katz und Maus*	both narrator and addressee share realms of existence with story world we-narratives: E. White, *Nocturnes for the King of Naples*	addressee as character (narrator only explicit or implicit address function): Farley, 'The House of Ecstasy'	authorial–figural continuum possible, too: Calvino, *If on a Winter's Night a Traveller*	peripheral you (in relation to a third-person protagonist): not found, but possible in principle	heterocommunicative you, you only protagonist, not addressee: Butor, *La Modification* (authorial–figural)	narrational level existentially divorced from story level; authorial and authorial–figural third person: Fielding, *Tom Jones* Joyce, *Portrait of the Artist as a Young Man* –↗

(B) Narrative with No Communicative Level

(reflector narrative and neutral narrative)
e.g. Ernest J. Gaines 'The Sky is Gray' (first person); Jean Muno, *Le Joker* and Jay McInerney, *Bright Lights, Big City* (second person); William Faulkner, 'Was' in *Go Down, Moses* (third person)

Figure 2 A revised typology of narrative person and communication

←——→ figural narrative

placed tags which serve the need of minimal disambiguation or by the excessive use of proper names in the manner of Gertrude Stein (e.g., in *The Autobiography of Alice B. Toklas* [1933] and especially in her *Three Lives* [1909]). The most radical consequence of this taboo on descriptive NPs can be observed in the increasing tendency to eschew naming at all. Thus a great number of recent texts, and not only first-person texts, refuse to legislate on the protagonist's name. This is very common for short stories but is becoming fairly frequent for the novel as well. For instance, one has a first-person novel with an unnamed protagonist in Margaret Atwood's *Surfacing* (1972);[46] a third-person novel (in the *man* form) in E.Y. Meyer's *In Trubschachen* (1973); and second-person novels with unnamed protagonists in Sunetra Gupta's *The Glassblower's Breath* (1993) and Edna O'Brien's *A Pagan Place* (1970).[47] It is much more difficult to find unnamed *he* or *she* protagonists for entire novels. One possible case might be Robbe-Grillet's *La Jalousie* (1957), but only if one accepts that the husband is the main protagonist (Frank and A. are, of course, named).

Here, too, one needs to consider matters in terms of a scale, a cline ranging from explicit and expository naming to the use of increasingly implicit and delayed information and ultimately to the refusal to name. In most reflectoral novels the protagonist's name turns up as if incidentally: in the dialogue, in somebody's interior monologue, in a letter.[48] A case of a near-refusal of naming occurs in Susan Sontag's *The Volcano Lover* (1992), where the eponymous hero is referred to throughout as 'the Cavaliere' and only historical knowledge supplies his identification with Alexander Hamilton. At the most extreme end of the scale no name is supplied at all, the protagonist remains an *I*, a *you* or a *he/she* without the crucial identificational mark of the proper name. In short fiction this has become a frequent ploy. Even more drastically, Jeanette Winterson's first-person narrator in *Written on the Body* (1992) is not only unnamed but also of indeterminate sex/gender.

Not that naming *per se* is absolutely necessary to evoking a story or a human subject – in fact the realistic parameter of personhood tends to be undermined much more forcefully by an alternation in pronouns referring to the same character, especially when that shifting is motivated by identificational problems of this character. Ambiguity and multi-referentiality are particularly difficult to handle typologically and can be processed successfully by readers only when situational frames (such as the attribution of insanity, temporary derangement, schizophrenia, loss of memory, sex change, etc.) can be applied to the fictional setup. Pronominal difficulties therefore tend to be resolved in terms of realistic storytelling parameters (where a narrator is primarily involved) and in terms of actantial or motivational (psychological) parameters where only the protagonists are concerned. Personhood, and particularly *identity*, is a fundamental presupposition about the real world. The deliberate flouting of a consistent portrayal of character therefore cries out for a compensatory recuperation in terms of motivation, or else the very foundations of the fictional world stand to slide into nothing.

My conclusions about the narratological category *person* therefore firmly wed that category to the cognitive concept of *personhood*, which operates as a frame. The story vs. discourse distinction which subtends traditional definitions of *person* is here argued to be already the *effect* of realistic narrativization whereby the frame of storytelling results in the postulation of a narrator figure (and/or a narratee) and basic-level actantial frames produce a level of interacting story existents (characters). The more schematically one conceives of the traditional model, the less it allows for the incorporation of non-realistic conceptions, with the known result of excluding second-person fiction and much else in recent experimental writing. If one conceives of story and discourse as parameters within a realistic frame of telling, viewing and experiencing, this helps to locate tellers and experiencers in motivated and re-cognizable frame situations and makes it possible to narrativize superficially recalcitrant materials with some elegance and ease. Second-person fiction, even texts with *one* and *it*, especially when deployed in reflector-mode narration, do not really create any serious problems: the *you*-protagonist is clearly an experiencer, and in some kinds of second-person narrative a quasi-realist situation of address may be projected. As we will see under 7.2, there are limits to narrativization, for instance where quasi-realistic storytelling situations are increasingly being undermined by various textual strategies of text generation. What matters most in the process of narrativization is consistency: one can easily learn to deal with a second-person protagonist if that protagonist is clearly presented as an experiencer; what is nearly impossible to visualize is a protagonist who disappears in protean fashion behind a barrage of shifting pronominal alignments and eludes the grasp of consistent identification. Such texts approach the redoubted realm of the unreadable.

6.3 TENSE AND NARRATION: UNDERMINING DEIXIS AS USUAL

6.3.1 The narrative present

> I am pregnant the first time I'm asked to do a training session on corporations.
> ('Body of Work'; Small, 1991: 30)

This is the beginning of a short story published in *The New Yorker* (8 July 1991). The present tense *I am*, evoking expectations of descriptive characterization (*I am a schoolteacher in Upper State New York*) or of habitual action (*I play tennis once a week, on Thursdays, with my boss*), here jars on the reader's nerves like a razorblade: *I am pregnant* sounds like a wife addressing her husband, not like a narrator addressing the reader or telling a story! Out of context, as a first line of fiction, the sentence does not even make sense as a historical present of sensational relevance (*So he offers me the job, and what happens, I'm pregnant the first time I'm asked to do a training session*). This is exactly the function of the present tense in this context, but it strikes one as extremely odd because historical presents do not usually initiate texts, and of course – as it turns out later – the entire story is written in the present tense. The recognition of a 'historical present-tense function' for the story onset therefore becomes a mere assumption of an underlying pattern in the narrative deep structure.

As one reads on in the text, the present tense in this short story starts to become quite natural; after all, present-tense narratives abound these days.[49] However, at the beginning of subsequent sections of Judith Small's 'Body of Work' one is again jolted out of one's readerly expectations. The second section starts with 'I want him to leave my office right now. He is too young, stands too close to me, looks me too easily in the eye, is too sure [...]' (ibid.: 31). This cannot even be explained as a historical present tense; it clearly renders what Deborah (whose name we learn only later when this intruder addresses her by her first name) *feels*: hence it is the equivalent of psycho-narration[50] or, possibly, interior monologue. Again, the section starts *medias in res*, at the point where Deborah's feelings erupt about the smart-alecky 'fresh-faced' young man 'straight out of Harvard or Stanford, clad in the shining raiment of his irrefutable logic' (ibid.).

The next two sections of the story employ a present progressive in their first sentences. This, again, is a highly unusual stylistic device since the present progressive, generally speaking, relates specific ongoing activities (settings[51]) on which one half-expects crucial events to intrude – but in this story no such incidences occur.

> A month later I'm driving through a pouring March rain, past the malls and condos of the suburbs to Tom Keaney's funeral.
>
> (ibid.: 31)

Deborah's filmic description of her drive gives rise, not to a surprising accident, but to her reminiscences about Tom. The present progressive, which one would expect to be used for current activities such as 'I'm learning Chinese', is here employed to pinpoint a very specific situation, and the temporal phrase at the beginning of the sentence in conjunction with the progressive again evokes familiar patterns of oral narrative[52] (*So at noon I'm driving along High Street, when who should run his bike across my way but Jim Fielding*), where the episode incipit and the setting-plus-incidence[53] points of conversational narrative have become conflated into one construction. Likewise, at the beginning of the final section we get: 'I'm watching the videotape of my talk' (ibid.: 32). Again the present progressive is used, although its oddity is here much muted by the specification of the situation: this is the videotape of the talk mentioned at the beginning of the story, so this must be the endpoint of the story, after all the deviational material that has been presented. The closure of the structural arc (temporal and thematic) is obvious. A second reason for the familiarity of 'I'm watching the videotape' relates to its assumed chronological status as the presumptive endpoint of the plot. One's immediate guess regarding the timing of this scene would tend to locate it at the 'here-and-now' point of narration: one expects the story to be told retrospectively from the viewpoint of the successful training session. This intuition is corroborated by the final lines of the text:

> Then the words begin to fade. I'm talking, and smiling, and then I'm talking very quietly, and then I turn my face to include some other listeners around the conference table and I'm moving my lips around silence. Then I smile again, turn my head another way, and the words come back, surging, receding, as if a wind were blowing through the tape. We are sitting around a table talking about corporations and suddenly we aren't; we are only mouth, hair, eyes, my dress the color of wine, somebody's sleeve, fingers, a smile, a coffee cup lifted, a head nodded. Somebody raises a hand.
>
> (ibid.)

This is a static view of what Deborah sees on the screen, film unrolling, description. The story ends *in medias res* with Deborah watching her successful session on video. The video cannot be reused because the tape falters into silence, leaving pictures – close-ups, just like the ones which the narrative has been offering in its own (linguistic) medium.

This is not the place to provide a list of even the best-known present-tense texts. Even among full-blown novels the number of present-tense texts has risen dramatically in the past two decades, and one would have to present a very extensive list indeed. Besides the early German instances of Franz Werfel's *Das Lied von Bernadette* (1941) and Ernst Wiechert's *Die Majorin* (1934), noted English examples are Robert M. Pirsig's *Zen and the Art of Motorcycle Maintenance* (1974), a good deal of Beckett's work (*Company* [1980], among others), J.M. Coetzee's *Waiting for the Barbarians* (1980), Pynchon's *Gravity's Rainbow* (1973), even George Garrett's historical novel *The Succession* (1983). *You*-texts are almost consistently written in the narrative present (compare Fludernik 1994d). The narrative present occurs most frequently in reflector-mode novels and is prominently employed in the short story. French examples are particularly common in the *nouveau roman* literature. See, for instance, Michel Butor's *La Modification* (1957) and most of Robbe-Grillet's novels, including *La Jalousie* (1957). Several recent German examples are noted in Petersen (1992: 73). Petersen also provides a historical abstract (1992: 88-9) which names Paul Scheerbart's novel *Rakkóx der Billionär* (1900) as the first novel with extensive present tense narrative. Petersen's first pure present-tense novel is Alfred Klabund's *Rasputin* (1929). Early English examples of the narrative present can be noted in Nathaniel Hawthorne's sketches (whose *narrative* qualities may, however, be open to doubt) and in several novels by Charles Dickens, where entire chapters are cast in the narrative present.[54] Judging from the notoriety of the Pirsig text and the narratological sensation caused by Coetzee's novels, I suspect that there are few early *novels* in English, although the number of early short stories is definitely greater but much less conspicuous since they can be read as descriptive sketches.

Present-tense narrative, as Dorrit Cohn has recently pointed out (Cohn 1993), is a most peculiar thing: one cannot realistically 'live' the story and narrate it at the same time or tell what one is currently experiencing *as a story* (it would tend to be ongoing commentary). The impossibility of simultaneous narration relates to a story schema which puts a premium on narrative's explanatory force (Adams 1993): narratives retrodictively[55] *explain why* (as well as *how*) things happened. This does not exclude the presentation of a mere registering of events as they obtrude on one's senses (Pamela's 'writing to the minute'; reporting in football or baseball or other sports); but that is not 'real' narrative.[56] Nor can the present tense here be equated with the use of the present in conversational narratives, since, as we have seen, it has no truck with the *historical* present tense. Present-tense narrative, in so far as it operates in a standard teleological fashion, attempts to square the circle, performing the blatantly impossible: it narrates 'as if' in the preterite, but does so in the present tense. The effect of such present-tense narrative, however – in contrast to the rather striking originality of Small's short story – is frequently one of surprising inconspicuousness; one hardly notices at all that the text employs the present tense.

The *narrative present*, as Stanzel and Cohn have named the form,[57] cannot simply be identified as an 'epic present' (Fries 1970: 338). As I have argued (cp. Fludernik 1993a: 47–51, 198–9), the epic *preterite* is constituted primarily, *not* by its status of fictionality (as Hamburger claimed), but by its reflectoral mediation (Stanzel): only for texts which have no *narrator's present* tense which is being contrasted with the *characters' past* can one posit an epic preterite, a preterite shorn of its deictic qualities. In accordance with this definition of the epic preterite as a past tense deprived of its deictic significance, an 'epic' *present tense* should be understood as an adeictic tense which would typically not be aligned with a speaking subject. It is here that Cohn's suggestion that narrative presents in first-person texts are more 'outrageous' than in third-person texts has its deictic grounding: only in first-person texts is the current speaker a deictic entity with existential properties. These existential properties are grounded in the first-person narrator's role as a personalized teller figure and its necessary embodiment. Third-person texts need not foreground the presence of a personalized narrator figure; the deictic opposition between the act of enunciation and the related events is consequently much muted in third-person narrative. However, much the same backgrounding of the deictic opposition also applies to first-person texts with reduced enunciational activity. Reflectoral first-person present-tense texts in fact document their quality of reflector narrative precisely, among other things, by their adeictic use of tense. Not only does the choice of a present tense or a past tense in reflectoral texts have no palpable effect of deictic differentiation; alternation between these tenses, too, frequently occurs without rhyme or reason and with little detectable impact on meaning.

I will return to the issue of tense alternation below. The deictic uprootedness of present-tense narrative derives especially from its collapsing of all tenses into the one present tense system and, more especially, from its inherent vagueness about circumstances of the act of narration or enunciation (Cohn 1993). Most present-tense texts, whether in the first, second or the third person, practise such deliberate refusal to situate the act of narration, and this becomes more striking and more puzzling when there is a garrulous and opinionated narrator, particularly a first-person narrator, on the scene. In Judith Small's story, for instance, the narrator Deborah is very much in the foreground as a chatty and sententious storyteller, but she is located in a temporal nowhere. This lack of a temporal point from which the first-person narrator views the experience radically affects the establishment of story meaning. Thus, in Coetzee's *Waiting for the Barbarians* (1980) the narrative moves along in chronological fashion but neither at the beginning nor at the end of the narrative is there a summary of the 'point' of the experience for the first-person narrator as a consistent interpretation of the events in their entirety. Nor does the text allow one to envisage a simultaneous situation of writing or speaking during which the protagonist could realistically be construed to indite (orally or in writing) the narrative of events as they occur to him. Some other present-tense texts can be read as simply reflections of what happens to the protagonist: as portrayals, that is, of a consciousness registering what happens to him or her. Such registering tends to suggest a neutral mode of narrative and a quasi-voyeuristic subtext, and it has recourse to 'ordinary' narrative techniques: descriptions (even of impressions and sense data) are traditionally cast in the present tense. Such uses are frequently compared (Petersen 1992: 68) with the *tabular present* (*tabularisches Präsens*). Hamburger (1968: 103, 1993: 123–4) used the term for Goethe's present tense passages in *The Elective Affinities*, and her analysis correctly outlines the pictorial quality of the device.[58] In yet other texts one finds a suggestion at their conclusion that the story is re-experienced by the dying protagonist as if on film: he has his life flash by before his eyes. This may also happen at crucial moments of a person's life. An example is Joyce Carol Oates's short story 'You', in which the story's 'I' appears to relive the events of the past few days in the split second before she meets her mother coming towards her down the gangway at the airport.[59]

A linguistic point to be noted about present-tense narratives is the fact that the present tense manifests a pronounced multi-functionality.[60] The present tense substitutes for *all* tenses except the present perfect and the future, which belong to the present-tense system (Benveniste 1971: 212). Flashbacks, which in past-tense narrative usually take the past perfect, are rendered in the past tense. Additionally, the present tense is of course also used for all situations in which past tense narrative already had a present tense: the narrator's commentary, meta-narrative reflections, gnomic pronouncements, proverbs and the like; characters' interior monologue and direct speech; the present as future; as well as for what would be the historical present if one had a past tense to contrast it with. Moreover, the narrative present naturally substitutes for all functions served by the preterite in past-tense narrative. Besides the preterite of narrative clauses, this includes sequence-of-tense preterites, including free indirect discourse forms,[61] anticipatory preterites (*he was to have done*) and sequence-of-tense conditionals (which show up as future-tense forms in present-tense narratives). The loss of the deictic distinction between present-tense *nows* and past-tense *thens* is therefore implicated in the loss of even more crucial narratological distinctions: that of story and discourse – i.e. the narrator's commentary is no longer temporally distinguished from reportative narrative – and that of narration vs. direct speech (interior monologue) or 'shifted' forms of present-tense free indirect discourse. Present-tense narrative therefore also radically blurs the line between external and internal events.

To illustrate the collapsing of these temporal distinctions let me quote a passage from the third chapter of Coetzee's *Waiting for the Barbarians*:

> The girl is bleeding, that time of the month has come for her. She cannot conceal it, she has no privacy, there is not the merest bush to hide behind. She is upset and the men are upset. It is the old story: a woman's flux is bad, bad for the crops, bad for the hunt, bad for the horses. They grow sullen: they want her away from the horses, which cannot be, they do not want her to touch their food. Ashamed, she keeps to herself all day and does not join us for the evening meal. After I have eaten I take a bowl of beans and dumplings to the tent where she sits.
>
> (iii; Coetzee 1982: 69)

The paragraph is on the plotline and all narrative clauses are in the present tense ('They grow sullen'). The present perfect of completion ('has come'), which – in a past-tense context – would have been shifted into the past perfect, remains a present perfect; likewise, anterior events in temporal clauses take the present perfect tense appropriate to the present-tense system: 'after I have eaten'. The men's dissatisfaction, which they utter in accusations about the evil the woman's menstruation will bring on them, is rendered in a condensed (narratorial) form of ironic, distancing free indirect discourse: 'It is the old story: *a woman's flux is bad luck, bad for the crops, bad for the hunt, bad for the horses*'.[62] The narrator's comments ('It is the old story' and 'she has no privacy') are indistinguishable from the reportative passages ('She cannot conceal it').

> The ducks, branded, enthralled, totter unsteadily away as you approach with Daniel and his son, he holds your sandwiches and a bottle of Chianti you have picked up along the way, the child clutches an enormous patterned cup and his greasy packet. Avishek, who has purchased, while you were waiting in McDonald's, a newspaper, and several bars of chocolate, takes a bench, in quite dangerous proximity, for the heady experience of having you practically brush past, as you climbed out of Trafalgar Square, half an hour ago, has left him eager to hover once more on the edge of discovery, to lurk in the brighter cone of shadow.
> (*The Glassblower's Breath*; Gupta 1994: IV, 104)

> Your hands clench under the sudden impact of the vehicle behind you, another double-decker of the same species, nosing the backside of its partner in some lurid mating ritual that forces London buses to always travel in clumps, an affinity that has proved indispensable, however, to Avishek, who sits nervously near the front of the bottom deck, his eyes glued to the orifice of the bus ahead, thankfully still in sight, still there are traffic lights,of course, and the not inconsiderable possibility that this one will try and outrun its predecessor, it will be a nail-biting journey for your cousin, a precarious sojourn through the isthmuses of chance.
> (ibid.: VI, 163)

In the first passage the use of the past tense for flashback sequences can be observed ('while you were waiting in McDonald's'; 'as you climbed out of Trafalgar Square, half an hour ago') whereas resultative anteriors, as above, remain in the present perfect. In the second passage Avishek's desperate calculations about whether or not he will lose sight of his cousin, whom he is shadowing, are rendered in the future tense, whereas in standard past-tense narrative they would be shifted into the conditional. The passage continues with a prognosticating comment by the narrator, indistinguishably also in the future tense: 'it will be a nail-biting journey for your cousin'. In a past-tense context this future tense would have been clearly marked as comment since its tense (present-tense system) would have stood out from the preterital context of the narration. Likewise, habitual presents ('some lurid mating ritual that forces London buses to always travel in clumps') are indistinguishable (except semantically and contextually) from narrative presents ('Your hands clench'). One can observe how, with the text all in present and future tenses, the reader has to invest much more interpretative effort into the reading.

256 *Virgin territories*

Although not usually recognized as an experimental technique, present-tense narrative therefore significantly departs from the traditional schemata of the real-world temporality of storytelling. Yet most present-tense narratives, however illogical, are easily recuperable as a story of events or as the representation of a mind reliving past experience as present. Hence the paradoxical situation that the narrative present is both a rather unknown oddity and a technique of unremarked-upon familiarity.

6.3.2 'Odd' narrative tenses

Besides narratives which are entirely written in the present tense, there also exist some experimental texts that employ even more outrageous narrative tenses. The extent of such writing is at present obscure. A few texts that I have come across are mentioned here, but the phenomenon may be much more extensive.

Let me start with the *future tense*. As far as I am aware this occurs fairly consistently throughout at least two English texts: Michael Frayn's *A Very Private Life* (1968) and Pam Houston's story 'How To Talk to a Hunter' (1990). The two uses are, however, entirely different. Frayn's future tense initially carries some deictic significance since the novel is a utopia situated in the future, although its deictic meaning soon evaporates. Pam Houston's story, on the other hand, uses no future tense (deictically speaking) at all, but the *will* morphology of verbal inflection that can be aligned with hypothetical discourse.

> The hunter will talk about spring in Hawaii, summer in Alaska. The man who says he was always better at math will form the sentences so carefully it will be impossible to tell if you are included in these plans.
> (Houston 1990: 99)

As Weinrich (1985: 57)[63] points out, the future tense belongs to the present-tense system of the language, and the sequence-of-tense rule therefore produces present-tense forms in 'simultaneous' subsidiary clauses: 'who *says*'; 'if you *are* included'. As a consequence, clauses of indirect discourse, free indirect discourse and all temporal, causal or conditional clauses also take the present tense, as do passages of interior monologue.

> He'll ask you to dance, and *before* you *can* answer he'll be spinning you around your wood stove, he'll be humming in your ear. *Before* the song *ends* he'll be taking off your clothes, setting you lightly under the tree, hovering above you with tinsel in his hair.
> (Houston 1990: 103)

With all these contexts that require a present tense the story has fewer future tenses than one would expect. Since the female protagonist's deictic centre predominates, *will* is almost consistently read as a hypothetical *will* rather than a future tense. The deictic significance of *will* is backgrounded in relation to the numerous present tenses of the text. The story reads like present-tense narrative with ample hypothetic speculation on the part of the female protagonist.

Although Michael Frayn's *A Very Private Life*, as a utopia situated in the future, embraces the full deictic weight of the *will* morphology, this text, too, soon lapses into the present tense, and it does so much less gracefully than Houston's short story. In the beginning Frayn exploits to the full the oddity of a narrative future tense by means of collocations with *once upon a time* and puns on the phrases *in the good old days* and *a long long while ago*:

> **Once upon a time there will be** a little girl called Uncumber.
> Uncumber will have a younger brother called Sulpice, and they will live with their parents in a house in the middle of the woods. There will be no windows in the house, because there will be nothing to see outside except the forest. While inside there will be all kinds of interesting things – strange animals, processions, jewels, battles, mazes, convolutions of pure shapes and pure colours – which materialise in the air at will, solid and brilliant and almost touchable. For ***this will be in the good new days a long, long while ahead***, and it will be like that in people's houses then.
>
> (Frayn 1981: 5)

Initially, Frayn restricts the present tense to subsidiary clauses and hence to their sequence-of-tense environment. However, as soon as a scene has been established, the present installs itself in the position of the narrative tense proper: temporal specifications (*one day*) coincide with the *will* future, but actions that occur in the wake of this episodic onset are rendered by means of the present tense:

> The fact that no one goes out and no one comes in doesn't mean that they ***won't see*** anyone, of course. They***'ll*** be seeing people all the time. [...] Particularly Aunt Symphorosa with the sad life and the perpetual smile; and Great-great-grandfather, who ***will*** make rather a habit of falling asleep while on transmission, so that Uncumber's father ***won't*** know whether he can politely switch him off or not. 'How can I watch the Battle of Borodino on the history channel while your blasted mother's grandfather is occupying the reception chamber?' he *complains* to his wife – a family joke.
>
> (ibid.: 6–7)

> ***One day*** she ***will*** hear the familiar clink of their tools on the other side of the wall, and their muffled talk and laughter, and she will say: 'The animals are there again!'
> It'***s*** all mixed up inside her head with some holovision programme she ***has seen***. She ***thinks*** people live inside, and animals outside.
> And she *takes* everything so seriously. ***One day*** her mother ***will*** find

her *tapping back* to the repairmen! [...] But when her mother gently **dissuades** her, Uncumber *is* furious. She **weeps** and **throws** herself on the floor and shouts that she wants to see the 'animals'.

(ibid.: 12–13)

In the second passage Uncumber's habitual actions (or the narrator's description of her character, if you will) are rendered in the present tense ('thinks'; 'takes'). Note also the present perfect 'has seen' for anterior clauses, which also ties in with the present-tense system to which the future tense belongs.

Frayn's narrative also has a narrator figure emerge early in the text, who sometimes voices 'his' or 'her' opinions:

This is the way children always repay the thoughtfulness of those who ordered them – particularly Uncumber! She *will* be a difficult child!

(ibid.: 14)

Statements such as 'She *will* be a difficult child' shift from a constantive statement about the future to an evaluative reading: 'She insists on being difficult'. Although the phrase occurs first as what appears to be her parents' estimation of Uncumber's character (ibid.: 8), it has now become an evaluative statement on the part of the narrator.

The *will* future in Frayn's novel, however, soon comes to lose its deictic, i.e. temporal, significance since it refers to a clearly hypothetical and fantastic future. Much of the description of Uncumber's world therefore appears much less prophetic than probabilistic, though the hypothetical tone is less pronounced than in the case of Houston's story:

Incidentally, their [the children's] father's name will be Aelfric, their mother's Frideswide. These names will seem ridiculous and embarrassing to Uncumber when she gets old enough to mind about such things. No doubt they *will* be rather old-fashioned by then. Why, she will wonder miserably, couldn't they have been called something sensible? Frumentius and Osyth, for instance, like her friend Rhipsime's parents.

(ibid.: 13–14)

Quite a few statements in *will* clauses concern habitual events (see, in my first quotation, the description of how Uncumber's people 'see' others over intercom). This use recalls the *will* construction that is used to designate recurring events in the future (and which corresponds to past tense *would*):

And they'll see a lot of the world. They'll have memorable family holidays together – weeks on a lonely shore where the sun shines all day, on and on, and the surf booms, and the fine salt spray drifts over them in the wind, riming their brown skins with white.

(ibid.: 8)

After the initial nine pages, however, the narrative shifts entirely into the present tense. At first the present introduces a recurring situation:

> Uncumber and Sulpice have this game they play, of *trying to get out*. It is one of their legends that somewhere a secret door exists into the outside world. They whisper about it together in corners, and draw up plans, and press and peer and pry among the soft, yielding surfaces of the walls and ceilings.
>
> (ibid.: 14)

The present then simply continues in the narration of the subsequent scene, although in the collocation *one day* plus present tense: 'But one day – when they are not even looking seriously – they find the secret panel!' (ibid.: 15). This, incidentally, is suggestive of an implied (deep-structural) historical present tense. The discovery constitutes a major incidence point. The next chapter starts with 'And then, one day when she is up in the little outside world at the top of the secret stairs, her elbow bangs against something sticking out' (ibid.: 17). After this the entire narrative is in the present tense, and the *will* future never recurs.

Another future-tense novel is Alberto Vanasco's *Sin embargo Juan vivía* (1947; *And Juan Lived After All*).[64] This is a second-person text (*tú*) with consistent future-tense narrative. I gather that the protagonist's actions are all referred to in the future tense, including even forms of the past in the future ('when you will have found the body' etc.). Unlike Houston's and Frayn's texts, Maurice Roche's *Compact* (1966), which we have already encountered as an example of alternating *pronominal* choices, utilizes the future tense as one of many tense options in a text that also plays with the alternation of tense. *Compact* juxtaposes narrative passages in the present tense, in the *imparfait*, in the future tense, the *conditionnel* and passages that employ only non-finite verbal forms. The future tense collocates with *tu*, whereas the conditional tense occurs only in the *vous* sections. No deictic significance attaches to these tenses at all – just as the various pronominal alternatives all refer to the unnamed protagonist, the various tense options are all narrative tenses referring to the story time – if story there is.

The conditional tense is also employed as a consistent tense option in Marguerite Duras's *La Maladie de la mort* (1982). In this novel the protagonist, consistently referred to as *vous*, engages in a plot that is highly fantastic, in fact something he imagines rather than actually lives through. The conditional is therefore an appropriate, duly hypothetical temporal choice for this text. A second book which employs the German *würde* conditional is E.Y. Meyer's novel *In Trubschachen* (1973), which I have already noted above (6.1). This text is written in the *man* form of the guidebook format and employs numerous *würde* passages to designate hypothetical (or narrative?) actions by the protagonist.

Schon durch den Umstand, daß man das Zimmer – damit es vom Zimmermädchen gemacht werden kann – jeden Morgen für ungefähr eine Stunde würde verlassen müssen, würde eine gewisse Regelmäßigkeit in den Tagesablauf hineinkommen, die später, wenn man – wie man es sich vorgenommen hat – auch arbeiten würde, in einen mehr oder weniger gleichbleibenden Tagesrhythmus würde übergehen können. Der je nachdem längere oder kürzere Spaziergang, den man sich deshalb – um die Zeit nicht sitzend in der Gaststube zu verbringen – jeden Morgen nach dem Frühstück zur Gewohnheit machen würde, würde aber nicht genügen, um sich die Bewegungsmenge zu verschaffen, die bei Vollpension und der Beschaffenheit des Essens im 'Hirschen' wünschenswert wäre, so daß man sich schon nach einem oder zwei Tagen auf alle Fälle für jeden späteren Nachmittag oder Abend noch einen längeren oder kürzeren Spaziergang würde vornehmen müssen, den man später – je nachdem, wie man mit der Arbeit vorankommen würde – auch auf die Zeit gleich nach dem Mittagessen oder auf den frühen Nachmittag würde verschieben können. Der Spaziergang am ersten Aufenthaltsmorgen würde einen jedenfalls zunächst einmal bei Tag den Weg durch das Dorf, den man am Vorabend vom Bahnhof her gekommen war, zurück- und dann der Haupt- oder Dorfstraße entlang weiter bis zur Bisquitfabrik KAMBLY AG am anderen Ende des Dorfes führen, so daß man zuerst einmal überhaupt einen Eindruck von diesem Dorf, in dem man sich zum ersten Mal aufhalten und das man vorher nur seinem Namen nach gekannt haben würde, und einen Überblick über seine Lage bekommen könnte.

(Meyer 1974: 26–7)[65]

The use of *würde* here is insistent and much more extensive than the future tense in Frayn's novel. Towards the end of the novel the *man* protagonist takes a hike with near-fatal consequences, all of which is rendered in the narrative *present*, but the conclusion of the novel returns to the conditional. Before the story of the hike, there is an extensive passage in the subjunctive which transcribes a series of tirades that the protagonist has to listen to in the village pub. This insert eases the formal transition from the rather conspicuous *würde* form to the present subjunctive and the present tense *per se*.[66]

I do not know any novels written entirely in the subjunctive form, but there is one experimental play by Ernst Jandl, *Aus der Fremde* (1979), that consistently employs the German subjunctive for its dialogue. The next section treats some even 'odder' temporal and modal devices.

6.3.3 Non-finite verb forms

As in Roche's text, which has sections of 'objective style', a few innovative novels have experimented with writing that employs **no *finite* verb** *forms*. Some of these experiments take the passive as their model, some eschew all verbal morphology or attempt verbless texts. For instance, in Roche's *Compact* one of the options is a kind of nominal style without verbs:

> BRIC-À-BRAC D'OÙ IL FALLAIT EXTRAIRE DES RESTES DISPARATES D'AVENTURES, FRAGMENTS DE TOUTES APPARTENANCES: IL DEVAIT ÊTRE POSSIBLE DE RECONSTITUER, PIÈCE PAR PIÈCE, CETTE FEMME PUZZLE FAITE DE BRIC ET DE BROC.
> (Roche 1966: 49)[67]

Verbless writing is practised also in Gertrude Stein's *Tender Buttons* (1914)[68] and Beckett's 'Ping' (1966).

Although I have not seen any consistent instances of it, **infinitival style** is probably another option for non-finite writing. Gabriele Wohmann's 'Gegenangriff' has passages which sound as if they are culled from a dictionary of German idioms, and they are all in the infinitive, but these infinitives do not tell a story; they are clearly quotations from the linguistic pool of German proverbs. Wohmann's text therefore employs non-finite verb forms in textual inserts rather than on the main story line (although that is difficult enough to trace, or rather define, in her work). Non-finite verb forms also occur in other textual insets in the novel of montage.[69] None of these options is likely to be employed consistently throughout a text, although the apparently much more disruptive deconstruction of syntax in Gertrude Stein or Djuna Barnes does actually occur in consistent fashion in what are texts of considerable length, comparatively speaking. Another interesting example is Simon Burt's 'Pisgah' (1994), a story that uses imperatives, present perfects and *how*-constructions: 'How, when I spent Sundays at my grandmother's, lunch was at one o'clock instead of the home time of midday, and how not even my grandmother could make the extra hour pass quickly' (ibid.: 228–9). This text also employs numerous passages that are entirely verbless.

A non-regular verbal form that has advanced to quite extensive use in recent times is that of the **imperative**. In much second-person fiction, for instance, imperatives play a crucial scene-setting role. Brian Richardson (1991b) has dubbed such texts as belonging to what he calls the 'subjunctive' mode, emphasizing their hypothetical quality. Above under 6.1.1 I have quoted some prominent imperative passages from Merwin's 'Simple Test'. The imperative exhorts the reader to imagine the fictional scene[70] and caters to the reader's eventual identification with the protagonist.[71]

> Arrive in some town around three, having been on the road since seven, and cruise the main street, which is also Route Whatever-It-Is, and vote on the motel you want. The wife favors a discreet back-from-the-road look, but not bungalows; the kids go for a pool (essential), color TV (optional), and Magic Fingers (fun). Vote with the majority, pull in,

and walk to the office. Your legs unbend weirdly, after all that sitting behind the wheel. A sticker on the door says the place is run by 'The Plummers', so this is Mrs. Plummer behind the desk. Fifty-fiveish, tight silver curls with traces of copper, face motherly but for the brightness of the lipstick and the sharpness of the sizing-up glance. In half a second she nails you: family man, no trouble. Sweet tough wise old scared Mrs. Plummer.

('How to Love America and Leave It at the Same Time'; Updike 1979: 40)

A fictional scene is here established by fiat, and the act of imperative enunciation openly generates a situation, projects a setting, the protagonists and, in due course, the story. Like present tense narrative with its unrealistic simultaneity of speaking and doing, the narrative imperative contravenes schemata of real-life storytelling by foregrounding the process of invention as it proceeds from a fictional positing of fictive 'reality'. Not only is second-person fiction 'impossible' in the sense of narrating to the reader or an addressee what that addressee *qua* story protagonist must know much better; by employing the imperative and the narrative present tense such second-person fiction additionally foregrounds the act of invention and illustrates how telling *generates* the story in the first place, rather than representing and reproducing in narrative shape a sequence of events that is prior to this act of linguistic creation.

6.3.4 Tense alternation

As with pronominal alternation, tense alternation in reference to the plot level is a common feature of recent writing. Tense alternation never signifies *temporally* as such, but signifies in relation to the narrator's (enunciator's) present. One can therefore distinguish between alternation that foregrounds and backgrounds the deictic distance between the act of narration and the story level, and alternation that does not induce a deictic shift. The latter correlates with internal focalization, and this is the most frequent case of irregular tense alternation in recent writing. In the vicinity of internal focalization the deictic quality of tense opposition evaporates, and both past and present tenses lose their temporal quality, which needs to be linked to a 'now' vs. 'then' opposition.[72] However, much superficial tense alternation actually involves a frequent shift from narrative into interior monologue and back, or from current perceptions to memories and fantasies. The alternation in these cases remains properly deictic and functional, but it conveys an effect of oscillation because the various levels alternate in rapid succession.

Texts with deictic tense alternation (past-tense vs. present-tense narratives) as a rule correlate with pronominal alternation – there is little realistic motivation for one and the same narrator to render the plot in alternately retrospective and presentifying segments. The one exception to this rule is the case of the historic present. Extended passages of the historic present tense in nineteenth-century literature typically experiment with presentification and descriptive close-ups. They may be considered as forerunners of later more extensive types of tense alternation.[73] In Dickens's *A Tale of Two Cities* (1859) the narrative twice moves into extended present-tense passages: at the point of Darnay's near-arrest when being smuggled out of revolutionary France (III, xiii; Dickens 1963: 347–50) and at the climactic execution scene (III, xv). In *Dombey and Son* (1848) five entire chapters (xxxi, xli, li, lvii, lxii) and parts of three others (xviii, xxxv, lix) are written in the narrative present, therefore qualifying the novel as an early example of tense alternation. Other Dickens novels that can be added to this list are *Our Mutual Friend* (1864–65) and *The Mystery of Edwin Drood* (1870). In *Our Mutual Friend* eight chapters are completely in the present tense (I, vii, x, xvii; II, iii, xvi; III, iii, xvii; IV, xvii) and I, ii and II, xvii have extensive present-tense passages. In *Drood*, Chapters i–v constitute a block of present-tense narrative, and xviii, xii, xiv, xix and xxii are also written entirely in the present tense. In each of these three novels the final chapter is cast in the present tense, although of course *Drood* just happens to break off at chapter xxii. Dickens's *Bleak House* (1853) is another example of true tense alternation (narrative present vs. 'standard' preterite), but it interacts with pronominal alternation (the authorial narrator's narrative present vs. Esther's first-person past-tense narrative).

In Fay Weldon's *Female Friends* (1974) present-tense sections in the third person (Marjorie, Grace, and Chloe) alternate with first-person chapters by Chloe written in the retrospective past tense and larded with her (necessarily present-tense) evaluations and observations about the status quo. The third-person sections utilize a *narrative* present, that is to say their presentness has no deictic significance; the first-person sections, on the other hand, use a markedly deictic preterite (*not* an epic preterite!) since they regularly contrast Chloe's present observations and gnomic speculations with the past of her own or her friends' experiences. Weldon's *The Life and Loves of a She-Devil* (1983) likewise alternates between third-person past-tense narrative (in which Ruth's story is rendered) and first-person sections whose present tense is, however, the present tense of direct speech (Ruth's harangue) and not a present tense of narration.

Tense alternation between the epic preterite and the narrative present can occur both in systematic and in unsystematic fashion. If alternation occurs systematically, it will do so chapter by chapter or in correlation with pronominal usage. Unsystematic uses of tense alternation, on the other hand, can occur in merely a few chapters or sections, as in *Dombey and Son*. In addition, such irregular tense shifts can also emerge on an even smaller scale for brief passages of a few lines or sentences at a time. Inserted passages of free indirect discourse or interior monologue in the present tense do not qualify as instances of a narrative present – they are of course meta-diegetic (Genette) or hypodiegetic (Rimmon-Kenan) material, hierarchically *embedded in* the surrounding past-tense narrative. Nevertheless, in some cases it may be extremely difficult to determine where exactly the presentation of action ceases and gives way to the quotation of embedded discourse. In the following passage from Susan Sontag's *The Volcano Lover* (1992) the description of the woman who later becomes Mrs Hamilton and of her views appears to belong to the narrative ('cannot imagine'), and the presentation of her thoughts therefore correlates with the narrative present of the frame:

> The young woman, who is only twenty-two, cannot imagine the man standing before her ever to have been someone her own age. He must be about the same age as Charles. Strange what happens to men. They don't care for being young.
>
> (Sontag 1992: 150)

Even more unsettling are the historical presents elsewhere in *The Volcano Lover*. These occur in quick alternation with the narrative past tense. At times the present is a present of the unshifted sequence-of-tense rule:

> His anger *keeps* him from going back to bed [...] *If only he could punish those who had wronged him, if only he could find an event that would answer to his sense of grievance and loss. Then he would return to England. After all, he has to live somewhere. How angry he feels. And how inconsolable.*
>
> (ibid.: 262)[74]

Here Napoleon is described as angry in the narrative present, and the final clauses of free indirect discourse (FID) naturally continue in the appropriate sequence of tenses. The central passage in this quotation is ambiguous between a shifted and an unshifted reading of the FID, but '*had* wronged him' probably clinches the case in favour of shifted FID. At other places the (free) indirect discourse has an unshifted tense (cp. Fludernik 1993a: 90–1, 178–86):

> Now that she knew how much she *wants* to touch him, her old freedom to touch him had become a self-conscious adventure of delicate, compensatory gestures.
>
> (ibid.: 237)

> She was also naturally very intelligent, which compounded the energy at her disposal. She asked for more lessons: she **wants** everything, starting with days, to be filled.
>
> (ibid.: 134)

> But she didn't want to give it up, she didn't want to lose the letter, which could be with him tomorrow, while she *is* here and *can't* be with him; and overcome by such a dizzying sense of loss, she burst into tears.

Suddenly space and time *make* no sense to her. Why *isn't* everything right here? Why *doesn't* everything happen at once?

(ibid.: 257)

At still other points the present tense refers to long-range processes or situations that extend beyond the point of time at which current plot action is situated:

That was the way the Cavaliere wanted her – not all the time of course, for then she would be bland and unseductive and without charm, but whenever he *opposes* her will or *disappoints* her. *She was not to complain when he left her, because he must leave her now, even though he doesn't want to, must join the King to hunt or play billiards.*

(ibid.: 135)

Someone in Naples <u>sent</u> him an amulet to ward off the evil eye. And someone in Positano who *has* the evil eye, and whose neighbors <u>were</u> piling offal nightly before his door, <u>asked</u> for protection.

(ibid.: 70)

From Switzerland, he <u>spoke</u> of the music *he* [William] *has been composing*.

(ibid.: 98)

In the entire ship, which *is* a little wider than and twice the length of a lawn tennis court, with some fifty passengers added to its crew of more than six hundred, there <u>were</u> only four latrines, all unusable.

(ibid.: 218)

The present tense in these examples is orientational. It cannot be explained either as a narrative present (there are too many narrative past tenses in the vicinity) or as a present of embedded discourse. Other uses of the present tense in *The Volcano Lover* present a kind of scenario of habitual actions and situations. This looks like a narrative present of sorts, or like a static descriptive historical present (since the text keeps alternating between past and present tenses).

She does not know who she is anymore, but she knows herself to be ascending. She sees how much the Cavaliere loves her. She feels her mastery. Skills fly in like birds and settle in her head. She drinks, she laughs loudly. She is hectic, full of blood. She warms the Cavaliere at night, he lays his angular head on her ripe soft bosom and slips his knees between hers.

(ibid.: 134–5)

The more expansive process gets the present tense:

He <u>tried</u> not to think of all that he had left behind in his magnificently furnished houses, which now *lie* unguarded, awaiting their plunderers.

(ibid.: 225)

266 *Virgin territories*

But then, can this not also signal his anxiety? Is this perhaps free indirect discourse in the present tense? The *now* could then be reinterpreted as a marker of subjectivity. At other times the present is utilized for character portraits or to present a vignette, a standstill of the plot:

> The Cavaliere's wife and the hero were listening attentively, respectfully. They *are* both genuinely interested in what the Cavaliere had to say. At the same time they *see* each other – they *spy* on each other – while the Cavaliere *goes* on talking.
>
> (ibid.: 251)

The alternation between presents and preterites in these examples seems less marked and cannot easily be identified with any one specific meaning effect. In particular, Sontag's novel does have a prominent narrator persona 'who' utters gnomic statements and evaluative comments galore so that the present tense does retain – at those points of narratorial intervention – a quality of deictic reliefing of *now* vs. *then*, of narratorial enunciation contrasted with story-world.

> Both as brave souls capable of throwing all caution to the winds. This relationship, which only rarely ends in bed, is one of the classic forms of heterosexual romantic love. In place of consummation there is elevation.
>
> (ibid.: 94)

> We admire, in the name of truthfulness, an art that exhibits the maximum amount of trauma, violence, physical indignity. (The question is: Do we feel it?) For us, the significant moment is the one that disturbs us most.
>
> (ibid.: 297)

Texts like Maurice Roche's *Compact*, on the other hand, where tense alternation occurs throughout for devious reasons, especially to indulge in the experimental foregrounding of linguistic possibilities, are in a different category altogether. Whereas slips into the present in Sontag occur almost as if on the sly, in Roche this is a technique of deliberate experimentation whose significance lies precisely in the alternation in and of itself. The alternation is between different tenses or morphological options (if one regards the conditional as perhaps not quite a 'tense'), whereas in Sontag it is still a question of deviation from the preterital norm, sometimes in unmarked fashion, and for a supposed set of effects which do, however, remain elusive.

6.4 DEIXIS IN ACTION

Like pronominal choices, tense links up with, and relates to, a speaker's (enunciator's) position. In the case of tense that deictic position is a temporal one, implying that telling comes after experiencing. However, since a great number of texts no longer simply employ a retrospective viewpoint – the exception being (quasi-)autobiographical fiction – this schema has gone out of fashion. The majority of recent novels adhere to a poetics of immediacy: to be as close to the fictional world as is possible, to present the story and the experience of protagonists *in actu*, to eschew evaluation at all costs. Such a poetics necessarily fosters a preference for present-tense narrative, even in novels where evaluation is still minimally present in the person of the first-person narrator (Coetzee's *Waiting for the Barbarians*), and it additionally encourages tense alternation as a consequence of deictic unmarkedness.

Whereas the temporal choice is rooted in the speaker function (if any) of the text, the pronominal options depend *both* on the extrapolation of a communicative level (narrator–narratee communication) *and* on the construction of a story-world, especially on the determination of dramatis personae. As I have attempted to show above, postmodernist texts frequently make the identification of the dramatis personae, especially their relative centrality to the 'plot' (if there is one), indeterminable or delay identification for the purposes of ambiguity or multivalency. The relationship between the enunciatory level and the story can only be specified if a story is extracted from the text; if the novel consists of a series of seemingly unrelated situations, it becomes nearly impossible to determine a consistent story and to specify whether alternative sections of *I*, *you* or *she* narrative fit themselves into one consistent scenario, whether they need to be arranged hierarchically (one discourse embedding the others), or whether they simply alternate as coequal originary segments in juxtaposition.

It needs to be emphasized that such disruptions of the story, unlike those typical of postmodernist fiction (cp. section 7.1), do not consist in the warping or deforming of plot structure or in the violation of readerly expectations of consistency but in the more radical refusal to specify the relationship between the dramatis personae and the represented fictional situations. To contrast: in Robert Coover's 'The Babysitter' (1969) a series of irreconcilable plot sequences is presented. Although these are contradictory, so that from a realistic perspective only *either* one *or* the other could have happened, the reader can naturalize these story lines as alternative developments of the plot. Fiction such as that of Christine Brooke-Rose, on the other hand, may disrupt realistic scenarios even more radically by a refusal to tell chronologically or provide motivational information. Much of the disorienting effect of *Out* (1964), for instance, stems from the lack of a narratorial presentation of explanatory connections between scenes. Brooke-Rose's work is also noteworthy for its presentation of counter-intuitive (indeed, illogical) scenarios. In her novel *Such* (1966), for example, the protagonist, Somebody, has a son who is a clock. Somebody splits open his brains to feed his offspring. Since the scenes in which the narrator-protagonist ('I') appears and in which he is represented as a psychiatrist who had a breakdown (who was returned to life after being pronounced dead) are fairly unrealistic, no naturalization on the lines of fantasy (Somebody fantasizes his family life; a deranged mind at work fantasizing itself as Somebody) adequately recuperates the textual parameters. Whereas in Brooke-Rose *some* dramatis personae remain constant throughout the text, even though the actions they perform are unrealistic, Thibaudeau's *Imaginez la nuit* (1968) or Nathalie Sarraute's *L'Usage de la parole* (1980) allow not even that much certitude about the fictional world. It is absolutely impossible to determine who is speaking in these texts; whether addressees or the persons denoted by *elle* and *ils*, etc., are stable for more than one section at a time. The setting and the text's dramatis personae remain radically open to interpretation.

The category person can therefore be said to depend directly on the construction of dramatis personae and, in a second move, on the relation of the story level to that of narrator–narratee communication. Categorizations such as first- or third-person narrative or even homo/ heterocommunicative narrative (Fludernik 1993b) therefore make sense only once a protagonist, and a focalizer, have been established for the text. Texts for which no streamlining of this sort can be established resist recuperation on the basis of such models, although – as we will see (7.2) – they then tend to be naturalized as one character's illogical or associative musings. Schemata of mimetic realism, one can note, again interfere with narratological categories.

Tense links up with person in so far as an enunciational level needs to be presupposed for a deictic anchoring of the past tense. If a text employs merely epic tenses, alternations become possible which may have little functional significance unless they also correlate with pronominal alternation. I have therefore argued that reflectoral narrative allows for a free variation in the categories of tense and person. This is no doubt connected with the fact that the standard past-tense narrative has mostly withdrawn to the realm of historical and autobiographical writing, whether of the factual or fictional type. The above analysis could not be more than a preliminary sally into virgin territory. Much ground-breaking research will yet have to be performed and a clearer theoretical framework developed before experimental uses of tense and pronouns can be given a convincing and satisfactory explanation.

7 Games with tellers, telling and told

In this chapter I wish to treat some of the most radical features of postmodernist texts in so far as they relate to the reader's visualizing of a story (plot) situation and/or a storytelling situation. In Chapter 6 I concentrated on the apparently *formal* or *grammatical* devices of pronominal usage and tense to illustrate how, in the process of interpretation, frames override microtextual oddities and allow a narrativization in terms of a second-person protagonist or in terms of quasi-simultaneous narration. Logical oddity or inconsistency of this sort ceases to be worrisome when the text can be read as a series of events, a story, or when it may be explained as the skewed vision of a ruling consciousness, that of a teller or that of a reflective or 'registering' mind. These reading processes which manufacture sense out of apparent nonsense are observed to apply even more radically when experimentation touches the core of narrative: the establishment of a fictional situation and/or the very language of storytelling. Narrativization is sorely tested at such points.

After a survey of postmodernist techniques in 7.1, I will in this chapter discuss four main types of text. In the first, textual inconsistencies are ascribed to the vagaries of the teller figure, the textual speaker-I (7.2). Although there may be little story to the narrative, readers are happy to narrativize this lack as part of the narrator-teller's narrative incompetence or as part of his or her deliberate strategy of self-reflexive writing. A related type of apparent breakdown occurs if no situation of storytelling can initially be construed, although the text may have very clear clues about such telling.[1] Reading texts as a speaker's utterance becomes quite impossible, however, in some radical experimental writing where the text consists of a number of competing discourses (7.3) which seem to be entirely unrelated to one another, so that their juxtaposition resists easy narrativization in terms of an arranger or a hierarchical ordering of discourses (for instance by means of embedding or even a circular structure). A third type of narrative in a very diverse number of manifestations is the typical postmodernist text which disrupts consistent story parameters. Consistency can sometimes be artificially (re-)established by the invocation of a consciousness which supposedly registers things in an illogical fashion. At other times, the reader can attempt to read against the grain of the text and reconstruct a story from what appears to be unpromising textual material (7.4). A standard case of the latter type is Joyce's 'Ithaca' episode from *Ulysses*, which is in question-and-answer format. The most radical refusal to 'make sense' in terms of narrative frames occurs in what I have called hermetic writing (7.5). Here the referential function of language itself is at risk, and this usually by means of an intentional destruction of grammatical and, particularly, syntactic structures. Like the texts of section 7.2 which juxtapose competing discourses, hermetic texts are extremely difficult to narrativize.

A few remarks are due at this point to clarify my neglect of plot-related disruptions in experimental fiction, to which I have refused anything like the centrality awarded them by most studies in literary postmodernism. As I have been arguing in this book, narrativity can be defined in terms of experiential parameters rather than merely on the basis of chronological event-related features. A disruption in chronology or event consitency does not therefore radically affect narrativity unless the inconsistency results in a downright failure to re-cognize a fictional situation. Modernist rearrangements of chronology, which struck contemporary readers as extremely radical, never undermined the presentation of narrative experience at all. Indeed, by forcing readers to exercise their ingenuity to recover a consistent chronology of events, or a structure of motivation for the characters, such literary techniques both supported the idea that there was something to uncover and recover behind or beyond the text and at the same time afforded a heightened reality effect. After all, 'real life' is a puzzle too; you don't get your 'story' presented to you by an authorial narrator who spoonfeeds you with reliable information. One reconstructs the case, albeit imperfectly, from disparate sources, and sometimes one has to follow up on initially unpromising leads.

Techniques which prove dangerous to the cognition of a text's narrativity do not therefore primarily relate to the disruption of a story's chronology but to the disturbance in consistency of frames and the logical relation *between* successive frames. Robert Coover's 'The Babysitter' (1969) disrupts a realistic story reading because the alternative stories cannot be recuperated within *one* simple and consistent plot. It is not the chronological rearrangement which flusters the reader but the contradiction and incompatibility between alternative story lines. Another type of narrative inconsistency that has been much analysed in studies of postmodernist writings concerns the cyclical short-circuit structure of some plots[2] and the transgressive crossings of story levels. Good examples of such writing are Gabriel Josipovici's 'Mobius the Stripper' (1974) or Ron Butlin's 'The Tilting Room' (1983). These texts are infinitely regressive, containing their own text within themselves in a Chinese box arrangement (Butlin), or they merge one text into the other by deliberately skewing textual hierarchies (Josipovici). The Chinese box format affects the constitution of a primary plot level by embedding the primary level on the secondary level, second and primary level on the third, and so on, thus refusing a firm ground for a primary story level. The Mobius loop model, on the other hand, juxtaposes two textual levels but radically disrupts attempts to hierarchize the two levels. Thus, in 'Mobius the Stripper' the story of Mobius can be but need not be the story that the first-person protagonist of the lower sequence is attempting to write. In Doris Lessing's *The Golden Notebook* the relations of embedding between the textual segments are impossible to ascertain, with the result that fact and fiction, story and fantasy within the fictional world become entirely indistinguishable. The transgression of story levels, with characters talking to their narrators (or authors), or readers becoming characters, etc., has also received a good deal of attention in critical studies, with Flann O'Brien's *At-Swim-Two-Birds* (1939) a frequently noted showpiece of the technique. More recent fiction on these lines includes texts such as Italo Calvino's *If on a Winter's Night a Traveller* (1979) or Carlos Fuentes's *Aura* (1962). However, none of these texts inevitably destroys narrativity; they merely rewrite story logic to include the fantastic and logically impossible. The most disruptive techniques of all are those that deconstruct the concept of a teller (the source of discourse), of the fictional persona (character), or of the fictional setting, with the elimination of sentence logic (between or within sentences) constituting a nadir of narrativity which is no longer recuperable except in terms of meta-narrative implications: the text then self-reflexively flaunts its practice of experimental writing.

7.1 NARRATOLOGICAL POSTMODERNISMS

Much work has been done on postmodernist writing, and at least one study attempts an exhaustive description of postmodernism's anti-realist strategies (W. Wolf 1993). McHale's (1987/1993, 1992a), Patricia Waugh's (1984) and Linda Hutcheon's (1988) classic studies of postmodernist phenomena are primarily concerned with the ideological and thematic properties of postmodernism, and they attempt to situate postmodernist writing in relation to Modernism, late Modernism or special types of postmodernist écriture such as surfiction or Tel Quel writing. Although McHale does note a number of narrative strategies that recur in postmodern texts, no systematic narratological (for instance Genettean) survey of such strategies is attempted. Within the aims of Hutcheon's or McHale's work, the decision has been not to establish in what ways precisely postmodernist texts contravene, say, Genettean parameters, but to concentrate on the rationale for postmodernist playfulness or on postmodernism's political persuasions (Hutcheon 1989). The results of McHale's and Hutcheon's studies are extremely illuminating because they tabulate figures of discourse and uses of language that directly correlate with poststructuralist and postmodernist aesthetic and critical positions. In particular, McHale's and Hutcheon's work has helped to place some major types of narrative experimentation in the limelight of critical attention. The most important among these have been postmodernism's tendency to disrupt narrative logic (plot sequence, motivation, the relation between plot and subplots), postmodernist texts' insistent privileging of the narratorial function over the plot function, and postmodernism's enthusiasm for self-reflexive metalinguistic play (metafiction). McHale's and Hutcheon's work concentrates on a substantial number of prominent metafictional techniques, all of which are designed to foreground the inventedness of the narrative discourse. They also provide a ground-breaking discussion of recent developments in the realm of historical fiction, introducing the postmodernist frame of historiographical metafiction.[3]

These textual strategies can be specified in much greater detail, enumerating all sorts of anti-illusionistic devices and properties. For instance, the plot value of a narrative can be endangered both on account of too meagre eventfulness ('nothing ever *happens*') and by an exaggerated amount of narrative action; consistency, likewise, may become anti-illusionistic through an excess of order and cross-referencing, just as pure coincidence[4] or randomness may result in an anti-illusionistic effect (W. Wolf 1993: sections 3.3.1, 3.4.3, 3.6.2, 3.6.3). Wolf's descriptive parameters, which are meant to cover *all* anti-illusionistic writing, not just the specific kind of anti-illusionism practised in postmodernist texts, concentrate on two aspects: on devices that affect the story level of narrative, its *signifié*; and on the foregrounding of the 'transmission' level ('die Auffälligkeit der Vermittlung') – i.e. the explicit, metafictional and metalinguistic uncovering of the text's fictionality. This complex spectrum includes the categories of too much order/too little order (incoherence); the non-narrative (descriptive, dramatic) tale; the reduction of plot; the use of illogical, impossible or incoherent plot items and plot relations; the destruction of the concepts of time or place or character as realistic elements in relation to the setting; the metaleptic jump between narrative levels; and the foregrounding of the narrative language and the narrative medium.

Although all of these anti-illusionistic elements can be found to occur regularly in postmodernist texts, this does not vouchsafe for their postmodernist quality. Indeed, Wolf's work documents that most of these techniques were employed as early as in *Tristram Shandy*, if not in *Don Quixote*. What happens in postmodernism is that these devices tend to cluster around the deconstruction of overall narrative coherence and to affect the most basic and fundamental properties of narrative discourse. It is for this reason that literary criticism dealing with postmodernism has concentrated on the progressive disintegration and dissolution of personal identity, the pervasive lack of realistic motivation, the destruction of cause-and-effect patterns. Postmodernist techniques therefore acquire their specificity through concentration and combination, through radicalization of current anti-illusionistic techniques, and on account of the ideological commitments which they display.

In the framework of this study, and owing to its narratological orientation, I would like to reshuffle some of Wolf's categories to make them more amenable to an updated narratological analysis. Thus, the most basic type of anti-illusionistic technique concerns those narrative strategies which affect plot structure. Whether there is a proliferation of irreconcilable event lines (Coover's 'The Babysitter'), impossible plots (Christine Brooke-Rose), or narratives with no plot at all (Beckett, some Sarraute texts), these disruptions of the plot level fundamentally affect narrativity. Incomplete story lines constitute another plot-related feature of narrative anti-illusionism, and there is also the case of chronological disruptions that make any consistent interpretation impossible (McHale 1993: 109). Besides this first category of plot *structure*, plot *consistency* should be mentioned. Violations of plot consistency are to be aligned with the disruption of cause-and-effect patterns or of motivational consistency. These aspects all link up with story verisimilitude and relate to the projection of action and character frames. Further basic narrative elements come under siege when the concept of character in its function as narrative agent or psychological function is affected. A third category of anti-illusionism, therefore, concerns the dissolution of story existents and of the setting. Story-world is most radically deconstructed when the constants of space, time and existence (cp. W. Wolf 1993: section 3.5.2) fall prey to the erosion of real-world parameters. Infractions of the law of identity should also be included in this category since they seriously disrupt the rock-bottom level of our narrative understanding.

As a consequence of such deconstruction, realistic parameters of agents acting in a setting or moving in recognizable space or time are no longer applicable and the interpretative reconstitution of story-world is seriously impaired if not made entirely impossible. By way of example, one can note Christine Brooke-Rose's novel *Out* (1964), in which the identity of the main protagonist (and the various versions of his story) are in doubt, or her novel *Such* (1966), in which the most fantastic events occur, and people and objects, this world and space world, mind and matter metamorphose into each other without logical or physical rhyme or reason. Yet even these radical texts do not completely disrupt the process of narrativization; they merely dilute constants of mimetic conceptualization to the point where realist frames become tenuous and are reduced to the notions of malleable or inconstant character, setting and event outlines.

A fourth level at which narratives disrupt their expected realistic frames relates to the establishment of story levels and the figure of the narrator. These are the frequently noted 'Chinese box' or *babushka* structures of experimental fiction (infinite regress of story-within-story) which I mentioned earlier, and to this category also belong the familiar types of metaleptic infractions: a storyteller becomes a character or a character engages in a harangue with his maker, the author. John Fowles's *Mantissa* (1982) is a prominent example of this kind of story-level infraction. More purely linguistic types of metafictionality can also be noted within this category of anti-realistic technique relating to the narrational level: deliberately odd syntax (McHale 1993: 154–5), metaphoric excrescences (ibid.: 135), the thematization of the act of writing, of linguistic play.

The infringements of realistic interpretation in the four categories therefore relate both to the story-world (action schemata, consistency, existents and setting) and to the storytelling frame, which involves disruptions of the who, the what and the how of narrating. They additionally undermine the story vs. discourse distinction on which all realistic concepts of storytelling and of story-world are based. The four areas of narrative experimentation that I wish to analyse in the following have not received any comparable critical attention, and they cut across the above technical distinctions. Rather than contravening the rules of realism and its cognitive parameters directly, these experiments obstruct the reader's attempts at narrativization on a more general interpretative level. The emphasis here is not on negative features ('no character', 'no plot', etc.) or on the infraction of neat boundary lines (as between narrative levels); on the contrary, some of the texts that I will analyse revel in a radical mode of heterogeneity which ultimately resists recuperation by means of plot or focalization in their traditional conceptualizations (7.5). The narratives that I will be looking at are not necessarily anti-illusionistic, but perhaps amorphous with regard to well-known realistic patterns of story-world on the one hand and storytelling frames on the other. By recuperating such texts, by narrativizing them, readers enforce a minimal holistic (cognitive) story shape on what is threatening to become unreadable, unshapable textual fluidity.

7.2 THE NARRATIVIZATION OF THE TELLER: NARRATION AS REFLECTIVE CONSCIOUSNESS

Real-world tellers operate under a number of constraints, most particularly those of their access to knowledge about the story-world. The acquisition of such knowledge depends on the requirement that they be participants or observers of the action recounted, or that they receive hearsay information about it. In the latter case, although narrators no longer need to have shared the story-world existentially, they do need to have heard about events by proxy, and there therefore exists a (sometimes very tenuous) existential link between the storyteller and the characters of the story along a chain of mediators. *Skaz*-type narrators[5] frequently portray just such a narrator who is associated with the setting of the story, usually his home town. See, for instance, the narrators of Gogol's 'Overcoat' (*Šinel,* 1842) and of Sherwood Anderson's *Winesburg, Ohio* (1919), who are both part of their fictional setup.

Much recent experimental or late-Modernist writing goes well beyond the authorial emancipation of the narrator in terms of eighteenth- or nineteenth-century omniscience – a stance that I characterized as transcending real-life parameters of storytelling. Reflectoral narrative and neutral narrative refine the textual speaker out of existence and therefore locate the fiction in the mind of a character or in the externally observable processes which evolve on the story line. Unlike these early twentieth-century experiments in fiction, late twentieth-century experimental fiction has tended to erase the apparent stance of objectivity implicit in camera-eye narrative and has come to critique the impassivity of an author function supposedly refined out of existence and paring its fingernails. The very metaphor of Joyce's characterization of the Flaubertian narrator is of course contradictory, attributing the all-too-human existential item of fingernails to a being that does not exist since it has allegedly been refined out of existence.

As if pointing out these very contradictions, experimental writers have started to foreground the artificiality and constructedness of fictional narrative, all the way from presenting clearly inept or unreliable narrator figures to a deliberate meta-narrative celebration of the act of narration. In such texts, writing is the main activity of the fictional character-*qua*-author, and the text usually plays with narrative levels in a very explicit manner. Some of John Barth's short fiction (especially 'Life story', 1967), Ronald Sukenick's prose and Raymond Federman's novels (for instance *Double or Nothing*, 1971) operate in this way, foregrounding the writer's activity of narration, invention and linguistic articulation. A second line of development can be traced in what one might call the passivization of the narrative voice. Instead of foregrounding the writing activity, the narrator reduces his or her involvement to the passive activity of reflection, registering thoughts and memories as they drift across his or her mind. Such narrators may be highly articulate quasi-oral tellers as in Beckett's trilogy, or they may experience narration as a series of fleeting images in a stream of consciousness emanating from the narrating mind.

An excellent example of the latter type is Juan Goytisolo's Juan trilogy, especially the final *Juan the Landless* (*Juan sin tierra*, 1973). In this novel the narrator experiences a series of visions and fantasies in which s/he at times participates as a *you*-protagonist. There is no 'story' to the entire novel, nor indeed does one find an explicit positioning of the act of narration. At the beginning of the novel the narrative *I* mentions that s/he is sifting through documentary evidence, but the scenes from the slave plantation which follow are clearly fantasized, and the evidence as to who exactly is the 'you' in these scenes remains ambiguous: 'you' is or is not Vosk, the vicar, who later turns out to be a woman (Goytisolo 1990: VI, 218); 'you' could be a second minister or teacher (ibid.: I, 34, 57). Nor does the narrator's remark about his or her putative slave ancestry come to much in terms of a consistent story either for the past or in the present:

the black woman's visitation by the Dove is cast in explicitly allegorical terms, and the offspring appears to have been engendered by the satyr-like *black* man, whereas the narrator is definitely a *white* person, and the reasons for his or her guilt remain somewhat puzzling. Does s/he feel guilty vicariously for the Spanish conquistadores? Or was his/her great-grandfather that 'you' who was involved in the oppression of blacks? Or, as elsewhere in the book, does blackness (and oppression) merely operate as a metaphor for the narrator's homosexuality – which is indeed merely *implied*, rather than discussed, by the narrative's repeated invocation of gay oppression and the use of a first-person plural morphology?

Indeed, no very clear line can be drawn between exclusively writer-oriented novels and exclusively consciousness-oriented texts. Goytisolo's novel ultimately remains ambivalent between these two explanatory or interpretative options. More clearly 'writerly' texts are Nicholson Baker's fairly 'realistic' novel *U and I* (1991) and Daphne Marlatt's *Ana Historic* (1988). In Baker's text 'I', *qua* 'Nicholson Baker the author', relates how he is writing the book we are currently reading, an encomium on John Updike. This writing activity consists, to start with, in 'Baker's' musings about what he could write, his putative memories about Updike, which are all fantasize and fiction, and his worries about the best marketing strategies. In Marlatt's book the main protagonist is the narrator Annie, who is her husband's research assistant. Instead of researching into the facts of a pioneer woman's life (Mrs Richards) in British Columbia, she starts to fantasize about Mrs Richards and begins to write fiction about her. Annie also rewrites mentally both her mother's life and the story of her relationship with her mother. The culmination of the novel (Annie's consummation of a lesbian relationship with a 'you' – a new acquaintance of hers) coincides with the narrative resolution on all these fronts. This narrative resolution hinges on Annie's abilities to write, to rework her experiences into language and to clarify them to herself in the process. The main plot of *Ana Historic* is therefore equivalent to the story of Annie's writing of herself in relation to others.

A lack of story material and the recuperation of narrativity in a re-cognization of the text as rambling or associative musing does not constitute as grave a departure from traditional forms (and norms) as one might be inclined to suspect. Sterne's *Tristram Shandy*, a precursor of much postmodernist (and even postcolonial)[6] writing, prefigures this type of discourse. In such writing little gets told or narrated; instead the text foregrounds both the narrator's act of producing *écriture* and the process of associative reflection by means of which it is composed, to the extent that it usurps the purely narrative function of the narrator's enunciation. Although this technique went briefly out of fashion with the conquest of narrative realism as practised in the traditional historical novel, in quasi-autobiography and mid-Victorian fiction, it reappeared long before the postmodern era in the early decades of this century. André Breton's novel

Nadja (1928) and Rainer Maria Rilke's *Die Aufzeichnungen des Malte Laurids Brigge* (1910) anticipate the excesses of postmodernist writing to stunning extent. Both of these novels are first-person texts. Rilke mimes a diary discourse in which the narrator engages in lengthy philosophical speculation. Later in the book scenes start to become unfixed, irrecuperable in terms of chronology or motivation, so that whatever story there is limits itself to the writer's associations and whims during the process of composition. André Breton's *Nadja* carries this process even further. Although *Nadja* is ostensibly a discourse about the eponymous heroine and the narrator's involvement with her, a technique that seems to marginalize the narrator, Nadja really serves as a mere pretext for the narrator's obsession with writing. If they are read as their narrator's rambling discourse, however, these two texts do not pose any serious threats to realistic recuperation.

More disorienting are novels like Jean Thibaudeau's *Une cérémonie royale* (1960) or *Imaginez la nuit* (1968), texts in which *je* does not necessarily provide a focal point of experientiality. In *Imaginez la nuit* a series of reflections by the 'I' alternates with a series of 'scenes' in which a number of unnamed protagonists are referred to as *tu, elle, il, elles,* and *ils*. There are even some *vous* passages, but these can arguably be construed as involving an actual addressee (narratee).[7] Unless one decides to treat these scenes as the fantasies or memories of the *je* protagonist, there is no way of naturalizing the various situations that are depicted in these pages. Thibaudeau's *Une cérémonie royale*, on the other hand, although perhaps technically more complex still, nevertheless easily lends itself to storification. The novel centres on a royal parade on the occasion of the princess's marriage. As in Coover's 'The Babysitter', disastrous alternative story lines are presented – including a scenario of assassination. At the same time the text juxtaposes a series of situations in which several groups of characters alternate: some scenes have the people gathered for the parade as their dramatis personae, some present a young woman and man who apparently fall in love with one another during the parade, and some passages describe the putative assassin. There are also a few sections in which the young woman is referred to by means of *you* and the couple as *we* – a pronominal choice that cannot be aligned with the remainder of the text without seriously disturbing the consistency of realistic parameters and frames. Although no unitary 'frame' of telling can be imposed on this novel, the various sections nevertheless individually allow themselves to be arranged in a mosaic of alternative viewpoints on the day of the ceremony. (In fact, the text resembles a film montage of alternative courses of events.) As an example of montage, Thibaudeau's *Une cérémonie royale* therefore belongs with texts discussed under 7.3 rather than with those foregrounding the speaker function of the narrator.

Recuperations on the basis of the speaker function require the presence of a salient textual *I* even if the bulk of the text does not have an

I: only the prominence of an *I* guarantees the hierarchical framing of other discourses as the *I*'s memories, fantasies or textual inventions, perceptions or thoughts. In Nathalie Sarraute's *L'Usage de la parole* (1980), the *I* is all-pervasive as an enunciator, an 'oral' voice whose function exhausts itself in the speaker position of the text. Although the novel delineates a number of dialogues (none of which allow the construction of a story), the succession of textual segments is structured on the pattern of a speaking voice, a voice that addresses two (different?) narratees, somebody referred to as *vous* and somebody addressed as *tu* ('mon chérie'). In the absence of any recuperability as story (in the sense of event sequence), this text is therefore naturalized in terms of a loquacious or even garrulous philosopher whose musings are directed at unnamed addressees and whose inventions (or memories)[8] include lengthy dialogue scenes.

Although from a plot-oriented perspective these texts constitute grave violations of the readerly code, they do not cause any major disruptions of narrativity; readers are able to naturalize them quite easily in terms of a ruling consciousness, transforming the 'story' into the depiction of the reflectional activities of the protagonist, the fictional *I*. The basic cognitive frame accessed is therefore that of REFLECTING. What I have been trying to trace is the reader's assimiliation of seemingly disparate materials (which afford little by way of a traditional 'story') by reinterpreting these textual givens as issuing from the active or passive consciousness of the storyteller, i.e. the figure of the writer who is the text's narrator persona and whose existence the reader projects from the textual *I*. This reading strategy may be actively encouraged by the text if the self-reflexive or meta-narrative mode is a prominent feature of that novel; or a text may require a more sophisticated interpretative activity, as is the case for Goytisolo's work. There are, however, quite a few novels where even this reading strategy on the lines of a storytelling frame (interpreting the text as unitary and narrative in so far as its experientiality relates to the establishment of a narrator figure) ceases to be a viable option. Where no unitary perspective can be forced on a text, the novel threatens to disintegrate into a congeries of unrelated discourses whose juxtaposition at best betrays the shaping hand of an arranger behind the scenes who is responsible for the montage.

7.3 THE USURPATION OF TELLING BY COMPETING DISCOURSES

Juxtaposition has been a feature of much traditional narrative, but has not been treated in terms of montage since juxtaposed material was usually handled with care to allow assimilation to the main story line. Subplots and multiple plotlines, owing to their 'well-made' integration into one overarching structure (an obvious example is the skilful plotting of *Bleak*

House or *A Tale of Two Cities*),⁹ rarely evoke the threat of 'mere' juxtaposition. Sixteenth- and seventeenth-century texts, on the other hand, are much looser in their politics of integration and – by later realist standards – neglect fully to articulate the precise relation between the discourses they juxtapose with one another. In Francis Kirkman's *The Counterfeit Lady Unveiled* (1673), for instance, one gets both a first-person and a third-person account of the eponymous conwoman's doings, all supposedly integrated under the umbrella of a fictional editor who pretends to have found the manuscripts and collected the information from the best authorities. Discourses that are apparently subsidiary to the main plotline, for instance framed narratives, in early texts frequently blossom into entire sub-narratives; they may be cast in the form of an exchange of letters or sometimes include a character's telling of her own or another's life story. (Compare, for instance, the narration of Prince Cesario's fate by Chevalier Tomaso in Behn's *Love-Letters* [1993: III, 230–341].) The epistolary novel, in and of itself, in so far as it combines several people's letters and a number of plots and counterplots, approaches a condition of juxtaposition, that is to say of apparent (surface-structure) randomness, that comes close to some of the less excessive games with juxtaposition in twentieth-century writing.

Juxtaposition, or *montage*, as it is also frequently called,¹⁰ emerges as a prominent feature in the Modernist novel of experimental cast, in Djuna Barnes, James Joyce, and John Dos Passos. In this respect Dos Passos is much more radical than Joyce. In Dos Passos' *U.S.A.* trilogy not all the strands of settings and characters come together to produce one big consistent mosaic. On the contrary, much of the material from the so-called camera-eye sections and from the ironical portraits of big men is appropriate to the thematic concerns of the book rather than to the plot, and the plot itself splits up into related and unrelated life stories. In *Ulysses* Joyce, by contrast, nearly always makes it possible for juxtaposed material to be read either as representing a character's probable thought material (this applies to the various insets in 'Scylla & Charybdis', which can be argued to symbolize Stephen's mental preoccupations) or as an 'arranger's' (Hayman 1970) playful interference with the text – an explanation that for instance suggests itself for the captions in 'Aeolus' and the prelude to 'Sirens'. Even in 'Circe' the dream metaphor operative for that chapter allows the recuperation of seemingly random juxtaposition as signifying the processes of associative dream logic.

In drama, too, juxtaposition is employed with great frequency. Juxtaposed material can, for instance, be used to provide a slot for memories or other 'mental' material. Harold Pinter, in his plays from the late 1960s and early 1970s, experimented with this technique (see Nischik 1993) and employed it to undermine realistic readings of the juxtaposed scenes. In Tom Stoppard's *Travesties* (1975), Henry Carr's random memories are arranged in sequence and (re)introduced by the recurring cuckoo-clock signal. As a relay point shifting between several memory sequences, this signal serves to mute somewhat the contrived artificiality of the dramatic arrangements.[11] Pinter's late plays, by contrast, no longer allow such easy resolutions, because their memory monologues fail to project a consistent reality (much less a plot). Whereas Stoppard's recurrent scenes are easily readable as different occasions on which Carr discussed the papers with his butler and then had a visit from Tristram Tzara or James Joyce, different instances of which are jumbled together in Henry Carr's memories, in Pinter's work the very personal memories of his characters do not accord or their fidelity is put in radical doubt. Thus, in *Silence* (1969) two men and one woman monologize in juxtaposition, but it never really emerges with any certainty whether the two men that the woman talks about in her monologue are to be identified with the two men we see on stage: that is a conclusion the viewer or reader may jump to, thereby going, in a manner of speaking, against the grain of the text. Nor does it ever become clear whether the man and the woman who monologize in *Landscape* (1968) are in fact a couple (their physical juxtaposition on stage suggests that they are), and whether their memories touch on their mutual experiences in her monologue: is she remembering how she first met him on the dunes, and he how he met her in the park? Consistency would seem to require that the couple remember how they first met, but the two stories do not match and each probably recalls their first great love *before* they met one another.[12] Likewise, in *Old Times* (1971), there is never any real confirmation of Anna's death in Kate's room in the bed in which she later seduces her husband-to-be, Deeley. The fictional 'reality' projectable from this play remains stubbornly contradictory: is Anna alive and visiting, or is she a ghost haunting the couple? One here arrives at precisely the kind of effect that one also encounters in Gabriel Josipovici's novel *Contre-Jour* (1982). As I have argued elsewhere (Fludernik 1994c), on a text-internal basis it cannot be determined whether the mother and daughter in that novel are merely fantasies projected each by the other, or whether within the fictional world at least one of them 'really' existed. (This question is resolved only on the basis of Part III of the novel, and then only in reference to the *extrafictional* biography of Pierre Bonnard.)[13] Such ontological inconsistencies already come closer to the kind of plot disruption practised in postmodern writing of the American school. In Coover's 'The Babysitter' – or in Pinter's *Silence* and *Landscape* – the story lines are incompatible. However, incompatibility in Josipovici and Pinter is of a much more radical kind than in the Coover story since it involves the ontology of the story existents, their identity and continuing identifiability over time. Anna's death in *Old Times* is a puzzle much on the lines of John Fowles's 'The Enigma' (1975) – an irretrievable piece of information. But where Fowles introduces a fairly common enigma, which is set in a detective frame, and then explodes this realism in the direction of metafictional invention – the missing person is said to have rewritten his life – Pinter's puzzle is more disturbing since Anna has been on stage and her flesh-and-blood appearance there is being negated by the revelations of Anna's and Kate's alleged student past. Whereas Fowles therefore merely undermines a realistic reading by means of metafictional devices, Pinter collapses the story within itself, although likewise from the perspective of the story's existential frames. The ambiguities of the text touch on the setting too, as we have already seen in Pinter's *Landscape*, where the existence of a shared past for the two protagonists seemed to be negated or at least put into radical doubt. In this kind of setup it becomes impossible to determine whether certain fictional 'landscapes' overlap chronologically and whether the characters share(d) a fictional world (*Silence*).

This problem of ontology can be radicalized even further, to the point where the text dissolves into mere metafictional invention (John Fowles's *Mantissa* [1982]), or into radical existential ambiguity (Richard Brautigan's *Trout Fishing in America* [1967]). I consider such texts as limit cases of narrativization. I have only briefly dealt with metafictional games under 7.1 since this has attracted a great deal of criticism already, but Brautigan's text requires more attention at this point. Unlike the novels I will deal with below, Brautigan's novel cannot simply be reduced to the formula of juxtaposition, although it shares a number of features with montage writing: it is episodic in structure; it lacks plot consistency (and even consistency in characters); it lacks realistic storytelling's progression of plot events towards and beyond one or several story climaxes. In Brautigan's text the ruling theme of trout fishing is subverted by the alternative (and incompatible) interpretation of that concept as applying (a) to a holiday activity or (b) to a *character* named *Trout Fishing in America*.[14] The novel consists of an unordered series of episodes about the activity of trout fishing juxtaposed in random fashion with an unordered series of scenes about Trout Fishing's experiences. The non-narrativizable aspect of the novel relates to the use of the metaphor of trout fishing, which, in quite disruptive manner, deconstructs the standard semantics of the genre. In one scene, trout streams can be bought by the yard ('The Cleveland Yard'; Brautigan 1972: 104), a description that de-naturalizes and commodifies nature just as the invention of a character named Trout Fishing foregrounds the textuality and playfulness of the novel.

Owing to these existential ambiguities Brautigan's book goes far beyond the more familiar postmodernist technique of juxtaposition and chronological chaos – as practised in, say, Joseph Heller's *Catch-22* (1961) or William Burroughs's *Naked Lunch* (1959). The montage strategy itself operates much more extensively, but to a lesser degree in, say, Vladimir Nabokov's *Pale Fire* (1962), Leonard Cohen's *Beautiful Losers* (1966) and John Barth's *Letters* (1979). These novels, besides playing with the juxtaposition of historical and fictional truth, additionally raise the question of narrative levels, of hierarchical embedding. In *Pale Fire*, for instance, the commentary on Slade's poem threatens neat existential separations. Brautigan's novel, by contrast, lacks an embedding context: the scenes describing the activity of trout fishing are on the *same* narrative level as those dealing with the character named Trout Fishing. From that perspective *Trout Fishing in America* is very close to the radical exercises in montage on which I want to concentrate in this section.

I will now turn to a few examples in English of what I have, in the section title, called the 'usurpation of telling by competing discourses'. Equivalent texts exist in German, French and Spanish. In the previous chapter I briefly noted Gabriele Wohmann's texts in *Gegenangriff* (1972), especially the sections 'Gegenangriff' and 'Selbstverteidigung'. There also exist entire novels in the montage mode, for instance Peter Chotjewitz's *Die Insel* (1968) or Otto Walter's *Die ersten Unruhen* (1972). For French, one can mention Maurice Roche's *Compact* (1966) and Nathalie Sarraute's *L'usage de la parole* (1980). Neither of these yields any plot at all, although some minimal scenarios can be gleaned from the text. Spanish texts which I have seen are perhaps less radical from a micro-textual point of view, but employ a number of interesting juxtapositional strategies. I have discussed Juan Goytisolo's Don Juan trilogy above under 7.2 and some passages of Cortázar's *62: A Model Kit* under 6.1.2. These texts anticipate the kind of radical juxtaposition with which I am concerned here but do not yet locate it on the level of discourse, juxtaposing plot segments rather than incompatible registers. As in Sarraute's *L'Usage de la parole* and Jean Thibaudeau's *Imaginez la nuit* (1968), Goytisolo's *Landscapes After the Battle* (1982), for instance, employs a series of internally consistent scenes which are, however, apparently unconnected with one another. The type of montage text that I want to present here employs juxtaposition on a sentence-by-sentence basis; it therefore affects narrative consistency on the micro-structural level.

I will first turn to Donald Barthelme's 'You Are as Brave as Vincent van Gogh' (1976) as a radical instance of the kind of text which I have in mind. Barthelme's five-page story from the collection *Amateurs* consists of numerous very brief paragraphs whose coherence (and cohesion) is violated throughout. The reader's attempts to construct a uniform scenario – a setting, a *you*-character 'who' is consistent for several paragraphs – are systematically foiled by the text. Even if the referent of *you* is taken to be consistent and identified as a woman and the *I*'s lover, irreconcilable information turns up in relation to nearly every other narrative parameter. Even if one tried to narrativize the text as the narrator's fantasies about the 'you', the resulting scenario would yield a very muddled narrator figure indeed. If the text is conceptualized as the utterance of a narrator, this enunciator jumps from one memory or imagined scene to another with barely any associative connection between them. The only indication, for instance, for identifying the *you* as a woman is provided by the paragraph that says 'Your husband, you say, is a saint' (1976: 169).

Games with tellers, telling and told 283

Inconsistencies immediately crop up as soon as one follows this up. If the *I* is the woman's lover (there are two references to her kicking the *I* in bed), then it is odd to learn at the end of the text that the *you* has got a baby whom she left on the lawn during a hailstorm while she was with her lover:

> You should not have left the baby on the lawn. In a hailstorm. When we brought him inside, he was covered with dime-size bruises.
>
> (ibid.: 171)

Where is the husband? Is it her baby at all? There is no way of deciding whether this is, quite simply, meant to be *absurd*. Compare:

> And the giant piece of yellow road-mending equipment enters the pool, silently, you are in the cab, manipulating the gears, levers, shove this one forward and the machine swims. Swims toward the man in the Day-Glo orange vest who is waving his Day-Glo orange flags in the air, this way, this way, here!
>
> (ibid.: 168–9)

Absurdity certainly operates as a textual strategy throughout, as in the descriptions which the narrator provides about the woman: 'You are as beautiful as twelve Hoppers' or 'You are as brave as Vincent van Gogh' (ibid.: 170). On the other hand, the repeated talk about fireworks can be given a sexual reading ('I make fireworks for you' and 'But there are fireworks in all movies, that is what movies are for – what they do for us', ibid.: 171), and then the 'realistic' scenario of the lovers' clandestine meeting becomes more suggestive – while they are having 'fireworks' in the bedroom, a hailstorm descends on the baby left out on the lawn.

A second parameter that is handled with blatant inconsistency is that of location. The situation of enunciation in this text is never specified – a narrative technique common in present-tense narration. Even more radically, the text jumps from one scenario to the other without any chronological signals. Much of the text, read as the narrator's reflections, must be fantasy or memory, but even that does not help to explain why even individual paragraphs are internally incoherent and deploy cohesive devices in definitely illogical manner. To illustrate, from the beginning of the text:

> You eavesdrop in three languages. Has no one ever told you not to pet a leashed dog? We wash your bloody hand with Scotch from the restaurant.
>
> Children. *I want one*, you say, pointing to a mother pushing a pram. And there's not much time. But the immense road-mending machine (yellow) cannot have children, even though it is a member of a family, it has siblings – the sheep's-foot roller, the air hammer.
>
> You ask: Will there be fireworks?

I would never pour lye in your eyes, you say.
Where do you draw the line? I ask. Top Job?
Shall we take a walk? Is there a trout stream? Can one rent a car? Is there dancing? Sailing? Dope? Do you know Saint-Exupéry? Wind? Sand? Stars? Night flight?

(ibid.: 167)

Even within the very first paragraph the sentences are linked only by the speaker and address function – they are formally cohesive but utterly incoherent. 'You eavesdrop in three languages' is a statement about the *you*'s habits, whereas the second sentence, which leads one to expect a rebuke for eavesdropping, refers to a quite different scenario – that of being bitten by a dog – and the third sentence seems to cohere with that. However, the restaurant scenario immediately evaporates; the only other passage in the text that could conceivably return to it occurs on the following page:

You are staring at James. James is staring back. There are six of us sitting on the floor around a low, glass-topped table. I become angry. Is there no end to it?

(ibid.: 168)

Since this passage follows 'You kick me in the backs of the legs while I sleep' (ibid.) and is succeeded by a description of a boy opening a fire hydrant, no textual information helps to clarify the narrator's 'Is there no end to it?', although one might take this to be implicitly about the narrator's sexual jealousy, if one takes James (whose name occurs here for the first and only time in the text) to be the addressee's husband. The restaurant scenario is furthermore negated by the information that the six are sitting around the table *on the floor*: unless this is a Japanese restaurant, the scene is hardly likely to be cohesive with the initial paragraph.[15]

To continue with the discussion of the beginning of the text as quoted above. The second paragraph of 'You Are as Brave as Vincent van Gogh' now presents us with a series of utterances by the *you*. Again there is a radical (logical) inconsistency when the topic moves from mother and children to the road-mending machine and its siblings, with a cohesive conjunction *but* that turns out to frustrate any attempts at establishing a convincing contrast between the two sentences. *But* would have to provide a counter-argument to 'And there's not much time', which is of course initially interpreted as referring to the narratee (and this provides another inconsistency with the ending of the text, where a baby is mentioned). The third sentence, then, allows one to reinterpret 'there's not much time' to refer, retroactively and quite absurdly, to the machine's (in)ability to conceive children.

The subsequent dialogue between the narrator and the narratee is likewise incoherent and noncohesive. It is a moot point whether 'Where do you draw the line' does or does not cohere with the previous 'I would never pour lye in your eyes'. Even the final paragraph of this extract, which initially suggests a scenario of holiday-making, becomes rather fanciful when one continues to interpret the one-constituent questions as still syntactically bound with the earlier *Is there ...?* or as objects of *Do you know ...?* ('[Do you know] night flight?').

Illogicalities in the use of conjuncts proliferate in the text. An example is the following passage, where *but* (highlighted for the reader's convenience) fails to make sense as an adversative:

> The salad chef moves in your direction, ***but*** you are lying on your back on the tennis court, parallel with and under the net, turning your head this way and that, applauding the players, one a tall man with a rump as big as his belly, which is huge, the other a fourteen-year-old girl, intent, lean stringy hair, sorry, good shot, nice one, your sunglasses stuck in your hair. You rush toward the mountain which is furnished with trees, ski lifts, power lines, deck chairs, wedding invitations, you invade the mountain as if it were a book, leaping into the middle, checking the ending, ignoring the beginning. And look there, a locked door! You try the handle, first lightly, then viciously.
>
> (ibid.: 170)

In the latter part of this paragraph, which is non-cohesive with the tennis court scene, a metaphor is developed which breaks down with the mention of locked doors – introducing yet another scenario linked to the Bluebeard topos. The text therefore juxtaposes a series of scenes and settings, none of which can be aligned with any of the others, much less arranged chronologically or fitted into a consistent plot sequence.

Donald Barthelme's 'story' therefore refuses to be narrativized on the grounds either of a consistent locus of enunciation or at least of a consistent presentation of setting. In spite of this, Barthelme's text can be recuperated or narrativized *thematically* in terms of an illicit love relationship in which the narrator projects for us a portrait of the narratee which is as incoherent as the narratee is fanciful and whimsical. The picture that emerges is that of a rather impetuous woman of thirty who has had little sexual experience (since her husband's sainthood, in collocation with the fireworks, implies that she may have failed to consummate her marriage). However, just as Vincent van Gogh was brave maybe only in the sense of having taken his own life, the narratee's character, as we glimpse it from this portrait of her in non-contiguous scenes, is a paradoxical one, a character that requires much fanciful interpretation and tends to elude the grasp of the beholder. In like manner the beauty of Hopper's art may be quite open to discussion. It certainly is not 'beauty' in the common sense of the term: brilliance? elegance? precision?

A comparable German text that I will not discuss at length is Konrad Bayer's 'novel' *der sechste sinn* (1966; 'The Sixth Sense'). In this text a similar discontinuity between sentences can be observed, and no consistent scenario or no consistent cast of characters is determinable.[16] Bayer's narrative language develops towards a juxtaposition of blocks of discourse that adumbrates some of the poetic destruction of language practised in Gertrude Stein (see below under 7.5.2). Yet in Bayer and Donald Barthelme the individual sentences themselves, read separately, are quite unexceptional; it is their enchainment into discourse that results in semantic inacceptability.

Another German example of the collage text, in which competing discourses vie for attention and refuse to be narrativized in terms of plot, setting or character(s), is Gabriele Wohmann's 1972 collection *Gegenangriff* ('Counter Attack'). The title story consists of a series of apparently unrelated discourses which include a dispute between a married couple, a harangue directed against somebody (evoking the context of a doctor-patient, nurse–old woman scenario), several newspaper clippings and, among these, the account of the former champion's challenge to the new champion (his counterattack). These ingredients are fairly ambiguous and indeterminate in themselves: one never learns much about the married couple or about the situation of the woman at whom the harangue is directed; and one cannot establish any realistic connection between these scenarios. Naturalization of the text therefore operates by means of the title as a metaphor: all the scenes deal with aggression, and so do the newspaper extracts and some of the linguistic idioms and clichés which are quoted in the text. The latter, mostly infinitives, tell even less of a story or trigger even less of a 'scene' since they are incohesive and incoherent, juxtaposed at random.

> Anstalten machen. Vorkehrungen treffen. Über die Minuten verfügen. Diesen Tag hintergehen. Den nächsten Tag reinlegen. Eine ganze Woche anschwindeln. Ringsum die abwartenden Nützlichkeiten.
> ('Gegenangriff'; Wohmann 1972: 161)[17]

Another story from the same collection, 'Selbstverteidigung' ('Self-Defense'), is structured around the scenario of having to defend oneself against repeated attacks by an aggressor who employs a variety of weapons. Interspersed with this self-help manual are newspaper clippings about all kinds of violence, and the recurring 'story' of 'little Bert' ('der kleine Bert'), who is retarded and kept in an institution where 'we' go and visit him sometimes. Other ingredients of this stylistic medley comprise medical and philosophical discourses, some of which centre on racial and ethical problems in connection with retardation (see the lengthy argument about the definition of what is a human being – *ein Mensch* – ibid.: 143).

An example of a montage text in which sections from several discourses are juxtaposed is Peter Chotjewitz's novel *Die Insel. Erzählungen auf dem Bärenauge* (1968). The entire novel consists of a diversity of narrative and non-narrative passages. These latter include lists of keywords for a putative 'table of contents', obituaries, texts of speeches and interviews, correspondence, diaries, etc. Like Brautigan's *Trout Fishing in America* (1967), *Die Insel* relies on a metaphor for its structure. The bear's eye (*Bärenauge*) is a metaphor applied to Berlin, which in terms of the novel is the 'eye' of (former) East Germany.[18] The text literalizes this metaphor and then applies it to other topics. The bear's eye is frequently mentioned in a sexual context (where it seems to denote the vagina), and it occurs in several political scenarios. Much of Chotjewitz's novel is taken up with quotations from other discourses, such as the obituary commemorating Rottenkopf's death, followed by the signatures of his friends and an R.I.P. passage, newspaper cuttings about the visit of the Shah to Germany, extracts from two novels and from diaries, and other written documents. In this respect Chotjewitz's book approaches another type of writing discussed below under 7.4, that of the non-narrative text which is narrativized by the reader in her urge to make sense of such writing *as a novel*, and hence as *narrative*.

One final example of macro-structural juxtaposition can be noted here, Otto F. Walter's *Die ersten Unruhen. Ein Konzept* (1972). Like Chotjewitz's novel this text consists of a collection of juxtaposed quotations from different kinds of discourses of all types of registers: newspaper reports, legal texts, philosophical discourse, a statistical table (1972: 60-1), chapters from folk tales in dialect, entries from encyclopedias, addresses to the audience of political meetings, and a *we*-narrative which represents the consciousness of the inhabitants of Jammers (the town which functions as the novel's setting). Although the individual segments initially appear to be non-contiguous, it eventually transpires that they trace the climate before and during the elections in Jammers, and that these documents help to explain the sudden upsurge in violence, which resulted in a kind of civil war between the Swiss-German and Swiss-Romanic population in Jammers. What initially appears to be sheer quotational juxtaposition can therefore be recuperated thematically and even chronologically to yield a story.

This section has presented some experiments in juxtaposition, concentrating on those kinds of juxtaposition that go beyond chronological jumbling and beyond the interweaving of different narrative lines. Such texts need not necessarily be non-narrative (descriptive, dramatic, lyric), but some of their montage elements usually are. The following section (7.4), on the other hand, deals with texts that are cast in entirely non-narrative shape. Narratives in the present section were no longer recuperable as the consciousness of a narrator figure because the juxtaposed material was too heterogeneous either stylistically or thematically to warrant integration as part of a verisimilar stream of consciousness. These texts therefore constitute a limit-case of narrativization where the unification of disparate material becomes impossible: neither a story and/or common situation nor a group of consistent characters, nor even a consistent narratorial voice can be projected from 'stories' like Donald Barthelme's 'You Are as Brave as Vincent van Gogh'. The texts for the most part remain series of individual items which are not even implicitly meaningful. Cohesion and coherence prove vitally affected in these examples, and the incipient dissolution of linguistic structures here approaches the situation of the downright destruction of language that is practised in the most recalcitrant texts of Joyce and Stein. For a discussion of these I refer the reader to section 7.5 below.

7.4 READING A STORY WHERE THERE IS NONE: AGAINST THE GRAIN OF THE TEXT

In this section I am basically repeating an argument which I proffered ten years ago in an essay on the 'Ithaca' episode of Joyce's *Ulysses* (Fludernik 1986) and now hope to integrate with the theoretical outline of this study. What I will be proposing is that texts which are by definition non-narrative texts, for instance texts in question-and-answer format (the 'Ithaca' episode, Jack Matthews's 'Questionnaire for Rudolph Gordon', Robert Pinget's *L'Inquisitoire*) or texts that consist of unmediated speech (the dramatic monologue or unframed interior monologue), are narrativized by the reader in terms of narrative schemata: in terms of a plot, in terms of a character's self-dramatization, in terms of a character's consciousness. This is basically what already happens with texts like Donald Barthelme's 'You Are as Brave as Vincent van Gogh', except that readers' strategies of importing meaning into such a text remain unsuccessful: no consistent meaning can be recuperated in terms of primary cognitive and narrative parameters: there is no story, no setting, and this is true even though references to the 'I' and the 'you' appear to be fairly consistent throughout.

Since in my model it is experientiality rather than plot that provides a cognitive ground for narrative, intractable texts that are built from non-narrative building blocks such as pure dialogue or (interior) monologue, description or argumentative prose *can* in principle be recuperated, *recognized*, that is, as *narratives*, even though this may be possible only with difficulty and texts have to be read against the grain of their non-narrative surface structure. In the case of Joyce's 'Ithaca' episode, for instance, the question-and-answer game is based on the presupposed existence of a series of events and actions in which Stephen and Bloom engage. The reader is forced to reconstruct these events and actions from the questionnaire, which linguistically and conceptually takes them for granted. Compare, for instance, questions such as 'What reminiscences temporarily corrugated his brow?' (Joyce 1984: III, 1479): this notifies the reader, first of all, *that* Leopold Bloom wrinkled his brows. Likewise, in Jack Matthews's 'Questionnaire for Rudolph Gordon' (1986) the questions reveal potential story matter much on the presuppositional lines of the notorious *When did you stop hitting your wife?* Thus, although no 'story' is 'told' in the ordinary sense of the terms, we are able to piece together some facts about the 'protagonist', and we reconstruct an ironical situation. The text implicitly evaluates Gordon's relationship to his parents, who send him a questionnaire in lieu of a letter.

3) How many of your father's paintings have you now sold?
4) Do you sense that you are nearing the end of your 'resources'?
5) Do you still dream of that little boat, nosing at the dock as if it were alive and waiting for you?
6) Did you sell the painting in which your father had put the boat?

(Matthews 1986: 83)

The questions presuppose a shared knowledge that the addressee, Rudolph Gordon, is hard up for money and selling his father's paintings to survive. The questionnaire proceeds to ask the whereabouts of one particular painting in an attempt to elicit memories about the scene depicted in it:

8) Do you remember that heavy cloth bathing suit, with its straps and the heavy, scratchy wool against your skin?

(ibid.)

Rudolph's deep-seated anxieties are then provoked by questions 13 and 14:

13) Was the woman truly your mother?
14) What if she lied to you; what if all your life she merely *pretended* to be your mother?

(ibid.)

Further on many more questions address Rudolph's memories:

28) Are you certain you cannot remember the shapes of the letters of her name, so that *now* you can read what was then only the mystery of print?

(ibid.)

Rudolph as a reader 'now' is being contrasted with Rudolph the child.

As in the 'Ithaca' episode some events in 'Questionnaire' are presupposed and the precise details about others are queried, thus implicitly affording the reader the information on what happened:

23) She was smaller than you, down below; and the man was smaller, too, because they existed far beneath your feet; what did you say when they begged for you to come down?
24) Why did you say 'never', instead of 'no'?

(ibid.)

Here Rudolph's feelings are taken for granted (but are new information to the reader) and Rudolph's answer to his parents is explicitly asked for, but later provided *implicitly* (again as presupposed material) in the subsequent question.

In some of the questions Rudolph's possible reactions to the content of this missive are also implied.

> 69) Why do you think you cannot answer such questions?
>
> (ibid.: 86)
>
> 97) When will you stop lying in your answers?
>
> (ibid.: 87)

At the end of the text, it 'turns out' that the questionnaire originates with Rudolph's dead parents:

> 98) Do you think even *this* would turn us away, if our hands and hearts and mouths were not packed with earth?
> 99) Do you truly believe that some things do not abide, beyond the habit and the way of the world?
> 100) Truly, this is enough for now, and somehow you must rest content with this personal questionnaire.
> Love always,
> Mom and Dad
>
> (ibid.)

The only *realistic* reading of the piece would therefore describe the questionnaire as a nightmare in which Rudolph's parents materialize to rebuke him:

> 61) Why do you need so much money to live?
> 62) Why can't you find a job?
>
> (ibid.: 85)

Narrativization for 'Questionnaire for Rudolph Gordon' therefore operates on two levels. As in the case of the 'Ithaca' episode a story about past events emerges from the presuppositions underlying the individual questions. Second, a reading that attempts to rationalize the *prima facie* fantastic situation of the 'letter from the grave' ends up by inventing a disturbed and guilty mind for Rudolph Gordon: the accusations levelled against him are then taken to be projections of his guilty conscience. On this reading, the text is therefore narrativized in terms of a ruling consciousness, and only secondarily in terms of 'story' material.

Another questionnaire text that tells a highly absurd (and entirely inconsistent) story is James G. Ballard's 'Answers to a Questionnaire' (1985).[19] This text consists exclusively of *answers* to a questionnaire, and from these one can imperfectly reconstruct the original questions. A quite fantastic story then emerges. Frequently it is nearly impossible to tell what the original questions might have been. Thus, the original question to answer No. 8 ('If I can avoid it'.) cannot be determined.[20]

1) Yes.
2) Male (?)
3) c/o Terminal 3, London Airport, Heathrow.
4) Twenty-seven.
5) Unknown.
6) Dr. Barnardo's Primary, Kingston-upon-Thames; HM Borstal, Send, Surrey; Brunel University Computer Sciences Department.
7) Floor cleaner, Mecca Amusement Arcades, Leicester Square.
8) If I can avoid it.
9) Systems Analyst, Sperry-Univac, 1979-83.
10) Manchester Crown Court, 1984.
11) Credit card and computer fraud.
12) Guilty.
13) Two years, HM Prison, Parkhurst.

(Ballard 1990: 81)

Verisimilar questions are difficult to come by for another reason, too. The answers indicate that this is no ordinary questionnaire (or, indeed, interrogation), and that the interrogatee is deliberately flouting the cooperative principle. For instance, (no. 14) ('Stockhausen, de Kooning, Jack Kerouac') suggests a question about the subject's favourite artists, and (no. 19) ('My greatest ambition is to turn into a TV programme') is clearly absurd. Neither answer fits a scenario of official enquiry.

The story that emerges from the subsequent answers deals with the circumstances of how the interrogatee met a 'genius' whom he later assassinates. That man was apparently a mad scientist, since by means of the public relations campaign of the interrogatee he has managed to get the entire population of the UK sterilized; the injections were supposed to induce immortality. Only the prisoner, as a man condemned to die for his assassination of the 'prophet', has been spared the medical treatment and is now officially asked to shoulder the burden of propagation. Since the prisoner appears to be gay, this constitutes a last ironic twist to a story that is already quite fantastic.

Besides such dialogic texts, formally non-narrative fiction also includes instances of dramatic monologues and autonomous interior monologues (Cohn 1978), as well as texts that parade as purely descriptive or argumentative prose. Texts which can be read as interior monologues are narrativized as pure consciousness, and I would therefore argue that instances of this type – such as Molly Bloom's monologue – do not require any story (i.e. event) material to be cognized as narrative. There clearly exists a fictional situation of Molly in bed thinking about a variety of problems, and this fictional situation in and by itself suffices to constitute the text's narrativity. I therefore endorse Cohn's view that autonomous interior monologue belongs with first-person narrative (Cohn and Genette 1992). On the stage, the simple fact of having one character out there, acting out his or her preoccupations, suffices to establish such a text's narrativity by means of the setting and the presence of this ruling consciousness. The narrative experience of the speaking or reflecting subject fully instantiates experientiality. Stage interior monologues include much of Beckett's dramatic oeuvre, especially his one-man plays. (See, for instance, *That Time* [1975].) Thomas Bernhard's *Einfach kompliziert* (1986) is another case in point. Since this play develops only a minimal action scenario, the implicit narrativity of the initial situation (protagonist on scene) is corroborated. Some monologic plays become dramatic monologues when the character on stage consistently addresses an unseen receiver of the discourse and inadvertently begins to disclose a story. An example of such a dramatic dialogue is Strindberg's one-person play *The Stronger* (1888).

The genre of the dramatic monologue, although *formally* pure dialogue, has clear affinities with narrative. Dramatic monologues frequently present an implicit story, but they are also narrativizable as a character's self-dramatization. In Robert Browning's 'My Last Duchess' the speaker inadvertently allows us to surmise that he was responsible for his wife's death, and the entire speech act can additionally be interpreted as characterizing the unacknowledged motives and obsessions of the speaker.[21]

Besides occurring in poetry, dramatic monologues can also be found in fiction and drama. There are several short stories that operate as dramatic monologues. Stanzel has already noted Katherine Mansfield's 'A Lady's Maid' (1920), Sinclair Lewis's 'Travel is So Broadening' (1928) and Dorothy Parker's 'Lady With a Lamp' (1944) (Stanzel 1984b: 226). I have elsewhere (Fludernik 1994c) discussed the function of the dramatic monologue in Gabriel Josipovici's novel *Contre-Jour* (1982), which juxtaposes two dramatic monologues invoking different versions of past events and therefore refracts each in the other's mirror. John Hawkes's novel *Travesty* (1976) is another very narrativizable instance of a dramatic monologue. In this text the speaker is taking his best friend and his daughter for a suicidal ride in his car with the avowed intent of killing them as well as himself. There is therefore a 'story level' concerning the speaker's actions (driving, talking) and sinister designs, but this story breaks off before the final crash occurs. One also learns much about the characters' past, glimpsing another 'story', this time of betrayal, seduction and jealousy. Traditional narratology would feel extremely uneasy about such a text: none of the events are 'told', and the formal characterization would need to be in terms of pure monologue – that is to say non-narrative material. This clearly bypasses the reader's interpretative investment in such texts since the reconstruction of the story outline and the suspense about the outcome (Will the car crash?) provide highlights of the reading experience.

Among formally 'non-narrative' texts purely descriptive instances are much rarer, although here, too, one finds some examples in Modernist prose.

Much of Virginia Woolf's or Katherine Mansfield's short fiction consists in descriptive ventures evoking a mood rather than any plot or a character's actual thought processes. This applies, for instance, to Virginia Woolf's story 'Kew Gardens' (1919) or to Eudora Welty's story-cycle *The Golden Apples* (1949), in which fictional situations rather than events take front stage. In so far as stories do get told in *The Golden Apples*, it is always between the lines, with the observations of a central (variable) consciousness focusing on occurrences whose full significance usually remains concealed from that character but provides fuel for the reader's detective ingenuity. Even more radical experiments in description have been provided by Alain Robbe-Grillet in his collection entitled *Instantanés* (1962). (See under 4.4 above.) Lists of all sorts, too, constitute typically non-narrative material, as do passages of argumentative prose. A text presented entirely in the shape of a list is Lucas Cooper's 'Class Notes' (1986), which consists in a set of annotations to the names of the writer's classmates. No story can be gleaned from this list, but the 'narrator's' preoccupation with disaster and envy suggests that this is another case of unwitting self-presentation. Perception always implies a perceiving consciousness, and thus descriptive texts frequently evoke a distinct observer persona. In Alain Robbe-Grillet's *La Jalousie* (1957), as we have seen under 4.4, the jealous husband seems to be responsible for the descriptions and their viewpoint. Perception even introduces itself into one of the most resolutely descriptive texts that I know, Heiner Müller's 'Bildbeschreibung' (1985), where a unitary perspective of an onlooker is deictically anchored in the text. I will return to this text below under 7.6 since I discuss it in connection with the lyric mode and genre distinctions in general.

James Joyce's *Finnegans Wake* (1939) can perhaps be mentioned, too, in this section of the present chapter. The *Wake* proves unreadable not simply and exclusively on account of its creative deformation of language, as discussed under 7.5. (As has frequently been noted, Wakean language obeys English syntax in many important respects and is therefore quite transparent on the syntactic level.) Where the *Wake* really begins to turn opaque is in the referential sector, since the transformation and creative collocation of lexical items fail to restrict the projection of connotation and denotation to unitary frames of reference. Wakean prose errs on the side of ambiguity and multivalence rather than stark non-referentiality. Despite such unpromising material, readers of the *Wake* have, however, been singularly adept at constructing all kinds of plots and significations. Readers' guides such as Campbell and Robinson's (1944/1986) propose that there are settings for the individual chapters and that characters can be identified across chapters even if their names undergo radical transformations. It has of course also been suggested that the entire *Wake* is to be read as a dream, with McEarwicker as the consciousness responsible for its content. One can here observe interpretation straining at the bit: one would like to read this text as a narrative, but the experience of reading the *Wake* is hardly conducive to such an undertaking. By forcing the reader to read against the very grain of such texts, by reimposing a story or at least a ruling consciousness on them, narrativization is imposed against all textual odds. Even after one has fixed a mythic outline for the *Wake*, and some fictional speakers have been allowed on the stage in parable-like settings (the Ant and the Grasshopper, the Moose and the Gripes), one's critical estimation of the *Wake* will tend to concentrate on the text's language as language, on the radical multi-levelled process of evoking meanings that proliferate and disperse rather than converge. The *Wake* therefore takes us to that category of writing which deconstructs ordinary language operations.

7.5 HERMETIC WRITING: THE DECONSTRUCTION OF THE REFERENTIAL FUNCTION OF LANGUAGE. WHERE EVEN THE MOST INTREPID READER FEARS TO TREAD

In this section I will treat a number of linguistic experiments in fictional prose. These texts attempt to hone linguistic expression down to its bare essentials, and even less than that, or they try to invent a new language by strategic repetition of a restricted number of linguistic units. Both techniques are inspired by musical precedent, Pater's dictum in *The Renaissance* (1893) that all art aspires towards the condition of music.[22] While Joyce and Woolf followed this lead and produced a poetic style that overlays referential meanings with additional patterns of lexical and phonological repetition, other writers in the more austere Modernist vein, inspired by Bauhaus architecture and cubist painting rather than music, started instead to dismantle language in an effort to lay bare its operations and workings. To the latter group belong Gertrude Stein and Samuel Beckett.

This second type of writing frequently develops into what I here call hermetic *écriture*: writing that resists easy accessibility not on account of its arcane, exuberant or flamboyant style – like Joyce's prose – but on account of its minimalism. The two styles have also been described in terms of late modernism vs. postmodernism (Fokkema and Bertens 1986; McHale 1987/1993, 1992a), and they roughly coincide with the opposition between Ihab Hassan's (1967) literature of silence for the minimalist style and the characterization of postmodern texts as language games or the 'literature of replenishment' (Barth 1980) for the more flamboyant experiments.[23] In this section I would like to concentrate on strategies of linguistic deconstruction. I will start with the expansive style of multifunctional punning and ambiguity (7.5.1) and proceed to a discussion of the reductionist techniques in Stein and Beckett (7.5.2).

7.5.1 Plenitude and multiplicity

In *Postmodernist Fiction* Brian McHale characterized Joyce's prose in the *Wake* as a montage of several registers which are superimposed on one another. Thus, in a discussion of III, iv, 564 McHale points out that the passage draws on the tourist-guide register and then introduces a number of connotations from the sexual realm (1993: 170-1). The implied referential *deers* of the park, for instance, show up as 'dears'.

> Finn his park has been much the admiration of all the stranger ones, grekish and romanos, who arrive to here. The straight road down the centre (see relief map) bisexes the park which is said to be the largest of his kind in the world. On the right prominence confronts you the handsome vinesregent's lodge while, turning to the other supreme piece of cheeks, exactly opposite, you are confounded by the equally handsome chief sacristary's residence. [...] In yonder valley, too, stays mountain sprite. Any pretty **dears** are to be caught inside but it is a bad pities of the plain. A scarlet pimparnell now mules the mound where anciently first murders were wanted to take root.
> (*Finnegan's Wake* III, iv; Joyce 1964: 564, 8-30)

As has been noted repeatedly in critical studies of the *Wake*, not least by Anthony Burgess (1972), this kind of punning can be extended to entire sentences and operate in a collocational manner like the notorious *nobirdy aviar*, which suggests an underlying syntagm of 'nobody ever' but at the discourse level overlays this with ornithological metaphors.[24] Joyce's syntax, even though at times convoluted and latinate in length, nevertheless stays perfectly transparent, with the paradigmatic punning shifting levels of reference but not syntactic mode. Besides the sexual innuendos and the nature imagery ('vinesregent' instead of *viceregent*), the passage also evokes the syntactic infelicities of guidebook language produced by not particularly proficient non-native speakers of English who tend to get lexemes mixed up (*you are confounded* for *you are confronted*).

The above is of course an oversimplification of Wakean language. Joyce also frequently spatializes his narrative by introducing complete lists whose individual items need to appear at crucial points of the relevant paragraph or page. Thus, the St Kevin episode (ibid.: IV, 604-5) runs through the hierarchy of church offices, a register that is implicit in a saint's life but is here arranged in quasi-geometrical fashion to draw attention to the pattern itself. Lists, as McHale has documented (1993: 162), are a favourite postmodernist device. The entire design of Wakean language is meant to make language go beyond the realistic level of sentence meaning aligned with a realistic story-frame, and the text does this by the multiple superimposition of contexts that add a metaphorical richness to the original base structure, allowing it to blossom (semantically speaking) in several directions at once.

In some postmodern sentence structures which McHale discusses (1993: 154) syntax is affected even more radically. Some syntagms fritter away into nothing, others suddenly go awry in mid-clause ('back-broke sentences', ibid.: 155):

> Having acquired in exchange for an old house that had been theirs, his and hers, a radio or more properly radio *station*, Bloomsbury could now play 'The Star-Spangled Banner', which he had always admired immoderately, on account of its finality, as often as he liked.
>
> (Donald Barthelme, 'The Big Broadcast of 1938';
> quoted McHale 1993: 154)

Here the placing of 'as often as he liked' is deliberately awkward, forcing the reader to reread and reinterpret. McHale's final example, which he does not characterize further, is perfectly naturalizable as a run-on sentence with further qualifications: back roads, which are mountainous and therefore nerve-shattering:

> The police are on their way now, over the fear-inducing back roads, many of them mountainous, that are known to be nerve-shattering even to the strongest nerves.
>
> (Gilbert Sorrentino, *Mulligan Stew*; quoted ibid.)

This sentence seems to me to be an instance of deliberately bad style (compare also the foreigner's guidebook language in the quote from the *Wake*), another common postmodernist technique in and of itself. Unlike the Joycean language of the *Wake*, therefore, where defamiliarization operates on the basis of semantic parameters, syntactic disruption in other postmodernist texts generally constitutes a recurring feature and serves to force the reader to reinterpret syntactic sequences, slowing down the reading process.

My next example text for the category of exuberant language play is Caryl Churchill's recent play *The Skriker* (1994), a dramatic text which continues Joyce's strategies from *Finnegans Wake* but also foregrounds the operations of language much more radically than does Joyce, deconstructing syntax and collocational expectations. Where Joyce, that is, simply piles one layer of meaning on the other in a vertical fashion, Churchill engages in punning on the syntagmatic plane, highlighting the radical openness of the linguistic and semantic structure and at the same time documenting the tenuousness of semantic constructions which proceed solely from formal aspects of language. The linguistic features on which I want to concentrate occur mainly in the soliloquies of the eponymous figure, the evil fairy called the Skriker.

> Heard her boast beast a roast beef eater, daughter could spin span spick and spun the lowest form of wheat straw into gold, raw into roar, golden lion and lyonesse under the sea, dungeonesse under the castle for bad mad sad adders and takers away. Never marry a king size well beloved. Chop chip pan chap finger chirrup chirrup cheer up off with you're making no headway. Weeps seeps deeps her pretty puffy cream cake hole in the heart operation. Sees a little blackjack thingalingo with a long long tale awinding. May day, she cries, may pole axed me to help her. So I

spin the sheaves shoves shivers into golden guild and geld and if she can't guessing game and safety match my name then I'll take her no mistake no mister no missed her no mist no miss no me no. Is it William Gwylliam Guillaume? Is it John Jack the ladder in your stocking is it Joke? Is it Alexander Sandro Andrew Drewsteignton? Mephistopheles Toffeenose Tiffany's Timpany Timothy Mossycoat? No 't ain't, says I, no tainted meat me after the show me what you've got. Then pointing her finger says Tom tit tot!

(Churchill 1994: 1)

There is a story told here, and one that we know well, the story of Tom Tit Tot or, in German, Rumpelstiltskin. The text presupposes the reader's knowledge of this story; in fact, without the recognition that a daughter asked to make gold from spinning straw can be aligned with that particular fairy-tale world, we would be at a loss to establish any textual cohesion. Since that story provides a sufficient semantic context, however, it becomes possible to unravel micro-structural elements and to observe how the sentences are structured on the collocation of idioms or common set phrases:

and if she can't guess
        guessing game
                game and safe
                      safety match
                            match my name
No 't ain't, says I
no tainted meat
        meet me after the show
                show me what you've got

Or:

Gobble gobble says the turkey turnkey key to my heart, gobbledegook de gook is after you. Ready or not here we come quick or dead of night night sleep tightarse.

(1994: 5)

Ready or not here we come
        come quick
           quick or dead
        [(in the) dead of night]
                    night sleep
                        sleep tight
                            tight arse

There are flashes of sense, but the general drift of the skriker's monologue pretends to tantalizing dark significance produced as a result of impenetrable incoherence. The skriker's magic is therefore also reflected in her verbal magic: the skriker's utterances are nonsensical rearrangements of available language material, and they have an effect similar to that of magic spells or of the incantations of, say, the three witches in *Macbeth*.

Churchill's text constitutes a limit-case of narrativization. A story is still being told, apparently, but its connection to the events on stage is purely metaphorical, evoking the skriker's bad-fairy background by means of an intertextual venture into British folktales, in which seduction, deceit and the eventual acquisition of wealth and power (through marriage to a rich husband, the prince) figure prominently (note the reference to Mossycoat), and which therefore links up with the plot of the play, fantastic as it may be.

I have come across one other text that employs the same strategy of syntactic portmanteau combination, 'Ansprache eines Entschlossenen an seine Unentschlossenheit' ('Address of a resolute man to his irresolution') from Michael Scharang's *Schluß mit dem Erzählen* (*Stop Telling Stories*; 1970). Unlike the initial passage from *The Skriker*, however, this text does not tell a story or allow narrativization, and it would probably tend to be read as a pure language game.

> Da wurde es mir
> zu viel
> Regen hat den Bahndamm unterspült
> [...]
> Kaum hatte ich
> das erste Wort
> läßt keinen Schluß auf das zweite zu
>
> (Scharang 1970: 35)

> Then for me it became
> too much
> water flooded the dam
> [...]
> Hardly had I spoken
> the first word
> is always the best[25]

Each of these three-line units can be read with the central line as a relay point. Line two continues the syntagm of the first line and then breaks off since line three cannot be integrated into the syntagm initiated in line one. At the same time, however, line two initiates a new syntagm that is completed by line three. Line two therefore has a double syntactic reading.

Overdetermination, although on a merely metaphorical level, occurs also in several texts that McHale (1993) discusses in his section 'Tropological Worlds'. As in Joyce, the literal and the figurative intertwine to the extent that it becomes impossible to decide whether a text is to be given a realistic or a metaphorical reading. McHale (1993: 135-7) quotes a passage from García Márquez's *The Autumn of the Patriarch* (1977) where one wonders whether the reference is to a case of cannibalism, or whether this is fantasy or sheer linguistic play. I would consider such cases to be precursors of Joyce's technique in the *Wake* in the sense that Joyce usually invokes two quite separate 'universes of discourse'[26] which yield different text worlds. In our earlier example, Joyce was playing the tourist guide-book register (in translation) against sexual topography. Márquez's passage, on the other hand, in prototypical metaphorical fashion, collapses cannibalism and sexuality into one, and this semantic connection (unlike the one offered by Joyce) makes perfect sense. Caryl Churchill, finally, goes beyond Joyce in stringing a multiplicity of purely linguistic contexts together, and these are only superficially reconcilable within the fairy-tale context – on a macro-structural level – whereas the idiomatic play works on a micro-textual level where no immediate cohesion or coherence can be construed. The situation is therefore similar to Wohmann's 'Gegenangriff' and 'Selbstverteidigung', since there, too, local incoherence is imperfectly counteracted by the application of global metaphor as reading strategy. Texts such as the ones discussed in section 7.3 therefore share this quality of contiguity or random juxtaposition with *The Skriker*, even if they employ montage in order to contrast larger textual segments and discourses, whereas linguistic disruption in *The Wake* and in *The Skriker* operates on the more minute scale of the idiom by idiom, syntagm by syntagm structure.

7.5.2 Language disassembled into words

The breaking down of ordinary syntactic patterns and of coherence and cohesion has a long tradition in the rhetoric of fiction: at emotional keypoints such failure to articulate within a received norm betokens an excess of emotion or a lack of control, a license to signify the unspeakable and inexpressible through a faltering of linguistic expression. In passages of interior monologue, on the other hand, the breakdown of standard syntax connotes the intrinsic non-verbal element of internal language, the rapidity of images as they fleet across the mind. Quite different, yet again, is the deliberate destruction of syntax by reduction and elimination as in Gertrude Stein's *Tender Buttons* (1914) or Samuel Beckett's 'Ping' (1967; 'Bing' 1966). And different, too, is the excessive use of repetition ad nauseam as it is employed in Stein's *Three Lives* (1909) or in *The Autobiography of Alice B. Toklas* (1933). Stylistic experiments of this latter type have no metafictional *content*, they are not *about* writing, at least not explicitly so; these texts do tell a story, but the excessive use of repetition or the extended techniques of linguistic emasculation serve implicitly to question a simple and naïve view of the representational potential of language.

Let me start with a passage from *The Autobiography of Alice B. Toklas*:

> The soldiers were all Kentucky, South Carolina etcetera and they were hard to understand.
>
> Duncan was a dear. He was supply-sergeant to the camp and when we began to find american soldiers here and there in french hospitals we always took Duncan along to give the american soldier pieces of his lost uniform and white bread. Poor Duncan was miserable because he was not at the front. He had enlisted as far back as the expedition to Mexico and here he was well in the rear and no hope of getting away because he was one of the few who understood the complicated system of army book-keeping and his officers would not recommend him for the front. I will go, he used to say bitterly, they can bust me if they like I will go. But as we told him there were plenty of A.W.O.L. absent without leave the south was full of them, we were always meeting them and they would say, say any military police around here. Duncan was not made for that life. Poor Duncan. Two days before the armistice, he came in to see us and he was drunk and bitter. He was usually a sober boy but to go back and face his family never having been to the front was too awful.
>
> (*The Autobiography*, vi; Stein 1990: 182–3)

Here the language seems to be uncontrived, moving along in a naïve structure of concatenation. This apparent simplicity, however, derives less from the syntactic or semantic properties of the passage than from the colloquial phrases with which it is sprinkled: 'Duncan was a dear'; 'Poor Duncan was miserable'; 'too awful'. Syntactically the passage is actually extremely complex since it attempts to represent spontaneous run-on speech, incorporates Duncan's utterances within Toklas's discourse ('here he was well in the rear and no hope of getting away') and additionally sneaks in Toklas's dialogue with A.W.O.L. soldiers hiding from the Americans into a sentence about advice given to Duncan:

> there were plenty of A.W.O.L. absent without leave the south was full of them, we were always meeting them and they would say, say any military police around here.
>
> (ibid.: 183)

The sentence runs on, incorporating Alice's explanation of the AWOL acronym and adding her exaggerated comment that there were large numbers of deserters about and that Gertrude Stein and she were 'bumping into them all the time'. Not only is this scenario unrealistic in the extreme, which is underlined by the linguistic clichés Alice employs, but the repetitiveness of these encounters ('always', 'they would say') fictionalizes the scenario even further. The little scene of Alice talking to AWOL soldiers is then garnished with a snatch from the dialogue: 'they would say, say [,] any military police around here [?]' The collocation of two instances of *say*, one interpretable as a finite verb, the other as a quotative device (Redeker 1990; Fludernik 1993a: 419), is initially odd but, once resolved as the clash of inquit phrase and quoted direct discourse, becomes another marker of colloquial style. Read from the perspective of Stein's more radically experimental writing, this additionally echoes her deliberate disruption of commonsense phrasing in works like *Tender Buttons* (1914).

Semantically, too, the passage betrays disturbing inconsistencies which are somewhat concealed by the realistic interpretation of the text: Toklas is naïve, and therefore she uses these collocations and unwittingly betrays her simplicity by linking items that have little connection with one another. Note, for instance, the oddity of 'find[ing] american soldiers here and there in french hospitals' (which connects with Stein and Toklas coincidentally running into deserters here and there) or the even more preposterous 'give the american soldier pieces of his lost uniform and white bread'. It remains entirely unclear whether 'his' in 'his lost uniform' refers to Duncan's or the sick soldier's uniform, and the collocation of uniform and bread debunks the putative symbolic importance of uniforms as indices of military valour by lowering them to the level of food crumbs, charity dispensed to the indigent.

In the following passage from *Tender Buttons* (1914) this odd juxtaposing of words and the use of repetitions without coherence have become the norm:

SAUSAGES
Sausages in between a glass.
There is read butter. A loaf of it is managed. Wake a question. Eat an instant, answer.
A reason for bed is this, that a decline, any decline is poison, poison is a toe a toe extractor, this means a solemn change. Hanging.
No evil is wide, any extra in leaf is so strange and singular a read breast.
('Food'; Stein 1972: 491)

This text is largely incoherent and non-cohesive. Coherence can be established merely on the microlevel of idioms which are evoked between two or three words and in the allusion to paradigmatic sets: *this, that*. Food allusions are everywhere, but they do not add up to a picture of a table laid with a recognizable selection of produce. There are sausages, a glass, butter and a loaf (of bread, one assumes), but the butter is red (like the sausage, the sausage resembles butter?) and both are in a text ('read'), and then a loaf 'of it' (the butter, the sausage, the unnamed bread?) is 'managed' – by us, the reader? or by the fictional persona who eats? There appears to be some dialogue going on ('question', 'answer') during the meal ('eat an instant'), and the consumer appears to be distracted from the conversation, needs to be exhorted to 'wake [up?]'

The third paragraph is even more mysterious. 'Bed' – which rhymes with 'red' and shares an assonance with 'breast' in the last paragraph, refers us back to 'wake'. 'Poison' goes with food, and 'decline' hovers uneasily between physical degradation (caused by poison?) and the gesture of declining, i.e. refusing, food. The paragraph goes on to evoke a context of crime: the poisoner's toe is extracted in torture and he is hanged – a 'solemn change' of context indeed!

'Evil' in the final paragraph obviously connects with this crime subtext, and food reappears in the change from 'loaf' to 'leaf'. 'Strange and singular' create another subcontext that links perhaps with the notorious mandrake said to grow underneath a hanged man's feet ('toe', 'poison is a toe'), and the final instance of 'red breast' can then be said to connote the blood of victim or murderer, or to refer back to the sausage or to the 'read' loaf of meat.

None of this suffices to constitute a consistent fictional scene, the individual items simply play with language as language. Stein's text therefore approaches the condition of opaque poetry or the quality of a musical score.

Similar experiments can be encountered in Gertrude Stein's so-called dramatic writings. The title *Four Saints in Three Acts* (1929) and the repeated mention of saints in the work of that name, for instance, in no way help towards a better understanding of the signification (or the non-signification) of the text:

> Might have as would be as would be as within within nearly as out. It is very close close and closed. Closed closed to letting closed close close close chose in justice in join in joining. This is where to be at at water at snow snow show show one one sun and sun snow show and no water no water unless unless why unless. Why unless why unless they were loaning it here loaning intentionally. Believe two three. What could be sad beside beside very attentively intentionally and bright.
>
> (1972: 582–3)

As in the 'say, say' collocation from *The Autobiography*, repetitions recur in this passage in great number and density. They are, however, irrecuperable as parts of different syntagms, or only just barely so:

> Might have
> as would be
> as would be as within
> within nearly as out
> It is very close
> close and closed.

And:

> This is where to be at
> at water

at snow
snow show
show one
one sun
and sun show
  (snow) show
and no water
no water unless
unless why unless
why unless
Why [,] unless they were loaning it here
loaning intentionally
what could be sa[i]d beside[s?]
beside[s] very attentively
        intentionally
        and bright

None of this makes any referential sense, and it therefore fails to relate to even the minimal requisites of narrative. Nor can one stipulate that, as a dramatic text, this is the portrayal of an aphasiac's mind or the depiction of a creative mind in the process of poetic composition (except for Stein's own process of writing this very text).

Beckett's late prose, except for 'Ping', retains some remnants of a speaker and some remnants of description, evoking, though minimally, a mind engaged in determining its own situation (location, identity) in a hostile, usually apocalyptic environment. Only 'Ping' reduces the linguistic function even further to the point where no definite personhood can be assigned to the producer of the text, no human being is necessarily designated as the topic of the discourse, and no even minimally verisimilar or utopian (dystopian) environment is evoked from the language. Although 'Ping' may not be as radical as Stein's work, it comes close to creating a musical piece in words, with the recurring lexeme (?) *ping* punctuating the rhythm of the prose.

> Light heat hands hanging palms front white on white invisible. Bare white body fixed ping fixed elsewhere. Only the eyes only just light blue almost white fixed front. Ping murmur only just almost never one second perhaps a way out. Head haught eyes light blue almost white fixed front ping murmur ping silence.
> ('Ping'; Beckett 1967: 165-6)

It is in texts like these that all attempts at referentiality utterly fail – no *situation* is any longer evoked, no setting, no dramatis personae, no minds, no speakers. Language exists in and of itself, disjoined from its referential anchorings, free-floating in proper Derridean fashion. What is at stake in writing of this kind is not only its narrativity, but also its fictionality –

no alternative world is projected because no topology and no existential items within such a topology have been created. If 'Ping' has been interpreted as the depiction of a mind at the point of dissolution, the linguistic analogue to the consciousness of a torture victim trying to battle against the agonies of overwhelming pain as it blossoms in the sores of the body, then this reading can be explained as a strategy of radical appropriation to the mimetic project, an intrepid move of sense-making against all linguistic evidence. Critics are confronted with a slippery ledge on which they rightly hesitate to tread for fear of losing their mental balance, and this ledge signifies the border area between language and fiction and the boundary line between the narrative and lyric genres. In the wake of this loss of referentiality, rationality, consistency and experientiality – where does one go?

7.6 NARRATIVE AND POETRY: THE CONDITION OF WRITING AS *ÉCRITURE*

In a recent paper by Brian McHale which deals with interpretations of experimental 'nonsense' poetry (1992b) McHale finds himself in a methodological quandary. Recuperations of three successive poems in terms of 'world', 'voice', and 'theme' increasingly turn out to be very partial or reduced readings, ignoring much else that is in the poem. The three poems resisted unitary reading strategies which tried to define them in terms of a fictional situation (world), in terms of the utterance (or mind) of a speaker (voice), or in terms of an image complex (theme). The one interpretative resolution that is then left, and which has indeed been suggested repeatedly by poststructuralists, is that of metafictional, metalinguistic reduction: the text is said to be, ultimately, about itself, about language, about its own production. When these interpretative strategies are applied to my previous section, McHale's argument repeats itself in my own presentation. Whereas the Beckett text ('Ping') was still at least *in nuce* recuperable as the description of a (tenuous) fictional situation or as the enactment of a fictional voice or mind, the passage from Gertrude Stein had to be reduced to thematic projections (food), but ultimately turned out to be about language and the free play of signifiers.

McHale attempts a move beyond this reductionism, claiming that, in order to read such texts in a *positive* way, one should conceive of the text 'as a map or model whose final constitution requires the reader's active response' (McHale 1992b: 27, quoting Bernstein 1986: 236). On the basis of Frederic Jameson's notion of 'cognitive mapping' (Jameson 1988), McHale proposes to read postmodernist nonsense poems as affording the reader opportunities for cognitive mapping, inviting the reader to engage creatively with the text, trying out a number of avenues of sense-making and, ultimately, asking the reader to read herself into the text:

These poems aspire, as Bernstein says, to project on to the world of human culture a map for the reader to read himself or herself into, a cognitive tool for finding our ways – and for finding our 'selves'? – in the hyperspace of postmodern culture.
(McHale 1992b: 29)

This conclusion certainly corresponds with the obsession of the reader with establishing sense, or – failing that – to establish patterns at all costs, against all obstacles. The problem with McHale's account (which is really Bernstein's) lies in another skirting of the actual reading process. Like metalinguistic explanations of experimental writing ('the text is about writing'), this meta-semiotic model ('the text is about interpretation') fails to capture the complexity of our literary response. McHale is correct in arguing that the reader herself establishes what can be claimed to be the locus of such texts' semiotic vectors. On the basis of readers' cognitions in the reading process guidelines are provided for possible but frequently irreconcilable avenues towards incompatible meanings.

McHale's vision of the text as a stimulant for the reader somewhat overlaps with another recent proposal which reposes on a poststructuralist poetics of heterogeneity and irruption. In his forthcoming book *Towards a Postmodern Theory of Narrative*, Andrew Gibson pleads for a narratology based on poststructuralist concepts such as 'filtration, percolation, blockages, connections and disconnections [...] and ceaselessly shifting mixtures and compounds' (A. Gibson, forthcoming, 'Introduction' 7-8; Serres 1993: 36–66). Gibson opposes these concepts to the rhetoric of continuities and radical breaks (chaos theory), and – in the narratological realm – to the 'essentialist' parameters of narrative levels, voice, focalization, etc. He pleads for a 'pluralization of the narratological imaginary, in which the idea of the unitary space of a given knowledge and the ideal of the dominant perspective from which it might all be surveyed, in Serres's words, are ruined together, and forever' (A. Gibson forthcoming: 31). Gibson's projected model wishes to dislocate the 'essential anthropos' (ibid.: 40) from his central position in the geometry of the narratological imaginary – a system that is enclosed in real-life essentialities such as the concepts of plot, character, voice, etc.

My own project in this book has been to insist on these essentialities, not in the traditional realist frame within a structuralist poetics but in the constructivist interpretation of their cognitive foundation (Nünning 1989b, 1990a; Jahn, under review; McHale 1992b). My approach does not locate postmodernist texts beyond the pale of narrative or of fictionality, where they are describable merely as departures from a realist and familiar model of the world. On the contrary, I argue, we tolerate a great measure of inconsistency, chaos and ambiguity when applying our cognitive parameters to our everyday experience. A cognitive and reader-oriented approach, such as is also traced in McHale's discussion of nonsense poetry, places a premium on creative reshuffling, on sense constitution. There are, however, some limits to this approach, and some texts (which I have called hermetic) do not lend themselves to recuperation as fictions or as narratives. My stance is that texts which maximally resist a realist or mimetic process of narrativization are important but rare examples of limit cases of experimental writing. I would have hesitated in such a claim ten years ago when fiction seemed in flux towards ever more sophisticated experiments, but the recent trend in experimental writing (in Pynchon, Umberto Eco and even in Josipovici) has been towards a return to late Modernist tendencies, towards a 'soft' experimentalism, and in particular towards a literature that is again *engagé* – historically (witness the resurgence of historical novels: Nünning 1995b) and politically (postcolonial, gay/lesbian and feminist texts). The most radical experiments in fiction appeared in the 1960s and 1970s (in the work of the surfictionists, Brooke-Rose, Josipovici, in the *nouveau roman* and Tel Quel writers like Queneau, Pinget, Perec or Sollers) or even at the beginning of this century (Dada, Gertrude Stein). This is not to say that current writing is intrinsically more realistic, but it is usually narrativizable to a greater extent, no longer geared towards radical areferentiality and semantic dispersal.

Radical tendencies have remained much more popular in poetry as far as I can see – a fact easily explainable as relating to the factor of textual length. What I would like to propose here is the thesis that in the realm of extremely experimental writing the traditional distinctions between genres have become erased to the point where texts like Gertrude Stein's *Four Saints in Three Acts*, Beckett's 'Ping' or some of Francis Ponge's poetry can equally be interpreted as poetic, dramatic or narrative writing without much affecting the ways in which such pieces are read. For drama the only criterion ultimately is that of stageability. Since Pinter's, Beckett's and Heiner Müller's experiments, stageability allows considerable reductivism; it suffices to have a speaker on stage (perhaps merely as a voice on tape or a visual image projected on a screen). The text that is then spoken or played can lack dramatic quality without seriously endangering the dramatic reception of the piece.

As an extreme example I would like to discuss Heiner Müller's 'residual play'[27] entitled 'Bildbeschreibung' (1985), which documents its residual nature most prominently in the lack of textual clues that might have helped to put a speaker *on stage*. For all its dialogic potential (Vogt 1995) the text therefore strongly resembles pure prose poetry or an experimental narrative text:

> Eine Landschaft zwischen Steppe und Savanne, der Himmel preußisch blau, zwei riesige Wolken schwimmen darin, wie von Drahtskeletten zusammengehalten, jedenfalls von unbekannter Bauart, die linke größere könnte ein Gummitier aus einem Vergnügungspark sein, das sich von seiner Leine losgerissen hat, oder ein Stück Antarktis auf dem

Heimflug, am Horizont ein flaches Gebirge, rechts in der Landschaft
ein Baum, bei genauerem Hinsehen sind es drei verschieden hohe
Bäume, pilzförmig, Stamm neben Stamm, vielleicht aus einer Wurzel,
das Haus im Vordergrund mehr Industrieprodukt als Handwerk,
wahrscheinlich Beton: ein Fenster, eine Tür, das Dach verdeckt vom
Laubwerk des Baumes, der vor dem Haus steht, es überwachsend, er
gehört einer andern Spezies an als die Baumgruppe im Hintergrund,
sein Obst ist augenscheinlich eßbar, oder geeignet, Gäste zu vergiften,
ein Glaspokal auf einem Gartentisch, halb noch im Schatten der
Baumkrone, hält sechs oder sieben Exemplare der zitronenähnlichen
Frucht bereit, aus der Position des Tisches, ein grobes Stück Handarbeit,
die gekreuzten Beine sind unbehauene junge Birkenstämme, kann
geschlossen werden, daß die Sonne, oder was immer Licht auf diese
Gegend wirft, im Augenblick des Bildes im Zenith steht, vielleicht steht
DIE SONNE dort immer und IN EWIGKEIT: daß sie sich bewegt, ist
aus dem Bild nicht zu beweisen, auch die Wolken, wenn es Wolken
sind, schwimmen vielleicht auf der Stelle, das Drahtskelett ihre
Befestigung an einem fleckig blauen Brett mit der willkürlichen
Bezeichnung HIMMEL, auf einem Baumast sitzt ein Vogel, das Laub
verbirgt seine Identität [...]

(H. Müller 1985: 7)[28]

Observation is constituted in this initial passage by a series of deictic
pronouns which correlate with a deictic centre, that of the observer.
References to *over*, *there* (*dort*), the *left*, to the foreground (*im
Vordergrund*) and background (*im Hintergrund*), and to an interpreting
mind (*augenscheinlich*; *kann geschlossen werden*) establish a vanishing
point from which the picture is being described. The characterization of
one of the clouds as being in the shape of a plastic toy pet from a funfair
which has escaped its leash provides the very first fanciful perspective on
the canvas and clearly introduces a subjective viewpoint.

As a prose text there are absolutely no problems with Heiner Müller's
piece: it is of course plotless, and it appears to have no characters 'on
stage', but – like Robbe-Grillet's *La Jalousie* – it allows itself to be recuperated as a human camera-eye text, a text to be filtered through an
observing, perceiving consciousness. And that consciousness emerges
explicitly towards the end of the text, where several instances of the first-
person pronoun show up in a passage where the observer becomes
involved in the objects depicted in the painting, identifying with the bird,
the woman, the man, etc.

Blut sprühend im Wirbel des Sturms, der die Frau sucht, Angst, daß
der Fehler während des Blinzelns passiert, der Schschlitz in die Zeit
sich auftut zwischen Blick und Blick, die Hoffnung wohnt auf der
Schneide eines mit zunehmender Aufmerksamkeit gleich Ermüdung
schneller rotierenden Messers, blitzhafte Verunsicherung in der

> Gewißheit des Schrecklichen: der MORD ist ein Geschlechtertausch, FREMD IM EIGNEN KÖRPER, das Messer ist die Wunde, der Nacken das Beil, gehört die fehlbare Aufsicht zum Plan, an welchem Gerät ist die Linse befestigt, die dem Blick die Farben aussaugt, in welcher Augenhöhle ist die Netzhaut aufgespannt, wer ODER WAS fragt nach dem Bild, IM SPIEGEL WOHNEN, ist der Mann mit dem Tanzschritt ICH, mein Grab sein Gesicht, ICH die Frau mit der Wunde am Hals, rechts und links in Händen den geteilten Vogel, Blut am Mund, ICH der Vogel, der mit der Schrift seines Schnabels dem Mörder den Weg in die Nacht zeigt, ICH der gefrorene Sturm.
>
> (ibid.: 14)[29]

As a narrative text, that is, Müller's 'Bildbeschreibung' poses absolutely no problems for narrativization, but as a dramatic text it does, since one would have to have a speaker utter this text, and the interpretation of this 'play' would depend crucially on how this was staged: as voice-over (one or several voices)? a monologue by an actor on stage? an actor reading the text? (I take it that the representation of the painting itself eludes realization on stage; the entire point of the text lies in its transmedial thematization of the visual through the verbal.) Compared to standard play scripts, Müller's text evokes the register of the stage direction, and it does so in typically postmodernist manner, using some of the techniques that Joyce employs in 'Circe'. The dreamscape of the painting is therefore what we are meant to visualize as stage action, and the observer's 'I' is likewise meant to stand in for the 'audience's' (reader's) stance in relation to this setting. One could therefore argue that the text is a dramatic text to the extent that it thematizes the audience (observer) position and conflates the text with the stage directions. However, to the extent that one reads this text as divorced from any possible staging, it necessarily becomes narrativizable only as a prose piece in which the perceiving consciousness turns out to be the main 'character' and the source of the description. The description itself then emerges as constituting, on a second level, at second remove, the fictional content of the perceiver-protagonist's mind.

These mergings of narrative and drama, which are observable in much radical writing for the stage, from Beckett to Pinter, Thomas Bernhard and Ernst Jandl, can be observed likewise on the borderline of narrative and poetry. There is of course the tradition of the prose poem, with Francis Ponge perhaps the most prominent representative. Ponge's poetry can easily be situated in the vicinity of the narrative genre. Narrative, i.e. fictional, situations can be found also in much poetry of a less experimental nature. Jonathan Holden (1980: 40–1, 50–2), for instance, discusses a poem by Philip Booth entitled 'Still Life', in which a second person's movements in a new nearly empty flat are detailed. It remains unspecified whether the 'you' is a woman or a man, what he or she is doing in this dump over Christmas, etc. The poem provides, precisely, a human still life much on the lines of a Hopper painting. Holden's second example is 'The Party to Which You Were Never Invited' by Stephen Dunn. Here the 'you' is a man ('You have dreamed of this moment,/ dreamed of a woman brave enough/ to embrace you'), and the scene of social ostracism is described in vivid colours. Such scenes are, of course, not restricted to poems with a second-person pronoun. Costello (1982: 502–3) quotes from John Ashbery's *Self-Portrait in a Convex Mirror*, another example of a 'narrative' scene in which the speaker imagines himself in a fictional setup.

Narrativization in poetry is very widespread indeed. Charles Tomlinson's poetry provides ample documentation of this. 'On the Hall at Stowey' (Tomlinson 1985) – a poem describing the speaker's visit to the old Elizabethan mansion – renders the perception of the speaker much in the same way as a fictional text might do. There is a succession of perceptions, thus even, *in nuce*, a story.[30] A second poem by Tomlinson, 'The Castle', is even more narrative: it presents the perceptions, *not* of the poem's speaker (the usual case) but of a third person subject, the castellan. Narrativity is here constituted on the basis of a third-person's consciousness – the prototypical case for fiction, but quite extraordinary for poetry.

> Directing his renovations, he sits alone;
> [...]
> But they finger the mysteries, as they unlink
> The pendants of chandeliers into their winking suds:
> He is easeless watching this process, they
> Sullen among their swaying burdens, remain
> Unmindful of the minuter jealousies he would haunt them with
> But which (since his power is nominal)
> He must mute into reprimands, or twist, unnoticed
> Round the stem of a candle-sconce, to suffer in person
> Those daily burnishings under a menial hand.
> He looks away. [...]
> ('The Castle', ll. 6, 12–21; Tomlinson 1985: 43)

Finally, one can also find proper fictional situations in poetry, situations that are not merely allegorical but seem to involve specific people under specific circumstances. Here, too, narrativization comes into operation:

> Recover, rising, the ease in which you came
>   Spreading on the grass your scarf and then yourself
> Laid on its crimson that would have challenged
>   Till you offset it, leaning there
> With the unconscious rectitude of grace
>   A little stiffly upon the elbow. [...]
> ('The Request', ll. 6–11; ibid.: 45)

The various details of the scarf's colour, for instance, operate much on the lines of a fictional *effet de réel*. Here, as in Heiner Müller's 'play' or in nonsense poetry, the boundaries between the genres blur.

Lyric poetry and narrative, in their less conventional forms, just like narrative and drama, merge here into one another formally and semantically, approaching that condition of music which poetry, in Pater's words, could best reproduce and which it was also the avowed aim of Modernist narrative to achieve. Since Virginia Woolf and James Joyce narrative has therefore tried to evoke the poetic mode ever more closely, and drama, in its mergers with prose narrative, has traced the same trajectory. Where experientiality resolves into words and their music, narrativity also finds its ultimate horizon. Where language has become pure language, disembodied from speaker, context and reference, human experience and narrativization by means of human experience recede into the background. Such texts, instead, foreground thematic issues, images, sounds and rhythms beyond any possible mimetic context. At this crossroads traditional generic configurations collapse to make way for fluid new shapes that are still in the process of creation. In this area of flux narratology must step carefully, deferring to the insights of literary criticism, and wait its turn.

8 Natural Narratology

In the previous chapters my approach has been to follow the history of English narrative from its supposed oral beginnings to its postmodern developments in the past thirty years, with brief excursions into German, French and Spanish literature. In this final chapter my double-pronged theoretical and historical method will need to be justified by its results, that is to say by the perspectives it affords for future research.

In Chapter 1 I proposed a new interpretation of what I call *narrativity* (and what Gerald Prince calls *narrativehood*).[1] Narrative at its fullest manifestation, I argue, correlates with human experientiality. Although this appears to be a fairly traditional view, my reconstitution of narrativity on the basis of experientiality allows for three important corollaries which depart from traditional understandings of narrative. For one, experientiality both subsumes and marginalizes plot. Events or actantial and motivational parameters in and of themselves constitute only a zero degree of narrativity, a minimal frame for the production of experientiality. (Compare below under 8.1.3.) This, in a second move, allows me to define a great number of plotless narratives from the twentieth century as narratives fully satisfying the requirement of experientiality since these texts operate by means of a projection of consciousness – the character's, that of the narrative voice, or the reader's – without necessarily needing any actantial base structure. Narrativity can therefore dispense with plot, but it cannot dispense with fictionality. There does need to be a fictional situation that consists in the presence of at least one *persona* and her consciousness. Neither existence *per se* nor plot *per se* constitute narrativity, but the crucial factor is that of human immundation, of situational embodiment. In experimental texts embodiment can be reduced to consciousness or perception with the setting dwindling to rudimentary implied contiguities. But consciousness there needs to be, because this is the locus of experientiality. A third corollary of my redefinition of narrativity is that it closely aligns narrativity with fictionality *per se*. As I have attempted to illustrate under 7.6, poetry can turn into narrative, it can become fictional, that is, precisely to the extent that a situation is depicted which then allows for the constitution of experientiality. Conversely, in so far as so-called narrative texts of a radically experimental nature undermine the last remnants of a fictional situation, in particular the possibility of locating an experiencer in it (whether *qua* agent or enunciator or experiencing consciousness/observer), they become indistinguishable from the purely lyric mode whose denotational framework operates in a-referential[2] manner.

In the following I would like to try and pull all the threads together by returning to a systematic recapitulation of the basic tenets of 'natural' narratology. This presentation can now rely on the sample studies conducted in earlier chapters and explicate the consequences of my redefinitions and reconceptualizations of the field of narratology. In a first section I will present an outline of the theoretical setup of the theory in which I will devote extensive space to situating my notion of narrativity in relation to that of other scholars (8.1). I will then proceed to a comparison of my model with standard narratological paradigms (8.2) and discuss the extent to which my own model is able to integrate the categories of classic narratology and where I have to leave them behind (8.3). Before my final conclusions I will branch out into two contiguous areas. I will at least briefly touch on the media of narrative and return for a last time to the questions of genre and text type (8.4). Second, I want to consider how a number of fashionable topics in literary theory interrelate with the narratological paradigm that I have been proposing. In 8.5 I will therefore briefly discuss the question of the usefulness or irrelevance of 'natural' narratology for ideological approaches to literature and for literary criticism that relies on an attitude of commitment.

8.1 WHAT IS NATURAL NARRATOLOGY? A THEORETICAL OUTLINE

In Chapter 1 I put forward a special reading of the term *natural* as I define it within a model called 'natural' narratology. The term *natural*, I argued, feeds from three areas of research. It adopts its fundamental concept of experientiality from spontaneous conversational storytelling. Natural linguistics, as the second influencing factor, contributes the realization that the semiotic system of language, and – here – of narrative, is founded on parameters relating to human environment and human embodiment within that environment. I have stressed in particular the factor of embodiment and the fact that linguistic and narrative repercussions of these origins can be observed and described linguistically. From natural linguistics, and from schema theory (or frame theory) in particular, I derive the insight that fictional situations are visualized in terms of re(-)cognizable real-world patterns which include the parameters of agency, perception, communicational frames, motivational explanation, and so forth. Within standard narrative typologies such basic-level frames can furthermore be argued to have been responsible for the projection of the fundamental discourse vs. story dichotomy. Moreover, these basic-level frames have been redeployed in narratology to produce a constitutive communicational model[3] whereby narrators, implied authors *et alii* 'talk to' narratees and readers of various descriptions. Natural linguistics and frame theory therefore enter at several levels of the model. Finally, my third inspiration for the term *natural* has come from Jonathan Culler's concept of naturalization, which I have rechristened *narrativization*. Narrativization, that is the re-cognization of a text as narrative, characterizes a process of interpretation by means of which texts come to be perceived *as narratives*. In the process of narrativization readers engage in reading such texts as manifesting experientiality, and they therefore construct these texts in terms of their alignment with experiential cognitive parameters. In other words, aspects one and two of this schema of natural narratology (the experientiality of natural narrative and the cognitive parameters inherent in natural linguistics) are subsumed in, and incorporated with, the processes of interpretation which constitute the third aspect or level of natural narratology, narrativization.

Natural Narratology[4] conceived in these terms is an explicitly constructivist (Watzlawick 1981; Luhmann 1984, von Glasersfeld 1989; Nünning 1989b; S. Schmidt 1989) model of narrative. Not only do readers construct the narrativity of a given text, thereby superseding any inherent or essentialist understandings of narrativity, but they also construct narrativity on the basis of real-world cognitive parameters (handled in a flexible manner), and they even enforce narrative readings for texts that have no evident experiential core. (The 'real world', in turn, is of course a primary-level construct.) Narrative texts are therefore, first and foremost, texts that are *read* narratively, whatever their formal make-up, although the fact that they are read in a narrative manner may be largely determined by formal and, particularly, contextual factors.[5] It is only in the context of publication, where a text is labelled a 'short story' or a 'novel', that narrativization will be elicited against the grain of an (apparently non-narrative) text. Generic classification therefore frequently determines the direction in which interpretation may move in the reading process.

Natural Narratology is, however, neither a purely theoretical nor a purely synchronic enterprise. Although I have just sketched a synchronic analysis of narrativization, historical or diachronic factors need to be incorporated into the theory as well. These historical aspects are meant to reflect the phylogenetic spread of storytelling parameters from orality into written narrative, and to document the discovery of the consciousness factor, which I interpret as a rediscovery of the deep-structural potentialities of the art of oral storytelling within the written medium. Natural Narratology therefore opens up a number of questions relating to the debate over orality and literacy, and it does so from a linguistic as well as a narratological angle. In fine-grained analyses of orality and literacy in medieval texts it becomes possible to discuss how specifically narrative functions change over time and how different linguistic manifestations develop in order to accommodate the changing requirements of storytelling.

The historical aspect of Natural Narratology moreover embraces a discussion of the history of narrative forms, a discussion that has so far largely lain dormant. I here continue the work of Elizabeth Deeds Ermarth and rely especially on the diachronic parts of F.K. Stanzel's seminal typology. As will be illustrated more fully below under 8.2 and 8.3.3, Stanzel's narrative situations, which trace a historical development from the predominance of first-person and authorial narrative to the invention of figural, i.e. reflectoral, narrative in the late nineteenth-century novel and its eventual hegemony in the Modernist canon, can now be supplemented by the much wider spectrum of narrative possibilities that has become available towards the end of the twentieth century. At the same time, Stanzel's three narrative situations, as I have argued, allow themselves to be redefined in terms of schema-theoretic cognitive frames. Other such schemata (for instance the perceptional and ideational one) can be added to this stock, so that a set of narrative situations emerges that are directly monitored by constitutive natural parameters and which in turn can be extended to cover increasingly 'odd' (or non-natural) configurations.

Natural Narratology is therefore designed to promote a fruitful exchange between critical theory and historical developments. It also moves one more step away from a merely evaluative analysis of narrative modes on the lines of research that has been privileging the Modernist canon against the 'loose baggy monsters' of yore. Questions of narrative value or quality, however, have not been entirely suspended. In the circumscribed realm of narrative function, for instance, comparisons between a number of different treatments are licit and potentially enlightening. I have, however, eschewed generalizing statements about the potential usefulness (or lack thereof) of postmodernist writing techniques, particularly in the attempt to transcend the current descriptive terminology, which is mostly of a negative kind: no plot, no setting, no characters. Nevertheless, at the point where natural parameters, even stretched to their utmost, no longer help to narrativize certain experimental texts, Natural Narratology will ultimately have to yield to a different model that is of a more poststructuralist orientation. Such a model would have to build from postmodernist reading and writing strategies that complement and transcend real-world parameters. I am thinking in particular of Andrew Gibson's stunning *Towards a Postmodern Theory of Narrative* (forthcoming), which promises to institute an entirely new conceptual apparatus for the discussion of narrative and non-narrative texts. It is too early to say[6] whether Gibson's theory will subsume Natural Narratology as the special case of an extended application of realist parameters or whether it will be able to account for realism differently within its own framework. That will also ultimately depend on one's understanding, i.e.

definition, of narrative. The model that I am proposing here deliberately incorporates much research from the philological, linguistic and narratological disciplines. Gibson, on the other hand, initiates a radical paradigm shift, forcing a fissure or discontinuity with structuralist precursors, where I myself attempt to preserve a continuity of sorts, even if that requires a subtle rhetoric of paradox and the strategic re-evaluation of traditional narratological lore.

8.1.1 The historical side of things: narrativization and its limits

Chapters 2 to 7 have traced a historical development of narrative forms and structures. This development has been presented from two very different perspectives. On the one hand, in the sections concerned with oral, medieval and early modern texts very specific linguistic signals have been analysed and related to an incipient alignment of narrative structures with the formal development from oral to written narratives. On the other hand, my text has brought into play very high-level cognitive parameters that support these surface-structure linguistic developments. These cognitive parameters are of a frame-creating nature – they induce a mode of interpretation which projects a realistic frame on the text and its enunciational properties, thereby aligning the text with well-proven cognitional schemata from our immediate everyday experience.

Cognitive parameters therefore become operative on two levels: on the macro-structural level, on which an encompassing frame is established in the course of reading; and on the microstructural level of linguistic surface structure, where specific signals can be argued to correlate with cognitively salient discourse points and therefore to textualize the structure projected by the larger narrative frame. As I have noted, neither the micro-structural signals in themselves nor the frame (which is inaccessible except as a projection) are essentialist entities, nor are they pre-established for the reader. On the contrary, the process of reading narrative *as narrative* inevitably involves an activity of narrativization on the reader's part. When one is concerned with the ordinary run-of-the-mill realistic text, this process of narrativization is quite automatic. Our expectations are fulfilled 100 per cent when we have somebody tell us of their experiences last Sunday at the races, since such stories cannot but conform to the natural givens of personal experience and endorse the narrator's self-presentation as both teller and experiencer of the events. Likewise, as I have argued, the very natural situation of traditional storytelling imperceptibly develops into the forms of history, the epic or romance, where the parameters of the hearsay narrative of vicarious experience become extended to cover much that exceeds realistic storytelling frames. In the model that I am here presenting narrativization therefore first 'strikes' in noticeable manner when the experientiality of story experience – which, in the oral mode, is aligned primarily with the first-person frame – becomes transferred on to the third-person realm. This extension, which engenders the narrativity of third-person narrative, has its roots in stories of vicarious experience, in jokes and anecdotes – all of these familiar types of natural narrative – and there is therefore no perceptible break with natural storytelling modes.

Narrativization relies on realistic story parameters. Within my model the concept of realism, even if of a decidedly constructivist kind, therefore plays a crucial, if not central, role. Narrativization reaches its limits precisely where realist modes of understanding cease to be applicable. Realist parameters can be stretched to a certain extent: one may experiment with different concepts of temporality or space, for instance, provided that this is taken either seriously (as in esoteric literature) or in an entirely non-serious or contrafactual fashion (comedy, parody, science fiction). Thus, disruptions of space and time in Marge Piercy's *Woman on the Edge of Time* (1976) are read straightforwardly as an indication of utopian virtualities, and in Thomas Pynchon's novels or Joseph Heller's *Catch-22* (1961) are interpreted as correlatives of the fictional world's pervasive illogicality and paradoxicality. To the extent that the concepts of character or individuality become affected in radically experimental texts, experiences of liminality (insanity, schizophrenia, shock or trauma) are frequently adduced to explain such disruptions of ordinary human experience. This is the strategy that makes much of Beckett's work readable as the vagaries of a deranged mind or as the agonized ruminations of a subject in the final stages of emotional and physical disintegration.

Realism, in the reading that it is given in this study (cp. 1.2.4) – although related to the construct of reality – has therefore exclusively constructivist and no imitational meanings. It is an interpretational strategy of mimeticism in accordance with which textual encounters are reinterpreted as relating to a fictive reality that shares a number of qualities with the 'real' world. Such representational equivalences may be equivalences of a symbolic and nominal/referential rather than of an iconic kind. That is to say, in the process of narrativization texts are *made to conform* to real-life parameters. This mimetic realism encompasses all kinds of verisimilitude: *effet de réel*, motivational *vraisemblance*, the instantiation of spatial or temporal coordinates, and the rock-bottom notions of identity, specificity or subjectivity. Texts such as Christine Brooke-Rose's *Such* (1966) are therefore resolutely anti-realistic, even though – reinterpreted generically as fantasy or science fiction, or indeed as the delusions of a schizophrenic – they ultimately become recuperable within the fold of narrativity. Realism is always an *effect* of interpretation, but this effect can be thwarted by radical inconsistencies in the represented fictional world. Alternative worlds, even in the realm of science fiction, are much less likely to prevent the application of natural parameters than are fissures and illogicalities within a basically realistic setup.

In the historical survey that I have presented narrativity has been demonstrated to undergo considerable fluctuations. In particular, it was argued that narrativity, which is at its lowest in narrative report, in contrast to its central importance in natural narrative, effectively recedes in early historical writing, where it persists at a merely minimal level of zero-degree narrativity. As a consequence, there is little extensive experiential narrative between the epic and the Elizabethan novel, with pseudo-historical writing in the pamphlet tradition uneasily hovering on the brink of narrativity. After a period when narrativity was practically reduced to zero-degree status in the prevailing (pseudo-)historical fiction of the day, experientiality and, with it, narrativity again resurface in the early novel literature. Narrativity properly comes into its own in the development of the consciousness novel. As I have attempted to show, the consciousness factor, already prominent in the eighteenth-century authorial novel, albeit in the shape of external perspective,[7] becomes central to the genre in the figural novel, as Stanzel calls it. The uncanny device of figuralization (Chapter 5) likewise depends for its effects on the consciousness factor, transposing the experientiality of the fiction from its roots in a human agent to that of an anonymous viewer who may or may not coincide with the reader's empathetic perspective. In addition, camera-eye narrative, notwithstanding its supposed objectivity, can be argued to rely on the projection of consciousness in nearly equal measure. Thus the texts of Robbe-Grillet or Dashiell Hammett repose on an implicit viewing position which is objective only in so far as the perceiver's emotions (their experientiality) remain unexpressed or are left implicit. Finally, narrativization by means of the named consciousness factor acquires an even more central status in the experimental writing tradition. Second-person fiction and other such 'oddities' rely very much on readers' establishment of experientiality (frequently on the lines of reflector mode narrative) for the second-person (or German *man*, etc.) protagonist. In so far as texts are cognized in unitary schemata, natural frames frequently serve to identify a central teller-figure whose mind restructures the story matter around her ideational orientation, or they project the workings of a diseased mind in the process of disassemblage, thereby recuperating disparities, inconsistencies and illogicalities of the narrational *récit*. Such narrativization can be complemented by projections of non-Aristotelian worlds and non-rationalistic philosophies of mind and matter – possibilities that are widely utilized in fiction that displays an ideological postmodernist orientation.[8]

When narrativization breaks down, whether incipiently or in full measure, it does so where the consciousness factor can no longer be utilized to tide over radical inconsistency, and this happens first and foremost where overall textual coherence or micro-level linguistic coherence (and cohesion) are at risk. Where texts have turned into a jumble of words without rhyme or reason and only imperfectly reflect a thematic common denominator, or where sentences are internally discontinuous or cohesively non-alignable in their sequence, narrativization is seriously impaired and semantic recuperation flounders even on the basic level of *linguistic*, referential naturalization. This does not prevent such texts from being interesting exercises in linguistic experimentation or from constituting highly ambitious examples of lyric poetry. Radical strategies of this sort therefore again take us to the very limits of generic concepts. I will return to these problems below under 8.4.

8.1.2 What is narrative? (Part one)

At this point it will be necessary to define more precisely how narrativization operates in relation to narrative. In particular the term *narrative* itself requires stricter delimitation. In Chapter 1 I provided an initial redefinition of narrativity on the basis of experientiality, but it is only now after having traced the historical development of narrative that I feel entitled to return to the question of how various types of narrative relate to one another.

My model derives its definition of narrativity from natural, i.e. oral, narrative and from the organic, dynamic process of narrative signification operative within that model. Already within the spectrum of oral forms of narration one can distinguish between report-like non-experiential narrative, which basically summarizes action or event sequences, and prototypical experiential narrative, that is narrative which renders one's own or another's experience within an evaluative frame. Experiential narrative, as we have seen, relates to the function of reportability, on the one hand, and the establishment of a narrative 'point', on the other. Its significance lies precisely in the dynamic interrelation between the newsworthiness of the story matter (tellability) and its significance for the current communicational situation ('point'). Report-like oral narrative, by contrast, serves to establish facts or background information rather than transporting any noteworthy meaning or entertaining the listener with the recounting of unexpected incidences.

There is therefore, I argue, a qualitative difference between two kinds of discourse even within conversational exchange, two kinds of discourse that are, however, traditionally lumped together under the heading of the text type (genre) and discourse mode *narrative*. If, as has traditionally been the case, one defines narrative as a text type that is based on 'telling a story', where story equals a set of events in chronological sequence, then these two kinds of narrative are, indeed, equivalent. However, if – as I have proposed – the factor of experientiality, of emotional involvement, evaluative or empathetic, is placed at the centre of one's analysis, then report-like narration does not qualify as narrative proper but comes to occupy a place closer to argumentative discourse. Report, I have argued, has closer affinities with logical sequencing (chrono-logy, after all, participates in the *logos*) than with the dynamics of experiential narrative. From this perspective, then, text types that develop directly from report sequences in oral discourse can be argued to have little or no narrativity and to be atypical for the generic constitution of narrative proper. This setup then ultimately leads to a re-evaluation of narrative genres. In the new schema natural narrative comes to be situated much closer to *belles lettres*, whereas historiographical discourse is relegated to the more reportative margins of the field.

Two aspects of narrative that have received considerable attention corroborate the above analysis: the recognition of the inherent fictionality of natural narrative; and the constitution of narrative temporality with its paradoxes and peculiarities.

Natural narrative shares with 'Literature' many of the qualities that are traditionally aligned with fictionality.[9] Thus, it has been documented that natural narratives restructure narrative material at each retelling, relying on cognitive schemata rather than perfect recall, reinventing and fictionalizing narrative experience. Chafe (1987, 1990a, 1990b), for instance, provides numerous examples of the restructuring of narrative episodes during consecutive retellings of narratives. It has also been noted that stories told by couples at dinner parties develop into performative repertory with a heavy fictional slant.[10] As Deborah Tannen has pointed out in several of her books, natural narrative also employs much fictionalized dialogue (and even interior monologue) that bears little relation to the realities of the 'original' discourse but which serves instead to foreground the narrator's emotional involvement with the story, the excitement of the experience, its reportability. In more narratological terms, one can translate this into evidence proving that even in oral narrative 'story' is transformed into discourse by means of chronological rearrangement, discourse-oriented rewriting and strategies of fictionalization. By the same token, it can be observed that report-like sequences, even in natural narrative, background the narrative's performance features (Wolfson 1982) and are low on emotionality and strategies of involvement. Hence, from the perspective of fictionalization, natural narratives of personal or vicarious experience – marked also by their specific temporal schemata (Harweg 1975a; cp. Fludernik 1991)[11] – can be separated from report-like narrative even on a formal linguistic level. Report-like narrative, for instance, typically employs a minimal episodic structure; it features an incipit and resolution point but frequently elides the incidence, and it fails to thematize the dynamic tension between the incidence and the *reaction* to it. Narrative experience, which becomes tellable only by distancing, lives precisely from this evocation of only retrospectively recuperable immediacy which the tension between incidence and reaction and the larger dialectics between reportability and point anchor within a formal frame.

Second, the affinity between natural narrative and literature can be documented also from an analysis of temporal structure. Recent discussions of narrative temporality have emphasized the paradoxical nature and dynamic tensions within the traditional notion of plot. Narrative temporality is no longer simply reducible to the sequence of an initial state, an onset of events and a final resolution point (new static situation) – a linear progression, that is; instead it is monitored by at least two levels of temporal cognition – that of teleology, which recognizes temporal sequence retrospectively, and that of the more mundane level of the actual succession of events in time (their chronology). A third level of the presentation of events in the discourse is also frequently added to this dyadic structure of chronology vs. teleology.[12] In an eye-opening essay, Ruth Ronen (1990b) has even outlined three basic approaches to narrative temporality, the first of which roughly corresponds with Adams's (1993) and other scholars' interest in different types of reconfiguration. Ronen distinguishes between the thesis that 'the temporality of fiction can be identified with the narrativity of fictional texts' (1990b: 29, 29–33), the proposal that it can be 'primarily attributed to the temporality of events and states of affairs projected or constructed by the fictional text' (ibid.: 29, 33–7) and the argument that 'the temporality of fiction can be primarily attributed to the temporality of the textual medium and of verbal presentation' (ibid.: 29, 37–41). Ronen's first thesis aligns narrative temporality with Dry's plot-propelling narrative clauses (Dry 1981, 1983) and Ricoeur's configurational designs; her second explanatory schema locates narrative temporality in the action sequences of real-world events (Ricoeur's Mimesis I) and the real-world frames of telling (my own level II). Ronen's third approach to narrative temporality concentrates on the reading process and the text's use of narrative tenses. It is important to keep these levels of analysis or conceptualization of temporality separate, and Ronen has performed an invaluable service to narrative theory by being the first to demonstrate the existence of these discrete viewpoints on temporality.

The most prominent and influential discussion of teleology and narrative dynamics in recent times has come from Jonathan Culler in his article 'Fabula and Sjuzhet in the Analysis of Narrative' (1980). In this paper, it will be remembered, Culler contrasted the necessity of tragic recognition in *Oedipus Rex* with the unlikelihood of this discovery within the surface structure of the plot. Oedipus kills the Sphinx, becomes king, the plague arrives and he tries to pacify the Gods by swearing he will avenge Laos' death. The reports by the messengers attempting to establish the facts of the murder are not conclusive, says Culler; what clinches the case is the obsessive necessity of the narrative to collapse the story of Laos with that of Oedipus, the necessity of the oracle to become truth. Culler's argument, which has given rise to a heated debate and has received some scathing criticism (Sturgess 1989, 1990, 1992; Adams 1989, 1993), collapses the levels of narrative (re)construction (Ricoeur's *emplotment*) and that of the discourse in its relation to the story (*histoire*). On the level of Oedipus-the-character, Oedipus delves into his past and discovers certain coincidences; but what he discovers has been in existence all along both on the level of the *histoire* – if he had not killed Laos he could not have discovered it now – *and*, iconically and proleptically, in the predictions of the Delphic oracle, which is *part* of the *histoire* as well as a proleptic *mise-en-abîme* of the *histoire*, a preliminary summary of the story that Oedipus will uncover. The play's central *anagnorisis* is therefore *not*, as Culler deconstructively argues, anterior to the plot, and it is not its determining factor; the oracle simply needs to precede the accomplishment of its predictions in the *histoire*, and the *histoire*, in its turn, unfolds in anagnoretic fashion. The level of the discourse is parallel to Oedipus' process of cognition. Culler's argument, which is based on the logical schema of cause and effect patterns, does not manage to deconstruct that dynamics except by rhetorical flourish; the reversals of Oedipal emplotment have their origin in the oracle, which has to be located prior to any attempts at self-definition on the part of the Sophoclean hero. What Culler's gesture of rhetorical reversal serves to indicate instead is the *aesthetic* primacy of teleology over chronological causalities.

Teleology also figures prominently in another recent analysis of narrative temporality and dynamics. In his seminal *Time and Narrative* (1983 85/1984 88) Paul Ricoeur treats this dichotomy in terms of its resolution in the *intrigue* on his level of Mimesis II, the level on which emplotment (the English translation of *intrigue*) is defined as 'draw[ing] a configuration out of a simple succession' (1984b: 65). This emplotment, as Ricoeur proposes, subsumes the dynamic factors of 'agents, goals, means, interactions, circumstances, unexpected results' (ibid.), which he had located on his level of Mimesis I. Emplotment therefore brackets the intentionality (as well as intensionality) of apparently sequential actions on the chronological plotline by relocating this dynamic potential, transferring it to the overarching teleological structure of narration. As Ricoeur notes, emplotment reflects and at the same time resolves the Augustinian paradox of time (the recognition that the *now* can be cognized as *now* only after it has receded into the past) by imposing on the heterogeneity of chronological sequentiality a unity of 'point' or 'theme', a 'sense of an ending'. This 'pressing together' of the disparate *accidentia* of plot provides narrative with the aesthetic closure which is the result of teleological emplotment (all ibid.: 66–8). Although Ricoeur does not treat oral types of narrative, he does concern himself with historiography, which, he argues, obeys the very same kinds of constraints as fiction. In Ricoeur, too, teleology is subsumed within a dynamic structure that specifically exceeds mere temporal sequentiality.

A recent proposal by Meir Sternberg (1992) likewise takes the temporality of narrative as the constitutive factor of narrativity and defines it in dialectic terms. Starting with Aristotle's *Poetics*, Sternberg contrasts the opposition of chronology vs. teleology within the story (*holos*) on the one hand and the plot (*muthos*) as restructured discourse representation on the other (ibid.: 474–9). In his reading, the proper cathartic effect of dramatic art arises precisely from the central dechronologization of the plot by way of discovery and/or reversal (ibid.: 476), and it is this contraction point that engenders the desired effect of pity and fear (ibid.: 479). As Sternberg correctly notes, the fundamental status of temporality remains implicit in this schema. The structuralist *reordering* of chronology into discourse, by contrast, loses sight of the holistic, dynamic and teleological quality of the Aristotelian model. In continuity with his earlier seminal work on the suspense element in narrative fiction (1978/1993, 1987), Sternberg goes on to define narrativity as constituted by three 'master strategies' which are relatable to the Augustinian concepts of recognition, retrospection, and prospection. These three strategies are: surprise, curiosity and suspense. The holistic arc of narrative temporality in his model therefore splits into three related experiential moments: the central coincidental encounter with the unexpected (surprise), which retrospectively turns out to be the uncanny familiar; a search for the origins of the coincidence (curiosity); and a movement forward to the anticipation of the resolution of the puzzle (suspense). In contrast to the dichotomous schemata of Chatman and his structuralist predecessors (Propp, Bremond, Todorov, Genette), Sternberg therefore in significant ways restructures the dynamics of narrativity and rewrites the definition of what is or is not a narrative:

> I define *narrativity* as the play of suspense/curiosity/surprise between represented and communicative time (in whatever combination, whatever medium, whatever manifest or latent form). Along the same functional lines, I define *narrative* as a discourse where such play dominates: narrativity then ascends from a possibly marginal or secondary role (e.g., as a temporal force governed by the space-making, descriptive function that always coexists with it [Sternberg 1981, 1983]) to the status of regulating principle, first among the priorities of telling/reading.
> (Sternberg 1992: 529)

Sternberg at the conclusion of his article then illustrates how different authors have privileged one of the three functions over the others. For instance, historiography, the anecdote, the folk tale and D.H. Lawrence as well as Trollope are said to favour suspense (ibid.: 534–5). At the present time it remains unclear whether, or to what extent, Sternberg may go on to separate historiography from fiction.[13] Even at this point it is, however, apparent that Sternberg locates the dynamics of narrative on the temporal plane of the reading process as it interacts with the paradoxes of chronology and teleology, whereas my own approach has been to situate narrativity in an organic frame of embodied and evaluative experientiality. Within my model temporality is a constitutive aspect of embodiment and evaluation, but it is secondary to the experience itself, which includes temporality as one of its parameters but – in my view – cannot be subsumed under the umbrella of temporality. If Sternberg and I part company here, this is on the basis of what I feel to be a nearly uncanny sympathy – a recognition of the what and the how of narrativity that could not, indeed, be closer.

Natural Narratology   323

I suspect that the reasons for our different trajectories can be found in what type of narrative Sternberg and I regard as prototypical and, equally, depend on our ulterior goals and ideological concerns. In contrast to Sternberg, I start out with oral narrative as my principal and originary narrational schema, and I also have to plead guilty to designs going beyond the indifferent categorization of literary narrative: after all, I am trying to propose a new typology of sorts, one which is maximally inclusive (despite *ex*cluding historical discourse). For these reasons narrative has here been defined in terms that respect narrative's enmeshment with temporality but locate that enmeshment within the notion of prototypical human experientiality.

It will now be incumbent on me to specify in more detail the range covered by my understanding of narrative and experientiality.

8.1.3 Degrees of narrativity, non-narrative texts and the question of historicity

How exactly, then, do I visualize the scale from non-narrative to minimally narrative to fully narrative texts? And to what extent is that scale defined generically, historically or merely theoretically (categorically)?

Let me start by briefly reviewing prominent definitions of narrativity. I begin with the time-old analysis of narrative as hinging on plot. As far as I can tell, the term *narrativity* was first used in a technical sense by Greimas (1970: 157–60/1987: 63–5),[14] where it seems to characterize the semiotic functioning of narrative as explicated in his semiotic square. (Greimas does not *define* his use of the term *narrativité*, whose meaning he seems to take for granted.[15]) The traditional formula in which narrativity correlates with a definition of narrative is usually illustrated in reference to a minimal plot of two or three events constructed on the lines of E.M. Forster's *The king died and then the queen died of grief* (1974: 60).[16] From this standard perspective, non-narrative texts are those without a plot function, for instance eventless texts (with just one event, or without triggering a change), without a proper conflict (therefore failing to instantiate the necessary parameters for the constitution of the semiotic square) or without a desirable diversification of incidents (M.-L. Ryan 1991: 119–20).[17] The latter criterion already adumbrates the slippage that occurs in G. Prince (1982), where narrativity, which originally designates 'the set of properties characterizing *narrative* and distinguishing it from nonnarrative; the formal and contextual features making a narrative more or less narrative, as it were' (G. Prince 1987: 64) begins to signify also the quality of good, tellable narrative:

> The degree of narrativity of a given narrative depends partly on the extent to which that narrative fulfills a receiver's desire by representing oriented temporal wholes (prospectively from BEGINNING to END and

retrospectively from end to beginning), involving a CONFLICT, consisting of discrete, specific, and positive situations and events, and meaningful in terms of a human(ized) project and world.

(ibid.)[18]

Prince's definition, despite this promising start, veers off into a number of tangents that trace this slippage from what narrative 'is' (with essential narrative 'features' attached) to what it 'does' to the receiver, and to the establishment of a scale of features that increase a text's narrativity. Thus Prince notes that 'narrative *is* the recounting of events rather than the discussion of their representation' (G. Prince 1982: 146), yet concedes, a page later, that '"The cat sat on the mat" is certainly not without interest but "The cat sat on the dog's mat" may be the beginning of a good story' (ibid.: 147). He also notes Culler's definition of narrative from *Structuralist Poetics* (Culler 1975: 143), according to which narrative 'presents temporal sequences of states and actions that make sense in terms of a human project and/or a humanized universe' (G. Prince 1982: 148). This latter qualification neither ties in with actionality *per se*,[19] nor exhausts (nor is presented as exhausting) the factor of 'human interest' or 'what makes a narrative interesting' in Prince's earlier remarks. Other criteria for narrativity, which Prince (1982) notes more or less at random, include:

- the 'discreteness and specificity of the (sequences of) events presented' (ibid.: 149)
- the 'extent to which their [the events'] occurrence is given as a fact (in a certain world) rather than a possibility or probability' (ibid.)
- the 'extent to which the events presented constitute (or pertain to) a whole, a complete structure with a beginning, a middle and an end' (ibid.: 151)
- the existence of a 'continuant subject' and of verisimilar causal relationships (ibid.)
- 'narrativity is a function of the possibility of viewing one event as dependent on a preceding one' (ibid.: 155) (this incorporates the teleological aspect of narrative)
- the 'point' of the narrative: 'Without desire on the part of the receiver and without the fulfillment of this desire, there can be no point to a narrative' (ibid.: 159)

The above criteria, which are not systematically related to one another, can easily be integrated into schema-theoretic understandings of event structures and action sequences such as the ones I started out from in Chapter 1. (G. Prince [1982] did not yet have the benefit of Ricoeur's ground-breaking proposal of a triple-layered model of mimesis.) According to Prince's framework, which reflects aspects of the tradition from Aristotle to the present, non-narrative texts have to be distinguished from texts with a low degree of narrativity. Thus the presence of events is a necessary condition, whereas wholeness and interest come in degrees of acceptability. Point, a non-formal criterion, curiously belongs with the necessary conditions: 'just as there can be no narrative – period – without desire on the part of a sender to produce one' (ibid.). Prince's non-narrative texts are therefore principally those without event sequences (such as pure interior monologue) or texts without a narrating instance (a criterion that is unaccountably missing from his definition of narrativity in Chapter 5 but occupies a central position in Chapter 1 of his book): drama as well as pure dialogue appears to be excluded from narrativity.[20] All of Prince's invented example sentences are moreover of the constantive type privileging past tense narrative and the standard realist *écriture*.

I have already noted how Chatman (1978, 1990) and Sternberg (1992) define narrativity in quite different structural terms: as an interplay of dynamic tensions (between story and discourse in Chatman's model; of suspense, curiosity and surprise in Sternberg's). These functionalist and non-essentialist approaches therefore give rise to quite different conceptualizations of the non-narrative. In Chatman's most recent proposals the non-narrative is located at the level of alternative discourse types (argument, description), whereas Meir Sternberg's narratological Other is as yet undefined (one will have to see what happens in the third instalment of 'Telling in Time'). It is difficult to judge what Sternberg will do with radically non-actional (post)modernist narrative, and I suspect that, like Prince, he might tend to exclude direct speech and thought representation from the realm of narrative proper. In contrast to Prince, Sternberg is, however, much more willing to accommodate narrative kernels if they contain a surprise or suspense element. As Sternberg correctly notes, even one-sentence constructs may blossom into a story (*Fire!* [1992: 520]) and conversational storytelling *in nuce* can be demonstrated in utterances such as *Guess what! The Thompsons have moved to Idaho*. Although I would not consider these utterances to *be* a narrative, they certainly provide the *source* for one; in fact, they could well be the abstracts of an ensuing narrative that elaborates on the surprise effect and point of those remarks. That is precisely what the second utterance promises: a story about the surprising news of the Thompsons' move, and the supplying of a narrative (i.e. conversational) point to this fact: the Thompsons being known as having a particularly sedentary disposition; the Thompsons having been expected to move to Washington; the speaker signalling the availability of a house next door which the interlocutor may wish to buy or rent. Compare also Prince's cat on the dog's mat (G. Prince 1982: 147), which provides an *opening* for a subsequent narrative rather than already the narrative itself.[21] Although such minimal units therefore have the makings of a more extended narrative, they do not fully deploy their dynamic or dialectic interrelation of reportability and point, serving instead as announcements of a theme, as *abstracts* of a story (Labov 1972) that may or may not be told thereafter. In fact, an opening gambit on the lines suggested by Sternberg may result in storytelling of an altogether different kind, with the interlocutor taking the opportunity to illustrate some of the Thompsons' peculiarities by telling of her weird experiences of them. By locating narrativity in the experientiality factor and by choosing natural narrative for my prototypical manifestation of it, I therefore decidedly disavow the fundamental importance of plot but by way of compensation attempt fully to integrate the theories of narrative's temporal dynamics.

Another recent suggestion has introduced the concept of *modes of narrativity* into the debate and in interesting ways parallels, as well as distances itself from, my own proposals. Marie-Laure Ryan (1992) relies on Gerald Prince's definition of 'narrativity' (in fact, Prince would call this narrativehood) as involving 'the presence in a text of a narrator telling a story', a frame to be supplemented by 'formulat[ing] the semantic properties of plots since plot is the supporting and constitutive structure of stories' (M.-L. Ryan 1992: 368). Since Ryan continues to see plot as fundamental to narrativity, her entire redefinition of narrativity and its modes, including the cognitive parameters that she proposes, necessarily develops in a direction very different from my own. Thus Ryan outlines three basic conditions of narrativity: (1) world creation (in the technical narratological sense of M.-L. Ryan [1991]); (2) the occurrence of changes of state to create a temporal dimension within the narrative world; and (3) the 'reconstruction of an interpretative network of goals, plans, causal relations, and psychological motivations around the narrated events' (M.-L. Ryan 1992: 371). Whereas for Ryan the third condition serves to give 'coherence and intelligibility to the physical events and turns them into a plot' (ibid.), this third condition – in my own model – very much relates to the underlying cognitive frames of human actionality (Ricoeur's level of Mimesis I). Since I also categorically dispense with the notion of plot, this leaves the world-creating situational parameter as the sole defining characteristic shared by our proposals. World-creating situations are endowed with potential actionality (from the ACTION frame supplemented with psychological motivation) and therefore engender plot sequences.

Ryan's model, whose cognitive leanings very much conform to my own methodological predispositions, comes very close to proposing a comparable notion of narrativization. Narrativity for her 'is not an intrinsic property of events' – and here, again, her concentration on plot as *the* central defining feature of narrative surfaces quite prominently – 'but a semantic network built around events by a reflecting consciousness' (ibid.: 376). Whereas in traditional narrative, the plot is filtered through the consciousness of the narrator, the reader in Ryan's model has to *construct* narrativity[22] from narratorless (but not non-narrative) texts such as ballet, drama or film: 'In underlying narrativity, by contrast, the narrative act of consciousness takes place in the mind of the receiver but skips the narratorial level' (ibid.: 377).[23] She likens this process of narrativization (in my terminology) to people's speculations about the experience of their fellow beings around them: 'We witness a fight, and we interpret it as an episode in an ongoing drama' (ibid.). Ryan therefore concludes by characterizing her 'modes of narrativity' as mental operations, as 'the games that the mind plays with narrative structures in the production and reception of texts'. She lists the following instructions for the reader:

> [. . .] embed them, combine them, multiply them, interleave them, dilute them with other ingredients, strip them of some of their basic elements, distort them, propose them for their own sake or use them in support of an argument, promise and defer them sometimes without guarantee of their eventual completion, derive them from the text by responding to a narratorial invitation, read them into the text on its implicit suggestion, and impose them on the text as an act of personal interpretation.
> (ibid.: 385)

These games with narrative structures elicit corresponding narrativizing actions on the part of the reader:

> Diluted narrativity asks the reader to sort out and condense information in order to retrieve the plot; on the contrary, embryonic narrativity makes the reader aware of what is missing for the text to achieve narrative coherence. In underlying narrativity, the reader must supply the interpretive network; in the figural mode, she must create individuated characters out of metaphors and collective entities; in exemplary narrativity, she must extract the point of the story and relate it to the general point of the text; and in deferred narrativity, she must integrate the events narrated by the text into a hypothetical global narrative structure encompassing both established past and possible future episodes.
> (ibid.: 384)[24]

This model therefore constitutes narrativity in the reading process, as I do myself for my own model, but it limits the reader's performance to the establishment of a plot, or to the acceptance of anti-narrativity (ibid.: 379–80). Both the various types of narrativity and their recuperation or mode of narrativization, as I would prefer to call it, firmly entrench the constitutive plot element and therefore – it seems to me – unjustifiably limit the possible range of responses to literature. Nevertheless, Ryan's proposals come closest to the spirit in which I am trying to combine narrative experientiality and the reader's narrativizations of textual material.

I wish to close this discussion of the term *narrativity* by pointing to one further study that crucially concerns narrativity: Philip J. M. Sturgess's book *Narrativity. Theory and Practice* (1992). Sturgess provides an invaluable discussion of early definitions of the notion, all of which centre on how narrative produces a *story* from different kinds of underlying material.[25] Sturgess's own proposal, however, locates narrativity on the *discourse* level of a story:

> Narrativity refers preeminently to the way in which a narrative *articulates* itself, the way in which each stage of its own extension creates what might be called a crisis or dilemma of the discourse, which is solved by its own furtherance in whatever form that happens to take.
> (Sturgess 1992: 26)

I cannot here go into Sturgess's 'logic' of narrativity, but it is important to stress that Sturgess's arguments concern literary narrative *exclusively*, so that, whatever the teleologic and holistic merits of his proposals, his terminology cannot be profitably integrated into my own approach. Although Sturgess's work is inspired by a more logical methodology, his results are closer to Sternberg's formulations than to Marie-Laure Ryan's or my own.

Having located narrativity in relation to other definitions of it, I now turn to the category of the non-narrative (cp. also below under 8.4) and to the question of a *grading* of narrativity. As I have argued throughout the book, experientiality is at its lowest in the presentation of merely a succession of events and their causal interdependence. It is therefore no coincidence that E.M. Forster's invented example sentence was *The king died and then the queen died of grief.* Here the queen's emotional predicament takes centre stage. Thus, even though the simple labelling of the causal connection by this reference to the queen's sentiments does not deserve to be called an index of experientiality, such experientiality is here indicated *in nuce*.

Historical narrative, on the other hand, I have argued, lacks the feature of surprise (in Sternberg's schema) or experientiality (in my own) and therefore only qualifies as zero-degree narrativity. Much narrative generally is reportative or historical in this sense, both in conversational language and in the written medium. Sequences of events without due regard to motivation, emotion or perception, without, that is, a due regard to characters' intensionality, do not in my model qualify as proper narratives. In so far as historical or reportative discourse instantiates action schemata that rely at least minimally on the empathizable notions of goal-directedness, perceptional parameters or intentional action, these texts can be recuperated as manifesting a low degree of narrativity. It is only where report usurps all potentially experiential functions of a narrative that, technically speaking, narrativity needs to be gauged at the zero mark. Terminologically, this involves me in some inconsistency: after all, I continue to refer to such texts of zero-degree narrativity as 'narratives' because common parlance prescribes this usage. There also is some precedent for similar terminological hassles, as in Hayden White's distinction between *narrating* and *narrativizing* (i.e. transforming the narration into a *story*) – an account which subsumes historiographical discourse under patterns of storification and sets aside the annals and chronicles (H. White 1981: 2). The real problem behind White's and my own attempts at counter-intuitive terminology lies in the much too general usage of the term *narrative*. Nevertheless, the embarrassments of terminological awkwardness are more than outweighed by the advantages of my re-evaluation of narrative properties, particularly when one regards the positive consequences of this reshuffling at the other end of the narrativity scale. The proposed reconstitution of narrativity on the lines of experiential rather than actantial parameters allows nothing less than a reintegration of some 80 to 90 per cent of hitherto marginalized literature from the Middle Ages to the twentieth century.

A word is here still due on the status of report sequences in the orality–literacy continuum. Just as description becomes a separate seemingly dispensable function in realist narrative, where it can be placed anywhere in the text, report, too, develops into separable textual chunks between scenes (though combinable with descriptive passages). This flexibility of positioning radically departs from the oral model. In natural narrative, description occurs in the function of either initial or delayed orientation but at no other points in the narrative. Delayed orientation, in turn, occurs quite freely within the oral narrative episode, but it is marked intonationally to indicate its complementarity. In parallel fashion, report sequences in conversational exchanges either are separate sequences unaligned with narratives of personal or vicarious experience, or are part of the initial orientation section (the preliminaries). Hence, report – unlike description – occurs both independently and as part of a narrative structure, and this correlates with its functional importance for the listener's informational uptake. That function is of course an extratextual or pragmatic one. Report, in my schema, is therefore not resolutely non-narrative *per se* but only when it usurps an entire narrative, in which case it constitutes a limit-case of zero-degree narrativity.

Before turning to more specifically narratological issues in the subsequent section I would like to conclude this section on narrativity by emphasizing the historical aspects of the model. Unlike the traditional narratological typologies of Genette, Bal, Bonheim, Lanser, Chatman, Prince or Greimas and Todorov, this model, like Stanzel's, is conceived as explicitly historical, as a synchronic descriptive frame that can be applied to the diachrony of narrative forms. This historical parameter allows for an additional level of generic development, of the move from new narrativizations (the third-person omniscient mode, the consciousness novel) to the constitution of current generic types. Once new generic types get installed, they are no longer perceived as non-natural and in need of narrativization. That is to say, there is no longer a need to reinterpret such textual constellations against the grain. Narrativization has become automatized.

I will come back to the relation between natural parameters and frames and the constitution of narrativity by means of narrativizational interventions in my final conclusion below under 8.6. It is important to stress, however, that, within the terms of my theoretical model, the *natural* relates exclusively to cognitive parameters, and to *naturally occurring* storytelling situations. Non-natural textual constellations refer to text types that are naturally *non-occurring*. For this reason new generic options (such as reflector-mode narrative) do not in the process of narrativization *become* natural, although they become *naturalized*, interpretable on the basis of a different set of natural parameters and naturalized in the Cullerian sense of availability as a new generic model. It is for this reason that I have replaced Culler's term *naturalization* with *narrativization*: narrativized non-natural text types do not ever *become* natural, although a new cognitive parameter (e.g. the EXPERIENCING parameter) may become available. Historicization therefore does not imply a tinkering with the natural, since the natural from the start was conceived as that which occurs in natural narrative, i.e. in natural storytelling situations or, abstractly, as part of a repertory of cognitive parameters that rely on embodiment and other prototypical frames operative within a natural human environment. I here insist on this distinction between static or permanent natural parameters and kinetic, historicizable processes of narrativization because some early responses to previous versions of this model as work in progress have tended to transfer the historical aspect into the very category of the natural – an illicit transference within my own construction of the theory.

8.2 STANDARD MODELS REVIEWED: HOW TO SQUARE THE CIRCLE

Now that the design of Natural Narratology can be more fully appreciated, it is time to ask what this new model *is doing*, what use it is and particularly how it relates to standard narratological paradigms. Why do we need a new model at all?

The foregoing discussion has already indicated that my model has been designed to subsume Stanzel's typology of three narrative situations in terms of special cases within the theory. Genette's typology, on the contrary, bears little immediate relation to my model since its categories are analytic and lack the synthetic, holistic setup of my own basic terms. Since Natural Narratology constitutes a development from Stanzel's theory, it has from the very outset opposed itself to the analytic descriptive narratologies of Genette, Prince, Bal, Bonheim, or Lanser. This does not mean, however, that the many useful conceptual tools made available by Genette and others are here simply ignored or dismissed without a proper hearing. On the contrary, as we will see, such analytic concepts are especially relevant to the fine-tuning of the model, even though its central categories are cognitive organic concepts rather than analytic or linguistic ones.

Before engaging with this fine-tuning, an initial discussion about the *areas of application* for my model is in order. Among different theories the comparison always tends to be in the direction of which theory covers more material or which theory provides better explanations of certain phenomena. Both Stanzel and Genette cover a wide range of texts within their respective methodologies. Stanzel should additionally be credited with a historical slant that allows the theory to be applied on a diachronic scale. His example texts range all the way from Elizabethan literature to the postmodernist novel,[26] although he concentrates on the classic periods of the novel, from the eighteenth century to the mid-twentieth century. Stanzel limits himself to *fictional* discourse, setting aside historiography or biography, and he remains firmly rooted in the study of Literature and the *written medium*, contrasting narrative (the novel and short story) with drama or film, which he treats as two entirely different (non-narrative) media. By contrast, Genette's range is much more restricted, although in *Fiction et diction* (1991) he actually broadens his approach to cover non-fictional narrative (history, biography), thereby significantly extending his range of texts in a direction left unaccounted for in Stanzel's corpus. Like Stanzel, however, Genette has little interest in oral narrative or simple narrative forms (i.e. Jolles's *einfache Formen*), nor does he deal with drama or film. Genette is even less concerned with medieval or early modern narrative and, oddly, discusses very little experimental writing. Thus, Genette only briefly notes the existence of second-person narrative and mentions other postmodernist writing merely in passing. Most important of all, Genette's typology is self-avowedly synchronic. Its categories are not examined from a diachronic perspective at all. However, in principle one could easily apply Genette's categories to the history of the novel, mapping out a diagram to show which combinations of narratological parameters were current in which successive historical periods. Unaccountably, this has, as far as I know, not yet been attempted. Genette's model has fed into the debates on larger narratological issues but has not sparked any historical analyses.

In the wake of Bonheim's ground-breaking *Literary Systematics* (1990) and his proposal to apply cladistics[27] to literary studies, historical engagements on the basis of Genette's or Lanser's system have recently become at least empirically possible. With the help of cladistics, if one wanted to apply it to narratology, one could produce diagrams that would represent in visual fashion how a number of narrative parameters cluster in individual works and how these clusters remain constant or shift their emphases and combinations on a diachronic plane. It is to be hoped that scholars from Cologne will produce a series of special studies on these lines which will then allow an empirical corroboration or refutation of organic models such as the ones proposed by Stanzel or myself. Bonheim, incidentally, has also been foremost among those discovering and analysing new forms of narrative such as second-person fiction (1982a, 1983, 1990: Chapter 15). His work therefore complements Genette's and Stanzel's in important aspects.

In contrast to Bonheim, Chatman's extensions of traditional narratology in *Coming to Terms* (1990) move in the direction of incorporating filmic narrative within the core corpus of narratives. In addition, Chatman contrasts narrative with two other text or discourse types, those of description and argument, integrating narrative in a broader spectrum of discourses. Moreover, Chatman presents some reconceptualizations in the area of focalization, a field that appears to have moved into a new phase of major redefinitions.[28] Chatman does not, however, branch out into diachrony, radically experimental types of narrative, or oral storytelling, and his range of texts largely coincides with Genette's: the eighteenth-century novel to Nabokov.

This summary demonstrates that Natural Narratology, as far as different types of narrative go, is able to cover more extensive ground than these other models. In addition to this diachronic range of narratives, Natural Narratology also in principle accommodates narrative in a diversity of media. Although I do not deal intensively with drama or film in this book, my theoretical setup explicitly embraces drama and film as well as ballets or cartoons, radio plays and video clips. I will be adding a few pertinent remarks on these different narrative genres below under 8.4. Besides significantly extending its *corpus* of literary texts as well as accommodating a diversity of media, Natural Narratology moreover extends its area of application to embrace conversational narrative. As a consequence of seeing conversational narrative as the central paradigmatic mode and medium of narration, Natural Narratology ends up deconstructing the fiction vs. non-fiction boundary, but redraws the lines on the issue of experientiality. As we have seen, this results in the exclusion of historiography from the realm of narrativity and it also eliminates from consideration much narrative report that belongs to the discourse-type narrative (Adams 1993). Finally, Natural Narratology also attempts to discuss a wide range of *experimental* writing.[29] The emphasis here, as already in *The Fictions of Language and the Languages of Fiction* (Fludernik 1993a), has been on the *availability* of certain options rather than on their precise description and placing within traditional models of narrative – a task performed by W. Wolf (1993). Instead, I have tried to supplement existing studies such as McHale (1992a, 1987/1993), P. Waugh (1984), Hutcheon (1988) or W. Wolf (1993), concentrating on narratologically relevant innovations which have received little attention.

To conclude. In comparison with the models of Genette, Stanzel, Bonheim or Lanser, Natural Narratology covers a significantly larger ground historically, generically and in relation to the media of narrative. It does so, however, at the price of a reconceptualization of what is narrative.

Regarding the second theoretical criterion of *explanatory power*, Natural Narratology can in at least some points also claim superiority over standard models. For one, by managing to integrate more experimental writing within its schema, Natural Narratology eschews the traditional effect of negative characterization (no plot, no characters, etc.) for experimental texts and thereby saves them from inevitable marginalization. Natural Narratology also provides a more comprehensive treatment of the questions of narrative person, voice and tense (see Chapters 5 and 6), a tactic that again ultimately allows the accommodation of yet more egregious 'oddities'. By presenting some, though perhaps controversial, answers to the debate about diachronic developments in the late medieval and early modern period, Natural Narratology can additionally lay claim to wider historical relevance. In particular, the beginnings of the novel have now become analysable from a number of new perspectives that will yet have to be more fully implemented and whose impact cannot at this point be assessed.

8.3 NARRATOLOGICAL CATEGORIES AND COGNITIVE PARAMETERS

8.3.1 Story vs. discourse reconsidered

The story vs. discourse distinction perhaps constitutes the most basic of all narratological axioms. It has been foundational to the narratological project since the Russian Formalists' distinction between *fabula* and *sjuzhet*. Chatman (1978, 1990) builds the very definition of narrative on the story vs. discourse distinction, and other models award a central position to this dyad, even though – like Genette and Bal – they incorporate it within a triad of narrative levels: story, text, and narration.[30] The classic dichotomy can be traced back as far as Aristotle's constitutive notion of plot (*muthos*), which may be argued to contrast with the triple structure of beginning, middle and end (*Poetics* 1451a) on the level of discourse presentation.[31] Aristotle's text actually implies the presence of at least three narrative levels: that of the story or *fabula* (the Oedipus myth); that of the restructuring of that story into a plot (Aristotle's *muthos*), which perhaps includes a subsidiary aspect of logicality (*logos*); and the discourse presentation itself with its whole (*to holos*) composed of beginning, middle and end. Aristotle's text explicitly relates beginning, middle and end to the action (*praxis*), but the implied reference is to the selection and discourse representation of the actantial substratum. It is a little remarked-upon fact that the discourse vs. story distinction is fundamental to the drama, too, and in the wake of narratology one has to remind oneself that, actually, Aristotle's model set out to discuss Greek *drama* and *not* narrative. Thus, paradoxically, narratology has taken its origin from a text of drama criticism, but this foundational frame has been repressed so successfully that drama has now frequently come to occupy the position of narratology's non-narrative Other.

In Chapters 6 and 7 I queried the general validity of the story vs. discourse distinction, or at least its status as an absolute of narratology.

I did so in view of what in recent experimental writing seems to me to be a move towards the deconstruction of the telling vs. story or text vs. story dichotomies. The story vs. discourse opposition seems to repose on a realist understanding of narration in which the concept of 'live now and tell later' inevitably splits experiential and narrational processes. In addition to these realist norms about telling and experiencing, the story vs. discourse dichotomy also brings into play the more sophisticated semiotic perspective of the *signifying text* on the one hand and the *signified object* (the story) on the other. The standard account of the story vs. discourse dichotomy in Genette (1972/1980), indeed, does *not* mention tellers or readers but proposes to describe textual structures (the *discours*) and their signifieds (the *histoire*). In a further move, Genette (1980) and Bal (1985) then *add* the production level of the discourse, *narration*, to the interface of the textual level of the *discours*.

The story vs. discourse dichotomy, usually conceptualized in terms of textualization that involves the option of temporal, causal and focalizational realignments, poses serious questions about the mediality of narration if narrative is conceived of as being necessarily based on plot. From the plot perspective, narrative comes to be equated with a basic story which is transmitted differently into fiction, drama or film. This is of course what Stanzel and Genette, Prince and Bal have always argued.[32] Chatman's insistence (1990: 124–38) on a cinematic narrator, by contrast – a proposal that has great elegance but is somewhat counter-intuitive – puts the question of mediality at the very centre of his argument and locates this mediality *not* in the language and the text but in the figure of the narrator (the teller, the producer of language or of screen material). Chatman's is therefore much closer to Stanzel's framework and his central notion of narrative *mediacy* than to Genette's semiotic formulations of the discourse signifying the story. Conceptualizing discourse as *text* (i.e. as a linguistic *product*), on the other hand, has great advantages over defining it in terms of production or mediality, since these differ across a variety of narrative forms and genres. Genette therefore need not feel constrained to invent cinematic narrators or *monstrateurs*, as do Chatman (1990) and Gaudreault (1988). Yet Genette promotes the status of the storyteller to a more central position when he comes to discuss historical narrative and biography. His discussion of fictionality in *Fiction et diction* (1991) centrally depends on the presence of a narrator and 'his' identity or non-identity with the main fictional protagonist and/or the author, respectively. Genette's semiotic system also implies that the text's signified always remains the *story*; this is what the text is *about*, its *raison d'être*. Although, from a commonsense perspective on prototypical narrative, there is little to take exception to in this formulation, it certainly raises the question of whether the story (and, if so, *what* story) is really the signified of narrative texts and how this scenario needs to be modified for twentieth-century texts that have no plot or story. A plot-oriented analysis of narrative is inevitably grounded in the communication model of literary speech acts, according to which the text appears to transport a meaning (i.e. the story) to the reader. Such an analysis certainly becomes questionable for a great many texts from the twentieth century, where there is little of a story but much analysis of consciousness and (social) circumstances; indeed, it fails even in the case of more traditional moralistic, didactic and allegorical writing where the story function can be argued to be backgrounded in relation to ulterior evaluative purposes.[33]

One reason for questioning the centrality of the story vs. discourse dichotomy as *the* central hub on which narratology is supposed to hinge therefore derives from my downgrading of story as a defining characteristic of narrative. Narrative is no longer pictured as either *communicating* a story or *signifying* a story and it is no longer regarded as the *product* of the narrative speech act. Even for quite traditional narratives one can pose the question of what precisely constitutes the story, and what, in particular, constitutes an *event* within such a story. Falling in love is a common story event in the novel and a crucial link in the causal chain of motivation, but events may also include sudden mental realizations on the part of a character (the recognition of somebody's treachery, for instance), speech acts (a face-threatening act, for example, which may entail retaliatory measures, as in William Godwin's *Caleb Williams*) or even tiny gestures, which in some plots acquire crucial significance. As in historiography, the notion of event is therefore a singularly fuzzy one and cannot be limited to notions of external agency. In fact the conception of what is or is not an event crucially depends on the *story* within which it occurs (H. White 1981: 19); the traditional definition of plot as consisting of at least two sequential events therefore turns out to be question-begging in a decidedly circular manner. Events have to be *functional* within the plot, subjected to its causality. But they can also operate merely as thematic units where plots are structured in less tightly motivational form. The above slippage between *story* and *plot* demonstrates the very fuzziness of the traditional model. If the narrative tells a story, does it not tell the *plot*? When a text is conceived in terms of enunciation, the narrator produces a discourse which signifies a plot, and then the plot implies a chronological sequence of events. The locution *to tell a story* clearly covers up treacherous indeterminacies which are laid bare by a questioning of the terminology.

A definition of what is or is not a story becomes nearly impossible in reference to the twentieth-century novel. Although all (post)modern texts most certainly have *discourse* reference (with or without a teller figure), what precisely (if anything) is their *story* (or plot) frequently cannot be delineated with any clarity. Events and stories are simply no longer central to the focus of what these texts are about. An obvious theoretical conclusion to this problem is of course simply to deny the label *narrative* to the bulk of twentieth-century fictions, to say, that is, that the norm for twentieth-century fiction is no longer instantiated by the narrative discourse type. The predominantly negative characterization of experimental fiction as contravening traditional story parameters (no plot, no character, no teleology, etc.) points in this direction, as do formulations on the lines of the 'death of the author'. Note also the prevalence of the label anti-narrative and M.-L. Ryan's proposal of the term *antinarrativity* (1992: 379-80).

However, in so far as certain traditional types of narratives can be visualized as contrasting a story-world with a situation of narration, the story vs. discourse distinction is certainly extremely useful. What I therefore propose to do within Natural Narratology is to subsume this distinction under the respective frames of a story schema (ACTION, fictional world) and a discourse schema (TELLING). Presentation of a fictional situation may be by means of a prominent narrational act, and in that case the traditional story vs. discourse distinction can usefully be employed to discuss focalization, the issues of presentational knowledge or ignorance (Füger 1978) and temporal chronology (the sequentialization of the experience itself, the narrator's rewriting of it and – on an intermediate level – the narrator's own order of knowledge).[34] In so far as story is taken to be a deep-structural aspect of narrative and narrative discourse is regarded as its mere medialization, the narrative text allows us to project a deep-structural story just as it allows us to project a teller figure on the enunciational plane. The *linguistic* presentation of experientiality, however, is not the privileged mode of narration. As we will see under 8.4, drama and film employ entirely different narrative strategies in order to present a 'discourse' in their medium, but this discourse need not entail a narrator or teller (shower) figure (*pace* Chatman [1990] and his cinematic narrator). Films and plays, after all, have a different kind of text(ure). Their relationship to the projection of a *fictional world*, however, is similar to that of written texts. Films and plays rely on the same cognitive parameters which are operative in the re-cognization of narrative structure in whatever medium.

Natural Narratology therefore does not entirely reject the story vs. discourse distinction but relegates it to those parameters which depend on a realistic cognization of both the story-world and the narrational act. In so far as a story is being *told* in 'realistic' terms and by a personalized narrator figure, it is clearly anterior to the telling and the constructed story can be suitably related to the narrational act. Recent experiments with simultaneous narration and second-person fiction make recuperation within such a teller scenario less worthwhile. Telling there is, but to visualize it in terms of prototypical scenarios only causes problems of interpretation. Simultaneous (present-tense) narrative, for instance, generally backgrounds the *act* of narration since its precise circumstances of utterance need to remain vague; likewise, some forms of second-person fiction quite openly *project* a fictional world by addressing, even exhorting, the *you*-protagonist. Both types of narrative, moreover, tend to blur the line between an intrafictional narratee and the implied reader figure (potentially a role that the real reader may want to empathize with). In second-person fiction this is most obvious, but present-tense narrative, too, implicitly erases the boundary between fiction and its textual recipient since the fiction is no longer situated in a clearly demarcated area which has been set apart from the recipient by means of the temporal deictic frame. To the extent that the act of narration becomes vague, the position of the addressee, too, is dislocated from a specific temporal and spatial point in relation to the story.

8.3.2 Tellers vs. reflectors, agents and readers: the dramatis personae of narratology

The story vs. discourse distinction also underlies much of the terminology that treats fictional agents: characters vs. narrators, reflectors vs. tellers. Indeed, story *world* cannot be conceived of without agents or fictional personae of one kind or another, and these are situated within a specific space and time. Likewise, any conceptualization of telling involves a narrational *act* and immediately invokes the figure of a teller and, ultimately, of a listener or reader. Within a realistic scenario, therefore, one has a communicative model of narration (teller → text → reader) and the projection by the text of a story-world that is typically anthropomorphic.

As Nilli Diengott (1987) has pointed out, the classic models of narratology all rely on such a realist frame. They typically impute agency to the structural positions within their respective schemas. Genette's distinction between homodiegesis and heterodiegesis, like his more recent analysis of fictionality in *Fiction et diction* (1991), crucially depends on the identity or non-identity of fictional and narrational agents. And the same is of course true for Stanzel, except that he contrasts the *fictional worlds* of the teller and the character, respectively – recognizing that personal identity relates fundamentally to being in time and space and can be established only in reference to the coordinates of personal development. Unlike Genette, therefore, Stanzel introduces the axis of temporality into his definition of homodiegesis: it is the protagonist's identity which develops across time and space from the fictional to the narrational world, an identity that changes and yet, by changing and recognizing itself as changing, reconstitutes itself as the same. Genette never touches on these dynamics of self-constitution of self-that-*is* through its other, the self-that-*was*, and that is of course typical of the synchronic, static and non-historical approach that he utilizes. As I have illustrated elsewhere, the same existential parameters that are applicable to first-person narrative become operative in reduplicated form in some types of second-person fiction where the teller and the protagonist-narratee share both the fictional world of the *then* and the communicative realm of the telling (*now*). In this setup there is continuity in the teller's and addressee's personalities, both of whom evolve from the *then* of shared experience to the *now* of current communicational exchange.[35]

The concepts of world or space also impinge on the configuration of realistic parameters. Where Stanzel allows for a grey zone of partial overlap between discourse world and story-world, introducing the figure of the peripheral narrator, Genette posits a theoretical dichotomy of identity and non-identity between the two realms, which is (logically) an absolute one. In practice Genette of course recognizes that there may be messy and fuzzy instances. In *Nouveau discours* Genette acknowledges the possibility of pronominal shifts, as in Thackeray's *Henry Esmond*, and allows for the figure of the chronicler as an intermediary form between the homodiegetic and the heterodiegetic realms (1983: 69–73/1988: 102–8). Stanzel proposes a contiguity, which allows for permeability between the past and the present, and therefore between the story-world and that of narration, whereas Genette's dichotomy reflects the logical irreconcilability between, on the one hand, the text as signifier and enunciation and, on the other hand, the story as its signified.

Much of the trench warfare that has been going on about the definitions of homodiegesis, with particular relation to the issue of focalization, can be explained as a consequence of the analytic, non-organic approach in mainstream narratological studies (what some people would call narratology's structuralist heritage). Stanzel's insight into the availability of *story-world* foregrounds two important facts. For one, it highlights the fictionality of the narrator figure. Although the first-person narrator has always been recognized as a fictional entity because s/he is also a character in the story, the heterodiegetic narrator persona (the 'Fielding' of *Tom Jones*) has been situated on the textual plane of the extradiegetic communication: this 'I' is an extradiegetic teller figure. This backgrounds (one could almost say: ignores) an evocation of the narrator's situationality within the fiction. In his dialogue with the narratee, 'I' appears to be part of a fictional world that pretends to homology with the Great Britain of Henry-Fielding-the-historical-author and his real readers. The very tension between the pseudo-factuality of that narrational frame and the purer fictionality of the plot (which is, of course, presented as an exercise in pseudo-historical writing) needs to receive central status in any discussion of the narrational dynamics of the authorial or omniscient novel. Genette and Mieke Bal fail to allow for this dynamic perspective in adequate ways. They conceive their categories of the extradiegetic and the heterodiegetic in terms of *either/or* options rather than pursuing the fruitful dialectic tensions and paradoxes which can be observed to operate in the narrative. The entire issue of extradiegetic narration (first or third person) becomes highly problematic in texts that do not foreground a separate act of narration or that consist of an enunciational act alone. Thus, the speaker of John Hawkes's *Travesty* (1976) tells a story only inadvertently – the diegetic plane of the text seems to lie in the fictional situation that is constituted by his speech act, by the tirade he is uttering and which the text pretends to transcribe. In such a context the distinction between extradiegesis and diegesis becomes useless.

The second crucial advantage of Stanzel's organicist schema is that his insistence on the presence of a narrational story-world welcomes both historical and reader-response-oriented approaches to the fictional text. From the point of view of literary history, the shifts between fictionality and factuality which prepare for the establishment of the novel as a genre (cp. McKeon 1987; L.J. Davis 1983; Hunter 1990) all centre around precisely this relationship between the teller figure (who pretends to be a contemporary of her historical readers) and her relationship to the story-world. This relationship is more often than not one of witness and attestation, even though the story itself does not deal with the personal experience of the teller. These insights can be incorporated into Natural Narratology, since its concept of a frame of telling allows for several real-world realizations of storytelling, such as hearsay, witness reports and the relation of well-known fables from times past. The analysis of this frame makes it possible to see the beginnings of the novel as building on oral patterns of everyday storytelling which are then artfully subverted and refined for the purposes of literature. Finally, this approach also manages to explain readers' (and critics') stubborn insistence on the presence of a teller figure in texts which do not linguistically warrant such an extrapolation. Purely textual analysis is superseded by the imposing of a communicational model of narrative which operates as the default frame for storytelling in general. Natural Narratology, furthermore, easily accommodates the well-known existential ambivalences of early narrative in which the narrator figure presents itself as a surrogate of the real author. Readers' inclination to equate narrators with the authors of texts simply derives from an ingrained habit, acquired from their real-world experience, and this interpretative move is deliberately fostered by the design of much early fiction. No wonder, then, that it takes grossly unreliable narrators to disabuse readers of their automatic strategies of identification, which they tend to impose as a matter of course.

Realistic frames, which include the distinction between tellers and agents, are only secondarily analytic categories; they actually constitute parameters of reading that project real-world cognitive frames on literary texts (which are taken to be mimetic). When such reading strategies break down, when no realistic scenarios can be projected, the telling frame as well as the story frame may be affected, both individually and with regard to their interdependence. Hence the theoretical necessity of putting the interpretative framework first, and of having stories and discourses, tellers and agents operate on a secondary level as instantiations of such interpretative strategies. The notions of characters, themes and plot, on the other hand, belong to a different level of narrative analysis. Character, plot and theme must not be confused with this distinction between agents and tellers, discourse and story levels. The latter are already situated on a more theoretical level, are the *result* of narratological *analysis*, and they interconnect with a text's interpretation. Characters, themes and plot, on the other hand, relate to a nearly pre-theoretical analysis of narrative, to the constituents of a narrative situation within the cognitive frames of Ricoeur's Mimesis I.

So far I have not yet talked about narratees and reflectors. These narrative instances are to some extent independent of the story vs. discourse distinction. That is to say, in so far as a text is posited to address a reader (or narratee), it does not need to have a story; in so far as a text can be argued to inscribe a reflector figure it does not necessarily have to have (in fact, in Stanzel's model, in its unadulterated form, it *must not have*) a narrational level of telling. Narratees and reflectors are therefore figures from quite different frames: texts which invoke a recipient role have a clear communicational paradigm; texts with a reflector character, by contrast, situate themselves in a story-world that appears to be 'given' in immediate fashion. Reflectors and narratees are therefore at opposite ends of a scale of narrative transmission or mediacy. What I have tried to do in my 'natural' framework is to reconceptualize reflectorhood within a different cognitive schema, that of pure experientiality and viewing. Reading reflectoral (i.e. internally focalized) texts as stories told within the customary frame of communication is self-contradictory and creates a whole string of theoretical problems. Traditional attempts to obviate these theoretical problems have resulted in the well-known models of focalization and in the positing of narrative transmission behind or beyond the illusion of immediacy. Such explanations, for instance, institute an apparatus of different types of focalization that in complex and empirically non-analysable ways[36] interacts with the category of voice and narrative level. Or – as in Chatman and Stanzel – they introduce a covert narrator persona, an implied author or arranger to account for the illusionist effect of the teller's absence. Shifting the emphasis to interpretation eschews these typological problems since the change to a different frame – that of reading from within the (deictic centre of the) fiction – prepares the way towards a cognition of narrative experientiality *in actu* and avoids the necessity of laborious typological gymnastics. Such a reconceptualization, which reinterprets the shift from teller to reflector-mode in terms of choosing a different cognitive frame (rather than inventing a new narrative persona, as the terminology proposes), has the additional advantage of historical adequacy. It manages to visualize reflectoral narrative as an ultimately natural rather than entirely non-natural setup, complementing earlier narrativizations of authorial omniscience. To the extent that omniscient authorial narrative exceeds real-life verisimilitude, it, too, can be regarded as non-natural in the normative sense. However, since such superseding of the limits of verisimilitude is (incipiently at least) a common technique in conversational storytelling and prevails already in the traditional epic, its non-naturalness should not be exaggerated. The same can be argued for reflectoral narrative which relies on the familiar cognitive parameters of viewing and experiencing. By instituting reflectoral narrative as a frame, one makes these parameters available and allows them to become accessible as complementary sources in the process of narrativization.

To summarize: the dramatis personae of narratology can be subsumed within the frames of Natural Narratology. They are anthropomorphized props attached to the frames employed in the process of narrativization. Thus, a holistic understanding of the frame of storytelling immediately projects a set of dramatis personae on the communicational level (tellers, listeners, i.e. narrators and narratees) just as it helps to conceptualize the fictional world in terms of a situation and/or plot complete with agents and experiencers, i.e. characters. The constitution of the plot configuration, on which the establishment of these dramatis personae depends, is likewise a function of an interpretative frame, although on a lower level of analysis.

Besides the agents of the plot and the narrators of the discourse levels of narrative, narrative theories have introduced a number of other categories of analysis, and it is to these that I will now turn in an attempt to sketch how many of the classic concepts of narratology can be preserved within the model of Natural Narratology.

8.3.3 Throwing out the baby and preserving the bath water: typological categories reconceptualized

In this section I want to deal with two narratological concepts or categories that have been profoundly influential and whose position within the new paradigm needs to be commented on. These are, first, the concept of narrative level and, second, narrative voice, focalization (and/or mode). What I wish to discuss in the following is in how far Natural Narratology subsumes these categories and to what extent they should be scrapped altogether.

Narrative level – in Genettean terminology the distinction between the extradiegetic, intradiegetic and metadiegetic levels of narrative – has been important in two areas of the analysis of narrative texts. The concept of narrative level helps to describe the important issues of, for one, the *tale within the tale* and, second, *frame narrative*. The concept of extradiegesis has been used repeatedly (by Bal and Genette) to discredit the existential continuity posited by Stanzel to obtain between a first-person narrator and her experiential character-self. The grounds for this critique lie in the presupposition that even in the first-person realm an unbridgeable gulf obtains between the narrating act and the story told. My own analysis of second-person fiction, however, clearly corroborates Stanzel's holistic view. Second-person texts illustrate the very same existential continuities that obtain in homodiegetic form. Homocommunicative narrative may (but need not) thematize the very dynamics of the *now* vs. *then* relationship *between*, on the one hand, the experiencing selves of the *I* and/or *you* in their shared past *and*, on the other hand, the present-day narrating or conative selves in their functions as teller and addressee on the communicative level.[37] Although the narrator or addressee may have a distanced relationship to their individual pasts, which may also be an evaluative one, the survival of narrator and narratee from their earlier story incarnations onto the communicational level of the narratorial plane demonstrates an uneasy contiguity of the fictional worlds of telling and experiencing. Since a preponderance of second-person fiction is additionally written in the narrative present tense, it decisively tends to undermine the story vs. discourse distinction and thereby affects the distinction between extradiegesis and diegesis as well.

To return to the questions of frame narrative and embedded narrative, i.e. the story-within-the-story format: the distinction between embedding and embedded narrative has proved to be highly useful and should be preserved intact. However, as criticism of Genette's term *metadiegetic* (for instance by Rimmon-Kenan)[38] has already noted, the relationship between the extradiegetic narrator and the (intra)diegetic story (i.e. the primary narrative that the narrator tells) cannot be equated completely with that between the intradiegetic storyteller and her metadiegetic story. The intradiegetic storyteller, *qua* character, belongs to the story level and his or her story is *by definition* part of characters' discourse and therefore belongs to a lower embedded level of narrative structure. This character's narrative enunciation, which constitutes a speech act (and thus plot element) of the story needs to be conceptualized additionally as a new corresponding extradiegetic level of narration which generates its own story signified (the meta-narrative). The hierarchical structure therefore comprises *four* rather than three levels. A relationship of embedding subsists between levels B and C, but not between levels A and B, or C and D.

A   extradiegetic level (heterodiegetic narrator)
B   story level (*histoire*, which includes C as its plot element)
C   character's discourse (embedded), e.g. the narration by the Man of the Hill in *Tom Jones*
D   story told by character (*histoire*, the life of the Man of the Hill)

Unlike the story-within-the-story, the specific structure of frame narrative, on the other hand, is never properly caught in these mathematical outlines. Although, technically speaking, a similar relation of embedding obtains, the constitution of stereotypical frame narrative needs to be connected with a proportional factor relating to the frame's length and significance. However structurally it is the case that both in a frame narrative and in an embedded narrative a character tells a story, usually in the setting of a frame narrative the framing primary story is quite marginal in relation to the embedded story, which takes up most of the text. Hence, indeed, the term *frame* narration, since the framing situation of storytelling merely serves to bracket the 'real' story and mirrors the reader's gradual access to the story proper. A story within the story, on the other hand, is usually of brief duration and tends to be employed as a *mise-en-abîme* or a symbolic analogue to the tale within which it is told as a *prima facie* digression. With regard to length, frame and inset are therefore in inverse proportion to the relation obtaining between a story and the embedded story within it. Frame narratives frequently thematize access to knowledge rather than highlighting thematic similarities and they also serve to authenticate the story, sometimes in the form of putative historical records which the frame narrator or editor pretends to have found.

The relationship between the frame and its inset is therefore a proportional one, which is very reminiscent of the relationship obtaining between peripheral homodiegesis and autodiegesis proper. In both cases one has to decide what the text is *about* in order to determine what the central relationships might be. In practice there usually tends to be little confusion because most texts weight their topics in a decisive manner. Theoretically speaking, one here has to do with a case of scale and of proportional quantity rather than a dichotomy or a qualitative relation; indeed the situation is one in which quantity turns into quality. No hard and fast rules apply; the situation is methodologically intractable, at least within a structuralist methodology. Holistic natural schemata, by contrast, have little difficulty with frame narratives or stories within stories since these are observable factors in real-world situations of storytelling. The specific function of a given tale and its relation to the discourse within which it is embedded can be extrapolated from the individual context: no absolutes of categorization need apply. Thus the very weighting that seems to be a consequence of the quantitative relationship in fact emerges as the triggering factor of the relative emphasis on textual proportions. If the tale is conceptualized as subsidiary to the primary story frame, a relationship of embedding obtains; if the primary story level serves as a mere introduction to the narrative proper, it will be perceived as a framing device. Such schemata, like parts and wholes, can be argued to belong with basic-level cognitive parameters (G. Lakoff 1987: 283).

Let me now turn to the issue of **voice, *focalization* and mode (*mood*)**. Genette restricts his definition of voice (*voix*) to the *narrator's* communicative function and therefore ends up opposing the narrator (who speaks) with the characters (who 'see'). Yet this fundamental distinction in Genette, which has justly become famous, involves itself in the problem of how to account for free indirect discourse and the internally focalized language that pretends to mimic characters' idioms and locutions. As Uspensky (1973) and Vološinov (1986) noted, it is, of course, precisely the linguistic signals of characters' language that alert the reader to the fact that the characters 'see'. If voice is defined as utterance or as a set of linguistic markers, the problem of voice in fictional texts can be dealt with easily. Voice can be attributed to the narrator and to the fictional personae in their dialogue; in texts without the presence of a first-person pronoun of a personalized narrator, voice can be inscribed by means of expressive features, linguistically definable as a deictic centre (Banfield 1982; Wiebe 1990; Fludernik 1993a). The issue of voice is therefore clearly separable from that of focalization if one regards voice as the linguistically generated *illusion* of a voice factor which can be defined empirically by a complex set of interrelated textual and contextual features and is corroborated by a mimetic reading of the text that stimulates this projection of a speaker or reflector function (Fludernik 1993a).

What is much more problematic than voice is the category of focalization or point of view, also variously termed mood (Genette) or mode (Stanzel).[39] The major problem with this category (whose precise definition has in any case never been agreed upon and is still open to remapping)[40] lies in its intermingling with the factor of voice (whether in my own or Genette's definition). On the one hand, as Genette and Bal have attempted to show, voice and focalization are two entirely different issues (*who sees* vs. *who speaks*). On the other hand, that neat distinction proves intuitively incorrect whenever one looks at the voice factor outside the narrator's language. Banfield's model (and my own extensions of it) demonstrate that in what Stanzel calls reflector-mode narrative the voice factor (deixis) is constitutive of the focalized interpretation (Banfield 1982; Fludernik 1993a), each supporting the other within a mimetic schema of interpretation. Indeed, the question of 'who speaks' can no longer be taken literally at all because in reflector-mode narrative there is no discernible speaker function in the text; yet the narrative implicitly suggests that the discourse emanates from the focalized consciousness of the reflector character, although that, of course, is the result of an illusionistic narrative technique.

Theories of focalization have started off from two different definitions: *source* of focalization and *entity focalized*, with some models combining the two. These distinctions are, however, untenable from a theoretical perspective. Focalization on the story level (i.e. one character observing another) does not properly belong to macro-focalization, i.e. the focalization of an entire text, but it is a small-scale management of the plot function. The only really important issue is that of the consistent or inconsistent rendering of the entire story by means of a particular slant or filter; and that, as Bal correctly notes, is a function that needs to be situated on the discourse level – on the same level as chronological rearrangement. Finally, options of focalization are not as varied or combinable as Genette and Bal maintain. A first-person narrator's presentation of her own story is usually fairly consistent and slippages are motivated by suspense, part of the narratorial rhetoric (as in omniscient fiction) rather than indicative of a change in focalization. Reflector-mode narrative or internal focalization is a specific and distinct option and likewise tends to be fairly consistent unless combined with an omniscient narrative frame. I have argued (Fludernik 1993b) that one should preserve Stanzel's term *figural narrative situation* precisely for such a setup, i.e. the combination of an evaluative, external narrative with long stretches of internal focalization. This is a historical type of transition between the earlier authorial narrative and the later reflector-mode texts, a transitional option which by hindsight can be said to have tested the feasibility of a large-scale presentation of consciousness. Although a transitional phenomenon within Stanzel's typology, figural narrative in this sense is actually a pervasive nineteenth- and twentieth-century type of narration, indeed a widespread one to judge from its prevalence in the work of Hardy, Meredith, Butler and others. A glance at Stanzel's typological circle likewise documents a panoply of texts on the authorial–figural continuum, as he calls it. The category therefore clearly seems to be an important one from a *historical* perspective.

In my opinion it is, however, quite wrong to treat any of these options as *focalizations*. What they involve, in terms of Natural Narratology, is a shift in the receptional frame from the frames of TELLING or ACTION-orientation to the parameters of VIEWING and EXPERIENCING, accompanied by a reduced involvement with traditional ACTION and storytelling parameters and an added emphasis on the presentation of consciousness. Focalization, although a useful terminological tool, has been particularly disruptive on account of its anthropomorphic conceptualizations since it seemed to require the presence of a see-er, i.e. Bal's focalizer, to become a proper narratological category. The extensive debate on focalization has really demonstrated that the category is an interpretative one and *not* exclusively a textual category. To put this differently: focalization ties in with frame, as Stanzel has already proposed for his narrative situations. TELLING frames and ACTION frames afford some kinds of focalizations, VIEWING frames quite different kinds of focalization. In particular, authorial aperspectivism (Genette's *focalisation zéro*) is simply a self-contradictory option since an authorial position of omniscience cannot be visualized in terms of a see-er: the narrator does not *see* the story (or parts of it); 'he' *produces* the story. What the narrative focalizes on on the story level is therefore the result of *selection* and not the result of *perception*. The person who 'sees' is the reader, but *à travers* the linguistic medium, and not in terms of *visual perception*. (Film, naturally, is a different matter altogether, but outside the visual medium readers *visualize* and *construct* the scene; they do not 'see' it.) Chatman's distinction between *slant* and *filter* (1990) therefore touches on a crucial point and provides an invaluable corrective to the standard conceptualizations of focalization. External focalization, as we have seen under 4.4, really relates to a refusal of inside views rather than connecting with the simple perceptional fact of observation – although the two aspects are of course related. What I am trying to suggest is that the perceptional metaphor has been a red herring. The crucial issue is that of the presentation of consciousness, and all visual and perceptional parameters are subordinate to this basic parameter. Perception centrally correlates with perceptional consciousness, and narratorial descriptions *either* invoke an evaluative frame of mind on the part of the narrator (*slant*), which has absolutely *no* truck with perception, *or* they illusionistically project a character's perceptions, and then are definitely relatable to a consciousness factor of what is traditionally termed internal focalization. On account of these inconsistencies it may be well to scrap the concept of focalization in its traditional configurations.

I will therefore propose that two sets of distinctions be salvaged from traditional accounts. The first set concerns what is properly termed focalization and distinguishes between an external and internal viewpoint (*vision sur* vs. *vision avec*)[41a] on non-human objects, that is to say it corresponds with an 'objective' vs. experiential focalization. Within Natural Narratology this is handled by the TELLING vs. EXPERIENCING and VIEWING frames. The second parameter concerns access to internality within a scale of knowledge. Here the two poles of the scale are complete access to another's consciousness and no access at all. This factor has no connection with viewpoint at all and really concerns teller-mode narratives exclusively: only in a narrative which is not internally focalized is there a *choice* between access or refusal of access to characters' consciousness. Within consistently focalized narratives (and this includes first-person texts) there cannot be a choice: as a human subject the reflector character or first-person protagonist can have access only to their own consciousness and perceptions. The recurrent combination (which is difficult to account for in the traditional models) of external views on *some* people and complete access to *others'* thoughts is a typically 'authorial' feature. A realistically conceived teller (first person) cannot read others' minds.

A much more important caveat concerns the grounding of these distinctions on the notion of a story level with its fictional givens. If it is unclear whether there is a story or a fictional situation and what precisely the discourse is meant to signify, parameters such as access to internality (whose internality?) or focalization on objects (who is there to observe what?) evaporate as applicable terminology. It is only when one has determined on a macro-frame (the text is an interior monologue, the text represents the jealous husband's observations) that one can then proceed to discuss *how* the details of this are handled in the discourse. Indeed, the very useful fine-tuning that the traditional terminology can perform (and to which I have had recourse throughout this study) becomes useful only when there is a specific story-world with characters and objects in a setting to describe, when these characters have something they can be said to perceive or there is something they can react to emotionally. Much of the descriptive toolbox that focalization has provided in fact correlates with *embedded* focalizations, that is to say with the shift in the narrative discourse between representations that project a character's visual or emotional viewpoint and representations that cannot realistically or mimetically be aligned to such a viewpoint, and which therefore – in the wake of the reader's inveterate anthropomorphizing – are then aligned with the narratorial stance. By retaining Stanzel's historical type of authorial narrative with heavy figural leanings as one prototypical genre, what I call *figural narrative* proper, this inconsistency then acquires a second-level motivation: experientiality is dealt with in the reflectoral sections of the narrative, and the presentative and evaluative frame is provided by the authorial omniscient report. The net effect of this combination comes close to an evocation of the dynamics of natural narrative in which windows on vicarious experience can be opened within the narrator's orientational and evaluative frame.

My facetious title for this section (throwing out the baby and preserving the bath water) can now be explicated as suggesting that the cherished distinctions of classic narratology can be dispensed with or reconceptualized with great facility. What needs to be preserved from the standard models is the postulation of a macro-narrative frame, a factor that is left inexplicit in most traditional accounts of narrative. The baby, the narrative typology, may safely be disposed of as long as one preserves the encompassing natural frames in which these typologies, *à leur insu*, used to be cradled.

8.4 THE MEDIUM OF NARRATIVE: GENRE REVISITED (WHAT IS NARRATIVE? PART TWO)

This section attempts at least a gesture towards discussing drama and film in a book that explicitly includes these genres within its definition of narrative but fails to treat them in the core of the text. When reconstituting narrativity along non-action-oriented lines, I not only excluded much material that is usually regarded as narrative but also broadened the application of narrative to include 'scenes' in poetry (7.6) and welcomed drama and film within the narrative fold. A more detailed argument for the narrativity of drama, film and some poetry is therefore necessary here in order to provide us with the arguments for a more precise redefinition of narrativity. I want, first, to return to a summary of the generic arguments proffered earlier, especially in section 7.6, clarifying more precisely how my definition of narrativity intersects with understandings of genre and fictionality. I will then present some brief reflections on the *specifics* of individual narrative genres without pretending to comprehensiveness. On the whole, quite an extensive number of distinguishing features between the novel, drama, and film have already been pointed out, most recently, for instance, by Lanser (1995) in relation to the possibilities afforded by the filmic medium.[41b] At the end of this section I will attempt a model of text and discourse types that embraces generic and functional aspects.

Before I turn to drama as the most important narrative genre whose narrativity needs to be documented, I want briefly to consider one other narrative genre that is frequently neglected in criticism. The *short story* and short fiction in general have received some critical attention but so far no consensus has been reached on the differences between the short story, other forms of short fiction and the novel.[42] Reid (1977) is characteristic of this general lack of criteria, and the discussion in Bremond *et al.* (1982) likewise implies a pervasive lack of agreement on how to distinguish between exempla, parables, fables, anecdotes and the like.[43]

> To anyone concerned with the evaluation and appreciation of literature, it is not crucial whether a particular work be a novel, a condensed novel, a novelette, a story, a tale, a sketch, an anecdote, an incident, a dramatic dialogue or whatever other term be applied. What does matter is whether a specific piece of writing provides the reader with an *experience*, whether it increases his or her understanding, intensifies his or her consciousness, provides the reader with pleasure and refreshment. All of the definitions with which I am familiar are arbitrary. And when we refer them to our actual experience in reading, we readily perceive how arbitrary they are. For instance, some of the experts tell us that the short story creates a *single* or a *unified* impression. What is the meaning here of single? Of unified? When we look at a work of art, we learn that there are not just *single* impressions to be gathered from it.
> (James T. Farrell, as quoted in Goetsch 1978: 111–12)

In the framework of Natural Narratology such terminological distinctions do not really matter either. What does require some analysis, however, is the significance of the factor of length and its repercussions on textual structure. I have noted repeatedly in Chapters 3 and 4 that elements such as description and report which have a fixed position within the episodic narrative structure become expandable but free-floating units as soon as episodic structure is modified in the wake of the explosion in story length. Orientational sections get blown up; description becomes a discourse unit in its own right; report sequences and scenes grow from elements that were originally situated within their fixed functional positions and eventually usurp the narrative episode *in toto*. This development was certainly prefigured in the lengthy medieval narratives, and it is probable that French patterns were responsible for many of the changes. An even more important factor must have been the necessity (born from the increase in textual length) to correlate a larger set of characters and to mediate between several places of action and several temporal planes.

What is peculiar about the short story from the cognitive perspective is that – unlike the fable, the parable, the anecdote or the joke – the

Natural Narratology 349

novella and the short story are decidedly *literary* forms.[44] They do *not* rely on the episodic structure of oral narration. That is as much as to say that the brevity of the short story, *cognitively* speaking, does not have a 'natural' quality of oral experientiality but serves a secondary, illusionistic re-evocation of orality. The short story is a written genre from the start, and its brevity is linked to artificial effects of epiphany, climactic development, the rendering of moods or sentiments. Naturally, as is frequently pointed out, short stories therefore lack the 'fullness' of presentation expected from a novel. But that criterion, besides being decidedly vague, is not very convincing in relation to the experimental novel, which may deliberately edit out any 'fullness of life' (as do Ronald Sukenick's novels). Finally, one may observe that the avowed peculiarity of much short fiction, especially of the short story (cp. Nischik 1985), has been to catch a moment of intensity, of epiphany, of significance. Such an intent correlates most uncannily with experiential parameters since that significance is a significance of mind, of perception, of understanding. The stories therefore frame for us a close-up of a character's or a perceiver's epiphany – and if the epiphany is not locatable in a character it can become an experience for the empathetic reader who is implied in the text's receptional framework. The short story, then, like much longer Modernist fiction,[45] perfects the representation of consciousness and constitutes an apogee of narrativity rather than a negligible or marginal genre. It is along these lines that future work on this highly popular genre may want to proceed.

Let me turn to **drama**. In narratological discussions drama is not generally accepted as a narrative genre. If drama is analysed exclusively in terms of the published text, drama easily becomes equatable with the conjunction of dialogue (which is of course a mimetic inset in fiction) and stage directions (which are not narrative discourse but instructional or descriptive prose). Such a reduction of drama to 'mere text' radically disavows drama's performative and visual qualities. Although, from the earliest theoretical analyses about narrative in Aristotle, drama has been represented as manifesting all the chronological finesses of plot that one meets with in epic narrative, more recent theoreticians have tended to oppose narrative and drama in terms of a dichotomy of the narrative vs. the non-narrative. This outlook is prominently espoused by Stanzel, Prince and Genette, since they foreground the textual nature of narrative and story mediation by means of a narrator's narrative discourse (*narration*). In so far as drama does not have an enunciator, a narrator figure, it cannot in the framework of these models be recuperated as a narrative genre. By contrast, Thomas Pavel (1985) and, implicitly, Chatman (1978, 1990) are quite open to the narrativity of drama. Pavel actually provides a representative analysis of dramatic plot for which he finds precedents in Bremond's typology of deep-structural narremes. In Chatman's case the narrativity of drama reposes on its story vs. discourse base; drama, it can be illustrated, frequently rearranges the chronological story sequence into quite different configurations on the level of the scenes on stage (drama's 'discourse'). The dramatic story/discourse opposition therefore mirrors the familiar categories of temporal realignment proposed by Genette.[46] Pavel and Chatman provide endorsements of the narrativity of drama by foregrounding plot-related features, whereas the rejections of drama's narrativity take their starting point in drama's lack of a level of narration (i.e. of narrator–narratee communication). Only secondarily do these theories consider drama's non-textual performative aspects as a disqualifying feature. Curiously enough, film is much more readily accepted as a narrative genre, a factor that seems to be based on drama's performativity and the relative stability of the filmic text (which does not change with each performance). Arguments *for* the narrativity of drama, then, first of all need to address the argument of drama's supposed lack of a narrational level.

There are a number of convincing counter-arguments to the view that drama lacks a communicative level. For one, the modern stage (and not only the modern stage) has seen the introduction of a narrator figure in the frame who 'narrates' the dramatic action. Brecht's plays famously employ such a speaker as one of the devices correlating with his technique of *Verfremdung*. Another well-known example is Thornton Wilder's *Our Town* (1938). The dramatic narrator or storyteller in these plays operates much like a filmic voice-over. However, since his physical presence on the stage inevitably puts him in the fiction, the stage narrator frequently has a function that resembles a *frame* narrator more than a standard extradiegetic narrator. The narrator persona can be homo- or heterodiegetic, and as a homodiegetic narrator fulfils many of the functions of a novelistic first-person narrator. He or she can indulge in memories or try to exculpate him/herself from various imputations (Henry Carr in Stoppard's *Travesties* [1975]), thus yielding a 'confessional increment' (Goldknopf 1969).

A second level at which drama's narrational qualities can be located is that of the stage directions. Most stage directions of course function simply as instructions, but as early as in closet drama and in the poetic drama of the Romantic period or, more famously, with Shaw one encounters extensive stage directions that go far beyond what is stageable. Some stage directions even narratively describe the character and the general habits of the dramatis personae in what amounts to an omniscient comment on the part of a narrator in a novel. Symbolist drama additionally indulges in stage directions that are cast in impressionistic style[47] and create visions of splendour (see, e.g. Villiers de l'Isle-Adam's *Axel* [1885–86]) that can only be evoked linguistically (and maybe filmed) but certainly not staged. Even Ibsen's stage directions, which are much more restrained, provide descriptions of how some characters appear to others – impressions which could scarcely 'get across' in a performance. A final twist in the development of stage directions has occurred recently in the new genre of the *cinéroman* or the film script-as-novel genre. In particular, work by Alain Robbe-Grillet (*Glissements progressifs du plaisir* [1974], *L'Année dernière à Marienbad* [1961]) and Susan Sontag (*A Duet for Cannibals* [1970], *Brother Carl* [1974]) can be noted in this connection. Many writers of fiction and drama have, moreover, recently started to produce scripts as a regular occupation (I am thinking in particular of Harold Pinter or George Garrett). Some (though not all) of these texts employ stage directions that significantly exceed what is presentable on stage or in a film. Although one can argue that these texts actually belong to an entirely different genre, the similarity with traditional excessive stage directions is more than striking.

From all these perspectives, one can see that drama (and indeed film) are not as devoid of narrational communication as one might have supposed, although the default case admittedly is that of drama having no narrator figure and purely functional stage directions. However, in so far as one takes the narrator figure to be a central feature of narrative, drama, like film, starts to cause conceptual problems since the visual medium represents its signified in non-enunciational form.

Another argument that would tend to emphasize drama's basically narrative nature bases itself on recent developments in drama and the novel. It can be observed that most anti-illusionistic techniques which are current in the postmodernist novel can be found also in experimental plays, and some of the earlier Modernist concentration on consciousness is equally traceable in the newer drama. Thus, where plot becomes inconsistent or is replaced by interior monologue, drama frequently follows suit. (One need only think of the plays of Peter Handke or the monologue plays of Thomas Bernhard.) In addition to extended soliloquy, Harold Pinter and Henry Miller have also experimented with the flashback presentation of memories. Some dramatic experiments even try to structure such memories on a pattern of association. (An example of this is the 'flashbacks' of Henry Carr's remembrances of Zurich in Stoppard's *Travesties* [1975].) (I have noted some examples of this type in Chapter 7.) Additionally there are dramatic texts that either completely eschew language (Beckett's *Breath* [1969]), consist of nonsense dialogues or incomprehensible actions reminiscent of ballet effects (Handke's *Das Spiel vom Fragen oder die Reise zum sonoren Land* [1989]) or employ description as a major technique (most consistently in Heiner Müller's 'Bildbeschreibung' [1985], in Alain Robbe-Grillet's 'stories' from *Instantanés* [1962], and in Laura Mulvey's films). From this perspective, then, experimental drama (and film) seems to attenuate the notions of plot, character and causality much in the same way as does the experimental novel, and this similarity of treatment immediately suggests that these all belong with the narrative genre.

If one replaces the traditional criteria for defining narrative (event sequence, narration and the story vs. discourse dichotomy) with the notion of experientiality, then the narrativity of drama and film is even more in evidence. Thus, monologic drama *qua monologue* can be neatly described as the situation of a character whose physical presence on stage already vouchsafes the basic experientiality of the setup. As with fiction, drama or film that cannot be recuperated experientially remains non-narrativizable. Laura Mulvey's films, which eschew a focused observer position, can here be noted as a typical example.[48] Mulvey's filmic experiments could therefore be understood as an instance of zero-degree narrativity. Her scenes present a camera view of actions and situations in progress which do not cohere into a 'whole', that is to say they do not link up with the experientiality of a character or even with a natural viewing position of the perceiver (the audience). Drama and film therefore also basically cover the same ground as fiction when described from the point of view of experiential narrativity.

Perhaps this is a good point at which to consider briefly how the *mediality* of film and drama affects their intrinsic narrativity. My basic assumption is that the *specifics* of drama and film need to be discussed separately from the novel, short story or tale. However, in so far as film and drama are narratives, they partake of the same stock of cognitive parameters and depend on the same receptional frames as do texts. It is only in the choice of one of these forms over the other that these media differ from written narratives. Where film and drama require the most differential treatment is on the level of the analytic toolbox. Narratologies, since they happen to deal with literary prose narratives, have so far concentrated on deictics, tense usage, focalization, etc.; film criticism, by contrast, needs to take account of cuts, close-ups, fades, shots, voice-over, etc. Some excellent work on these lines is already available for film (Bordwell 1985, 1989; Gaudreault 1988; Kozloff 1988; Branigan 1992). As regards the stage, drama criticism likewise has already provided quite extensive treatments both of the more generally narratological aspects of the genre (Pfister 1977/1988; Werling 1989) and of the specifically performance-oriented issues relating to the semiotics of visual presentation and the gestural realm (which is called *proxemics*). There is therefore little need for me to dwell on these issues in the framework of the present study.

To anticipate my conclusions at the outset: narrativity can be established with equal felicity in all the named media (except perhaps the cartoon with its necessarily highly stylized graphic and linguistic styles). Having said that, however, it is still important to point out that some kinds of narrativization can be achieved more easily in one medium than in another. As Lanser (1995) has demonstrated with such verve in relation to Jeanette Winterson's non-sexed and non-gendered narrator in *Written on the Body* (1992), written texts in some languages manage to leave the narrator's (or a character's[49]): sex unspecified, but this cannot easily be done in film and only barely so on the stage. Of course one can dress up characters in a manner that disguises their sex, and one can film a sequence in which one never sees the protagonist's face or hears his or her voice. However, indefiniteness is not equivalent to ambiguity; visual representations of people are taken to be *either* male *or* female persons: ambiguity tends to cause serious discomfort. Of course some films deliberately play with the refusal to present a protagonist from the front,[50] and some detective movies use the slouching hat or the turned-up collar to delay identification of, say, the murderer. The murderer may then even turn out to be a woman.[51]

It is fairly obvious that the cinema has a near monopoly on representing perception and on representing action – but some of this can be done well in drama, too. On the other hand, drama does worst in directly[52] representing motivation and consciousness, and one can even argue that an action-oriented spectacle with little focusing on a major character – as, for instance, was common on the Renaissance stage – shares with early fiction some of its low-degree narrativity. Such drama behaves like mere report. Drama and fiction in the Renaissance period certainly occupied a continuum of generic forms, and the repertory comprised soliloquies as much as grand scenes. What is entirely different for the stage and the book as media concerns less the performance factor (though that is certainly relevant)[53] but the visual impact of performances – an aspect of crucial aesthetic import – and the fact of a quasi-iconic representational mode: actors as characters. Film is most obtrusive in this respect, allowing little space for the viewer's own creative input, whereas drama is specific in some things but fairly schematic in others. Props on the stage and dramatic space in general tend to be symbolic, whereas film has great problems getting away from precise instantiations of objects, rooms or landscapes.

This is not the place to go into an extensive analysis of these genres and their comparative merits and disadvantages.[54] Much excellent work has already been done on the narrative specifics of film (Bordwell 1985, 1989; Branigan 1992; Kozloff 1988; Fleishman 1992), and there is ample literature on drama, too.[55] What I want to emphasize at this point is merely the ways in which narrativity can be constituted in all three media and on the basis of the same set of cognitive parameters, even though some of these parameters appear to be privileged over others within one medium or the other. In particular, the telling function, although possible in film and sometimes in drama, does traditionally tend to restrict itself to fiction. In a wider view of the full range of narrative possibilities, this constraint on generic diversification seems less embarrassing than one might have thought: after all, TELLING can be dispensed with in fiction as a frame just as ACTION can be dispensed with in all of these narrative genres. My conclusion would therefore be that mediality affects narrative in a number of important ways but on a level of specific representations only. In general, narrativity can be constituted in equal measure in all textual and visual media.

In section 7.6 I also opened the boundary that has remained most adamantly closed to extensions of narrativity and suggested that some *poetry* can be treated as narrative from the point of view of experientiality. Narrative poetry (*Rime of the Ancient Mariner*) or narrative in verse, of course, have always been recognized as belonging to the narrative genre.

In Chapter 7 I noted that some poems describe a poetic persona's perceptions (in Tomlinson's 'The Hall at Stowey' and 'The Castle'), thus rendering the text equivalent to an *in nuce* first-person narrative or putting an observer on the scene whose perceptions can be cognized in terms of the VIEWING frame. Poems can also depict a situation involving specific characters at a specific point in time, and they may additionally employ a great deal of descriptive realism. The comparison of so-called 'fiction' with poetry enables me to define the concept of narrativity more closely. Much that *appears* to be narrative in poetry does not actually qualify as such because it does not concern specific fictional personae but posits a hypothetical or allegorical scenario:

> I beheld her on a day,
> When her look out-flourished May;
> And her dressing did out-brave
> All the pride the fields then have;
> Far I was from being stupid,
> For I ran and called on Cupid,
> [...]
> I, foolhardy, there up took
> Both the arrow he had quit
> And the bow; with thought to hit
> This my object. But she threw
> Such a lightning, as I drew,
> At my face, that took my sight
> And my motion from me quite;
> So that there I stood a stone,
> Mocked of all; and called of one
> (Which with grief and wrath I heard)
> Cupid's statue with a beard,
> Or else one that played his ape,
> In a Hercules-his shape.
>
> (Ben Jonson, 'How He Saw Her', ll. 1–6, 20–32; H. Maclean 1974: 46–7)

In so far as Cupid is here introduced within a parable designed to characterize the narrator–narratee relationship, this parable does not really tell a story or openly manifest experientiality. What is missing from the scenario is specificity – the poem is not *about* a particular person calling on Cupid but projects a hypothetical scene that serves as a metaphor for the speaker's frustrated love relationship. The experience of the speaker is entirely allegorical. Nevertheless, the above poem does have a narrative kernel of actionality, and – although the story is an allegorical one – could conceivably be read in fictional terms. Indeed, if one defines narrative in terms of a series of *actions* and *events*, this poem scores high on the scale of narrativity. William Blake's 'The Sick Rose', on the other hand, addresses an imaginary rose but beyond this hypostasization neither a specific fictional situation nor a person's consciousness (even the rose's in anthropomorphic reinterpretation) can be made out. This is not of course to say that the symbol has not given rise to a variety of situational naturalizations that have, precisely, imported a narrative reading into this poem. Again, such readings are entirely metaphorical: they see the rose as a woman, they interpret the sickness as sexual guilt, and so on.

Much of the specificity of standard narrative, one can now observe, derives from fiction's evocation of a real-world setting and from the positing of particularity within that setting. The apostrophic mode of 'Rose thou art sick' – an enunciation by a speaker out of time and space – contributes to the dislocation of the scenario (however one wants to visualize it) from a specific point in space and time; these remain resolutely indefinite. Even the past tense of Jonson's poem cannot entirely help to instantiate narrativity since the scenario eschews location on a chronological axis relative to the narrating (or, rather, speaking) voice. If one, then, starts with the requirement of experientiality which obviates the named difficulties, other thematic problems emerge. One classic poetic situation that seems to refute poetry's typical lack of experientiality (and hence narrativity) is that of the prevalence in poetry of the reflections and enthusings on the part of the speaker of a poem. But that speaker never becomes a character in her own right, never begins to exist within an alternative fictional world. Indeed, lyric poetry is generally taken to be 'concerned with general truths rather than with particular facts' (M.-L. Ryan 1992: 386). Unless the reflections are clearly part of a person's specific experience at a specific (fictional) moment in time, one cannot describe this setup in terms of experientiality. Fictional situations therefore need to be situated at a particular (even if indefinite) moment in time, and the story-world, too, needs to be locatable as a non-hypothetical realm. There are many poems which veer towards the narrative text type and many so-called narrative texts that move towards the lyric or poetic mode. Since specificity and embodiment and the experientiality that develops from them are graded concepts, an entire area of more or less narrative texts can be made out on the borderlines of the lyric genre.

A final redefinition of narrativity would therefore outline the fact that experientiality is intimately linked to perceptional parameters and to consciousness, to the frames that I have argued to be relevant: ACTION (goal-orientation, motivation), VIEWING, EXPERIENCING, TELLING, REFLECTING. These can only surface in specific anthropomorphic individuals who necessarily live at a specific time and place, even if that time and that place are merely imaginary. Within my conception of narrative, fictional world and perceptional focus are therefore organically (i.e. schematically) interrelated and constitute a situational kernel which is open to narrative developments. Imaginary scenarios in poetry may be quite similar to fictional ones; the boundary line is definitely permeable with a cline proceeding from the extremely narrative to the tenuously narrative and to the absolutely non-narrative text.

It now becomes possible to attempt an integration of narrative texts within a model of other basic text types. The lyric mode, which may perhaps be defined as deploying a pure voice factor for the purposes of an essentially metalinguistic preoccupation with sensibilia, constitutes one such meta-genre or text type, alongside others like description, argument and spontaneous conversational interaction. I have here named an open list that requires more research before it could be specified in absolute terms. Chatman (1990), it will be remembered, distinguished three basic text types: narrative, argument and description. Adams (1993) concurs but has exposition besides narrative and description and calls these *discourse* types, reserving the term text type for what is traditionally called *genre*. The set that I have named above cannot be allowed to stand as such. Purely descriptive texts are fairly rare, as are purely lyrical ones, whereas narrative, argument (or exposition) and conversational exchange occupy very important areas of linguistic expression both quantitatively and in relation to their functional centrality. In addition – *pace* Adams – I tend to conceive of these categories as macro-genres (text types) rather than discourse types, although description, exposition and narrative (i.e. event report) operate extensively as subsidiary elements within narrative, expository and conversational texts. It is worth noting that descriptive and lyric texts are much less heterogeneous, particularly descriptions. Poetry, as a particularly ill-defined genre, does indeed accommodate narrative and descriptive modes; with poetry the distinction between genre (poetry) and discourse type (the lyric) therefore becomes particularly problematic. Moreover, the concept of fictionality, although an important constituent of narrative texts (including oral narrative), cannot profitably be applied to conversations, argumentative prose or poetry, where it contrasts with 'truth' or 'non-fiction'. Expository writing can deal with fictional entities, just as fiction may employ persuasive argument (a fact Chatman dwells on with justification). It is for this reason that literary and linguistic attempts to define text types on essentialist grounds have failed woefully.[56] In particular, the results of more functional and pragmatic approaches demonstrate the very different status that argument and description as discourse types have in, say, conversation and written texts, particularly in literature.

Conversational exchange is perhaps the most indigenous text type, one that is empirically traceable and easily set apart from more rhetorical types of oral performance (incantations, prayers, orations, oral poetry, oral narrative). Yet even conversational exchange, once one starts to analyse it more carefully, embraces a great diversity of different genres, from telephone conversations to teatime chats, from doctor–patient exchanges to small talk at business meetings. No wonder then that written modes prove to be even more intractable, since they are so heterogeneous and diversified.

The solution to the genre vs. discourse mode approach therefore lies in the separation of meta-genres (conversation, narrative, argument, instruction/description) from micro-textual discourse types that characterize not entire *classes* of texts but parts or *segments* of specific texts. Historical genres or what I will now call text types (telephone conversation, hymn, instruction manual) are located on an intermediary level between these meta-genres and the discourse types. In my model description, argument and conversation, *as discourse types*, are *part of* natural narrative: orientational sections are intrinsically descriptive; argument occurs (if at all) in narratorial comment, in the abstract and evaluation sections; and conversation is rendered by means of fictional dialogues. Report sections, finally, which correlate with zero-degree narrativity, constitute the 'narrative' parts (discourse mode) of the genre (text type) natural narrative. Report, then, is exclusively a discourse type but neither a genre (text type) nor a meta-genre. Meta-genres such as conversation, narrative, argument or instruction have very specific pragmatic functions (phatic communication, the narrative reworking of experience, rhetorical suasion, and practical orientation),[57] whereas in the prototypical frame of natural narrative the individual discourse types function within one holistic structure that keeps them in separate slots within one unitary frame. I have noted in Chapters 3 and 4 how the medial and conceptual transcoding of oral texts into written genres (Habermalz, forthcoming) affects this originally functional distribution of discourse types within the mould of natural narrative and results in a refunctionalization of some elements (the moving of the central schema of incidence to the former incipit position) and the reconceptualization of narrative structure in relation to other elements (the restructuring of episode sequences into report-cum-scene sequences). Since historical genres are obviously in continual flux, the generic level of text types cannot but be inconsistent and resistant to theoretical delimitation. The novel, the short story and the poem consist of a wide spectrum of heterogeneous constituents which include the full range of discourse types from the lyric mode to pure report sequences lacking experientiality; one even finds the monopolization of one discourse type to the near exclusion of the others.

Narrative's experiential function can now be argued to serve a deep-seated human need to grasp the meaning of immundation, of one's experiences, sufferings and actions. As a *discourse mode*, however, narrative can be identified as that mundane informational output that provides basic-level temporal information about events. The discourse mode *narrative* equals the category report sequence. Zero-degree narrativity therefore merely defines texts that extend the discourse-mode *narrative* over the entire text to the exclusion of other discourse modes and thereby reduce the potentialities of organicist textual structure to a minimal enchainment of events. Narrativity, on the other hand, is a characteristic of entire texts and of genres, and it is constituted meta-generically in its basic function of experiential reappropriation. The model that I have presented in this study therefore locates the notion of experientiality and narrativity on a level of basic-level cognitive meta-frames and meta-functions of human linguistic interaction. The three generic levels of meta-genres, text types and discourse types which I have proposed are conceived as a model that should help to explain the paradoxes of narrative essentiality and narrative all-pervasiveness, of the fundamental human importance of storytelling on the one hand and its mechanical craft-like deployment in many texts on the other. The above reflections will presumably require further modification in the future; no doubt I have here arrived at the limits of theorization and should lapse into philosophical silence.

One further point may, however, need clarification. I have resisted the temptation to include poetry among the four meta-genres although there are persuasive arguments for doing so. My reservations or anxieties touch on the problematics of definition for the lyric mode as a meta-genre. To propose poetry as a meta-genre, as the pure lyric so to speak, immediately raises the question of metalinguistic utterance and of language play. As I have argued elsewhere (Fludernik, forthcoming) *all* texts have a level of metalinguistic commentary. It would therefore be highly problematic to equate this *general* structural feature of texts with one meta-genre, even if poetry does indeed award much space to metalinguistic reflection. Should one perhaps characterize the poetic speech act as the use of language in a kind of Jakobsonian poetic function rather than defining it in terms of lyricism or metalinguistic play? I am no poetry specialist, and I hesitate to trespass on territory that to me looks much like a terminological and conceptual wilderness. The signs demarcating the natural process of poetic effusion for me read *No trespassing*. I will leave the mystery of poetic invocation to reside peacefully in its domain beyond the pale of humdrum linguistic speech-acting. There it shall remain, beckoning across the abyss of the unspeakable to infuse our domesticated articulations with aspirations towards transcendence.

8.5 THE POLITICS OF NARRATIVE: FEMINISM, POSTCOLONIALISM AND THE DISCOURSE OF AUTHORIAL POWER

Recently more adventurous studies in narrative theory have increasingly started to incorporate thematic and poststructuralist concerns, moving away from the formalist setup of the structuralist mode of Stanzel, Genette, Bal, Chatman, Lanser (1981), Bonheim, Sternberg, Pavel or Prince. This development can be said to have started with Brooks (1984/1985) and Chambers (1984), and has recently found full expression in Lanser's *Fictions of Authority* (1992), Chambers's *Room for Maneuver* (1991) and Andrew Gibson's *Towards a Postmodern Theory of Narrative* (forthcoming).[58] These approaches attempt to combine ideological frameworks (of feminism, of power, of the economy of discourse) with the more formal concerns of narratology. In the following I want to discuss three areas of ideological criticism which can lay claim to some representativeness within the current scenario of theoretical debate: on the question of *écriture féminine* and its narratological relevance; on the status of ethnic and postcolonial studies within narratology; and on the significance of Foucauldian approaches to discourse.

8.5.1 *Écriture féminine* and the place of narratology in feminist studies

Lanser's concern in her *Fictions of Authority* is not directly with *écriture féminine* but with narrative voice, and she develops insights presented by Robyn Warhol in her study of the engaging narrator (1989). In a recent article in *Narrative* (1995) Lanser has additionally tried to (re)introduce the concept of the gendered (and sexed) narrator. This is a particularly fruitful aspect for narrative study and one which has been neglected for a long time. As Lanser points out, texts by women are underrepresented in the example passages of most narrative theories, as are – one may want to add – such other 'underdog' categories as ethnic fiction, gay/lesbian fiction or postcolonial writing. Second, much too little attention has been paid to the construction of default gender. It is an undeniable fact that the determinable sex of the empirical author (Jane Austen, John Updike) tends to predispose readers to attributing the same sex to the omniscient narrator, and – I would argue – even more strongly to the sex of an *unnamed* first-person narrator of ambivalent (non-explicit) gender. Jeanette Winterson's *Written on the Body* (1992), which Lanser takes as her example case of the latter category, inevitably produces 'lesbian' readings of the unnamed narrator figure on the basis of (a) the empirical author's (i.e. Winterson's) biological sex and (b) her previous work about lesbian issues. This unnamed narrator is presented as bisexual in the second half of the book, so that both readings ('the narrator is male' and 'the narrator is female') disrupt a standard heterosexual interpretation of the plot. The disruption will be more forceful for those readers – male?? readers perhaps – who may initially have opted for a 'straight' reading of the opening situation in terms of '(male) narrator has love affair with married woman', and it will tend to be less surprising for those who have taken the narrator to be a woman since that second reading already starts out with the assumption of a lesbian relationship. The reader will perhaps experience the narrator's bisexuality as less scandalous because cultural prejudice tends to include all forms of 'deviant' sexuality within one seemingly unitary category of non-default sexuality. That the lesbian narrator *also* sleeps with men will therefore have much less of a shock value.

Lanser never properly defines the difference between gender and sex in relation to narrators or narratees (one of G. Prince's [1995] valid points of criticism). The idea seems to be that natural authors have determinable sex and so do most first-person narrators. Third-person narratives, on the other hand, may have personalized narrators whose sex is revealed at some point in the text (for instance, as in Ronald Sukenick's or John Barth's stories, the narrator's wife may be introduced), but in the majority of cases what is or is not implied by the narrator's discourse about himself tends not to deserve the label *sex* (since it does not relate to the narrator's biological make-up) but projects instead the narrator's *gender*. For instance, as Barbara Hardy has documented, gender typification in George Eliot's novels is sometimes consistently male, and sometimes inconsistent, with sometimes male and at other times female attributes (B. Hardy 1982: 131–40).[59] Empirical studies of literature could help to clarify some of these issues. In particular, in novels by authors whose sex is unknown to the reader (a frequent case with non-European authors or émigré writers from non-European countries whose exotic first names obstruct automatic gender decoding), the *reader's biological sex* and internalized gender (do men tend to expect a male narrator? women a female narrator?) and, sometimes, the *protagonist's* sex may determine the reader's constructions of the narrator's genderization. In fact, when the author's name does not carry explicit markers of sex and/or gender for the reader, even the *protagonist's* sex, particularly in novels cast in the reflector-mode or in novels with a non-personalized covert narrator figure, tends to influence the reader's gender construction of the *empirical author's* sex. Thus Nuruddin Farah's *Maps* (1986), which has a male protagonist, may suggest to some readers that the author must be male (which is correct). I still remember the first time I read Leslie Silko's *Ceremony* (1977), which was proposed to me as an example of Native American literature, and took Silko to be a male author – a supposition reinforced by the fact that there was a male protagonist. (As it turned out, much to my surprise, Leslie Silko happens to be a woman.)

Genderization of the narrator figure shows most explicitly in the use of anaphoric pronouns in critical discourse. Narrators in books by male authors are referred to by the masculine pronoun: *the narrator ... he* (commonly for Dickens, Hardy, Trollope, Scott and others); whereas with women authors the narrator is frequently referred to by means of anaphoric *she* (for Jane Austen, the Brontës, Virginia Woolf). Various strategies to counteract this tendency have been undertaken on the part of narratologists in order to emphasize the non-coincidence of the author and narrator figure. Besides the traditional use of gender-nonspecific *he* even, say, for Jane Austen's narrators, there has also been Bal's (1985) attempt to institutionalize *it* (*the narrator ... it*) as an alternative non-gendered option, and more recently *she* (in lieu of gender-nonspecific *he*) is gaining ground (the option I have chosen for this book). It is a moot point which of these three non-gendered pronouns serves its purpose best. In particular, trying to insist on the non-gendered reading of the narrator position actually *obscures* the dynamics and generation of gender construction which is rooted in readers' empirical reactions to texts. This can be observed with great ease in the common type of second-person narrative where the *you* protagonist remains unnamed. Particularly at the beginning of second-person texts one often encounters radical gender indeterminacy. Strategies for obscuring gender relations additionally include the invention of gender-nonspecific pronouns (June Arnold's *na* in *The cook and the carpenter* [1973]) and/or the gender-nonspecific naming of protagonists (ditto in Arnold).[60]

Gender issues therefore have far-reaching narratological consequences and need to be studied in great depth. The above remarks, however, also indicate that gender is a category that requires a model opposing explicit markings of gender on the one hand and the default construction of gender (or – alternatively – an area of indeterminacy) on the other. Unless there is explicit textual marking, that is, all gender constructions are interpretative moves, and much more research needs to be done to determine the forces regulating these interpretative moves. One will also have to come to some agreement on the very use of the terms *gender* and *sex* in this kind of discussion, perhaps limiting the term *sex* to explicitly embodied narrators. However, since the construction of the narrator's sex so frequently relies on the implicit and metaphorical genderizations of the narrator position, the term *gender* is also difficult to eschew in the context.

A most hotly contested area in feminist studies has been that of *écriture féminine*, that is to say the issue of whether or not there is such a thing as 'female' writing that can be distinguished (linguistically if possible) from 'male' writing. Put differently, can one determine the biological sex of the author from his or her work? Although an author's *gender*, in the sense of authorial outlook and values, may perhaps be construed from the supposed 'message' of a text (frequently aligned with the position of the notorious 'implied author'),[61] feminist debates on this issue have for the most part centred on linguistically verifiable aspects of the text such as syntactic or pronominal structures, textual coherence and the lack thereof, lexical choice, repetition and the like. However, even at this level, ideological commitments tend to interfere with descriptive parameters. 'Feminist' *écriture* is pictured as organic, syncretic and whole (in contrast to the supposed analyticism of so-called 'male' discourse), described as flamboyantly anti-rationalist (as opposed to 'male' logic or phal-logocentrism), and as processual, in flux or all-encompassing (in contrast to the alleged tendency towards disparateness in 'male' categorizations of linguistic entities).

Linguistic analyses have yielded no really adequate results about the existence or non-existence of women's language. As Spender (1980) and others have noted, prototypically 'feminine' linguistic behaviour, although widespread among women (R. Lakoff 1975/1989), does not need to betoken femininity as such but frequently serves to signal a number of specific discourse strategies (such as ingratiation, deliberate downtoning, politeness, non-assertiveness, non-authoritarian openness, willingness to save the interlocutor's face) which are apparently connected with cultural mores and women's observably more cooperative discourse tactics designed to create intimacy (Tannen 1990). A feminist reinterpretation of these typically feminine discourse strategies therefore reveals a tactics of deliberate, cooperative and interactive 'public relations' management where a traditional perspective of female stereotyping inevitably tended to register only weakness, vagueness, rambling illogicality or even stupidity.

A comparable result is reached when one analyses passages in fictional texts that purport to illustrate so-called *écriture féminine*. That this style of writing is not peculiar to women has been pointed out already by Julia Kristeva (1974/1984), whose prime exemplars of *écriture féminine* are James Joyce and Jean Genet. Indeed, the typically rambling discourse of Molly Bloom's interior monologue or the naïvety and stylistic monotony of the narrative discourse of Gertrude Stein's *Three Lives* (1909) or *The Autobiography of Alice B. Toklas* (1933) easily compare with the chattiness of some postmodernist fiction written by men:

> [...] he got up and went into the kitchen, coming back for no reason with an opened can of sardines in his hand, placed it at the foot of his wife's chair saying, Cats like sardines, and she suddenly looked up, startled, saying, Oh my god, my sardines, snatching them up just as the cat leaped down, That's my lunch, putting them on his desk, then reached out picking one from the can with her fingers saying I like sardines, eating from her hand, licked her fingers, then reached out for another, as he had done once – where was it? – when he had lived for two weeks on sardines and Wheaties until some nice girl had come along to among other things feed him, Chicago, and then some money had come, he took a sardine, ate it and discovered he was hungry, or was it L.A., the hotel permeated by the smell of urine like rotting spinach, no Chicago where he was going to college that time because L.A. was only a trip with Banally that crass son of a bitch who never believed anything and took it for granted no questions asked and who drove off and left him stranded in of all places Needles, California because he was trying to make some girl he had picked up and he got back hitch-hiking to Chicago just in time to pack up and move to Boston, You want to get that bread?

he asked her, to start the school year because he was following the money then and somebody was offering him more in Boston where he almost married black-eyed Lillian, it would have been easier to take rat poison, faster and less painful, she came back with the bread and a knife and they finished the sardines [...]

('The Permanent Crisis'; Sukenick 1969: 5)

One can compare this text with passages from Sunetra Gupta's *The Glassblower's Breath* (1993) where one likewise has several levels of memory intertwined in a barely separable way. The syntax in Gupta's novel also at times resembles that of Sukenick's prose. Both passages employ run-on structures which package the embedded layers of memory into a series of coordinated and subordinated clauses that are not structured in immediately clarifying or obviously logical ways.

And so you had waited, as the shadows deepened, mute shadows, fresh evening wind scattered the steam that lingered upon her [the sister's] lifeless lips, parted in half-smile in the heavy dimness, you dreamt, that night, that those lips were compressed in terrified resignation to death, and you woke, remembering that you had begun to write of her death long before it had become a reality, long before you were drawn back into the shadows that had been your home, to watch her die, smiling, on a winter afternoon, her palms streaked with the dark mockery of her long lifeline, carved against the contours of her exaggerated mound of Venus, she would be lucky in love, the hoary soothsayer had told her, dragging his filthy nails across the cushion of flesh into the sallow valley where her heart line dipped and dispersed, but her health, he had said, gravely palpating the bony hollow, her health would always trouble her.

(Gupta 1994: 5-6)

Gupta's syntactic simplicity, of course, belies the profundity of the emotion registered, and it therefore does not produce the effect of jauntiness that Sukenick's prose conveys. That Sukenick's style is strategic and not merely a mimetic representation of naïvety can be argued by recourse to surfictionists' pronouncements on their aesthetic. Thus Raymond Federman in the *Surfiction* manifesto proposes that '[the] most striking aspect of the new fiction will be its semblance of disorder' and he goes on to describe the new fiction as 'illogical, unrealistic, nonsequitur, and incoherent' (quoted in Friedman and Fuchs 1989b: 5).

Linguistic descriptions of such run-on syntax tend to take as comparative standard a text with default values of lucidity and easy processing – values that have indeed been rejected quite deliberately by Gupta and Sukenick. From a literary point of view, however, it makes little sense to characterize this kind of language exclusively in terms of illogicality, lack of structure, lack of proper cohesion and coherence, etc., as a standard linguistic description might prompt. One can analyse such experimental texts much more fruitfully if their opposition to 'logocentrism' is acknowledged, if their apparent illogicality is reinterpreted as a deliberate attempt to circumvent ingrained expectations of clarity, cohesion and hierarchical structures of embedding. Such language flaunts its liberation from the fetters of culturally required conformity to 'good writing', and it does so in order to compel a re-evaluation of the current ideology. Feminist texts may want to foreground organicism and syncretism, miming the incessant flow of experience by means of a non-discrete handling of linguistic units, by proposing a holistic and metaphoric approach to the relation of language to represented world. For instance, Anaïs Nin emphasizes the subversive potential of digression, but (unlike Laurence Sterne) exploits it for holistic purposes: 'By obeying the improvisations born of emotions, by abandoning myself to digressions and variations, I found an indigenous structure, a form born of organic growth, like crystal formations' (quoted in Friedman and Fuchs 1989a: vii). In Sukenick's case, on the other hand, one will be tempted to interpret the selfsame syntactic markers quite differently, aligning the author's strategy with a revolutionary spirit of opposition to tradition in general. One may regard this use of language as indicative of the *laissez-faire* personality of the protagonist, who seems to belong to the beat generation, (maybe) indulges in drugs, and tries to liberate himself from culturally determined self-alienation. Whereas the interpretation of the Gupta passage was therefore read as signifying oppositionality in accordance with the *author's* ideological tendencies (which are of a feminist slant), the quotation from Sukenick was taken to indicate *both* potential commitments on the part of the author *and* the worldview of the third-person protagonist. Since Gupta's novel is written in the reflectoral mode and its unnamed second-person protagonist is a woman, one can tentatively extend the feminist interpretation of the noted linguistic features to apply also to the character's (prototypically female?) experience. The syntax, then, *signifies* an experience of flow and indeterminacy on the story level.

Although both of the quoted passages utilize very similar syntactic techniques, the liberating and oppositional effects of the texts, as we have seen, can be interpreted differently in the case of the male and the female writer. Even more importantly, it emerged that both types of empathetic readings ultimately derive from text-*external* ideological positions and cannot be *objectively* recuperated by a linguistic analysis in and of itself.

As for the more ideological definitions of *écriture féminine*[62] such as practised and theoretically propounded by Luce Irigaray (1985) or Hélène Cixous (1976/1981), these concentrate on the textual make-up of writing which corresponds to poetic norms proposed by Julia Kristeva in her *Revolution in Poetic Language* (1974). Kristeva's example texts are, however, by male writers; conversely, the very metaphoric descriptions of *écriture féminine* especially by Irigaray and Cixous, do not empirically lend themselves to linguistic recuperation and objective analysis (deliberately so, of course). They are intentionally poetic and a-logical:

> I love you: body unshared, undivided. Neither you nor I severed. There is no need for blood shed, between us. No need for a wound to remind us that blood exists. It flows within us, from us. Blood is familiar, close. You are all red. And so very white. Both at once. You don't become red by losing your candid whiteness. You are white because you have remained close to blood. White and red at once, we give birth to all the colors: pinks, browns, blonds, greens, blues ... For this whiteness is no sham. It is not dead blood, black blood. Sham is black. It absorbs everything, closed in on itself, trying to come back to life. Trying in vain ... Whereas red's whiteness takes nothing away. Luminous, without autarchy, it gives back as much as it receives.
> (Irigaray 1985: 206–7)

The practice of *écriture féminine* resists definition for strategic political reasons:

> It is impossible to *define* a feminine practice of writing, and this is an impossibility that will remain, for this practice can never be theorized, enclosed, coded – which doesn't mean that it doesn't exist. But it will always surpass the discourse that regulates the phallocentric system; it does and will take place in areas other than those subordinated to philosophico-theoretical domination. It will be conceived of only by subjects who are breakers of automatisms, by peripheral figures that no authority can ever subjugate.
> (Cixous 1981: 253)

In fact, even feminists themselves find it hard to locate their speaking in relation to the symbolist order which – according to feminist Lacanian lore – makes autonomous female speech impossible:

> If the 'woman' is precisely the Other of any conceivable Western theoretical locus of speech, how can the woman as such be speaking in this book? Who is speaking here, and who is asserting the otherness of the woman? If, as Luce Irigaray suggests, the woman's silence or the repression of her capacity to speak, are constitutive of philosophy and of theoretical discourse as such, from what theoretical locus is Luce Irigaray herself speaking in order to develop her own theoretical discourse about women? Is she speaking *as* a woman, *in the place of* the (silent) woman, *for* the woman, *in the name of* the woman? Is it enough to *be* a woman in order to *speak as* a woman? Is 'speaking as a woman' a fact determined by some biological *condition* or by a strategic, theoretical *position*, by anatomy or by culture? What if 'speaking as a woman' were not a simple 'natural' fact, could not be taken for granted?
> (Felman 1975: 3; quoted Moi 1985: 138)

Indeed, female speech is seen to operate subversively, in the interstices of male discourse, subverting it in the very act of using language against the grain of its patriarchal inscriptions. The methodology of feminist discourse is therefore describable in terms of the strategies that Chambers (1991) observes to operate in *Room for Maneuver*: tactics that are observably equivalent to standard discourse – here experimental male writing – but redeploy these linguistic devices with feminist interests in mind for ulterior feminist purposes.

One can therefore conclude that, for Natural Narratology, the issue of gender is crucial exclusively on the plane of what, in my model, is level IV: narrativization. In order to read certain texts more mimetically, one may want to fill in on the important factor of the narrator's gender (and/or sex). As regards the more precisely ideological framework of *écriture féminine*, it should now be apparent that one cannot immediately extrapolate the subtending ideology from the linguistic make-up of the text. Knowledge of the author's ideological commitments, though, tends to impinge on one's interpretation of a text, but it need not determine readings in definitive and delimiting ways.

8.5.2 Ideology and power

In this section I would like briefly to outline two areas of what are basically cultural and ethnic studies and discuss their potential connection with narratological analysis.

One such area is the wide field of ethnic and postcolonial studies. In this a number of issues could be analysed from a narratological perspective. Foremost among these is the choice of language, dialect or idiom for the narrator's language and for the represented dialogue (Mair 1992). Whereas the colonial novel (Joyce Cary's *Mister Johnson* [1939]; E.M. Forster's *A Passage to India* [1924]) employed non-standard English only in the dialogue of the natives, institutionalizing the narrator's language as a 'white British' voice, more recent postcolonial texts have started to use native English idiom – which reflects a local cultural *norm* – for the narrator's discourse, thereby subverting, and sometimes *in*verting, the old colonial hierarchies. British English, in this context, can come to signal definitely negative evaluations, such as implying a betrayal of indigenous cultural norms on the part of the speaker using 'proper' English or suggesting that such speakers are (political) conformists or opportunists in the colonial or postcolonial context. Even more recent 'new' literatures extend the use of native languages to embrace a postmodernist aesthetic of *bricolage* in which several different idiolects and sociolects are juxtaposed. Texts of this type therefore offer an appealing polyvocality and multi-ethnicity that serves as a political manifesto of cross-cultural tolerance. See, for instance, the work of Salman Rushdie or Rohinton Mistry (*Tales from Firozsha Baag*) as examples of such a Bakhtinian meeting of tongues.

A second area of narratological interest in postcolonial literature and ethnic or minority literature in general is that of formal innovation. It is quite noticeable that a great majority of texts playing with 'odd' pronouns, especially second-person fiction, have decidedly ideological concerns. Some of these concerns are clearly postcolonial, as in Jamaica Kincaid's *A Small Place* (1988) or Nuruddin Farah's *Maps* (1986); others are oppositional from a political perspective (Oriana Fallaci's *Un uomo* [1979]; Julio Cortázar's 'Graffiti' [1979]); and yet others play with gender indeterminacy in order to establish a form–content correlation in the portrayal of gay/lesbian relationships. (See, for instance, Jane Rule, *This Is Not For You* [1970]; Edmund White, *Nocturnes for the King of Naples* [1978]; Daphne Marlatt, *Ana Historic* [1988]; June Arnold, *The cook and the carpenter* [1973]; Christopher Isherwood, *A Single Man* [1964]; Monique Wittig, *L'Opoponax* [1964].)[63] Technical innovation, however, does not necessarily signify in the ideological realm. Several second-person texts, for example, exploit the oddity of the pronominal alignments in order to delineate rifts in a character's personality[64] (the Farah text (1986); Fuentes's *A Change of Skin* [1967]; Rex Stout's *How Like a God* [1929]), and yet others employ it to reflect typical tensions in familial (mother–daughter) and erotic (love) relationships. Although texts that foreground technical innovation draw attention to their strategic use of these formal devices, such innovation can become automatized to the extent of complete habitualization. Many recent second-person texts, for instance, employ the second-person mode with a familiarity that betokens a loss of its erstwhile originality and 'oddity'. As a consequence these texts also lose their semantic impact and ideological force. (Only if the formal device is conspicuous will there be a need to lavish disproportionate interpretative attention on it.)

I have dealt with these issues in Chapter 6, but exclusively in connection with pronominal and temporal choice. There is of course extensive innovation in other areas as well. An in-depth study of oppositional modes and their political significance might yield a hefty chapter in a narratological history of fiction. Are all oppositional texts innovative from a narratological perspective? And if not, as appears to be the case, can any specific purposes be aligned with the use of certain strategies? How political, for instance, are Sukenick's postmodernist tactics? What, if any, is the ideological significance of Christine Brooke-Rose's work? Are these texts simply surfictionist self-reflexive textual play or do they not meta-textually signify political revolt as well as cultural non-conformism? As Suleiman (1990) and Friedman and Fuchs (1989a) illustrate, one needs to be wary of over-easy form–content correlations. Much ethnic protest literature, as is well known, has utilized traditional modes of narration, and some experimental fiction is inveterately esoteric and *dégagé*.

Besides the named postcolonial, political and gender issues I would also like to comment briefly on a recent debate between Dorrit Cohn, Mark

Seltzer and John Bender (Cohn 1995b, Bender 1995; Seltzer 1995). In her article in the second anniversary issue of *New Literary History* Cohn criticizes recent accounts of the nineteenth-century novel where Foucault's metaphor of penitential surveillance strategies is exploited to 'prove' the Victorian novel's alleged authoritarianism. The authorial narrator is said to survey 'his' (the texts are all by male authors and/or have a male narrator figure) characters in a manner reminiscent of the Benthamite prison guard supervising his charges in a panoptic setup, controlling them, exposing them to his privileged gaze which they cannot reciprocate. As Cohn correctly points out, the authorial narrator may be controlling the discourse linguistically, but it is the author (or, more correctly, the text's evaluational instance *qua* implied author) that is responsible for the effectual control of the characters; surely, shifting the onus of control onto the *narrator* constitutes a regression from the painfully won distinction between narrators and authors. Second, Cohn is understandably worried about the imputation of tyranny to such narrators, particularly since it is maintained that this tyranny surfaces in (of all places!) passages of free indirect discourse. Even in cases where the narrator appears to rewrite characters' discourse, I would agree with Cohn that merely the choice of free indirect discourse over indirect speech or speech report signals a willingness to incorporate otherness rather than merely objectify or reify it (as is implied by the metaphor of the panopticon). That Bakhtin's characterization of Dickens's work as typically polyphonic (a tradition accessible in Vološinov 1986) should here be completely turned on its head surely makes one pause. Bender's response characterizes free indirect discourse as typically 'a disembodied presence' (Bender 1995: 30), which is not only oxymoronic from a linguistic perspective (presence does imply embodiment) but simply incorrect as far as descriptions of free indirect discourse go. In free indirect discourse it is, on the contrary, the narrator's language that is disembodied, and the text's expressivity subverts the narrative's supposed objectivity and neutrality by infiltrating the fiction of narratorial disembodiment with expressive elements locatable in the (decidedly bodied) characters. Despite Bender's sarcasms about 'making the world safe for narratology' one can therefore observe a great necessity on the part of lax thinkers and spouters of metaphorical discourse to devote a little bit of time to getting their nitty-gritty details right.

Seltzer's and Bender's *ripostes*, although downtoning the application of the prison metaphor, actually transfer the political implications of narrative discourse to an altogether different plane. Seltzer does admit that the 'process of vision' is not reducible to 'disembodied, panoptic objectification' (Seltzer 1995: 23). What he is really interested in is discovering structural homologies between enunciational hierarchies in the narrational realm and the *societal* power structures which are allegedly reflected in them. This homology can be argued to obtain on a symbolic plane where representational strategies and the relationship of language to its signified are at issue. Narrative language has full control over its objects of representation. But these mechanisms of control lie beyond the purlieu of a personalized narrator's rhetorical strategy and – failing the presence of an 'implied author' position – can be attributed only to the creative interventions of the author. Yet, and here Seltzer's model turns out to refute his own argument, the author herself can be argued to be determined in her linguistic and semantic choices by the linguistic system and its rules and regulations. These rules allow for creative redeployment and subversive reappropriation but they do nevertheless set a frame of delimitation and control on what language can be made to mean. The author herself can control the fiction by excluding options rather than by constraining interpretation in any one direction.

Nor is the metaphor of the panopticon particularly apt to characterize the narrator's role as a puppet master, as in Thackeray's famous formulations. The full horror of Jeremy Bentham's panoptic vision lies in the prisoners' subjection to complete surveillance and a resultant loss of even minimal pockets of privacy. Puppets on a string, by contrast, are made to act and express their individuality. They are not human beings turned into lifeless objects as a result of sinister strategies of pacification, but – quite to the contrary – lifeless puppets inspired with anthropomorphic afflatus by the puppetmaster's skilful manipulation of the strings. Nor is the puppet theatre's audience in a position that would in any way reflect the prison guard's relation to his inmates. The audience of a puppet play, as any audience, enjoys the illusion of the puppets' free agency, it does not want to annihilate their humanity by exercising absolute punitive power over the actors on stage. Indeed, the Benthamite prison model derives its horrors of inhuman exposure to the wardens' controlling vision not merely from the resultant lack of privacy; although that, surely, can be apprehended as subtle psychological torture. The full cruelty of this treatment consists precisely in the implicit threat of punitive measures which are to be unleashed on the prisoners as soon as they do anything not prescribed by the penitentiary's regulations. Full omniscient vision acquires its sinister force only to the extent that it uses that vision to acquire complete knowledge to be used for active intervention that will necessarily result in adverse action on the inmates' bodies.

Whereas the pretence of all drama is that one *overhears* the characters, who are acting unconstrainedly and are blithely unaware of their exposure to the audience's judgmental vision, the Benthamite prison dystopia operates most perniciously in its effects on the inmates' recognition that they are being controlled by the implacable eye of the prison guard, which – in a manner resembling God's vision of human subjects as outlined in theology – lies beyond the universe within which the prisoners have been confined. (Foucault quotes an inscription on the walls of the carceral cell where it says 'in black letters: "God sees you"' [1979: 294].) The inmates' situation is therefore one of triple constraint. They are subjected to physical imprisonment, thus losing the faculty of self-determined agency and physical movement; they are additionally subjected to the ineluctable gaze of the prison guard, who thereby acquires complete knowledge[65] about them (although this is only *external* knowledge!); and they are, on a third level, completely exposed to the prison regime and its unlimited leverage of power, including, specifically, the mechanisms of brute force that can be inflicted on prisoners' bodies. Although, like all penal procedures, this triple subjection affects only the prisoner's body and cannot directly impinge on the mind and conscience of the prison subject, the ulterior effect of this policy is, of course, to force the convict into the complete denial of his own personality and individuality. Where earlier beliefs about the accessibility of the soul through inscription on the body (Foucault 1975/1979) had justified physical torture both as a means of eliciting the truth and as a demonstration of the judiciary's disciplinary powers, the Benthamite strategy of coercion has the same ulterior purpose of forcing the prisoner to turn his inside out. Where resistance collapses in the wake of physical abuse under torture, the prisoners experience the humiliation of complete hysterical self-surrender to the will of the tormentor, moulding their mental selves in obedience to the controlling force of the torturer's conceptual designs.[66] In the Benthamite scenario, likewise, the non-violent pressures exerted on the inmates' bodies result in such acute mental discomfort and persistent fear of impending punishment that their desired psychological effect will equally be one of voluntary surrender to the moral dictates of the prison regime. Those dictates veil their commerce with the ideologies of power since they adopt a discourse of Christian ethics, endorsing precepts that require the recognition of one's own guilt, and they institutionalize the subsequent acceptance of self-inflicted penance and self-mortification.

Whereas the omniscient narrator of the Victorian novel is omniscient merely to the extent of knowing the story by means of a panoptic vision of the fictional world, the Benthamite penitentiary adopts a theological reading of God's omniscience that does not limit itself to the benevolent access to knowledge of past, present and future but very explicitly alludes also to the enactment of divine wrath, with its threat of irreversible damnation that this access to complete knowledge may come to provoke. Bentham's penitentiary, as Bender (1987) was quick to point out, projects a vision of state paternalism that corresponds to a patriarchal authoritarian version of the regime of a wrathful Christian God. Divine retribution persists as a constant threat behind the benevolent image of the father figure whose mild measures of penal correction are figured as the all-seeing light within whose compass man needs to abide and beyond which he can stray only at his own risk, the risk of falling into the pit of darkness, incurring damnation. God, like the nineteenth-century omniscient narrator figure, of course has access to his subjects' most secret thoughts, but the omniscient narrator is far from wielding the same kind of absolutist powers over his creatures.

Natural Narratology 371

The narrator cannot threaten his characters, nor will they be physically compelled to obey his will. Poetic justice, which mirrors the Christian doctrine of divine retribution, on the other hand, belongs within the jurisdiction of the *author*, whose shaping designs determine the course of events and in the final act mete out deserved punishment to those who have offended against the prevailing moral code. The design of the Benthamite panopticon can therefore be disclosed as a fantasy of divine omnipotence, as an attempt to constrain inmates by the subtle exercise of veiled external force without, however, in actual fact affording the privilege of divine omniscience which the panopticon was originally devised to imitate. The omniscient narrator, by contrast, enjoys the full privilege of access to his characters' most private thoughts but lacks the Benthamite prison's machinery of disciplinary resources. It is these policies of relentless surveillance and absolute control which turn the potentially benign faculty of all-encompassing vision into the oppressive horrors of the Panopticon where they serve to subject the incarcerated to their dehumanizing effect of abject humiliation.

8.6 PULLING THE THREADS TOGETHER: FINISHING TOUCHES TO THE DESIGN OF NATURAL NARRATOLOGY

In section 1.3 I presented a four-level model comprising three categories of natural (and cultural) frames and, a fourth, the process of narrativization, explaining how narrativity emerges from an interpretative mediation through consciousness-related frames. Having moved through the history of narrative forms in Chapters 2 to 7, it is now time to integrate our findings within the model and to explicate more fully how natural frames and parameters are accessed within it.

So far I have used the terms *frame* and *parameter* more or less interchangeably, a usage that was designed to reflect their functional dependence on each other: frames accommodate a number of related parameters. The notion *frame* itself may now have to be differentiated in accordance with the various levels and related to the process of recognization. Finally, those areas of literary interpretation which go beyond a reconstitution of the fictional world in the process of narrativization – the extraction of metaphoric levels of meaning, thematic units, political and philosophical messages, and so on – also need to find a place at the horizons of Natural Narratology. Like most traditional narratological models, Natural Narratology concentrates on the techniques by which a mimetic illusion is engendered in narrative. The strategies of interpretation (which are constitutive of Natural Narratology), however, also need to embrace more traditionally interpretative areas at the periphery of narratology even if this wider semantic field manifests more general textual intentions applicable not merely to narrative but also to poetry, philosophical or political writing.

Levels, frames, parameters

Above, I distinguished between four levels on which natural categories can be located: level I, of real-life schemata of action and experience; level II, of natural frames, including those of ACTION, VIEWING, EXPERIENCING, TELLING and REFLECTING; level III, of narratological and generic concepts (extrapolated from the parameters operative at level II); and level IV, of the process of narrativization which combines all of these levels and produces narrativity by means of a mediation through consciousness. That mediating consciousness can be situated on the level of the fictional world, in a protagonist; on the level of narration (in a teller or self-reflexive authorial voice); or even in the reader (or her proxy). Consciousness therefore shows up on the plane of the represented world, in its re-cognization by means of basic frames and, third, in the constitution of story experience as *narration*, in the mediational process that results in the establishment of the mimetic illusion, of narrativity.

Natural categories on level II are holistic frames that comprise a number of natural parameters which belong to level I. Thus, the make-up of the ACTION frame feeds from level I, where the parameters of goal-oriented action, motivational choice and of chronological and teleological configuration are located within the frame of real-life actionality. Likewise, the VIEWING and EXPERIENCING frames include such parameters as the perception of incidence, observational viewpoint (or perspective), temporal and spatial coordinates, and so on. And in the same way, the TELLING frame comprises the notion of a teller, structural features of enunciation, the figure of a virtual addressee, etc. Similarly, the REFLECTING frame can be said to invoke the parameters of rumination, arguing, memory, self-criticism, and so forth. Since frames are holistic entities, they encompass a prototypical scenario in its entirety; the individual parameters or elements linked to the frame, though, may be an open set. In some circumstances one set of features may become relevant, in different circumstances quite another set.

Narratological frames on level III are extrapolated from levels I and II, and they are ultimately historically determined interpretative tools much like the genres which I also situated on level III. Genres and narratological categories are not necessarily 'natural' *per se*, although some oral genres, historical writing, poetry and even drama, and narrative as a macro-genre can certainly lay claim to transcultural and trans-historical validity. However, more specific generic types such as the novel or the dramatic monologue or the revenge tragedy certainly depend on cultural and historical conventions and norms, which makes for another open set.

What I have tried to achieve in this book does not concern the invention of yet another typological model with categories and subcategories all specified ad nauseam. I leave that to more categorically minded souls. My main intention, on the contrary, has been to incorporate the insights of narratology within a more encompassing frame that can accommodate a wider spectrum of texts and which manages to remove some of the problem areas detectable in current models. The model also serves to supersede macro-focalization frames ('the novel of internal focalization') and Stanzel's narrative situations and go in the direction of a number of larger narrative frames which partly overlap with Stanzel's narrative situations. Most important of all, the model has attempted to emphasize the receptional and creative aspect of narrativity, discussing the generation of narrativity in the process of narrativization. In the framework of this study I have concentrated on the *narrative* side of interpretation, which is only part of a range of more general interpretative strategies. Narrativization reads texts *as narrative* and therefore reduces their potential metaphorical or philosophical or argumentative meanings to the projection of a fictional world, to embodied experientiality within it and to the specifics of individuality. Plot-oriented models of narrative have reduced the field of narrative significance even further. So, although Natural Narratology relegates metaphoricity and other semantic areas of interpretation to the margins or the superstructure of narrativization, it nevertheless opens the field at least a little further than do traditional narratologies that centre on a character-plus-plot constellation. Finally, fiction that emphasizes metaphoric structure, such as the texts by Gertrude Stein which I analysed in Chapter 7, is perceived as moving in the direction of lyric poetry, and thus inevitably seems to downplay its narrative and experiential qualities.

A note is here due on the form vs. function issue. Although the cognitive parameters and frames within which I operate and the mediational processes that I have proposed are not empirical in their design, nevertheless I do revert to empirical textual data when discussing the development of narrative structure: tense usage, discourse markers, pronouns or syntactic peculiarities. This emphasis on linguistic data suggests that there is a fundamental correlation between form and function, that, ultimately, one can detect some homology between signifiers and signifieds. I have noted in the course of the text how certain linguistic markers correlate with the experiential schema of oral narrative and how other linguistic markers indicate a projection of consciousness features. I have also noted the importance of deictic elements in the constitution of perceptional and expressive frames and have introduced some remarks on the status of pronouns and tense for the creation of new types of narrative. Although no one-to-one correlation can be said to obtain between any of these linguistic features and a specific cognitive or semantic function, structural points of reference (the incipit, for instance) *are* indeed invariably marked by one type of feature or the other; and the choice of certain odd pronominal or temporal features also seems to imply a specific meaning effect even if that meaning effect is not constant over a variety of texts using the same device. What I therefore try to perform in this book is a last-ditch effort to make linguistics meaningful within a wider narratological and critical arena.

Let me turn to a final gesture of pulling all the threads of the theory together. In Natural Narratology consciousness plays a crucial role. It both mediates narrativity and constitutes one of its signifiers. Since the real-life author of a text never coincides with the personae of the narrative (except in history and autobiography), all narrative in my definition of the term fundamentally represents *another's consciousness*, a proposal that reiterates the Hamburgerian schema of fictionality. Unlike Hamburger, however, the use that I make of consciousness relates not only to characters' direct emotional or mental experience but also to the level of mediation, and on that level both to the manner and to the process of mediation. Perceptional viewpoint in the VIEWING frame and direct apperception, cognition and ideation in the EXPERIENCING frame, for instance, locate consciousness both on the figural level and on the level of reception. By transferring her deictic centre to the coordinates of another's mentality, the reader indirectly participates in the fictional process and recuperates or re-cognizes characters' experientiality in a vicarious manner. At the same time perceptional perspective or ideation of course belong directly with the parameters of real-life structural schemata and refer to the experiential setup of cognition and perception, not only to the mediating process, which only becomes possible on the basis of these basic-level concepts. In passages of figuralization (Chapter 5), moreover, the reader is led to empathize with the projection of an intrafictional viewpoint whose experientiality is supplied by projection into the text. Texts such as these cohere on the basis of a blank which is filled in by the reader in the process of interpretation, just as missing narrative structures are imported into the text by readers when they read texts against their non-narrative grain (Chapter 7).

Consciousness operates on two further levels within the model. Thus, all narration and all narrative experience inevitably entail a consciousness factor. Narration involves the conscious re-cognization of one's experience, the correlation of reportability and point. In natural narrative's dynamics of evaluation versus the reliving of personal experience (point vs. reportability), the factor of memory and of imaginative projection is very strong, and it mediates what was experienced in body and mind and transfers it to the here and now of narrative recuperation and transmission. Literary narrative extends this basic potential of grasping the meaning of one's embeddedness in a human context by allowing a more sophisticated and also more variegated reshaping and projection of narrative experience. By placing natural schemata and natural parameters at the foundation of its theoretical architecture, Natural Narratology centrally incorporates consciousness as the basic factor of human cognition, emotion and experience.

Ultimately, narrative conceptualizations of immundation provide the most natural, basic-level approach to human confrontation with the human condition. The consciousness factor and the four-level model of cognitive schemata, moreover, mirror the processes observable in the constitution of radial categories in cognitive linguistics. Thus, as I have argued, basic-level parameters and schemata operate in prototypical manner and are accessible as prototypes whose application to new contexts allows for the functional extension of the original concepts. Just as the primary-level parameters of actionality become incorporated into the schemata on level II, where they operate within a holistic frame of re-cognization, generic and narratological schemata in turn deploy these basic-level concepts in creative ways and institute new schemata that become available to readers. In the process of narrativization, finally, all these various types and levels are accessed and combined to produce workable interpretations and creative interventions, all of which are contextually monitored and functionally embedded within the reader's active engagement with the text. Natural Narratology therefore traces cognitive processes on each and every level, including the level on which Natural Narratology itself constitutes itself theoretically and pragmatically. It is for this reason that Natural Narratology can be argued to propose the most 'natural' approach to narrative since it attempts to foreground human embodiment and its cognitive consequences on all levels of narrative and narrational experience.

In lieu of an epilogue

Let us consider, not a trip into the domesticated wilderness of Yosemite National Park, but a far less strenuous pastime, a visit to the movie theatre. On screen you witness a climb, though this time the ascent is not up a trail in California's most popular national park, but instead the conquest of another national monument, Manhattan's most famous architectural landmark, the Empire State Building. You watch the scaling, not of a cast-iron stairway leading towards a splendid view of Nevada Falls, but the mounting of craggy skyscraper surface to a roof that will reward you with a prospect of the cityscape below. You recall where it all started, visualizing the camera's entry into the womb of Nature, past a huge wooden gate whose ritual opening for the sacrificial victim and our own riveted gaze provided access to the heart of darkness and to the realm of its dreaded master. The image of this monarch of the wilderness evokes the memory of how he was captured and carried back to the American wilds, a jungle that consists of man-made trunks of concrete-and-glass palaces. Our gaze also re-encounters the scene in the theatre where the giant ape was displayed in chains to serve as a spectacle of primeval horror. This trip into the wilderness has been a story of striking commercial success: Nature, first colonized and enslaved, is now being commodified in the music hall. Yet the brute beast of the forest cannot be contained; he pulls the pillars of the commercial temple on the gaping crowd and, like Samson, regains his virility, mounting to the top of Empire's phallic tower, the colonizers' symbol of absolute control.

From Muir's genteel invocation of the wilderness designed to inspire the reader with Wordsworthian sentiments of aesthetic pleasure, we have turned to a confrontation with the deadly forces of the Other and have been titillated by its powerful sexual symbolism. Instead of contemplating the wilderness, a mere waterfall, across an abyss that benevolently saves one from direct contact with the Other, in the movie we are kept at a safe distance from, yet directly involved with, the horrors of Nature. The film traces an inverse path to the trail followed by Greenblatt's hypothetical visitor to Yosemite National Park. In the cinema we trail the camera team into the very heart of the jungle and observe them take back, not a photo of the giant ape, but the monster itself, the embodied Other. King Kong, at whose feet the spectator cringes in fascinated ravishment much as the fey Ann Darrow (impersonated by Fay Wray) does on screen, represents Nature in the raw. With the captured Kong we journey back to the heart of civilization, here symbolized by Manhattan's downtown cityscape, which, for the ape, must be America's heart of darkness, the site of capitalism's commercial Real. This wilderness is later conquered and partly destroyed by Kong as soon as he liberates himself and can fully exercise the brute power of his superior strength.

In the film this conquest of the civilized world by the creature of the wilderness is offset by the ape's sentimental love for his victim, an emotion that lowers his resistance and fatally exposes him to the hands of the Americans. (Even Kong is subjected to the truism of *Cherchez la femme*.) In the film, Nature as that primeval Other that both fascinates and awes the civilized subject becomes domesticated in the wake of its anthropomorphization and is portrayed in the figure of Kong the gullible and victimized *ingénu*. Kong is enthralled by that most potent weapon, the charms of American womanhood, and his enslavement effectively signifies his emasculation at the hands of Darrow's civilizing forces. That Darrow herself occupies the position of the victim exposed to the camera's pornographic gaze, that she is hung in (flower) chains to be 'fed' to the ape – all of this clearly underlines her substitutability with the monster. Darrow is used as a tool for catching the beast so that it can be commodified, just as she in turn has been quite literally 'bought' by the director so that he can feed her image to the hungry gaze of the movie-going public. The woman and the ape are therefore exchangeable commodities, and this parallelism implies in turn that the woman epitomizes the destructive powers of Nature and like Kong has to be domesticated by art's civilizing mission.

Whereas Greenblatt's wilderness in the park remains resolutely Other and resists recuperation except by aesthetic proxy, Kong succumbs to the sway of the symbolic both internally and externally: internally because he becomes human in his love for Ann Darrow; externally because he is conquered by the Americans and has their definitions of him inscribed upon his body. The natural, therefore, becomes recuperable, controllable and linguistically definable as soon as it is humanized. King Kong in his progress towards the heart of civilization *removes* human signposts, clearing the way for a powerful impact of himself as the primal signifier of the Other. Only when he is most human does Kong fully signify this otherness. As long as he remains off limits in the wilderness, he seems to impersonate that untouchable and elusive signified beyond the abyss of language which is situated in the mythic realm of the heart of darkness. From Greenblatt's disembodied exemplum belonging to the domain of signification, we have therefore made an incursion into the realm of the wilderness embodied on screen. Both tales tell their stories of commodification, but only in the fate of Kong does the natural become human and the human become naturalized. In contrast to a picturesque view of Nevada Falls, *King Kong* treats us to a powerful series of images that inscribe human physiology on to the wilderness' body and, in significant juxtaposition, to a sequence of shots that project human anatomy on Manhattan's architectural jungle, too.[1] From the womb of Nature in which Ann Darrow is imprisoned (as her fragile body later finds itself encaged in the round circumference of Kong's fingers), we shift to the symbolic architecture of the Empire State Building scaled by a re-immasculated Kong. Human anatomy and the natural, although victimized and commodified by the commercial spirit, reassert themselves with a vengeance. The site of the Natural, as we have known all along, is after all coextensive with the human habitat of man's 'natural' environment.

Notes

PROLOGUE IN THE WILDERNESS

1 See the debate between Searle and Derrida (Derrida 1977a, 1977b; Searle 1977).
2 Compare Fludernik (1993a: Chapter 8).
3 Greenblatt's pattern mirrors other famous journeys into the wilderness' heart of darkness which are characterized by an intensification of linguistic recuperation but are eventually confronted with speechless horror, or the very horror of inarticulation. The heart of darkness is the site at which language is maximally deployed but fails to signify, provoking speechless terror.
4 Compare the dictum: 'Realism, whose only definition is that it intends to avoid the question of reality' (Jean-François Lyotard, *The Postmodern Condition*; quoted Kearns 1992: 857).
5 In the original: 'Le simulacre n'est jamais ce qui cache la vérité – c'est la vérité qui cache qu'il n'y en a pas. / Le simulacre est vrai (L'Ecclésiaste)' (Baudrillard 1981: 9).

1 TOWARDS A 'NATURAL' NARRATOLOGY

1 Constructivism, a sociological methodology, is linked with the name of Alfred Schütz. See, for instance, Schütz (1960) or Schütz and Luckmann (1975). For recent literary applications see also S. Schmidt (1989, 1992) and von Glasersfeld (1989).
2 G. Prince (1995: 80). See G. Prince (1982: 145–61) for his definition of *narrativity* as a scalar concept of what makes good narrative. In his *Dictionary of Narratology* Prince's definition of narrativity is, however, closer to my own understanding of the term, which appears to be shared by other critics: 'The set of properties characterizing NARRATIVE and distinguishing it from nonnarrative; the formal and contextual features making a narrative more or less narrative, as it were' (1987: 64; s.v. narrativity).
3 The reference is to professional storytellers recounting traditional tales, but not epic poems (i.e. oral poetry). For Indian equivalents see Tedlock (1983). Traditions of oral folk tales are also widespread in Ghana (Anthony Appiah, personal communication). Materials such as the ones Tedlock presents have been incorporated into literary narrative, as for instance in the work of Leslie Silko. The practice of communal oral storytelling is no doubt fairly general in oral cultures. It is, however, frequently impossible for me to distinguish between the epic genre of oral poetry and the storytelling of the folk tale kind when I do not have very clear information about the linguistic make-up of these orally produced texts. Thus, for languages with which I am not familiar

I cannot tell whether the original is in verse or prose (an aspect many translations pass over in silence), and categorization then becomes dangerous. This is why I have refrained from naming any more sources for putative traditions of folk tales.
4 See Euler (1991) and under 2.3.1.
5 For the classic distinction between medial and conceptual orality see Koch and Österreicher (1985). Folk tales, in the shape that we have come to know them, belong to a *written* genre with very spurious oral substrata.
6 Claimed, mostly, not by Forster himself but by his structuralist epigones.
7 Compare Sturgess (1992).
8 For those who have skipped the Prologue, I should point out that it is there that I provide an extensive argument on these lines.
9 Such notions were of course current in structuralist linguistics, but have been superseded in the work of discourse analysis.
10 See also, earlier: 'verbal acts of real persons on particular occasions in response to particular sets of circumstances' (B. Smith 1983: 15).
11 See Searle (1975) and Ohmann (1972).
12 For another proposal that *opposes* natural narrative to fiction see Richardson (1987: 306–7).
13 Prototype effects (cp. G. Lakoff 1987: Chapter 3) include notions such as markedness, default values or radial categories.
14 See Schütz and Luckmann (1975: 44): 'Nach den Beispielen schiene es, als ob die alltägliche Lebenswelt einen gewissen Vorrang hätte. In der Tat stellt sie den Urtypus unserer Realitätserfahrung dar. Im täglichen Ablauf werden wir wiederholt in sie zurückgeholt, und mit einer gewissen Einschänkung können wir die anderen Sinngebiete als Modifikationen der alltäglichen Lebenswelt auffassen.'
15 See Dressler (1989, 1990), Dressler *et al.* (1987) and the literature quoted there, as well as Dziubalska-Kołaczyk (forthcoming).
16 See G. Lakoff (1987) for an introduction.
17 See Dressler (forthcoming), Haiman (1985a, 1985b), Landsberg (1996), and L. Waugh (1993).
18 See Kellermann *et al.* (1989). The acronym MOP stands for 'memory organization packet'.
19 The reference is to Minsky's *frames* (1975), Schank and Abelson's *scripts* (1977), and Rumelhart's *schemas* (1975).
20 See G. Lakoff (1987: 45–8).
21 Scripts need not actually be universal. The attractiveness of the restaurant script lies in most readers' familiarity with the restaurant as an accessible institution.
22 Compare: 'Ein Schema unserer Erfahrung ist ein Sinnzusammenhang unserer erfahrenden Erlebnisse, welcher zwar die in den erfahrenden Erlebnissen fertig konstituierten Erfahrungsgegenständlichkeiten erfaßt, nicht aber das Wie des Konstitutionsvorganges, in welchem sich die erfahrenden Erlebnisse zu Erfahrungsgegenständlichkeiten konstituierten' (Schütz 1960: 87–8).
23 Compare G. Lakoff (1987: 265–80).
24 For an excellent illustration of this see Wierzbicka (1985). See also Schütz and Luckmann (1975): 'Der weitaus größte Bereich lebensweltlicher Typisierungen ist sprachlich objektiviert' (p. 233); 'Kurzum, die Sprache kann als die Sedimentierung typischer Erfahrungsschemata, die in einer Gesellschaft typisch relevant sind, aufgefaßt werden' (ibid.); 'Entsprechend können wir sagen, daß die semantische Gliederung einer Sprache den in einer Gesellschaft vorherrschenden typisch relevanten Erfahrungsschemata weitgehend entspricht. Sie entspricht daher auch weitgehend der Typik, die im subjektiven

Wissensvorrat des in diese Gesellschaft und Sprache sozialisierten einzelnen angelegt ist' (ibid.: 234).
25 See, especially, Haiman (1985a, 1985b). Syntactic considerations have sparked some interest also among prototype scholars. See, for instance, case study 3 in G. Lakoff (1987) on *there*-constructions, or Charles Fillmore's case grammar, in which the valency spectrum can be argued to be a syntactic application (or, rather, anticipation) of prototype theory.
26 Also called 'isomorphic iconicity', diagrammatic iconicity refers to the structural isomorphism between form and meaning. Most simplistically, this can be described in terms of 'form-meaning biuniqueness or the one form-one meaning principle' (L. Waugh 1993: 75).
27 For a recent collection of essays tracing the subversion of the paradigmatic opposition of nature vs. culture in literary texts from the nineteenth and twentieth centuries see the *Festschrift* in honour of Paul Goetsch (Groß *et al.* 1994).
28 Compare in G. Prince's *Dictionary of Narratology*: '[...] some narratologists (Labov, Prince, Rimmon-Kenan) have defined it [narrative] as the recounting of at least two real or fictive events [...] neither of which logically presupposes or entails the other' (1987: 58; s.v. narrative).
29 See also M.-L. Ryan (1987).
30 The term *implied author* is here employed as an abbreviation for the narrative's overall meaning structure, for what Nünning (1989a) characterizes as his level N3: the construction of meaning outside the purview of a personalized narrative instance.
31 Compare, however, the merited criticism of Culler's unjustified fusion of narrative levels in Sturgess (1989, 1990) and Adams (1989, 1993).
32 For the fictionalization of historical discourse see also H. White (1978) and Rigney (1988, 1990).
33 Ricoeur does, of course, introduce the terms quasi-plot (1984b: 181), quasi-character (ibid.: 200), quasi-event (ibid.: 224) and even 'quasi-causal explanation' (ibid.: 139–41). See also (ibid.: 230).
34 See the handy presentation of this transformation from data into story in H. White (1981).
35 This raises the question of narrative's relationship with poetry. Paradoxical as this may seem, the very closeness of radically consciousness-oriented types of the Modernist novel to poetry (a feature deliberately produced by Woolf and Joyce) corroborates my analysis. Poetry which is narrativizable can be argued to be practically narrative, and some narrative which is purely metalinguistic can be treated as belonging, in effect, to the realm of poetry. See Chapters 7 and 8 for more extended argument. See also below on the crucial feature of embodiment for narrative which is, precisely, missing from poetry.
36 i.e. a Keatsian ability of empathy with what is not naturally available for empathy.
37 Chatman's institution of a narrator for film as well as fiction bears some superficial resemblance to Stanzel's proposal.
38 i.e. what is traditionally called the historical present tense for nineteenth-century fiction and historical writing. Note, however, that this use of the present is different from the *oral* type of historical present (Schiffrin 1981; Fludernik 1991). For an example of freezing see, for instance, Aphra Behn's 'scenes' such as the following:

> 'He [Octavio's uncle] was all Eyes and Ears, and had use of no other Sense but what inform'd those: He *gazes* upon her [Sylvia], as if he waited and listen'd what she would farther say; and she stood waiting for his Reply, till asham'd, she turn'd her Eyes into her Bosom, and knew not how to proceed.

Octavio views both by turns, and *knows* not how to begin the Discourse again, it being his Uncle's Cue to speak: But finding him altogether mute – he *steps* to him, and gently pull'd him by the sleeve – but *finds* no Motion in him; he *speaks* to him, but in vain; for he [the uncle!] could hear nothing but *Sylvia*'s charming Voice; nor saw nothing but her lovely Face, nor attended any thing but when she would speak again, and look that way.'

(*Love Letters*; Behn 1993: III 286)

39 See also Branigan (1992: 7).
40 In Schütz's work the familiarization of the strange is also seen as one of the crucial factors triggering interpretation. The *a-typical* which refuses to be appropriated by familiar schemata is correctly perceived as threatening (Schütz and Luckmann 1975: 234–5).
41 The reference is to Todorov's three-fold explanation of *vraisemblance* (1968: 1–2).
42 Compare Prendergast (1986: 12) on the *doxa* of realism.
43 Compare Prendergast (1986: 64).
44 See '[...] il faudrait réinterpréter le réalisme, car paradoxalement ce qu'on appelle couramment le réalisme est un genre littéraire qui rejette le code d'accréditement. Dans Balzac et dans Flaubert il n'y a pas d'accréditement et c'est pour cela en un sens que c'est réaliste' (Barthes 1978: 84). In translation: '[...] realism ought to be reinterpreted, for, paradoxically, what is normally called realism is a literary genre that rejects the code of accreditation. In Balzac and in Flaubert there is no accreditation, and in a way that is what makes them realists' (Furst 1988: 102).
45 'And how should Dorothea not marry? – a girl so handsome and with such prospects? Nothing could hinder it but her love of extremes, and her insistance [sic] on regulating life according to notions which might cause a wary man to hesitate before he made her an offer, or even might lead her at last to refuse all offers. A young lady of some birth and fortune, who knelt suddenly down on a brick floor by the side of a sick labourer and prayed fervidly as if she thought herself living in the time of the Apostles – who had strange whims of fasting like a Papist, and of sitting up at night to read theological books! Such a wife might awaken you some fine morning with a new scheme for the application of her income which would interfere with political economy and the keeping of saddle-horses: a man would naturally think twice before he risked himself in such fellowship. Women were expected to have weak opinions; but *the great safeguard of society and of domestic life was, that opinions were not acted on. Sane people did what their neighbours did, so that if any lunatics were at large, one might know and avoid them.*' (*Middlemarch*, i; Eliot 1986: 9–10). See Pannenberg (1983: 30) on the prototypical equation of religious faith with the irreal or counterfactual.
46 Compare M.-L. Ryan's category of 'underlying narrativity' (1992: 376–7).
47 A distinction is made here between self-*reflective* consciousness and the general feature of self-*reflexive* writing in the postmodernist mode. The latter includes self-reflexive strategies such as juxtaposition, allusion or iconicity, which may exceed the limits of the ruling narrational or reflectoral consciousness.
48 This thesis is, however, critiqued in Lamarque and Olsen (1994: 31–8).
49 See the wonderful anecdote about the transmission of cultural knowledge by means of stories which frames the *Pañcatantra* as cited in Haug (1991). The exempla of the *Pañcatantra* teach the stupid sons of the king what all school teaching failed to inculcate in them: wisdom.
50 This has been discussed at length in Clanchy (1979), Stock (1983) and Ermarth (1983).

51 This has already been proposed by some feminist critics (Duffy 1977; Gardiner 1989).
52 My use of the term *realist* therefore roughly corresponds to what W. Wolf (1993) calls *aesthetic illusion*.
53 B.H. Smith (1983: 24–30) is somebody who extends the application of the fictional to any imagined context, including poetry.
54 Randall Walton's examples of play do not thematize the situational feature of embodiment which he so prominently invokes (Walton 1990).
55 For a recent discussion of this issue see Engler and Müller (1994).
56 Compare also Hempfer (1990: 130 footnote 75).
57 Compare Hempfer (1990: 117).
58 See, for instance, Hamburger (1968: 103; 1993: 123–4).
59 See also the argument in Hempfer (1990: 127): 'Mir schiene es also möglich, Fiktionalität als eine Als-ob-Struktur dergestalt zu definieren, daß sich fiktionale Texte über eine bestimmte Menge von Strukturen konstituieren, die sie hinsichtlich dieser Strukturen isomorph zu bestimmten Typen nichtfiktionaler Diskurse erscheinen lassen, daß sie aber gleichzeitig über Strukturen verfügen, die diese Isomorphie als eine nur scheinbare ausweisen.'
60 This is true for Greek antiquity and for the Middle Ages, but may have to be qualified for Latin prose.
61 Hempfer quotes a memorable passage from Gautier's *Capitaine Fracasse*: 'Nous commettrons cette incongruité dont les auteurs de tous les temps ne se sont pas fait faute, et sans rien dire au petit laquais qui serait allé prévenir la camériste, nous pénétrerons dans la chambre à coucher, sûrs de ne déranger personne. L'écrivain qui fait un roman porte naturellement au doigt l'anneau de Gygès, lequel rend invisible' (Hempfer 1990: 129 footnote 71).
62 Compare G. Lakoff (1987: 83–4).
63 Compare Mathieu-Colas (1986), who rehearses inconsistencies of definition and application in the presentation of narratology's subject matter in the writing of Genette and other structuralist narratologists.

2 NATURAL NARRATIVE AND OTHER ORAL MODES

1 G. Prince (1982) is an exception to the rule since he adopts the concept of narrative 'point' from Labov (1972).
2 On the short story and the short short story see Bonheim (1982b), Nischik (1985), Lohafer and Clarey (1989) and the special issue of *Style* 27.3 edited by Sarah Hardy (1993).
3 Compare de Jong (1989) on Homer, Ryding (1971) on the French *chansons de geste*, and recent work on medieval literature, especially Fleischman (1990), as well as Kittay and Godzich (1987), Vitz (1989) and Kinney (1992).
4 This view is not incompatible with Stempel's point (1964) that orality elements function in an intrinsically different manner in written texts and that they lose their original functions immediately *on insertion* into a written discourse, an insertion that immediately results in a complete restructuring of the oral pattern. 'Oral' elements, that is, may be linguistically definable structures which have their observable *origin* in the spoken language even if they 'do' entirely different things once they occur in written texts.
5 The allusion is to André Jolles's *Einfache Formen* (Jolles 1930/1969).
6 See the report published by this research group: *Sieben Jahre Sonderforschungsbereich 321: 'Übergänge und Spannungsfelder zwischen Mündlichkeit und Schriftlichkeit.' Eine Zwischenbilanz 1. Juli 1985–30. Juni 1992*. University of Freiburg: SFB 321, D-79085 Freiburg, Germany. Fax: 0049-761-203-2025. The most recent manifesto from Freiburg is included in de Gruyter's hand-

book *Writing and Its Use*. See Raible (1994) and Koch and Österreicher (1994).
7 The Koch and Österreicher model (1985) can be compared with Douglas Biber's influential study of oral linguistic features (Biber 1988).
8 See Österreicher (1993) for the original proposal and Habermalz (forthcoming) for the English terminology.
9 For the term *faction* and the *non-fiction novel* see Hollowell (1977) and B. Foley (1986). Noted examples of the non-fiction novel are Norman Mailer's *The Armies of the Night* (1968) and *The Executioner's Song* (1979) and Truman Capote's *In Cold Blood* (1965).
10 However, as Rossi (1985) argues, Boccaccio's narrative is already a fully literary one – an assessment which I can only endorse emphatically. The episodic structures outlined by Todorov do not correspond to my own more linguistic definition of the narrative episode. Todorov relies on the deep structure whereas I concentrate on the linguistic surface structure.
11 For models that incorporate the reading process into their plot analyses see M.-L. Ryan (1987, 1991) and Adams (1993).
12 In fact applicability to the novel is hindered for reasons of textual length – it is not (in principle) rejected. Marie-Laure Ryan's approach would be highly useful in the analysis of individual scenes of chapters of a novel. See also M.-L. Ryan (1991) for a more complex presentation of her views.
13 See Tannen (1982c, 1984, 1989) and Fludernik (1993a: especially Chapter 8).
14 The term *reflector-mode narrative* (Stanzel 1984b) roughly corresponds to the novel of consistent internal focalization.
15 Research in progress on narrative structure between 1250 and 1750 analyses a large corpus of texts and does so genre by genre. Owing to the vastness of the material, results are so far available only for those patches which I have been able to till myself. For a final completion of the project I am waiting for the results from a number of M.A. and Ph.D. theses in progress whose authors are working through complementary parts of the corpus.
16 As Hilary Dannenberg pointed out to me, yet another TV genre has recently emerged in which people watch a film representation of their own experiences on TV while commenting on them by way of storytelling (*Hearts of Gold*, BBC Television).
17 One should probably distinguish among a number of different types of jokes, some of which would have a more anecdotal structure. Weber (1993), for instance, cites numerous anecdotes which have a punch line or whose climax is witty repartee quite on the model of jokes.
18 For documentation see Tedlock (1983) and Anthony Appiah on Ghanaian spider tales (personal communication). In many accounts of oral storytelling it remains unclear to the non-initiated whether these utterances are prose or verse narratives, i.e. whether they belong to 'epic poetry' (oral poetry) on Homeric lines or to the more mundane type of institutionalized storytelling which I am talking about.
19 On oral epic poetry see also J.M. Foley (1990) and Zumthor (1990).
20 Compare, e.g. the contrast between Studs Terkel's war interviews and his more recent book on attitudes of Americans towards race (Terkel 1990, 1992).
21 See, for instance, *This is Your Life* (ITV/BBC TV) or *Desert Island Discs* (BBC radio). Thanks go to Hilary Dannenberg for providing this information.
22 Compare E. Prince (1979, 1981).
23 See, for example, the special issue of *Text* 7.3 on this question, with work by Johnstone (1987a), Norrick (1987) and Tannen (1987a). See also Bublitz (1989) and Fischer (1994).

24 See also Adato (1979) for another example: '*So I says* "What happened to *you.*" [...] But anyway, that's immaterial. – *So I says* "What happened to *you* [...]"' (1979: 173).
25 In an early article Chafe (1968) voiced some dissatisfaction with the transformationalist account of idiomaticity (see also Bolinger 1976). His later studies of oral discourse now suggest an even more radical reassessment of generative grammar – at least for the purposes of the spoken language. It would seem that the unit to be generated is no longer the sentence but the idea unit. However, recent revisions of EST after X-bar theory might be able to deal with idea units in a much better way than original S or S" structures could. It might be possible to analyse idea units such as XPs or, at most, CP + IP, with an optional coordination slot that could incorporate either conjunctions (*and, or, because*) or discourse markers (*well, why*). Such an arrangement could generate the spoken-language tokens as well as the more complex written material.
26 See the discussion on subordination in Matthiessen and Thompson (1988). For plot-initiating *when* clauses see Tomlin (1985) and Couper-Kuhlen (1988). An example of such a contraction is: *We were sipping our whisky, when in comes Jo and says* ...
27 In this place I do not discuss post-incidental situatives because they would distract from the main points of the argument. (Compare Fludernik 1992b.)
28 Diacritics above stand for intonational categories in Halford's (1993) notation.
29 *So* here seems to resume the incipit function of *but* after too extensive direct discourse.
30 Most notations have been eliminated except for pauses (dashes and dots) and capitals (for extra emphasis).
31 Stanzel (1984b: 204–9). See also Genette's remarks in his update of *Narrative Discourse* (1988: 102–4).
32 Compare Labov and Waletzky (1967) or an example from Couper-Kuhlen's corpus: 'What are the .. the strangest things that've .. happened to .. you during your career as a public analyst?' (1994, 'The Missing Sparrow').
33 'I'm giving you all these details. I don't know if you want them. [1.2 [.6] U-m [.2]] the .. the reason I'm giving you the details is cause I don't know what the point of the movie was' (Chafe 1980: 302). Numbers in square brackets refer to the length of pauses measured in seconds.
34 That is, excepting the devotional literature, much of which was taken down by clerks on the basis of oral elicitation (see, for instance, the early thirteenth-century *Life* of Christina of Markyate and Margery Kempe's *Book*). Even where the narrative is actually in the first-person, as in Julian of Norwich's *Revelations of Divine Love*, descriptions of the vision prevail over experiential parameters. The dream poem should also be excepted from a true autobiographical reading, and so should narrative frames (*Canterbury Tales*).
35 See McKeon (1987: Chapters 4–6) and de Certeau (1988: 270).
36 Prison writings cited in Foxe's *Actes and Monuments* (*Book of Martyrs*) tend to portray the victims' doubts about their worthiness to suffer much more insistently than is customary in contemporary recusant texts. John Gerard's sufferings, for instance, are depicted with an equanimity that behoves a saint in a hagiographical text rather than a struggling soul under persecution (Gerard 1609/1951).
37 A film about a man picking pears was shown to several informants who then had to summarize the 'story'.
38 Numbers in square brackets refer to the length of pauses.
39 It is therefore no coincidence if episode beginnings and endings have been numbered among the sites of what for traditional philologists looked like the historical present tense (Graef 1889; Roloff 1921; Bauer 1970).

40 Compare Weinrich (1985). For a brief summary see Fludernik (1993a: 45–52).
41 See Bonheim (1982b: 18–32).
42 I here deliberately ignore description in postincidental situatives (Harweg 1975a) which are perceptional rather than orientational in function.
43 This is very well illustrated by the story quoted in Johnstone (1987b). In this narrative the driver employs her faculty for repartee against a policeman.
44 Compare also *Margo 2*, where the third (stupid) character, in imitation of earlier examples of natural disaster which distracted the firing squad from executing his fellow prisoners, cries 'Fire' (Euler 1991: 215–16).
45 See, e.g., *Jonathan 1* (Euler 1991: 198).
46 The joke is told twice, in Freud's *Traumdeutung/Interpretation of Dreams* (1972: 138–9) and in *Der Witz und seine Beziehung zum Unbewußten* (Freud 1970: 61).
47 Also in *Der Witz* (Freud 1970: 109). The interlocutor speaks the truth, but the traveller accuses him of lying by uttering the truth when he expects him to be lying.
48 The hagiographical patterning of Roper's biography in fact at times bars the view of more mundane and pragmatic concerns. See Crewe's superlative chapter on Roper's biography in which he uncovers an indirect critique of More (Crewe 1990).
49 The precise words of the text are: '[. . .] if I shall than say to all you agayn, maisters, I went once for good company with you, which is the cause that I goe nowe to hell, play you the good felowes nowe agayn with me, as I went than for good companye with you, so some of you goe now for good company with me' (More 1910: 300). Compare the scene in Robert Bolt's *A Man for All Seasons*, which fictionalizes the anecdote as More's quip under interrogation:

> NORFOLK [. . .]: 'Can't you do what I did, and come with us, for fellowship?'
> MORE: 'And when we stand before God, and you are sent to Paradise for doing according to your conscience, and I am damned for not doing according to mine, will you come with me, for fellowship?'
> (Bolt 1990: 132)

50 Roper, on the latter point, has an anecdote which contradicts More's bland encomia of the goodness of the king. Early on he has More admit quite realistically and cynically that the king would be willing to sacrifice him for worldly acquisitions (More 1910: 216). Later in the text More's exemplary forgivingness (motivated by the typological requirements) is dwelled on insistently.
51 But see Crewe (1990) for a different psychoanalytic reading of that episode.
52 In the anecdote, criticism of these 'friends' is muted: they are warned against unnamed procurers of their virginity and never openly accused of attempting to procure More.

3 FROM THE ORAL TO THE WRITTEN: NARRATIVE STRUCTURE BEFORE THE NOVEL

1 Work in progress on narrative structure from roughly 1250 to 1750 will take up these important questions in more detail than is possible in the current context.
2 There seems to be a lack of complete consensus on these texts' status as *prose* narrative.
3 The comparison is only valid up to a point. The English case affords cardinal insights into syntactic management and the structuring of narrative episodes, whereas the unrhyming examples discussed by Kittay and Godzich (1987) are

noteworthy primarily for the complete reshuffling of the temporal system – a fact that is closely linked to the loss of an oral context.
4 Passus VI in Langland's *Piers Plowman* (C-Text) is an incipient first-person text, and there apparently exist some German examples (Alois Wolf, personal communication).
5 On More see, for instance, the biographies by Roper (More 1910), Harpsfield (1963), Stapleton (1966) and 'Ro.Ba' (Ba 1950).
6 A preliminary study of narrative in sermons included the analysis of the following three collections: *Early English Homilies* (EETS O.S. 152), *Middle English Sermons* (EETS O.S. 209), and *Mirk's Festial* (EETS O.S. 96; Mirk 1905). The sermons by John Fisher or John Donne only rarely have narrative excursuses.
7 The reference is to André Jolles's *Einfache Formen* (1930/1969), a seminal (though now somewhat dated) study of myth, legend, anecdote, the joke, the fairy tale, etc.
8 See J. Schmidt (1986: 269–71) for examples.
9 One may perhaps disagree with this evaluation and point out that these (verse) retellings of saints' lives appear to be in very 'oral' style and were obviously meant to serve, not the monastic community which is the target audience of the early Katherine Group (cp. Horstmann 1881; Wolpers 1964; Bugge 1975), but the populace at large, although there appears to be little historical evidence of public 'market place' or church festival performances. However, if Chaucer's depiction of storytelling pilgrims has any sort of realistic background, it would indeed support the argument that saints' legends (in ballad form) had a fairly wide popular currency beyond narrowly liturgical settings.
10 'As to this matter, I remember a story that accords with it. There was once a man who had four friends. And three of them he loved very affectionately, but for the fourth he had but little affection. So it one time came to pass (befell) that he offended against the king of the country and broke the law in such a manner that he was sentenced to death. And when he was arrested and the sentence was to be executed he implored those who had arrested him to allow him to talk to his friends before his death.

'He came to his first friend whom he trusted most and implored him to help him and intercede for him with the king. And this first friend answered him as follows: I will neither side with nor defend someone who is a proved felon against the king; you have deserved to die. Therefore I would buy the shroud for you to be buried in. Any other answer he did not get. Then he left in great dejection and set out to try his second friend beseeching him to intercede for him with the king, so that the king would reprieve him. And he answered him saying that the only favour he would do for a felon to the king was to help himself to deliver the traitor to death. Then when he achieved no success with the second friend, he set out to try his third and came to him and implored him to go with him and intercede for him with the king so that he would forgive him his offence. And he answered him and said that he would not help him but instead, since he had committed treason against the king, he would help to hang him. Then he set out to try his fourth friend, in whom he had least hope, and implored him to go with him and beseech the king to forgive him his offence. And then he answered him and said: Since you ask me so openly I will go with you to the king, even though you have not deserved it, and ask the king to forgive you your offence, and rather than that they execute you, I am willing to die for you in my own person.' (Referential ambiguities in the original have been preserved in my translation.)
11 'Das Motiv der Kästchenwahl' (Freud 1913/1982).
12 Euler's collection has numerous examples (1991).

13 I have not quoted the exegesis of this exemplum.
14 See Enkvist (1986), Enkvist and Wårvik (1987), and Riehl (1993) for German.
15 Moreover, in the St Margaret text, all instances of clause-initial *þa* occur after a preposed prepositional phrase which can be argued to blur the effect of the traditional pattern that marks onset both formally and structurally. For examples and further details on *þa* (ME *þo*) see Fludernik (1995b).
16 'Once it came to pass (*it befelle*) that the entire province of St Nicholas suffered very badly from hunger because nearly all of them lacked sustenance. And then God's servant heard that ships which were loaded with wheat had arrived at the port. And then he immediately went there and implored the seamen to help the starving people with 100 bushels of wheat from each ship. And then they said in reply: "Holy father, we dare not, because we get the wheat in measured quantities and we have to supply the emperor's granaries in Alexandria with exactly that quantity." And then the holy man said to them: "Do as I have asked you and I promise you by God's goodness that you won't have less when you get to the granaries." And after they had given him the wheat, they came to Alexandria and delivered the full quantity of what they had originally received. And then they told this miracle to the emperor's servants and they all praised God and his servant very much. And then (meanwhile) this holy man distributed the wheat to everyone according to their need so that not only was it sufficient to live on for two years but there was also left enough for sowing.' (My translation.)
17 The ships, in the Latin source, actually go from Alexandria to the emperor (cp. in the notes, *Three Lives from the Gilte Legende* 1978: 89), but this was mistranslated already in the *Légende Dorée*, the French source of the English translation.
18 In some MSS. the location of the miracle is *Nice*, but Nicholas is still the Bishop of Myra.
19 'So when the duke and his wife came to the king, peace was made between them by the intercession of high-ranking nobility. The king liked and loved the lady well and he feasted the couple beyond measure and (then) asked the lady to sleep with him. But she was an outstandingly virtuous woman and refused to accede to the king's demands.

'And then she told this to her husband the duke and said to him:

"I suspect that it was to dishonour me that we were sent for. Because of that, my husband, I advise you that we should leave this place immediately so that we can ride to our own castle during the night."

'And just as she had counselled they left so that neither the king nor anyone among his retainers were aware of their departure. As soon as king Uther found out about their sudden departure, he became terribly angry; then he called together his privy council and told them about the sudden departure of the duke and his wife. Then they advised the king to send for the duke and his wife by means of a challenge:

'"And if he refuses to come at your request then you can do what you think best; then you have cause to make war on him."

'In this manner (*soo*) it was done, and the messengers got their answer which was this, in short, that neither he nor his wife would come to him. Then the king became terribly angry, and then the king again sent him clear terms calling upon him to get ready and to prepare and fortify himself, for he would fetch him out of his biggest castle within forty days. As soon as (when) the duke had received this warning, he immediately (*anone*) set out to fortify and garrison two strong castles one of which was called Tintagl and the other one Terrabyl.' (My translation.)

20 'But Merlin had performed such magic unto king Pellinore that he did not see king Arthur and (so) passed by him without saying anything.' (My translation.)
21 '"Well," said Arthur, "I will prepare for him shortly."
   'Then king Arthur sent for all the children born on May Day that were begotten by lords and conceived by ladies. For Merlin had told king Arthur that the man who would kill him and destroy the whole country was to be born on May Day. So he sent for them all on pain of death and so many sons of lords and many sons of knights were found out, and all of them were sent to the king. And so Mordred was sent by king Lottis's wife. And all of them were put to sea in a ship. And some (children) were four weeks old and some even younger. And so by stroke of fate the ship drifted towards a castle and (capsizing) was all destroyed and most of the party were killed except for Mordred who was cast ashore. And a good man found him and brought him up till he was 14 years old and then he brought him to court, as will be told later towards the ending of the MORTE D'ARTHUR.
   'But many lords and barons of this kingdom were offended at the manner in which their children's lives had been lost and many blamed Merlin for it rather than Arthur. So (but?) out of fear and for love of Arthur they kept their peace. But when the message came to king Royns, (then) he became exceedingly furious, and he prepared a large army, as is told later in the BOOK OF BALYNE THE SAVAGE which follows, that is, the story of how Balyne got the sword.' (My translation.)
22 Compare above in Chapter 2 (pp. 62-3) for similar features in oral narrative.
23 Editorial italics in the original have been eliminated in all quotes in this section. Translation: 'Then Maxcene called upon his gaoler/to arrest the young woman/and put her in prison/while he was to make the wheels./And before the end of the third day/they were specially wrought for her; they were so horrifying to look at/that they caused many a man to tremble with fear.' (My translation.)
24 'Old and young, I ask you earnestly to abandon your wicked behaviour;/Think of God who endowed you with the capacity to atone for your sins!/Now I will recount to you with good and sweet words/the life of a virgin that was called Maregrete (Margaret).' (My translation.)
25 Compare my discussion of this and the quotes from Chafe (1980) in the previous chapter.
26 See W. Wolf (1993: 591) on a passage in Charlotte Brontë's *Shirley*: '[...] while he [Mr Yorke] sits leaning back [...] I will snatch my opportunity to sketch the portrait of this French-speaking Yorkshire gentleman.'
27 'The sorrow that Alla feels night and day/for his wife and also for his child/ is so great that no-one would be able to describe it./But now I will switch to Custance/who has been floating (present) on the sea in anguish and in sorrow/for more than five years in accordance with God's dispensation/before her ship finally approached land.' (My translation.)
28 'The constable was not the lord of the place/I was talking about, where he found Custance/but ruled it with strength for many years/under Alla, King of the whole of Northumberland,/who was very wise and brave in the battles/against the Scots, as is well known./But I will (now) return again to my (proper) subject matter.' (My translation.)
29 For a more extensive discussion of the use of *þo* see Fludernik (1995b).
30 See the editions by the Early English Text Society, O.S. 87 for the *Early SEL* and O.S. 235, 236, 244 for Corpus Christi Cambridge MS 145 and British Museum MS Harley 2277.
31 "When the young man had heard the answer/of blessed Agnes, he became very sad,/and so dearly did blind Love grieve him/that, suffering both mental

and physical pains,/he fell ill and lay down in his bed;/But on account of his heavy sighs this was overheard/by the doctors who told his father what had happened./And when he (i.e. the father) realized that the affection/that his son bore to Agnes was set so irretrievably,/he repeated all his former offers/in all respects and even offered her more./But surely his efforts were all in vain/for she said plainly that under no circumstances/would she betray the pledge of her first spouse./And since he stood at that time in the prefecture/in a high social position of great dignity,/he thought that no one beside himself/exceeded him in worth,/and therefore he wondered who it was/by whom Agnes enhanced her social position (beyond his score)/and of whose wealth she boasted so much.' (My translation.)

32 'And when he saw that this did not cause her any pain,/[he had] chains of iron made in haste./With these she was bound straight away/and at once thrown into prison./And as she was there alone,/the devil, in order to tempt her, took [present perfect] on/the shape of an angel by his magic/and came to her shining brightly/and said to her: "Julienne,/I am one of God's angels,/and He sent me to admonish you/that, rather than be tormented further,/you should sacrifice to the [heathen] gods."' (My translation.)

33 One can speculate whether these became popular in the fourteenth century as a result of French influence, since *quant* was a prominent conjunction in the French prose sources.

34 'Then the fire was banked up. She was sitting very quietly in the flames./The fire could not burn her even a little. It did not hurt her at all./Then they very quickly took and heated pitch and sulphur/and threw it boiling on her naked tender body/and all the time the young woman was sitting quietly. It did not hurt her at all./ But she kept on preaching all the time with a merry heart (talking) of Jesus, the king of heaven./Then the wicked justice did not know what else he could do./When (it became clear that) he could not overcome this virtuous little soul with his craft/he ordered her throat to be pierced by a sharp and keen blade/so that she would lose the faculty of speech and also her holy life./When her throat was pierced (however) she spoke even more vehemently/and preached eagerly of Jesus Christ. And she laughed scornfully. "Ye," she said, "that are Christians, be ye glad and merry. [. . .]"' (My translation.)

35 'When the emperor saw this/he conceived great anger in his heart./He commanded that the clever young woman/should be brought to him at once./And though he was angry in his heart/he spoke to her in a courteous manner:/"Well, worthy young woman, who are praised so much [. . .]"' (My translation.)

36 'Then the tyrant became furious/and he ordered great torments to be inflicted on Katherine./He ordered his men to take her immediately/ and strip her naked both back and side./Then they beat her with scorpions,/and inflicted many other great pains on her./But all this he saw did not avail,/it could not get her to weaken in her faith./Then they put her in prison/where she was completely shrouded in darkness/and he had reliable men guard her (to make sure)/that she got neither drink nor food./In this wise she was supposed to have no sustenance/until twelve days were over and gone./But every day angels came to her,/(and) she received full measure of food from heaven./So at this time she was thrown into prison,/And at the same time the following came to pass [. . .]' (My translation.)

37 Compare Boureau (1986), who distinguishes various steps in the inexorable progression of the physical battle between tyrant and virgin martyr, here Maxentius and St Katherine.

38 'Now Floris, who has set out for his father's house/arrives there./He alights in his father's hall./His father greeted him at once/and also his mother, the queen./But it was nearly impossible for him/not to ask where his beloved was;/He does not

wait for the answer/and immediately he leaves,/(and) into (her) room he comes./He asked the young woman's mother right away,/"Where is Blauncheflour, my sweetheart?"/"Sir," she said, "to tell you the truth,/I don't know where she is.!"/She bethought herself of the lie /which the king had arranged./"You are deceiving me," he answered then;/"It hurts me very much that you deceive me!/Tell me where my dear one is!"/Crying profusely she then said,/"Sir," she said, "dead." "Dead!" said he./"Sir," she said, "yes indeed."/"Alas, when did that dear girl die?"/"Sir, less than a fortnight ago/she was covered with earth,/and she had died for the love of you."/Floris, who was so handsome and gentle,/then fainted, he really did./The Christian woman began to call/on Jesus Christ and Holy Mary./The king and the queen heard her cry (and)/in haste they came running into her room,/and the queen saw before her,/the child she had given birth to lying in a swoon./The king was deeply worried/when he saw what happened to his son for love.' (My translation.)

39 See, for instance, ll. 113–23 (Sands 1993: 285).

40 'This Troilus was present/when they demanded Criseyde in exchange for Antenor,/as a result of which his face began to change rapidly/since he nearly died from these words;/but nevertheless he did not say anything/so that no-one should notice his feelings;/with manly courage he attempted to bear up to his grief/and with great anguish and terrible fear/he waited for what the lords would say;/and if they agreed – which God forbid – /that she should be exchanged, he determined on two things:/firstly how to save her honour and second in which way/he could best prevent her exchange./Very quickly he considered the situation.' (My translation.)

41 'When, as I have recounted, the Greeks/were besieging Troy with strength,/it happened one day when Phaebus was/in the first part of the Lion of Hercules,/that Hector and many bold noblemen/were setting a date to fight with the Greeks,/since he tried to cause them as much distress as possible.

'I cannot tell whether it was soon or later between/the time they met and the day on which they wanted to fight;/but, one day well armed, bright and shining/Hector and many honourable men went out/with spears in their hands and their big bows ready,/and face to face without any delay/their enemies met them in the field at once.

'All day long with spears well-sharpened,/with arrows, spears, swords and cruel clubs/they fought and threw horses and men to the ground/and dashed their brains with their axes./But in the last assault, to tell the truth,/the Trojans conducted themselves so badly/that they were defeated and fled homeward at night.' (My translation.)

42 See Casparis (1975).

43 'This Troilus began to founder in tears/that welled like alcohol out of a bottle;/ and Pandarus stopped talking,/cast his eyes to the ground./But anyway, in the end he thought:/ "For God's sake, before my friend dies/I will say a few words more to him."' (My translation.)

44 The demonstrative noun phrase had always been one possible choice at incipit points of narrative episodes, but occurred only rarely in comparison to incipits featuring *þo* and other discourse markers. *Troilus*, for the first time, generalizes the construction, to an extent much beyond its use in Capgrave and other texts of the period.

45 I am here deliberately excluding the verse narrative of this period, which on the whole remains faithful to traditional models, with some of Dryden's and Pope's work not radically different *structurally* from the Spenserian tradition. There appears to be an unbroken tradition, particularly in respect of the use of the historical present. Spenser and Capgrave employ the historical present extensively in contexts that are static, or cast entire action sequences in the

historical present. This mode then recurs in Dryden and Pope, particularly in their verse translations of epic material.
46 See Stanzel (1984b: 204–9).
47 Compare Greenblatt's excellent discussion (1980) of More's humanistic playfulness in *Utopia*.
48 Underlining signals past tenses in the result sections. Other emphases in bold italics.
49 Thomas Dangerfield is frequently mentioned as the putative author of this rogue's tale, which would make the text into an autobiography with alternating first- and third-person narration.
50 Present participles are emphasized in italics. All original emphases have been eliminated.
51 Relative *the which* is prominent in Caxton but also occurs frequently in the prose of Fisher. The *Book of Common Prayer* also has a liking for the construction: '*Who*, in the same night that he was betrayed, took bread ...' The use of the present perfect is a typical case of an incipient integrating device according to Wolfgang Raible's aggregation vs. integration schema (Raible 1992).
52 See, for instance, the ruse by means of which Pointz betrays Tyndale as he passes through a narrow lane before Philips (Foxe 1967: 184).

4 THE REALIST PARADIGM: CONSCIOUSNESS, MIMESIS AND THE READING OF THE REAL

1 See DeJean (1991) for Behn's French sources and Day (1966) for the avatars of epistolary fiction.
2 Another French import, as Madame de La Fayette's *La Princesse de Clèves* (1678) documents.
3 It is therefore fully justified to name Behn as the first novelist (Gardiner 1989: 201; Duffy 1977: viii).
4 But see M. Smith (1995) for a contrary argument.
5 Supplementary functions of description, particularly its symbolic uses, are a late development in the history of the novel.
6 Volume 3 of the Pickering edition of Behn's works only appeared after the completion of the manuscript, so that references could not be rewritten to cite this authoritative edition.
7 More recently, *Don Tomazo* has been attributed to Thomas Dangerfield. See Salzman (1991: xix–xxi).
8 Compare, for instance, a particularly 'dramatic' exchange in which Moll outdoes herself in witty repartee (Defoe 1971: 46–7).
9 Historical presents are printed in bold italics, participle constructions in italics, (resultative) past tenses have been underlined, and expressive features highlighted in bold underline. All original emphases have been deleted.
10 Compare the examples from Chaucer and Caxton's *The Golden Legend* which I quoted under 3.2.
11 Thomas Middleton's *A Trick to Catch the Old One* (1604–06) starts with a *prose* 'interior monologue' by the protagonist Witgood. Although half of what Witgood utters are proverbs, this is the most verisimilar representation of internal discourse from the period that I have so far come across.
12 Besides the purely dramatic scene and the scene in which dialogue prevails.
13 See Wulf Österreicher (1993). *Verschriftung* designates the mechanic transcription of oral material into written form, whereas *Verschriftlichung* involves the cognitive reshaping of the oral text into a written format, a structural and cognitive remedialization of the oral story. The term *con-ceptual transcoding* (for *Verschriftlichung*) is used by Sabine Habermalz (forthcoming).

14 This, incidentally, is sheer slander on the narrator's part (or the opinion of those who pity Tarquin) since Miranda has been portrayed as flirtatious but not as promiscuous until that point of the narrative. There is indeed little in the text to support that she is not still, technically speaking, a virgin at the time of her marriage.
15 Thus, in 'The Fair Jilt', the narrator gives us a glowing description of Tarquin and adds, 'I have seen him pass the Streets' (Behn, 1967: 98). On the relationship of Behn's narrators to the historical Aphra Behn see below under 4.2.2.
16 Compare Pearson (1991) for a discussion of Behn's ambiguous presentation of female deceitfulness and vice.
17 Cohn (1978) defines psycho-narration as the narratorial description of characters' minds, what Stanzel (1984b) calls *thought report* and Leech and Short (1981) term the 'narrative report of thought acts' ('NRTA').
18 Such soliloquies very frequently centred on an internal debate or a moral quandary. See W.G. Müller (1991: 98) for a particularly instructive passage from Lyly's *Euphues* (1578).
19 All Middle English examples of free indirect discourse with which I am familiar, even when they represent a character's thoughts, have a 'spoken' quality about them as if they are uttered dramatically, or they are ambiguous with regard to their internality. The same holds for the handful of Renaissance passages which also seem to involve a soliloquial utterance on the reporter's part.
20 In the previous paragraph Henault is described as turning his face towards her 'with love', which she contrasts with 'shewing her face': Henault acts like the sun towards which she turns, replacing the eyes of the world with the privileged glance of her beloved. (This conceit, which is very common in the poetry of the period, may have found its way into the story from Behn's lyric oeuvre.)
21 Behn's attitude towards Catholicism, however, cannot be gauged in such simple terms. Narratorial presentations of religiosity (e.g. in the description of Octavio's ceremony when taking his vows – *Love-Letters* III, 379–83) foreground the external trappings of the Catholic religion, the ritual and glamour of it rather than any devotional aspects. Behn-the-narrator (as well as Behn-the-author?) herself seems to have held views similar to those attributed to Isabella.
22 Compare my examples in Fludernik (1993a: 94–6).
23 i.e. sympathetic towards the character's perspective. See Cohn (1978) for the definition of this term.
24 Compare, for example, Fludernik (1993a: 162–3) for examples of this construction.
25 And from the popularity of the mock-chivalric mode as in, say, Charlotte Lennox's *The Female Quixote* (1752).
26 See Brinkmann (1969, 1977). Starting with Scott, the historical novel had a first heyday in the mid-nineteenth century with work by Thackeray (*Henry Esmond*), Dickens (*A Tale of Two Cities*), Kingsley (*Westward, Ho*) or Eliot (*Romola*) in the forefront of that tradition.
27 For an excellent discussion see Schabert (1981).
28 See my remarks on this point under 1.2.4.
29 See also Fowler (1981: 103–6) for French examples of the construction. Thanks go to Brian McHale for pointing out this parallel.
30 McKeon links Miranda's new-found virtue to the discovery of Tarquin's low birth (his nobility has been an imposture): 'Forced to confront the persistence of her love in the absence of his title, Miranda, chastened and newly chaste, reforms her own heart' (1987: 259).

31 On the centrality of chance in the realist novel see Bell (1993).
32 Aristotle's distinction between the verisimilar and the historical in the *Poetics* (1460a) still holds.
33 The term *fantastic* is here used in the sense of Todorov's *marvellous* (Todorov 1970/1993).
34 See Greenblatt's *Marvellous Possessions* (1992) and Hulme and Whitehead (1992) for examples.
35 The lengthy soliloquies of the epic and the Renaissance romance are externalized signifiers of interiority but their general availability to the narrator clearly cannot but be fictive.
36 For those unfamiliar with the story: Isabella marries again after a long absence of her husband, believed to have died abroad, only to have him come back once she is happily settled in her new marriage and has ceased to love him. She ends up murdering both her first and her second husband.
37 Cp. Barthes (1984b: 61, 63–4), where the death of the author is linguistically defined in terms of the 'death' of the narrator of the narrative's enunciatory level of the text.
38 Sternberg's concept of the 'omnicommunicative author' (Sternberg 1978: 259–61, 268–74) foregrounds the narrational or representational choices in *focalisation zéro*, which operates on the basis of access to complete knowledge.
39 See Humphrey (1954), Stanzel (1971), Cohn (1978), and *passim* in Oppel (1965). For the linguistic devices employed to effect this 'mind style' see Nischik (1991a) and Busch (1970); the last provides impressive documentation for signals of narrated perception, free indirect discourse and other indices of reflector narrative.
40 See Kittel (1990, 1991).
41 See, e.g. Stanzel (1984b: 211, 270 footnote 56). See also Fielding's caricature of this in *Shamela*, where the heroine writes to her mother while lying in bed with Squire Booby (Fielding 1970: 330). For a French example see a passage from *La Nouvelle Héloïse* quoted in Husson: 'Il me semble entendre du bruit [...] On ouvre! ... on entre! ... c'est elle! c'est elle! je l'entrevois, je l'ai vue, j'entends refermer la porte' (Husson 1991: 304).
42 The text here varies drastically from edition to edition, with the Everyman library preserving more free indirect discourse than the Penguin edition, which follows the novel's first edition of 1747–48.
43 This is not to say that free indirect discourse passages do not also render scenes of extreme emotional upheaval, especially in the more spectacular writing of the Brontës, Wilkie Collins, or in some of George Eliot's fiction (*The Mill on the Floss*). But there is frequently a taint of unreason (if not *déraison*) attached to such excesses.
44 This is the standard reading of *La Jalousie* as given in Hamburger (1968: 103/1993: 123–4), Whiteside (1982) or Epps (1987). But see Ermarth (1992: 72–84) for a reading that refuses any realistic interpretations of jealousy.
45 For a good discussion of Stanzel's ambiguities about neutral narrative and the proposal to reintroduce a neutral narrative situation see Broich (1983). See also Meindl (1994).

5 REFLECTORIZATION AND FIGURALIZATION: THE MALLEABILITY OF LANGUAGE

1 *Skaz* is a form of storytelling that imitates, parodies and stylizes oral storytelling. It can be used to narrate both in a first- and in a third-person mode. The term was coined by Boris Eichenbaum and is now a standard critical term

in Russian and Formalist literary criticism. Examples of *skaz* in literature in the English language are, for instance, the 'Cyclops' episode narrative by the unnamed first-person narrator in *Ulysses*, or some of the work by Mark Twain, Ring Lardner or James Thurber (*Huckleberry Finn*, 'Haircut'). See Eichenbaum (1971a, 1971b), Titunik (1977), and Vinogradov (1972).
2 See below for definitions and examples of Stanzel's term *reflectorization*.
3 For the term compare Goetsch (1985) and Koch and Österreicher (1985).
4 See especially Tristram (1996).
5 For another discussion of this passage see van Gunsteren (1990), who disagrees with Stanzel's explanation but does not propose a very convincing analysis herself when making the extradiegetic narrator responsible for the juxtaposition of variable focalizations in 'The Garden Party'. (See 1990: 96–100).
6 Van Gunsteren (1990: 97) agrees with this estimation.
7 i.e. the world view that the reader constructs for the text as a whole.
8 For a definition of psycho-narration, i.e. the narrative's external description of characters' thought processes, see footnote 17 in Chapter 4.
9 I will come back to the establishment of observer positions in section 5.2 below.
10 See Banfield (1982: 30–1).
11 'The characters whom Einfried has sheltered! Even a writer is here, an excentric person, who bears the name of some kind of mineral or precious stone and who fritters the Lord's days away here' (quoted in Stanzel 1984b: 182).
12 'Suddenly something startling happened. The woman stopped playing abruptly, putting her hand above her eyes to peer into the gloom, and Mr Spinell turned around quickly in his seat. The door *back there*, which led to the corridor, had opened, and a dark figure *came in*' (quoted in Stanzel 1984b: 183).
13 For a more extensive discussion see Stanzel (1984b: 181–4) and Fludernik (1993a: 390–1).
14 Transferential deixis is a sign of empathy by means of which the speaker transfers herself into an imaginary position in relation to which s/he then perceives visibilia (Bühler 1934). Textual deixis figures as only one kind of such imaginary transference of schematic *hic et nunc*.
15 Stanzel (1984b: 173–8).
16 'Der Geist der Erzählung', an extended metaphor used by the narrator at the beginning of Thomas Mann's *Der Erwählte* (Mann 1980: 7–8).
17 The story is a case of variable internal focalization in Genette's terms.
18 Another similar passage in which Alice, in her thoughts, refers to Mrs Stubbs's 'photers': 'How many there were! There were three *dozzing* at least' (section 8, Mansfield 1984: 459) is discussed in Reid (1988: 29–30).
19 'And after all the weather was ideal. They could not have had a more perfect day for a garden-party if they had ordered it' (Mansfield 1984: 487).
20 For a more thematic analysis of these passages see Reid (1992: 134–42).
21 'When she saw the old sheep-dog [...] "Ugh! What a coarse, revolting creature!" said Florrie' (Mansfield 1984: 442).
22 This fable-like feature recurs in section 11, where Florrie the cat welcomes the onset of darkness (ibid.: 466).
23 Compare also 'And now they had passed the fisherman's hut, passed the charred-looking little *whare* where Leila the milk-girl lived with her old Gran' (ibid.: 443).
24 If one reads the final sentence ('Perhaps if you had waked up') as the observer's soliloquy.
25 Compare, for instance, 'after all'; 'if they had ordered it'; 'you could not help feeling'; 'yes, literally hundreds'.
26 See Nünning (1993).

27 My attention was first drawn to this passage during a lecture course on Dickens which F.K. Stanzel gave in the winter term of 1976–77. He was at the time writing the first (German) version of his *Theory of Narrative*. During the discussion in class Stanzel emphasized the observer position which is projected by the text, but he did not suggest any connection with the issue of reflectorization or figuralization.

28 For reasons of brevity I have elided the long paragraph that reiterates the stillness and quietude theme and have numbered the paragraphs to facilitate reference in the following discussion.

29 Indeed, since we are dealing with present-tense narrative, the paragraph could even be labelled free indirect discourse rather than direct speech, but – for lack of conclusive evidence – I will leave that question pending. (On free indirect discourse in the present tense and the resultant problems of delimitation, see Fludernik 1993a: 89–91).

30 See also Gerald Prince's category of the 'disnarrated' (1992: 28–38) and Herman's 'hypothetical focalization' (1994).

31 Lady Dedlock's despair is quite explicitly commented on by Mr Tulkinghorn in his thoughts: '*She* cannot be spared. Why should she spare others?' (Dickens 1962: 660). Her question as to his whereabouts later that night (ibid.: 661) further helps to incriminate Lady Dedlock in the eyes of the reader.

32 On 'Death in Venice' and Cohn's interpretation of it, see also Stanzel (1992).

33 '[...] and [he] felt his heart throb with terror, yet with a longing inexplicable' (Mann 1936: 6).

34 'He was overwrought by a morning of hard, nerve-taxing work, work which had not ceased to exact his uttermost in the way of sustained concentration, conscientiousness, and tact [...]' (Mann 1936: 3).

35 'Gustav Aschenbach was the poet-spokesman of all those who labour at the edge of exhaustion; of the overburdened, of those who are already worn out but still hold themselves upright; of all our modern moralizers of accomplishment, with stunted growth and scanty resources, who yet contrive by skilful husbanding and prodigious spasms of will to produce, at least for a while, the effect of greatness. There are many such, they are the heroes of the age. And in Aschenbach's pages they saw themselves; he justified, he exalted them, he sang their praise – and they, they were grateful, they heralded his fame' (Mann 1936: 12).

36 'Heroismus [...] der Schwäche' (Mann 1989: 18).

37 Compare the later sarcastic echo of this passage in section v (Mann 1994: 94; 1936: 71–2).

38 For an excellent recent narratological paper on *Maisie* see G. Moore (1994 for 1989). Moore also holds that the narrator's and the characters' voices cannot simply be assigned with the dichotomy of 'who sees' and 'who speaks'.

39 In fact, the passage continues: 'If she knew her instructress was poor and queer she also knew ...'

40 See Golding (1955: 106). Another famous example of this type is Tolstoy's description of Natasha's first evening at the opera in *War and Peace* (VIII, ix). A stylistic equivalent of such defamiliarization may be noted in Joyce's description of a tin of sardines in the 'Oxen of the Sun' episode of *Ulysses*.

6 VIRGIN TERRITORIES: THE STRATEGIC EXPANSION OF DEICTIC OPTIONS

1 See Cohn (1989, 1990).
2 For work on second-person fiction see the special issue on second-person narrative by *Style* (28.3), which I guest-edited (Fludernik 1994b) and the separate

bibliography of second-person fiction in *Style*'s subsequent bibliographical issue (Fludernik 1994d).
3 The issues presented in this section have been the subject of a number of recent and forthcoming articles. See B. Richardson (1991b), Margolin (1994, 1996), Fludernik (1993b, 1994a, 1994b, 1994c) and especially – on the question of alternating multiple-person texts – Korte (1989), Peel (1989), Nischik (1994) and B. Richardson (1994).
4 Plural *you*, i.e. the equivalent of Spanish *ustedes* or German *ihr*, can of course refer to two very different sets of protagonists: *you* + others, or *you* + *you* (see Margolin 1994). In the first reading, *you* occurs intermittently in second-person fiction, just as *we* and *they* do in first- and third-person narrative. The only text I know which employs such *you* (*ustedes*) for extended sections of the narrative is Fuentes's *Cambio de piel (A Change of Skin)*. You + *you*, which is the standard address form to couples in epistolary writing, I have not come across at all, but again there may be treasures out there of whose existence I am not yet aware.
5 An exception is Fuentes's 'Alma Pura', in which the golden childhood of brother and sister is related in extended *we*-passages.
6 Margolin (1994) devotes some space to the problem and is currently working on *we* narratives (Margolin 1996). Margolin's discussion of different deictic constellations which are in principle possible for *we*-narratives suggests a great diversity of forms, but the as yet rather sparse corpus of *we*-texts does not include the full range of these theoretically available options. Pierre Silvain's *Les Éoliennes* was first noted as an instance of *we*-narrative in Didier Coste's *Narrative as Communication* (1989) but Raja Rao's *Kanthapura* (1970) is a much more interesting *I/we*-narrative.
7 Notations *sic* in the original.
8 Note the narrative parenthetical 'her friends knew' in the first sentence of my extract and the 'expressive' quality of 'the right thing', 'seen eye to eye', 'which was sweet' or 'naturally'.
9 For the moment I exclude nineteenth-century instances and earlier anticipations of second-person narrative as discussed in Fludernik (1994a).
0 My bibliography (Fludernik 1994d) of second-person fiction includes works by Samuel Beckett, Edna O'Brien, Joyce Carol Oates, John Updike and Thomas Wolfe.
11 To this type belong novels such as Jay McInerney's *Bright Lights, Big City* (1984), Edna O'Brien's *A Pagan Place* (1970) or Jean Muno's *Le Joker* (1971).
12 An example of this is Günter Grass's *Katz und Maus* (1961).
13 Thus, initially, in Cortázar's 'Graffiti' (1979). See also Alice Munro's 'Tell Me Yes or No' (1974), Edmund White's *Nocturnes for the King of Naples* (1978) or Gloria Naylor's *Mama Day* (1988).
14 Compare my 'Second-Person Narrative as a Test Case for Narratology' (Fludernik 1994c).
15 See, for instance, Papadiamantis's 'Around the Lagoon' or Julio Cortázar's 'Graffiti' as treated in Fludernik (1994a) and Kacandes (1994).
16 This is particularly true of Lillian Smith's *Strange Fruit*. See also Meindl (1994).
17 For an extensive list of such texts see Gnutzmann (1983).
18 Compare Morrissette (1965) and Fludernik (1993b) for a list of such contexts.
19 In a seminar on second-person fiction which I taught in Freiburg in the winter term of 1994/95 students noted their increased empathy for *you* protagonists. Only one text, Jay McInerney's *Bright Lights, Big City* (1984), created empathy problems: half of my (female) students resented the protagonist's attitudes and felt increasingly aggravated by the novel.

20 Compare Fludernik (1995c).
21 See the examples for *one*, German *man* and French *on* cited in Steinberg (1971).
22 Italics to highlight free indirect discourse.
23 Fludernik (1995a, 1995c).
24 I only recently came across Zeller (1992) who discusses these texts. Thanks are due to Paul Goetsch, who kindly referred me to this study.
25 'One is thinking of Sacco and Vanzetti, Nicola Sacco and Bartolomeo Vancetti [sic]. It's a mystery why precisely Sacco and Vanzetti should occur to one. And when thinking of Sacco and Vanzetti, one thinks, one would have to ponder that perhaps no-one anywhere on the entire globe is thinking about Sacco and Vanzetti at the very moment, that no-one is remembering the early film about them. And one goes on to ask: Well, how was it with Sacco and Vanzetti? In one's mind's eye one sees oneself as a boy, the circus in the middle of that night, that circus which brought the film about Sacco and Vanzetti to the countryside at the beginning of the great times of the film [...]' (My translation.)
26 'Incidentally, he argued, one couldn't look at Caspar David Friedrich's Bohemian landscapes without mentioning the sky in these paintings. Friedrich hardly ever produced any that were stiller or more motionless.' (My translation.)
27 'One is departing.
On one's way to the station one is struck by the following: [...]
One crosses the plain on the local train. One notes that the bush of wild roses, to see which one sat down specially on the right side of the aisle, has been cut down.
One crosses streets, meadowed valleys, passes houses that have been pulled down as well as renovated buildings, one remembers the fate of their inhabitants, their kin.
While driving through the forest one imagines oneself transferred to Russia. [...]
One changes into the express train.' (My translation.)
28 'One will arrive.
In the parks there will still be roses, nasturtiums.
The figure on the monument will stare in the direction of the arched bridge, from where the splash of the body won't sound any louder than the rapping of two knuckles. The south wind will waft the fragrance of nasturtiums across the canal.' (My translation.)
29 The reference is to Gerhard Meier's trilogy *Toteninsel* (1979), *Borodino* (1982) and *Die Ballade vom Schneien* (1985). So strong is the 'we' reading for these *man* (one) passages that Zeller (1992) actually claims that these texts are instances of *ich/wir* (I/we) narration.
30 Manfred Jahn has kindly pointed out to me that some experimental science fiction texts actually employ reflectorized *it* in reference to a robot-protagonist. One example of this is Walter M. Miller's 'I Made You' (1954). The protagonist of 'I Made You', although initially introduced as 'it' ('It had disposed of the enemy' – Miller 1974: 485), eventually acquires a name, Grumbler, which is first mentioned on the intercom. Whereas the active Grumbler operates under the cover of 'it', 'its' human antagonist is referred to as 'the feeble thing in the cave' (ibid.). Grumbler's feelings are described by means of psycho-narration ('It hated sound and motion' – ibid.; 'And it knew the nature of the world' – ibid.: 487) and quite extensive passages of free indirect discourse: 'Tomorrow, when the enemy was gone, it would drag the trailer back to the main feeders for recharging, when the sun rose to drive the generators once again' (ibid.: 493).
31 Italics highlight instances of free indirect discourse.
32 For an example passage see Fludernik (1993a: 86).

33 Stanzel (1984b: 100–4) had analysed the first/third-person alternation in Thackeray's *Henry Esmond*, and Nischik (1991a: 161–9; published separately in 1994) discusses instances of *I/she* alternation in Atwood's short fiction, most notably in 'The War in the Bathroom' (from the Canadian edition of *Dancing Girls*).
34 Nischik (1994: 233, 240) distinguishes between *successive* and *simultaneous* pronominal alternation in texts with *invariant* focalization ('invariante Fokalisierungsinstanz'). Her examples, unlike *Henry Esmond*, are all reflector-mode narratives.
35 I here concur with Cohn's position *contra* Genette in their epistolary exchange (Cohn and Genette 1985/1992).
36 For criticism on Farah's book see Cobham (1992) and B. Richardson (1994: 318–9).
37 The third-person sections include, for instance, the thoughts of Artemio's son.
38 Even Susan Suleiman throws up her hands in despair when it comes to *Compact* (1990: 44–50).
39 See Stanzel (1984b: 104–10).
40 See Rimmon-Kenan (1992: 105–7).
41 The spelling of the title is somewhat of a puzzle. The British paperback edition which I was using has capital *H* in *Ana Historic*, but the copyright notice gives the title with small *h*: *Ana historic*, which is a spelling that keeps recurring in the critical literature, too.
42 Compare Green and LeBihan (1994) and the criticism quoted there.
43 Compare Diengott's ground-breaking discussion of this (1987).
44 Stanzel's distinction is, of course, a scalar concept *in practice*.
45 See Fludernik (1993b) for illustrations of second-person homodiegesis and heterodiegesis.
46 For further examples see Cohn (1989: 15) and Nischik (1991b). A prominent case is, of course, Ralph Ellison's *The Invisible Man* (1952).
47 Reflectoral *he* or *she* novels with unnamed protagonists are quite rare. There is Beckett's *Ill Seen Ill Said* (1981/1982) – a *she* text – and the *elle* sections in Duras's *Le Vice-consul* (1966).
48 Compare Sylvia Plath's *The Bell Jar* (1966: 22, 32), where in two different conversations Esther Greenwood is addressed first as 'Miss Greenwood' (although also as 'Elly', which is incorrect) and later as 'Esther'. See also Raymond Chandler's *Farewell, My Lovely* (1992: 17) for a first-person text in which the narrator's name is first mentioned in a telephone conversation. For the third person see, for instance, Nathalie Sarraute's *Le Planétarium* (1959), in which the identity of the first section's reflector character is clarified only in the dialogue of section 2 (Sarraute 1965: 15).
49 *The New Yorker* of 1991–93 has over 20 per cent present-tense stories. Greiner (in progress) has counted 28 present-tense stories out of 123 (= 22.7 per cent) in issues between March 1991 and February 1993. Other short story collections have even higher percentages of narrative presents. Lorrie Moore's *Self-Help* (1985) consists of present-tense stories only, although there are many imperative texts and one that uses imperatives and *will* exclusively ('The Kid's Guide to Divorce'). Among a small selection of anthologies of recent fiction, stories in the narrative present made up a percentage of 31 per cent. (In one collection the percentage was as high as 38 per cent.)
50 I.e., the narrator's description of the character's thoughts and feelings.
51 Compare my definition of the term in Chapter 2, p. 66 above.
52 See Couper-Kuhlen (1995) for recent uses of the present progressive in conversational narrative.
53 Compare my definition of these terms in Chapter 2.

54 See below under 6.3.4.
55 Ricoeur (1984b: 135).
56 On sports reports, see M.-L. Ryan (1993).
57 The term *narrative present* is used by Frey (1946).
58 Casparis (1975) offers a similar analysis.
59 Compare Fludernik (1993b).
60 See the discussion of this in Neumann (1990, 1991) and Cohn (1993).
61 See Fludernik (1993a: 89–91, 191–6).
62 Italics to mark free indirect discourse.
63 See also Benveniste's 'Les relations de temps dans le verbe français' (1966: 246; 1971: 212).
64 The novel is quoted in Gnutzmann (1983). Unfortunately this novel was only available to me in Spanish (which I do not read). The following description of the text relies on information received from Markus Schäffauer (Freiburg), whom I would like to thank for his help with Spanish literature.
65 'The very fact that every morning one would have to leave the hotel room for an hour or so to make it accessible to the chambermaid, would bring a certain regularity into one's daily schedule, which – once one had started to do some work, as was one's intention – would develop into a more or less constant daily rhythm. With the three-cooked-meals-a-day high-calorie catering at the 'Hirschen' the exercise afforded by the longer or shorter (as the case might be) walk which one would take every morning after breakfast so as not to spend the time sitting in the hotel restaurant would not be sufficient exercise, and after a day or two already one would therefore absolutely have to schedule another longer or shorter walk each late afternoon or evening, which – depending on the progress one would make with one's work – one could also shift to the time immediately after lunch or to the early afternoon.

One's first morning one would start by passing through the village in daytime, taking the road one had taken from the station the evening before, and then proceed along the main road to the cake factory KAMBLY AG at the other end of the village, and this stroll would help one to orient oneself and to get an initial impression of the village, in which one would be staying for the first time and which one would previously have known only by name.' (My translation.)
66 Another brief, nearly consistent conditional text is Richard Barlow's 'The Phone Would Ring' (1994).
67 'BITS AND PIECES FROM WHICH IT WAS NECESSARY TO EXTRACT THE UNMATCHED REMAINS OF AFFAIRS, FRAGMENTS OF ALL SORTS OF THINGS: IT MUST HAVE BEEN POSSIBLE TO RECONSTRUCT, LITTLE BY LITTLE, THIS PUZZLE-WOMAN MADE OF PIECES AND BITS' (Roche 1988: 37).
68 Compare also 7.5 below.
69 See below under 7.3, where I briefly deal with Peter Chotjewitz's novel *Die Insel* (1968).
70 Quite a few second-person texts have an initial *imaginez* command placed at the very beginning of the text: Beckett's *Imagination Dead Imagine*; Larbaud's 'Mon Plus Secret Conseil'; Jean Thibaudeau's *Imaginez la nuit*.
71 See Fludernik (1994a, 1994c).
72 For the discussion of afunctional tense alternation in reflector-mode writing see Stanzel (1981b).
73 I here disregard the case of the 'oral' historical present which operates in the shape of short-stretch tense alternations, taking up less than a paragraph (usually only a few clauses) before modulating back into the preterite (Schiffrin 1981; Fludernik 1991).
74 Narrative past tenses are highlighted by means of underlining; italics mark free indirect discourse.

7 GAMES WITH TELLERS, TELLING AND TOLD

1. Address frequently operates as such a marker of the reintroduction of a speaker function. A stunning example of this technique is Sunetra Gupta's *The Glassblower's Breath* (1993), where the discourse that was originally non-attributable eventually turns out to be the enunciation of the jealous husband.
2. I am referring to Douglas Hofstadter's concept of 'strange loops' (1979: 684–719). The term *short circuit* (*narrativer Kurzschluß*) is used by W. Wolf (1993: 356–72). For an excellent discussion of the figures of the loop and the Mobius strip in English experimental fiction see Berressem (1995). See also M.-L. Ryan's categories of 'the never-finished picture', 'the scrambled picture', 'the crazy quilt', etc. in M.-L. Ryan (1992).
3. For an excellent recent collection of essays on this genre see Engler and Müller (1994).
4. I am using the term in its non-specialized sense. (Compare Dannenberg [in progress] on a more technical definition of coincidence.)
5. On *skaz* see Chapter 5, note 1 (p. 394).
6. See Hawes (1993) for an excellent account of the significance of *Tristram Shandy* for Salman Rushdie's *Midnight's Children*.
7. In Nathalie Sarraute's *L'Usage de la parole* a similar constellation can be observed. At one point, however, the *vous* gets arrested: here a story is apparently being told involving the *vous* as a protagonist (1980: 143–4).
8. Certainly the section 'Le mot Amour' (Sarraute 1980: 67–83). The section 'Et pourquoi pas?' (ibid.: 35–45), on the other hand, may be a hypothetical scene: 'Voici deux autres interlocuteurs.'
9. See Nischik (1981) for an excellent discussion of multi-plotline structure in the novel in English.
10. See Fritz (1993).
11. See, for instance, the sequence in Act I (Stoppard 1982: 27–36).
12. Compare Goetsch (1976) for a reading that sees the two stories as parallel but separate. See also B. Richardson (1991a).
13. The letter, which constitutes Part III, is a near-verbatim version of a historical document, a letter Bonnard wrote to Henri Matisse.
14. For instance, Trout Fishing receives fan mail and writes a letter to 'Dear Ardent Admirer', signed 'Trout Fishing in America' ('A Return to the Cover of This Book'; Brautigan 1972: 76–7).
15. In fact, the 'Scotch from the restaurant' need not imply anything about the characters' location; the bottle could simply have been *bought* in the restaurant.
16. See Petersen (1992: 84–5) for a brief description.
17. 'Making preparations. Taking precautions. Having the minutes at one's disposal. Deceiving this day. Cheating the next day. Lying to an entire week. All around expectant amenities.' (My translation.)
18. The bear is also the heraldic symbol of Berlin.
19. Thanks go to Manfred Jahn for sending me a photocopy of this short story.
20. Affirmative questions would require an answer that is preceded by *not* (*Not if I can avoid it*), but negative questions are hard to come by: *But you prefer not to do manual labour?* would be possible but does not seem very convincing to me either.
21. Browning himself pretended to some ambiguity on this point, saying that he 'meant the commands were that she [the Duchess] should be put to death', but retracting this in the next sentence (Corson 1886: viii). For a recent account see Osterwalder (1992).

22 'All art constantly aspires towards the condition of music' (Pater 1980: 106).
23 Note, however, that Barth's earlier term 'literature of exhaustion' does not necesssarily coincide with late modernism but seems to characterize surfictionist writings (Barth 1967).
24 See 'Amengst menlike trees walking or trees like angels weeping nobirdy aviar soar anywing to eagle it! But rocked of agues, cliffed for aye!' (*Finnegans Wake* III, iii; Joyce 1964: 505, 16–18)
25 My translation. The second triplet uses a pun on a proverb which I could not translate literally.
26 The allusion is to a passage from Donald Barthelme's *Snow White* (1967): 'You and I, Mr. Quistgaard, are not in the same universe of discourse' (quoted McHale 1993: 167).
27 The final note on the text describes it as 'abgestorben[e] dramatisch[e] Struktur' (H. Müller 1985: 14), a 'withered dramatic structure'.
28 'A landscape between steppe and savanna, the sky Prussian blue, two huge clouds are swimming in it, as if held together by wire skeletons, or in any case of unfamiliar design, the larger one on the left could be a rubber toy animal from a funfair that has torn itself loose from its lead, or a piece of the Antarctic (viewed) on the flight home, on the horizon a flat mountain range, on the right of the landscape (there is) a tree, upon closer inspection three trees of different height, mushroom-shaped, bark to bark, perhaps (growing) from one root, the house in the forefront (looks) as if produced industrially rather than by craftsmanship, probably concrete: a window, a door, the roof hidden by the foliage of the tree which stands in front of the house, overgrowing it, it belongs to a species different from that of the group of trees in the background, its fruit is apparently edible or suitable for poisoning guests, a glass bowl on a garden table, still half in the shadow of the treetop, in it are six or seven pieces of the lemonlike fruit, from the position of the table, a rough piece of handicraft, the crossed legs are made of raw young birch stems, one can conclude that the sun, or whatever throws light on this area, is at its height at the moment of the painting, perhaps THE SUN is there always FOR ALL ETERNITY: impossible to tell from the painting if it moves, also the clouds, if they are clouds, are perhaps swimming on the spot, the wire skeleton attaching them to a speckled blue board with its random designation SKY, on a branch a bird is sitting, the leaves hiding its identity [...]' (My translation.)
29 'Blood spraying in the whirl of the tempest, which seeks the woman, fear that the mistake might happen while blinking, when the eye slits up in the moment between glance and glance, hope dwells on the edge of a knife quickly rotating with increasing attention and fatigue, a flash of insecurity born of the certainty of horror: the MURDER consists of a sex change, ALIENATION IN ONE'S OWN BODY, the knife is the wound, the neck is the hatchet, does the fallible guard belong to the design, on which apparatus has the lens been fixed that is sucking the colours from the view, in which eye socket has the retina been fixed, WHO or WHAT is asking after the painting, TO LIVE IN THE MIRROR, is this ME the man with the dancing step, his face my grave, the woman with the wound in the neck is this ME, holding the dissected bird in my right and left hands, blood on its (her?) mouth, ME the bird writing with its beak the message that points the way into the night for the murderer, ME the frozen tempest [...]' (My translation.)
30 See especially the first two stanzas, where the castle comes into view, and the final two stanzas, where the speaker's impressions of its interior and his last glimpses of the house as he turns away are described.

8 NATURAL NARRATOLOGY

1. G. Prince (1995: 80).
2. *A-referential* in the sense of having non-specific, i.e. general, reference. See below under 8.4 for further argument.
3. See Coste (1989) and, most recently, O'Neill (1994).
4. Now that the model has become reality and I can drop the inverted commas around *'natural'*, the label will be capitalized.
5. What Reid (1992: 44–6) treats as circumtextual and extratextual reading frames. See also O'Neill (1994: 121–3).
6. At the time of my final redaction of this book I had only seen Chapter 1 of Gibson's manuscript. Gibson generalizes procedures of postmodernist experimentalism which are best characterized in a poststructuralist framework and attempts to make the theoretical categories of such a poststructuralist paradigm available for the discussion of more traditional narrative, too. The toolbox that he uses most has recently been presented in fascinating comprehensiveness by Hanjo Berressem (1995).
7. In the majority of eighteenth-century texts consciousness is represented by means of dissonant psycho-narration.
8. Compare Ermarth's *Sequel to History* (1992) and McHale's excellent *Constructing Postmodernism* (1992a).
9. Compare, however, Lamarque and Olsen (1994) for a decisive separation of the notions of *literature* and *fiction*.
10. See, for instance, Mandelbaum (1993) and Aronsson and Cederborg (1994).
11. Note, particularly, the preference for the perfect tense in German report sequences (Harweg 1975a).
12. See Adams (1993), who uses a first-person narrative (*The Great Gatsby*) for demonstration, thus instituting a third level of temporal cognition (the order of Nick Carraway's experience, how he comes to learn of the story).
13. The third instalment of 'Telling in Time' is presumably soon due in *Poetics Today* but had not yet appeared when this manuscript was completed.
14. See G. Prince (1987: 64, s.v. *narrativity*). Brooks (1984/1985), Prince's first reference, does not contain a definition of narrativity. Prince also fails to mention the collection edited by Tiffeneau (1980), which uses the term in its title(!) and contains an article by Ricoeur with his explication of narrativity (*la narrativité*) as it was later incorporated into *Temps et récit*. (See Mitchell [1981] for the English version of this article.) A contemporary paper by Kloepfer (1980) defines narrativity on the basis of a structural feature, namely the dynamic interrelation of three levels of narrative rather than Chatman's two (story and discourse). Sturgess (1992) lists further roughly contemporaneous uses of the term in Keith Cohen (1979: 91–2), Hayden White (1981) – originally published in *Critical Inquiry* in 1980 – and in Scholes (1982).
15. Rimmon-Kenan (1983: 7) interprets the term as referring to 'an immanent story structure'.
16. Gerald Prince, on whose proposals I will concentrate here, also provides constructed sample sentences (1982: *passim*).
17. Compare also the discussion in Dannenberg (1995).
18. Compare G. Prince's explication of degrees of narrativity, which he identifies with degrees of telling 'a better story' (1982: 145).
19. Oddly, G. Prince cites Culler under his category of 'event description'.
20. G. Prince (1987: 58, s.v. *narrative*) explicitly excludes drama.
21. But see below under 8.4 for a more extensive discussion of situations (and descriptions thereof) as incipiently experiential narrative kernels.

22 A comparable model is proposed in Scholes (1982: 60) where he introduces *narrativity* as 'the process by which a perceiver actively constructs a story from the fictional data provided by any narrative medium'. Narrativity applied to *narration* yields *story*. Not only has the term narrativity in narratological studies been used consistently to refer to an entity or construct rather than a *process*; but Scholes also seems to locate the effects of narrativity (i.e. my narrativization) in the establishment of a story and therefore joins M.-L. Ryan in privileging plot as the central defining characteristic of narrative. See also Sturgess (1992: 14–15) on Scholes.
23 What M.-L. Ryan calls 'the unmediated narrativity of drama, movies, ballet, or of dialogue novels' (1992: 377).
24 For lack of space the various categories of *narrativity* (not *narratives*!) which are here referred to cannot be explained, and I must ask the reader to consult Ryan's essay (M.-L. Ryan 1992: 371–8).
25 Sturgess discusses White (1981) and Scholes (1982) at length.
26 See, for instance, his discussions of Max Frisch or Ingeborg Bachmann (Stanzel 1981b, 1984b: 104–5, 108).
27 Cladistics methodologically derives from biology and provides a visual model for the mapping of featural dependencies. Cladistics therefore offers a kind of a visual analogue to a statistics of feature interdependence. For details see Bonheim (1990: Chapter 9).
28 Compare recent work by Edmiston (1991), Herman (1994) and Jahn (forthcoming).
29 For another recent sketch on how traditional narratology 'does' for postmodern texts see Vitoux (1992).
30 For a discussion of the various deep-structural levels of narrative see Korte (1985) and my discussion of this issue in section 1.5 in Fludernik (1993a: 58–65). Compare also O'Neill (1994: 21).
31 The *muthos* is contrasted with *logos* which seems to cover the logical connections between plot elements (see Aristotle 1982: 1460a).
32 See also M.-L. Ryan (1992).
33 Ryan feels constrained to introduce a mode of 'instrumental narrativity' (1992: 380–1) to account for the genres of the *exemplum* or the illustrative anecdote.
34 See Adams (1993) for the distinction.
35 Compare texts like Jane Rule's *This Is Not For You* (1970). Most second-person texts, however, have existential continuity only for one of the 'interlocutors', the teller *or* the narratee. The most common case is that of a narrator who has survived and addresses her discourse to the dead narratee, as in Oriana Fallaci's *Un uomo* (1979) or Edmund White's *Nocturnes for the King of Naples* (1978). See Fludernik (1994a) for further examples.
36 This is certainly the case for Bal's and Genette's models, whose different categories of focalization are arranged schematically side by side with tense and voice in Genette, and alongside sequential ordering and characterization in Bal. (Bal has the narrator on a superior level of her model.) See Jahn (1995: 36–8) for a critique of Genette's refusal to link the various categories.
37 For the terms *homocommunicative* and *conative*, compare under 6.2 and Fludernik (1993b; 1994a, 1994c).
38 See Rimmon-Kenan (1983: 91–2). Rimmon-Kenan replaces *metadiegetic* by *hypodiegetic*, a term first introduced in Bal (1977).
39 For more recent discussions in the wake of Genette and Bal, see Berendsen (1984), Vitoux (1982, 1984), Cohan (1986), Cordesse (1988), Nelles (1990), Ronen (1990a), Edmiston (1991), Husson (1991), O'Neill (1992), Herman (1994) and Jahn (forthcoming).

40 See Chatman's recent attempt at an entirely new terminology in *Coming to Terms* (1990). For an even more recent reconceptualization see Nünning (1995a).
41a My *vision sur* corresponds to Jean Pouillon's (1946) *vision du dehors*, i.e. external focalization. His *vision par derrière* (zero focalization) is excluded from consideration.
41b On the novel vs. film see also Chatman (1980) and Scholes (1982: Chapter 4).
42 Bonheim (1982b) finds that none of the current definitional features of the short story is excluded from novelistic literature. His only positive conclusion is that short stories tend to begin *in medias res* and to prefer open endings. (See also N. Friedman [1989: 18-9].) For a recent survey of the novel vs. short story problematic see *Style* 27.3 (Fall 1993), as well as May (1976), Lohafer (1983), Lohafer and Clarey (1989) and Pasco (1991). Brooks's promising 'The Tale vs. the Novel' (1988) unfortunately does not deal with the issue of textual length or with the tricky question of definition. There are obviously too many different kinds of short fiction to fit comfortably into any *one* definition of the short story or the tale.
43 On the factor of length see the quotations collected in Goetsch (1978), as well as work by Zumthor (1983), Lohafer and Clarey (1989) and Pasco (1991).
44 See the enlightening discussion of the Griseldis story from the *Decameron* by Rossi (1985).
45 It is a moot point whether *all* short stories lend themselves to an epiphanic reading or whether only Modernist short stories can be described in these terms. If the latter, the epiphanic characterization would need to be identified as a mere period marker.
46 For detailed presentations of chronological rearrangement see Pfister (1977/ 1988) and B. Richardson (1987).
47 Indeed, some impressionist prose sounds very much like the stage directions in symbolist drama. Busch (1970: 75) quotes passages from Alphonse Daudet's novel *La Belle-Nivernaise* which evoke a scene precisely in the sketchy terms of dramatic stage directions: 'Une rue étroite comme un égout, des ruisseaux stagnants, des flaques de boue noire, des odeurs de moisi et d'eau sale sortant des allées béantes.' ('A street as narrow as a sewer, stagnant brooks, puddles of black mud, smells of mould and dirty water coming out of the wide-open avenues.' My translation.) Note the absence of finite verbs throughout the entire passage which Busch quotes, as well as the unstageability of the described objects.
48 Mulvey, for instance, presents sequences of camera moves that focus on a non-human visual perspective fixed at about a metre's height from the floor. She thereby defies the default eye-level constraint that is one of the basic conventions operative in descriptive shots.
49 An especially interesting case has recently come to my attention. In Maureen Duffy's *Love Child* (1971) neither the sex of the narrator nor that of the lover of the narrator's mother can be determined.
50 An interesting case is Robert Montgomery's *Lady in the Lake* (1946), based on Chandler's novel, in which Phillip Marlowe's point of view is constitutive of the entire film, with the exception of the very beginning of the film, several views of Marlowe in the mirror and the final scene when one again gets a view of the detective's face. (See Branigan 1992: 142-6.)
51 A recent instalment of the Austrian TV crime series *Rex* (the name of the detective's Alsatian) had a case of two murders performed (as it turned out) by a fake-invalid who, much to the viewer's surprise, was able to leave her wheelchair and even walk. The murders were filmed from a perspective that only showed an indistinct outline of the murderer's shape or concentrated on hands covered in heavy-duty gloves. The sex of the murderer was thus kept indeterminate until the final scenes of the film.

52 Overhearing asides, however, gives the audience great satisfaction and the illusion of control.
53 One can, however, also argue that each reading of the same book constitutes a separate experience.
54 For an insightful comparison of novels and films see, for instance, Chatman (1980).
55 See Alter (1990), Aston and Savona (1991), Carlson (1990) and Fischer-Lichte (1992).
56 See, e.g., Virtanen (1992). Gumbrecht (1982) presents a very interesting discourse-operational approach to text types which is based on Luckmann's constructivist model (Schütz and Luckmann 1975). His schema comprises only three meta-genres, those of narrative, description and argument.
57 Gumbrecht (1982: 207) characterizes his genres *narrative* and *argument* in terms similar to those I have employed: 'Durch *Erzählen* werden die in subjektiven Bewußtseinsabläufen vollzogenen *Thematisierungssequenzen* intersubjektiv; durch *Beschreibungen* die Ergebnisse der *Interpretation* von thematisierten Wahrnehmungsgegenständen; durch *Argumentation* werden subjektiv konstituierte *Handlungsmotive* zur intersubjektiven Übernahme bereitgestellt. Anders formuliert: *Erzählen* ist auf Intersubjektivität des *Erlebens*, *Beschreiben* auf Intersubjektivität vollzogener *Erfahrung*, Argumentieren auf Intersubjektivität des *Handelns* gerichtet.' I do not necessarily agree that description always correlates with perception; on the contrary, I have characterized instruction on the operational lines that Gumbrecht reserves for *argument*.
58 Reid (1992) is a not so successful attempt to combine economics with narrative theory.
59 See also Graver (1984: 284–6) and my discussion of the issue in Fludernik (1992c: 168–70).
60 All of these strategies, as Lanser (1995) correctly notes, are possible only in languages that fail to specify gender in the concordance of participles and adjectives. Among standard Indo-European languages German is most suited to the blurring of gender relations since it does not use the type of concordance employed in the Romance and Slavic languages, and English is also quite conformable. German and English do retain traces of gender concordance in possessive pronouns: e.g. *his/her* hat. Unlike German, English additionally requires the use of a possessive (and genderized) pronoun when referring to body parts (*he shook his head*), where German can make do with the definite article which does not reveal the subject's sex: *er schüttelte den Kopf*.
61 Nünning's level N3 in Nünning (1989a).
62 See especially 'Quand nos lèvres se parlent' ('When Our Lips Speak Together') in Irigaray (1985: 205–18) and Cixous (1981).
63 For further examples and a discussion of the issue see Fludernik (1994a, 1994c, 1994d).
64 See also the examples discussed in Korte (1989).
65 From a 'Lacanian perspective' Foucault characterizes 'a gradual shift from a politics of the discourse of the master to one of the discourse of knowledge, in which the shift from direct punishment to discipline and penalization describes the passage of the subject from slave to a disciplined and normalized surface of knowledge [...]' (Berressem 1993: 215).
66 For the dynamics of quasi-mystical self-surrender under torture see de Certeau (1986) and Scarry (1985).

IN LIEU OF AN EPILOGUE

1 See Berressem (1992: 117–8) for the 'city as body' nexus in postmodern culture.

References

TEXTS

Saints' legends

The Book of Margery Kempe. Ed. W. Butler-Bowdon. EETS O.S. 212. London: Oxford University Press, 1940.

The Early South-English Legendary or Lives of the Saints. Ms. Laud, 108, in the Bodleian Library. Ed. Carl Horstmann. EETS O.S. 87. London: Trübner & Co., 1887.

Legends of the Saints in the Scottish Dialect of the Fourteenth Century. Ed. W.M. Metcalfe. Scottish Text Society. 4 parts. London: Blackwood & Sons, 1891.

The Life of Christina of Markyate, a Twelfth-Century Recluse. Ed. and trans. C.H. Talbot. Oxford: Clarendon Press, 1987.

The Liflade ant te Passiun of Seinte Iuliene. Ed. S.R.T.O. d'Ardenne. EETS O.S. 248. Oxford: Oxford University Press, 1961.

The Lives of Women Saints of our Contrie of England, also some other liues of holie women written by some of the auncient fathers (c. 1610–1615). Ed. from MS. Stowe 949, by C. Horstmann. EETS O.S. 86. London: Trübner & Co., 1886.

Medieval English Saints' Legends. Ed. Klaus Sperk. English Texts, 6. Tübingen: Niemeyer, 1970.

The Northern Homily Cycle. See Horstmann (1881).

Seinte Marherete, the Meiden ant Martyr. Re-edited from MS. Bodley 34, Oxford and MS. Royal 17A xxvii, British Museum, by Frances M. Mack, BA PhD. EETS O.S. 193. London: Oxford University Press, 1934. Rprt. with corrections 1958.

Seinte Katerine. Re-edited from MS Bodley 34 and the other Manuscripts. Ed. S.R.T.O. d'Ardenne and E.J. Dobson. EETS S.S. 7. Oxford: Oxford University Press, 1981.

The South English Legendary. Eds Charlotte D'Evelyn and Anna J. Mill. EETS O.S. 235, 236. 1956. London: Oxford University Press, 1967. Reprint.

Three Lives from the Gilte Legende. Ed. from MS. B.L. Egerton 876, by Richard Hamer. Middle English Texts. Heidelberg: Carl Winter, 1978.

For further saints' lives see under Capgrave, Caxton, Bokenham, Julian of Norwich, Lydgate and Horstmann.

Other texts

Adam, Villiers de l'Isle. See Villiers.
Aichinger, Ilse. 'Spiegelgeschichte'. *Meine Sprache und Ich. Erzählungen.* Frankfurt am Main: Fischer, 1978. 46–54.

Aleshovsky, Yuz. 'From the Book of Final Statements'. *Partisan Review* 51 (1984): 367–74.
Anderson, Sherwood. *Winesburg, Ohio* [1919]. Penguin Classics. Harmondsworth: Penguin, 1983.
Arnold, June. *The cook and the carpenter. a novel by the carpenter.* Plainfield, VT: Daughters, Inc., 1973.
Atwood, Margaret. *Surfacing* [1972]. New Press Canadian Classics. Toronto: General Publishing Co, 1983.
Atwood, Margaret. 'The War in the Bathroom'. *Dancing Girls and Other Stories.* Toronto: McClelland and Stewart, 1977. 7–18.
Ba., Ro. *The Life of Syr Thomas More Sometymes Lord Chancellour of England.* Eds Elsie Vaughan Hitchcock and P.E. Hallett. EETS O.S. 222. Oxford: Oxford University Press, 1950.
Baker, Nicholson. *U and I.* New York: Random House, 1991.
Ballard, James G. 'Answers to a Questionnaire' [1985]. *War Fever.* London: Collins, 1990. 81–5.
Barlow, Richard. 'The Phone Would Ring'. *New Writing 3*. Eds Andrew Motion and Candice Rodd. London: Minerva, 1994. 140–5.
Barnes, Djuna. *Nightwood* [1937]. New York: New Directions, 1961.
Barth, John. *Letters* [1979]. London: Granada, 1981.
Barth, John. 'Life-Story' [1967]. *Lost in the Funhouse. Fiction for print, tape, live voice* [1968]. New York: Bantam, 1981. 116–29.
Barth, John. *Sabbatical.* London: Panther, 1982.
Barthelme, Donald. *Snow White* [1967]. New York: Atheneum, 1972.
Barthelme, Donald. 'You Are as Brave as Vincent van Gogh'. *Amateurs.* New York: Farrar, Straus & Giroux, 1976. 167–71.
Barthelme, Frederick. 'Moon Deluxe'. *The New Yorker* 57 (February 15, 1982): 41–4; Rprt. *Moon Deluxe. Stories.* New York: Penguin, 1983. 61–72.
Bayer, Konrad. *der sechste sinn. ein roman* [1966]. In *das gesamtwerk.* Reinbek bei Hamburg: Rowohlt, 1977. 335–444.
Beckett, Samuel. 'Breath' [1969]. *Collected Shorter Plays.* London: Faber & Faber, 1984. 209–11.
Beckett, Samuel. *Company.* London: Calder, 1980.
Beckett, Samuel. *Ill Seen Ill Said* [1981/1982]. In *Nohow On.* London: Calder, 1992. 55–97.
Beckett, Samuel. *Imagination Dead Imagine.* London: Calder, 1965.
Beckett, Samuel. *Not I* [1972]. In *Collected Shorter Plays.* London: Faber & Faber, 1984. 213–23.
Beckett, Samuel. 'Ping' ['Bing' 1966]. *No's Knife. Collected Shorter Prose 1946–1966.* London: Calder & Boyars, 1967. 165–8.
Beckett, Samuel. *That Time* [1975]. In *Collected Shorter Plays.* London: Faber & Faber, 1984. 225–35.
Behn, Aphra. 'Agnes de Castro' [1688]. *The Works of Aphra Behn.* Ed. Montague Summers. Vol. 5. New York: Phaeton, 1967. 209–56.
Behn, Aphra. 'The Dumb Virgin' [1698]. *The Works of Aphra Behn.* Ed. Montague Summers. Vol. 5. New York: Phaeton, 1967. 415–44.
Behn, Aphra. 'The Fair Jilt, or: The Amours of Prince *Tarquin* and *Miranda*' [1688]. *The Works of Aphra Behn.* Ed. Montague Summers. Vol. 5. New York: Phaeton, 1967. 67–124.
Behn, Aphra. 'The History of the Nun, or: The Fair Vowbreaker' [1689]. *The Works of Aphra Behn.* Ed. Montague Summers. Vol. 5. New York: Phaeton, 1967. 257–325.
Behn, Aphra. *Love-Letters Between a Nobleman and his Sister* [1684–87]. Ed. Janet Todd. In *The Works of Aphra Behn.* Vol. 2. London: William Pickering, 1993.

Behn, Aphra. 'The Lover's Watch'. *The Novels of Mrs Aphra Behn*. With an intr. by Ernest A. Baker, MA. London: Routledge/New York: Dutton, 1905. 203–69.
Behn, Aphra. 'The Lucky Mistake' [1689]. *The Works of Aphra Behn*. Ed. Montague Summers. Vol. 5. New York: Phaeton, 1967. 349–98.
Behn, Aphra. *Oroonoko* [1688]. In *The Works of Aphra Behn*. Ed. Montague Summers. Vol. 5. New York: Phaeton, 1967. 125–208.
Behn, Aphra. 'The Unfortunate Bride' [1698]. *The Works of Aphra Behn*. Ed. Montague Summers. Vol. 5. New York: Phaeton, 1967. 399–414.
Behn, Aphra. 'The Unfortunate Happy Lady: A True History' [1698]. *The Works of Aphra Behn*. Ed. Montague Summers. Vol. 5. New York: Phaeton, 1967. 35–65.
Bernhard, Thomas. *Beton*. Frankfurt: Suhrkamp, 1982.
Bernhard, Thomas. *Einfach kompliziert*. Frankfurt: Suhrkamp, 1986.
Bokenham, Osbern. *Legendys of Hooly Wummen*. Ed. from MS. Arundel 327 by Mary S. Serjeantson. EETS O.S. 206. London: Oxford University Press, 1938.
Bolt, Robert. *A Man for All Seasons* [1962]. New York: Vintage, 1990.
Borges, Jorge Luis. 'Epilogo'. *Obras completas*. Buenos Aires: Emecé, 1974. 1,141–5.
Brautigan, Richard. *Trout Fishing in America* [1967]. New York: Laurel, 1972.
Breton, André. *Nadja*. Paris: Gallimard, 1928.
Brooke-Rose, Christine. *The Christine Brooke-Rose Omnibus: Out/Such/Between/Thru*. Manchester: Carcanet, 1986.
Brown, Charles Brockden. *Edgar Huntly; or, Memoirs of a Sleepwalker* [1799]. The Masterworks of Literature Series. New Haven, College and University Press, 1973.
Burroughs, William S. *Naked Lunch* [1959]. New York: Grove, 1966.
Burt, Simon. 'Pisgah'. *New Writing 3*. Eds Andrew Motion and Candice Rodd. London: Minerva, 1994. 223–42.
Butlin, Ron. 'The Tilting Room'. *The Tilting Room*. Edinburgh: Canongate, 1983. 59–66.
Butor, Michel. *A Change of Heart*. Trans. Jean Stewart. New York: Simon & Schuster, 1959. Trans. of *La Modification*.
Butor, Michel. *La Modification*. Paris: Minuit, 1957.
Calvino, Italo. *If on a Winter's Night a Traveller* [1979]. Trans. William Weaver. London: Picador, 1982.
Capgrave, John. *The Life of St Katharine of Alexandria*. Ed. Carl Horstmann. EETS O.S. 100. 1893. Millwood, Kraus Reprint Co., 1973.
Capote, Truman. *In Cold Blood. A True Account of a Multiple Murder and Its Consequences*. New York: Random House, 1965.
Cary, Joyce. *Mister Johnson* [1939]. New York: Time Incorporated, 1962.
Caxton, William. *The Golden Legend* [*The Golden Legend or Lives of the Saints as Englished by William Caxton*, 1483]. Ed. F.S. Ellis. The Temple Classics. New York: AMS Press, 1973. From the edition of 1900, London: J.M. Dent.
Caxton, William. *Paris and Vienne. Translated from the French and printed by William Caxton* [1485]. Ed. MacEdward Leach. EETS O.S. 234. London: Oxford University Press, 1957.
The Cely Letters, 1472–1488. Ed. Alison Hanham. EETS O.S. 273. London: Oxford University Press, 1975.
Chandler, Raymond. *The Big Sleep* [1939]. London: Hamish Hamilton, 1967.
Chandler, Raymond. *Farewell, My Lovely* [1940]. London: Hamish Hamilton, 1992.
Chaucer, Geoffrey. *The Canterbury Tales*. Ed. A.C. Cawley. Everyman's Library. London: Dent, 1970.
Chaucer, Geoffrey. *The Riverside Chaucer*. Ed. Larry D. Benson. New York: Mifflin, 1987. Third edn.

Chaucer, Geoffrey. *Troilus and Criseyde*. Ed. John Warrington. Rev. and intr. Maldwyn Mills. Everyman's Library. London: Dent, 1974.
Chotjewitz, Peter O. *Die Insel. Erzählungen auf dem Bärenauge*. Reinbek bei Hamburg: Rowohlt, 1968.
Churchill, Caryl. *The Skriker*. London: Nick Hern Books, 1994.
Coetzee, J.M. *Waiting for the Barbarians* [1980]. King Penguin. Harmondsworth: Penguin, 1982.
Cohen, Leonard. *Beautiful Losers* [1966]. Toronto: McClelland & Stewart, 1991.
Collins, Wilkie. *The Woman in White* [1860]. Ed. Harvey Peter Sucksmith. London: Oxford University Press, 1975.
Cooper, Lucas. 'Class Notes'. *Sudden Fiction: American Short-Short Stories*. Eds Robert Shapard and James Thomas. Salt Lake City: Peregrine Smith, 1986. 122–5.
Coover, Robert. 'The Babysitter' [1969]. *Pricksongs and Descants. Fictions by Robert Coover*. New York: New American Library, 1970. 206–39.
Cortázar, Julio. 'Graffiti' [1979]. *We Love Glenda So Much and Other Tales*. Trans. Gregory Rabassa. New York: Knopf, 1983. 33–8.
Cortázar, Julio. *62: A Model Kit. A Novel* [1968]. Trans. Gregory Rabassa. London: Marion Boyars, 1994.
Couper-Kuhlen, Elizabeth. Corpus of conversational stories. Unpublished manuscript of transcriptions. 1994.
Davis, Lydia. 'Old Mother and the Grouch'. *Partisan Review* 60.1 (1993): 129–37.
Defoe, Daniel. *The Fortunes and Misfortunes of the Famous Moll Flanders, &c.* [1722]. Ed. G.A. Starr. London: Oxford University Press, 1971.
Defoe, Daniel. *Robinson Crusoe* [1719]. Penguin Classics. Harmondsworth: Penguin, 1985.
Deloney, Thomas. *The Works*. Ed. Merritt E. Lawlis. Bloomington: Indiana University Press, 1961.
Dickens, Charles. *Bleak House* [1853]. London: Oxford University Press, 1962.
Dickens, Charles. *Dombey and Son* [1848]. London: Oxford University Press, 1974.
Dickens, Charles. *Great Expectations* [1860–61]. The Clarendon Dickens. Oxford: Oxford University Press, 1993.
Dickens, Charles. *The Mystery of Edwin Drood* [1870]. London: Oxford University Press, 1972.
Dickens, Charles. *Our Mutual Friend* [1864–65]. London: Oxford University Press, 1952.
Dickens, Charles. *A Tale of Two Cities* [1859]. New York: Signet, 1963.
Don Tomazo, or the Juvenile Rambles of Thomas Dangerfield [1680]. In Peterson (1961): 177–289.
Dos Passos, John. *U.S.A.* [1938]. Harmondsworth: Penguin, 1978.
Drummond, William. *The History of the Lives and Reigns of The Five James's Kings of Scotland, From the Year 1423 to the Year 1542* [1655]. In *The Works* [1711]. Anglistica & Americana, 60. Hildesheim: Georg Olms, 1970. xix–116.
Duffy, Maureen. *Love Child*. New York: Knopf, 1971.
Duras, Marguerite. *La Maladie de la mort [The Sickness Unto Death]*. Paris: Minuit, 1982.
Duras, Marguerite. *Le Vice-consul*. Paris: Gallimard, 1966.
Early English Homilies from the Twelfth Century MS. Vesp. D. XIV. Ed. Rubie D.-N. Warner. EETS O.S. 152. New York: Kraus Reprint, 1971.
Echenoz, Jean. *Nous trois. Roman*. Paris: Minuit, 1992.
Edgeworth, Maria. *Castle Rackrent* [1800]. World's Classics. Oxford: Oxford University Press, 1980.
Eliot, George. *Middlemarch* [1871]. Ed. David Carroll. Oxford: Clarendon Press, 1986.

Eliot, George. *The Mill on the Floss* [1860]. Ed. Gordon S. Haight. Oxford: Clarendon Press, 1980.
Eliot, George. *Romola* [1863]. Ed. Andrew Brown. Oxford: Clarendon Press, 1993.
Fallaci, Oriana. *Un uomo*. Milan: Rizzoli, 1979.
Farah, Nuruddin. *Maps*. Pantheon Modern Writers. New York: Pantheon, 1986.
Farley, Ralph Milne. 'The House of Ecstasy'. *Alfred Hitchcock's Fireside Book of Suspense*. Ed. Alfred Hitchcock. New York: Simon & Schuster, 1947: 144–53.
Faulkner, William. *As I Lay Dying* [1930]. Harmondsworth: Penguin, 1986.
Federman, Raymond. *Double or Nothing. a real fictitious discourse*. Chicago: Swallow Press, 1971.
Fielding, Henry. *The History of the Adventures of Joseph Andrews [. . .] and An Apology for the Life of Mrs. Shamela Andrews*. London: Oxford University Press, 1970.
Fielding, Henry. *The History of Tom Jones. A Foundling* [1749]. 2 vols. Ed. Fredson Bowers. Oxford: Clarendon Press, 1974.
Fisher, John. *The English Works of John Fisher, Bishop of Rochester*. Ed. John E.B. Mayor. EETS E.S. 27. London: Trübner & Co., 1876.
Fisher, John H., Malcolm Richardson, and Jane L. Fisher. Eds. *An Anthology of Chancery English*. Knoxville, TN: University of Tennessee Press, 1984.
Floris and Blancheflour. In Sands (1993): 279–309.
Forster, E.M. *A Passage to India* [1924]. London: Edward Arnold, 1978.
Fowles, John. 'The Enigma' [1975]. *The Ebony Tower*. London: Jonathan Cape, 1984. 185–239.
Fowles, John. *A Maggot* [1985]. London: Picador, 1991.
Fowles, John. *Mantissa*. London: Jonathan Cape, 1982.
Foxe, John. *Fox's Book of Martyrs. A History of the Lives, Sufferings and Deaths of the Early Christian and Protestant Martyrs* [1563]. Ed. Byron Forbush. Clarion Classics. Grand Rapids, MI: Zondervan, 1967.
Frayn, Michael. *A Very Private Life* [1968]. London: Fontana, 1981.
Frisch, Max. 'Burleske'. *Max Frisch: Gesammelte Werke in zeitlicher Folge, 1944–1949*. Vol. 2. Frankfurt: Suhrkamp, 1976. 556–61. 12 vols.
Frisch, Max. *Mein Name sei Gantenbein* [1964]. In *Max Frisch: Gesammelte Werke in zeitlicher Folge, 1944–1949*. Vol. 5. Frankfurt: Suhrkamp, 1976. 5–320. 12 vols.
Fuentes, Carlos. 'Alma pura' [1964]. *Cuerpos y ofrendas. Antologia*. Madrid: Alianza Editorial, 1972. 101–21.
Fuentes, Carlos. *Aura* [1962]. Trans. Lysander Kemp. New York: Farrar, 1965.
Fuentes, Carlos. *A Change of Skin* [1967]. Trans. Sam Hileman. New York: Farrar, 1986.
Fuentes, Carlos. *The Death of Artemio Cruz* [1962]. Trans. Sam Hileman. New York: Farrar, 1988.
Gaines, Ernest J. 'The Sky is Gray'. *Bloodline*. New York: Norton, 1976. 83–117.
Gallant, Mavis. 'With a Capital T'. *79 Best Canadian Stories*. Eds Clark Blaise and John Metcalf. Ottawa: Oberon Press, 1979. 38–51.
Garrett, George. *The Succession. A Novel of Elizabeth and James*. New York: Doubleday, 1983.
Gascoigne, George. *The Pleasant Fable of Ferdinando Jeron[i]mi and Leonora de Valasco* [1575]. In *The Posies*. Ed. John W. Cunliffe. Cambridge: Cambridge University Press, 1907.
Gerard, John. *The Autobiography of an Elizabethan* [1609]. Trans. from the Latin by Philip Caraman. Intr. Graham Greene. London: Longmans, Green & Co., 1951.
Gibson, Margaret. 'Leaving'. *Love Stories by New Women*. Eds Charleen Swansea and Barbara Campbell. Charlotte, NC: Red Clay Books, 1978. 90–4.
Godden, Rumer. 'You Need to Go Upstairs'. *Gone. A Thread of Stories*. New York: Viking, 1968: 143–52.

Godwin, William. *Caleb Williams* [1794]. World's Classics. Oxford: Oxford University Press, 1991.
Gogol, Nikolai. 'The Overcoat' [1842]. *Diary of a Madman and Other Stories*. Penguin Classics. Harmondsworth: Penguin, 1987.
Golding, William. *The Inheritors*. London: Faber & Faber, 1955.
Goldsmith, Oliver. *The Vicar of Wakefield* [1766]. In *Collected Works of Oliver Goldsmith*. Vol. 4. Ed. Arthur Friedman. Oxford: Clarendon Press, 1966. 3–185. 5 vols.
Goytisolo, Juan. *Juan the Landless* [1973]. Trans. Helen R. Lane. London: Serpent's Tail, 1990.
Goytisolo, Juan. *Landscapes after the Battle* [1982]. Trans. Helen Lane. New York: Seaver Books, 1987.
Goytisolo, Juan. *The Virtues of the Solitary Bird* [1988]. Trans. Helen R. Lane. London: Serpent's Tail, 1991.
Grass, Günter. *Katz und Maus*. Neuwied am Rhein: Luchterhand, 1961.
Greene, Robert. *Greens Groats-worth of Wit, bought with a Million of Repentaunce* [1592–96]. In *The Life and Complete Works in Prose and Verse of Robert Greene, M.A.* Ed. Alexander B. Grosart. Vol. 12. The Luth Library. New York: Russell & Russell, 1964. 95–150.
Gupta, Sunetra. *The Glassblower's Breath* [1993]. London: Penguin, 1994.
Hall, Radclyffe. *The Well of Loneliness* [1928]. London: Virago, 1982.
Hammett, Dashiell. *The Glass Key* [1931]. London: Cassell, 1974.
Hammett, Dashiell. *The Maltese Falcon* [1930]. London: Cassell, 1974.
Handke, Peter. *Das Spiel vom Fragen oder die Reise zum sonoren Land*. Frankfurt: Suhrkamp, 1989.
Harpsfield, Nicholas. *The life and death of Sr Thomas More, knight, sometymes Lord high Chancellor of England*. EETS O.S. 186. London: Oxford University Press, 1963. Reprint.
Hawkes, John. *The Lime Twig*. New York: New Directions, 1961.
Hawkes, John. *Travesty*. New York: New Directions, 1976.
Hawthorne, Nathaniel. 'Foot-prints on the Sea-shore'. *Tales and Sketches*. New York: The Library of America, 1982. 561–70.
Hawthorne, Nathaniel. 'The Haunted Mind'. *Twice-Told Tales*. Vol. 2. Boston: Houghton Mifflin, 1900: 93–100.
Hawthorne, Nathaniel. *Hawthorne's Short Stories*. Ed. Newton Arvin. New York: Vintage, 1946.
Haywood, Eliza. *Betsy Thoughtless* [1751]. Intr. Dale Spender. London: Pandora, 1986.
Heller, Joseph. *Catch-22* [1961]. New York: Dell, 1985.
Helprin, Mark. 'North Light – A Recollection in the Present Tense'. *Ellis Island & Other Stories*. New York: Delacorte Press/Seymour Lawrence, 1981. 63–7.
Holinshed, Raphael. *Holinshed's Chronicles. Richard II 1398–1400, Henry IV, and Henry V* [1587]. Eds R.S. Wallace and Alma Hansen. Westport, CA: Greenwood Press, 1971. Rprt. 1978.
Horstmann, C. *Altenglische Legenden. Neue Folge*. Heilbronn: Henninger, 1881.
Houston, Pam. 'How to Talk to a Hunter'. *The Best American Short Stories 1990*. Selected From US and Canadian magazines by Richard Ford with Shannon Ravenel. Boston: Houghton Mifflin Co., 1990. 98–104.
Isherwood, Christopher. *A Single Man*. London: Methuen, 1964.
Ishiguro, Kazuo. *The Remains of the Day* [1989]. London: Faber & Faber, 1990.
James, Henry. *What Maisie Knew* [1897]. In *The Novels and Tales of Henry James*. New York Edition, 11. New York: Charles Scribners, 1908. Rprt. 1936.
Jandl, Ernst. *Aus der Fremde* [1979]. In *Gesammelte Werke. Band 3: Stücke und Prosa*. Ed. Klaus Srblewski. Darmstadt: Luchterhand, 1985. 255–336.

Janowitz, Tama. *Slaves of New York*. New York: Crown, 1986.
Johnson, B.S. *Albert Angelo*. London: Constable, 1964.
Jong, Erica. *Fear of Flying* [1973]. New York: Signet, 1974.
Josipovici, Gabriel. *Contre-Jour. A Triptych for Pierre Bonnard* [1982]. Manchester: Carcanet, 1986.
Josipovici, Gabriel. *In a Hotel Garden*. Manchester: Carcanet, 1993.
Josipovici, Gabriel. 'Mobius the Stripper. A Topological Exercise' [1974]. *Steps. Selected Fiction and Drama*. Manchester: Carcanet, 1990. 133–52.
Josipovici, Gabriel. 'Second Person Looking Out' [1976]. *In the Fertile Land*. Manchester: Carcanet, 1987. 15–21.
Joyce, James. *Finnegans Wake* [1939]. London: Faber & Faber, 1964.
Joyce, James. *Ulysses. A Critical and Synoptic Edition*. 3 vols. Ed. Walter Gabler. New York: Garland, 1984.
Julian of Norwich, *Revelations of Divine Love; Shewed to a devout ankress by name of Julian of Norwich*. Ed. Dom Roger Huddleston. London: Burns, Oates & Washbourne, 1952. Second edn.
Kafka, Franz. 'Eine kleine Frau'. *Sämtliche Erzählungen*. Ed. Paul Raabe. Frankfurt: Fischer, 1970. 177–84.
Kempe, Margery. *The Book of Margery Kempe*. See under Saints' legends.
Kincaid, Jamaica. *A Small Place* [1988]. New York: Penguin-Plume, 1989.
King Horn. In Sands (1993): 15–54.
King Kong. Dir. Merian C. Cooper and Ernst B. Schoedsack. RKO, 1933.
Kirkman, Francis. *The Counterfeit Lady Unveiled* [1673]. In Peterson (1961): 1–102.
Kirsch, Sarah. 'Blitz aus heiterm Himmel'. *Geschlechtertausch: Drei Geschichten über die Umwandlung der Verhältnisse*. Darmstadt: Luchterhand, 1980. 5–24.
Klabund, Alfred [Alfred Henschke]. *Rasputin. Ein Roman-Film* [1929]. In *Klabunds Gesammelte Werke in Einzelausgaben*. Vol. 2. Wien: Phaidon, 1930. 203–75.
Koch, Stephen. *Night Watch*. New York: Knopf, 1969.
La Fayette, Madame de. *La Princesse de Clèves*. Paris: Gallimard-Folio, 1972.
Langland, William. *The Vision of William Concerning Piers the Plowman. Together with Vita de Dowel, Dobet et Dobest. Secundum Wit et Resoun. Text C*. Ed. Walter W. Skeat. EETS O.S. 54. London: Oxford University Press, 1873.
Larbaud, Valéry. 'Mon Plus Secret Conseil' [1921]. *Amants, heureux amants*. In *Oeuvres complètes de Valéry Larbaud*. Vol. 6. Paris: Gallimard, 1952. 176–287.
Lardner, Ring. *Round Up. The Stories of Ring Lardner*. New York: Charles Scribner, 1929.
Lawrence, David Herbert. 'England, My England' [1915]. *The Complete Short Stories*. Vol. 2. London: William Heinemann Ltd, 1955. 303–33.
Lennox, Charlotte. *The Female Quixote* [1752]. World's Classics. Oxford: Oxford University Press, 1989.
Lessing, Doris. 'What Price the Truth'. *The New Yorker* (25 March, 1991): 30–3.
Lewis, Sinclair. 'Travel Is So Broadening'. *The Man Who Knew Coolidge. Being the Soul of Lowell Schmaltz, Constructive and Nordic Citizen*. New York: Harcourt, Brace, & Co., 1928.
Lish, Gordon. 'The Merry Chase'. *Sudden Fiction: American Short-Short Stories*. Eds Robert Shapard and James Thomas. Salt Lake City: Peregrine Smith, 1986. 50–4.
Lispector, Clarice. *The Stream of Life* [1973]. Trans. Elizabeth Lowe and Earl Fritz. Minneapolis: University of Minnesota Press, 1989.
Lodge, Thomas. *Lodge's 'Rosalynde' Being the Original of Shakespeare's 'As You Like It'* [1590]. Ed. W.W. Greg. Folcroft: Folcroft Library, 1971. Facsimile of 1907 edition (New York: Duffield/London: Chatto & Windus).
Lydgate, John. *The Minor Poems of John Lydgate*. Part I. Ed. Henry Noble MacCracken. 1911. EETS E.S. 107. London: Oxford University Press, 1962. Reprint.

McCarthy, Mary. 'The Genial Host'. *The Company She Keeps*. New York: Harcourt, 1942. 137–63.
McCarthy, Mary. *The Group*. New York: Harcourt, Brace & World, 1963.
McGahern, John. *The Dark* [1965]. London: Penguin, 1983.
McInerney, Jay. *Bright Lights, Big City*. New York: Vintage, 1984.
Maclean, Hugh, Ed. *Ben Jonson and the Cavalier Poets*. A Norton Critical Edition. New York: Norton, 1974.
Mailer, Norman. *The Armies of the Night. History as a Novel. The Novel as History*. New York: The American Library, 1968.
Mailer, Norman. *The Executioner's Song*. Boston: Little, Brown & Co., 1979.
Malamud, Bernard. 'In Kew Gardens'. *Partisan Review* 52 (1985): 536–9.
Malory, Sir Thomas. *Works*. Ed. Eugène Vinaver. London: Oxford University Press, 1971. Second edn.
Mann, Thomas. *'Death in Venice' and Seven Other Stories*. Trans. H.T. Lowe-Porter. New York: Knopf, 1936.
Mann, Thomas. *Der Erwählte* [1951]. Frankfurt: Fischer, 1980.
Mann, Thomas. 'Der Tod in Venedig' [1912]. *Der Tod in Venedig und andere Erzählungen*. Frankfurt: Fischer, 1989.
Mansfield, Katherine. 'At the Bay' [1921]. *The Stories of Katherine Mansfield*. Auckland: Oxford University Press, 1984. 441–69.
Mansfield, Katherine. 'Feuille d'Album' [1917]. *The Stories of Katherine Mansfield*. Auckland: Oxford University Press, 1984. 266–70.
Mansfield, Katherine. 'The Garden Party' [1922]. *The Stories of Katherine Mansfield*. Auckland: Oxford University Press, 1984. 487–99.
Mansfield, Katherine. 'A Lady's Maid' [1920]. *The Stories of Katherine Mansfield*. Auckland: Oxford University Press, 1984. 382–6.
Marlatt, Daphne. *Ana Historic* [1988]. London: The Women's Press, 1990.
Mason, Mike. 'The Van'. *79 Best Canadian Stories*. Eds Clark Blaise and John Metcalf. Ottawa: Oberon Press, 1979. 84–94.
Matthews, Jack. 'A Questionnaire for Rudolph Gordon'. *Sudden Fiction: American Short-Short Stories*. Eds Robert Shapard and James Thomas. Salt Lake City: Peregrine Smith, 1986. 83–7.
Meier, Gerhard. *Der schnurgerade Kanal* [1977]. In *Werke*. Vol. 2. Berne: Zytglogge, 1987. 205–374.
Merwin, W.S. *The Miner's Pale Children*. New York: Athenaeum, 1969.
Merwin, W.S. 'Simple Test'. *Scenes from American Life. Contemporary Short Fiction*. Ed. Joyce Carol Oates. New York: Random, 1973. 245–6.
Meyer, E.Y. *In Trubschachen. Roman* [1973]. Frankfurt: Suhrkamp, 1974.
Middle English Sermons. Edited from British Museum MS. Royal 18 B. xxiii. Ed. Woodburn O. Ross. EETS O.S. 209. London: Oxford University Press, 1940.
Middle English Verse Romances [1986]. Ed. Donald B. Sands. Exeter Medieval English Texts and Studies. Exeter: University of Exeter Press, 1993.
Middleton, Thomas. *A Trick to Catch the Old One* [1604–06]. In *Five Plays*. Penguin Classics. London: Penguin, 1988. 1–69.
Milburn, George. 'The Apostate'. *No More Trumps and Other Stories*. New York: Harcourt, Brace, & Co., 1933. 38–46.
Miller, Walter M., Jr. 'I Made You' [1954]. *The Penguin Science Fiction Omnibus*. Ed. Brian Aldiss. London: Penguin, 1974. 485–96.
Mirk, John. *Mirk's Festial. A Collection of Homilies, by Johannes Mirkus (John Mirk)*. Ed. Theodor Erbe. Part I. EETS E.S. 96. London: Trübner & Co., 1905.
Mistry, Rohinton. *Tales from Firozsha Baag* [1987]. London: Faber & Faber, 1992.
Moore, Lorrie. *Self-Help. Stories by Lorrie Moore* [1985]. New York: Plume, 1986.

More, Sir Thomas. *The Utopia of Sir Thomas More. Ralph Robinson's Translation with Roper's Life of More and Some of his Letters*. Ed. George Sampson. London: G. Bell & Sons, 1910.
Morris, John. *The Troubles of Our Catholic Forefathers Related by Themselves*. Third Series. London: Burns and Oates, 1877.
Morrison, Toni. *The Bluest Eye* [1970]. New York: Washington Square Press, 1972.
Morrison, Toni. *Sula* [1973]. New York: Plume, 1982.
Müller, Heiner. 'Bildbeschreibung'. *Shakespeare Factory I*. In *Texte*, 8. Berlin: Rotbuch, 1985. 7–14. 11 vols, 1974–89.
Muno, Jean. *Le Joker. Roman* [1971]. Brussels: Editions Labor, 1988.
Munro, Alice. 'Tell Me Yes or No'. *Something I've Been Meaning to Tell You. Thirteen Stories*. New York: McGraw Hill, 1974.
Mush, John. *Mr. John Mush's Life of Margaret Clitherow*. In Morris (1877): 331–440.
Nabokov, Vladimir. *Pale Fire* [1962]. Penguin Modern Classics. London: Penguin, 1988.
Nashe, Thomas. *The Unfortunate Traveller* [1594]. In *Pierce Penniless his Supplication to the Devil, Summer's Last Will and Testament, The Terrors of the Night, The Unfortunate Traveller and Selected Writings*. Ed. Stanley Wells. The Stratford-upon-Avon Library, 1. London: Edward Arnold, 1964. 187–278.
Naylor, Gloria. *Mama Day* [1988]. New York: Vintage, 1989.
Norfolk, Lawrence. *Lemprière's Dictionary*. London: Sinclair-Stevenson Ltd, 1991.
Oates, Joyce Carol. 'Master Race'. *Partisan Review* 52 (1985): 566–92.
Oates, Joyce Carol. 'You'. *The Wheel of Love and Other Stories*. New York: Vanguard, 1970. 362–87.
O'Brien, Edna. *A Pagan Place* [1970]. London: Weidenfeld & Nicolson, 1990.
O'Brien, Flann. *At-Swim-Two-Birds* [1939]. Penguin Modern Classics. Harmondsworth: Penguin, 1960.
'Of þe vox and of þe wolf'. *Middle English Humorous Tales in Verse*. Ed. George H. McKnight. Boston: Heath, 1913. 25–37.
Paltock, Robert. *Peter Wilkins* [1750]. The World's Classics. Oxford: Oxford University Press, 1990.
Papadiamantis, Alexandros. 'Oloyira sti limni [Around the Lagoon]' [1892]. *Apanta* [Collected Works]. Ed. N.D. Triantafillopoulos. Vol. 2. Athens: Ekdosis Domos, 1982. 379–400.
Parker, Dorothy. 'Lady With a Lamp' [1944]. *The Collected Dorothy Parker*. London: Duckworth, 1974. 246–53.
Paston Letters and Papers of the 15th Century. Ed. Norman Davis. Oxford: Clarendon Press, 1971.
Perec, Georges. *Les Choses*. Paris: Julliard, 1965.
Peterson, Spiro. Ed. *The Counterfeit Lady Unveiled and Other Criminal Fiction of Seventeenth-Century England*. Garden City, NY: Anchor Books, 1961.
Piercy, Marge. *He, She, and It*. New York: Knopf, 1991.
Piercy, Marge. *Woman on the Edge of Time* [1976]. London: The Women's Press, 1987.
Pinget, Robert. *The Inquisitory* [1963]. Trans. Donald Watson. London: Calder & Boyars, 1966.
Pinter, Harold. *Landscape* [1968]. In *Plays: Three*. London: Faber & Faber, 1991. 165–88.
Pinter, Harold. *Old Times* [1971]. In *Plays: Four*. London: Faber & Faber, 1993. 1–71.
Pinter, Harold. *Silence* [1969]. In *Plays: Three*. London: Faber & Faber, 1991. 189–209.
Pirsig, Robert M. *Zen and the Art of Motorcycle Maintenance. An Inquiry into Values* [1974]. New York: Bantam, 1981.

Plath, Sylvia. *The Bell Jar* [1963]. London: Faber & Faber, 1966.
Plenzdorf, Ulrich. *Die neuen Leiden des jungen W.* Frankfurt: Suhrkamp, 1973.
Plumpton Correspondence. A Series of Letters, Chiefly Domestical Written in the Reigns of Edward IV, Richard III, Henry VII, and Henry VIII. Ed. Thomas Stapleton. Camden Society, 4. London: Camden Society, 1839. New York: Johnson Reprint, 1968.
Poe, Edgar Allan. 'Bon-Bon'. *Poetry and Tales.* New York: Library of America, 1984. 164–80.
Ponge, Francis. *Pièces.* Le Grand Receuil. Paris: Gallimard, 1961.
Pynchon, Thomas. *Gravity's Rainbow.* London: Picador, 1973.
Queneau, Raymond. *Exercises de style* [1941]. Paris: Gallimard, 1963.
Radcliffe, Ann. *The Mysteries of Udolpho* [1794]. The World's Classics. Oxford: Oxford University Press, 1970.
Rao, Raja. *Kanthapura* [1970]. Delhi: Orient Paperbacks, 1993.
Richardson, Samuel. *Clarissa, or the History of a Young Lady* [1747–48]. In *The Works of Samuel Richardson.* Vol. 4. Edinburgh: Ballantyne, 1883.
Rilke, Rainer Maria. *Die Aufzeichnungen des Malte Laurids Brigge* [1910]. In *Sämtliche Werke.* Vol. 6. Frankfurt: Insel, 1966.
Robbe-Grillet, Alain. *L'Année dernière à Marienbad. Ciné-roman.* Paris: Minuit, 1961.
Robbe-Grillet, Alain. 'La chambre secrète'. *Instantanés.* Paris: Minuit, 1962. 97–109.
Robbe-Grillet, Alain. *Glissements progressifs du plaisir. Ciné-roman.* Paris: Minuit, 1974.
Robbe-Grillet, Alain. *La Jalousie.* Paris: Minuit, 1957.
Robbe-Grillet, Alain. 'La plage'. *Instantanés.* Paris: Minuit, 1962. 63–73.
Robbe-Grillet, Alain. *Le Voyeur.* Paris: Minuit, 1955.
Roche, Maurice. *Compact. Roman.* Paris: Seuil, 1966.
Roche, Maurice. *Compact.* Trans. Mark Polizzotti. New York: Knopf, 1988.
Roper, William. *The Life of Sir Thomas More* [publ. 1626]. In More (1910): 203–71.
Roth, Joseph. *Radetzkymarsch. Roman* [1932]. Cologne: Kiepenheuer & Witsch, 1989.
Roth, Joseph. *The Radetzky March.* Trans. Eva Tucker based on an earlier translation by Geoffrey Dunlop. Woodstock, NY: Overlook Press, 1983.
Rule, Jane. *This is Not for You* [1970]. Tallahassee: Naiad, 1988.
Rushdie, Salman. *Midnight's Children.* London: Jonathan Cape, 1981.
Rushdie, Salman. *Shame* [1983]. London: Picador, 1984.
Salzman, Paul. Ed. *An Anthology of Seventeenth-Century Fiction.* The World's Classics. Oxford: Oxford University Press, 1991.
Sands, Donald B. Ed. *Middle English Verse Romances* [1986]. Exeter Medieval English Texts and Studies. Exeter: University of Exeter Press, 1993.
Sarah, Robyn. 'Wrong Number'. *The Fiddlehead* 105 (Spring 1975): 22–4.
Sarraute, Nathalie. *The Planetarium* [1959]. Trans. Maria Jolas. London: Calder, 1965.
Sarraute, Nathalie. *Tu ne t'aimes pas. Roman.* Paris: Gallimard, 1989.
Sarraute, Nathalie. *L'Usage de la parole.* Paris: Gallimard, 1980.
Sarraute, Nathalie. *You Don't Love Yourself.* Trans. Barbara Wright. New York: George Braziller, 1990. Trans. of *Tu ne t'aimes pas.*
Sayers, Dorothy. *Gaudy Night* [1936]. New York: Avon, 1968.
Scharang, Michael. 'Ansprache eines Entschlossenen an seine Unentschlossenheit'. *Schluß mit dem Erzählen und andere Erzählungen.* Neuwied: Luchterhand, 1970. 35–7.
Scheerbart, Paul. *Rakkóx der Billionär. Protzenroman* [1900]. Frankfurt: Insel, 1976.

Senesi, Mauro. 'The Giraffe'. *Harper's Magazine* 226 (no. 1352, January 1963): 80–2.
Settle, Elkanah. *The Complete Memoirs of the Life of That Notorious Impostor Will. Morrell* [1694]. In Peterson (1961): 291–372.
Sidney, Sir Philip. *The Countess of Pembroke's Arcadia (The New Arcadia)* [1593]. Ed. Victor Skretkowicz. Oxford: Clarendon Press, 1987.
Sidney, Sir Philip. *The Old Arcadia*. The World's Classics. Oxford: Oxford University Press, 1994.
Silko, Leslie. *Ceremony* [1977]. New York: Penguin, 1988.
Silvain, Pierre. *Les Éoliennes*. Paris: Mercure de France, 1971.
Small, Judith. 'Body of Work'. *The New Yorker* (July 8, 1991): 30–2.
Smith, Lillian. *Strange Fruit*. New York: Reynal & Hitchcock Publ., 1944.
Sontag, Susan. *Brother Carl; a filmscript*. New York: Farrar, Straus & Giroux, 1974.
Sontag, Susan. *A Duet for Cannibals. A screenplay* [1970]. London: Allen Lane, 1974.
Sontag, Susan. *The Volcano Lover*. New York: Farrar, Straus, Giroux, 1992.
Spark, Muriel. *The Driver's Seat*. New York: Knopf, 1970.
Stapleton, Thomas. *The Life and Illustrious Martyrdom of Sir Thomas More* [1588/1612]. Trans. from the Latin of Philip E. Hallett, ed. and annotated by E.E. Reynolds. London: Burns & Oates, 1966.
Stein, Gertrude. *The Autobiography of Alice B. Toklas* [1933]. New York: Vintage, 1990.
Stein, Gertrude. *Four Saints in Three Acts* [1929]. In *Selected Writings of Gertrude Stein*. Ed. Carl Van Vechten. New York: Vintage, 1972. 511–40.
Stein, Gertrude. *Tender Buttons* [1914]. In *Selected Writings of Gertrude Stein*. Ed. Carl Van Vechten. New York: Vintage, 1972. 458–509.
Stein, Gertrude. *Three Lives* [1909]. New York: Vintage, 1986.
Stoppard, Tom. *Travesties* [1975]. London: Faber & Faber, 1982.
Stout, Rex. *How Like a God*. New York: Vanguard, 1929.
Strindberg, August. *The Stronger. A Scene* [1888]. Trans. Edwin Bjorkman. In *Fifty One-Act Plays*. Ed. Constance M. Martin. London: Gollancz, 1934.
Styron, William. *Lie Down in Darkness*. Indianapolis: Bobbs-Merrill, 1951. 9–11.
Suarez, Virgil. *Latin Jazz*. New York: Morrow, 1989.
Sukenick, Ronald. *The Death of the Novel and Other Stories*. New York: Dial, 1969.
Survey of English Usage, University College London, Gower Street.
Terkel, Studs. *'The Good War.' An Oral History of World War Two* [1984]. New York: Ballantine, 1990.
Terkel, Studs. *Race. How Blacks and Whites Think and Feel About the American Obsession*. New York: New Press, 1992.
Thibaudeau, Jean. *Imaginez la nuit. Roman*. 'Tel Quel'. Paris: Seuil, 1968.
Thibaudeau, Jean. *Une cérémonie royale*. Paris: Minuit, 1960.
Thompson, Kent. 'Shotgun'. *Canadian Short Stories. Third Series*. Toronto: Oxford University Press, 1978. 295–311.
Thorpe, Adam. *Ulverton*. London: Secker & Warburg, 1992.
Thurber, James. 'You Could Look it Up' [1941]. *My World – And Welcome To It*. New York: Harcourt, Brace, & World, 1969. 85–110.
Tomlinson, Charles. *Collected Poems*. Oxford: Oxford University Press, 1985.
Tournier, Michel. 'The Fetishist'. *Partisan Review* 51 (1984): 327–46.
Tournier, Michel. *Vendredi ou les Limbes du Pacifique*. Paris: Gallimard, 1967.
Updike, John. 'Flight' [1959]. *Pigeon Feathers and Other Stories*. New York: Knopf, 1962. 49–73.
Updike, John. 'How To Love America and Leave It at the Same Time'. *Problems and Other Stories*. New York: Knopf, 1979. 40–6.

Vanasco, Alberto. *Sin embargo Juan vivía* [*And Juan Lived After All*]. Buenos Aires: HIGO Club, 1947.
Vargas Llosa, Mario. *La casa verde* [*The Green Mansion*]. Barcelona: Editorial Seix Barral SA, 1965.
Villiers de L'Isle-Adam, Philippe-Auguste Mathias de. *Axël* [1885–86]. In *Oeuvres Complètes*. Vol. 2. Ed. Alan Raitt. Bibliothèque de la Pléiade. Paris: Gallimard, 1986. 531–677.
Voragine, Jacobus a. *Jacobi a Voragine Legenda Aurea vulgo historia lombardica dicta*. Ed. Th. Graesse. 7 vols. Lipsiae: Impensis librariae Arnoldianae, 1850.
Walpole, Horace. *The Castle of Otranto* [1765]. London: Oxford University Press, 1964.
Walter, Otto F. *Die ersten Unruhen. Ein Konzept.* Reinbek: Rowohlt, 1972.
Warren, Robert Penn. *All the King's Men* [1946]. San Diego: Harcourt Brace Jovanovich, 1982.
Weldon, Fay. *The Cloning of Joanna May*. London: Collins, 1989.
Weldon, Fay. *Female Friends* [1974]. Chicago: Academy, 1988.
Weldon, Fay. *The Life and Loves of a She-Devil* [1983]. New York: Balantine, 1990.
Weldon, Fay. 'Weekend' [1978]. *Watching Me, Watching You*. London: Sceptre/Hodder & Stoughton, 1993. 183–201.
Welty, Eudora. *The Golden Apples* [1949]. In *The Collected Stories of Eudora Welty*. New York: Penguin, 1983. 259–461.
Werfel, Franz. *Das Lied von Bernadette* [1941]. Frankfurt: Fischer, 1992.
White, Edmund. *Nocturnes for the King of Naples*. New York: St Martin's, 1978.
Wiechert, Ernst. *Die Majorin* [1934]. Frankfurt: Ullstein, 1990.
Wilder, Thornton. *Our Town* [1938]. In *Three Plays*. London: Longmans Green & Co., 1958. 1–103.
Winterson, Jeanette. *Written on the Body* [1992]. London: Vintage, 1993.
Wittig, Monique. *Le Corps lesbien*. Paris: Minuit, 1973.
Wittig, Monique. *L'Opoponax*. Paris: Minuit, 1964.
Wittig, Monique. *The Opoponax*. Trans. Helen Weaver. London: Peter Owen, 1966.
Wohmann, Gabriele. 'Fahrplan' [1968]. *Gegenangriff*. Neuwied: Luchterhand, 1972. 145–8.
Wohmann, Gabriele. 'Gegenangriff' [1971]. *Gegenangriff*. Neuwied: Luchterhand, 1972. 161–81.
Wohmann, Gabriele. 'Selbstverteidigung' [1971]. *Gegenangriff*. Neuwied: Luchterhand, 1972. 132–44.
Wolf, Christa. *Kindheitsmuster* [1976]. Frankfurt: Luchterhand, 1988.
Wolf, Christa. *A Model Childhood*. Trans. Ursula Molinaro and Hedwig Rappolt. New York: Farrar, Straus, Giroux, 1980. Trans. of *Kindheitsmuster*.
Woolf, Virginia. *Jacob's Room* [1922]. London: The Hogarth Press, 1976.
Woolf, Virginia. 'Kew Gardens' [1919]. *A Haunted House and Other Short Stories*. New York: Harcourt Brace Jovanovich, 1972. 28–36.
Woolf, Virginia. *The Waves* [1931]. London: The Hogarth Press, 1963.
Zamyatin, Yevgeny. *We* [1924]. Trans. Bernard Guilbert Guerney. London: Jonathan Cape, 1970.

CRITICISM

Adams, Jon-K. (1989) 'Causality and Narrative'. *Journal of Literary Semantics* 18: 149–62.
Adams, Jon-K. (1993) 'Narrative Explanation. Aspects of a Theory of Narrative Discourse'. Habilitation, University of Freiburg, Germany.
Adato, Albert (1979) 'Unanticipated Topic Continuations'. *Human Studies* 2: 171–86.

References 419

Aercke, Kristiaan P. (1988) 'Theatrical Background in English Novels of the Seventeenth Century'. *Journal of Narrative Technique* 18: 120-36.
Alter, Jean (1990) *A Socio-Semiotic Theory of Theatre*. Philadelphia: University of Pennsylvania Press.
Aristotle (1982) *Aristotelous peri poiètikès/The Poetics*. With an English translation by W. Hamilton Fyfe. Loeb Classical Library, 199. London: Heinemann.
Aronsson, Karin, and Ann-Christin Cederborg (1994) 'Conarration and Voice in Family Therapy: Voicing, Devoicing and Orchestration'. *Text* 14.3: 345-70.
Aston, Elain, and George Savona (1991) *Theatre as Sign System: A Semiotics of Text and Performance*. London: Routledge.
Bäuml, Franz H. (1985) 'The Theory of Oral-Formulaic Composition and the Written Medieval Text'. In J.M. Foley (1985a): 29-45.
Bal, Mieke (1977) *Narratologie. Essais sur la signification narrative dans quatre romans modernes*. Paris: Klincksieck.
Bal, Mieke (1985) *Narratology. Introduction to the Theory of Narrative*. Trans. by Christine van Boheemen. Toronto: University of Toronto Press.
Banfield, Ann (1982) *Unspeakable Sentences. Narration and Representation in the Language of Fiction*. Boston: Routledge & Kegan Paul.
Banfield, Ann (1987) 'Describing the Unobserved: Events Grouped Around an Empty Centre'. In Fabb et al. (1987): 265-85.
Barth, John (1967) 'The Literature of Exhaustion'. *The Atlantic Monthly* 220 (August): 29-34. Rprt. *The Novel Today*. Ed. Malcolm Bradbury. Contemporary Writers in Modern Fiction. Manchester: Manchester University Press, 1977. 70-83.
Barth, John (1980) 'The Literature of Replenishment. Postmodern Fiction'. *The Atlantic Monthly* 245 (January): 65-71.
Barthes, Roland (1968) 'L'Effet de réel'. *Communications* 11: 84-9.
Barthes, Roland (1978) *Prétexte: Roland Barthes*. Paris: Union générale d'éditions.
Barthes, Roland (1981) *Camera Lucida: Reflections on Photography* [1980]. Trans. Richard Howard. New York: Hill & Wang.
Barthes, Roland (1982) 'Le discours de l'histoire'. *Poétique* no. 49: 15-21.
Barthes, Roland (1984a) *Essais critiques IV. Le Bruissement de la langue*. Paris: Seuil.
Barthes, Roland (1984b) 'La mort de l'auteur'. In Barthes (1984a): 61-7.
Baudrillard, Jean (1981) 'La précession des simulacres'. *Simulacres et simulation*. Débats. Paris: Galilée, 9-68.
Baudrillard, Jean (1988) *Selected Writings*. Ed. Mark Poster. Stanford, CA: Stanford University Press.
Bauer, Gero (1970) *Studien zum System und Gebrauch der Tempora in der Sprache Chaucers und Gowers*. Wiener Beiträge zur englischen Philologie, 73. Vienna: Braumüller.
Bauman, Richard (1986) *Story, Performance, and Event. Contextual Studies of Oral Narrative*. Cambridge Studies in Oral and Literate Culture. Cambridge: Cambridge University Press.
Bell, David F. (1993) *Circumstances. Chance in the Literary Text*. Lincoln, NE: University of Nebraska Press.
Bender, John (1987) *Imagining the Penitentiary. Fiction and the Architecture of Mind in Eighteenth-Century England*. Chicago: University of Chicago Press.
Bender, John (1995) 'Making the World Safe for Narratology: A Reply to Dorrit Cohn'. *New Literary History* 26.1: 29-34.
Bentham, Jeremy (1791) *Panopticon; or, the Inspection-House*. Dublin: T. Payne.
Benveniste, Emile (1966) *Problèmes de linguistique générale, 1*. Paris: Gallimard.
Benveniste, Emile (1971) *Problems in General Linguistics*. Miami Linguistics Series, 8. Coral Gables, FL: University of Miami Press.

Berendsen, Marjet (1984) 'The Teller and the Observer. Narration and Focalization in Narrative Texts'. *Style* 18.2: 140–58.
Bernstein, Charles (1986) *Content's Dream. Essays 1975–1984*. Los Angeles: Sun and Moon Press.
Berressem, Hanjo (1992) 'The City as Text: Some Aspects of New York in Contemporary Art and Fiction'. *Amerikastudien/American Studies* 37: 107–21.
Berressem, Hanjo (1993) *Pynchon's Poetics. Interfacing Theory and Text*. Urbana, IL: University of Illinois Press.
Berressem, Hanjo (1995) 'Moebius-Strips and Time-Loops: Topological and Temporal Metaphors in Twentieth-Century American Art and Literature'. Habilitation, University of Aachen.
Bertinetto, Pier Marco (1993) 'Due tipi di Presente "storico" nella prosa letteraria'. *Omaggio a Gianfranco Folena*. Eds M.A. Cortelazzo, E. Leso, P.V. Mengaldo, G. Peron and L. Renzi. Padua: Editoriale programma, 2, 327–44.
Biber, Douglas (1988) *Variation across Speech and Writing*. Cambridge: Cambridge University Press.
Black, Elizabeth (1989) 'The Nature of Fictional Discourse: A Case Study'. *Applied Linguistics* 10.3: 281–93.
Blumenfeld-Kosinski, Renate, and Timea Szell (1991) *Images of Sainthood in Medieval Europe*. Ithaca, NY: Cornell University Press.
Bolinger, Dwight (1976) 'Meaning and Memory'. *Forum linguisticum* 1: 1–14.
Bolinger, Dwight (1977) *Meaning and Form*. London: Longman.
Bond, Clinton (1994) 'Representing Reality: Strategies of Realism in the Early English Novel'. *Eighteenth-Century Fiction* 6.2: 121–40.
Bonheim, Helmut (1982a) 'Conative Solicitude and the Anaphoric Pronoun in the Canadian Short Story'. *Sprachtheorie und angewandte Linguistik. Festschrift für Alfred Wollmann zum 60. Geburtstag*. Ed. Werner Wolte. Tübinger Beiträge zur Linguistik, 195. Tübingen: Narr. 77–86.
Bonheim, Helmut (1982b) *The Narrative Modes. Techniques of the Short Story*. Cambridge, UK: D.S. Brewer.
Bonheim, Helmut (1983) 'Narration in the Second Person'. *Recherches anglaises et américaines* 16: 69–80.
Bonheim, Helmut (1990) *Literary Systematics*. Cambridge, UK: D.S. Brewer.
Booth, Wayne C. (1983) *The Rhetoric of Fiction* [1961]. Chicago and London: Chicago University Press. Second edn.
Bordwell, David (1985) *Narration in the Fiction Film*. Madison, WI: University of Wisconsin Press.
Bordwell, David (1989) *Making Meaning. Inference and Rhetoric in the Interpretation of Cinema*. Cambridge, MA: Harvard University Press.
Bourdieu, Pierre (1986) *Outline of a Theory of Practice* [1972]. Trans. Richard Nice. Cambridge Studies in Social Anthropology, 16. Cambridge: Cambridge University Press.
Boureau, Alain (1986) 'Les structures narratives de la *Legenda aurea*: de la variation au grand chant sacré'. *Legenda Aurea: Sept Siècles de Diffusion. Actes du colloque international sur la* Legenda aurea: *texte latin et branches vernaculaires à l'Université de Québec à Montréal 11–12 mai 1983*. Ed. Brenda Dunn-Lardeau. Montreal: Editions Bellarmin/Paris, 57–76.
Branigan, Edward (1992) *Narrative Comprehension and Film*. London: Routledge.
Bremond, Claude (1973) *Logique du récit*. Paris: Seuil.
Bremond, Claude, Jacques Le Goff, and Jean-Claude Schmitt (1982) *L' «Exemplum»*. Typologie des Sources du moyen âge occidental. Fasc. 40. Turnhout, Belgium: Brepols, 1–164.
Brinkmann, Richard (1969), ed., *Begriffsbestimmung des literarischen Realismus*. Darmstadt: Wissenschaftliche Buchgesellschaft.

Brinkmann, Richard (1977) *Wirklichkeit und Illusion. Studien über Gehalt und Grenzen des Begriffs Realismus für die erzählende Dichtung des neunzehnten Jahrhunderts*. Tübingen: Niemeyer. Third edn.
Brinton, Laurel J. (1992) 'The Historical Present in Charlotte Brontë's Novels: Some Discourse Functions'. *Style* 26.2: 221–44.
Broich, Ulrich (1983) 'Gibt es eine "neutrale Erzählsituation"?' *Germanisch-Romanische Monatsschrift* 33: 129–45.
Bronzwaer, W.J.M. (1970) *Tense in the Novel. An Investigation of Some Potentialities of Linguistic Criticism*. Groningen: Wolters-Noordhoff.
Bronzwaer, W.J.M. (1978) 'Implied Author, Extradiegetic Narrator and Public Reader: Gérard Genette's Narratological Model and the Reading Version of *Great Expectations*'. *Neophilologus* 63: 1–18.
Brooks, Peter (1985) *Reading for the Plot. Design and Intention in Narrative* [1984]. New York: Vintage.
Brooks, Peter (1988) 'The Tale vs. The Novel'. *Novel* 21.2-3: 285–92.
Bublitz, Wolfram (1988) *Supportive Fellow Speakers and Cooperative Conversations*. Amsterdam: Benjamins.
Bublitz, Wolfram (1989) 'Careless or Cooperative? Repetition in Spoken Discourse'. Paper read at Vienna University.
Bühler, Karl (1934) *Sprachtheorie. Die Darstellungsfunktionen der Sprache*. Jena: Gustav Fischer.
Bugge, John (1975) *Virginitas. An Essay in the History of a Medieval Ideal*. International Archives of the History of Ideas, Series Minor, 17. The Hague: Nijhoff.
Burgess, Anthony (1972) 'The *Ulysses* Sentence'. *James Joyce Quarterly* 9: 423–35.
Burke, Peter (1969) *The Realist Sense of the Past*. New York: St Martin's Press.
Busch, Frieder (1970) 'Katherine Mansfield and Literary Impressionism in France and Germany'. *Arcadia* 5: 58–76.
Button, Graham, and John R.E. Lee (1987), eds, *Talk and Social Organization*. Intercommunication, 1. Clevedon, Avon (England): Multilingual Matters Ltd.
Campbell, Joseph, and Henry Morton Robinson (1986) *A Skeleton Key to Finnegans Wake. Joyce's Masterwork Analyzed* [1944]. New York: Penguin.
Carlson, Marvin (1990) *Theatre Semiotics: Signs of Life*. Bloomington: Indiana University Press.
Casparis, Christian Paul (1975) *Tense Without Time. The Present Tense in Narration*. Schweizer Anglistische Arbeiten 84. Berne: Francke.
Centineo, Giulia (1991) 'Tense Switching in Italian: The Alternation Between *passato prossimo* and *passato remoto* in Oral Narratives'. In Fleischman and Waugh (1991): 55–85.
Cerquiglini, Bernard (1981) *La Parole médiévale. Discours, syntaxe, texte*. Paris: Minuit.
de Certeau, Michel (1986) *Heterologies. Discourse on the Other*. Trans. Brian Massumi. Theory and History of Literature, 17. Minneapolis: University of Minnesota Press.
de Certeau, Michel (1988) *The Writing of History* [1975]. New York: Columbia University Press.
Chafe, Wallace L. (1968) 'Idiomaticity as an Anomaly in the Chomskyan Paradigm'. *Foundations of Language* 4: 109–25.
Chafe, Wallace L. (1973) 'Language and Memory'. *Language* 49: 266–81.
Chafe, Wallace L. (1977a) 'Creativity in Verbalization and Its Implications for the Nature of Stored Knowledge'. In Freedle (1977): 41–55.
Chafe, Wallace L. (1977b) 'The Recall and Verbalization of Past Experience'. *Current Issues in Linguistic Theory*. Ed. Roger W. Cole. Bloomington, IN: Indiana University Press, 215–46.

Chafe, Wallace L. (1979) 'The Flow of Thought and the Flow of Language'. In Givón (1979): 159–81.
Chafe, Wallace L. (1980), ed., *The Pear Stories. Cognitive, Cultural, and Linguistic Aspects of Narrative Production*. Advances in Discourse Processes, 3. Norwood, NJ: Ablex.
Chafe, Wallace L. (1987) 'Cognitive Constraints on Information Flow'. *Coherence and Grounding in Discourse*. Ed. Russell Tomlin. Amsterdam: John Benjamins, 21–51.
Chafe, Wallace L. (1990a) 'Repeated Verbalizations as Evidence for the Organization of Knowledge'. *Proceedings of the XIVth International Congress of Linguists, Berlin 1987*. Ed. Werner Bahner. Berlin: Akademie Verlag, 57–69.
Chafe, Wallace L. (1990b) 'Some Things That Narratives Tell Us About the Mind'. *Narrative Thought and Narrative Language*. Eds Bruce K. Britton and Anthony D. Pellegrini. Hillsdale, NJ: Lawrence Erlbaum, 79–98.
Chafe, Wallace L. (1994) *Discourse, Consciousness, and Time. The Flow and Displacement of Conscious Experience in Speaking and Writing*. Chicago: University of Chicago Press.
Chambers, Ross (1984) *Story and Situation. Narrative Seduction and the Power of Fiction*. Theory and History of Literature, 12. Minneapolis: University of Minnesota Press.
Chambers, Ross (1991) *Room for Maneuver. Reading Oppositional Narrative*. Chicago: Chicago University Press.
Chase, Cynthia (1978) 'The Decomposition of the Elephants: Double-Reading *Daniel Deronda*'. *PMLA* 93: 215–27.
Chatman, Seymour (1978) *Story and Discourse. Narrative Structure in Fiction and Film*. Ithaca: Cornell University Press.
Chatman, Seymour (1980) 'What Novels Can Do That Films Can't (and Vice Versa)'. *Critical Inquiry* 7: 121–40.
Chatman, Seymour (1986) 'Characters and Narrators. Filter, Center, Slant, and Interest-Focus'. *Poetics Today* 7.2: 189–224.
Chatman, Seymour (1990) *Coming to Terms. The Rhetoric of Narrative in Fiction and Film*. Ithaca, NY: Cornell University Press.
Cixous, Hélène (1981) 'The Laugh of the Medusa' [1976]. In Marks and Courtivron (1981): 245–64.
Clanchy, M.T. (1970) 'Remembering the Past and the Good Old Law'. *History* 55: 165–76.
Clanchy, M.T. (1979) *From Memory to Written Record. England 1066–1307*. London: Edward Arnold.
Cobham, Rhonda (1992) 'Misgendering the Nation: African Nationalist Fictions and Nuruddin Farah's *Maps*'. *Nationalisms and Sexualities*. Eds Andrew Parker, Mary Russo, Doris Sommer and Patricia Yaeger. New York: Routledge, 42–59.
Cohan, Steven (1986) 'A Review Essay: Point of View in Narrative'. *Modern Language Studies* 16.3: 345–50.
Cohen, Keith (1979) *Film and Fiction*. New Haven, CT: Yale University Press.
Cohn, Dorrit (1978) *Transparent Minds. Narrative Modes for Presenting Consciousness in Fiction*. Princeton, NJ: Princeton University Press.
Cohn, Dorrit (1981) 'The Encirclement of Narrative: On Franz Stanzel's *Theorie des Erzählens*'. *Poetics Today* 2.2: 157–82.
Cohn, Dorrit (1983) 'The Second Author of "Der Tod in Venedig"'. *Probleme der Moderne. Studien zur deutschen Literatur von Nietzsche bis Brecht. Festschrift für Walter Sokel*. Eds Benjamin Bennett, Anton Kaes and William J. Lillyman. Tübingen: Niemeyer, 223–45.
Cohn, Dorrit (1989) 'Fictional *versus* Historical Lives: Borderlines and Borderline Cases'. *The Journal of Narrative Technique* 19.1: 3–30.

Cohn, Dorrit (1990) 'Signposts of Fictionality: A Narratological Approach'. *Poetics Today* 11.4: 775–804.
Cohn, Dorrit (1993) '"I doze and I wake": The Deviance of Simultaneous Narration'. *Tales and 'their telling difference'. Zur Theorie und Geschichte der Narrativik. Festschrift zum 70. Geburtstag von Franz K. Stanzel*. Eds Herbert Foltinek, Wolfgang Riehle and Waldemar Zacharasiewicz. Heidelberg: Winter, 9–23.
Cohn, Dorrit (1995a) 'Optics and Power in the Novel'. *New Literary History* 26.1: 3–20.
Cohn, Dorrit (1995b) 'Reply to John Bender and Mark Seltzer'. *New Literary History* 26.1: 35–7.
Cohn, Dorrit, and Gérard Genette (1992) 'A Narratological Exchange' [1985]. In Fehn *et al.* (1992): 258–66.
Cole, Peter (1981), ed., *Radical Pragmatics*. New York: Academic Press.
Cordesse, Gérard (1988) 'Narration et focalisation'. *Poétique* no. 76: 487–98.
Cornis-Pope, Marcel (1991) *Hermeneutic Desire and Critical Rewriting. Narrative Interpretation in the Wake of Poststructuralism*. London: Macmillan. New York: St Martin's Press, 1992.
Corson, Hiram (1886) *An Introduction to the Study of Robert Browning's Poetry. Subtlest Assertor of the Soul in Song*. Boston: D.C. Heath.
Coste, Didier (1989) *Narrative as Communication*. Theory and History of Literature, 64. Minneapolis: University of Minnesota Press.
Costello, Bonnie (1982) 'John Ashbery and the Idea of the Reader'. *Contemporary Literature* 23: 493–514.
Couper-Kuhlen, Elizabeth (1988) 'On the Temporal Interpretation of Postposed *When*-Clauses in Narrative Discourse'. *Papers on Language and Mediaeval Studies Presented to Alfred Schopf*. Eds Richard Matthews and Joachim Schmole-Rostosky. Neue Studien zur Anglistik und Amerikanistik, 37. Frankfurt: Lang, 363–72.
Couper-Kuhlen, Elizabeth (1994) Corpus of conversational stories. Unpublished manuscript of transcriptions.
Couper-Kuhlen, Elizabeth (1995) 'On the Foregrounded Progressive in American Conversational Narrative: A New Development?' *Anglistentag 1994 Graz. Proceedings*. Eds Wolfgang Riehle and Hugo Keiper. Tübingen: Niemeyer. 229–45.
Couturier, Maurice (1991) *Textual Communication. A Print-based Theory of the Novel*. London: Routledge.
Crewe, Jonathan (1990) *Trials of Authorship. Anterior Forms and Poetic Reconstruction from Wyatt to Shakespeare*. Berkeley: University of California Press.
Culler, Jonathan (1975) *Structuralist Poetics. Structuralism, Linguistics and the Study of Literature*. London: Routledge & Kegan Paul.
Culler, Jonathan (1980) 'Fabula and Sjuzhet in the Analysis of Narrative. Some American Discussions'. *Poetics Today* 1.3: 27–37.
Dannenberg, Hilary P. (1995) 'Story and Character Patterning in Jane Austen's Plots'. *Sprachkunst* 26.1: 75–103.
Dannenberg, Hilary P. (in progress) 'Coincidence and Parallelism in the Novel'. Habilitation, University of Freiburg, Germany.
Davis, Lennard J. (1983) *Factual Fictions. The Origins of the English Novel*. New York: Columbia University Press.
Day, Robert Adams (1966) *Told in Letters. Epistolary Fiction Before Richardson*. Ann Arbor, MI: University of Michigan Press.
DeJean, Joan (1991) *Tender Geographies: Women and the Origins of the Novel in France*. New York: Columbia University Press.
Derrida, Jacques (1977a) 'Signature, Event, Context'. *Glyph* 1: 172–97.
Derrida, Jacques (1977b) 'Limited Inc'. *Glyph* 2: 162–254.

Diengott, Nilli (1987) 'The Mimetic Language Game and Two Typologies of Narrators'. *Modern Fiction Studies* 33.3: 523–34.
van Dijk, Teun A. (1985), ed., *Handbook of Discourse Analysis. I–IV.* Orlando: Academic Press.
Dressler, Wolfgang U. (1989) *Semiotische Parameter einer textlinguistischen Natürlichkeitstheorie.* Österreichische Akademie der Wissenschaften. Philosophisch-Historische Klasse. Sitzungsberichte, 529. Vienna: Verlag der ÖAW.
Dressler, Wolfgang U. (1990) 'The Cognitive Perspective of "Naturalist" Linguistic Models'. *Cognitive Linguistics* 1.1: 75–98.
Dressler, Wolfgang U. (forthcoming) 'Parallelisms between Natural Textlinguistics and other components of Natural Linguistics'. In Dziubalska-Kołaczyk (forthcoming).
Dressler, Wolfgang U., Willi Mayerthaler, Oswald Panagl, and Wolfgang U. Wurzel (1987) *Leitmotifs in Natural Morphology.* Studies in Language Companion Series (SLCS), 10. Amsterdam: John Benjamins.
Dry, Helen Aristar (1981) 'Sentence Aspect and the Movement of Narrative Time'. *Text* 1.3: 233–40.
Dry, Helen Aristar (1983) 'The Movement of Narrative Time'. *Journal of Literary Semantics* 12.2: 19–53.
Duffy, Maureen (1977) *The Passionate Shepherdess. Aphra Behn, 1640–1689.* London: Cape.
Duncan, Starkey (1974) 'On the Structure of Speaker–Auditor Interaction During Speaking Turns'. *Language in Society* 2: 161–80.
Dunn-Lardeau, Brenda (1986), ed., *Legenda Aurea: Sept Siècles de Diffusion. Actes du colloque international sur la* Legenda aurea: *texte latin et branches vernaculaires à l'Université de Québec à Montréal 11–12 mai 1983.* Montreal: Editions Bellarmin/Paris: Librairie J. Vrin.
Duyfhuizen, Bernard (1992) *Narratives of Transmission.* London: Associated University Presses.
Dziubalska-Kołaczyk, Katarzyna (forthcoming), ed., *Naturalness Within and Across Components. Papers from the Kraków Workshop on Natural Linguistics.* Sprachtypologie und Universalienforschung (STUF). Leipzig: Akademie Verlag.
Edmiston, William F. (1989) 'Focalization and the First-Person Narrator: A Revision of the Theory'. *Poetics Today* 10.4: 729–44.
Edmiston, William F. (1991) *Hindsight and Insight. Focalization in Four Eighteenth-Century French Novels.* University Park, PA: Pennsylvania State University Press.
Ehlich, Konrad (1980), ed., *Erzählen im Alltag.* Frankfurt: Suhrkamp.
Ehrlich, Susan (1990) *Point of View. A Linguistic Analysis of Literary Style.* London: Routledge.
Eichenbaum, Boris (1971a) 'Wie Gogols "Mantel" gemacht ist' [1918]. *Russischer Formalismus. Texte zur allgemeinen Literaturtheorie und zur Theorie der Prosa.* Ed. Jurij Striedter. UTB. Munich: Fink, 125–59.
Eichenbaum, Boris (1971b) 'Die Illusion des *skaz*' [1918]. *Russischer Formalismus. Texte zur allgemeinen Literaturtheorie und zur Theorie der Prosa.* Ed. Jurij Striedter. UTB. Munich: Fink, 161–7.
Engler, Bernd, and Kurt Müller (1994), eds, *Historiographic Metafiction in Modern American and Canadian Literature.* Paderborn: Schöningh.
Engler, Bernd, and Kurt Müller (1995a), eds, 'Einleitung: Das Exemplum und seine Funktionalisierungen'. In Engler and Müller (1995b): 9–20.
Engler, Bernd, and Kurt Müller (1995b) *Exempla. Studien zur Bedeutung und Funktion exemplarischen Erzählens.* Berlin: Duncker & Humblot.
Enkvist, Nils Erik (1986) 'More about the Textual Function of the Old English Adverbial *þa.* *Linguistics across Historical and Geographical Boundaries. In Honour of Jacek Fisiak on the Occasion of His Fiftieth Birthday.* Vol. 1.

Linguistic Theory and Historical Linguistics. Eds Dieter Kastovsky and Aleksander Szwedek. Trends in Linguistics. Studies and Monographs, 32. Berlin: Mouton de Gruyter, 301-9.

Enkvist, Nils Erik, and Brita Wårvik (1987) 'Old English þa, Temporal Chains, and Narrative Structure'. *Papers from the Seventh International Conference on Historical Linguistics*. Eds Anna Giacalone Ramat, Onofrio Carruba and Giuliano Bernini. Current Issues in Linguistic Theory, 48. Amsterdam: John Benjamins, 221-37.

Epps, Rosalind (1987) 'L'Objet et la subjectivité dans *La Jalousie* d'Alain Robbe-Grillet'. *Essays in French Literature* 24: 94-102.

Ermarth, Elizabeth Deeds (1981) 'Realism, Perspective, and the Novel'. *Critical Inquiry* 7: 499-520.

Ermarth, Elizabeth Deeds (1983) *Realism and Consensus in the English Novel*. Princeton, NJ: Princeton University Press.

Ermarth, Elizabeth Deeds (1992) *Sequel to History. Postmodernism and the Crisis of Representational Time*. Princeton, NJ: Princeton University Press.

Erzgräber, Willi, and Sabine Volk (1988), eds, *Mündlichkeit und Schriftlichkeit im englischen Mittelalter*. ScriptOralia, 5. Tübingen: Narr.

Euler, Bettina (1991) *Strukturen mündlichen Erzählens. Parasyntaktische und sententielle Analysen am Beispiel des englischen Witzes*. ScriptOralia, 31. Tübingen: Narr.

Fabb, Nigel, Derek Attridge, Alan Durant, and Colin MacCabe (1987), eds, *The Linguistics of Writing. Arguments between Language and Literature*. New York: Methuen.

Farrell, Thomas B. (1985) 'Narrative in Natural Discourse: On Conversation and Rhetoric'. *Journal of Communication* 35.4: 109-27.

Fehn, Ann, Ingeborg Hoesterey, and Maria Tatar (1992), eds, *Neverending Stories. Toward a Critical Narratology*. Princeton, NJ: Princeton University Press.

Felman, Shoshana (1975) 'The Critical Phallacy'. *Diacritics* 15: 2-10.

Fineman, Joel (1989) 'The History of the Anecdote: Fiction and Fiction'. In Veeser (1989): 49-76. Rprt. *The Subjectivity Effect in Western Literary Tradition. Essays Toward the Release of Shakespeare's Will*. Cambridge, MA: MIT Press, 1991. 59-87.

Finney, Gail (1992) 'Crossing the Gender Wall: Narrative Strategies in GDR Fictions of Sexual Metamorphosis'. In Fehn *et al.* (1992): 163-78.

Fischer, Andreas (1994), ed., *Repetition*. SPELL, 7. Tübingen: Narr.

Fischer-Lichte, Erika (1992) *The Semiotics of Theatre*. Bloomington: Indiana University Press.

Fisher, John H. (1985) 'Chaucer and the Written Language'. *The Popular Literature of Medieval England*. Ed. Thomas J. Heffernan. Tennessee Studies in Literature, 28. Knoxville, TN: University of Tennessee Press, 237-51.

Fleischman, Suzanne (1990) *Tense and Narrativity. From Medieval Performance to Modern Fiction*. Texas Linguistics Series. Austin, TX: University of Texas Press.

Fleischman, Suzanne, and Linda R. Waugh (1991), eds, *Discourse Pragmatics and the Verb. The Evidence from Romance*. London: Routledge.

Fleishman, Avrom (1992) *Narrated Films. Storytelling Situations in Cinema History*. Baltimore: Johns Hopkins University Press.

Fludernik, Monika (1986) '"Ithaca" - An Essay in Non-Narrativity'. *International Perspectives on James Joyce*. Ed. Gottlieb Gaiser. Troy, NY: Whitston, 88-105.

Fludernik, Monika (1991) 'The Historical Present Tense Yet Again: Tense Switching and Narrative Dynamics in Oral and Quasi-Oral Storytelling'. *Text* 11.3: 365-98.

Fludernik, Monika (1992a) 'The Historical Present Tense in English Literature: An Oral Pattern and its Literary Adaptation'. *Language and Literature* 17: 77-107. (Crosscurrents issue, 1992.)

Fludernik, Monika (1992b) 'Narrative Schemata and Temporal Anchoring'. *The Journal of Literary Semantics* 21: 118–53.
Fludernik, Monika (1992c) 'Subversive Irony: Reflectorization, Trustworthy Narration and Dead-Pan Narrative in *The Mill on the Floss*'. *Yearbook of Research in English and American Literature [REAL]* 8: 159–84.
Fludernik, Monika (1993a) *The Fictions of Language and the Languages of Fiction. The Linguistic Representation of Speech and Consciousness*. London: Routledge.
Fludernik, Monika (1993b) 'Second Person Fiction: Narrative YOU as Addressee and/or Protagonist. Typological and Functional Notes on an Increasingly Popular Genre'. *Arbeiten aus Anglistik und Amerikanistik [AAA]* 18.2: 217–47.
Fludernik, Monika (1993c) 'Review Essay: Narratology in Context'. *Poetics Today* 14.4: 729–61.
Fludernik, Monika (1994a) 'Introduction: Second-Person Narrative and Related Issues'. *Style* 28.3: 281–311.
Fludernik, Monika (1994b), ed., *Second-Person Narrative*. Special issue. *Style* 28.3.
Fludernik, Monika (1994c) 'Second-Person Narrative as a Test Case for Narratology: The Limits of Realism'. *Style* 28.3: 445–79.
Fludernik, Monika (1994d) 'Second-Person Narrative: A Bibliography'. *Style* 28.4: 525–48.
Fludernik, Monika (1994e), rev. Fleischman, Suzanne, and Linda R. Waugh, eds, *Discourse Pragmatics and the Verb. The Evidence from Romance*. London: Routledge, 1991. In *Journal of Literary Semantics* 23.2: 132–41.
Fludernik, Monika (1995a) 'Erzähltexte mit unüblichem Personalpronominagebrauch: engl. *one* und *it*, frz. *on*, dt. *man*'. *Erlebte Rede und impressionistischer Stil. Europäische Erzählprosa im Vergleich mit ihren deutschen Übersetzungen.* Ed. Dorothea Kullmann. Göttingen: Wallstein, 283–308.
Fludernik, Monika (1995b) 'Middle English *þo* and Other Narrative Discourse Markers'. *Historical Pragmatics*. Ed. Andreas Jucker. Pragmatics and Beyond, NS 35. Amsterdam: John Benjamins, 359–92.
Fludernik, Monika (1995c) 'Pronouns of Address and "Odd" Third Person Forms: The Mechanics of Involvement in Fiction'. *New Essays in Deixis. Discourse, Narrative, Literature.* Ed. Keith Green. Amsterdam: Rodopi, 99–129. [The printed version of this essay has undergone drastic cutting and reformulation for which there is no consent from the author. The appalling number of typos and errors in documentation are the responsibility of the editor, who never sent out proofs.]
Fludernik, Monika (1995d), rev. of Virtanen (1992). *Language and Literature* 4.1: 64–7
Fludernik, Monika (forthcoming) 'Linguistics and Literature: New Horizons in the Study of Prose'. *Journal of Pragmatics* 26.3 (1996).
Fokkema, Douwe, and Hans Bertens (1986), eds, *Approaching Postmodernism. Papers Presented at a Workshop on Postmodernism, 21–23 September 1984, University of Utrecht.* Amsterdam: John Benjamins.
Foley, Barbara (1986) *Telling the Truth. The Theory and Practice of Documentary Fiction.* Ithaca, NY: Cornell University Press.
Foley, John Miles (1985a), ed., *Comparative Research on Oral Traditions: A Memorial for Milman Parry.* Columbus, OH: Slavica Publishers.
Foley, John Miles (1985b) 'Reading the Oral Traditional Text: Aesthetics of Creation and Response'. In J.M. Foley (1985a): 185–212.
Foley, John Miles (1990) *Traditional Oral Epic. The Odyssey, Beowulf, and the Serbo-Croatian Return Song.* Berkeley: University of California Press.
Fontanille, Jacques (1989) *Les Espaces subjectifs. Introduction à la sémiotique de l'observateur (discours – peinture – cinéma).* Langue Linguistique Communication. Paris: Hachette.

Forster, E.M. (1974) *Aspects of the Novel* [1927]. London: Edward Arnold.
Foucault, Michel (1977) *Discipline and Punish. The Birth of the Prison* [1975]. New York: Vintage.
Foucault, Michel (1983) *This Is Not a Pipe* [1982]. Berkeley: University of California Press.
Fowler, Roger (1981) 'Chapter Six: The Referential Code and Narrative Authority'. *Literature as Discourse. The Practice of Linguistic Criticism*. London: Batsford Academy, 96–128.
Frank, Joseph (1945) 'Spatial Form in Modern Literature. An Essay in Two Parts'. *Sewanee Review* 53: 221–40; 433–56; 643–53.
Frank, Joseph (1963) *The Widening Gyre. Crisis and Mastery in Modern Literature*. Bloomington, IN: Indiana University Press.
Freedle, Roy O. (1977), ed., *Discourse Production and Comprehension*. Advances in Discourse Processes, 1. Norwood, NJ: Ablex.
Freeman, Donald C. (1981), ed., *Essays in Modern Stylistics*. London: Methuen.
Freud, Sigmund (1970) *Der Witz und seine Beziehung zum Unbewußten. Psychologische Schriften* [1905]. Studienausgabe, 4. Frankfurt: Fischer, 9–219.
Freud, Sigmund (1972) *Die Traumdeutung* [1900]. Studienausgabe, 2. Frankfurt: Fischer.
Freud, Sigmund (1982) 'Das Motiv der Kästchenwahl' [1913]. *Bildende Kunst und Literatur*. Studienausgabe, 10. Frankfurt. Fischer, 181–93.
Frey, John R. (1946) 'The Historical Present in Narrative Literature, Particularly in Modern German Fiction'. *Journal of English and Germanic Philology* 45: 43–67.
Friedman, Ellen G., and Miriam Fuchs (1989a), eds, *Breaking the Sequence. Women's Experimental Fiction*. Princeton, NJ: Princeton University Press.
Friedman, Ellen G., and Miriam Fuchs (1989b) 'Contexts and Continuities: An Introduction to Women's Experimental Fiction in English'. In Friedman and Fuchs (1989a): 3–51.
Friedman, Norman (1989) 'Recent Short Story Theories: Problems in Definition'. In Lohafer and Clarey (1989): 13–31.
Friedman, Susan Stanford (1993) 'Spatialization: A Strategy for Reading Narrative'. *Narrative* 1.1: 12–23.
Fries, Udo (1970) 'Zum historischen Präsens im modernen englischen Roman'. *Germanisch-Romanische Monatsschrift* 51: 321–38.
Fritz, Horst (1993), ed., *Montage in Theater und Film*. Tübingen: Narr.
Füger, Wilhelm (1978) 'Das Nichtwissen des Erzählers in Fieldings *Joseph Andrews*. Baustein zu einer Theorie negierten Wissens in der Fiktion'. *Poetica* 10: 188–216.
Furst, Lilian R. (1988) 'Realism and Its "Code of Accreditation"'. *Comparative Literature Studies* 25.2: 101–26.
Gardiner, Judith Kegan (1989) 'The First English Novel: Aphra Behn's *Love Letters*, the Canon, and Women's Tastes'. *Tulsa Studies in Women's Literature* 8.2: 201–21.
Gaudreault, André (1988) *Du littéraire au filmique. Système du récit*. Paris: Meridiens Klincksieck.
Genette, Gérard (1969) *Figures II*. Paris: Seuil.
Genette, Gérard (1972) 'Discours du récit'. *Figures III*. Paris: Seuil.
Genette, Gérard (1980) *Narrative Discourse. An Essay in Method*. Trans. Jane E. Lewin. Ithaca, NY: Cornell University Press.
Genette, Gérard (1983) *Nouveau Discours du récit*. Paris: Seuil.
Genette, Gérard (1987) *Seuils*. Paris: Seuil.
Genette, Gérard (1988) *Narrative Discourse Revisited*. Trans. Jane E. Lewin. Ithaca, NY: Cornell University Press.
Genette, Gérard (1990) 'Fictional Narrative, Factual Narrative'. *Poetics Today* 11.4: 755–74.

Genette, Gérard (1991) *Fiction et diction*. Paris: Seuil.
Genette, Gérard (1993) *Fiction and Diction*. Trans. Catherine Porter. Ithaca, NY: Cornell University Press.
Gibson, Andrew (forthcoming) *Towards a Postmodern Theory of Narrative*. Edinburgh: Edinburgh University Press.
Givón, Talmy (1979), ed., *Syntax and Semantics 12. Discourse and Syntax*. New York: Academic Press.
Glasersfeld, Ernst von (1983) 'On the Concept of Interpretation'. *Poetics* 12.2-3: 207-18.
Glasersfeld, Ernst von (1989) 'Facts and the Self from a Constructivist Point of View'. *Poetics* 18.4-5: 435-48.
Gnutzmann, Rita (1983) 'La novela hispanoamericana en segunda persona' ['The Hispano-American Novel in the Second Person']. *Iberoromania* ns 17: 100-20.
Goetsch, Paul (1976) 'Harold Pinter: *Old Times*'. *Das englische Drama der Gegenwart. Interpretationen*. Ed. Horst Oppel. Berlin: Erich Schmidt, 206-21.
Goetsch, Paul (1978) 'Aussagen über die Kürze'. *Studien und Materialien zur Short Story*. Schule und Forschung. Frankfurt: Diesterweg, 104-14.
Goetsch, Paul (1985) 'Fingierte Mündlichkeit in der Erzählkunst entwickelter Schriftkulturen'. *Poetica* 17.3-4: 202-18.
Goldknopf, David (1969) 'The Confessional Increment: A New Look at the I-Narrator'. *Journal of Aesthetics and Art Criticism* 28: 13-21.
Goldsmith, Marcella Tarozzi (1991) *Nonrepresentational Forms of the Comic. Humor, Irony, and Jokes*. American University Studies, 117. New York: Lang.
Goodwin, Charles (1981) *Conversational Organization. Interaction Between Speakers and Hearers*. New York: Academic Press.
Goodwin, Charles, and Marjorie Goodwin (1987) 'The Interactive Construction of Conversational Stories'. Paper given at Harvard University's Center for Literary Studies, 6 January.
Goody, Jack (1987) *The Interface Between the Written and the Oral*. Cambridge: Cambridge University Press.
Graef, A. (1889) 'Die präsentischen Tempora bei Chaucer'. *Anglia* 12: 532-77.
Graver, Suzanne (1984) *George Eliot and Community. A Study in Social Theory and Fictional Form*. Berkeley: University of California Press.
Green, Keith, and Jill LeBihan (1994) 'The Speaking Object: Daphne Marlatt's Pronouns and Lesbian Poetics'. *Style* 28.3: 432-44.
Greenblatt, Stephen (1980) *Renaissance Self-Refashioning. From More to Shakespeare*. Chicago: University of Chicago Press.
Greenblatt, Stephen (1989) 'Towards a Poetics of Culture'. In Veeser (1989): 1-14.
Greenblatt, Stephen (1992) *Marvellous Possessions. The Wonder of the New World* [1991]. Oxford: Oxford University Press.
Greimas, Algirdas Julien (1970) *Du Sens*. Paris: Seuil.
Greimas, Algirdas Julien (1983) *Structural Semantics. An Attempt at a Method* [1966]. Lincoln, NB and London: University of Nebraska Press.
Greimas, Algirdas Julien (1987) *On Meaning. Selected Writings in Semiotic Theory*. Theory and History of Literature, 38. Minneapolis: University of Minnesota Press.
Greiner, Agnes Vera (in progress) 'Die Erzählung im Präsens: Ausgewählte amerikanische Kurzgeschichten der Gegenwart'. MA thesis, University of Freiburg, Germany.
Groß, Konrad, Kurt Müller, and Meinhard Winkgens (1994), eds, *Das Natur/ Kultur-Paradigma in der englischsprachigen Erzählliteratur des 19. und 20. Jahrhunderts. Festschrift zum 60. Geburtstag von Paul Goetsch*. Tübingen: Narr.
Gumbrecht, Hans Ulrich (1980) 'Erzählen in der Literatur – Erzählen im Alltag'. In Ehlich (1980): 403-19.

Gumbrecht, Hans Ulrich (1982) 'Über den Ort der Narration in narrativen Gattungen'. In Lämmert (1982): 202–17.
Gunsteren, Julia van (1990) *Katherine Mansfield and Literary Impressionism*. Amsterdam: Rodopi.
Habermalz, Sabine (forthcoming) '"Signs on a White Field": A Look at Orality in Literacy and James Joyce's *Ulysses*'. *Oral Tradition* (1996).
Haiman, John (1985a), ed., *Iconicity in Syntax. Proceedings of a Symposium on Iconicity in Syntax, Stanford, June 24–26, 1983*. Typological Studies in Language, 6. Amsterdam: Benjamins.
Haiman, John (1985b) *Natural Syntax. Iconicity and Erosion*. Cambridge: Cambridge University Press.
Halford, Brigitte K. (1993) 'The Structure of Spoken Canadian English. A Core-Linguistic Approach to Oral Communication'. Habilitation, University of Freiburg, Germany. To appear as *Talk Units. The Structure of Spoken Canadian English*. ScriptOralia, 87. Tübingen: Narr, 1996.
Halford, Brigitte K., and Herbert Pilch (1990), eds, *Syntax gesprochener Sprachen*. ScriptOralia, 14. Tübingen: Narr.
Halliday, M.A.K. (1981) 'Linguistic Function and Literary Style: An Inquiry into the Language of William Golding's *The Inheritors*'. In Freeman (1981): 325–60.
Halliday, M.A.K., and Ruqaiya Hasan (1976) *Cohesion in English*. English Language Series, 9. London: Longman.
Hamburger, Käte (1968) *Die Logik der Dichtung* [1957]. Stuttgart: Klett. Second edn.
Hamburger, Käte (1993) *The Logic of Literature* [1973]. Trans. Marilynn J. Rose. Preface by Gérard Genette (trans. Dorrit Cohn). Bloomington, IN: Indiana University Press. Second, revised edn.
Hardy, Barbara (1982) *Particularities. Readings in George Eliot*. London: Peter Owen.
Hardy, Sarah (1993), ed., *The Short Story: Theory and Practice*. Special issue of *Style*. 27.3 (Fall 1993).
Harweg, Roland (1975a) 'Perfekt und Präteritum im gesprochenen Neuhochdeutsch: Zugleich ein Beitrag zur Theorie des nichtliterarischen Erzählens'. *Orbis* 24.1: 130–83.
Harweg, Roland (1975b) 'Präsupposition und Rekonstruktion: Zur Erzählsituation in Thomas Manns *Tristan* aus textlinguistischer Sicht'. In Schecker and Wunderli (1975): 166–85.
Hassan, Ihab (1967) 'The Literature of Silence: From Henry Miller to Beckett and Burroughs'. *Encounter* (January): 74–82.
Hassan, Ihab (1971) *The Dismemberment of Orpheus. Towards a Postmodern Literature*. New York: Oxford University Press.
Haubrichs, Wolfgang (1977), ed., *Erzählforschung 2*. Zeitschrift für Literaturwissenschaft und Linguistik, Beiheft 6. Göttingen: Vandenhoeck & Ruprecht.
Haug, Walter (1991) 'Exempelsammlungen im narrativen Rahmen: Vom *Pañcatantra* zum *Dekameron*'. In Haug and Wachinger (1991): 264–87.
Haug, Walter, and Burghart Wachinger (1991), eds, *Exempel und Exempelsammlungen*. Tübingen: Niemeyer.
Hawes, Clement (1993) 'Leading History by the Nose: The Turn to the Eighteenth Century in *Midnight's Children*'. *Modern Fiction Studies* 39.1: 147–68.
Hayles, N. Katherine (1991) 'Constrained Constructivism: Locating Scientific Inquiry in the Theater of Representation'. *New Orleans Review* 18.1: 76–85.
Hayman, David (1970) *'Ulysses'. The Mechanics of Meaning*. Englewood Cliffs, NJ: Prentice Hall.
Heise, Ursula K. (1992) '*Erzählzeit* and Postmodern Narrative: Text as Duration in Beckett's *How It Is*'. *Style* 26.2: 245–69.

Hempfer, Klaus W. (1990) 'Zu einigen Problemen einer Fiktionstheorie'. *Zeitschrift für französische Sprache und Literatur* 100: 109–37.
Henrich, Dieter, and Wolfgang Iser (1983), eds, *Funktionen des Fiktiven*. Poetik und Hermeneutik, 10. Munich: Fink.
Herget, Winfried, Klaus Peter Jochum, and Ingeborg Weber (1986), eds, *Theorie und Praxis im Erzählen des 19. und 20. Jahrhunderts. Studien zur englischen und amerikanischen Literatur zu Ehren von Willi Erzgräber*. Tübingen: Narr.
Herman, David (1994) 'Hypothetical Focalization'. *Narrative* 2.3: 230–53.
Hoffbauer, Brigitte (1991) 'Diskurssignale in spontanen mündlichen Erzählungen'. MA Thesis, University of Freiburg, Germany.
Hofstadter, Douglas R. (1979) *Gödel, Escher, Bach: An Eternal Golden Braid. A Metaphorical Fugue on Minds and Machines in the Spirit of Lewis Carroll*. New York: Vintage.
Holden, Jonathan (1980) 'The Abuse of the Second-Person Pronoun'. *The Rhetoric of the Contemporary Lyric*. Bloomington: Indiana University Press, 38–56.
Hollowell, John (1977) *Fact & Fiction. The New Journalism and the Nonfiction Novel*. Chapel Hill, NC: University of North Carolina Press.
Hopper, Paul J. (1979a) 'Aspect and Foregrounding in Discourse'. In Givón (1979): 213–41.
Hopper, Paul J. (1979b) 'Some Observations on the Typology of Focus and Aspect in Narrative Language'. *Studies in Language* 3.1: 37–64.
Hulme, Peter, and Neil L. Whitehead (1992), eds, *Wild Majesty. Encounters with Caribs from Columbus to the Present Day*. Oxford: Oxford University Press.
Humphrey, Robert (1954) *Stream of Consciousness in the Modern Novel*. Perspectives in Criticism, 3. Berkeley: University of California Press.
Hunter, J. Paul (1990) *Before Novels. The Cultural Contexts of Eighteenth-Century English Fiction*. New York/London: Norton.
Husson, Didier (1991) 'Logique des possibles narratifs. Etude des compatibilités entre les variables du récit'. *Poétique* 22 (no. 87): 289–313.
Hutcheon, Linda (1988) *A Poetics of Postmodernism. History, Theory, Fiction*. London: Routledge.
Hutcheon, Linda (1989) *The Politics of Postmodernism*. New Accents. London: Routledge.
Irigaray, Luce (1985) *This Sex Which is not One* [1977]. Ithaca, NY: Cornell University Press.
Iser, Wolfgang (1993) *The Fictive and the Imaginary. Charting Literary Anthropology* [1991]. Baltimore: Johns Hopkins University Press.
Jahn, Manfred (1995) 'Narratologie: Methoden und Modelle der Erzähltheorie'. *Literaturwissenschaftliche Theorien, Modelle und Methoden. Eine Einführung*. Ed. Ansgar Nünning. WVT-Handbücher zum literaturwissenschaftlichen Studium, 1. Trier: Wissenschaftlicher Verlag Trier, 29–50.
Jahn, Manfred (forthcoming) 'Windows of Focalization: Deconstructing and Reconstructing a Narratological Concept'. *Style* 30.3 (1996).
Jahn, Manfred (under review) 'Frames, Preferences, and the Reading of Third-person Narratives: Towards a Cognitive Narratology'. Manuscript.
Jahn, Manfred, and Ansgar Nünning (1994) 'Forum. A Survey of Narratological Models'. *Literatur in Wissenschaft und Unterricht* 27.4: 283–303.
Jameson, Frederic (1988) 'Cognitive Mapping'. *Marxism and the Interpretation of Culture*. Eds C. Nelson and L. Grossberg. Urbana and Chicago: University of Illinois Press, 347–60.
Jankofsky, Klaus P. (1986) '*Legenda aurea* Materials in *The South English Legendary*: Translation, Transformation, Acculturation'. In Dunn-Lardeau (1986): 317–29.

References 431

Jankofsky, Klaus P. (1991) 'National Characteristics in the Portrayal of English Saints in the *South English Legendary*'. In Blumenfeld-Kosinski and Szell (1991): 81–93.
Jankofsky, Klaus P. (1992), ed., *The South English Legendary. A Critical Assessment*. Tübingen: Francke.
Johnstone, Barbara (1987a) 'An Introduction'. *Text* 7.3: 205–14.
Johnstone, Barbara (1987b) '"He says . . . so I said": Verb Tense Alternation and Narrative Depictions of Authority in American English'. *Linguistics: An Interdisciplinary Journal of the Language Sciences* 25.1: 33–52.
Jolles, André (1969) *Einfache Formen. Legende, Sage, Mythe, Rätsel, Spruch, Kasus, Memorabile, Märchen, Witz* [1930]. Darmstadt: Wissenschaftliche Buchgesellschaft.
de Jong, Irene J.F. (1989) *Narrators and Focalizers. The Presentation of the Story in the Iliad* [1987]. Amsterdam: Grüner. Second edn.
de Jong, Irene J.F. (1991) 'Narratology and Oral Poetry: The Case of Homer'. *Poetics Today* 12.3: 405–24.
Kacandes, Irene (1993) 'Are You In the Text?: The "Literary Performative" in Postmodernist Fiction'. *Text and Performance Quarterly* 13: 139–53.
Kacandes, Irene (1994) 'Narrative Apostrophe: Reading, Rhetoric, Resistance in Michel Butor's *La Modification* and Julio Cortázar's "Graffiti"'. *Style* 28.3: 329–49.
Kahler, Erich (1973) *The Inward Turn of Narrative* [1970]. Trans. Richard and Clara Winston. Bollingen Series, 83. Princeton, NJ: Princeton University Press.
Kearns, Katherine (1992) 'A Tropology of Realism in *Hard Times*'. *English Literary History* 59: 857–81.
Kellermann, Kathy, Scott Broetzmann, Tae-Seop Lim, and Kenji Kitao (1989) 'The Conversation MOP: Scenes in the Stream of Discourse'. *Discourse Processes* 12: 27–61.
Kinney, Clare Regan (1992) *Strategies of Poetic Narrative. Chaucer, Spenser, Milton, Eliot*. Cambridge: Cambridge University Press.
Kittay, Jeffrey, and Wlad Godzich (1987) *The Emergence of Prose. An Essay in Prosaics*. Minneapolis: University of Minnesota Press.
Kittel, Harald (1990) 'An Innovative Mode of Literary Self-Revelation: Free Indirect Discourse in Charles Brockden Brown's *Edgar Huntly* and in Its German Translation'. *Amerikastudien/American Studies* 35: 53–66.
Kittel, Harald (1991) 'Revolutionäre Formen perspektivischen Erzählens in einem quasi-autobiographischen Ich-Roman: William Godwins *Caleb Williams*'. *Frühe Formen mehrperspektivischen Erzählens von der Edda bis Flaubert. Ein Problemaufriß*. Eds Armin Paul Frank and Ulrich Mölk. Berlin: Erich Schmidt, 34–53.
Kloepfer, Rolf (1980) 'Dynamic Structures in Narrative Literature. The Dialogic Principle'. *Poetics Today* 1.4: 115–34.
Kloepfer, Rolf, and Gisela Janetzke-Diller (1981), eds, *Erzählung und Erzählforschung im 20. Jahrhundert. Tagungsbeiträge eines Symposiums der Alexander von Humboldt-Stiftung Bonn-Bad Godesberg. Veranstaltet vom 9. bis 14. September 1980 in Ludwigsburg*. Stuttgart: Kohlhammer.
Knott, John R. (1993) *Discourses of Martyrdom in English Literature, 1563–1694*. Cambridge: Cambridge University Press.
Koch, Peter, and Wulf Österreicher (1985) 'Sprache der Nähe – Sprache der Distanz. Mündlichkeit und Schriftlichkeit im Spannungsfeld von Sprachtheorie und Sprachgeschichte'. *Romanistisches Jahrbuch* 36: 15–43.
Koch, Peter, and Wulf Österreicher (1994) 'Funktionale Aspekte der Schriftkultur'. *Schrift und Schriftlichkeit/Writing and Its Use. Ein interdisziplinäres Handbuch internationaler Forschung/An Interdisciplinary Handbook of International*

Research. Eds Hartmut Günther and Otto Ludwig. Vol. 1. Berlin: de Gruyter, 587–604.

Koch, Walter A. (1994), ed., *Simple Forms. An Encyclopedia of Simple Text-Types in Lore and Literature*. Bochum: Brockmeyer.

Korte, Barbara (1985) 'Tiefen- und Oberflächenstrukturen in der Narrativik'. *Literatur in Wissenschaft und Unterricht* 18: 331–52.

Korte, Barbara (1989) 'Spielarten der Distanzierung: Zum Personenwechsel im Erzählwerk'. *Literatur in Wissenschaft und Unterricht* 22.2: 158–71.

Kozloff, Sarah (1988) *Invisible Storytellers. Voice-Over Narration in American Fiction Film*. Berkeley: University of California Press.

Kristeva, Julia (1984) *Revolution in Poetic Language* [1974]. New York: Columbia University Press.

Kroeber, Karl (1992) *Retelling/Rereading. The Fate of Storytelling in Modern Times*. New Brunswick, NJ: Rutgers University Press.

Labov, William (1972) *Language in the Inner City. Studies in the Black English Vernacular*. Philadelphia: University of Pennsylvania Press.

Labov, William, and Joshua Waletzky (1967) 'Narrative Analysis: Oral Versions of Personal Experience'. *Essays on the Verbal and Visual Arts*. Ed. J. Helms. Seattle: University of Washington Press, 12–44.

Lämmert, Eberhard (1982), ed., *Erzählforschung. Ein Symposium*. Stuttgart: Metzler.

Lakoff, George (1987) *Women, Fire, and Dangerous Things. What Categories Reveal about the Mind*. Chicago: University of Chicago Press.

Lakoff, Robin T. (1989) *Language and Woman's Place* [1975]. New York: HarperCollins.

Lamarque, Peter, and Stein Haugom Olsen (1994) *Truth, Fiction, and Literature. A Philosophical Perspective*. Oxford: Clarendon Press.

Landsberg, Marge (1996), ed., *Iconicity in Syntax*. Berlin: Mouton de Gruyter.

Langacker, Ronald W. (1985) 'Observations and Speculations on Subjectivity'. In Haiman (1985a): 109–50.

Langacker, Ronald W. (1990) 'Subjectification'. *Cognitive Linguistics* 1.1: 5–38.

Lanser, Susan Sniader (1981) *The Narrative Act: Point of View in Prose Fiction*. Princeton, NJ: Princeton University Press.

Lanser, Susan S. (1986) 'Toward a Feminist Narratology'. *Style* 20.3: 341–363.

Lanser, Susan S. (1988) 'Shifting the Paradigm: Feminism and Narratology'. *Style* 22.1: 52–60.

Lanser, Susan S. (1992) *Fictions of Authority. Women Writers and Narrative Voice*. Ithaca, NY: Cornell University Press.

Lanser, Susan S. (1995) 'Sexing the Narrative: Propriety, Desire, and the Engendering of Narratology'. *Narrative* 3.1: 85–94.

Leech, Geoffrey N., and Michael H. Short (1981) *Style in Fiction. A Linguistic Introduction to English Fictional Prose*. London: Longman.

Löffler, Arno (1986) 'Die wahnsinnige Heldin: Charlotte Lennox' The Female Quixote'. *Arbeiten aus Anglistik und Amerikanistik [AAA]* 11.1: 63–81.

Lohafer, Susan (1983) *Coming to Terms with the Short Story*. Baton Rouge: Louisiana State University Press.

Lohafer, Susan, and Jo Ellyn Clarey (1989), eds, *Short Story Theory at a Crossroads*. Baton Rouge/London: Louisiana State University Press.

Lord, Albert B. (1960) *The Singer of Tales*. Cambridge, MA: Harvard University Press.

Luhmann, Niklas (1984) *Soziale Systeme*. Frankfurt: Suhrkamp.

McHale, Brian (1992a) *Constructing Postmodernism*. London: Routledge.

McHale, Brian (1992b) 'Making (Non)sense of Postmodernist Poetry'. *Language, Text and Context. Essays in Stylistics*. Ed. Michael Toolan. Interface. London: Routledge, 6–36.

McHale, Brian (1993) *Postmodernist Fiction* [1987]. London: Routledge.
McKeon, Michael (1987) *The Origins of the English Novel, 1600–1740*. Baltimore: Johns Hopkins University Press.
Maclean, Marie (1991) 'Pretexts and Paratexts: The Art of the Peripheral'. *New Literary History* 22.2: 273–80.
McMahon, Katherine G. (1992) 'St. Scholastica – Not a Wife!' In Jankofsky (1992): 18–28.
Mair, Christian (1992) 'Literary Sociolinguistics. A Methodological Framework for Research on the Use of Nonstandard Language in Fiction'. *Arbeiten aus Anglistik und Amerikanistik [AAA]* 17.1: 103–23.
Mandelbaum, Jenny (1993) 'Assigning Responsibility in Conversational Storytelling: The Interactional Construction of Reality'. *Text* 13.2: 247–66.
Maratschniger, Martina (1992) 'Zur Implementierung der natürlichkeitstheoretischen Syntax in TURBO-Prolog'. Paper given at the annual conference of Austrian Linguists, Innsbruck, 25 October 1992.
Margolin, Uri (1991) 'Reference, Coreference, Referring, and the Dual Structure of Literary Narrative'. *Poetics Today* 12.3: 517–42.
Margolin, Uri (1994 for 1990) 'Narrative "You" Revisited'. *Language and Style* 23.4: 425–46.
Margolin, Uri (1996) 'Telling Our Story: On "We" Literary Narratives'. Forthcoming. *Language and Literature* 5.2. In print.
Marks, Elaine, and Isabelle de Courtivron (1981), eds, *New French Feminisms. An Anthology* [1980]. New York: Schocken Books.
Mathieu-Colas, Michel (1986) 'Frontières de la narratologie'. *Poétique* no. 65: 91–110.
Matthiessen, Christian, and Sandra A. Thompson (1988) 'The Structure of Discourse and "Subordination"'. *Clause Combining in Grammar and Discourse*. Eds John Haiman and Sandra A. Thompson. Typological Studies in Language, 18. Amsterdam: Benjamins, 275–329.
May, Charles E. (1976), ed., *Short Story Theories*. Athens, OH: Ohio University Press.
Mayerthaler, Willi (1992) 'Aspekte der natürlichkeitstheoretischen Syntax'. Paper given at the annual conference of Austrian Linguists, Innsbruck, 25 October 1992.
Mecke, Jochen (1990) *Roman-Zeit. Zeitformung und Dekonstruktion des französischen Romans der Gegenwart*. Mannheimer Beiträge zur Sprach- und Literaturwissenschaft, 16. Tübingen: Narr.
Meindl, Dieter (1994) 'A Model of Narrative Discourse along Pronominal Lines'. Manuscript.
Minsky, Marvin (1975) 'A Framework for Representing Knowledge'. *The Psychology of Computer Vision*. Ed. Patrick Henry Winston. New York: McGraw Hill, 211–80.
Mitchell, W.J.T. (1981), ed., *On Narrative*. Chicago: Chicago University Press.
Moi, Toril (1987) *Sexual/Textual Politics. Feminist Literary Theory* [1985]. New Accents. London: Routledge.
Moore, Gene (1994 for 1989) 'Focalization and Narrative Voice in *What Maisie Knew*'. *Language and Style* 22.1: 3–24.
Morrissette, Bruce (1965) 'Narrative "You" in Contemporary Literature'. *Comparative Literature Studies* 2: 1–24. Rprt. and expanded in *Novel and Film: Essays in Two Genres*. Chicago: University of Chicago Press, 1985. 108–40.
Morton, Donald (1993) 'The Crisis of Narrative in the Postnarratological Era: Paul Goodman's *The Empire City* as (Post)Modern Intervention'. *New Literary History* 24.2: 407–24.
Mosher, Harold F., Jr (1991) 'Toward a Poetics of "Descriptized" Narration'. *Poetics Today* 12.3: 425–46.

Müller, Wolfgang G. (1979) 'Charlotte Lennox' *The Female Quixote* und die Geschichte des englischen Romans'. *Poetica* 11: 369–93.

Müller, Wolfgang G. (1981) 'Implizite Bewußtseinsdarstellung im behavioristischen Roman der zwanziger und dreißiger Jahre: Hammett, Chandler, Hemingway'. *Amerikastudien/American Studies* 26: 193–211.

Müller, Wolfgang G. (1982) 'Das Ich im Dialog mit sich selbst. Bemerkungen zur Struktur des dramatischen Monologs von Shakespeare bis zu Samuel Beckett'. *Deutsche Vierteljahrsschrift* 56.2: 314–33.

Müller, Wolfgang G. (1991) 'The Rhetoric of the Soliloquy in the Novel'. *Anglistentag 1990 Marburg. Proceedings*. Eds Claus Uhlig and Rüdiger Zimmermann. Tübingen: Niemeyer, 96–108.

Nelles, William (1990) 'Getting Focalization into Focus'. *Poetics Today* 11.2: 365–82.

Neumann, Anne Waldron (1990) 'Escaping the "Time of History": Present Tense and the Occasion of Narration in J.M. Coetzee's *Waiting for the Barbarians*'. *Journal of Narrative Technique* 20.1: 65–86.

Neumann, Anne Waldron (1991) 'Present Tense and the Occasion of Narration in Margaret Atwood's *The Handmaid's Tale*'. Paper read at the Nice Conference of the Association for the Study of Narrative Literature, June 1991.

Nischik, Reingard M. (1981) *Einsträngigkeit und Mehrsträngigkeit der Handlungsführung in literarischen Texten*. Tübinger Beiträge zur Anglistik, 1. Tübingen: Narr.

Nischik, Reingard M. (1985) *Short Short Stories. Analyses and Additional Material*. Paderborn: Schöningh.

Nischik, Reingard M. (1991a) *Mentalstilistik. Ein Beitrag zu Stiltheorie und Narrativik. Dargestellt am Erzählwerk Margaret Atwoods*. Tübingen: Narr.

Nischik, Reingard M. (1991b) ' "Où maintenant? Quand maintenant? Qui maintenant?" Die namenlose Ich-Erzählfigur im Roman'. *Poetica* 23.1–2: 257–75.

Nischik, Reingard M. (1993) 'Montage intermedial: Strukturelle Bezüge und Funktionen von Montage in Harold Pinters Arbeiten für Film, Fernsehen und Theater'. *Montage in Theater und Film*. Ed. Horst Fritz. Tübingen: Narr, 275–311.

Nischik, Reingard M. (1994) 'Sukzessive und simultane Aufspaltung der Erzählinstanz im Erzählwerk Margaret Atwoods'. *Orbis Litterarum* 49: 233–51.

Norrick, Neal R. (1987) 'Functions of Repetition in Conversation'. *Text* 7.3: 245–64.

Nünning, Ansgar (1989a) *Grundzüge eines kommunikationstheoretischen Modells der erzählerischen Vermittlung. Die Funktionen der Erzählinstanz in den Romanen George Eliots*. Horizonte, 2. Trier: Wissenschaftlicher Verlag.

Nünning, Ansgar (1989b) 'Informationsübertragung oder Informationskonstruktion? Grundzüge und Konsequenzen eines konstruktivistischen Modells von Kommunikation'. *Humankybernetik* 30.4: 127–40.

Nünning, Ansgar (1990a) 'Bausteine einer konstruktivistischen Erzähltheorie. Die erzählerische Umsetzung konstruktivistischer Konzepte in den Romanen von John Fowles'. *Delfin* 7.1 (no. 13): 3–17.

Nünning, Ansgar (1990b) '"*Point of view*" oder "*focalization*"? Über einige Grundlagen und Kategorien konkurrierender Modelle der erzählerischen Vermittlung'. *Literatur in Wissenschaft und Unterricht* 23: 249–68.

Nünning, Ansgar (1992) 'Mimesis und Poiesis im englischen Roman des 18. Jahrhunderts: Überlegungen zum Zusammenhang zwischen narrativer Form und Wirklichkeitserfahrung'. *Neue Lesarten, neue Wirklichkeiten: Zur Wiederentdeckung des 18. Jahrhunderts durch die Anglistik. Symposium zu Ehren von Ulrich Suerbaum*. Eds Gerd Stratmann and Manfred Buschmeier. Trier: Wissenschaftlicher Verlag, 46–69.

Nünning, Ansgar (1993) 'Renaissance eines anthropomorphisierten Passepartouts oder Nachruf auf ein literaturkritisches Phantom? Überlegungen und

Alter- nativen zum Konzept des "*implied author*"'. *Deutsche Vierteljahrsschrift* 67.1: 1-25.

Nünning, Ansgar (1995a) 'On the Perspective Structure of Narrative Texts: Steps Towards a Constructivist Narratology'. Forthcoming in *Narrative Perspective: Cognition and Emotion*. Eds Seymour Chatman and Willie van Peer.

Nünning, Ansgar (1995b) *Von historischer Fiktion zu historiographischer Metafiktion*. 2 vols. Trier: Wissenschaftlicher Verlag Trier.

Österreicher, Wulf (1993) '*Verschriftlichung* und *Verschriftung* im Kontext medialer und konzeptioneller Schriftlichkeit'. *Schriftlichkeit im frühen Mittelalter*. Ed. Ursula Schaefer. ScriptOralia, 53. Tübingen: Narr, 267-92.

Ohmann, Richard (1972) 'Speech, Literature, and the Space Between'. *New Literary History* 4 (1972): 47-64.

Olney, James (1993) 'Memory and the Narrative Imperative: St. Augustine and Samuel Beckett'. *New Literary History* 24.4: 857-80.

O'Neill, Patrick (1992) 'Points of Origin: On Focalization in Narrative'. *Canadian Review of Comparative Literature* 19.3: 331-50.

O'Neill, Patrick (1994) *Fictions of Discourse. Reading Narrative Theory*. Toronto: University of Toronto Press.

Oppel, Horst (1965), ed., *Der moderne englische Roman. Interpretationen*. Berlin: Erich Schmidt.

Osterwalder, Hans (1992) 'Poet and Persona in "My Last Duchess"'. *Yearbook of Research in English and American Literature [REAL]* 8: 183-93.

Pannenberg, Wolfhart (1983) 'Das Irreale des Glaubens'. In Henrich and Iser (1983): 17-34.

Parry, Adam (1971) *The Making of Homeric Verse. The Collected Papers of Milman Parry*. Oxford: Clarendon Press.

Pasco, Allan H. (1991) 'On Defining Short Stories'. *New Literary History* 22.2: 407-22.

Pater, Walter (1980) *The Renaissance. Studies in Art and Poetry. The 1893 Text.* Ed. Donald L. Hill. Berkeley: University of California Press.

Pavel, Thomas G. (1985) *The Poetics of Plot. The Case of English Renaissance Drama*. Theory and History of Literature, 18. Minneapolis: University of Minnesota Press.

Pearson, Jacqueline (1991) 'Gender and Narrative in the Fiction of Aphra Behn'. *Review of English Studies* ns 42 (no. 165): 40-56; 42 (no. 166): 179-90.

Peel, Ellen (1989) 'Subject, Object, and the Alternation of First- and Third-Person Narration in Novels by Alther, Atwood, and Drabble: Toward a Theory of Feminist Aesthetics'. *Critique* 30.2: 107-22.

Petersen, Jürgen H. (1992) 'Erzählen im Präsens. Die Korrektur herrschender Tempus-Theorien durch die poetische Praxis in der Moderne'. *Euphorion* 86: 65-89.

Pfister, Manfred (1988) *The Theory and Analysis of Drama* [1977]. European Studies in English Literature. Cambridge: Cambridge University Press.

Polanyi, Livia (1978) 'False Starts can be True'. *Berkeley Linguistics Society* 4: 628-39.

Polanyi, Livia (1982) 'Literary Complexities in Everyday Storytelling'. In Tannen (1982b): 155-70.

Polanyi, Livia (1985) *Telling the American Story. A Structural and Cultural Analysis of Conversational Storytelling*. Norwood, NJ: Ablex.

Pollak, Wolfgang (1988) *Studien zum Verbalaspekt. Mit besonderer Berücksichtigung des Französischen* [1960]. Berne: Lang. Second edn.

Pouillon, Jean (1946) *Temps et roman*. Paris: Gallimard.

Pratt, Mary Louise (1977) *Toward a Speech Act Theory of Literary Discourse*. Bloomfield and London: Indiana University Press.

Preisendanz, Wolfgang, and Rainer Warning (1976), eds, *Das Komische*. Poetik und Hermeneutik. Arbeitsergebnisse einer Forschungsgruppe, 7. Munich: Fink.
Prendergast, Christopher (1986) *The Order of Mimesis. Balzac, Stendhal, Nerval, Flaubert*. Cambridge: Cambridge University Press.
Prince, Ellen F. (1979) 'On the Given/New Distinction'. *Chicago Linguistic Society* 15: 267–78.
Prince, Ellen F. (1981) 'Toward a Taxonomy of Given-New Information'. In P. Cole (1981): 223–55.
Prince, Gerald (1982) *Narratology. The Form and Functioning of Narrative*. Berlin: Mouton.
Prince, Gerald (1987) *A Dictionary of Narratology*. Lincoln and London: University of Nebraska Press.
Prince, Gerald (1991) 'Narratology, Narrative, and Meaning'. *Poetics Today* 12.3: 543–52.
Prince, Gerald (1992) *Narrative As Theme. Studies in French Fiction*. Lincoln, NE: University of Nebraska Press.
Prince, Gerald (1995) 'On Narratology: Criteria, Corpus, Context'. *Narrative* 3.1: 73–84.
Propp, Vladimir (1968) *Morphology of the Folktale* [1928]. Trans. Laurence Scott. Austin, TX: University of Texas Press. Second edn.
Quasthoff, Uta M. (1980) *Erzählen in Gesprächen. Linguistische Untersuchungen zu Strukturen und Funktionen am Beispiel einer Kommunikationsform des Alltags*. Kommunikation und Institution, 1. Tübingen: Narr.
Raible, Wolfgang (1992) *Junktion. Eine Dimension der Sprache und ihre Realisierungsformen zwischen Aggregation und Integration*. Sitzungsberichte der Heidelberger Akademie der Wissenschaften. Philosophisch-historische Klasse. Bericht 2. Heidelberg: Carl Winter.
Raible, Wolfgang (1994) 'I. Allgemeine Aspekte von Schrift und Schriftlichkeit/General Aspects of Writing and Its Use'. *Schrift und Schriftlichkeit/ Writing and Its Use. Ein interdisziplinäres Handbuch internationaler Forschung/An Interdisciplinary Handbook of International Research*. Eds Hartmut Günther and Otto Ludwig. Vol. 1. Berlin: de Gruyter, 1–17.
Ray, William (1990) *Story and History*. Oxford: Blackwell.
Redeker, Gisela (1990) 'Ideational and Pragmatic Markers of Discourse Structure'. *Journal of Pragmatics* 14: 367–81.
Reid, Ian (1977) *The Short Story*. The Critical Idiom, 37. London: Methuen.
Reid, Ian (1988) 'Genre and Framing: The Case of Epitaphs'. *Poetics* 17: 25–35.
Reid, Ian (1992) *Narrative Exchanges*. London: Routledge.
Richardson, Brian (1987) 'Time is Out of Joint. Narrative Models and the Temporality of the Drama'. *Poetics Today* 8.2: 299–310.
Richardson, Brian (1988) 'Point of View in Drama: Diegetic Monologue, Unreliable Narrators, and the Author's Voice on Stage'. *Comparative Drama* 22.3: 193–214.
Richardson, Brian (1991a) 'Pinter's *Landscape* and the Boundaries of Narrative'. *Essays in Literature* 18: 37–45.
Richardson, Brian (1991b) 'The Poetics and Politics of Second Person Narrative'. *Genre* 24: 309–30.
Richardson, Brian (1994) 'I etcetera: On the Poetics and Ideology of Multipersoned Narratives'. *Style* 28.3: 312–28.
Richardson, Brian (forthcoming) 'Chapter Three. Temporal Sequence, Causal Connection, and the Nature of Narrative: Disjunction and Convergence in *Mrs. Dalloway* and Pinter's *Landscape*'. *Unlikely Stories: Causality, Ideology, and Interpretation in Modern Narrative*. Forthcoming. University of Delaware Press.
Ricoeur, Paul (1983) *Temps et récit I*. Paris: Seuil.

Ricoeur, Paul (1984a) *Temps et récit II. La Configuration dans le récit de fiction*. Paris: Seuil.
Ricoeur, Paul (1984b) *Time and Narrative*. Vol. 1. Trans. Kathleen McLaughlin and David Pellauer. Chicago, IL: Chicago University Press.
Ricoeur, Paul (1985a) *Temps et récit III. Le temps raconté*. Paris: Seuil.
Ricoeur, Paul (1985b) *Time and Narrative*. Vol. 2. Trans. Kathleen McLaughlin and David Pellauer. Chicago, IL: Chicago University Press.
Ricoeur, Paul (1988) *Time and Narrative*. Vol. 3. Trans. Kathleen McLaughlin and David Pellauer. Chicago, IL: Chicago University Press.
Riehl, Claudia Maria (1993) *Kontinuität und Wandel von Erzählstrukturen am Beispiel der Legende*. Göppinger Arbeiten zur Germanistik, 576. Göppingen: Kümmerle.
Riffaterre, Michael (1990) *Fictional Truth*. Baltimore: Johns Hopkins University Press.
Rigney, Ann (1988) 'Du récit historique. La prise de la Bastille selon Michelet (1847)'. *Poétique* no. 75: 267–78.
Rigney, Ann (1990) *The Rhetoric of Historical Representation. Three Narrative Histories of the French Revolution*. Cambridge: Cambridge University Press.
Rigney, Ann (1992) 'The Point of Stories: On Narrative Communication and Its Cognitive Functions'. *Poetics Today* 13.2: 263–84.
Rimmon-Kenan, Shlomith (1983) *Narrative Fiction. Contemporary Poetics*. New Accents. London: Methuen.
Rimmon-Kenan, Shlomith (1992) 'Interpretative Strategies, Interior Monologues'. In Fehn *et al.* (1992): 101–11.
Roloff, Hans (1921) *Das Praesens historicum im Mittelenglischen*. Gießen: von Münchow.
Ronen, Ruth (1990a) 'La focalisation dans les mondes fictionnels'. *Poétique* no. 83: 305–22.
Ronen, Ruth (1990b) 'The Semiotics of Fictional Time: Three Metaphors in the Study of Temporality in Fiction'. *Style* 24: 22–44.
Rosenwasser, David (1986) 'The Idea of Enclosure: Prisons and Havens at the Rise of the Novel'. *DAI* 46.12: 3,728A.
Rossi, Luciano (1985) 'Das *Dekameron* und die romanische Tradition: die außerordentliche Geduld der Griselda'. *Vox Romanica* 44: 16–32.
Rowse, Alfred Leslie (1950) *The English Spirit. Essays in History and Literature*. London: Macmillan.
Rumelhart, David E. (1975) 'Notes on a Schema for Stories'. *Representation and Understanding. Studies in Cognitive Science*. Eds Daniel G. Bobrow and Allan Collins. Language, Thought, and Culture: Advances in the Study of Cognition. New York: Academic Press, 211–36.
Ryan, Judith (1992) 'Fictionality, Historicity, and Textual Authority: Pater, Woolf, Hildesheimer'. In Fehn *et al.* (1992): 45–61.
Ryan, Marie-Laure (1987) 'On the window structure of narrative discourse'. *Semiotica* 64.1–2: 59–81.
Ryan, Marie-Laure (1991) *Possible Worlds, Artificial Intelligence, and Narrative Theory*. Bloomington, IN: Indiana University Press.
Ryan, Marie-Laure (1992) 'The Modes of Narrativity and Their Visual Metaphors'. *Style* 26.3: 368–87.
Ryan, Marie-Laure (1993) 'Narrative in Real Time: Chronicle, Mimesis and Plot in the Baseball Broadcast'. *Narrative* 1.2: 138–55.
Ryding, William W. (1971) *Structure in Medieval Narrative*. The Hague: Mouton.
Sacks, Harvey (1986) 'Some Considerations of a Story Told in Ordinary Conversations'. *Poetics* 15: 127–38.
Sacks, Harvey (1987) 'On the Preferences for Agreement and Contiguity in Sequences in Conversation'. In Button and Lee (1987): 54–69.

Salzman, Paul (1991), ed., *An Anthology of Seventeenth-Century Fiction*. The World's Classics. Oxford: Oxford University Press.
Sasaki, Toru (1994) 'Towards a Systematic Description of Narrative "Point of View": an Examination of Chatman's Theory with an Analysis of "The Blind Man" by D.H. Lawrence'. *Language and Literature* 3.2: 125–38.
Scarry, Elaine (1985) *The Body in Pain. The Making and Unmaking of the World*. Oxford: Oxford University Press.
Schabert, Ina (1981) *Der historische Roman in England und Amerika*. Erträge der Forschung, 156. Darmstadt: Wissenschaftliche Buchgesellschaft.
Schank, Roger C., and Robert P. Abelson (1977) *Scripts, Plans, Goals and Understanding. An Inquiry into Human Knowledge*. The Artificial Intelligence Series. Hillsday, NJ: Lawrence Erlbaum Association.
Schecker, Michael, and Peter Wunderli (1975), eds, *Textgrammatik. Beiträge zum Problem der Textualität*. Konzepte der Sprach- und Literaturwissenschaft, 4. Tübingen: Niemeyer.
Schegloff, Emanuel A. (1992) 'In Another Context'. *Rethinking Context. Language as an Interactive Phenomenon*. Eds Alessandro Duranti and Charles Goodwin. Studies in the Social and Cultural Functions of Language. Cambridge: Cambridge University Press, 193–227.
Schiffrin, Deborah (1981) 'Tense Variation in Narrative'. *Language* 57.1: 45–62.
Schiffrin, Deborah (1987) *Discourse Markers*. Studies in Interactional Sociolinguistics, 5. Cambridge: Cambridge University Press.
Schmidt, Josef (1986) 'Golden Legends during the Reformation Controversy: Polemical Trivialization in the German Vernacular'. In Dunn-Lardeau (1986): 267–75.
Schmidt, Siegfried J. (1989) 'On the Construction of Fiction and the Invention of Facts'. *Poetics* 18.4–5: 319–35.
Schmidt, Siegfried J. (1992) 'The Logic of Observation: An Introduction to Constructivism'. *Canadian Review of Comparative Literature/Revue Canadienne de Littérature* 19.3: 295–311.
Scholes, Robert (1982) *Semiotics and Interpretation*. New Haven, CT: Yale University Press.
Schreiner, Klaus (1966) 'Zum Wahrheitsverständnis im Heiligen- und Reliquienwesen des Mittelalters'. *Saeculum* 17: 131–69.
Schütz, Alfred (1960) *Der sinnhafte Aufbau der sozialen Welt. Eine Einleitung in die verstehende Soziologie* [1932]. Wien: Springer. Second edn.
Schütz, Alfred, and Thomas Luckmann (1975) *Strukturen der Lebenswelt*. Darmstadt: Luchterhand.
Schütz, Alfred, and Thomas Luckmann (1989) *The Structures of the Life-world*. 2 vols. Evanston, IL: Northwestern University Press.
Searle, John R. (1975) 'The Logical Status of Fictional Discourse'. *New Literary History* 6.2: 319–32.
Searle, John R. (1977) 'Reiterating the Differences: A Reply to Derrida'. *Glyph* 1: 198–208.
Seltzer, Mark (1995) 'The Graphic Unconscious: A Response'. *New Literary History* 26.1: 21–8.
Serres, Michel (1993) *Les Origines de la géométrie. Tiers livre des fondations*. Paris: Flammarion.
Sieben Jahre Sonderforschungsbereich 321: 'Übergänge und Spannungsfelder zwischen Mündlichkeit und Schriftlichkeit.' Eine Zwischenbilanz 1. Juli 1985–30. Juni 1992. Sonderforschungsbereich 321, Albert-Ludwigs-Universität Freiburg im Breisgau. Werthmannplatz. D-79085 Freiburg, Germany. Tel. 0049–761–203-2026. Fax: 0049–761–203 2025.
Silk, Sally M. (1992) 'When the Writer Comes Home: Narrative Failure in Butor's *La Modification*'. *Style* 26.2: 270–86.

Smith, Barbara Herrnstein (1983) *On the Margins of Discourse. The Relation of Literature to Language* [1978]. Chicago: University of Chicago Press.
Smith, Barbara Herrnstein (1992) 'Making (Up) the Truth: Constructivist Contributions'. *University of Toronto Quarterly* 61.4: 422-9.
Smith, Mack (1995) *Literary Realism and the Ekphrastic Tradition*. University Park: Pennsylvania State University Press.
Söll, Ludwig (1969) 'Zur Situierung von *on* "nous" im neuen Französischen'. *Romanische Forschung* 81: 535-49.
Spencer, Jane (1986) *The Rise of the Woman Novelist. From Aphra Behn to Jane Austen*. Oxford: Blackwell.
Spender, Dale (1980) *Man Made Language*. London: Routledge.
Stanzel, Franz Karl (1969) *Die typischen Erzählsituationen im Roman. Dargestellt an Tom Jones, Moby-Dick, The Ambassadors, Ulysses u.a.* [1955]. Wiener Beiträge zur englischen Philologie. Vienna: Braumüller. Fourth edn.
Stanzel, Franz Karl (1971) *Narrative Situations in the Novel. Tom Jones, Moby-Dick, The Ambassadors, Ulysses*. Trans. J.P. Pusack. Bloomington, IN: Indiana University Press.
Stanzel, Franz Karl (1972) *Typische Formen des Romans* [1964]. Göttingen: Vandenhoeck.
Stanzel, Franz Karl (1977) 'Die Personalisierung des Erzählaktes im *Ulysses*'. *James Joyces 'Ulysses'. Neuere deutsche Aufsätze*. Ed. Therese Fischer-Seidel. Frankfurt am Main: Suhrkamp, 284-308.
Stanzel, Franz Karl (1978a) 'Towards a "Grammar of Fiction"'. *Novel* 11: 247-64.
Stanzel, Franz Karl (1978b) 'Zur Konstituierung der typischen Erzählsituationen'. *Zur Struktur des Romans*. Ed. Bruno Hillebrand. Darmstadt: Wissenschaftliche Buchgesellschaft, 558-76.
Stanzel, Franz Karl (1981a) 'Teller-Characters and Reflector Characters in Narrative Theory'. *Poetics Today* 2.2: 5-15.
Stanzel, Franz Karl (1981b) 'Wandlungen des narrativen Diskurses in der Moderne'. In Kloepfer and Janetzke-Diller (1981): 371-83.
Stanzel, Franz Karl (1982) *Theorie des Erzählens* [1979]. UTB 904. Göttingen: Vandenhoeck & Ruprecht. Second, revised edn.
Stanzel, Franz Karl (1984a) 'Linguistische und Literarische Aspekte des erzählenden Diskurses'. *Österreichische Akademie der Wissenschaften. Philosophisch-Historische Klasse*. Sitzungsberichte, 437. Vienna: Verlag der Österreichischen Akademie der Wissenschaften.
Stanzel, Franz Karl (1984b) *A Theory of Narrative*. Cambridge: Cambridge University Press.
Stanzel, Franz Karl (1991) 'Zur Problemgeschichte der "Erlebten Rede". Eine Vorbemerkung zu Yasushi Suzukis Beitrag "Erlebte Rede und der Fall Jenninger"'. *Germanisch-Romanische Monatsschrift* 41.1: 1-4.
Stanzel, Franz Karl (1992) 'Consonant and Dissonant Closure in *Death in Venice* and *The Dead*'. In Fehn *et al.* (1992): 112-23.
Steinberg, Günter (1971) *Erlebte Rede. Ihre Eigenart und ihre Formen in neuerer deutscher, französischer und englischer Erzählliteratur*. Göppingen: Alfred Kümmerle.
Stempel, Wolf-Dieter (1964) *Untersuchungen zur Satzverknüpfung im Altfranzösischen*. Archiv für das Studium der neueren Sprachen und Literaturen, Beiheft 1. Braunschweig: Westermann.
Sternberg, Meir (1978) *Expositional Modes and Temporal Ordering in Fiction*. Baltimore: Johns Hopkins University Press. Rprt. Bloomington: Indiana University Press, 1993.
Sternberg, Meir (1981) 'Ordering the Unordered: Time, Space, and Descriptive Coherence'. *Yale French Studies* 61: 60-88.

Sternberg, Meir (1983) 'Deictic Sequence: World, Language and Convention'. *Essays on Deixis*. Ed. Gisa Rauh. Tübingen: Narr, 277-316.
Sternberg, Meir (1987) *The Poetics of Biblical Narrative. Ideological Literature and the Drama of Reading*. Bloomington: Indiana University Press.
Sternberg, Meir (1992) 'Telling in Time (II): Chronology, Teleology, Narrativity'. *Poetics Today* 13.3: 463-541.
Stierle, Karlheinz (1972) 'L'Histoire comme exemple, l'exemple comme histoire. Contribution à la pragmatique et à la poétique des textes narratifs'. *Poétique* no. 3: 176-98.
Stock, Brian (1983) *The Implications of Literacy. Written Language and Models of Interpretation in the Eleventh and Twelfth Centuries*. Princeton, NJ: Princeton University Press.
Striedter, Jurij, and Wolf-Dieter Stempel (1972), eds, *Texte der russischen Formalisten. Band I: Zur allgemeinen Literaturtheorie und zur Theorie der Prosa*. Theorie und Geschichte der Literatur und der schönen Künste, 6.1. Munich: Fink.
Sturgess, Philip J.M. (1989) 'A Logic of Narrativity'. *New Literary History* 20.3: 763-83.
Sturgess, Philip J.M. (1990) 'Narrativity and Double Logics'. *Neophilologus* 74: 161-77.
Sturgess, Philip J.M. (1992) *Narrativity. Theory and Practice*. Oxford: Clarendon Press.
Suleiman, Susan Rubin (1990) *Subversive Intent. Gender, Politics, and the Avant-Garde*. Cambridge, MA: Harvard University Press.
Survey of English Usage, University College London, Gower Street.
Svartvik, Jan, and Randolph Quirk (1979), eds, *A Corpus of English Conversation*. Lund Studies in English, 56. Lund: C.W.K. Gleerup.
Tannen, Deborah (1982a), ed., *Analyzing Discourse. Text and Talk*. Georgetown University Round Table on Languages and Linguistics 1981. Washington, DC: Georgetown University Press.
Tannen, Deborah (1982b), ed., *Spoken and Written Language. Exploring Orality and Literacy*. Norwood, NJ: Ablex.
Tannen, Deborah (1982c) 'Oral and Literate Strategies in Spoken and Written Narratives'. *Language* 58.1: 1-21.
Tannen, Deborah (1984) *Conversational Style. Analyzing Talk Among Friends*. Norwood, NJ: Ablex.
Tannen, Deborah (1987a) 'Repetition in Conversation as Spontaneous Formulaicity'. *Text* 7.3: 215-43.
Tannen, Deborah (1987b) 'Repetition in Conversation: Toward a Poetics of Talk'. *Language* 63: 574-605.
Tannen, Deborah (1989) *Talking Voices. Repetition, Dialogue, and Imagery in Conversational Discourse*. Studies in Interactional Sociolinguistics, 6. Cambridge: Cambridge University Press.
Tannen, Deborah (1990) *You Just Don't Understand. Women and Men in Conversation*. New York: William Morrow.
Tedlock, Dennis (1983) *The Spoken Word and the Work of Interpretation*. Philadelphia: University of Pennsylvania Press.
Terkel, Studs (1990) *'The Good War'. An Oral History of World War Two* [1984]. New York: Ballantine.
Terkel, Studs (1992) *Race. How Blacks and Whites Think and Feel About the American Obsession*. New York: New Press.
Tiffeneau, Dorian (1980), ed., *La Narrativité. Receuil*. Paris: Editions du Centre National de la Recherche Scientifique.
Titunik, Irwin R. (1977) 'Das Problem des *skaz*. Kritik und Theorie'. In Haubrichs (1977): 114-140.

References 441

Todd, Janet (1989) *The Sign of Angellica. Women, Writing, and Fiction, 1660-1800*. London: Virago.
Todorov, Tzvetan (1966) 'Les catégories du récit littéraire'. *Communications* 8: 125-51.
Todorov, Tzvetan (1968) 'Introduction'. *Communications* 11: 1-4.
Todorov, Tzvetan (1993) *The Fantastic. A Structural Approach to a Literary Genre* [1970]. Trans. Richard Howard. Foreword Robert Scholes. Ithaca, NY: Cornell University Press.
Tomlin, Russell S. (1985) 'Foreground-Background Information and the Syntax of Subordination'. *Text* 5: 85-122.
Toolan, Michael (1994), rev. of Fludernik (1993a). *Language and Literature* 3.3: 223-8.
Tristram, Hildegard L.C. (1988) 'Aggregating versus Integrating Narrative: Original Prose in England from the Seventh to the Fifteenth century'. In Erzgräber and Volk (1988): 53-64.
Tristram, Hildegard L.C. (1996), ed., *(Re)Oralisierung*. ScriptOralia, 84. Tübingen: Narr.
Turner, Mark (1991) *Reading Minds. The Study of English in the Age of Cognitive Science*. Princeton, NJ: Princeton University Press.
Uspensky, Boris A. (1973) *A Poetics of Composition. The Structure of the Artistic Text and Typology of a Compositional Form*. Berkeley: University of California Press.
Vance, Eugene (1987) *From Topic to Tale. Logic and Narrativity in the Middle Ages*. Theory and History of Literature, 47. Minneapolis: University of Minnesota Press.
Vauchez, André (1981) *La Sainteté en Occident aux derniers siècles du Moyen Age. D'après le procès de canonisation et les documents hagiographiques*. Rome: Ecole Française de Rome.
Veeser, H. Aram (1989) *The New Historicism*. London: Routledge.
Viègnes, Michel (1990) '*Mimesis* et catégories universelles: les limites du réalisme objectif dans le récit'. *French Literature Series* 17: 15-25.
Vinogradov, Viktor (1972) 'Das Problem des *skaz* in der Stilistik' [1925]. In Striedter and Stempel (1972): 169-207.
Virtanen, Tuija (1992) *Discourse Functions of Adverbial Placement in English. Clause-Initial Adverbials of Time and Place in Narratives and Procedural Place Descriptions*. Åbo: Åbo Akademi.
Vitoux, Pierre (1982) 'Le jeu de la focalisation'. *Poétique* no. 51: 358-68.
Vitoux, Pierre (1984) 'Notes sur la focalisation dans le roman autobiographique'. *Etudes littéraires* 17.2: 261-72.
Vitoux, Pierre (1992) 'Narratology in Postmodern Times'. *Yearbook of Research in English and American Literature [REAL]* 8: 117-23.
Vitz, Evelyn Birge (1989) *Medieval Narrative and Modern Narratology. Subjects and Objects of Desire*. New York: New York University Press.
Vogt, Beate (1995) 'Die Enden des Dialogs. Dialogizität als strukturbildendes Verfahren in den Dramen von Elfriede Jelinek, Heiner Müller und Thomas Bernhard'. Dissertation, University of Freiburg. Manuscript.
Vološinov, V.N. (1986) *Marxism and the Philosophy of Language* [1929]. Trans. Ladislav Matejka and I.R. Titunik. Cambridge, MA: Harvard University Press, 1973. Reprint.
Walton, Kendall L. (1990) *Mimesis as Make-Belief. On the Foundations of the Representational Arts*. Cambridge, MA: Harvard University Press.
Warhol, Robyn R. (1989) *Gendered Interventions. Narrative Discourse in the Victorian Novel*. New Brunswick: Rutgers University Press.
Watt, Ian (1957) *The Rise of the Novel*. Berkeley: University of California Press.

Watzlawick, Paul (1981), ed., *Die erfundene Wirklichkeit. Wie wissen wir, was wir zu wissen glauben? Beiträge zum Konstruktivismus*. Munich: Piper.

Waugh, Linda R. (1993) 'Against Arbitrariness: Imitation and Motivation Revived'. *Diacritics* 23.2: 71–87.

Waugh, Patricia (1984) *Metafiction. The Theory and Practice of Self-Conscious Fiction*. New Accents. London: Methuen.

Weber, Volker (1993) *Anekdote. Die andere Geschichte*. Stauffenberg Colloquium, 26. Tübingen: Stauffenberg.

Weinrich, Harald (1985) *Tempus. Besprochene und erzählte Welt* [1964]. Sprache und Literatur, 16. Stuttgart: Kohlhammer. Fourth edn based on the second, revised edn of 1971.

Werling, Susanne (1989) *Handlung im Drama. Versuch einer Neubestimmung des Handlungsbegriffs als Beitrag zur Dramenanalyse*. Studien zur Deutschen Literatur des 19. und 20. Jahrhunderts, 12. Frankfurt: Lang.

White, Hayden (1978) *Tropics of Discourse. Essays in Cultural Criticism*. Baltimore: Johns Hopkins University Press.

White, Hayden (1981) 'The Value of Narrativity in the Representation of Reality'. In Mitchell (1981): 1–23.

Whiteside, Anna (1982) 'Enonçiation et je(ux): L'Exemple de *La Jalousie* de Robbe-Grillet'. *French Forum* 7.2: 157–72.

Wiebe, Janyce M. (1990) 'Recognizing Subjective Sentences: A Computational Analysis of Narrative Text'. Dissertation SUNY Buffalo, Department of Computer Science, March 1990. Technical Report No. 90–03.

Wierzbicka, Anna (1985) 'Oats and Wheat: The Fallacy of Arbitrariness'. In Haiman (1985a): 311–42.

Wolf, Werner (1993) *Ästhetische Illusion und Illusionsdurchbrechung in der Erzählkunst. Theorie und Geschichte mit Schwerpunkt auf englischem illusionsstörenden Erzählen*. Tübingen: Niemeyer.

Wolfson, Nessa (1982) *CHP. The Conversational Historical Present in American English Narrative*. Topics in Socio-Linguistics, 1. Dordrecht: Foris.

Wolpers, Theodor (1964) *Die englische Heiligenlegende des Mittelalters. Eine Formgeschichte des Legendenerzählens von der spätantiken lateinischen Tradition bis zur Mitte des 16. Jh.* Tübingen: Niemeyer.

Wright, Susan (1992) 'Subjectivity and Experiential Syntax'. Paper presented at the conference of the Association for Literary Semantics, University of Canterbury, 1 August 1992.

Yacobi, Tamar (1987) 'Narrative Structure and Fictional Mediation'. *Poetics Today* 8.2: 335–72.

Zeller, Rosemarie (1992) *Der Neue Roman in der Schweiz. Die Unerzählbarkeit der modernen Welt*. SEGES, 11. Fribourg: Universitätsverlag.

Zumthor, Paul (1983) 'La brièveté comme forme'. *Formation, codification et rayonnement d'un genre médiéval. La Nouvelle. Actes du colloque international de Montréal (McGill University, 14–16 octobre 1982)*. Eds Michelangelo Picone et al. Montreal: Plato Academic Press, 3–8.

Zumthor, Paul (1990) *Oral Poetry. An Introduction*. Trans. Kathryn Murphy-Jody. Theory and History of Literature, 70. Minneapolis, MN: University of Minnesota Press.

Author index

Collated by Hilary P. Dannenberg

Anonymous works are listed in the subject index.

Abelson, Robert P. 17
Adams, Jon K. 320, 356, 403 n12
Adato, Albert 385 n24
Anderson, Sherwood 274
Aristotle 333, 349
Arnold, June 236, 361, 367
Ashberry, John 309
Atwood, Margaret 243, 248
Austen, Jane 48, 170

Bachmann, Ingeborg 237
Baker, Nicholson 276
Bakhtin, Mikhail 368
Bal, Mieke 215, 334, 338, 341, 344–5, 361, 404 n36
Ballard, James G. 290–1
Banfield, Ann 50, 169, 175, 178, 186, 192, 194–7, 201, 204, 217–18, 220, 223, 344, 361
Barlow, Richard 400 n66
Barnes, Djuna 261
Barth, John 224, 275, 281, 402 n23
Barthelme, Donald 282–5, 288, 296, 402 n26
Barthelme, Frederick 227, 229
Barthes, Roland 3–4, 31–3, 197, 382 n44
Baudrillard, Jean 8–9
Bayer, Konrad 285–6
Beckett, Samuel 49, 239, 251, 261, 273, 292, 294, 299, 303–4, 306, 316, 351
Behn, Aphra 37, 48, 56, 130–2, 136, 139–42, 144–58, 161–2, 164–6, 169, 393 n21; 'Agnes de Castro' 145; 'The Dumb Virgin' 145, 162; 'The Fair Jilt' 142, 144, 148–51, 153, 161, 393 n15; 'The History of the Nun' 136, 140–1, 153–7, 166; *Love Letters Between a Nobleman and his Sister* 130, 142, 144–5, 153, 157–8, 161, 166, 279, 381–2 n38; 'The Lucky Mistake' 136, 145, 161; *Oroonoko* 145–8, 161, 162; 'The Unfortunate Bride' 145, 162; 'The Unfortunate Happy Lady' 139–40
Bender, John 367–8, 370
Bentham, Jeremy 368–71
Bernhard, Thomas 292, 351
Bernstein, Charles 304–5
Berressem, Hanjo 401 n2, 406 n65
Blake, William 355
Boccaccio 56, 384 n10
Bokenham, Osbern 110–11
Bolinger, Dwight 18
Bolt, Robert 386 n49
Bonheim, Helmut 244, 331–2, 405 n42
Booth, Philip 308–9
Booth, Wayne C. 222
Branigan, Edward 20, 26
Brautigan, Richard 281–2
Brecht, Bertolt 350
Bremond et al. 85–6, 348
Bremond, Claude 21–2, 29
Breton, André 276–7
Brinkmann, Richard 38
Brontë, Charlotte 389 n26
Brooke-Rose, Christine 49, 267–8, 273, 317, 367; *Out* 273; *Such* 273, 316

Brooks, Peter 405 n42
Brown, Charles Brockden 48, 171
Browning, Robert 292
Bublitz, Wolfram 61, 64
Burroughs, William 281
Burt, Simon 261
Butlin, Ron 270
Butor, Michel 251

Calvino, Italo 271
Capgrave, John 117, 120
Cary, Joyce 366
Caxton, William 102, 107, 132–6, 142; *The Golden Legend* 96–7, 109; *Paris and Vienne* 132–5
Chafe, Wallace L. 62, 78–9, 319, 385 n25, n33
Chambers, Ross 366
Chandler, Raymond 173, 399 n48
Chatman, Seymour 26, 245, 325, 332–4, 340, 345, 349–50, 356, 381 n37
Chaucer, Geoffrey 79; 'The Man of Law's Tale' 109–10; *Troilus and Criseyde* 117–20
Chotjewitz, Peter 282, 286–7
Churchill, Caryl 296–9
Cixous, Hélène 364–5
Coetzee, J.M. 251, 253–5, 267
Cohen, Leonard 281
Cohn, Dorrit 41, 48, 55, 174–5, 211, 222, 252–3, 291, 367–8, 393 n17, 399 n35
Collins, Wilkie 152
Compton-Burnett, Ivy 49
Cooper, Lucas 293
Coover, Robert 267, 270, 273, 280
Cortázar, Julio 241–2, 282, 367
Couper-Kuhlen, Elizabeth 61, 63–4, 73, 385 n32
Crewe, Jonathan 386 n48
Culler, Jonathan 20, 22, 31–5, 45–6, 313, 320–1, 330

Daudet, Alphonse 405 n47
Defoe, Daniel 238, 392 n8
Derrida, Jacques 4
Dickens, Charles 218, 252; *Bleak House* 207–11, 217, 237–8, 263; *Dombey and Son* 263; *Great Expectations* 219; *Our Mutual Friend* 263; *The Mystery of Edwin Drood* 263; *A Tale of Two Cities* 237, 263

Diengott, Nilli 337
Dos Passos, John 279
Dry, Helen A. 320
Dryden, John 391–2 n45
Duffy, Maureen 405 n49
Duncan, Starkey 64
Dunn, Stephen 309
Duras, Marguerite 259

Echenoz, Jean 224
Edgeworth, Maria 168
Eliot, George 162, 217–18, 360; *The Mill on the Floss* 152, 202–3; *Romola* 161, 182–4, 202–3, 216
Engler, Bernd 86
Enkvist, Nils Erik 101
Ermarth, Elizabeth D. 78, 130, 314, 394 n44
Euler, Bettina 82–3

Fallaci, Oriana 367, 404 n35
Farah, Nuruddin 237, 239, 360, 367
Farrell, James T. 348
Faulkner, William 243
Federman, Raymond 275, 363
Felman, Shoshana 365
Fielding, Henry: *Tom Jones* 151–2; *Shamela* 394 n41
Fineman, Joel 3, 85
Fleischman, Suzanne 54
Fludernik, Monika 63, 252, 280
Forster, E.M. 14, 22, 323, 328, 366
Foucault, Michel 369–70
Fowles, John 235–6, 274, 280–1
Foxe, John 95, 127–8, 385 n36, 392 n52
Frayn, Michael 256–9
Freud, Sigmund 85, 386 n46
Fries, Udo 252
Frisch, Max 230, 243
Fuentes, Carlos 227, 231, 239, 271, 367
Furst, Lilian R. 29, 32, 382 n44

Garrett, George 238, 251
Gascoigne, George 135–6, 139
Gautier, Théophile 383 n61
Genette, Gérard 31–3, 41, 55, 150, 175, 215, 244, 330–1, 334, 337–8, 341–5, 349–50, 399 n35, 404 n36
Gerard, John 385 n36
Gibson, Andrew 305, 314–15, 403 n6
Godden, Rumer 229
Godwin, William 48, 335
Godzich, Wlad 386 n3

Gogol, Nikolai 274
Golding, William: *The Inheritors* 215
Goldknopf, David 350
Goldsmith, Oliver: *The Vicar of Wakefield* 152
Goody, Jack 59
Goytisolo, Juan 240, 275–6, 282
Greenblatt, Stephen 1–11, 376–8
Greene, Robert: *A Groats-worth of Wit* 142
Greimas, Algirdas J. 323
Gumbrecht, Hans Ulrich 406 n56, n57
Gunsteren, Julia van 395 n5
Gupta, Sunetra 248, 255, 363–4, 401 n1

Halford, Brigitte 66–9
Hall, Radclyffe 230–1
Hamburger, Käte 27, 169, 222, 252–3, 374
Hammett, Dashiell 317; *The Maltese Falcon* 173–4
Handke, Peter 351
Hardy, Barbara 360
Hardy, Thomas 162
Harweg, Roland 65–6, 71, 192
Haug, Walter 86
Hawkes, John 230, 292, 338–9
Hawthorne, Nathaniel 252
Haywood, Eliza 170
Heller, Joseph 281, 316
Hemingway, Ernest 173
Hempfer, Klaus W. 383 n59
Hoffbauer, Brigitte 66–9
Hofstadter, Douglas 401 n2
Holden, Jonathan 308
Homer 59
Horstmann, C. 97, 108, 113
Houston, Pam 256
Husson, Didier 172, 394 n41
Hutcheon, Linda 271–2

Ibsen, Henrik 350
Irigary, Luce 364–5
Iser, Wolfgang 35, 42–3
Isherwood, Christopher 235, 367
Ishiguro, Kazuo 232

Jahn, Manfred 219
James, Henry 213, 217; *The Turn of the Screw* 238; *What Maisie New* 214–6
Jameson, Frederic 304
Jandl, Ernst 260

Janowitz, Tama 239
Johnson, B.S. 238–9
Jolles, André 85
Jong, Erica 243
Jonson, Ben 354–5
Josipovici, Gabriel: *Contre-Jour* 280, 292; *In a Hotel Garden* 49; 'Mobius the Stripper' 270–1; 'Second Person Looking Out' 239
Joyce, James 294, 310, 362; *Finnegans Wake* 293–6, 299; *Ulysses* 49, 196–7, 270, 279, 288

Kearns, Katherine 32–3
Kincaid, Jamaica 230, 367
Kirkman, Francis: *The Counterfeit Lady Unveiled* 279
Kirsch, Sarah 243
Kittay, Jeffrey 386 n3
Klabund, Alfred 252
Kloepfer, Rolf 403 n14
Koch, Peter 54
Korte, Barbara 243
Kristeva, Julia 362, 364

Labov, William 54, 65–6, 73, 76
Lamarque, Peter 40–2
Langacker, Ronald W. 75–6
Langland, William 387 n4
Lanser, Susan S. 347–8, 352, 359–60
Lawrence, David Herbert 217; 'England, My England' 184–8, 216–17
Leech, Geoffrey 393 n17
Lennox, Charlotte: *The Female Quixote* 170–1
Lessing, Doris 271
Lewis, Sinclair 292
Lispector, Clarice 243
Lodge, Thomas 147; *Rosalynde* 158
Lord, Albert B. 59
Luckmann, Thomas 380 n14, n24, 382 n40

McCarthy, Mary 224–5, 239
McGahern, John 237, 239
McHale, Brian 271–3, 294–6, 298–9, 304–6
McInerney, Jay 397 n19
McKeon, Michael 131, 159, 393 n30
Malory, Sir Thomas 102–7
Mann, Thomas: 'Death in Venice' 211–13, 219; *The Magic Mountain* 196–7; "Tristran' 192–3, 196

Mansfield, Katherine 218, 292; 'At the Bay' 198–203, 217; 'Feuille D'Album' 198, 204–5, 218–19; 'The Garden Party' 179–82, 184, 196, 201–2, 205, 217–18
Margolin, Uri 397 n6
Marlatt, Daphne 244, 276, 367
Mathieu-Colas, Michel 383 n63
Matthews, Jack 288–90
Meier, Gerhard 234–5
Merwin, W.S. 228, 261
Meyer, E.Y. 235, 248, 259–60
Middleton, Thomas 392 n11
Miller, Henry 351
Miller, Walter M. 398 n30
Mistry, Rohinton 366
Moore, Gene 396 n38
Moore, Lorrie 228–9, 399 n49
More, Sir Thomas 85–91, 386 n49, n50, 387 n5
Müller, Heiner 293, 306–8, 351
Müller, Kurt 86
Mulvey, Laura 351–2, 405 n48
Munro, Alice 228

Nabokov, Vladimir 281–2
Nashe, Thomas: *The Unfortunate Traveller* 125, 142, 147–8
Nin, Anaïs 364
Nischik, Reingard M. 237, 243, 399 n33, n34
Nünning, Ansgar 183, 381 n30

O'Brien, Edna 248
O'Brien, Flann 271
Oates, Joyce Carol 253
Olsen, Stein Haugom 40–2
Österreicher, Wulf 54, 392 n13

Parker, Dorothy 292
Parry, Milman 59
Pater, Walter 294, 402 n23
Pavel, Thomas 349–50
Peel, Ellen 238
Perec, Georges 224
Petersen, Jürgen H. 251–2
Piercy, Marge 236, 316
Pinget, Robert 288
Pinter, Harold 279–81, 351; *Landscape* 280–1; *Old Times* 280–1; *Silence* 280
Pirsig, Robert M. 251
Plath, Sylvia 399 n48
Polanyi, Livia 61

Ponge, Francis 306, 308
Pope, Alexander 391–2 n45
Pouillon, Jean 405 n41a
Prince, Gerald 12, 311, 323–5, 349, 379 n2, 381 n28, 383 n1, 403 n14, n20
Propp, Vladimir 53
Pynchon, Thomas 251, 316

Quasthoff, Uta M. 73
Quirk, Randolph 72

Radcliffe, Ann 48
Reid, Ian 348
Richardson, Brian 236, 243, 261
Richardson, Samuel 170; *Clarissa* 171
Ricoeur, Paul 22–4, 28, 34, 43, 45, 55, 320–1, 324
Riehl, Claudia 101
Riffaterre, Michael 160–1
Rilke, Rainer Maria 277
Robbe-Grillet, Alain 251, 317, 351; *La Jalousie* 46, 173–4, 248, 251, 293, 394 n44; *Instantanés* 176, 293, 351
Roche, Maurice 233, 239, 259, 260–1, 266, 282, 400 n67
Ronen, Ruth 320
Roper, William 85–91
Rossi, Luciano 384 n10
Roth, Joseph 233
Rousseau, Jean-Jacques 394 n41
Rule, Jane 367, 404 n35
Rushdie, Salman 366
Ryan, Marie-Laure 56, 326–7, 336, 355, 382 n46, 401 n2, 404 n33

Sacks, Harvey 64
Sarah, Robyn 227
Sarraute, Nathalie 243, 268, 273, 399 n48; *L'Usage de la parole* 278, 282, 401 n7–8; *Tu ne t'aimes pas* 49
Sayers, Dorothy 233
Schank, Roger C. 17
Scharang, Michael 298
Scheerbart, Paul 251–2
Schiffrin, Deborah 66
Schmidt, Siegfried J. 43
Scholes, Roberts 404 n22
Schütz, Alfred 17, 73, 380 n14, n22, n24, 382 n40
Searle, John R. 16
Seltzer, Mark 367–9
Senesi, Mauro 224
Settle, Elkanah 132, 142; *Will Morrell* 124–5, 136–9, 143–4

Short, Michael H. 393 n17
Sidney, Sir Philip 122–3, 128, 147, 158
Silko, Leslie 360
Silvain, Pierre 224
Small, Judith 249–51, 253
Smith, Barbara H. 16, 383 n53
Smith, Lillian 230
Sontag, Susan 248, 264–6, 351
Sorrentino, Gilbert 296
Spark, Muriel 49
Spender, Dale 362
Spenser, Edmund 391 n45
Stanzel, F.K. 27–8, 47–8, 73, 131, 169, 175, 179–81, 192, 196, 199, 201–2, 217–18, 220, 223, 237, 242, 244, 246, 252, 314, 330–1, 334, 337–41, 344–5, 347, 349, 373, 393 n17, 396 n27, 399 n33
Stein, Gertrude 248, 261, 294, 299–304, 306, 362
Stempel, Wolf-Dieter 383 n4
Sternberg, Meir 321–3, 325–6
Stoppard, Tom: *Travesties* 279–80, 350–1
Stout, Rex 231, 367
Strindberg, August 292
Sturgess, Philip J.M. 22, 327–8, 403 n14
Styron, William 230
Suarez, Virgil 236–8
Sukenick, Ronald 275, 362–4, 367
Svartvik, Jan 72

Tannen, Deborah 64–5, 319
Tedlock, Dennis 379 n3
Terkel, Studs 29, 76, 384 n20
Thackeray, William 237
Thibaudeau, Jean: *Imaginez la nuit* 240, 268, 277; *Une cérémonie royale* 277
Todorov, Tzvetan 31, 33, 384 n10
Tolstoy, Leo 16
Tomlinson, Charles 309–10
Tournier, Michel 238

Updike, John 243, 262
Uspensky, Boris A. 343–4

Vanasco, Alberto 259
Vargas Llosa, Mario 231
Viègnes, Michel 39
Villiers de L'Isle-Adam, Philippe 350
Volosinov, V.N. 343–4

Wachinger, Burghart 86
Waletzky, Joshua 54, 73
Walpole, Horace 48
Walter, Otto 282, 287
Walton, Kendall L. 383 n54
Warren, Robert P. 230
Wårvik, Brita 101
Watt, Ian 29, 37, 131, 159
Waugh, Linda R. 18, 271, 381 n26
Waugh, Patricia 271
Weber, Volker 85
Weinrich, Harald 71, 80, 256
Weldon, Fay: *The Cloning of Joanna May* 238; *Female Friends* 238, 263; *The Lives and Loves of a She-Devil* 263; 'Weekend' 188–91, 203, 217
Welty, Eudora 293
Werfel, Franz 251
White, Edmund 367, 404 n35
White, Hayden 34, 36, 328–9
Wiechert, Ernst 251
Wilder, Thornton 350
Winterson, Jeanette 248, 352, 359–60
Wittig, Monique 233, 236, 367
Wohmann, Gabriele 224, 243–4, 261, 282, 286, 299
Wolf, Christa 243
Wolf, Werner 271–3, 383 n52, 401 n2
Wolfson, Nessa 63, 73
Woolf, Virginia 216, 218, 293–4, 310; *Jacob's Room* 205–7; *The Waves* 192–8, 217–18
Wright, Susan 155

Zamyatin, Yevgeny 224

Subject index

Collated by Hilary P. Dannenberg

Page numbers in **bold** indicate where technical terms are defined.

abstract (Labov) 65-6, 81, 325
achrony (Genette) 138
addresses to the audience 109, 115
adverbial deixis 194
agency, agent 26-7, 74-5, 245, 273, 337-41; agents vs. characters 339-40
allegory 354-5
alterity 3-9, 33, 376-8
analepsis (Genette) see flashback
anecdote 58, 82-4, 85-91, 384 n17
aperspectivism 138, 345; see also zero focalization
argument as text type 356-7
as clause 111
attribution of discourse 186-92, 198, 202-6, 215-18, 225, 264-6, 401 n1
author see narrator/author coidentity
authorial-figural continuum (Stanzel) 246
authorial intrusions 109
authorial narrative 165-8, 207-10, 368-71; see also omniscience
authorial narrative situation (Stanzel) 47-8
autobiography 47, 77, 95
autodiegesis vs. homodiegesis 343

biography 24, 25, 86, 95
but 284-5

camera eye see neutral narrative
centre of consciousness (Henry James) see reflector character/deictic centre
character 245, 273; see also agency, existence

chronology 20-1, 270; see also temporality
cladistics 331, 404 n27
cognitive frames 12, 15, 22-3, 27-8, 43-52, 163, 231, 245, 303, 312-23, 358, 371-5; and focalization 345; see also frame (theory), natural frames
cognitive linguistics 17
cognitive parameters 12, 15, 19, 22-3, 43-52, 211-13, 305-6, 313-15, 343, 352, 371-5
cognitive principles see narrativization
commentary 65, 80, 97
communal perspective 179-92, 198-9, 208, 210, 213, 217, 219
concordance 406 n60
conditional tense 259-60
configurality (Ricoeur) see Author index
consciousness 26-7, 48, **49-50**, 197, 223-44, 278, 374-5, 382 n47; access to character's 150, 177, 346; as cognitive frame 221, 278, 291-2, 311-13, 317, 355-6, 372-4; representation of 147-8, 150-1, 153-9, 161, 169-72, 194, 346, 349, 374
consciousness novel 130-1, 164, 168-72, 317
consciousness scene 131, 147-8, 153-9, 170
consistency see narrativization, plot
consonance see dissonance (D. Cohn)
constructivism 12, 305-6, 313, 379 n1
conversation as text type 356-7

Subject index 449

conversational storytelling *see* natural narrative
coordination vs. subordination 62, 107, 133–6, 141
criminal biography 79, 101–2, 124–8
cultural studies 366–71

deictic centre 75–6, 156, **169**, 178, 192–207, 218, 223–44, 256–7, 266, 307, 344; *see also* empty centre
deixis 192–7, 217–18, 242, 262–3, 266–8; and present-tense narrative 252–4; temporal deixis *see* tense; transferential deixis/*Deixis am Phantasma* (Bühler) 196–7
dérimage 93–4
description 80, 132, 150–1, 176, 329, 348, 392 n5, 406 n57; and perception 293; as text type 356–7
diachrony *see* novel, history of
dialogue novel 175
didactic aspect of literature 25
discours indirect libre see free indirect discourse
discourse analysis 16, 60–81
discourse markers (Schiffrin) 62–3, 70, 101–14
discourse mode/type 318, 336, 356–8
discourse vs. story *see* story vs. discourse
discursive vs. narrative texts *see* text type
dissonance vs. consonance (D. Cohn) 157, 202
Don Tomazo 125–6, 143
drama 28, 130, 145, 279–81, 291–2, 302–3, 306–8, 333, 347, 349–53, 369–70, 403 n20; drama vs. novel 142–8; and experiential narrative 351–2; and narrativity 306–8, 349–53; narrative in the form of drama *see* dramatic narrative; symbolist drama 350; *see also* stage directions
dramatic monologue 144, 288, 291–2
dramatic narrative 49

écriture féminine 359–66
effet de réel (Barthes) 3, 4, 8, 31–3, 37–8, 131, 150, 159–63, 172
ekphrasis 131
embedded discourse 264–6
embedded narrative 281–2, 342–3; *see also* narrative level

embedded orientation *see* orientation
embodiment 17–19, 30, 203–4, 211–13, 217, 252–3, 311, 312, 322, 355
emplotment (Ricoeur) *see* Author index
empty centre (Banfield) 175–6, 178, 192–207, **192, 195–6**, 218
epic preterite (Hamburger) 222, 252
epic (as a genre) 53, 55, 165
episode *see* narrative episode
episodic narrative vs. teleological narrative 56
epistolary fiction 48, 130, 279
erlebte Rede *see* free indirect discourse
event 335
event sequences 20
exemplum 85–91, 82–4
existence, existent 26–7, 132, 203, 245–9, 267, 271, 274, 354–5
experiencing vs. narrating self (Stanzel) 337, 341–2
experientiality **12–13**, 20–30, 24–5, **28–30**, 70, 94, 99, 120, 127, 158, 163, 170, 173, 176, 195, 197, 245, 270, 277–8, 288, 292, 310, 311, 312, 313, 322–3, 327–8, 349, 351–2, 354–8, 373; lack of 103, 99; in second-person texts 226–9; transfer from first- to third-person text 79, 99, 120, 315–16
experimental writing 35, 269–310, 351, 367; *see also* postmodernism
expository writing *see* argument
expressivity *see* deictic centre, reflectorization
external focalization 175, 184–5, 345–6; *see also* neutral narrative

faction 384 n9
fairy tales 56
familiarizing article (Bronzwaer) 193–4
fantastic, the 33, 162
feminism 236, 358–66, 376–8; *see also écriture féminine*, gender
fictionality 9–10, 36, 38–43, 311, 319, 347, 383 n53; markers of 80; and narrativity 38–9, 303–4; and poetry 39–40
fictive discourse (B.H. Smith) 16
fictive vs. hypothetical 39–42
figural narrative (situation) (Stanzel) 48, 169, 179, 317, 345, 347; *see also* reflector-mode narrative

450 Subject index

figural narrative (Fludernik) 246, 347
figuralization 178–222, *esp.* 192–207, **197–8, 201–4**
figuralization vs. reflectorization *see* reflectorization
film 28, 345, 347, 351–3, 376–8
film script as novel (*cinéroman*) 351
fingierte Mündlichkeit see pseudo-orality, *skaz*
first-person narrative 47–8, 94, 224, 249–53, 337–8, 359; *see also* homodiegetic
first-person novel 168
first- vs. third-person narrative 122, 252–3, 315–16, 337–8; in neutral narrative 174–5; in present-tense texts 252
flashback 150, 151, 254, 351
Floris and Blancheflour 115–17
focalization 340, 343–7, 404 n28; *see also* communal perspective, figural narrative, reflector mode
folk tale 14, 53–4, 56, 59, 379 n3, 380 n5
foregrounding 60–1, 80
form–function correlation 53–128 *passim*, 373
frame narrative 342–3; *see also* embedded narrative
frame, frame theory 17–19, 162, 312–13
free indirect discourse 70, 76, 153, 155–8, 169, 171, 191–202, 215, 225, 229, 231–3, 254, 264–6, 343, 368–71, 394 n43, 398 n30; in Middle English 155, 393 n19; and reflectorization 180–4, 189, 194, 202, 219–20
freezing (Casparis) 28
future tense 256–9

gay/lesbian texts 275–6, 291, 352–3, 367, 359–60
gender 151, 236, 243, 248, 359–61, 366, 367, 406 n60; of narrator 248, 352–3, 359–61, 405 n49; *see also* pronouns gender-nonspecific
generic present tense 230
generic *you see you*
genre 45, 304–10, 313, 318–23, 329, 347–58, 372
Gilte Legende, The 102–3, 106–7
Gothic novel 170, 172

hagiography 86–91, 93, 95, 98–9, 127, 386 n48; *see also* saints' legend

hermetic writing 294–9
heterocommunicative (Fludernik) *see* homocommunicative
heterodiegetic (Genette) *see* homodiegetic
historical narrative *see* historiography
historical novel 24, 25, 160, 393 n26
historical present *see* present tense
historicity 328–30
historiography 24–6, 38–40, 87–91, 96, 166, 319, 328, 335; anecdote as 3–4, 85–91
historiographical metafiction 272
homocommunicative vs. heterocommunicative (Fludernik) 245–7, 342
homodiegetic vs. heterodiegetic (Genette) 240, 245, 337–8
how 156–7
humanistic prose 121
hypothetical discourse 228–30, 256, 259, 261, 354–5, 401 n8; *see also* fictive discourse

iconicity 18, 381 n26
idea units (Chafe) 62
identity *see* personhood
ideological criticism and texts 358–71
imperative 261–2
impersonal *on* 232–3, 246
implied author 22, 47, 361, 381 n30; and reflectorization 181, 183–4, 196, 203, 218; and unreliability 211–13
impressionist prose 350, 405 n47
incidence **66**, 69, 74–5, 82, 114, 125–6, 148, 372; lack of 100–1, 111, 115, 120, 123
incidence schema (Pollak) 29, 75, 152
incipit **65–6**, 70, 82, 120, 123–4, 130, 148, 152
incompatiblity 280–1
insanity 316
institutionalized storytelling 77–81
interior monologue 153, 208, 230–1, 250, 288, 291, 392 n11; on stage 351, 353
internal focalization 153, 155–6, 158, 169–70, 172, 262–3, 345; *see also* figural narrative, reflector mode
intonation 61
inversion 70
irony 89–90, 181–3, 189–90, 202–3, 213, 215, 217, 220

Subject index 451

irreal 382 n45
it 235-6, 398 n30

joke 58, 81-5
jongleur ('bard') 47, 77, 165
juxtaposition *see* montage

King Horn 115
King Kong 376-8

legal texts 95
legend *see* saints' legend, hagiography
length of text *see* text length
letters 95
life story (oral biography) 59-60
linguistic method 373
Lives of Woman Saints, The 126-7

macro-episode 145-51
macro-genre *see* meta-genre
man (German) 232-5, 246, 259-60
mediacy/mediation, *Mittelbarkeit* (Stanzel) 27-8, 333-7, 372-4
mediality 352-3
medieval narrative 53, 92-120, 155; in prose 93-107; in verse 107-20
medium of narrative 333-7; *see also* drama, film
metafiction(ality) 272-5, 280-1, 304; *see also* self-reflexiveness
meta-genre 356-8, 372; *see also* text type
metalepsis (Genette) 273-4
Middle English *see* medieval narrative
Middle English Sermons 99-101
mimesis 9-10, 35-8, 159, 162, 220, 304, 316; and cognitive restraints 19; Mimesis I/II/III (Ricoeur) *see* Author index; mimesis vs. diegesis *see* diegesis
mimicry 182
mind style 394 n39
Modernism 170-2, 270, 271, 279, 314
montage 277-88, 299
multiple subjects 224-36

naming of narrator/protagonist 246-8, 359
narratee 227, 340; *see also* address to the audience
narrative as a text type 304-10, 318-23, 356-8
narrative episode 100-28; agent in 129; development of 110, 114, 120, 124-8, 129-31, 142-53, 163-4; junctures 78-9, 109-10, 113, 115; management of 113; structure of 65-85, 144, 349
narrative levels 270-1, 273-4, 275, 281-2, 338-9, 341-3; *see also* story vs. discourse, metalepsis, plotline vs. off-plotline
narrative of personal experience, and of vicarious experience *see under* natural narrative
narrative present *see* present tense
narrative report 58, 71-7
narrative situations (Stanzel) 47-8, 131, 168-9, 314, 330, 373
narrative structure 103; macrostructure vs. microstructure 114, 120, 128, 129-31, 145-53, 163; *see also* narrative episode, episodic vs. teleological
narrative tense *see* tense, narrative
narrativity 2, 12-15, 20-30, **26**, 36, 38, 41, 49, 270-1, 273, 276, 278, 291, 303-4, 309, 311, 316-17, 321-2, 323-30, 347, 349, 352-6, 372-4, 379 n2, 403 n14, 404 n22; and consciousness 49-50, 148, 173; degrees of 355-6; and discourse 327-8, 358; in drama and film 349-53; modes of (Ryan) 326-7; and plot 20, 270, 273, 323-7, 404 n22; zero degree of 28, 311, 317, 328-9, 358
narrativization 20, 31-5, **34-5**, 45-6, 174-7, 219-21, 223, 232, 240, 248-9, 267-310, 313, 315-18, 326-7, 341, 352, 366, 371-4; and genre 329-30; impossibility of 244
narratology 55-6, 305
narratology, standard models 292, 330-33
narrator/author coidentity/equation 164, 339, 360-1
narrator 197, 207-17, 243, 245, 252-3, 282, 366; covert 340; personalized 47, 151; on stage in drama 350; as teller figure 109, 115, 274-8
natural, the 3-11, **10-12**, 15-17, 19, 43, 312, 330; opposites of 5-11, 12
natural discourse (Smith) 16
natural frames 43-51, 164-5, 176, 221, 231-2, 238, 248-9, 268, 274-8
natural linguistics, 17-19, 312-13
natural narrative **13-17**, 53-91, 312, 318-19, 329, 357; interactional

features 64–5; narrative of personal experience **57**, 63–70, 72–3, **75**; narrative of vicarious experience **57**, 71–7, 84, 316; *see also* observational narrative, jokes
natural narratology 217–21; defined 12–52, *esp.* 19; reviewed 311–78, *esp.* 332–3
natural parameters 131, 163–5
naturalization (Culler) 20, 31, 33–4, 45–6, 223, 267–8, 304, 313; *see also* narrativization
Natürlichkeitstheorie (natural linguistics) 17–19
neutral narrative 28, 48–50, 131, 164, 172–6, 219, 247, 275, 307, 317
non-communicative texts 246–7
non-narrative texts 326–7; in relation to standard definitions of narrativity 49, 287–94, 323, 325, 349–52; in relation to my definition of narrativity 36, 49, 328–30
non-natural **11**, 12
norm (vs. deviation) 5–6
Northern Homily Cycle 101, 112–14
novel, history of 128, 129–77, 313–18, 329, 339
novel of letters *see* epistolary fiction
novella 349
now 115–17, 156, 254, 265–6

observational narrative 58, 71–7, **74**, 98, 127
observation 28, 196; *see also* observational narrative, perception
observer 186, 192, 194–6, 198, 204, 207–17, 218, 220, 293, 307–8
Of þe Vox and of þe Wolf 101
omniscience 48, 151, 165–8, 275, 359, 368–71
on (French) *see* impersonal *on*
one 205–6, 222, 232–3, 246
oral history 60, 91
oral narrative 13–14, 53–91; *see also* natural narrative
oral poetry 14, 55, 59, 77, 384 n18
orality 14, 55
orality vs. literacy 15, 44–5, 53–7, 79, 90–1, 92–128, 313, 383 n4
orientation 65–6, 82, 131–42, 145–6, 150, 265, 348, 357; delayed orientation 141; embedded orientation 63, 65, 80
other(ness) *see* alterity

panopticon (J. Bentham) 368–71
parable 86
parataxis 55, 141
past progressive 148, 151–2, 155
past perfect tense 132, 145–7, 149, 150, 194–5, 254
past tense/preterite 126
perception 28, 69, 74–6, 150, 153 194–7, 204, 345–6, 355, 368–71
peripheral first-person narrative 73, 122, 343
person 222–68, 277; alternation 236–44, 277
personhood 245, 248–9, 316
personal experience, narratives of *see* natural narrative
Personalisierung (Stanzel) 179
perspective *see* focalization
picaresque novel 124–8, 130, 132, 136–9, 142, 145, 147, 148, 150, 162
plot 20–3, 162, 270, 272–3, 311, 319–22, 334–5; consistency of 273; in drama 145, 349–50; *see also* narrativity
plotline vs. off-plotline 62–3, 66, 132
poetry 39–40, 302, 304–8, 308–10, 354–6, 358, 381 n35, 383 n53
point of view *see* focalisation
point (Labov) 29, 63, 70, 81
political texts 367
postcolonialism 366–7
postmodernism 178, 269–310, *esp.* 271–4, 305–6; 314, 382 n47
poststructuralism vs. structuralism 305, 315, 359
pragmatics 357
present participle 126–7, 144
present perfect tense 258
present tense 223, 253–4, 256–9; historical present 28, 84, 115–17, 126, 144, 155–6, 250, 263–6, 391–2 n45; narration 253, 283–5, 336–7, 396 n29; narrative present tense 223, 249–56, 257–9, 263–4, 267, 299 n49; present progressive 250; present tense vs. historical present 252; tabular present 119, 253, 266
preterite/past tense *see* tense, epic preterite
pronouns, personal 222–68; gendered 236, 360–1; gender-nonspecific 222, 361; indefinite 232; invented 236, 361; odd 223–44, 367; plural

Subject index 453

pronouns 222; pronoun alternation 236–44, 262
prototype, prototype theory 16–19, 51, 323, 357, 372–5
pseudo-orality (*fingierte Mündlichkeit*) 178, 205, 349
psycho-narration 153, 157–8, 170, 182–3, 215, 250, 393 n17

reader 201, 304–5, 337–41, 359–61, 374; see also narratee
realism 10, 29, 35–8, **37–8**, 97–8, 129–77, **131**, **159**, 159–62, 178, 203, 223, 241, 273–4, 276, 314–16, 329, 346–7, 382 n44
realist frame 245, 249, 273–4, 305, 315–16, 346–7
realist novel 37, 130, **131**, 132, 153, 159–63, 165–77, 188, 246
referential noun phrases 246
reflector character/mode (Stanzel) 27–8, 153, 179, 181, 213, 223, 229, 247, 275, 340–1, 345, **384 n14**; and present-tense narrative 251, 253; and pronominal alternation 242; see also figural narrative situation
reflectorization (Stanzel) 179–81, 192
reflectorization (Fludernik) 178–222 esp. 179–92, **184**, 199, **202–3**, 209–10, 216–17, 224–5; consonance vs. dissonance 202; consonant reflectorization 213–17
reflectorization vs. figuralization 201–7, 210–11, 217–20
relative clauses (*the which*) 121, 126, 133, 141
reliability 151, 165–8
religious texts, devotional literature 77–8, 86–90, 385 n34; see also saints' legend
Renaissance literature 79–80, 120–8
repetition 61, 93
report 130, 163, 318, 329, 353, 357
report-cum-scene structure see macro-episode
reportability see tellability
representation 2–11
resolution (as end point of natural narrative structure) 65–6, 82, 147
result (as part of episodic narrative structure) 65–6, 70, 81–2, 125–6, 148
romance: eighteenth-century romance 159; Elizabethan romance 121–4, 127, 148; medieval verse romance 94, 115–20; prose romance 95; romance tradition 150, 166

St Katherine Group (c. 1230) 93, 95, 101, 388 n15
saints' legend 78, 94–9, 107–14
scene 78, 123, **142**; dialogue scene **142–3**, 145; dramatic scene 131, **142**, 142–53, 171; narrative scene 127, 130, 151, 163; see also consciousness scene
schema of incidence see incidence
Scottish Legendary, The 111
second-person fiction 4, 219, 222, 226–32, 245, 251, 261–2, 275–6, 282–5, 341–2, 361, 367
self-address see you
self-reflexiveness 50–1, 271–2; vs. self-reflective consciousness 382 n47
sequence of tenses 254–7, 264–6
sequentiality 21–2, 26
sermons 84, 95, 99–101, 387 n6
setting 62, 271, 274, 281–4; in experiential narrative **66**, 82
setting-plus-incidence unit 146–54
short story 53, 348–9, 405 n42, n45
simultaneous narration 252
simple forms 53–4, 96
skaz 178, 205, 218, 274, **394 n1**
slant vs. filter (Chatman) 345
so 103–7
soliloquy 147–8, 158, 394 n35 see also consciousness scene
South English Legendary 97, 101, 110, 112
specificity 203, 316, 354–5
speculative narrative 209
speech, representation of: in free indirect discourse 156; in indirect discourse 144, 147
stage directions 350–1
story vs. discourse 56, 204, 274, 312–13, 333–7, 349–50; and personhood 245, 249; and second-person fiction 228, 336–7, 342; and present-tense narrative 254, 336–7
story vs. plot 335
stream of consciousness 169
style 300–1
subjectivity see consciousness, reflectorization
subject verb inversion see inversion
'subjunctive' mode 228, 261
subjunctive narrative 260

subordination *see* coordination
surfiction 178, 271
Survey of English Usage 224
syntax 108, 121, 133–5, 141, 295–9, 299–301, 302–3, 362–4; (prepositional phrase) preposing 70; in the oral language 15–16, 62, 385 n25; *see also* coordination vs. subordination, inversion, present participle

tall tale 77
teleology 20–2, 24, 130, 320–2
tellability 24–5, 29, 63, 70
teller mode 27, 47, 167, 247
teller vs. reflector (mode) 27–8, 169, 204, 220, 274–5, 337–41; in relation to reflectorization 179–81; *see also* internal focalization, narrator
tellers/teller figure 252–3, 271, 274–8; in reflectorization 185, 217–19; *see also* narrator
temporal markers 66
temporality 21, 319–22
tense, narrative 84, 222–68; infinitival style 261, 286; non-finite verb forms 260–2; odd narrative tenses 256–60; tense alternation 66, 259, 262–6; tense shift in episodic narrative 119, 144; verbal deixis 194–5, 262–3, 266–8; *see also* individual tenses
text length 348
text type 60, 318, 356–8; new definition of 357–8; *see also* genre
þa, þo 101, 110, 112
that + NP 161
then 254; and then 101–7; *þan(ne)* 101–2, 112–13; *than(ne), then(ne)* 102–6
they 224–5
third-person narrative 47–8; *see also* heterodiegetic, authorial narrative
this + NP 391 n44

thought report *see* psycho-narration
thus, þus 113–14, 116–17
transfiguralization (Stanzel) 196
translations 95
transcoding *see* Verschrift(lich)ung
turn-taking 63
typicalization, typicality 182, 217, 220, 162; in FID 184, 208
typology 246–8, 341–7, 372–3

unreliability (Booth) 168, 275; and reflectorization 211–13
utopian fiction 316

verbless texts 261
verisimilitude 4, 31–3, 37, 159–63, 273, 316
Verschriftlichung (conceptual transcoding) 54, 148
Verschriftung (medial transcoding) 54
verse narrative 53, 55, 59, 78, 93, 107–20, 391–2 n45
verse vs. prose genres 92–4, 120
vicarious experience, narratives of *see* natural narrative
voice (Genette) 343–7
voice effect 178–221
voice-over 350

we 224, 287
when 62, 112; *whan(ne)* 104–5, 111, 113
witness 73, 75–6, 99, 164, 168, 207–11, 339

you 197–8, 200–1, 204–6, 226–32, 251, 282–5, 308–9; generic *you* 204–5, 229–30; self-address 230–1

zero degree of narrativity *see* narrativity
zero focalization (Genette) 167, 345; *see also* aperspectivism

An environmentally friendly book printed and bound in England by www.printondemand-worldwide.com

PEFC Certified
This product is from sustainably managed forests and controlled sources
www.pefc.org
PEFC/16-33-415

Mixed Sources
Product group from well-managed forests, and other controlled sources
www.fsc.org Cert no. TT-COC-002641
© 1996 Forest Stewardship Council

This book is made entirely of chain-of-custody materials

#0442 - 071111 - C0 - 234/156 - PB